An African Slaving Port and the Atlantic World

This book traces the history and development of the port of Benguela, the third largest port of slave embarkation on the coast of Africa, from the early seventeenth century to the mid-nineteenth century. Benguela, located on the central coast of present-day Angola, was founded by the Portuguese in the early seventeenth century. In discussing the impact of the trans-Atlantic slave trade on African societies, Mariana P. Candido explores the formation of new elites, the collapse of old states, and the emergence of new states. Placing Benguela in an Atlantic perspective, this study shows how events in the Caribbean and Brazil affected social and political changes on the African coast. This book emphasizes the importance of the South Atlantic as a space for the circulation of people, ideas, and crops.

Mariana P. Candido is Assistant Professor at Princeton University. She is the author of *Fronteras de Esclavización: Esclavitud, Comercio e Identidad en Benguela, 1780–1850* (2011) and co-edited *Crossing Memories: Slavery and African Diaspora* (2011) with Ana Lucia Araujo and Paul E. Lovejoy. Her articles have appeared in the *Journal for Eighteenth-Century Studies, Slavery & Abolition, African Economic History, Portuguese Studies Review, Cahiers des Anneaux de la Mémoire,* and *Brésil(s). Sciencies Humaines et Sociales.*

African Studies

The African Studies series, founded in 1968, is a prestigious series of monographs, general surveys, and textbooks on Africa covering history, political science, anthropology, economics, and ecological and environmental issues. The series seeks to publish work by senior scholars as well as the best new research.

A list of books in this series will be found at the end of this volume.

An African Slaving Port and the Atlantic World

Benguela and Its Hinterland

MARIANA P. CANDIDO

Princeton University

CAMBRIDGE
UNIVERSITY PRESS

32 Avenue of the Americas, New York NY 10013-2473, USA

Cambridge University Press is part of the University of Cambridge.

It furthers the University's mission by disseminating knowledge in the pursuit of
education, learning and research at the highest international levels of excellence.

www.cambridge.org
Information on this title: www.cambridge.org/9781107529748

© Mariana P. Candido 2013

First published 2013
First paperback edition 2015

A catalogue record for this publication is available from the British Library

Library of Congress Cataloguing in Publication data
Candido, Mariana P. (Mariana Pinho), 1975– author.
An African slaving port and the Atlantic world : Benguela and its
Hinterland / Mariana Candido, Princeton University.
pages   cm. – (African studies ; 124)
Includes bibliographical references and index.
ISBN 978-1-107-01186-1
1. Benguela (Angola)–Economic conditions.   2. Slave trade–Africa,
West–History.   I. Title.
HC950.Z7B46   2013
387.109673´4–dc23   2012033211

ISBN 978-1-107-01186-1 Hardback
ISBN 978-1-107-52974-8 Paperback

Contents

List of Maps and Images		*page* viii
Acknowledgments		ix
	Introduction	1
1.	Contacts, Competition, and Copper: Benguela until 1710	31
2.	The Rise of an Atlantic Port, 1710–1850	89
3.	Benguela and the South Atlantic World	143
4.	Mechanisms of Enslavement	191
5.	Political Reconfiguration of the Benguela Hinterland, 1600–1850	237
	Conclusion	313
Bibliography		323
Index		351

Maps and Images

Maps

1. Benguela and the Atlantic world   *page* xiv
2. West Central Africa and the ocean currents   30
3. Portuguese fortresses south of the Kwanza River   34
4. Benguela and its interior   276

Images

1. "Perspectiva da Pequena Cidade de São Philippe de Benguella, vista do ancoradouro da Bahia de Santo António," in José Joaquim Lopes de Lima, *Ensaios sobre a Statística das Possessões Portuguezas*, vol. 3, part 2 (Lisbon, 1846), between pp. 26–27.   2

2. São Felipe de Benguela. (*Source:* AHU, Iconografia 001, doc. 317.)   88

3. Nossa Senhora do Pópulo, Benguela. (Photo by Mariana P. Candido.)   124

4. Benguela Bay. (*Source:* AHU, Cartografia 001, doc. 268.)   142

5. Caconda. (*Source:* AHU, Iconografia 001,doc. 267.)   172

6. Nossa Senhora da Conceição, Caconda. (Photo by Mariana P. Candido.)   259

Acknowledgments

This book began to take shape during the months of July and August 2009 while I was at the Arquivo Histórico Ultramarino and the Torre do Tombo in Lisbon. This was when I finally realized that I had enough material to write a history of Benguela from its foundation in the seventeenth century. Although I have been working on the history of Benguela since 2000, I had not dared to extend my research before 1780, when most scholars agree that the port played a crucial role in the trans-Atlantic slave trade. Some of the ideas presented in my doctoral dissertation are still here, such as the mechanisms of enslavement and the fact that some people were captured not far from the coast. However, this is a different study, the result of extensive research done in 2007 and 2009 and subsequent reflection on the importance of the port of Benguela and its interior to the Atlantic world.

I am most grateful to the many colleagues and friends who have encouraged me at different moments and in different locations. Workshops and lectures in Vancouver, Paris, Mexico City, and Ann Arbor in 2010 were crucial to refining some ideas while I was writing the manuscript. Thor Burnham, Jennifer Spears, Martha Jones, James Sweet, Jean Hébrard, Rebecca Scott, Butch Ware, Bertie Mandelblatt, Silvia Marzagalli, María Elisa Velázquez, and Rina Cáceres, as well as other members of these colloquia, asked me tough questions and pushed me in new directions.

At the Department of History at Princeton University I am fortunate to have generous and extraordinary colleagues who read an earlier draft and provided me with their insights. I am particularly grateful for the careful reading of Molly Green, Jeremy Adelman, and Emmanuel Kreike, who suggested new directions. Zack Kagan-Guthrie helped to locate many of the cases in the parish records used in this study. He also read early drafts of chapters and made valuable suggestions. Samila Xavier de Queiroz, Ana Eliza Santos Rodrigues, and Kássia Pereira da Costa also have provided valuable help collecting data in Minas Gerais. I am very grateful for the assistance and research skills of Zack, Samila, Ana, and Kássia.

Thanks to an academic leave from Princeton in 2009–10, I was able to do more research on the seventeenth century and conceptualize and write most of this book. The chair of the department, Bill Jordan, facilitated several requests for research expenses and leave time, allowing me to go once again to Portugal, Angola, and Brazil. Tsering W. Shawa, from the Princeton GIS Library, generously drew the maps that illustrate this book. I also enjoyed tremendous support from my previous department at the University of Wisconsin–La Crosse. Among many wonderful colleagues, I have to acknowledge the support of the chair of the department, Charles Lee, and the friendship of Victor Macías-Gonzalez. Both helped me to go to Angola to do research in the summer of 2007, which allowed me to consult many of the parish records used in this study.

Generous fellowships allowed me to finish my research and write during my academic leave. The Luso-American Foundation funded two months of research in the Torre do Tombo in 2009. I was extremely lucky to have Hugh Cagle, Drew Thompson, and Cláudia Sousa as research companion and shared with them many of the ideas presented in this book. I am also thankful for the financial support of the Fundação Calouste Gulbenkian, a University of Wisconsin–La Crosse Research Grant, and the CNPq/ Pro-Africa Project, "Acervo Digital Angola Brasil-PADAB," under the leadership of Mariza de Carvalho Soares. At the John Carter Brown Library I met a community of scholars who helped me to start writing the manuscript. Conversations with Ana Valdez, Karen Graubart, and Diego Pirillo suggested that I place Benguela in an Atlantic context. At the Gilder Lehrman Center (GLC) at Yale University I enjoyed four very productive months in the company of Emma Christopher, Dana Schaffer, and Melissa McGrath. The GLC staff constantly cheered me up, provided chocolate, and offered real conversations, at a time when I was immersed in my bubble and isolated from the world. Stuart Schwartz's generous feedback on seventeenth-century Iberia helped me to feel more confident about my incursion into early Benguela.

Beatrix Heintze read several chapters and commented extensively, saving me from errors and pushing me in new directions. A marvelous historian, Beatrix has been extremely supportive of my work, and I am very grateful for her support over the years. Joseph Miller, José Curto, Walter

Hawthorne, Mariza de Carvalho Soares, Renée Soulodre–La France, Silvia Lara, Olatunji Ojo, Stacey Sommerdyk, Bashir Salau, David Wheat, and Jennifer Lofkrantz read early versions of some chapters and helped me to refine many of the ideas I present in this book. Roquinaldo Ferreira, Roberto Guedes, Daniel Domingues da Silva, Mariza de Carvalho Soares, and David Wheat shared their own research with me, in a clear indication that there is more generosity in the academic world than one might think. Acknowledgment is also due to Marcia Schenck, Morgan Robinson, Edna Bonhomme, and Kristen Windmuller, who read the manuscript and offered valuable suggestions.

In the summer of 2011, I was able to return to Lisbon, Luanda, Benguela, and Rio thanks to the support of the Tuck Fund, the Program in Latin American Studies (PLAS), Princeton University, and the "Angolan Roots of Capoeira" project, funded by the University of Essex, United Kingdom, and under the coordination of Matthias Rohrig Assunção. In Lisbon, Cláudia, Amanda, and Nuno became special friends and offered me a place to stay. António Mendes also made his Alfama available, and I thanked him every day for allowing me to see the Tejo while writing. Research is always more interesting when you can discuss it with friends after the archives are closed, and I thank Jelmer Vos, Antônio Wilson Silva de Souza, Marina Torre, Vanessa Oliveira, Ana Paula Madeira, Pablo Gomez, Cristobal Delgado Matas, Ana Flávia Ciccheli Pires, Augusto Nascimento, and Eugénia Rodrigues for discussing many of the ideas present here over dinner, lunch, a bica, or a *fino* over the past several years. I also have to express my thanks to the staff of the Portuguese archives, particularly Jorge Fernando do Nascimento, who microfilmed and digitized many of the documents from the Arquivo Histórico Ultramarino, as well as Fernando José de Almeida, Mário Pires Miguel, and Octávio Félix Afonso.

In Angola, I owe a great debt of gratitude to the staff of the *Arquivo Histórico Nacional*, in particular Domingos Mateus Neto, who always makes my research easier and more entertaining. Rosa Cruz e Silva, formerly director of the archive, now the Minister of Culture, also provided much-needed support at different stages. I also benefited from the help of Bernardo Sá, Bonga, and Fernando Miguel Gonçalo. Massalo, Jean-Michel Mabeko-Tali, Carla, and Hermínia Barbosa kindly hosted me in Luanda over the years. Paulo Valongo, Armando Jaime Gomes, and Kajibanga shared with me their knowledge and helped me to navigate Benguela's archives and libraries. São Neto, Paula Russa, Aida Freudenthal, and Massalo helped to make my trip to Caconda, Dombe

Grande, and Quilengues possible in 2011. Visiting Caconda would not have been possible without the help of Francisco Quina, who offered me a place to stay, fresh bread, and stories of his home town and the recent civil war. Quina also drove me to Lubango and Huíla, making it possible for me to travel further south. Archbishop Dom Damião António Franklin kindly allowed me to do research in the religious archives in Luanda, opening a window into the lives of people usually excluded from official documents. I am very grateful for all those who helped me in Angola, many of whom will remain anonymous but who had a significant impact on my experience there, helping me to navigate markets, archives, churches, kimbos, and libraries. Massalo, Hermínia, Marcia, and Jelmer made my stay in Luanda in 2011 one of the most enjoyable, filled with cheerful conversations accompanied by funge, carapaus, and mufetes.

Kathleen Sheldon read the entire manuscript and helped me to present it in better English. I am especially grateful for her generous insights and suggestions. Eric Crahan at Cambridge University Press has guided me through the process of getting this book published, with lots of attention and patience. Martin Klein and John Thornton, at one time anonymous readers, also read the manuscript carefully and made several suggestions to improve the final result. Paul Lovejoy and Richard Roberts offered me invaluable feedback. I am very thankful for the suggestions and support I have received from these great scholars. I cannot forget the immense support and assistance I have received over the years from archivists and librarians in Angola at the Biblioteca Municipal de Luanda, Arquivo do Arçobispado de Luanda, Arquivo Histórico Nacional, the Biblioteca da Província de Benguela, and the Comarca Judicial de Benguela. In Lisbon, I am grateful to the staff of the Torre do Tombo, Biblioteca Nacional, Sociedade de Geografia de Lisboa, and Arquivo Histórico Militar. I also have to express my gratitude to the librarians and archivists in Rio de Janeiro at the Arquivo Nacional, Instituto Histórico e Geográfico Brasileiro, Arquivos da Cúria Metropolitana, and the Biblioteca Nacional, as well as the Arquivo da Câmara Municipal de Mariana in Minas Gerais. The staff of the Interlibrary Loan and Article Express Offices at Firestone Library also made my research easier while away from Princeton, as well as while at Princeton, quickly locating books and articles from around the world.

Many friends kept me sane during the process of writing, revision, and final submission. Susana Draper shared many of the anxieties and joys of the process. She helped me to put things in perspective, and I am very thankful for her optimism. My colleagues in the history department also offered camaraderie and support, in particular Vera Candiani, Bhavani Raman, Tera Hunter, Jonathan Levy, Katya Pravilova, and Helmut Reimitz. Old and new friends in Brazil, Canada, the United States, Portugal, and Angola also kept me grounded and never let me forget that there is life beyond the archives and my computer screen. Alessandra Carvalho, Gabriela Medina, Hermínia Barbosa, Adriana Trindade, Samantha Quadrat, Cláudia Souza, Mônica Lima, Valesca Cerki, Ana Lucia Araujo, and Wendy Belcher offered me rich friendship and were generous enough to forget my silences, missed calls, and the e-mails I never answered. As always, my parents, Roseli M. Valente Pinho and Roberto José de Alagão e Candido; my sisters, Isabela, Fernanda, Joana, and Marcia; and my grandparents, Alberto José do Carmo Pinho and Nilza Valente Pinho, managed to cheer me up and comfort me despite the distance. I am always grateful for their constant support over the years, especially when studying African history was thought to be a bad career choice in Brazil more than ten years ago. More than anyone, Yacine Daddi Addoun has offered me support, comprehension, and friendship, providing a critical reading of my work and helping me to be a better scholar and person. My thinking and most of this book are owed to innumerable conversations, exchanges, and readings with Yacine.

I dedicate this book to all those who supported me, especially my family and Paul Lovejoy, my mentor and academic role model, who has offered me more help than I could have ever imagined or dared to request. Paul Lovejoy has showed me the importance of fair, collaborative work and a commitment to African history. I hope one day to do justice to him and to be as generous a scholar as he has always been to all those around him.

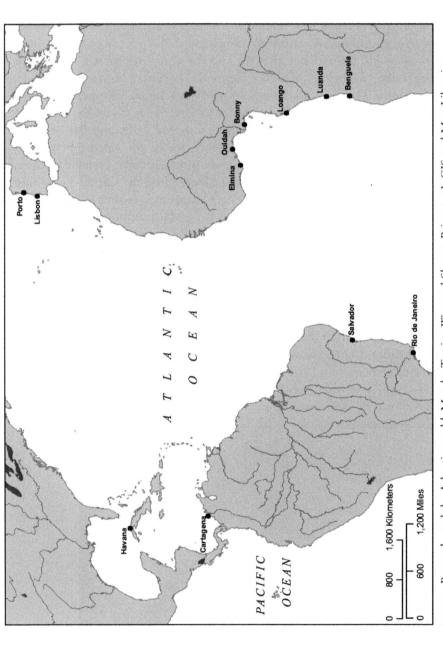

MAP 1. Benguela and the Atlantic world. Map by Tsering Wangyal Shawa, Princeton's GIS and Map Librarian.

Introduction

The port of Benguela was a major outlet for the departure of slaves in the era of the trans-Atlantic slave trade. Scholarship on the slave trade, however, has been focused on the part of the Atlantic and the African continent north of the equator. This book shows that the trans-Atlantic slave trade was a story of the South Atlantic and that Benguela and its population played a major role in that trade. Benguela was at the center of this story, and as I show throughout this book, became integrated into the world economy in the early seventeenth century. From the seventeenth century to the mid–nineteenth century, coastal and inland populations joined the Atlantic commerce, which had a profound effect on the subsequent history of the region and of West Central Africa as whole. In this study I move my analysis inland, following the pattern of both foreign merchants and the Atlantic commerce itself. The result is an analysis of the effects of the trans-Atlantic slave trade not only on the societies along the coast but also on those located inland, exploring political, economic, and social changes, moving away from a scholarship centered on demographic analysis. Although important, quantitative studies have disregarded changes brought about by the slave trade: shifts in how people organized and identified themselves, for example, or how gender dynamics were altered as a result of the sex imbalance. In exploring the political and social effects of the trans-Atlantic slave trade, I engage with a number of themes familiar to specialists on the slave trade and slavery in Africa, including the impact of climate and disease on local and foreign populations, the nature of colonialism and slavery and its intimate link with the slave trade, questions of new social groups and identities, and the overall significance

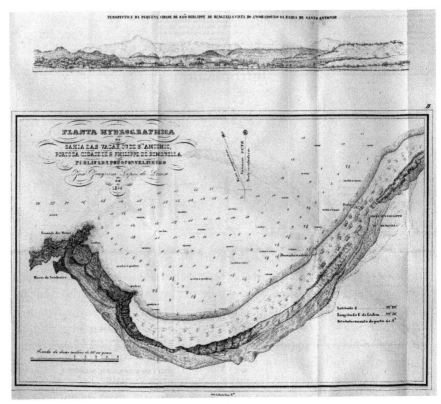

IMAGE 1. "Perspectiva da Pequena Cidade de São Philippe de Benguella, vista do ancoradouro da Bahia de Santo António," in José Joaquim Lopes de Lima, *Ensaios sobre a Statística das Possessões Portuguezas*, vol. 3, part 2 (Lisbon, 1846), between pp. 26–27.

of the trans-Atlantic slave trade on African societies. This study is the first full-length history of Benguela and its hinterland to appear in English. Older histories, notably Ralph Delgado's studies published in Portuguese in the 1940s, defended Portuguese colonialism, reflecting the era in which they were written, when Angola was still under colonial rule.[1] Although Portuguese officials and foreign traders are part of this story, a major role is given to the local African people who inhabited Benguela and its interior.

---

[1] Ralph Delgado, *O Reino de Benguela: do Descobrimento à Criação do Governo Subalterno* (Lisbon: Beleza, 1945); Ralph Delgado, *A Famosa e histórica Benguela. Catálogo dos Governadores, 1779 a 1940* (Lisbon: Cosmos, 1940).

Situated on the central coast of present-day Angola, an indigenous settlement existed in what is now Benguela before the Portuguese invasion in 1617. From the early seventeenth century to 1975, Benguela was a Portuguese colony, sometimes autonomous from the central administration in Angola but generally under Luanda's control. Today, Benguela is the fourth-largest city in Angola, after Luanda, Huambo, and Lobito, with important fishing and agricultural industries. Unlike the castles on the coast of Ghana at Elmina and the Cape Coast, there is no remaining evidence of the fortress that once stood in Benguela, which was destroyed in the twentieth century despite its historical importance. In the beginning of the seventeenth century, soldiers and colonial administrators lived within the fortress. Later on, the settlement expanded beyond the fortress' walls, and in the eighteenth century, new administrative buildings were erected. Although the fortress is gone, reminders of a past that is intimately linked with the trans-Atlantic slave trade can still be seen in Benguela in the Nossa Senhora da Misericórdia Hospital and the Nossa Senhora do Pópulo Church. Regardless of the lack of monuments memorializing the slave trade and the near invisibility of Benguela in the historiography, this past should not be forgotten. The importance of this port in the Atlantic economy is reflected in the presence of people identified as "Benguela" in Brazil and elsewhere in the African diaspora, such as Cuba, Colombia, and Peru. Despite the wealth of historical evidence attesting to its importance, most of the scholarship on the trans-Atlantic slave trade has focused on ports north of the equator. The region where Benguela is situated is referred to as West Central Africa, which incorporates Benguela along with distinct ports such as Loango, Malembo, Cabinda, Ambriz, and Luanda.[2] This broader lens does not reflect how local people organized themselves or even how Europeans identified this region during the era of the slave trade. Rather, it is a cultural unity identified by scholars in the twentieth century and applied retroactively.[3] An

---

[2] Scholars describe West Central Africa as a unified region, although recognizing the plurality of languages, ethnicities, political organizations, and backgrounds. See, for example, David Eltis and David Richardson (eds.), *Extending the Frontiers: Essays on the New Transatlantic Slave Trade Database* (New Haven, CT: Yale University Press, 2008), 19–22; Stephanie E. Smallwood, *Saltwater Slavery: A Middle Passage from Africa to American Diaspora* (Cambridge, MA: Harvard University Press, 2007), 104–5. Stacey Sommerdyk's dissertation discusses some of the incongruences of joining Loango, Luanda, and Benguela as part of the same region, when the organization of the slave trade was profoundly distinct. See "Trade and the Merchant Community of the Loango Coast in the Eighteenth Century," PhD dissertation, Hull University, 2011.

[3] John K. Thornton, *Africa and Africans in the Making of the Atlantic World, 1400–1800* (Cambridge: Cambridge University Press, 1998), 191, 194.

Africanist perspective on the slave trade forces Benguela to be studied in isolation in order to better explore its uniqueness. Only with specific studies will we be able to understand the specificity of the slave trade in different regions of the continent.[4] Thus this book is a contribution to a growing scholarship on African slave ports, redirecting our gaze to the South Atlantic by focusing on the importance of Benguela to the history of Africa, the African diaspora, and the Atlantic world.[5]

The study spans over 200 years. It starts with the first Portuguese expedition in what became known as "Benguela Velha" in the fifteenth century and traces developments until the mid–nineteenth century. In 1850, the Brazilian government banned slave imports, resulting in the decline of Benguela and its population in the Atlantic economy. The emphasis is on African agency, stressing the role of the local population in the transformations during the era of the slave trade. This study dialogues with the literature about African history and the Atlantic world, filling gaps in the scholarship, particularly when related to the role of Benguela in the South Atlantic.[6] The evidence and narrative presented here engage

[4] Lisa A. Lindsay, *Captives as Commodities: The Transatlantic Slave Trade* (Upper Saddle River, NJ: Pearson Prentice-Hall, 2007). For studies emphasizing specificity, see Stacey Sommerdyk, "Rivalry on the Loango Coast: A Re-examination of the Dutch in the Atlantic Slave Trade," in *Trabalho Forçado Africano: O Caminho de Ida*, ed. Arlindo Manuel Caldeira (Porto: CEAUP, 2009), 105–18; and Mariana P. Candido, *Fronteras de Esclavización: Esclavitud, Comercio e Identidad en Benguela, 1780–1850* (Mexico City: El Colegio de Mexico Press, 2011).

[5] See Phyllis Martin, *The External Trade of the Loango Coast, 1576–1870: The Effects of Changing Commercial Relations on the Vili Kingdom of Loango* (Oxford, UK: Clarendon Press, 1972); Robin Law, *Ouidah: The Social History of a West African Slaving "Port" 1727–1892* (Athens: Ohio University Press, 2004); Kristin Mann, *Slavery and the Birth of an African City: Lagos, 1760–1900* (Bloomington: Indiana University Press, 2007). For studies with a strong African perspective on the Atlantic world, see Linda M. Heywood and John K. Thornton, *Central Africans, Atlantic Creoles, and the Making of the Foundation of the Americas, 1585–1660* (New York: Cambridge University Press, 2007); Gwendolyn Midlo Hall, *Africans in Colonial Louisiana: The Development of Afro-Creole Culture in the Eighteenth Century* (Baton Rouge: Louisiana State University Press, 1992); James H. Sweet, *Recreating Africa: Culture, Kinship, and Religion in the African-Portuguese World, 1441–1770* (Chapel Hill: University of North Carolina Press, 2003); Paul E. Lovejoy and David V. Trotman, "Enslaved Africans and their Expectations of Slave Life in the Americas: Towards a Reconsideration of Models of 'Creolisation'," in *Questioning Creole: Creolisation Discourses in Caribbean Culture*, ed. Verene Shepherd and Glen L Richards (Kingston, Jamaica: Ian Randle, 2002), 67–91.

[6] For North Atlantic approaches, see, among others, Peter C. Mancall, *The Atlantic World and Virginia, 1550–1624* (Chapel Hill: University of North Carolina Press, 2007); Toyin Falola and Kevin D. Roberts (eds.), *The Atlantic World, 1450–2000* (Bloomington: Indiana University Press, 2008); and Paul Gilroy, *The Black Atlantic: Modernity and Double Consciousness* (Cambridge, MA: Harvard University Press, 1993). Some

with wider debates about the impact of the trans-Atlantic slave trade on African societies and the economic, political, and cultural development of the South Atlantic system. Instead of a place seen as peripheral, Benguela occupies center stage in this analysis, in which the political, economic, and social changes that altered the region affect not only those who lived there but also the more than 700,000 slaves deported from its port. This book makes several contributions. First, it is the first book-length analysis of the history of Benguela and its hinterland. Second, this study is one of the few in English to emphasize the centrality of the South Atlantic during the era of the trans-Atlantic slave trade. Third, it examines the importance of Brazil and Brazilian-born traders as merchants, colonial administrators, and military personnel, as well as slavers, emphasizing bilateral connections between Portuguese colonies. Fourth, the study demonstrates how involvement in the Atlantic economy led to a series of radical transformations in settlement patterns, political systems, and identities in the hinterland. In short, this book reexamines the effects of the trans-Atlantic slave trade in West Central Africa, moving away from a scholarship that has downplayed its impact. In so doing, it discusses the mechanisms of enslavement and identity formation in the interior of Benguela. Lastly, this is a contribution to the role of women in African history before the mid–nineteenth century. In this study, women are key historical agents, as traders and slaves, and they are not restricted to a single chapter. They are everywhere in this book, which simply acknowledges the fact that there is abundant information on women in Portuguese colonial sources. Women

scholars, mainly writing in Portuguese, have emphasized the specificity of the South Atlantic; see Fernando A. Novais, *Estrutura e Dinâmica do Antigo sistema Colonial (Séculos XVI-XVIII)* (São Paulo: CEBRAP, 1974); José H. Rodrigues, *Brasil e África: outro horizonte* (Rio de Janeiro: Civilização Brasileira, 1961); Manuel dos Anjos da Silva Rebelo, *Relações entre Brasil e Angola, 1808–1830* (Lisbon: Agência Geral do Ultramar, 1970); Corcino M. dos Santos, "Relações de Angola com o Rio de Janeiro (1736–1808)," *Estudos Históricos* 12 (1973): 7–68; and Pierre Verger, "The Influence of Africa on Brazil and of Brazil on Africa," *Journal of African History* 3 (1962): 49–67. For some studies in French, see Pierre Verger, *Flux et Reflux de la traite des Negres entre le Golfe de Benin et Bahia de Todos os Santos, du XVIIe au XIXe siècle* (Paris: Mouton, 1968); and Frederic Mauro, *Le Portugal, le Bresil et L'Atlantique au XVII siecle (1570–1670)* (Paris: Fundação Calouste Gulbenkian, 1983). For some studies in English, see Joseph C. Miller, *Way of Death: Merchant Capitalism and the Angolan Slave Trade, 1730–1830* (Madison: University of Wisconsin Press, 1988); Lauren Benton, "The Legal Regime of the South Atlantic World, 1400–1750: Jurisdictional Complexity as Institutional Order," *Journal of World History* 11, no. 1 (2000): 27–56; Ana Lucia Araujo, *Public Memory of Slavery: Victims and Perpetrators in the South Atlantic* (Amherst, NY: Cambria Press, 2010); and Walter Hawthorne, *From Africa to Brazil: Culture, Identity, and an Atlantic Slave Trade, 1600–1830* (New York: Cambridge University Press, 2010).

traders were in many cases in charge of trade negotiations, serving as a vanguard of colonialism and Atlantic commerce. Each one of these points will be expanded throughout this book and will receive the attention it deserves in subsequent chapters.

The history of Angola and, more specifically Benguela forces us to read-dress the use of conventional labels such as "precolonial" African history in reference to events on the continent before the Berlin Conference in 1884–5 and the partition of Africa among European powers. Like the Cape Colony, Luanda, and Algeria, the indigenous population of Benguela and its hinterland was under colonial subjugation well before the end of the nineteenth century. Thus this book is a history of early Portuguese impe-rialism. Yet it is also a study of the integration of Benguela into the world economy and how this process led to political and social changes in this region. The collapse and emergence of new states inland of Benguela, such as Kakonda and Viye, can only be understood in a context of expanding Portuguese colonialism and the trans-Atlantic slave trade. Although slav-ery probably existed before the arrival of the Portuguese in the region, their demand for captives altered the institution. Slave use expanded, as did raids and other mechanisms employed to capture people. The colo-nial zone on the coast and the establishment of the Portuguese fortress inland altered the landscape, introduced a new language and legal code, and contributed to the development of a local elite associated with the colonial state.

As an Atlantic port, Benguela was one of the major centers of the slave trade for more than 200 years, yet it was a small town with a pop-ulation of only 1,500 to 3,000 people during the period under consid-eration. From 1600 to 1850, the relationship of this port town with the Atlantic world faced changes. It started as an alternative route to the copper mines and inland slave market, but soon it became a major port on its own. Ocean currents favored its development. It was located close to Luanda, the main Portuguese settlement in the African continent. Yet it was difficult to reach Benguela from Luanda. While captains were forced to sail to Benguela to access the northerly coastal currents that would take them toward the port of Luanda, it was extremely difficult to sail from north to south along the coast. Land routes also were a challenge because Kissama, the region between Luanda and Benguela, remained outside Portuguese control for most of the period analyzed here. Thus the population in Benguela, including colonial administrators, foreign and local merchants, and the free and enslaved Ndombe and other groups who moved into the Portuguese zone, enjoyed an unsupervised lifestyle.

Benguela was a Portuguese colony that remained almost completely outside metropolitan control. Even the authorities stationed in Luanda had a difficult time overseeing and controlling the actions of Portuguese officers in Benguela. The governor of Benguela, judges, and other colonial bureaucrats in many ways relished their autonomy to make decisions on the collection of tax, the waging of war, and the punishment of criminals. Conversely, the presence of corrupt officials interested more in personal gain than in colonial consolidation represented a threat to the Portuguese Crown. Officials willing to break the law also were a menace to African rulers and their subjects.

This book engages with a series of debates in the historiography, which its contributions seek to reshape. I will introduce them briefly here and spend the next pages analyzing these major interventions. The first contribution is to reassess the impact of the trans-Atlantic slave trade on African societies. Throughout the book, these effects will be discussed, particularly the growing and devastating power of Atlantic pressure, which favored the decline of old chiefdoms and the growth of new communities and states associated with the Atlantic world. The effects can also be noted in the spread of diseases and environmental crises, as well as in the changing nature of alliances between Portuguese and African rulers. The second cluster of the historiography this study engages concerns the nature of the cultural changes provoked by colonial encounters, which focuses on the debate around creolization in the Atlantic world. As part of colonialism and the expansion of Atlantic commerce, Luso-African societies were formed along the coast and in the interior. This led to the emergence of new social groups, transformed family and household compositions, and eventually remade sexual roles. In sum, contact with the Atlantic world provoked changes to gender relations, as well as the interaction between landlords and strangers. The third debate revolves around the effects of Portuguese colonialism and the expansion of slave societies. The Portuguese presence introduced a new dynamic, linked to association with a global empire and the imposition of colonialism. Local trade was transformed not only in being reoriented toward the coast but also in the nature of the goods desired and the volume of production demanded. The slave trade, which predated arrival of the Portuguese, achieved a new status as the basis of commerce, trade, political ascension, and social relationships. It also accelerated changes to gender roles. The fourth historiographic debate this book engages relates to the expansion of enslavement and slave exports. Cycles of violence had a major impact on African and colonial societies constantly under the threat of warfare. Persistent instability transformed the polities within the Benguela hinterland and was directly connected to changes in commerce and local institutions. I will explain each one of these contributions and show how this study reshapes these debates in the next few pages.

The first historiographic contribution is a major reassessment of the impact of the trans-Atlantic slave trade on African societies. Benguela was not an empty land before the arrival of Portuguese explorers; thus the people who inhabited this territory were profoundly affected by the Portuguese presence and the subsequent pressure of the Atlantic commerce. The largest group that lived along the coast was the Ndombe, who were organized under different chiefdoms along Cattle Bay (Baía das Vacas) and did not constitute a homogeneous group. Agropastoralists, they fished, hunted small birds and animals, and traded with groups established inland. The arrival of Portuguese explorers was probably seen as part of the normal movement of traders, not as an event that would forever alter relationships between the Ndombe and the outside world. The ruler of the state of Peringue,[7] living in what is now the urban center of Benguela, granted the Portuguese the right to trade after receiving a payment of tribute. This was initially seen as a commercial partnership; he did not expect the new arrivals to settle for the long term. Yet the Portuguese had already established merchant communities along the coast of West Africa, including building the fortress of Elmina, and they expected to do the same on the coast of West Central Africa. They failed in Kongo but were successful along the coast of the state of Ngola, where Luanda is now found. Thus, while the ruler of Peringue expected a short-term visit, the Portuguese explorer Manoel Cerveira Pereira intended to settle and establish a Portuguese colony. Different perceptions of trade agreements marked the foundation of the Portuguese colony south of the Kwanza River; however, the local population resisted territorial penetration. Gradually, autonomous states around Benguela entered into contact with the small Portuguese population stationed in the fortress. While most contacts were peaceful and based on exchanging trade goods, in the later seventeenth century, episodes of armed conflict shaped the interactions between the Ndombe and the Portuguese. While some Ndombe rulers managed to remain outside the influence of the Portuguese colony, others signed vassalage treaties that guaranteed

---

[7] Portuguese sources use the same term to refer to both the ruler and the political territory being ruled. Thus the chiefdom and the head of the group are identified by the same term, *Peringue*.

easy access to imported commodities and brought them protection by the Portuguese army, including its firearms, cannons, and gunpowder. Similar to what had happened in the New World, where Spaniards were seen as allies by minor rulers against Aztec expansion, rulers of smaller African communities welcomed Portuguese support against stronger neighbors with whom they were in competition.

The alliances proved to be fatal and represented the end of autonomous political life for most rulers located along the bay of Benguela, demonstrating how the Portuguese presence led to political and economic instability. Yet specialists in West Central African history have claimed that the Atlantic economy and the trans-Atlantic slave trade had only minor impacts on local societies in West Central Africa.[8] Departing from this suggestion of continuity grounded in demographic studies, this book engages with the consequences of the trans-Atlantic slave trade in African societies. This study explores political changes, the collapse of old states and the emergence of new ones, and the subsequent shifts in the ways that people identified themselves. Societies in the interior of Benguela faced violent upheavals associated with the slave trade from its inception. Rulers were killed, removed from power, and co-opted into the trans-Atlantic slave trade from the early seventeenth century through the mid–nineteenth century. Constant competition for resources, subjects, power, and markets threatened alliances between African rulers and imposed fragmented polities with different degrees of connection to the colonial apparatus and the trans-Atlantic slave trade.

Treaties with the Portuguese required the payment of tribute, in most cases in the form of slaves. Rulers also were forced to open their territories to traders and their caravans and to welcome Catholic priests and colonial authorities. In exchange, they gained access to imported commodities. In the short term, this might have resulted in the survival of local political elites. However, in the long term, treaties with the Portuguese allowed the expansion of colonialism; brought about African dependence on imported commodities with a short lifespan, such as alcohol, gunpowder, and textiles; and led to the imposition of new elites who relied on their strong ties to Atlantic commerce. The violence that was

---

[8] John Thornton, "The Slave Trade in Eighteenth Century Angola: Effects of Demographic Structure," *Canadian Journal of African Studies* 14, no. 3 (1980): 417–27; Joseph C. Miller, "The Significance of Drought, Disease and Famine in the Agriculturally Marginal Zones of West-Central Africa," *Journal of African History* 23, no. 1 (1982): 17–61; Joseph C. Miller, *Way of Death: Merchant Capitalism and the Angolan Slave Trade, 1730–1830* (Madison: University of Wisconsin Press, 1988).

required to generate the captives of war who fed the expanding need for cheap labor in the mines of the New World provoked political instability, displaced people who became refugees, and negatively affected agricultural production. Although political competition and warfare predated the arrival of the Portuguese, the level of violence was elevated to previously unknown levels and, once introduced, lasted more than 300 years. The continuous disruption of raids, warfare, and other acts of violence forced the Ndombe and neighboring African groups to restructure the institutions that organized their lives, but they did so without achieving the level of security and prosperity that might have been expected from their involvement in international trade. The demands and transformations imposed by the trans-Atlantic slave trade had a devastating impact on the hinterland of Benguela. As Walter Rodney, Paul Lovejoy, Joseph Inikori, Walter Hawthorne, and Toby Green have shown, we cannot separate economic decline, dependency, and political instability on the African continent at the end of the nineteenth century from the long history of the trans-Atlantic slave trade.[9]

The second historiographic debate this book discusses is the cultural transformation that the inhabitants of this region faced during this tumultuous period, which tends to be called "creolization" in the scholarship.[10] Acknowledging concern about the use of the term "Creole/

---

[9] Walter Rodney, *History of the Upper Guinea Coast: 1545–1800* (New York: Monthly Review Press, 1980); Paul E. Lovejoy, *Transformations in Slavery: A History of Slavery in Africa*, 3rd ed. (Cambridge: Cambridge University Press, 2011); Joseph Inikori (ed.), *Forced Migration: The Impact of the Export Slave Trade on African Societies* (London: Hutchinson, 1982); Walter Hawthorne, *Planting Rice and Harvesting Slaves: Transformations Along the Guinea-Bissau Coast, 1400–1900* (Portsmouth, NH: Heinemann, 2003); Toby Green, *The Rise of the Trans-Atlantic Slave Trade in Western Africa, 1300–1589* (Cambridge: Cambridge University Press, 2011).

[10] Kamau Brathwaite, *The Development of Creole Society in Jamaica, 1770–1820* (Oxford, UK: Clarendon Press, 1971); Ira Berlin, "From Creole to African: Atlantic Creoles and the Origins of African-American Society in Mainland North America," *The William and Mary Quarterly* 53, no. 2, Third Series (April 1996): 251–88; Ira Berlin, *Generations of Captivity: A History of African-American Slaves* (Cambridge, MA: Belknap Press of Harvard University Press, 2003), 24–36; Paul Lovejoy and David Trotman, "Enslaved Africans and their Expectations of Slave Life in the Americas: Toward a Reconsideration of Models of 'Creolisation,'" in *Questioning Creole: Creolisation Discourses in Caribbean Culture*, ed. Verene Shepard and Glen L. Richards (Kingston, Jamaica: Ian Randle, 2002); Roquinaldo Ferreira, "Ilhas Crioulas: O Significado Plural da Mestiçagem Cultural na África Atlântica," *Revista de História* 155, no. 2 (2006): 17–41; Linda M. Heywood and John K. Thornton, *Central Africans, Atlantic Creoles, and the Making of the Foundation of the Americas, 1585–1660* (New York: Cambridge University Press, 2007), 49–106; Jane Landers, *Atlantic Creoles in the Age of Revolutions* (Cambridge, MA: Harvard University Press, 2010).

Crioulo," which has a derogatory meaning in Portuguese,[11] I recognize that these processes of cultural exchange and creation took place. Perhaps the most evident aspect was the formation of Luso-African societies in Benguela and its interior. Men born in Portugal and Brazil crossed the Atlantic, married local women, and gave shape to a mixed generation of Luso-Africans who identified themselves with the colonial state. The descendants of Portuguese and Brazilian men were socially perceived as Portuguese or white. In a region deeply affected by slaving operations, a social classification as Portuguese, white, or a vassal of the Crown protected people from enslavement. The adoption of the Portuguese language and the practice of baptism or marriage in the Catholic Church sometimes were sufficient to mark an individual as a *filho da terra*, or "locally born white," as some Luso-Africans were known. The inability to attract Portuguese women, allied with the high mortality rate of recently arrived foreigners, forced the Portuguese Crown to incorporate the African population into the colonial administration. In Benguela and its interior, Luso-Africans occupied key positions in the administration, exercising the role of captain-major in the inland fortresses, for example, and shaping the way colonialism was inserted into the local population.

I explore the role of creolization and its intimate relations with the slave trade and colonialism. Creolization is understood here as a sociocultural transformation, not the incorporation of Western values or acculturation, as it is often used in an Atlantic context.[12] Presenting sociocultural

---

[11] See the discussion in Chapter 2, as well as Maria da Conceição Neto, "Ideologias, Contradições e Mistificações da Colonização de Angola no Século XX," *Lusotopie* (1997): 327–59; and Beatriz Heintze, "Hidden Transfers: Luso-Africans as European Explorers' Experts in 19th Century West Central Africa," in *The Power of Doubt: Essays in Honor of David Henige*, ed. Paul Landau (Madison: University of Wisconsin Press, 2011), 19–40.

[12] See the excellent discussion on creolization in the Introduction of James H. Sweet, *Domingos Alváres, African Healing, and the Intellectual History of the Atlantic World* (Chapel Hill: University of North Carolina Press, 2011). For influential studies on creolization, see, among others, Linda M. Heywood, "Portuguese into African: The Eighteenth Century Central African Background to Atlantic Creole Culture," in *Central Africans and Cultural Transformations in the American Diaspora*, ed. Linda Heywood (New York: Cambridge University Press, 2002), 91–114; Paul E. Lovejoy and David Vincent Trotman (eds.), "Ethnic Designations of the Slave Trade and the Reconstructions of the History of Trans-Atlantic Slavery," in *Trans-Atlantic Dimensions of Ethnicity in the African Diaspora* (London: Continuum, 2003), 9–42; Hawthorne, *From Africa to Brazil*; Green, *The Rise of the Trans-Atlantic Slave Trade*; Kalle Kananoja, "Healers, Idolaters, and Good Christians: A Case Study of Creolization and Popular Religion in Mid-Eighteenth Century Angola," *International Journal of African Historical Studies* 43, no. 3 (2010): 443–65.

transformations as a unidirectional route can serve to emphasize the Westernization of Africans and deny the fact that most people living in West Central Africa, deliberately or not, ignored Christianity and the adoption of Portuguese names. They also resisted allying themselves with the colonial state and identifying themselves as Portuguese vassals. However, some did, such as the rulers who signed political and commercial treaties and the donas, wealthy merchant women who accumulated human capital, emphasized by Joseph Miller as a characteristic of societies in West Central Africa. Both actors guaranteed protection under Portuguese law and continued to accumulate dependents, mixing different conceptions of power and social capital.[13] While these changes were deeply connected to the presence of Portuguese colonial agents and expansion of the global economy, they simultaneously reflected local processes of transformation, such as the collapse of old states and the emergence of new ones. Political allegiances and the markers by which people identified themselves were altered. The Ndombe and others adopted values associated with the Portuguese presence, whereas at the same time the colonial state incorporated local institutions. For instance, the local ceremony of *undar* was appropriated by the colonial state and served to legitimize Portuguese vassal treaties in the eyes of local people. Originally, it was employed when newly selected rulers assumed power, but political and social pressure transformed the institution, as explored further in Chapter 1. The local *mucano* tribunal, in charge of legal cases and the arbitration of conflicts (and analyzed in Chapter 4), was also adopted by the colonial state. Thus creolization is not understood here as a one-way process but as one in which different actors negotiated elements of each other's culture, adopting those they found relevant in a world facing ongoing transformation.

The significance of creolization is that adjusting to sociocultural changes and new political organizations was not new or unusual for West Central Africans who were captured and exported to the Americas. Like their peers who remained on the African continent, they were used to ongoing social and political transformations; thus the trans-Atlantic venture was another set of experiences in a region in constant reconfiguration. Identity should not be read as synonymous with ethnicity, as Toby Green has warned, but as related to kin, lineage, and connections with

---

[13] For more on the concept of human capital, see Miller, *Way of Death*, 43–53. For more on social capital, see Pierre Bourdieu, *Outline of a Theory of Practice* (Cambridge: Cambridge University Press, 2004), 178–80.

political alliances.[14] People adopted new identities when confronted with expansionist states because they were incorporated by those powerful entities, or were enslaved, or were forced to relocate elsewhere. Identities related to state or language affiliation were superimposed on those of village and lineage, showing how people had multiple identifiers rather than the single one attributed to them by Europeans who could not conceive of identities as flexible and socially constructed. The Ndombe, Kakonda, Viye, and Mbailundu were identifiers related to political allegiance and subject to change, yet Portuguese agents read them as fixed identities, creating the illusion of ethnicities incapable of change, which had devastating effects in the twentieth century.

The third historiographic debate addressed here is the emergence of a slave society on the African continent and the effects of Portuguese colonialism. Benguela and the colonial centers inland became slave societies, where slave labor was not only the main export but also the foundation of the economic and social order.[15] Invested in the Atlantic economy, local traders were the primary impetus for the expansion of slavery and the creation of a colonial society that did not differ much from others around the Atlantic. Like colonial officers, merchants made ample use of slaves in household and commercial activities. In addition, they helped to spread the Portuguese language and Portuguese customs: They were baptized and married in the Catholic Church; they wore pants and shoes; they consumed manioc flour and *cachaça*, an alcoholic beverage produced by slave labor in Brazil; and they carried muskets and handguns.[16] Itinerant traders who traveled inland, surrounded by slaves working as porters and security personnel, represented the Lusophone culture through their

---

[14] Green, *The Rise of the Trans-Atlantic Slave Trade*, 62–3. See also Linda Heywood and John K. Thornton, *Central Africans, Atlantic Creoles, and the Making of the Foundation of the Americas, 1585–1660* (New York: Cambridge University Press, 2007).

[15] For more on slave societies, see Ira Berlin, "Time, Space, and the Evolution of Afro-American Society on British Mainland North America," *American Historical Review* 85, no. 1 (1980): 53–4; and Paul E. Lovejoy, *Transformations in Slavery: A History of Slavery in Africa* (Cambridge: Cambridge University Press, 2000), 1–5.

[16] For the role of merchants as cultural diffusers, see Philip D. Curtin, *Cross-Cultural Trade in World History* (Cambridge: Cambridge University Press, 1984); and Peter Mark, *"Portuguese" Style and Luso-African Identity: Precolonial Senegambia, Sixteenth to Nineteenth Centuries* (Bloomington: Indiana University Press, 2002). For studies on Angola, see Beatrix Heintze, "A Lusofonia no interior da África Central na era pré-colonial. Um contributo para a sua História e Compreensão na Actualidade," *Cadernos de Estudos Africanos* 6–7 (2006): 191–3; Ferreira, "Ilhas Crioulas," 17–41; and Mariana P. Candido, "Merchants and the Business of the Slave Trade at Benguela, 1750–1850," *African Economic History* 35 (2007): 1–30.

lifestyle and became a model for people who lived miles away from the coast. It is easier to quantify the demographic impact of the trans-Atlantic slave trade than to access the social effects of the emergence of a slave society as a result of colonialism. Both provoked the imposition of a new diet, such as the adoption of corn and manioc, and the introduction of new consumption habits, such as the demand for Asian textiles and Brazilian alcohol. Evidence suggests that by the eighteenth century, the population living in the highlands – more than 300 km inland – cultivated New World crops, drank *cachaça*, relied on slave labor for production, baptized their children in small Catholic chapels, and were deeply involved in the Atlantic economy; in short, they had been profoundly transformed. The trans-Atlantic slave trade modified marriage and naming practices, altered eating and dressing habits, and converted merchants into political elites. While acknowledging the importance of demographic studies in revealing the trends and patterns of the trans-Atlantic slave trade, this study emphasizes social, political, and economic changes, particularly the effects of becoming a slave society in the Atlantic basin. Quantitative studies that analyze population exports, natural reproduction, and food production tend to neglect social transformations, such as the dependence of societies on slave labor.[17] Institutions were profoundly altered during the era of trans-Atlantic slave trade, ranging from the emergence of new military and commercial elites, to the introduction of credit, the appearance of new crops, and the rise of innovative patterns of consumption to changes in such personal markers as naming practices, the ways of identifying oneself, and slavery itself.[18]

---

[17] For some of the quantitative-based studies, see Philip D. Curtin, *The Atlantic Slave Trade: A Census* (Madison: University of Wisconsin Press, 1969); David Eltis, *Economic Growth and the Ending of the Transatlantic Slave Trade* (New York: Oxford University Press, 1987); John Thornton, "The Slave Trade in Eighteenth Century Angola: Effects of Demographic Structure," *Canadian Journal of African Studies* 14, no. 3 (1980): 417–27; José C. Curto and Raymond R. Gervais, "The Population History of Luanda during the Late Atlantic Slave Trade, 1781–1844," *African Economic History* 29 (2001): 1–59; David Eltis, Philip Morgan, and David Richardson, "Agency and Diaspora in Atlantic History: Reassessing the African Contribution to Rice Cultivation in the Americas," *American Historical Review* 112, no. 5 (2007): 1329–58.

[18] Several studies have explored institutional changes associated with the slave trade. Among them, see Lovejoy, *Transformations*; Patrick Manning, *Slavery and African Life: Occidental, Oriental, and African Slave Trades* (Cambridge: Cambridge University Press, 1990); José C. Curto, *Enslaving Spirits: The Portuguese-Brazilian Alcohol Trade at Luanda and its Hinterland, c. 1550–1830* (Leiden: Brill Academic Publishers, 2004); Heywood and Thornton, *Central Africans, Atlantic Creoles*; Heintze, "A Lusofonia no interior da África Central," 179–207; Green, *The Rise of the Trans-Atlantic Slave Trade*; George E. Brooks, *Eurafricans in Western Africa* (Athens: Ohio University Press,

These slave societies were ruled by an elite of enslavers and slave merchants who benefited from regional political fragmentation. The emergence of a slave society should be seen as a product of the slave trade – in fact as one of the transformations it provoked, along with intermarriage and the cohabitation of European men with African women, as well as the co-optation of local traders into a system of credit and commerce that required adapting to the demands of the Atlantic trade. As people had previously learned to live with periods of drought and famine, they later had to find ways to survive the threat of warfare, raids, and enslavers' activities.

Colonialism relied on violence. In this book I explore how violence was intrinsic and omnipresent in Benguela, imposing order not only over slaves but also, and perhaps even more dramatically, over free people.[19] In Benguela, as in other slave societies, the use of violence or simply the threat it represented helped to maintain power relationships in which colonial officials and masters terrorized dependents, free and slave, who relied on wealthier and more powerful people for their own survival. Free people feared enslavement and deportation to the Americas and avoided confrontation with the colonial regime at all costs. In Chapter 1, for example, I explain how colonial armies were not only tasked with imposing order in the territories around Benguela during the seventeenth century but also responsible for keeping neighboring rulers at bay. During the eighteenth and nineteenth centuries, colonial force also was employed to maintain order within the colonial center among free people and slaves, as explored in Chapter 2. Power and violence were employed daily through different mechanisms and were integrally connected to the economic structure of a society whose expansion was based on slave raids. The expansion of violence could only exist in a context where that same violence was viewed as acceptable and necessary by the actors involved. Power and violence were inherent to the colonial

---

2003); and Toyin Falola and Paul E. Lovejoy (eds.), *Pawnship in Africa: Debt Bondage in Historical Perspective* (Boulder, CO: Westview Press, 1994).

[19] I am particularly influenced by the studies of Pierre Bourdieu, *Outline of a Theory of Practice* (Cambridge: Cambridge University Press, 2004); Orlando Patterson, *Slavery and Social Death: A Comparative Study* (Cambridge, MA: Harvard University Press, 1982); Boubacar Barry, *Senegambia and the Atlantic Slave Trade* (Cambridge: Cambridge University Press, 1998); Gwendolyn Midlo Hall, *Social Control in Slave Plantation Societies: A Comparison of St. Domingue and Cuba* (Baltimore: Johns Hopkins University Press, 1971); Lovejoy, *Transformations in Slavery*; and Aida Freudenthal, *A Recusa da Escravidão: Quilombos de Angola no século XIX* (Luanda: Museu Nacional de Escravatura, 1996).

state; their use justified and legitimized slavery, colonialism, and social hierarchies. Violence became a central feature within social relations and defined social control and governed interactions between Europeans and local Ndombe in Benguela as well as between African states, slave masters and slaves, whites and blacks, men and women, Luso-Africans and people not integrated into the Atlantic economy. An emphasis on quantitative analysis fails to recognize the prevailing force of violence and its devastating effects on West Central African societies.

The consolidation and expansion of these slave societies were intimately related to the rise and collapse of states in the interior of Benguela. This study shows how people organized their societies, including the calculations and strategies employed by rulers to gain and maintain political control of their territories. It also stresses how women and men of different social status and from different birthplaces interacted in a historical moment of change, conflict, and trade. For the interior states, such as Kalukembe, Mbailundu, and Viye, for example, it is possible to explore how power and prestige were gained and how commercial control was exercised and eventually lost or displaced by the emergence of a new political power. In sum, a broad range of institutions, from chiefdoms to marriage, is seen in a historical perspective not as static, emphasizing change rather than continuity. In this analysis, the period between 1617 and 1850 was marked by human movement, slave raids, and conflict and changes among existing forces. Migration and political reorganization affected the way people associated themselves with their homelands and their rulers, ultimately transforming identities, which have continued to be interpreted in the historiography as fixed and unchanged.[20] Moving away from a historiography that persists in portraying local identities as ahistorical and stable, I show how the Ovimbundu did not constitute a unified group in Benguela's interior during the era of the trans-Atlantic slave trade, challenging Jan Vansina's idea that a dynastic web emerged in this region after 1600 and gave way to a centralized pan-Ovimbundu confederation.[21] Rather than relying on ethnographic data from the early

---

[20] David Birmingham, *Central Africa to 1870: Zambezia, Zaire and the South Atlantic* (Cambridge: Cambridge University Press, 1981), 83–7; Jan Vansina, "Long-Distance Trade Routes in Central Africa," *Journal of African History* 3 (1962), 375–90; Maria Emilia Madeira Santos, *Nos Caminhos da Africa: Serventia e Posse* (Lisbon: IICT, 1998); T. J. Desch Obi, *Fighting for Honor: The History of African Martial Art Traditions in the Atlantic World* (Columbia: University of South Carolina, 2008), 48–50; Heywood and Thornton, *Central Africans*, 94.

[21] Vansina, *How Societies Are Born*, 253–4.

twentieth century, I use contemporary evidence, such as parish records, slave registers, and colonial reports, to explore how people who lived in Benguela and its hinterland identified themselves. The result is the possibility of exploring changes associated with the expansion and transformation of the slave society that in many ways are linked to creolization and cultural changes. Throughout this book I explore how societies were transformed and how cultural changes were perceived by actors in West Central Africa not as an imposition but rather as a way of negotiating a world in flux, which explains why so many people, including those living outside areas nominally controlled by Portugal, baptized their children, as explored in Chapter 5.

A study of Benguela and its links to the interior of West Central Africa allows us to view the dynamics of the slave trade as this small town served as a funnel through which many enslaved Africans moved into the Atlantic world. This leads to the last historiographic debate this study engages: the mechanisms of enslavement and the process of slave export. Unlike other parts of the African continent, where Europeans were limited to the coast and failed to conquer territory, Portuguese officials in Benguela were directly involved in raids, warfare, and other processes of capture. This study challenges the idea that the Portuguese involvement in the process of capture and in the slave trade was minimal and superficial.[22] For the past four decades, historians have steadily emphasized the participation of African rulers and merchants in the slave trade. As a result, the role of Portuguese officers in kidnapping and other violent strategies to reduce Africans to bondage has been minimized.

Cycles of violence and the incessant warfare imposed instability and transformed the polities within the Benguela hinterland. The Atlantic economy and the pressures of enslavement affected political life, judicial systems, and notions of right and wrong. Slave raiding altered the geopolitics of the region. Despite an emphasis in the literature on the gradual movement inland of the slaving frontier, the examples explored in this book, and more specifically in Chapter 4, show that people were captured and enslaved along the coast.[23] The data do not allow me to make

---

[22] The public contest "Maravilhas de Origem Portuguesa no Mundo" in 2009 and the publication of Jonuel Gonçalves, *A Economia ao Longo da História de Angola* (Luanda: União dos Escritores Angolanos, 2011) were the most recent examples of efforts to minimize the Portuguese involvement with the trans-Atlantic slave trade. See Chapter 3 for more details.

[23] For the concept of slaving frontier, see Joseph C. Miller, *Way of Death: Merchant Capitalism and the Angolan Slave Trade, 1730–1830* (Madison: University of Wisconsin Press, 1988), 140–69; and David Birmingham, *Trade and Conflict in Angola: The Mbundu*

definitive quantitative claims, yet the evidence reveals that the majority of people exported as slaves from regions along the coast were primarily enslaved through processes of random violence such as kidnapping. The hinterland of Benguela and the port itself were enmeshed in slave raids from coastal and inland forces that had profound repercussions on political and commercial organization throughout the period. This study ultimately challenges the idea that most people exported from West Central Africa by the nineteenth century came from inland regions by demonstrating how an important number of the people kidnapped were originally from regions along the coast, thus presenting a major revision to the concept of slave frontier in West Central Africa.

Slavery is not seen as social death in this book. The pioneering study of Orlando Patterson explored the violence of the slavery system, although his emphasis on powerlessness, dishonor, and isolation denied the ability of slaves to assert their humanity.[24] Slavery was understood as an institution, and examples explored in this study dismiss the idea of social death. Coastal and inland residents acted, resisted, coped, and transformed their lives in the context of enslavement. Rather than social annihilation, I see invention and adaptation in a very constructive process where African agency is emphasized. The Ndombe, Kakonda, and Mbailundu did not give up and accept enslavement. They continued to live their lives and find meaning in the changes to how they did so. Even when captured, they challenged their enslavement. Although affected by horrifying labor conditions, colonialism, warfare, displacement, and economic deprivation, the inhabitants of Benguela and its interior, as well as those who ended up in the Americas, made their own world.[25]

By studying how slavery and enslavement operated in both Benguela and its interior, we can see how sharply identities diverged between the two. Political allegiance to local rulers or to the Portuguese Crown was

---

and Their Neighbours under the Influence of the Portuguese, 1483–1790 (Oxford, UK: Clarendon Press, 1966); and the discussion in Chapter 4.

[24] Orlando Patterson, *Slavery and Social Death: A Comparative Study* (Cambridge, MA: Harvard University Press, 1982). For a more recent contribution to the idea of slavery as social death, see Smallwood, *Saltwater Slavery*. Other scholars, however, have moved away from the idea of social annihilation, and I am profoundly influenced by their work, especially Audra Diptee, *From Africa to Jamaica: The Making of an Atlantic Slave Society, 1775–1807* (Gainesville: University Press of Florida, 2010), as well as the contributions in Paul E. Lovejoy and David V. Trotman (eds.), *Trans-Atlantic Dimensions of Ethnicity in the African Diaspora* (London: Continuum, 2003); and Hawthorne, *From Africa to Brazil*.

[25] Eugene D. Genovese, *Roll, Jordan, Roll: The World the Slaves Made* (New York: Vintage Books, 1976).

the main source of identification in Benguela. The main characters of this narrative saw themselves as subjects of the rulers of Ndombe, Kakonda, Kilengues, Viye, or Wambu. Sometimes they also saw themselves as Portuguese subjects, *filhos da terra*, or Luso-Africans. The inhabitants of Benguela's hinterland were not members of the same political or social community, a fact that is essential to understanding enslavement in the region. As in other regions, only on a very few occasions did people enslave fellow citizens, and when it happened, it was mainly due to judicial condemnation. Criminals were enslaved and banished overseas in the same way that Europeans exported their criminals to their colonies. In most cases, however, slavers captured enemies, people who spoke a different language, worshiped different ancestors, or held different political allegiances. People enslaved outsiders, not fellow countrymen and women. Thus the political fragmentation of Benguela's hinterland and the absence of a unified sense of community help to explain the more than 200 years of involvement in the trans-Atlantic slave trade. Although the work of missionaries and anthropologists has emphasized cultural and linguistic homogeneity before the twentieth century, available evidence indicates that the same did not apply to political identity.[26] In the seventeenth, eighteenth, and the first half of the nineteenth centuries, the people who inhabited the land between the coast and the highlands lived under a variety of polities, of different sizes and organizational structures. People were not seen as part of the same linguistic or political group, which explains why they raided each other. The sense of unity came about after the trans-Atlantic slave trade and probably was shaped by the arrival of missionaries in the late nineteenth century and early twentieth century, although no study has yet historicized the construction of the Ovimbundu ethnicity. Thus "Ovimbundu," "Nyaneca," and other ethnic labels familiar to any Angolan or Angolan specialist were the result of historical processes subsequent to the end of the trans-Atlantic slave trade and were absent from the documents consulted in this study.

Whereas much of the literature on the trans-Atlantic slave trade focuses on the coast, the Middle Passage, and the arrival in the New

---

[26] For some studies that emphasize unity, see Gladwyn M. Childs, "Chronology of the Ovimbundu Kingdoms," *Journal of African History* 11 (1970): 241–8; Wilfrid D. Hambly, *The Ovimbundu of Angola* (Chicago: Field Museum of Natural History, 1937); Jan Vansina, *Paths in the Rainforest: Toward a History of Political Tradition in Equatorial Africa* (Madison: University of Wisconsin Press, 1990); and John K. Thornton, *Africa and Africans in the Making of the Atlantic World, 1400–1800* (New York: Cambridge University Press, 1998), xxxv–xxxvi.

World, this book takes us deep into the African interior and allows us to see the very beginning of what would be the long journey to slavery on the opposite side of the Atlantic.[27] The role of Benguela in the Atlantic economy was evident from its foundation in the early seventeenth century. The Portuguese *asientos* in Spanish America allowed the deportation of war captives and initiated the trans-Atlantic slave trade. The history of Benguela and its hinterland cannot be understood in isolation from the Atlantic world. In this book, the movement across the Atlantic and the effect it had on local societies, both on the coast and in the interior, cannot be disassociated from Brazil's outsized presence in the local imagination. Brazil, the only Portuguese colony in the Americas, was the destination of most of the people forcibly exported through the port of Benguela. In return, colonial officials, traders, and *degredados*, the infamous exiles of the Portuguese empire, regularly arrived in Benguela. The colony of Brazil was a model for Portuguese administrators, who copied its slave society in colonial centers in West Central Africa. For the African population of Benguela and its interior, Brazil was a threat, a place to be avoided.

This book contributes to a larger discussion on the Atlantic world, slavery, imperialism, and identity formation. It is heavily indebted to the works of specialists on West Central Africa and to those who have worked on slavery and the slave trade in Africa and in the diaspora, who have propelled the debates I raise here. This study is also a contribution to a past that most people in Benguela, preoccupied and traumatized by the civil war that devastated Benguela's interior, do not see as relevant. Although local rulers and merchants actively participated in the capture, sale, and deportation of more than 700,000 people from the port of Benguela, those were not fair exchanges, and they lost much more than they gained

---

[27] Smallwood, *Saltwater Slavery*; Law, *Ouidah*; Kristin Mann, *Slavery and the Birth of an African City: Lagos, 1760–1900* (Bloomington: Indiana University Press, 2007); and William St. Clair, *The Door of No Return: The History of Cape Coast Castle and the Atlantic Slave Trade* (New York: BlueBridge, 2007). For other titles that have explored changes in inland societies, see G. Ugo Nwokeji, *The Slave Trade and Culture in the Bight of Biafra: An African Society in the Atlantic World* (Cambridge: Cambridge University Press, 2010); Walter Hawthorne, *Planting Rice and Harvesting Slaves: Transformations Along the Guinea-Bissau Coast, 1400–1900* (Portsmouth, NH: Heinemann, 2003); Robin Law, *The Oyo Empire, c.1600–c.1836: A West African Imperialism in the Era of the Atlantic Slave Trade* (Oxford, UK: Clarendon Press, 1977); Olatunji Ojo, "Warfare, Slavery and the Transformation of Eastern Yorubaland c.1820–1900," PhD dissertation, York University, 2003; Jan Vansina, "Ambaca Society and the Slave Trade c. 1760–1845," *Journal of African History* 46, no. 1 (2005): 1–27; and Joseph C. Miller, *Kings and Kinsmen: Early Mbundu States in Angola* (Oxford, UK: Clarendon Press, 1976).

in bottles of alcohol, beads, and textiles. Their agency made them victims of the trans-Atlantic slave trade, whose violent consequences left no one untouched. Much has been written about the agency of Africans in the slave trade, which risks underrepresenting the motivations and role of Europeans. This study stresses the participation of Portuguese- and Brazilian-born agents in processes of capture and enslavement, along the coast and in the interior, challenging the idea that the Portuguese involvement in the process of capture and in the slave trade was minimal and a side effect of the availability of captives of war. This perspective is not to deny that some rulers enslaved enemies or criminals. Rather, it is an effort to reach a more balanced appraisal of the role of all actors and see the past as a shared responsibility. Although slavery probably existed before the arrival of the Portuguese in the region, the Portuguese demand for captives altered the institution and incited violence. As in other cases, colonialism in Benguela was intimately related to slavery, the control over women's and men's bodies, circulation, and rights.[28] Slavers and slaves labored to produce wealth elsewhere. Although their names are not remembered in history books or monuments, their cultural legacy and the presence of their descendants are a testimony to their importance in West Central Africa and in the African diaspora. And their actions should not be forgotten or dismissed.

The research for this book was an Atlantic enterprise involving archives and libraries in Angola, Portugal, Brazil, Canada, and the United States. I relied on colonial documents produced by Portuguese, Brazilian, and African agents. Reports, official letters, censuses, export data, parish records, and official chronicles revealed interesting details about the lives of those who resided in and around Benguela. Although I made use of the published oral traditions collected by missionaries and anthropologists in the early twentieth century, I opted to focus my attention on the rich archives available in Luanda and Benguela, which provided written documents for the early history of West Central Africa. The decades of anticolonial and civil armed conflict in Angola affected my research as much as the work of the many other historians who have preceded me. Unable to visit some of the towns and villages mentioned extensively in this book until July 2011, I centered my research in the Arquivo Histórico Nacional,

---

[28] Pamela Scully, *Liberating the Family?: Gender and British Slave Emancipation in the Rural Western Cape, South Africa, 1823–1853* (Portsmouth, NH: Heinemann, 1997), 9–11; and Edna G Bay, *Wives of the Leopard: Gender, Politics, and Culture in the Kingdom of Dahomey* (Charlottesville: University of Virginia Press, 1998), 142–53.

the Biblioteca Municipal, and the Arquivo do Arçobispado de Luanda, all located in Luanda. Caconda, Quilengues, and many of the locations in the interior of Benguela had been surrounded by land mines until recently, which inevitably made any research a risk and, moreover, resulted in the migration and displacement of the inhabitants of the highlands. I did research in the Comarca Judicial de Benguela and in the Biblioteca da Província de Benguela in Benguela, but most documents found there referred to the end of the nineteenth century, a period not covered in this book. Peace and the repair of the roads, as well as an increasing sense of security, certainly will reveal more documents produced not only by colonial agents but also by African courts.[29] My work draws heavily on archival records in part because few studies have focused on Benguela. I have made use of some of the official colonial histories from the early twentieth century, such as those organized by Ralph Delgado, but the focus of this study is not to celebrate Portuguese colonialism.

Aware of the limitations of the colonial documents, I focused on the information they contained about Africans, although most of the available evidence presents a very partial view of the past. It was a great surprise to find so many references to women and slaves in these documents. For many decades, historians have believed that it was difficult, perhaps even impossible, to include women and slaves in precolonial African history. Portuguese documents, however, are filled with references to both groups. Although this book is not a history of women, they play a central role in my analysis. Enslaved or free, rich or dispossessed, women shaped the history of Benguela and its interior and played a major role in integration of the region and its population into the Atlantic world. Court cases and parish records provide significant space and scope to women, slaves, and other groups absent from most documents.

Portuguese colonial documents also reveal information on groups that have long since disappeared. Oral traditions collected in the early twentieth century provide information on the formation of the major states in the central highlands. Yet they were silent on the history of groups and states that had disappeared. Civil war in the twentieth century forced

---

[29] Catarina Madeira Santos, "Écrire le Pouvoir en Angola. Les archives Ndembu (XVIIe–XXe siècles)," *Annales. Histoire, Sciences Sociales* 4 (2009): 767–95; Ana Paula Tavares and Catarina Madeira Santos, *Africæ monumenta: Arquivo Caculo Cacahenda* (Lisbon: Instituto de Investigação Científica Tropical, 2002); and Evá Sebestyén, Jan Vansina, and Manoel Correia Leitão, "Angola's Eastern Hinterland in the 1750s: A Text Edition and Translation of Manoel Correia Leitão's 'Voyage' (1755–1756)," *History in Africa* 26 (1999): 299–364.

the inhabitants of Benguela's highlands to relocate elsewhere, showing that the continuous wave of migrations had not ended with abolition of the trans-Atlantic slave trade. Twentieth-century wars in Angola resulted in the premature death of the members of younger and older generations, altering how oral traditions are remembered. Thus important *sobas* (rulers) disappeared from collective memory and are currently considered unimportant, such as Joanes Gaspar, a Ndombe ruler from Dombe Grande who is discussed in greater detail in Chapter 4.[30] Portuguese accounts, however, reveal the existence of *sobas* in earlier times and sometimes report their disappearance. Through official reports we can follow the rise and decline of states, although these sources are limited and focus only on the ruling class. In order to construct a social history of the region, I have relied on myriad sources. The data, however, do not necessarily answer every question. Much of the African past remains blurred since documents were produced by Europeans who were not concerned with topics of interest to historians today.[31] However, the gaps and silences are revealing, indicating what may have been destroyed, transformed, and created by the actors involved.

In this study, written documents are seen as artifacts of knowledge, as defined by Michel Foucault, shaping and mediating relationships between colonizers and colonized, subjects and rulers, creating a clean-cut binary world that dismissed the struggles, clashes, and negotiations that characterized power struggles.[32] As with all history, my interpretation of the

[30] I was able to interview Vivo Maquiqui, from Cangombe Inglês, and Gonçalves Paulo, from Dombe Grande, and neither recalled any ruler beyond four generations. No one remembered Joanes Gaspar, who ruled in Dombe Grande in the 1840s and was a major ally of the Portuguese. This example demonstrates how in certain circumstances the only way to reconstruct the past is to rely on written documents. I am very thankful to Matthias Assunção, who brought to my attention these two *sobas*; Paula "Russa" Gomes, who facilitated the interviews; and Marcia C. Schenck, who helped me in the process. For more on the Ndombe, see Candido, "Slave Trade and New Identities in Benguela," 59–75.

[31] See Peter Burke (ed.), *New Perspectives on Historical Writing* (University Park: Pennsylvania State University Press, 2001); Jacques Le Goff and Pierre Nora (eds.), *Constructing the Past: Essays in Historical Methodology* (Cambridge: Cambridge University Press, 1985); Jan Vansina, *Kingdoms of the Savanna* (Madison: University of Wisconsin Press, 1966); Jan Vansina, *Living with Africa* (Madison: University of Wisconsin Press, 1994); Eric Hobsbawn, "History from Below: Some Reflections," in *History from Below: Studies in Popular Protest and Popular Ideology in Honour of George Rude* (Montreal: Concordia University, 1985).

[32] Michel Foucault, *La Arqueología del Saber* (Buenos Aires: Siglo XXI, 2002). See also Ann L. Stoler, *Along the Archival Grain: Epistemic Anxieties and Colonial Common Sense* (Princeton, NJ: Princeton University Press, 2009); Bhavani Raman, "The Familial World of the Company's *kacceri* in Early Colonial Madras," *Journal of Colonialism and Colonial History* 9, no. 2 (2008).

documents recreates a story, a constructed narrative that tries to imagine order from a mass of primary sources, not necessarily organized and cataloged. I selected the documents to be incorporated and the format of the narrative, giving shape to the past. This narrative is a "verbal fiction," as defined by Hayden White, profoundly influenced by my vision of the world, my place of origin, my political opinions, and the story I felt compelled to tell.[33] This study is the result of my reflections on the importance of an Afrocentric approach to history, which grew out of my discontent with how Africans and Africa are frequently portrayed in North America. African societies are almost invisible, and when they receive some attention, it is as a place of poverty, exoticism, sensuality, and foreign intervention. This book is also my intervention in a historiography dominated by a North-South approach, where non-Anglophones tend to play minor roles, the African past is seen as essentially a space where great men took action, and women and slaves are seen as minor actors.

Examining the slave trade at Benguela contributes to the history of slavery and the history of West Central Africa by reconstructing the experiences of the affected population in an effort to understand the complexity of the political, social, and economic transformations imposed by the trans-Atlantic slave trade. These sources reveal that Benguela is not an exception. Like the changes that affected Senegambia or southern Africa, Benguela and its hinterland were a region deeply transformed by the Atlantic economy. Migration and violence were constant features of life for the people who lived in the region. This study offers a detailed history of the port and its hinterland, particularly of the people who made these places and inserted them into the global economy.

The Chapters

The first two chapters of this book offer a chronologic history of Benguela, laying the groundwork for a more thematic approach in the remaining three chapters. Chapter 1 focuses on the early history of Benguela, including the abandoned settlement of Benguela-Velha, from the sixteenth to the early eighteenth centuries. It traces the chronology of the Portuguese

---

[33] Hayden V. White, *Metahistory: The Historical Imagination in Nineteenth-Century Europe* (Baltimore: Johns Hopkins University Press, 1973), 1–42. For more on the role of the historian on language selection and the creation of the narrative, see, among others, Paul Ricoeur, *Time and Narrative*, vol. 1 (Chicago: The University of Chicago Press, 1984), 52–75; and Natalie Zemon Davis, *Fiction in the Archives: Pardon Tales and Their Tellers in Sixteenth Century France* (Stanford, CA: Stanford University Press, 1987).

relationship with local rulers, the lure of copper, and the first slave raids. I explain how colonial armies were responsible for imposing order in the territories around Benguela during the seventeenth century and keeping neighboring rulers at bay. The chapter discusses the importance of Benguela in the seventeenth century and how it related to Portuguese conceptions of overseas empire. I also resuscitate the debate on the *jagas*, dormant since 1981; explore the Dutch attacks in the 1640s; and examine the formation of a colonial society with strong links to Brazil and the African interior. The analysis reveals the existence of disputes, fissures, and tensions between colonial authorities in Benguela, in Luanda, and in Lisbon. The internal conflicts help to clarify the history of the colony in the seventeenth century, where the Portuguese used some of the same strategies that characterized colonies in other parts of the Portuguese empire, such as Brazil and Goa, but also shows the implementation of structures, such as indirect rule, seen in the late nineteenth century in Africa.

Chapter 2 traces the history of Benguela from 1710 to 1850, using the cessation of attacks by competing European powers as a beginning point and the termination of slave imports in Brazil as an ending marker. The chapter deals with the relationship between the colonial center and neighboring polities. It explores how changes in Portugal in the eighteenth century, including increased fiscal control over the overseas territories, led to the expansion of colonial bureaucracy and administration. The chapter also focuses on the population who inhabited the area surrounding the port. During the eighteenth and nineteenth centuries, colonial force maintained order within the colonial center among free people and slaves. Power and violence were employed daily through different mechanisms and were integrally connected to the economic structure of a society whose expansion was based on slave raids. In Chapter 2 I also discuss the establishment of a slave society and a Luso-African community, both connected to and influenced by events in the Atlantic and in the interior. Violence was crucial in the process and shaped the nature of the relationships between colonial officers and local Ndombe people, African rulers and subjects, slave owners and slaves, and men and women – in short, the entire population, including those not directly participating in the Atlantic world. The chapter also explores the increasingly close links between Benguela and Brazilian ports during the eighteenth century and the early nineteenth century, consolidating a South Atlantic partnership of elites.

The focus of Chapter 3 is the role of Benguela in the Atlantic economy. The analysis is centered on the participation of traders and residents of

Benguela in the South Atlantic world. It explores how the location of the port favored its emergence. Through an analysis of the length of slave voyages and the resulting mortality rates, it becomes clear how slave traders came to prefer exporting captives from Benguela to Brazil, a practice that reinforced their bilateral connections. The chapter also discusses trade with Spanish America in the seventeenth century and its transformation in the subsequent centuries to rely primarily on Brazilian ports. Moreover, the chapter follows the circulation of imported goods in the central highlands and demonstrates how slave routes imposed new habits and styles in the interior. In this chapter I also show how the reliance of the scholarship on demographic analysis has mistakenly emphasized continuity rather than rupture. My attention is on the social changes associated with expansion of the trans-Atlantic slave trade: changes in gender dynamics with the enrichment of female traders; the adoption of new crops, such as maize and manioc, and the new dietary patterns that resulted; and new consumption habits, such as the growing demand for *cachaça*, Portuguese wine, Asian textiles, beads, gunpowder, cloth items, and paper. Through a variety of examples, I show how even those societies located far away from the coast were deeply affected by the Atlantic market and the new habits it engendered. The role of colonial officials in the expansion of violence inland is also analyzed, as well as their involvement in raids, slave acquisition, negotiations, and transport to the littoral. Europeans were not limited to the coast, as in other parts of Africa before the mid–nineteenth century. In Benguela, Portuguese officials conquered territory, helped to expand the limits of the Portuguese empire, and were directly involved in raids, warfare, and other processes of enslavement.

In Chapter 4 I discuss the mechanisms of capture and enslavement in Benguela and its interior. While warfare was an important mechanism that combined colonial expansion with raids and enslavement, some cases from the second half of the eighteenth century and first half of the nineteenth century reveal the prevalence of kidnapping and debt enslavement in regions not far from the port. Places of enslavement close to the coast meant that many of the people who were deported from Benguela had been exposed to colonialism and the Atlantic economy before arriving in the Americas. The cases detailed in this chapter also allow us to see enslavement in its concrete details rather than as an abstract process, including through legal cases where people regained their freedom. Moreover, it demonstrates that social and political networks and institutions at times could react quickly to protect loved ones and dependents. Contributing to and benefiting from a historiography that has focused on the demographic analysis of the trans-Atlantic slave trade, I explore how raids and enslavement affected individuals rather than groups, which will be the focus of Chapter 5. Portuguese colonialism and the Atlantic demand for a constant supply of slaves generated violence, which was endemic in Benguela and its hinterland. Structures were put in place to protect against "illegal enslavement," creating an arbitrary division between those who could and could not be enslaved.

Chapter 5 focuses on the interior of Benguela, particularly on Caconda, exploring the political changes around this Portuguese fortress and in the central highlands. While Chapter 4 explored cases of enslavement, Chapter 5 deals with political reconfigurations in the context of the Atlantic economy. Primary sources reveal the composition of the society established 200 km inland at Caconda, which permits an investigation into the effects of the Atlantic slave trade on societies located away from the coast. The chapter also analyzes how the transfer of Caconda to the Katala region in the 1760s altered the landscape and favored an expanded Portuguese presence. The last sections of the chapter deal with three major states in the central plateau, Wambu, Mbailundu, and Viye, and their historical interactions with colonialism and the trans-Atlantic slave trade. The analysis reveals the lack of a unified identity or any sense of belonging to a common political, cultural, or economic group. Competition and warfare emphasized animosity and prevented the formation of a unified coalition against the expanding Atlantic pressure. No sense of Ovimbundu identity existed in Benguela's hinterland before 1850, which certainly affected how the people exported from these regions organized their lives in the diaspora.

This chapter also explores how creolization moved inland, looking at the expansion of new naming and marriage practices in Caconda, Kitata, and Ngalangue, indicating that creolization was not limited to the coast. Moreover, this chapter stresses the expansion of creolization into areas beyond the control of the Portuguese Crown, where people living under autonomous rulers chose to baptize their children, suggesting that such practices could be used as mechanisms of protection against the threats of violence and enslavement. Assuming new identities – as Portuguese vassals, Luso-Africans, or Catholics – therefore was a means through which individuals in Benguela's hinterland could protect themselves against the dangers generated by the Atlantic economy. There have been decades of debate over conceptions of ethnicity on the African continent, but specialists on Angolan history have failed to engage with these ideas before the end of the nineteenth century. In this book I emphasize how the reconfiguration of identity was a constant process in Benguela and its hinterland during the era of the trans-Atlantic slave trade. People assumed new allegiances and inscribed themselves into new communities, forging new social, political, and economic networks as a means of protection from raids, warfare, and enslavement. Yet the resulting identities were fluid and subject to change, depending on a series of variations, offering the important point that the major ethnic groups that came to dominate Angolan politics in the twentieth century were absent as coherent and unified forces prior to 1850.

In sum, this study explores the history of the port of Benguela from the initial relationship established between the local Ndombe population and the Europeans beginning in the mid–sixteenth century. It shows how slave exports to Spanish America and copper exploitation were the driving forces in the early colonial era. The study follows the rise of Benguela as a slaving port in the eighteenth century, which was intimately related to the expansion of slavery in Brazil, and explores the formation of a slave society with strong links to the Atlantic world. I also examine the role of warfare, kidnapping, judicial cases, and debt, among other mechanisms, in reducing people to bondage. Another important factor was the participation of colonial agents, mainly those born in Europe and Brazil, in the processes of enslavement. The study concludes with an examination of the rearrangement of the political landscape around Benguela and its interior, which resulted in the collapse of old polities and the emergence of new states deeply involved in the capture and sale of slaves. In short, this book reexamines the effects of the trans-Atlantic slave trade in West Central Africa, stressing how local societies were profoundly transformed by their contact with the Atlantic world. In so doing, *An African Slaving Port on the Atlantic World* "re-Capricornizes the Atlantic,"[34] emphasizing the importance of bilateral connections in the South Atlantic in order to understand trends and paradigms in Atlantic history beyond those based on a North Atlantic perspective.

Note on Spelling

Colonial sources present different spellings for the same location and are inaccurate if compared with modern maps. Language and spelling are, naturally, the result of historical circumstances; many toponyms in

---

[34] Peter Beattie, "'ReCapricorning' the Atlantic," *Luso-Brazilian Review* 45, no. 1 (2008), 1–5.

Umbundu could be spelled in different ways. When referring to places and towns that still exist, I have employed their present-day spelling in Portuguese, as used in current maps of Angola. For example, I use Caconda or Quilengues to refer to the Portuguese colonial settlements. When referring to places that are not present in current maps of Angola, I have followed the spelling used in recent publications by other scholars. For political organizations, people, and titles, I have followed the orthographic conventions of African languages. Thus it is Kakonda and Kilengues when referring to the state and its subjects, as well as Wambu and Mbailundu. I am aware that the characters of the history recounted here did not necessarily employ the terms used in sources and in this book to designate a state, its ruler, or subjects. It is not clear how the subjects of Peringue, Kikombo, or Sokoval referred to themselves. The spelling of group names was determined by colonial officials, not by the speakers themselves.

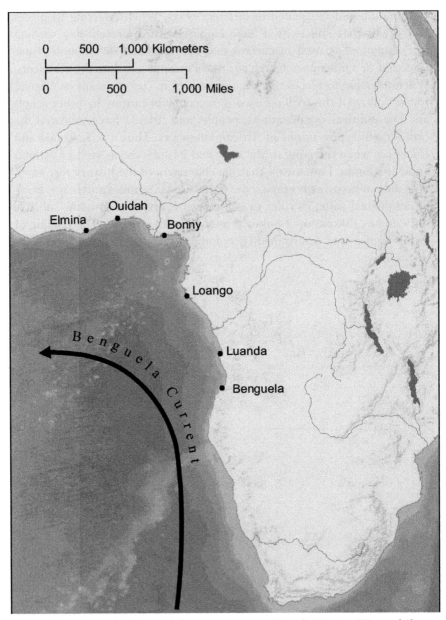

MAP 2. West Central Africa and the ocean currents. Map by Tsering Wangyal Shawa, Princeton's GIS and Map Librarian.

Contacts, Competition, and Copper

Benguela until 1710

Interactions of local populations with outsiders marked the early history of what came to be known as Benguela. Later on, the arrival of Europeans added to this mix of cultural contacts, accommodation, and competition. Limited sources contain information on the inhabitants of Benguela before its foundation, and they were produced by outsiders. Yet they emphasize fluidity and mobility of the population. No local written sources have been located, and archeological diggings and research have been affected by armed conflict and land mines in the recent past.[1] Oral traditions suggest the place was known as *ombaka*, literally "commercial entrepot" in Umbundu, before the arrival of the Portuguese, revealing its importance as a place of interactions in early times. Another interpretation claims that *ombaka* referred to the title of a woman who ruled among the Ndombe, not exactly the territory.[2] Site of a market, the location was a space where different people met, interacted, and exchanged goods. It also suggests that trade between the coast and the interior predates

---

[1] Teams of the Museu Nacional de Arqueologia, based in Benguela, have been excavating around Benguela and the Baía Farta since 2007, after decades of interruption during the armed conflict in Angola. Yet more diggings and analysis have to be performed to increase our knowledge about Benguela's past before the sixteenth century. I am very grateful to the director of the museum, Paulo Valongo, who kindly received me in Benguela during the summer of 2011. Paula Gomes also offered invaluable help. Carlos Ervedosa's studies are key for the archeology in Benguela. See Carlos Ervedosa, *Arqueologia Angolana* (Lisbon: Edições, 70, 1980), 70.

[2] See Luis Figueira, *África Bantu: Raças e tribus de Angola* (Lisbon: Fernandes, 1938), 239; and A. Hauenstein, "Noms accompagnés de proverbes, chez les Ovimbundu et les Humbi du Sud de l'Angola," *Anthropos* 57, nos. 1–2 (1962): 107.

the Portuguese arrival, even if based on relay trade similar to what was happening in Western Africa and Southern Africa.[3]

This chapter presents the early history of the port as marked by strong contacts with neighboring populations. The goal is to present a narrative that recaptures the history of Benguela in the sixteenth and seventeenth centuries, which in many ways shaped the subsequent interactions of Portuguese colonial agents with the local population. Founded to supply the Portuguese empire with copper and slaves, at various times the port was invaded by both European and African forces. Despite that insecurity, the port became the administrative center of the colony. At the mouth of the Catumbela River, the early settlement was located in a natural bay whose abundance of fish, mammals, and birds attracted people. Archeological research shows that the Bay of Benguela and Farta Bay, located a few miles away, were inhabited by people who used hand axes and chopping tools, knew metallurgy, and produced ceramic pots. They hunted small birds and fish along the coast.[4] Reports from the nineteenth century refer to people sailing on fishing canoes south of Benguela and collecting mollusks, yet it is not clear if ocean sailing was common in this region of West Central Africa before the arrival of the Portuguese.[5] Thus, when the Portuguese arrived there, they did not find an empty land, but a territory occupied by communities ruled by local systems of governance. In fifteenth-century Portuguese documents, the name Benguela did not designate the place known today by that name. It referred to a port founded by the Portuguese in 1587, north of the Cuvo River, an early settlement that was soon abandoned. Only in 1771 did the Portuguese return to that port and rename it Porto Amboim. In 1617, a new Benguela was founded south of the Catumbela River. Thus all references to Benguela before 1617 refer to what later became known as Benguela-Velha, old Benguela, and, in the eighteenth century, Porto Amboim.

[3] Philip D. Curtin, *Cross-Cultural Trade in World History* (Cambridge: Cambridge University Press, 1984), 25–7; Toby Green, *The Rise of the Trans-Atlantic Slave Trade in Western Africa, 1300–1589* (Cambridge: Cambridge University Press, 2011), 35–52.

[4] There is very little archeological research done in Benguela. See Luís Joaquim Marques Pais Pinto, "Arqueologia da Faixa Sedimenral de Benguela. A Idade da Pedra e do Ferro," *Leba* 7 (1992): 203–20.

[5] John Purdy, *The New Sailing Directory for the Ethiopic or Southern Atlantic Ocean* (London: R. H. Laurie, 1844), 414–5. On sailing before contact with the Portuguese, see Maria Emilia Madeira Santos, "Os Africanos e o mar: Conhecimento e Práticas à Época da chegada dos Portugueses," *Africa: Revista do Centro de Estudos Africanos* 20–1 (1997–8): 79–92; John K. Thornton, *Africa and Africans in the Making of the Atlantic World, 1400–1800* (Cambridge: Cambridge University Press, 1998), 19–20; Francisco Travessos Valdez, *Six Years in a Traveler's Life in Western Africa* (London: Hurts and Blackett, 1861), 74–6.

The first contact between the Portuguese and the people who lived on the littoral south of the Kwanza River occurred in the late sixteenth century. The Portuguese Regimento (government orders) of 1546 referred to a Kingdom of Benguela, south of the Kingdom of Angola, where "many kings and heathen lords lived."[6] In 1563, the priest António Mendes mentioned land disputes between the King of Benguela and the King of Angola, as if there was a single ruler south of the Kwanza River.[7] By 1586, the ruler of Benguela, although it is not clear which one and who he was, requested "friendship" with the King of Portugal and was described as having control of a "wealthy land, with many mines."[8] Following this political alliance, new expeditions were sent south of the Kwanza. Yet little is known about the exact location of the so-called Kingdom of Benguela or the people who lived there. From the few sixteenth-century reports available, it is clear that the Portuguese assumed that there was a single ruler in the region, in a fashion similar to what they had met in the region north of the Kwanza River in Kongo, Ngola, or Ndongo. However, seventeenth-century official correspondence indicates the existence of multiple rulers in the region and a wide variety of polities, from centralized large-scale states to chiefdoms, which were smaller political organizations in scale and population that often exhibited cyclic instability. Both structures, however, relied on hierarchies and social complexity.[9]

Unaware of the difference between Kongo, Ndongo, and the population south of the River Kwanza, Portuguese agents proceeded with the same approach of identifying a ruler and working on his conversion and

---

[6] Ilídio do Amaral, *O Reino do Congo, os Mbundu (ou Ambundos), o Reino dos "Ngola" (ou de Angola) a Presença Portuguesa de Finais do Século XV a Meados do Século XVI* (Lisbon: Instituto de Investigação Científica Tropical, 1996), 85–6.

[7] António Brásio, *Monumenta Missionária Africana*, vol. 2 (Lisbon: Agência do Ultramar, 1953), 495; "Carta do Irmão António Mendes ao Padre Geral," May 9, 1563. Linda M. Heywood and John K. Thornton, *Central Africans, Atlantic Creoles, and the Making of the Foundation of the Americas, 1585–1660* (Cambridge: Cambridge University Press, 2007), 51–4; Ralph Delgado, *O Reino de Benguela: Do Descobrimento à Criação do Governo Subalterno* ([S.l: s.n.], 1945), 16; Amaral, *O Reino do Congo*, 199.

[8] Brásio, *Monumenta Missionária*, vol. 3, 332; "Carta do Padre Diogo da Costa ao Provincial de Portugal," May 31, 1586.

[9] For a discussion on chiefdoms, see Igor Kopytoff, "Permutations in Patrimonialism and Populism: The Aghem Chiefdoms of Western Cameroon," in *Beyond Chiefdoms: Pathways to Complexity in Africa*, ed. Susan Keech McIntosh (Cambridge: Cambridge University Press, 1999), 88–96; and Jan Vansina, "Pathways of Political Development in Equatorial Africa and Neo-evolutionary Theory," in McIntosh, *Beyond Chiefdoms*, 166–72. For a more evolutionary approach, see Timothy K. Earle, "The Evolution of Chiefdoms," in *Chiefdoms: Power, Economy, and Ideology* (Cambridge: Cambridge University Press, 1991), 1–15.

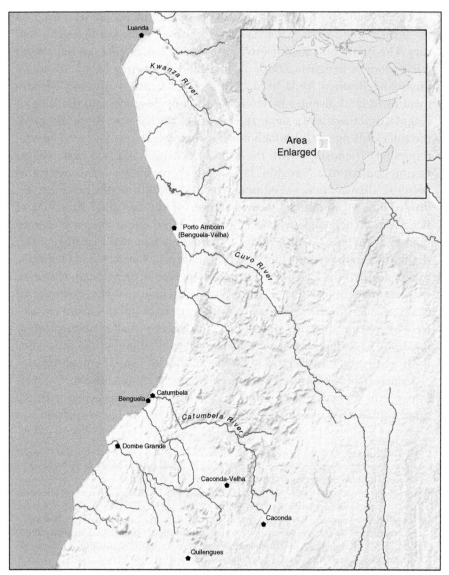

MAP 3. Portuguese fortresses south of the Kwanza River. Map by Tsering Wangyal Shawa, Princeton's GIS and Map Librarian.

subjugation. Religious conversion was important because the Portuguese empire was acting in the name of and enjoying full support of the Catholic Church. Reports of the early contacts between the Portuguese and the population along the coast are numerous but restricted to the Portuguese side because there is no account concerning how local Africans perceived and understood these early exchanges. The sources discuss Portuguese activities, battles, and interactions with local rulers and are silent on the relationship among African rulers or the internal conflicts within local states. Local political organizations were designated *sobados* in Portuguese documents, regardless of their size. The term is a derivation of *soba*, in Kimbundu, to designate "chief." Portuguese employed the term in non-Kimbundu-speaking regions, such as Benguela and its interior, despite the fact that a local term, *sòmá*, existed in Umbundu-speaking regions.[10] Yet, despite the limitations, Portuguese accounts allow us to read between the lines to understand or at least get some clues regarding the internal situation and the strengths and weaknesses of political entities in West Central Africa.[11]

When Henrique Pais reached Benguela-Velha in 1546, he had already heard about large numbers of people living along the coast. He was supposed to gain access to mines and establish trade agreements "all in peace and friendship."[12] Benguela-Velha was a "steep, black, rugged, and stony point, with white cliffs to the south."[13] A small bay provided a natural harbor. Henrique Pais' main goal was to establish commercial contacts with the local population. The sixteenth century was a time when the Portuguese and the Spanish fought to conquer new lands and people in order to control access to metals in a true mercantilist mode of accumulation and state wealth.[14] The arrival of the Portuguese on the African

[10] The naming of African rulers is a topic that will be explored later. In the region of Benguela, the Portuguese used the term *soba* to indicate the highest African authority, sometimes translated as "chief" or "king." Joseph Miller employs *soba* as "Portuguese appointed chief." See Joseph C. Miller, *Kings and Kinsmen: Early Mbundu States in Angola* (Oxford, UK: Clarendon Press, 1976), 302. In some dictionaries, the Kimbundu word is translated as "king" or "petty king" (*rei* or *régulo* in Portuguese). See António da Silva Maia, *Lições de Gramática de Quimbundo (Português e Banto)* (Cucujães, Portugal: Tipografia das Missões, 1964), 168.

[11] Beatrix Heintze, "The Extraordinary Journey of the *Jaga* through the Centuries: Critical Approaches to Precolonial Angolan Historical Sources," *History in Africa* 34 (2007): 69. For a discussion on principalities, chiefdoms, states, *soba*, and *soma*, see Jan Vansina, *How Societies are Born: Governance in West Central Africa before 1600* (Charlottesville: University of Virginia Press, 2004), 163.

[12] Delgado, *O Reino de Benguela*, 19; A. de Albuquerque Felner, *Angola: Apontamentos sobre a Colonização dos Planaltos e Litoral do Sul de Angola* (Lisbon: Agência Geral das Colônias, 1940), 410–11; "Carta de Doação a Paulo Dias de Novais," September 6, 1571; David Birmingham, *The Portuguese Conquest of Angola* (Oxford University Press, 1965), 2.

[13] Purdy, *New Sailing Directory*, 412.

[14] Glenn J. Ames, "An African Eldorado? The Portuguese Quest for Wealth and Power in Mozambique and the Rios de Cuama, c. 1661–1683," *International Journal of African*

coast is best understood in a context of expansion and empire building. More concerned with the profitable trade in Asia, the Portuguese exploitation of Benguela should be seen as a step to strengthen their power in Indian Ocean commerce. In Benguela, they could acquire copper, essential for the Asian market, and *nzimbu* shells, in demand in the Kingdom of Kongo.[15]

This chapter explores the first century of the foundation of Benguela, emphasizing the interaction of the Portuguese with local populations. In search of minerals that could be sent to India in exchange for spices, Portuguese explorers hoped to find copper and silver in Benguela. Yet the wealth of Benguela was not its natural resources, although they were important, but its people. A gateway to densely populated areas, Benguela became an important slave port. Copper, birds, and animals filled Portuguese ships and decorated rooms in Lisbon and other European cities. But it was the commerce in human beings that transformed this region. The seventeenth century was the time when the South Atlantic commerce in slaves started to take shape, generating competition among the actors involved. Dutch, English, and French traders challenged the Portuguese power, conquering ports and smuggling people and minerals. The people around Benguela joined the Atlantic trade in different capacities, sometimes as trade partners, more often as slaves. They also played an important role in limiting the actions of the Portuguese to the coast. This chapter also engages with the debate on the *jagas*, a heated academic discussion in the 1960s and 1970s that has not received much attention after Anne Hilton's contribution in 1981.[16] The identity of the *jagas* is of particular importance in West Central Africa and, as I will show later, is more about Portuguese perceptions of Africans than an accurate name

---

Historical Studies 31, no. 1 (1998): 91–110. See also Stuart Schwartz, "Prata, Açucar e Escravos: de como o império restaurou Portugal," *Tempo* 12, no. 24 (2008): 202–23; and Robert W. Harms, *The Diligent: A Voyage Through the Worlds of the Slave Trade* (New York: Basic Books, 2002), 35–7.

[15] Sanjay Subrahmanyam, "Holding the World in Balance: The Connected Histories of the Iberian Overseas Empires, 1500–1640," *American Historical Review* 112, no. 5 (2007): 1362–63; A. J. R. Russell-Wood, *A World on the Move: The Portuguese in Africa, Asia, and America, 1415–1808* (Manchester, UK: Carcanet, 1992), 145; Stuart B. Schwartz, "Luso-Spanish Relations in Hapsburg Brazil, 1580–1640," *The Americas* 25, no. 1 (1968): 41–3. For the use of *zimbo* in Kongo, see David Birmingham, *Central Africa to 1870* (Cambridge: Cambridge University Press, 1981), 28–30; and Jan Hogendorn and Marion Johnson, *The Shell Money of the Slave Trade* (Cambridge: Cambridge University Press, 2003), 101–2.

[16] Anne Hilton, "The *Jaga* Reconsidered," *Journal of African History* 22, no. 2 (1981): 191–202.

associated with a particular group. Moreover, this first chapter claims that Benguela was already important in the Portuguese empire in the seventeenth century, giving rise to discussions of colonialism and the intrusion of Benguela into the world-system economy.[17]

The First Benguela

Diogo Cão was probably the first Portuguese to visit the region between Benguela-Velha and Benguela in 1483. He traveled to the mouth of the Catumbela River and a bay located south of it, probably Benguela or Farta, and named it St. Maria.[18] Successive explorers did not necessarily recognize the places visited by their predecessors; they often provided new names, which makes it more challenging to identify places mentioned in historical documents. When King Infante D. Henrique of Portugal granted Paulo Dias de Novais the captaincy of Angola in 1574, he fully expected new expeditions to Benguela-Velha. As a captain, Dias de Novais was given full jurisdiction over local mines and taxation, and he also enjoyed trading privileges over any natural resources, such as spices or minerals.[19] As soon as he landed in Luanda, Dias de Novais sent his nephew, Lopes Peixoto, to Benguela-Velha to find sources of gold and silver and to continue the trade partnerships initiated by Henrique Pais. Although Peixoto did not find the mines, the mission was successful because he traded "with heathens for provisions, cows, vegetables, slaves, ivory, and rings and bracelets made of copper."[20] Lopes Peixoto established commercial relationships and started the construction of a temporary fortress to protect the seventy soldiers under his command. As a result of the trade cooperation, the ruler identified as the King of Benguela requested "friendship" and subjugation to the King of Portugal in 1586, as mentioned earlier, probably related to its ongoing competition with the Ndongo state located north. Father Diogo da Costa, a

---

[17] Immanuel Wallerstein, *World-Systems Analysis: An Introduction* (Durham, NC: Duke University Press, 2004).

[18] Ernest G. Ravenstein, *The Voyages of Diogo Cão and Bartholomeu Dias, 1482–88* (London: W. Clowes and Sons, 1900), 7–8.

[19] António Henrique R. de Oliveira Marquês, *History of Portugal* (New York: Columbia University Press, 1972), 1, 377; Delgado, *O Reino de Benguela*, 20. For trading privileges of individuals in the precharter companies that characterized the Atlantic world before 1620, see Cátia Antunes and Filipa Ribeiro Da Silva, "Cross-Cultural Entrepreneurship in the Atlantic: Africans, Dutch and Sephardic Jews in Western Africa, 1580–1674," *Itinerario* 35, no. 1 (2011): 54–7.

[20] Anonymous, *Benguela e seu sertão, 1617–1622* (Lisbon: Impressa Nacional, 1881), 7.

priest who visited the region, described the ruler of Benguela as a "very understanding [man] and in control of a kingdom with extreme mineral wealth."[21]

While the ruler of Benguela saw the Portuguese as a coequal trade ally, Lopes Peixoto understood the alliance as subjugation. These different understandings of their political and commercial alliance led to a series of conflicts between African and Portuguese forces throughout the centuries. The ruler of Benguela did not realize that by signing a treaty with the Portuguese he was giving up his sovereignty. He had agreed to allow the Portuguese to settle along the coast and to build a fortress, where personnel and trade goods could be stored and protected from pillage or attacks. However, he did not surrender to Portuguese control.[22] The initial relationships were peaceful, but they soon turned sour. After some days, subjects of the Benguela ruler attacked Portuguese soldiers who were fishing and, in control of the weapons, killed the remaining soldiers in the fortress, sparing the lives of two men who escaped to Luanda.[23] In the attack, Lopes Peixoto was killed, an action that temporarily halted the colonization fever south of the Kwanza. Facing conflicts in the Kongo at the same time, the Portuguese Crown ceased sending more troops to Benguela-Velha and, until 1617, focused on its relationship with the political and economic elites of Ndongo and Kongo.[24] Although the captaincy system was short-lived in Angola, it established the practice where governors and captains enjoyed a range of trading privileges and treated local people and land as their personal property, rather than the Crown's, mixing private and public. This practice led to a series of conflicts later

[21] Brásio, *Monumenta Missionária Africana*, vol. 3, doc. 87, "Carta do Padre Diogo da Costa ao Provincial de Portugal," May 31, 1586, 332. See also Delgado, *O Reino de Benguela*, 21–2; Linda M. Heywood and John K. Thornton, *Central Africans, Atlantic Creoles, and the Making of the Foundation of the Americas, 1585–1660* (Cambridge: Cambridge University Press, 2007), 52–4.

[22] For similar cases in West Africa, see the account of John W. Blake, *Europeans in West Africa—1450–1560* (London: The Hakluyt Society, 1942), 18–60. See also Harvey M. Feinberg, *Africans and Europeans in West Africa: Elminans and Dutchmen on the Gold Coast during the Eighteenth Century* (Philadelphia: American Philosophical Society, 1989); and M. D. D. Newitt, *A History of Portuguese Overseas Expansion, 1400–1668* (New York: Routledge, 2005), 25–6.

[23] Brásio, *Monumenta Missionária Africana*, vol. 4, "História da Residência dos Padres da Companhia de Jesus em Angola e Coisas Tocantes ao Reino e Conquistas," May 1, 1594, 571–7; and Domingo de Abreu e Brito, *Inquérito da Vida Administrativa e Economica de Angola* (Coimbra: Imprensa da Universidade, 1931), 24. See also Delgado, *O Reino de Benguela*, 23; Heywood and Thornton, *Central Africans, Atlantic Creoles*, 89.

[24] Linda Heywood, "Slavery and Its Transformation in the Kingdom of Kongo: 1491–1800," *Journal of African History* 50 (2009): 6.

on between colonial authorities who had different understandings of personal and official rights.[25] Men on the spot and authorities based in Luanda and Lisbon had different and sometimes competing interpretations of colonial policies, missions, and goals. Based on circumstances on the ground, administrators in Benguela, allied with the locals recruited as colonial forces and intermediaries, adapted colonial policies with a certain degree of autonomy.[26]

By the early seventeenth century, geographic and trade conditions pushed the Portuguese to rethink their strategies, and they once again turned their expansionist eyes to the south of the Kwanza. Ocean currents and winds in the South Atlantic forced ship captains to sail south before landing in Luanda, which allowed them to see the coast and report back to Lisbon authorities. Between the places now known as Lobito and Benguela, the littoral is made up of a series of cliffs and small beaches that offered a natural harbor for large and small vessels. Ships usually made single stops along the littoral wherever a captain and his crew could find safe anchorage and acquire supplies of fresh water and food from the local population. They also could repair any damage to the ships before heading to Luanda or Cabinda.[27]

The unification of the Iberian Crowns between 1580 and 1640 favored acceleration of the expansion of the slave trade in West Central Africa. During that time, the Hapsburg family ruled both Iberian empires and challenged the Treaty of Tordesilla that separated the lands conquered by them. The Joint Iberian Crown was interested in gaining access to slaves and mines, so it funded expeditions and studies to expand its knowledge

---

[25] I will explore this further in Chapters 3 and 4. See also Mariana P. Candido, "African Freedom Suits and Portuguese Vassal Status: Legal Mechanisms for Fighting Enslavement in Benguela, Angola, 1800–1830," *Slavery & Abolition* 32 (2011): 447–59.

[26] "Men on the spot" were a specific set of colonial agents different in their backgrounds, motivations, and aims from the metropolitan government, which could include soldiers, low-ranking bureaucrats, translators, and Africans transformed into colonial intermediaries. In the case of Benguela, I also employ the concept to refer to the governor of Benguela. For more on the idea of "men on the spot," see Kanya-Forstner, "French Missions to the Central Sudan in the 1890s: The Role of Algerian Agents and Interpreters," *Paideuma* 40 (1994): 15–32; Justin Willis, "'Men on the Spot,' Labor, and the Colonial State in British East Africa: The Mombasa Water Supply, 1911–1917," *International Journal of African Historical Studies* 28, no. 1 (1995): 25–48; Benjamin Nicholas Lawrance, Emily Lynn Osborn, and Richard L. Roberts (eds.), *Intermediaries, Interpreters, and Clerks: African Employees in the Making of Colonial Africa* (Madison: University of Wisconsin Press, 2006).

[27] Joseph C. Miller, *Way of Death: Merchant Capitalism and the Angolan Slave Trade, 1730–1830* (Madison: University of Wisconsin Press, 1988), 15–17; Thornton, *Africa and Africans*, 194.

of the region. Domingos Abreu de Brito, for example, visited the colony of Angola in 1590–1 and reported on the importance of the trade with Benguela-Velha. In his report, Brito recommended that the Portuguese Crown separate the taxes collected in the ports of Benguela-Velha and Luanda in order to access the exact value and importance of the slave trade from those ports. He also advised the Portuguese to nominate a governor autonomous from Angolan affairs and acquire three *galeotas* (light vessels) to carry on trade between Benguela-Velha and Luanda.[28] Reports of ivory and gold and silver mines pushed the Portuguese Crown to consider sending new missions to reoccupy the port.[29] By 1611, King Felipe II (or Felipe III in Spain) reported on the abundance of copper in Benguela-Velha. According to him, copper "could be sent to Brazil in slave ships, without any extra cost. In the port [of Benguela-Velha] slaves could be acquired for a better profit than in Angola, for the privilege of the Crown." He also mentioned that the high population density favored capturing slaves and that the ivory could find markets elsewhere.[30]

Even though expeditions of exploration were sent, the place known as Benguela remained outside of Portuguese control until 1617. Located between the rivers Longa and Cuvo, Benguela-Velha was abandoned by the Portuguese after Lopes Peixoto was killed. An English sailor, Andrew Battell, visited Benguela-Velha in 1600–1 and wrote an account that "should be read as his oral reminiscences recorded by others," as Vansina reminded us.[31] According to his report, the population that lived there was called Endalanbondos, had no form of government, and had been profoundly affected by Imbangala attacks and raids that targeted people and cattle. The local inhabitants were also described as "very treacherous, and those who trade with these people must stand upon their own guard."[32] On the few occasions when the Imbangala were mentioned

---

[28] Brito, *Inquérito à Vida Administrativa*, 3, 12.

[29] Brito, *Inquérito à Vida Administrativa*, 39; Brásio, *Monumenta Missionária*, vol. 4, "Memórias de Jerônimo Castanho a el-Rei," September 5, 1599, 599.

[30] Brásio, *Monumenta Missionária Africana*, vol. 6, doc. 8, "Regimento do Governador de Angola," September 22, 1611, 32–3.

[31] Jan Vansina, "On Ravenstein's Edition of Battell's Adventures in Angola and Loango," *History in Africa* 34 (2007): 323.

[32] Ravenstein, E. G., *The Strange Adventures of Andrew Battell of Leigh, in Angola and the Adjoining Regions* (London: Hakluyt Society, 1901), 17. Battell's account was collected and published first in Samuel Purchas, *Purchas His Pilgrimage, or Relations of the World and the Religions Observed in All Ages and Places Discovered, from the Creation unto the Present* (London, 1613); and Samuel Purchas, *His Pilgrimage* (London, 1625). Like most scholars, I made use of Ravenstein's edition. For more on the problems with Ravenstein's edition, see Vansina, "On Ravenstein's Edition," 321–47.

in primary sources, it was often in relationship to Benguela-Velha, not Benguela, as this case demonstrates. Portuguese documents on Benguela are silent on the Imbangalas, suggesting that they were not an important force in Benguela. Scholars who have worked on the Imbangala focused mainly on the regions north of the Kwanza River or around Benguela-Velha.[33] Despite reporting no form of government, Battell referred to the local ruler as the Prince Hombiangymbe.[34] Battell also offered one of the few seventeenth-century descriptions of styles of dress. "Men of this place wear skins about their middles and beads about their necks." Women wore "a ring of copper about their necks; ... about their arms little rings of copper that reach their elbows; about their middle a cloth of the Insandie tree, which is neither spun nor woven; on their legs rings of copper that reach to the calves of their legs."[35] The importance of beads also was described by other travelers and explorers in later periods, which helps to explain the central role of beads in the late eighteenth and early nineteenth centuries. They were used not only for fashion but also to barter for cattle and later to purchase captives.[36] More important was Battell's description of jewelry made of copper. He also reported on the large number of captives. According to him, "[W]e loaded our ship with slaves in seven days, and bought them so cheap that many did not cost

---

[33] For discussions of the Imbangala, mostly north of Kwanza or in the region of Benguela-Velha, see Jan Vansina, "The Foundation of the Kingdom of Kassanje," *Journal of African History* 4, no. 3 (1963): 355–74; David Birmingham, "The Date and Significance of the Imbangala Invasion of Angola," *Journal of African History* 6, no. 2 (1965): 143–52; Joseph C. Miller, "The Imbangala and the Chronology of Early Central Africa," *Journal of African History* 13, no. 4 (1972): 549–74; John Thornton, "The African Experience of the '20s and Odd Negroes Arriving in Virginia in 1619," *William and Mary Quarterly* 55, no. 3, series 3 (1998): 427–8; and Henriques, *Percursos da Modernidade*, 153–7.

[34] Ravenstein, *Strange Adventures*, 21.

[35] Insandie trees were identified by the editor of Battell's account as wild fig trees. See Ravenstein, *Strange Adventures*, 17–18.

[36] Ravenstein, *Strange Adventures*, 17. For reports on the demand for beads in the interior of Benguela, see Instituto Histórico Geográfico Brasileiro (IHGB), DL31,09, October 25, 1797, "Ofício de Fernando da Silva Correia, tenente regente, a d. Miguel António de Melo, [governador de Angola], comunicando o envio do mapa das pessoas de artilharia da Fortaleza de Novo Redondo." See also Arquivo Histórico Ultramarino (AHU), Angola, caixa 89, doc. 25, October 25, 1798. For the number of beads imported by the late eighteenth century, see Arquivo Histórico Ministério de Obras Públicas, Transporte e Comunicações, Superintendência Geral de Contrabando, Balança Geral do Comércio de Portugal e Seus Domínios, L. SGC 4, 1776, L. SGC 5, 1777, and L. SGC 6, 1798. For more on beads and their importance to the slave trade, see Mariana P. Candido, "Merchants and the Business of the Slave Trade at Benguela, 1750–1850," *African Economic History* 35 (2007): 10–16.

one real, which were worth in the city of Luanda twelve thousand *reis*."[37] Tales of many captives and a large amount of copper certainly worked as a motivation for later explorers.

News about the region and its population soon arrived in Lisbon, probably brought by different traders. Brito had reported that there were more mineral deposits in the interior of Benguela than in Peru.[38] Believing in Brito's assessment and hoping that enough silver could be found, the Portuguese Crown developed new interest in Benguela-Velha. During the seventeenth century, the Portuguese elite imported silver from Spanish territories in the Americas. Thus, if mines were available in Benguela-Velha, there was a chance they could become self-reliant and not need to depend on the silver available in the Spanish colonies. The Joint Iberian Crown so strongly desired mineral wealth that it sent the explorer Manoel Cerveira Pereira to conquer new lands. Lured by the mineral fever, the Crown issued instructions to Cerveira Pereira to separate the new colony to be founded from the existing Angolan administration. Cerveira Pereira had already participated in several attacks in the interior of Angola, including the battle of Cambambe, and the wars against Axila Mbanza and Mosseque in 1603. With previous experience on the ground and credited with the defeat of the ruler of Kambambe, he was the ideal candidate to establish a colony south of the Kwanza. Yet he was a controversial choice. The governor of Angola charged him with illegal activities and had him arrested in 1607.[39] Among other accusations, he was suspected of smuggling slaves to Rio de la Plata traders, of sexual abuse of female residents, of personal interests in the attacks on the *soba* of Axila Mbanza, and of taking royal taxes for himself. Despite these accusations, King Dom Felipe II of Portugal requested his presence in Madrid and nominated him as governor, conqueror, and settler of the Kingdom of Benguela (*Governador, Conquistador e Povoador do Reino de Benguela*). Probably following the advice of Domingos de Abreu Brito, the King divided the two provinces, stating, "[T]he Governor of Angola, from today onward, has nothing to do with the jurisdiction

---

[37] Ravenstein, *Strange Adventures*, 20.

[38] Abreu e Brito, *Inquérito da Vida administrativa*, 14–15, 39.

[39] AHU, Angola, caixa 1, doc. 20, March 11, 1612. Cadornega also describes the Manoel Cerveira Pereira expedition and the Kambambe attacks. See António de Oliveira de Cadornega, *História Geral das Guerras Angolanas, 1680–1681* (Lisbon: Agência-Geral das Colónias, 1940), 61. For more on the founding of Benguela, see Stefan Goodwin, *African Legacy of Urbanization: Unfolding Saga of a Continent* (Lanham, MD: Lexington Books, 2008), 185.

of Benguela."⁴⁰ His goals were to provide autonomy to the governor in Benguela and not disrupt the trade in Angola. The nomination of Cerveira Pereira highlights the clear intention to establish a colony, not a *feitoria* (trading post). Settlers, colonial officers, and the indigenous population became part of an 'imagined community' of the Portuguese empire, where Christian values prevailed over local customs and religious systems, although the port of Benguela was still very much vulnerable to the military and political power of the polities around it and in its hinterland. As Frederick Cooper stated, "Overseas empires provided, ever since Magellan's circumnavigation of the earth, a space of imagination that was global, but a field of power that was limited and delicate."⁴¹ The fact that in the seventeenth century Benguela was perceived as a colony in the minds of bureaucrats in Lisbon does not mean that territorial control was guaranteed. As in other places, colonial settlement was under constant negotiation with local rulers and merchant elites. On his return to Angola, Cerveira Pereira prepared to travel to Benguela by collecting information about the land and its people. In a letter to the King, he requested two priests to convert the local heathens, two skilled miners who could locate mineral mines, a superintendent of the treasury, and a secretary. He also requested 300 soldiers, including two barbers, with the recommendation that most of soldiers should come from Kongo or Angola because troops coming from Portugal tended to become sick and die. To help in the conquest, he believed that twenty horses equipped with forty protective cotton coverings were necessary. For his troops, he asked for 100 spears for the horsemen; 400 handguns, 100 muskets, and sufficient gunpowder; axes and hoes; and medical supplies. He did not receive everything he requested in part because the governor of Angola refused to cooperate.⁴² Yet it shows his intentions to carry out King

---

⁴⁰ AHU, Angola, caixa 1, doc. 20, March 11, 1612; and AHU, Angola, caixa 1, doc. 33, February 14, 1615. See also Delgado, *Reino de Benguela*, 33–5, 43. On Abreu Brito's advice, see his *Inquérito à Vida Administrativa*, 3.

⁴¹ Frederick Cooper, *Colonialism in Question: Theory, Knowledge, History* (Berkeley: University of California Press, 2005), 166; Benedict Anderson, *Imagined Communities: Reflections on the Origin and Spread of Nationalism* (London: Verso, 2006), 21–3. For the tenuous situation of Portuguese colonialism, focusing on the case of Brazil, see Alida C. Metcalf, *Go-Betweens and the Colonization of Brazil, 1500–1600* (Austin: University of Texas Press, 2005), 55–65.

⁴² This incident was the first clash between Angolan and Benguelan authorities that continued throughout the 1617–1850 period. For details, see AHU, Angola, caixa 1, doc. 20, March 11, 1612; and AHU, Angola, caixa 1, doc. 53, February 20, 1616. For more on Cerveira Pereira's previous experience in the hinterland of Angola, see Miller, *Kings and Kinsmen*, 196–7. Barbers acted as bleeders and performed medical procedures and

Dom Felipe II's orders to conquer and settle in Benguela, with the priests representing the support of the Catholic Church for an expansion very much focused on securing access to mineral accumulation.

The Foundation of Benguela and the Early Portuguese Settlement

On April 11, 1617, Manoel Cerveira Pereira left Luanda with 130 soldiers to conquer the land south of Kwanza. He stopped at the Benguela-Velha port established earlier by Lopes Peixoto. Pereira decided to look for a better natural harbor, away from the place that had been devastated by African forces decades before. He chose the bay between the Catumbela and Marimbondo (Cavaco) rivers and disembarked his people. He ordered the immediate construction of a fortress and named the village São Felipe de Benguela, in honor of King Felipe. The patron was São Lourenço.[43] Arriving during the *cacimbo*, the cooler dry season that takes place in West Central Africa from May to August, Cerveira Pereira did not realize that they had settled close to swamps and at the mouth of the Catumbela River, a place that favored the proliferation of mosquitoes during the rainy season. In the first weeks, the troops faced mild and dry weather, which led the new governor to report that the climate was excellent. He also was satisfied with the abundance of fish, cattle, and land suitable for agriculture. For the cattle wealth, the bay became known as *Baía das Vacas*, or Cattle Bay.[44]

The initial fortress was established in a naturally protected area, with a cliff close by and between two streams that provided fresh water. Nearby, Ndombes, called "Mundombes" in the sources, watched the arrival of the Portuguese. The initial Portuguese settlement was small, but in official correspondence it claimed control of the Kingdom of Benguela "limited by the land of the Sumbe and, in the interior by the land of the Genge,

---

dental care. See Mariza de Carvalho Soares, "A Biografia de Ignácio Montes: O Escravo que virou Rei," in *Retratos do Império: Trajetórias Individuais no Mundo Português nos séculos XVI a XIX* (Niterói, Rio de Janeiro: Eduff, 2006), 47–68; and A. C. Saunders, *História Social dos Escravos e Libertos Negros em Portugal (1441–1555)* (Lisbon: Imprensa Nacional, 1994), 196.

[43] AHU, Angola, caixa 1, doc. 74, August 28, 1617. See also Delgado, *O Reino de Benguela*, 61; and Felner, *Angola*, 333. Delgado claims that Benguela was founded in May rather than August. Cerveira Pereira, however, stated August 10, São Lourenço's day. See also José Joaquim Lopes de Lima, *Ensaios Sobre a Statistica das Possessões Portuguezas na Africa Occidental e Oriental* (Lisbon: Imprensa Nacional, 1844), xxiii, 3.

[44] Felner, *Angola*, 325. For more on the importance of cattle south of the Kwanza, see Miller, *Kings and Kinsmen*, 262.

filled with Quilombos of *jagas*, called by the name of Quilengues."[45] The nearby population and the ruler, *soba* Peringue, certainly did not view the arrival of the Portuguese in the same way. Peringue had agreed to the presence of Cerveira Pereira and his men after he received some unspecified gifts. The payment of tributes, or gifts, as the Portuguese officially termed such exchanges, sealed diplomatic relationships and represented the right to settle temporarily in the territory.[46] Eight days after disembarking, Cerveira's black soldiers went to cut timber to be used in building the fortress. A few miles from the beach, two men were killed and six captured by Peringue's soldiers. Cerveira Pereira retaliated and organized an attack with fifty men. The village hosting Peringue and his men was burnt. The attack resulted in thirty-one people killed and the capture and subsequent enslavement of forty more. Seventy cows also were stolen.[47]

The first year was marked by ongoing hostilities in part because Pereira and Peringue had different ideas regarding the Portuguese presence. Armed conflict dominated the period, contributing to exhaustion of the European troops and a sense of insecurity along the littoral. After fifteen days, Cerveira Pereira organized a failed assault on Peringue, who escaped before the Portuguese troops arrived. Pereira reported that the land was empty, except for the presence of one woman. She was captured and informed the Portuguese that Peringue had moved his subjects to another Ndombe chiefdom, probably the land of Kizamba, located in the bay of São Francisco, nine miles away from Cattle Bay.[48] Peringue

[45] Cadornega, *História Geral*, 3, 168. Centuries later, Joachim Monteiro also described the Ndombe as the inhabitants of Benguela and as pastoralists; Joachim John Monteiro, *Angola and the River Congo* (New York: Macmillan, 1876), 265–6. See also Delgado, *Reino de Benguela*, 62; *Benguela e seu Sertão*, 17. In the twentieth century, the Quilengues were two ethnic groups (divided into Quilengue-Humbe and Quilengue-Musho) belonging to the greater linguistic group Nhaneka-Humbe-Va-nyaneka-lunkumbi), whereas the Ndombe (in the sources with Bantu prefixes: Mundombe, Vandombe) belonged to the linguistic group of the Umbundu. See José Redinha, *Distribuição Étnica de Angola: Introdução, Registo Étnico* (Luanda: Centro de Informação e Turismo de Angola, 1962), 16–19. See also Gladwyn Murray Childs, "The Peoples of Angola in the Seventeenth Century According to Cadornega," *Journal of African History* 1, no. 2 (1960): 271–9.

[46] On the right of rulers to allocate access to land and the common practice of receiving visitors and traders, see Mahmood Mamdani, *Citizen and Subject* (Princeton, NJ: Princeton University Press, 1996), 44–7; and Jeff Guy, "Analyzing Pre-Capitalist Societies in Southern Africa," *Journal of Southern African Studies* 14, no. 1 (1987): 18–37. The initial diplomatic and commercial relationships south of Kwanza resembled the previous experience north of the river. See Miller, *Kings and Kinsmen*, 177–9.

[47] AHU, Angola, caixa 1, doc. 87, July 2, 1618. Delgado also mentions this episode in his *O Reino de Benguela*, 67; Felner, *Angola*, 333.

[48] AHU, Angola, caixa 1, 87, July 2, 1618. For the Kizamba and the Dombe Grande, see Maria Alexandra Aparício, "Política de Boa Vizinhança: os Chefes Locais e os Europeus

remained away for some time, though some of his people returned to the area close to the bay and requested Cerveira Pereira's authorization to resettle on their own land, which was by then occupied by the conqueror's troops.[49]

Soon Cerveira Pereira faced problems that resulted from his poor decision regarding the location of the new Benguela. Summer months brought rains and high humidity, with serious effects on his troops. By 1618, 38 of the initial 130 soldiers had already died, including Pereira's brother, son-in-law, and a nephew. His troops then were reduced to ninety-two men, including six who had brought their wives and eighty black soldiers from Angola, among them sixty personal slaves.[50] His problems were not only the environment but also the resistance of the local ruler and population, who did not want the Portuguese to settle permanently on their land. When Peringue realized that the Portuguese were not planning to leave any time soon, he organized an attack. The sound of Portuguese handguns and muskets frightened the Ndombe forces, who moved away from the coast. Enjoying the peace, Portuguese soldiers started building the initial fortress with sticks and mud, a technique known as *pau a pique*, with straw roofs to protect the soldiers and the goods from the sun.[51]

By 1618, the Portuguese colony of Benguela was no more than a fortress. Yet traders from the interior continued to travel to the coast and exchange goods. In official correspondence, Peringue was named a *fidalgo* ("nobleman") probably because he had been baptized and had given control over his land to the Portuguese. Another nearby ruler, Kitumbela, requested an alliance with the Portuguese in part because he was threatened by hunter and gatherer Kwandu groups ("Moquimbas" in the sources) located three days' travel south of Benguela.[52] Farmers and herders, who raised cattle, goats, and sheep, visited the fortress and sold their products to the personnel stationed there. Colonial agents

em Meados do século XIX. O Caso do Dombe Grande," in *II Reunião Internacional História de Angola* (Lisbon: CNCDP, 2000), 109. For tribute paid by other Europeans along the West African littoral, see Harms, *The Diligent*, 205–7.

[49] Delgado, *O Reino de Benguela*, 67.

[50] Abel Augusto Bolota, *Benguela, Mãe de Cidades* (Benguela: Câmara Municipal de Benguela, 1967), 24; Delgado, *Reino de Benguela*, 65–6, Felner, *Angola*, 334.

[51] Bolota, *Benguela, Mãe de Cidades*, 19.

[52] AHU, Angola, caixa 1, 87, July 2, 1618. For more on the Kwandu, see E. Westphal, "A Re-Classification of Southern African Non-Bantu Languages," *Journal of African Languages* 1 (1962); and Carlos Estermann, "Les Twa du Sud-ouest de l'Angola," *Anthropos* 57 (1962).

began to provide credit for local traders who were fueling commerce.[53] A few months after his arrival, Cerveira Pereira reported on the mineral wealth, especially copper, and on the large number of cattle available. The search for minerals was a constant concern for the Portuguese colonial state. Colonial authorities were lured by tales of mines, inland Eldorados, and their ability to rescue the Portuguese empire from the constant need to obtain silver and gold coins from the Spanish empire.[54] Copper was essential in the Asian market. In Malabar, for example, it was used in exchange for pepper. Dutch traders reported acquiring copper from Chinese and Japanese markets and using it in Gujarat in exchange for spices and textiles.[55] Copper also was important in the nascent sugar industry established in São Tomé and Brazil, where it was a component used in the clarification of sugar. Stuart Schwartz claimed that, on average, a sugar mill used 2.5 tons of copper in each boiler.[56] Most of the copper was acquired from Sweden, but the possibility of finding copper mines in Benguela allowed the Portuguese empire to dream of becoming autonomous and no longer relying on imports to support its sugar production in Brazil. Copper also was used in artillery bullets and could be used in coin production. The Portuguese elite, in serious distress over the lack of mineral resources in its colony in the Americas, hoped to find new mines soon, and the exploitation of Benguela represented hope.

Curious about the mines, Cerveira Pereira commanded inland excursions to the land of Cbo Kalunda, where supposedly the copper mines were located.[57] The mission failed in its goal of finding copper mines,

[53] AHU, Angola, caixa 1, 87, July 2, 1618. See also Brásio, *Monumenta Missionária*, vol. 6, 315–18. For similar developments along the coast in the seventeenth century, see Feinberg, *Africans and Europeans in West Africa*, 25–7. People along the coast and the interior continued to raise cattle into the late nineteenth and early twentieth centuries, although how wealth was perceived and transmitted probably changed. See Carlos Estermann, *The Ethnography of Southwestern Angola* (New York: Africana Publishing, 1976), 2, 151–2.

[54] Pascoal Leite de Aguiar, *Administração Colonial Portuguesa no Congo, em Angola e em Benguela* (Lisbon: Sociedade Histórica da Independência de Portugal, 2006), 1, 152. See also João Medina and Isabel de Castro Henriques, *A Rota dos Escravos. Angola e a Rede do Comércio Negreiro* (Lisbon: Cegia, 1996), 83. For the use of silver from Spanish America in Portugal, see C. R. Boxer, "Brazilian Gold and British Traders in the First Half of the 18th Century," *Hispanic American Historical Review* 49, no. 3 (1969): 455.

[55] Sanjay Subrahmanyam, *The Political Economy of Commerce: Southern India, 1500–1650* (Cambridge: Cambridge University Press, 2002), 84–5, 245.

[56] Stuart Schwartz, "Prata, Açúcar e Escravos: de como o Império Restaurou Portugal," *Tempo* 12, no. 24 (2008): 222.

[57] AHU, Angola, caixa 1, doc. 86, June 15, 1618. Pedro Neto de Melo, the highest magistrate in the colony, also mentioned Cbo Calunda. See Felner, *Angola*, 556, "Auto que Mandou fazer o Ouvidor Geral e Provedor da Fazenda Pedro Neto de Melo," June 15, 1618.

but the relationship between the Portuguese explorers and local Ndombe changed. Portuguese officials suspected locals were hiding information about the mines, whereas rulers located inland, including Cbo Kalunda, were not happy to see their territories invaded by foreign forces, and clashes took place. Portuguese forces started to seize people and raid villages in a process not unlike what had happened earlier in Kongo.[58] By 1618, although in a precarious condition with few residents, the fortress of Benguela started to operate as a slaving center. Knowledge of the early contacts is based on the documents written by the Portuguese explorers, which tend to emphasize Portugal's abilities rather than its weaknesses. However, it becomes clear that the failure to find copper altered the initial diplomatic contacts. In 1618, after the failed expedition to the mines of Cbo Kalunda, Cerveira Pereira reported that two ships left Benguela with slaves and cattle.[59] Thus Benguela was more than "a minor outpost engaged in local commerce in foodstuff," as Linda Heywood and John Thornton claimed in 2007.[60] From that point onward, one year after its foundation, the departure of war captives became Benguela's main economic activity, even though Luanda was the official port of embarkation to the trans-Atlantic slave trade.

From that inauspicious beginning, Benguela rose to become one of the most important slaving ports in the South Atlantic. There, Portuguese merchants acquired slaves, in warfare or through the hands of African traders, and *nzimbu* shells, used as currency in Kongo.[61] The shoreline and its natural harbor allowed ships to sail close to the coast and dock in the bay. The nine miles of beach offered safe anchorage to ships, protected by the troops ashore. Up to thirty vessels could dock at the Catumbela Bay in the vicinity of the port of Benguela.[62] Additionally,

---

[58] José C. Curto, "Luso-Brazilian Alcohol and the Slave Trade at Benguela and Its Hinterland, c. 1617–1830," in *Négoce Blanc en Afrique Noire: L'évolution du Commerce à Longue Distance en Afrique Noire du 18e au 20e Siècles*, ed. H. Bonin and M. Cahen (Paris: Publications de la Société française d'histoire d'outre-mer, 2001), 353; John K. Thornton, *The Kingdom of Kongo: Civil War and Transition, 1641–1718* (Madison: University of Wisconsin Press, 1983), 6–7, 44; Joseph C. Miller, "The Paradoxes of Impoverishment in the Atlantic Zone," in *History of Central Africa*, ed. David Birmingham and Phyllis Martin (London: Longman, 1983), 131–45.

[59] Adriano A. T. Parreira, "A Primeira 'Conquista' de Benguela (Século XVII)," *História*, 28 (1990): 67.

[60] Heywood and Thornton, *Central Africans, Atlantic Creoles*, 116.

[61] For the use of *zimbo* in Kongo, see Birmingham, *Central Africa to 1870*, 28–30; Hogendorn and Johnson, *The Shell Money of the Slave Trade*, 101–2.

[62] Heintze, *Fontes para a Historia de Angola*, 1, 184, "Descrição dos Portos de Luanda e Benguela," January 8, 1630.

currents and winds forced ship captains to stop by the port, creating the opportunity to provide the variety of services required by visitors. In 1624, the newly appointed governor of Angola, Fernão de Sousa, spent nine days in Benguela on his way to Luanda.[63] In 1667, Capuchin missionary Giovanni Antonio Cavazzi described a trip from Pernambuco, Brazil, to the port of Luanda via Benguela. Because of the currents and strong winds the ship faced in November, the captain of the ship was forced to sail south. The ship landed in Benguela and, a few days later, in Luanda.[64] Location and ocean currents helped to expand trade and insert the port into the world economy, where slave exports became the organizing force of accumulation and wealth.[65]

The multiplicity of rulers and the Portuguese goal to expand and acquire slaves resulted in low-level warfare strategies that men on the spot employed to guarantee territorial control and to generate captives to meet the demand in the Spanish colonies in the Americas, a topic I will cover in more detail in Chapter 3. Metropolitan and Luanda authorities insisted on the importance of advancing territorial conquest throughout the seventeenth century, and the men on the spot continued to negotiate expansion at the expense of neighboring *sobas*. Roquinaldo Ferreira, however, claims that "efforts to stake out control over the interior of Benguela were neglected" owing to the focus on Luanda's hinterland.[66] As we will see in the next section, agents on the ground in Benguela continuously made efforts to occupy the interior, enjoying a degree of autonomy their location granted them. The official correspondence mentions few encounters with the local Ndombe population. By 1626, two of the Ndombe chiefdoms located at the Bay of Benguela, under Peringue and Kizamba, were vassals of the Portuguese. Both provided food, cattle, and slaves to the settlement of Benguela from the early seventeenth century.[67]

---

[63] Heintze, *Fontes para a Historia de Angola*, 1, 23, 184, "Descrição dos Portos de Luanda e Benguela," January 8, 1630.

[64] Giovanni Antonio Cavazzi, *Descrição Histórica dos Três Reinos do Congo, Matamba e Angola* (Lisbon: Junta de Investigações do Ultramar, 1965), 2, 282, L. VII, para. 172.

[65] Wallerstein, *World-Systems Analysis*. For the use of world-systems analysis before the nineteenth century, see Terence K. Hopkins and Immanuel Wallerstein, "Commodity Chains in the World-Economy Prior to 1800," *Review (Fernand Braudel Center)* 10, no. 1 (1986): 157–70.

[66] Roquinaldo Ferreira, "Slaving and Resistance to Slaving in West Central Africa," in *The Cambridge World History of Slavery. AD 1420–AD 1804*, vol. 3, ed. David Eltis and Stanley L Engerman (New York: Cambridge University Press, 2011), 118.

[67] AHU, Angola, caixa 2, doc. 103, July 16, 1626; and Francisco Travassos Valdez, *Six Years of a Traveller's Life in Western Africa* (London: Hurst and Blackett, 1861), 320. See also Miller, *Kings and Kinsmen*, 211–13; and Aparício, "Política de Boa Vizinhança," 109.

In the 1680s, Portuguese official António de Oliveira Cadornega claimed that the Ndombe were the "the most loyal vassals of the Portuguese in the province [of Benguela]."[68] Men on the spot and Benguela visitors relied on the local population to feed them and provide soldiers, even when considering them primitive or savage.[69] From official correspondence it is clear that there was no single centralized political power in the region. There were "many lords of their lands and vassals."[70] Several rulers controlled access to land, trade, and their subjects; still their power was restricted to small territories, and warfare was constant in part because the power of the leaders relied on their ability to conquer new communities and tax them. Portuguese accounts refer to the poor conditions of the settlements and to diseases affecting the population more than to the organization of African polities or the customs of the Ndombe who lived around the fortress. Africans were portrayed in the official records as people without any valuable skills. Yet they controlled access to copper mines, manufactured jewelry that enticed the Portuguese, cultivated the food eaten by colonial agents, collected *nzimbu* shells, exploited salt mines, and raised cattle.[71] All these items became very important for the survival of Portuguese agents in West Central Africa and beyond.

The Art of Naming People: *Sobas, Jagas,* the Portuguese, and the Vassal Treaties

Portuguese expansion required the signing of treaties of vassalage with local rulers to guarantee access to land and trade routes and to protect Portuguese settlers. While plunder was constantly used, it was recognized

[68] Cadornega, *História Geral*, 3, 172. António de Oliveira Cadornega lived in Luanda for more than forty years and left one of the earlier accounts on the Portuguese presence in Angola, the three volumes of *História de Angola*. See Beatrix Heintze, *Angola nos séculos XVI e XVII. Estudo sobre Fontes, Métodos e História* (Luanda: Kilombelombe, 2007).

[69] Karen Graubart makes a similar comparison with the Spanish presence in Peru. See her "Indecent Living: Indigenous Women and the Politics of Representation in Early Colonial Peru," *Colonial Latin American Review* 9, no. 2 (2000): 213. For more on Portuguese reliance on *sobas'* cooperation to provided troops, see Thornton, "The African Experience of the '20s," 424–5.

[70] Cadornega, *História Geral*, 3, 172. See also Vansina, *How Societies Are Born*, 190.

[71] Cadornega, *História Geral*, 3, 171. See also Heintze, *Fontes para a História de Angola*, 1, 213, "A Angola Portuguesa e Regiões Circunvizinhas: Descrição Topográfica e História da Ocupação Portuguesa," after August 4, 1630; Brásio, *Monumenta Missionária*, 7, 436, "Relação da Conquista de Benguela," April 22, 1626; and Cavazzi, *Descrição Histórica dos três Reinos*, 1, 25, L. I, para. 20. For more on warfare as a characteristic of chiefdoms, see Earle, *Chiefdoms*, 6.

as a limited practice with serious consequences in the long run. Alliances with local rulers were seen as key to the success of trade and the colonial presence, yet the imposition of a new order made use of metaphors of savagery and barbarity to justify the use of violence. Political and economic alliances had been established already elsewhere along the African coast and reveal the inclusion of African rulers in this new and expanding Atlantic world. Treaties signed between Portuguese authorities and African rulers reproduced European categories of vassalage, including their terminology. They also adapted local ceremonies, such as the *undar*.[72] In a formal ceremony borrowed from the transmission of power in the state of Ndongo, subjects and elders recognized the acceptance of a new authority associated with supernatural power. *Undar*, according to contemporary witnesses, was performed when a prospective ruler lay down on the floor and dust or flour was thrown over his body. This dust then was spread over his chest and arms, marking his rise to power and his acceptance by the elders of the community. In the case of the *undamentos* under the auspices of the governor of Benguela, the governor himself threw the dust or flour over the soon-to-become *soba*. After receiving the dust or flour, the newly inaugurated *soba* agreed to subject himself and his followers to the Portuguese Crown. Mixing local and foreign practices, a letter, in Portuguese, was signed by all involved to indicate that they agreed to the contract, showing the importance of writing in the colonial world. African rulers who accepted vassalage declared a solemn oath of obedience and loyalty, and the Portuguese promised protection and recognized the legitimacy of the ruler.[73] In this

[72] The most important works on vassal treaties in Angola are Beatrix Heintze, "The Angolan Vassal Tributes of the 17th Century," *Revista de História Económica e Social* 6 (1980): 57–78; and Beatrix Heintze, "Luso-African Feudalism in Angola? The Vassal Treaties of the 16th to the 18th Century," *Separata da Revista Portuguesa de História* 18 (1980): 111–31. See also her *Angola nos Séculos XVI e XVII. Estudos sobre Fontes, Métodos e História* (Luanda: Kilombelombe, 2007), chap. 7. Vassal treaties were also employed with the Amerindian population of Brazil. See Angela Domingues, *Quando os Índios eram Vassalos. Colonização e Relação de Poder no Norte do Brasil da segunda metdade do Século XVIII* (Lisbon: Comissão Nacional para as Comemorações dos Descobrimentos Portugueses, 2000); see also Manuela Carneiro da Cunha and Francisco Salzano, *História dos Índios no Brasil* (São Paulo: Companhia das Letras, 1992). For examples elsewhere, see Green, *The Rise of the Trans-Atlantic Slave Trade*, 152–3.

[73] For more on *undar*, see Felner, *Angola*, 472. See also Heintze, "Luso-African Feudalism in Angola?" 116; Catarina Madeira Santos, "Escrever o Poder. Os Autos de Vassalagem e a Vulgarização da Escrita entre as Elites Africanas Ndembu," *Revista de História* 155, no. 2 (2006): 86–8; Ana Paula Tavares and Catarina Madeira Santos, *Africæ*

way, Portuguese agents incorporated a local practice, *undar*, and added to it new elements, in the same way that local chiefdoms adopted the ceremony to reinforce their power vis-à-vis their neighbors and subjects. Vassalage in itself reveals the ongoing process of creolization taking place in Benguela by the early seventeenth century, a topic I will explore further in Chapter 2. Creolization is understood here not as Westernization, as James Sweet fears, but as adoption of new values, which assumed new meanings to all the actors involved. As Toby Green has explained, "[E]ach of the groups involved in this cross-cultural trade borrowed from one another's practices in order to find a mutual territory of shared understanding and communication."[74]

In the eighteenth century, during the vassalage ceremony, African rulers received a royal stamp on the left side of their chest "to be respected by their subjects, and be recognized as vassal of the Portuguese Majesty" in a form similar to the physical stamps put on exported slaves.[75] It is not clear if the physical mark was done in the seventeenth century. Vassals had to pay tribute, usually in the form of captives. They also allowed the incursion of traders and armies into the territory under their control. In addition, they hosted colonial officials and provided men as soldiers and porters. Vassals had to refrain from violence and could not take in slaves who had run away from white settlers or any other resident in the Portuguese settlements. It was a diplomatic, political, and commercial treaty employed by the Portuguese until 1920.[76] Portuguese administrators recognized and incorporated local rulers into the colonial

monumenta: Arquivo Caculo Cacahenda (Lisbon: Instituto de Investigação Científica Tropical, 2002); Linda Heywood and John Thornton, "Central African Leadership and the Appropriation of European Culture," in *The Atlantic World and Virginia, 1550–1624*, ed. Peter C. Mancall (Chapel Hill: University of North Carolina Press, 2007), 220–4; and Pélissier, *História das Campanhas de Angola*, 63–4.

[74] Green, *The Rise of the Trans-Atlantic Slave Trade in Western Africa, 1300–1589*, 154. For James Sweet's remarks, see his *Domingos Álvares, African Healing, and the Intellectual History of the Atlantic World* (Chapel Hill: University of North Carolina Press, 2011), 5–6.

[75] See ANTT, Conde de Linhares, Mç. 46, doc. 4, July 9, 1765. For an example of vassal treaties in the nineteenth century, see "Auto de Undamento e Vassalagem que prestou o soba Iundo Aquembi em 1838," *Angola, Mensário Administrativo* 7 (1948): 40; and Santos, "Escrever o Poder," 81–95.

[76] For the obligations of vassals, see Heintze, "The Angolan Vassal," 57–78; Catarina Madeira Santos, "Écrire le Pouvoir en Angola. Les archives Ndembu (XVIIe -Xxe Siècles)," *Annales. Histoire, Sciences Sociales* 4 (2009): 776–7; and Rosa Cruz e Silva, "The Saga of Kakonda and Kilengues," in *Enslaving Connections. Changing Cultures of Africa and Brazil during the Era of Slavery*, ed. José C. Curto and Paul E. Lovejoy (New York: Humanity Books, 2004).

state. Called *sobas*, as in their previous experience north of the Kwanza River, local rulers were perceived as native authorities by the Portuguese Crown, and they were responsible for tax collection and army recruitment.[77] Their function in the Portuguese empire was not different from the "chiefs" employed by the British in Northern Nigeria or in East Africa in the late nineteenth and early twentieth centuries. Vassals became colonial intermediaries, in search of new opportunities that could preserve their position in the context of colonial conquest.[78]

Vassal treaties recognized political, geographic, and physical rights of *sobas* and their subjects and also set a boundary that recognized Africans who were allies and protected them from others who were not.[79] After his vassalage in 1618, the *soba* of Peringue, for example, was forced to provide Cerveira Pereira with slaves to be employed in public service, including responsibility for security at the port and its surroundings. Some of them also were used as domestic servants. Although originally foreign, these treaties resonated with African rulers because they used similar strategies in their diplomatic and political alliances and made use of practices familiar to them, such as the *undar*.[80] With the vassalage treaties, populations living in regions under Portuguese rule were subjects of the Portuguese Crown, and colonial officials had to protect them. In order to be considered a vassal from the mid–seventeenth century onward, rulers and their subjects were expected to convert to Christianity. As vassals and allies of the colonial state, their enslavement and deportation to the Americas should have been prevented by the Portuguese Crown, although vassalage and Christianity did not protect many people in Angola.[81]

---

[77] Miller, *Kings and Kinsmen*, 258.

[78] Michael Crowder, "Indirect Rule: French and British Style," *Africa: Journal of the International African Institute* 34, no. 3 (1964): 197–205; Cooper, *Colonialism in Question*, 164–5, 184–5; Benjamin N. Lawrance, Emily Osborn, and Richard L. Roberts (eds.), *Intermediaries, Interpreters, and Clerks: African Employees in the Making of Colonial Africa* (Madison: University of Wisconsin Press, 2006), 7–10.

[79] AHU, Angola, caixa 9, doc. 25, April 10, 1666. On classification and the language of rights, see Pamela Scully, *Liberating the Family? Gender and British Slave Emancipation in the Rural Western Cape, South Africa, 1823–1853* (Portsmouth, NH: Heineman, 1997), 34–46; and Graubart, "Indecent Women," 223–4.

[80] For the *soba* of Peringue's obligations, see Delgado, *O Reino de Benguela*, 67. For the similarities between Portuguese and West Central African political and diplomatic institutions, see Heywood and Thornton, *Central Africans, Atlantic Creoles*, 106–7, 119; and John Thornton, "'I Am the Subject of the King of Congo': African Ideology in the Haitian Revolution," *Journal of World History* 4 (1993): 181–214; Heywood and Thornton, "Central African Leadership," 194–224.

[81] Heintze, "Angolan Vassal Tributes," 57–78. See also Candido, "African Freedom Suits and Portuguese Vassal Status," 447–59. On Catholic Africans in the Americas, see

Vassalage altered naming practices and became important as an identifier in the region, reinforcing creolization and making it accessible to more people. At the same time, vassalage became a product of the process of cultural pluralism and creolization. The ruler of Peringue, for example, was called *jaga* in the colonial documents before he signed a treaty with the Portuguese Crown. In 1618, while he resisted Portuguese control, the ruler was referred to as the *jaga* of Peringue. In the same year, Cerveira Pereira invaded Peringue's territory and seized 200 people and 150 head of cattle.[82] After the defeat, Peringue declared vassalage to the Portuguese and, for the first time, was called *soba* in the Portuguese correspondence. This account shows how African rulers and Portuguese officials had different interpretations of vassalage and dependency and how naming practices in the correspondence classify Africans and their subjects as allies or not. Being a *jaga* or a *soba* was positional and could change depending on the relationship between colonial authorities and African forces. Both terms were imposed on the local population by the colonial agents in part because the designations were foreign (probably Kimbundu) and referred to previous encounters of the Portuguese with populations located north of the Kwanza River. Portuguese explorers and administrators called most African rulers they encountered in West Central Africa, if they were not *mani* or *dembo*, a *soba*.[83] Rulers simultaneously profited from the situation, demonstrating how it was a mutually beneficial commercial and political alliance. Men on the spot reinforced the power of *sobas* because vassal rulers became privileged intermediaries

Hein Vanhee, "Central African Popular Christianity and the Making of Haitian Vodou Religion," in *Central Africans and Cultural Transformations in the American Diaspora*, ed. Linda Heywood (Cambridge: Cambridge University Press, 2001), 243–64; Heywood and Thornton, *Central Africans, Atlantic Creoles*; Thornton, *Africa and Africans*; John K. Thornton, "On the Trail of Voodoo: African Christianity in Africa and the Americas," *The Americas* 44 (1988): 261–78; and James H. Sweet, *Recreating Africa: Culture, Kinship, and Religion in the African-Portuguese World, 1441–1770* (Chapel Hill: University of North Carolina Press, 2003), 109–15, 191–215. For the reception of Catholicism among Central Africans, see Wyatt MacGaffey, *Religion and Society in Central Africa: The BaKongo of Lower Zaire* (The University of Chicago Press, 1986), 191–216.

[82] AHU, Angola, caixa 1, 87, July 2, 1618; Delgado, *O Reino de Benguela*, 70–2.

[83] *Mani* was the local title employed in the kingdom of Kongo and Ndongo. See Joseph C. Miller, "Central Africans During the Era of the Slave Trade, c. 1490s–1850s," in *Central Africans and Cultural Transformations in the American Diaspora* (Cambridge: Cambridge University Press, 2001), 40–3; and Beatrix Heintze, "Written Sources and African History: A Plea for the Primary Source. The Angola Manuscript Collection of Fernão de Sousa," *History in Africa* 9 (1982): 77–103. *Dembo* was the title of the rulers of the Ndembu, principalities along the Kwanza River. See Santos, "Escrever o Poder," 82–3. See also Vansina, *How Societies are Born*, 187–90.

in the commerce between the coast and the interior and had access to imported commodities. Moreover, traders had to pay tribute to *sobas* while crossing their territories, bringing additional economic advantages beyond what the movement of a caravan could provide. Colonial classifications of local rulers as *sobas* or *jagas* also were influenced by economic activities and lifestyle. Farmers, for example, were seen as less threatening than cattle owners with their transhumance and nomadic pastoral lifestyle. In this the Portuguese colonial experience in the seventeenth century is not different from French or British colonialism two centuries later, when the pastoralist Fulani became a major source of political conflict over economic rights.[84]

After Peringue declared vassalage in 1618, Governor Cerveira Pereira was visited by "the neighboring *jaga*" of Kangombe. Again, Pereira did not explain the meaning of the term *jaga* or the exact location of Kangombe, although it seems that the Kangombe territory was located north, close to Catumbela. According to Pereira's account, "[T]his black man said he was an enemy of the local unconverted ruler [Peringue]."[85] The *jaga* of Kangombe approached the Portuguese forces in order to get support to defend his people and engage in expansionist conquest. The ruler saw the Portuguese as a possible ally who could offer weapons and support. Governor Pereira initially welcomed Kangombe, but eventually his power became a threat to the Portuguese presence along the littoral. Kangombe hosted runaway slaves of Portuguese settlers, which was a clear violation of the vassalage treaty. Kangombe refused to return runaway slaves

---

[84] A. G. Adebayo, "Jangali: Fulani Pastoralists and Colonial Taxation in Northern Nigeria," *International Journal of African Historical Studies* 28, no. 1 (1995): 125–7.

[85] AHU, Angola, caixa 1, 87, July 2, 1618. *Ngombe* means "cattle" in several Bantu languages, including Umbundu; thus the name was probably used by several rulers in the region and did not necessarily refer to the same group. Childs claimed that Kangombe was a tributary of the *soba* of Bié, thus living in the central highlands by the nineteenth century, although Kangombe declared vassalage to Captain Dom Antonio de Alencastre (1772–9) in an earlier period. See Gladwyn M. Childs, *Umbundu Kinship and Character* (Oxford University Press, 1949), 198. In the 1880s, Sanders, a missionary stationed in Viye, stated that *Kangombe* was the title of the ruler of Viye. See *The Missionary Review of the World* (Princeton, NJ: Missionary Review Publishing, 1882), 476. In the early twentieth century, the missionary Luíz Keiling claimed that Kangombe was an Ngalange *soba*. See Luiz Keiling, *Quarenta anos de África* (Braga: Edição das Missões de Angola e Congo, 1934), 110. During the summer of 2011, I visited one region known as Candombe Inglês, located between Dombe Grande and the coast, southwest of Benguela. I asked several people if Candombe and Kangombe could be the same place, but no one was able to provide a convincing explanation that the *soba* of Kamgombe in 1618 was living on land around Dombe Grande nowadays, some 65 kilometers southeast of Benguela.

and accused "whites of being women ashore," adding that "they [whites] were men only in the sea."[86] Through an ambassador, he renounced Christianity and broke away from Portuguese control. Cerveira Pereira threatened Kangombe and requested the return of the runaway slaves. He reminded him of the vassal agreement; otherwise, he "would show if the whites were men or women." The behavior of Kangombe opened space for a "just war," a rationalization for attacking the unfaithful that had been used in Portugal since the fourteenth century to justify attacks against Muslims and Jews. Legitimization of war through a religious lens crossed the Atlantic and was used in actions against Muslims in North Africa, Amerindians in Brazil, and Africans, showing how experiences elsewhere shaped the Portuguese actions in Benguela.[87]

After the heated exchange between Cerveira Pereira and Kangombe, the governor gathered sixty soldiers and headed to Catumbela to defeat the *jaga* in battle. The troops crossed the Catumbela River and arrived at Kangombe's land, capturing Kangombe and his subjects. For fifteen days the Portuguese troops stayed in Kangombe's land, looting villages and seizing people as part of the booty of war. A law from 1570 allowed the enslavement of captives of a "just war against the heathens, with authorization [of the King] or of the governor of the land."[88] The debate on the legality of the war was designed to prevent illegal enslavement of vassals. A war could be "just" from the perspective of the Portuguese jurists if it was done against "Moors and Turks" or "unfaithful" people who prevented the work of missionaries and traders evangelizing the heathens. In the case of the conflict with Kangombe, Portuguese troops enslaved captives of war and seized food stock and cattle herds. Acting as the governor of the land, Cerveira Pereira ordered Kangombe to be beheaded, in a clear attempt to show the strength of the Portuguese forces and serve as an example to other rulers. Indeed, five days after returning to Benguela,

---

[86] AHU, Angola, caixa 1, 87, July 2, 1618.
[87] Beatriz Perrone-Moisés, "A Guerra Justa em Portugal no Séc. XVI," *Sociedade Brasileira de Pesquisa Histórica* 5 (1989–90): 6; Ligia Bellini, "Notas sobre Cultura, Política e Sociedade no mundo Português do séc. XVI," *Tempo* 7 (1999): 13–17; Angela Domingues, "Os Conceitos de Guerra Justa e Resgate e os Amerindios do Norte do Brasil," In *Brasil: Colonização, Escravidão*, Maria B. N. Silva (ed.) (Rio de Janeiro: Nova Fronteira, 2000); Lauren Benton, "The Legal Regime of the South Atlantic World, 1400–1750: Jurisdictional Complexity as Institutional Order," *Journal of World History* 11, no. 1 (2000): 46–8.
[88] For the war on Kangombe, see AHU, Angola, caixa 1, 87, July 2, 1618; also described in Delgado, *Reino de Benguela*, 67–9. For the 1570 law, see Perrone-Moisés, "A Guerra Justa em Portugal," 6.

Pereira received the ambassador of the ruler of Kitumbela, who requested the friendship of Governor Cerveira Pereira.[89] After becoming a vassal, the ruler of Kitumbela was called a *soba*, and as such, he obtained weapons and gunpowder from the Portuguese as tribute. The firearms were used to attack the decentralized Kwandu groups. In alliance with Portuguese forces, Kitumbela captured more than 1,000 cattle and 94 copper bracelets from that conflict.[90]

These attacks and vassalage treaties signed in the initial years of colonial settlement illustrate some patterns of Portuguese expansion in Benguela. First, they demonstrate the limitations of the colonial state and the importance of political alliances with local rulers to guarantee territorial control. Second, they reveal the intense cultural exchange between the actors involved and how creolization was central to Portuguese colonialism and expansion of the slave trade. Third, they display how armed conflict was endemic and perceived in terms of strategic alliances and even masculinity. Fourth, they also indicate the existence of several polities of different sizes and structures around Benguela. Cerveira Pereira employed the terms *jaga* and *soba* several times without explaining their meaning, indicating that they were concepts that were self-evident in the Portuguese world of the seventeenth century. Scholars, however, have been debating the meaning of *jaga* for decades. In the seventeenth century, *jaga* had a derogatory meaning. Andrew Battell, who visited Benguela-Velha in 1601–2 and traveled among the *jagas*, described them as "the greatest cannibals and man-eaters in the world, for they feed chiefly upon man's flesh [notwithstanding their] having all the cattle of that country."[91] Descriptions of non-Europeans as cannibals filled the travel narratives of the early centuries of European expansion. Cannibals, for example, could be attacked in just wars because anthropophagy was a "horrible sin against nature."[92] Battell described the *jagas* as nomadic pastoral people

---

[89] AHU, Angola, caixa 1, 87, July 2, 1618. See also Felner, *Angola*, 336–7.

[90] AHU, Angola, caixa 1, 87, July 2, 1618.

[91] Ravenstein, *Strange Adventures*, 21. For other seventeenth-century accounts describing the *jagas* as cannibals, see Beatrix Heintze, "Contra as Teorias Simplificadoras. O 'Canibalismo' na Antropologia e História da Angola," in *Portugal não é um País Pequeno. Contar o "Império" na Pós-Colonidade*, ed. Manuela Ribeiro Sanches (Lisbon: Cotovia, 2006), 223–4. The association between *jagas* and cannibalism is still strong. *The Dictionary of Portuguese-African Civilization*, published in 1995, defined *jagas* as "savage groups from southeast of the Congo and Cuango Rivers who c. 1580 repeatedly attacked and ransacked São Salvador and other settlements." See Benjamin Núñez, *Dictionary of Portuguese-African Civilization* (London: Hans Zell, 1995), 1, 223.

[92] Perrone-Moisés, "A Guerra Justa em Portugal," 8–9. On canibalism as an excuse to justify the disappearance of smuggled slaves, see Miller, *Kings and Kinsmen*, 197,

who migrated in search of water sources. He also mentioned that they did not consume meat but fed themselves with milk.[93] *Jagas* were portrayed as people without faith, king, or order, as bands of nomads who pillaged the people they encountered. Officials who were unhappy with the tight control of Cerveira Pereira, for example, preferred to join the *jagas* than remain in Benguela.[94] In 1618, the Portuguese Baltasar Rebelo de Aragão referred to the *jagas* as

Aliens who wander in the interior. They attack and rob people, and are organized in large groups. Some of them served the Portuguese, especially the governors, who employed them to control sobas who rebelled against Portuguese control. The Portuguese, however, do not control the Jagas, and when they tried to do it, the Jagas rose up and seized many slaves.[95]

Jagas were said to come originally from the interior of the continent and have been associated with the Imbangala hordes. In all cases they were portrayed as savage, violent anthropophagics.[96] Rather than natural lords of the land, the *jagas* were tyrants who engaged in cannibalism.

244–51. For an interpretation of Europeans as cannibals, see Heintze, "Contra as Teorias Simplificadoras," 221–2; Beatrix Heintze, "Propaganda Concerning 'Man Eaters' in West Central Africa in the Second Half of the Nineteenth Century," *Paideuma* 49 (2003): 125–32; and John Thornton, "Cannibals, Witches, and Slave Traders in the Atlantic World," *William and Mary Quarterly* 60, no. 2 (2003): 273–94. For more on how the idea of cannibalism shaped European encounters with the "other," see Nigel Rigby, "Sober Cannibals and Drunken Christians: Colonial Encounters of the Cannibal Kind," *Journal of Commonwealth Literature* 27 (1992): 171–82; Robin Law, "Human Sacrifice in Pre-colonial West Africa," *African Affairs* (1985): 58–9. On West Central Africans seen as cannibals in the Americas, see Kathryn Joy McKnight, "Confronted Rituals: Spanish Colonial and Angolan 'Maroon' Executions in Cartagena de Indias (1634)," *Journal of Colonialism and Colonial History* 5, no. 3 (2004). For a different time period, see Luise White, *Speaking with Vampires: Rumors and History in Colonial Africa* (Berkeley: University of California Press, 2000).

93 On cattle societies in West Central Africa, see Jan Vansina, *How Societies Are Born, Governance in West Central Africa before 1600* (Charlottesville: University of Virginia Press, 2004), 121–31.

94 Paulo Jorge de Sousa Pinto, "Em Torno de um Problema de Identidade. Os 'Jagas' na História do Congo e Angola," *Mare Liberum*, nos. 18–19 (1999–2000): 230; see also the account of the Dutch geographer Olfert Dapper in Robert O. Collins, *Central and South African History* (Princeton, NJ: Markus Wiener Publishers, 1990), 33–7.

95 Cited in Ilídio do Amaral, *O Rio Cuanza (Angola), Da Barra a Cambambe: Reconstituição de Aspectos Geográficos e Acontecimentos Históricos dos Séculos XVI e XVII* (Lisbon: Ministério da Ciência e da Tecnologia, 2000), 37–8.

96 Cavazzi, *Descrição Histórica dos Três Reinos*, 1, 173–5, L. II, para. 1; Ravenstein, *Strange Adventures*, 18–20; Cadornega, *História Geral*, 1, 11, 14. For more on this, see Amaral, *O Reino do Congo*, 225–6; and Miller, *Kings and Kinsmen*, 182–3; Miller, *Way of Death*, 4–5; and Thornton, "The African Experience of the '20s," 428–30.

On some occasions, they were said to be rulers neighboring the Kingdom of Angola.[97]

The debate on the *jagas* is long standing among scholars. Jan Vansina claimed that the *jagas* were the Imbangala and that they emerged around the Kilengues area. They were a small pastoral group that migrated north, incorporating warriors along the way.[98] Beatrix Heintze located several *jagas* north and south of the Kwanza in the seventeenth century. Heintze and Vansina agree that the *jagas* originally were pastoral groups from the south who, after joining several operating bands, migrated north. Their interpretation is based on Cadornega's account from the late seventeenth century, which reported *jaga* military camps in the interior of Benguela.[99] In agreement with Vansina's and Heintze's use of sources, Paulo Jorge de Souza Pinto asserts the existence of "many *jagas*," although he recognized that all these different people who were called *jagas* in the Portuguese documentation were not necessarily the same group.[100] From seventeenth-century accounts about Benguela, it is clear that the *jagas* did not represent a single group. *Jagas* seem to be a Portuguese creation, incorporating several groups who resisted the Portuguese advance. The multiplicity of *jagas*, sometimes placed in Kongo and at other times in the Benguela central highlands or in Kassange, indicates that they were not the same group, except in the mind of the Portuguese colonialists.[101] Anne Hilton claimed that the *jagas* were dislocated Kongo or Tio groups, ancestors of the Yaka, who raided Kongo in 1568 and attempted to break Kongo's monopoly on the slave trade.[102] Yet she also claims that in the Kongo the term *jaga* was employed to refer to the "other," not necessarily

[97] Vansina, "On Ravenstein's Edition," 343.

[98] Vansina, *How Societies Are Born*, 197; see also David Birmingham, "The Date and Significance of the Imbangala Invasion of Angola," *Journal of African History* 62, no. 2 (1965): 143–52; and Heywood and Thornton, *Central Africans, Atlantic Creoles*, 94.

[99] Heintze, "Critical Approaches," 83; and Beatrix Heintze, "Translocal Kinship Relations in Central African Politics of the 19th Century," in *Translocality. The Study of Globalising Processes from a Southern Perspective*, ed. Ulrike Freitag and Achim von Oppen (Leiden: Brill, 2010), 189. See also Cadornega, *História Geral*, 3, 249–50.

[100] Heintze, "Critical Approaches," 83; and Pinto, "Em Torno de um Problema," 196.

[101] Lopes de Limas placed the *jagas* in the Mbailundu and Libolo, in the interior of Benguela, but also in Zenze and Cafuxe, in the Luanda hinterlands. See Lima, *Ensaios Sobre a Statistica*, 3, xxxv, 200–1.

[102] Hilton, "The *Jaga* Reconsidered." According to sources from the 1660s, the *jagas* were neighbors of the Queen Njinga in Matamba, and by the 1700s, they occupied the territory east of Kwango. See R. Avelto, "Les Grandes Mouvements de Peuple en Afrique. Jagas et Zimba," *Bulletin de Geographie Historique et Descriptive* 27, 1–2 (1912): 137.

to a specific group. Joseph Miller also indicates that the portrayal of the *jagas* was shaped by Portuguese ideas of people they considered barbarous, cruel, and uncivilized.[103] Alfredo Margarido and later on Isabel de Castro Henriques reveal that the Portuguese called other groups *jagas*, including some in Senegambia.[104] It seems that in seventeenth-century Benguela, the Portuguese employed the term, derived from their experience in the Kongo in 1568 with the so-called *jaga* invasions, to refer to any group that was not under Portuguese control.[105] Thus, rather than referring to a specific group of people in Benguela, *jaga* was employed to refer to nameless enemies, whose political and social structure was foreign to the Portuguese. In sum, they only existed in the mind of the Portuguese, unable to identify differences among different groups. A parallel situation was found with the *zimba*, a term used by the Portuguese to refer to any "bellicose group" in East Africa.[106] Portuguese agents represented the African population living around Benguela by reference to classifying systems they had experienced earlier. Yet the term gained a life of its own, and the *jagas* have received the attention of a number of scholars.

The acknowledgment of differences and similarities with an entity that was already known, however, brings its own classification and hierarchy. The language employed in the official correspondence is highly formalized and expressed stereotypes that the Portuguese employed when they encountered new or unknown people. The only kinds of political structures the Portuguese could understand were those similar to their own monarchy, which explains their relative success in Kongo, for example, or in the Ndongo. When facing small entities that were not as centralized as those groups north of the Kwanza or pastoral groups, the Portuguese assumed that they were backward, which justified the use of the term *jaga* to represent the unknown.[107] From these cases it seems that the term *jaga*

---

[103] Joseph C. Miller, "Requiem for the *Jaga*," *Cahiers d'Etudes Africaines* 13, no. 49 (1973): 122–3.

[104] For more on the *jagas*, see Isabel da Castro Henriques, *Percursos da Modernidade em Angola* (Lisbon: IICT, 1997), 192–5.

[105] Hilton, "The *Jaga* Reconsidered," 196; and John Thornton, "A Resurrection for the *Jaga*," *Cahiers d'Études Africaines* 18, nos. 1–2 (1978): 223–7. Miller, however, associates the 1568 events in Kongo with internal conflicts and political disputes about who was a legitimate ruler. See his "Requiem for the *Jaga*," 146–7; and François Bontinck, "Un Mausolée pour les Jaga," *Cahier d'Études Africaines* 20, no. 3 (1980): 387–9.

[106] See Miller, "Requiem for the *Jaga*," 125; and Edward Alpers, "The Mutapa and Malawi Political Systems to the Time of the Ngoni Invasions," in *Aspects of Central African History*, ed. Terence Ranger (London: Heineman Educational Books, 1968), 21.

[107] Heintze, "Critical Approaches," 69.

was employed in Benguela to refer to any African authority that did not recognize Portuguese power and not to a specific group. By the end of the sixteenth century, in the conflict that resulted in the abandonment of the colonial attempt in Benguela-Velha, Portuguese authorities referred to local people who raided the village as *jagas*. Thus it seems that use of the term *jaga* in Benguela did not refer to a specific group but to people seen as a threat, to enemies of the Portuguese, people who resisted commercial alliances and conversion to Christianity. The ruler of Kissama, for example, was repeatedly called *jaga* in Portuguese documentation until he was subject to Portuguese power at the end of the seventeenth century. By 1694, the ruler of Kissama declared that he wanted to accept "the light of the church and the holy baptism."[108] Only then was he called *soba* and not *jaga*, emphasizing the shifting and positional meaning of the term *jaga* to describe rulers not subject to Portuguese power. Yet historians wrote about these groups as if they had meaning for local population in the past, overlooking the fact that they might as well be a mere creation of men on the spot.[109]

Mineral Failure and Improvising a Colony, *ca.* 1617–1640

By the 1620s, the Benguela settlement was surrounded by a fence of wooden posts reinforced with thorns. In the village, Ndombe and other groups participated in the economy created by the Portuguese presence, selling locally produced food, as well as fish, vegetables, and fruit.[110] Although small and vulnerable, the initial settlement expanded beyond the fortress's walls, showing the commitment of the Portuguese to stay there for a long time, in their attempt to establish an overseas empire.[111] Few Portuguese lived in this small Atlantic port. The local population was composed initially of Ndombe, expanded later by the arrival of people

[108] AHU, Angola, caixa 15, doc. 8, March 13, 1694. For more on the link between Christianity, Portuguese expansion, and warfare, see Amaral, *O Reino do Congo*, 80–1.

[109] For more on the idea of men on the spot versus metropolitan officials, see Justin Willis, "'Men on the Spot,' Labor and the Colonial State in British East Africa: The Mombasa Water Supply, 1911–1917," *International Journal of African Historical Studies* 28, no. 1 (1995): 25–48.

[110] AHU, Angola, caixa 1, 87, July 2, 1618; AHU, Angola, caixa. 2, doc. 104, June 18, 1626.

[111] A. J. R. Russell-Wood, "Patterns of Settlement in the Portuguese Empire, 1400–1800," in *Portuguese Oceanic Expansion, 1400–1800*, ed. Francisco Bethencourt and Diogo Ramada Curto (New York: Cambridge University Press, 2007), 161–3; and Delgado, *O Reino de Benguela*, 72.

from other groups, some of them enslaved. Ndombe and Portuguese lived and worked in close contact. The initial population of Benguela was composed of 130 Portuguese men; however, malaria, *paludismo*, reduced the initial contingent to 10 Portuguese officers. They were assisted by 80 Africans employed in the *guerra preta*, the troops recruited by different *sobas* who provided arms to Portuguese officials.[112] The colonial documents do not reveal the number of Ndombe who lived in the initial settlement and who did not serve as soldiers. Although restricted in the extent of their domination, men on the spot were in constant search of new ways to expand their territorial control, and recruiting neighboring populations was a common strategy.

The initial decades of the seventeenth century were a period of "improvising the empire," as defined by Sanjay Subrahmanyam. The Portuguese searched for copper, attacked the Ndombe population, subjugated some rulers, and were constantly redefining priorities and policies. Although slaves were already being exported from Luanda, the main Portuguese interest in the region south of the Kwanza initially rested on mines rather than on slaves. If the goal were simply to export slaves, there would have been no need to establish a colony, dispatch a governor, and install a colonial bureaucracy. The Portuguese had been trading along the Bight of Benin since the early fifteenth century without establishing a fortress, in a clear indication that the commerce in slaves did not require a European settlement.[113] Thus the occupation of Benguela in the early seventeenth century had more to do with the Portuguese conception of empire, including locating mines to secure state wealth and converting non-Christians.

[112] Bolota, *Benguela, Cidade*, 25. On the effects of disease on European troops, although focused on the nineteenth century, see Philip D. Curtin, *Disease and Empire* (Cambridge: Cambridge University Press, 1998). On black troops, see Hebe Mattos, "'Black Troops' and Hierarchies of Color in the Portuguese Atlantic World: The Case of Henrique Dias and his Black Regiment," *Luso-Brazilian Review* 45, no. 1 (2008): 6–29. See also Roquinaldo Ferreira, "The Supply and Deployment of Horses in Angola Warfare (17th and 18th Century)," in *Angola on the Move: Transport Routes, Communications and History*, ed. Beatrix Heintze and Achim Von Oppen (Frankfurt: Lembeck, 2008), 49–51. See also Douglas L. Wheeler, "The Portuguese Army in Angola," *Journal of Modern African Studies* 7, no. 3 (1969): 425–6; Carlos Couto, *Os Capitães-Mores em Angola no Século XVIII: Subsídios para o Estudo para a sua Actuação* (Lisbon: Instituto de Insvestigação Científica de Angola, 1972), 256–8.

[113] Sanjay Subrahmanyam, *Improvising Empire: Portuguese Trade and Settlement in the Bay of Bengal, 1500–1700* (Delhi: Oxford University Press, 1990), 219–25. The Portuguese founded the fortress of São João Batista da Ajuda at Ouidah, in the Bight of Benin, in 1721. See William St. Clair, *The Door of No Return: The History of Cape Coast Castle and the Atlantic Slave Trade*. New York: BlueBridge, 2007, 30–1; Heintze, *Angola nos Séculos XVI e XVII*, 169–71.

And in order to maintain the cross and sword policy, soldiers and priests were sent to Benguela. However, most of the colonial officials were dissatisfied with the living conditions and the threat of Dutch, French, and English traders. Authorities faced revolts by lower-ranking officials and other residents who often had serious health problems and who were not happy with their pay or with the tight control to which they were subjected; in addition, they continually feared that they would be attacked by their African neighbors. In 1617, seventy of the initial settlers tried to leave Benguela, probably tired of the demands of its first governor, Cerveira Pereira. A few months later, another escape was planned by Gaspar, a convict from Portugal. In addition to dealing with individuals who wanted to flee colonial control, Governor Pereira discovered that one of his captains was plotting his murder.[114] Colonial officials stationed in Benguela also faced a series of conflicts with authorities based in Luanda that went back to the separation of the two kingdoms by King Felipe III, when the governor of Angola interpreted the autonomy of Benguela as an affront to his power and authority. The governor of Angola, Luis Mendes de Vasconcelos, and Cerveira Pereira were in constant dispute in the 1620s.[115]

In 1621, Cerveira Pereira showed interest in invading and occupying the territory of Sumbe Ambuila in the north in order to impose vassalage treaties on the local ruler. Sumbe Ambuila had been acting as a middleman in the slave trade, selling captives to European interlopers. He requested that the governor of Angola supply soldiers, horses, a barber "to take care of the sick people," and a *tendala* ("a translator") to facilitate communication.[116] His forces in Benguela were limited (fifty-three soldiers and some exiled civilians), which affected his projects. The lack of doctors was a chronic problem in Benguela. In the early years, Simão

[114] Delgado, *O Reino de Benguela*, 73–4. On the conflicts with neighboring rulers, see Cerveira Pereira's report in AHU, Angola, caixa 2, doc. 1, October 4, 1621.

[115] Delgado, *O Reino de Benguela*, 76–9; Felner, *Angola*, 345.

[116] AHU, Angola, caixa 2 doc. 3, November, 7 1621; Delgado, *O Reino de Benguela*, 95–6; and Felner, *Angola*, 341. For more on the *tendala* and the roles played by this skilled interpreter, cultural broker, and negotiator, see Beatrix Heintze, "Ethnographic Appropriations: German Exploration and Fieldwork in West-Central Africa." *History in Africa* 26 (1999): 105–7; and Tavares and Santos, *Africæ monumenta*, 440. For the function of *tendalas* in Angola during the sixteenth and seventeenth centuries, see Heintze, *Fontes para a História*, 1, 128–9; and Beatrix Heintze, *Angola nos Séculos XVI e XVII. Estudo Sobre Fontes, Métodos e História* (Luanda: Kilombelombe, 2007), 221–3. For more on Sumbe Ambuila's role in Atlantic commerce, see Miller, *Kings and Kinsmen*, 217.

Ferraz worked as a doctor, attending the demands of the residents, although at this point medicines available in Angola were so old that they killed more than cured the sick.[117] Health care was in the hands of barbers, who, as in Portugal and Brazil, performed medical operations, including dental care.[118]

The death of Cerveira Pereira in 1621 created a power vacuum in Benguela. António Pinto and later Cristovão Rodrigues ruled the town temporarily, while the governor of Angola and authorities in Lisbon struggled to find a replacement for the most important position south of the Kwanza River. Bento Banha Cardoso, former governor of Angola, refused his nomination, claiming that Benguela was not an "important part of his majesty's conquered lands. There were no mines, nor any important slave trade. The fortress was located in a risky place, unprotected and vulnerable to any Dutch attack." Besides, Cardoso claimed not to have enough funds to support a local garrison of soldiers. Lopo Soares Lasso accepted the mission as the captain-major of Benguela; though not a governor, he was the highest authority. He arrived in Benguela in 1627, with "72 soldiers, some of them married to help to expand the settlement; some black troops, weapons, gunpowder, ammunition, and boats." Most of the people were paid by Soares Lasso himself because the King provided only weapons and ammunition.[119] The incipient urban center, however, continued to attract inland caravans. By the 1620s, traders from the interior were stopping at Benguela to acquire gunpowder, alcohol, and weapons.[120]

---

[117] AHU, Angola, caixa 2, doc. 3, November, 7 1621; and Bolota, *Benguela, Cidade*, 25. On medical practices, see Brito, *Inquérito à Vida Administrativa*, 21. On the limits of medical knowledge, see also Carlos Alberto Cunha Miranda, *A Arte de Curar nos Tempos da Colônia: Limites e Espaços da Cura* (Recife: Secretaria de Cultura, 2004).

[118] For the role of barbers in Brazil and Portugal, see Tania Salgado Pimenta, "Barbeiros-Sangradores e Curandeiros no Brasil (1808–28)," *História, Ciências e Saúde* 2 (1998): 353; Márcia Moisés Ribeiro, "Nem Nobre, nem Mecânico. A Trajetória Social de um Cirurgião na América Portuguesa do Século XVIII," *Almanack Braziliense* 2 (2005): 71–2; and A. C. de C. M. Saunders, *História Social dos Escravos e Libertos Negros em Portugal (1441–1555)* (Lisbon: Imprensa Nacional-Casa da Moeda, 1999), 196. African barbers were also employed on Portuguese slave ships; see Mariana P. Candido, "Different Slave Journeys: Enslaved African Seamen on Board of Portuguese Ships, c. 1760–1820s," *Slavery & Abolition* 31, no. 3 (2010): 395–409. It is not clear if Africans with some knowledge of treatment were in charge of surgeries as in colonial Brazil. See Mary Karasch, *Slave Life in Rio de Janeiro, 1808–1850* (Princeton, NJ: Princeton University Press, 1987), 203; Manuela C. da Cunha, *Negros estrangeiros. Os Escravos Libertos e a sua volta à África* (São Paulo: Brasiliense, 1985), 32; Sweet, *Recreating Africa*, 139–43.

[119] Delgado, *O Reino de Benguela*, 115–17.

[120] Beatrix Heintze, *Fontes para a História de Angola no Século XVII*, 2 vols. (Stuttgart: F. Steiner Verlag Wiesbaden, 1985–1988).

By 1627, the newly arrived Captain Lopo Soares Lasso found three vassal *sobas* living adjacent to Benguela, the rulers of Peringue, Mani Berro, and Kizamba. He also mentioned "a *soba* of the beach," probably in reference to Kitumbela. In the following years, the new captain-major engaged in several low-level conflicts in the area close to Benguela, and in 1629, he reached the copper mines in the region of Sumbe, near the Cuvo River, but was unable to gain access to it. Soares Lasso also mentioned the subjugation of the ruler of Kakonda located close to the Kupololo River, 40 *légoas* inland, or almost 180 km. The Portuguese colony in Benguela maintained friendly relationships with the "blacks of Kambamba [possibly Cambambe] and Molundo."[121] During the rule of Lopes Soares, several punitive expeditions, or "just wars," were launched against enemies of the *sobas* of Peringue and Mani Berro. The attacks targeted the *jagas* of Anguri, Kissange, and Bisansongo. In the space of a few months, Lopo Soares organized several raids around Benguela, which probably resulted in captives and loss of life, though the extent of loss on the African side is not clear. Portuguese sources refer to the death of five or six slaves of Francisco Dias Quilão, a *tendala*, and a Portuguese soldier, besides a large number of wounded forces. By September 1628, Lopo Soares waged a "just war" against "the most powerful and fearful Black [ruler], Kambamba, who refused to declare obedience to the Portuguese."[122] From the account, it is not clear where the ruler of Kambamba was located, although reports indicate that many subjects of Kambamba were enslaved and killed, and between 4,000 and 5,000 cows were seized.[123] Lopo Soares Lasso's activities in Benguela's surroundings in the 1620s were perceived as strengthening the renown of the Portuguese empire, at a time when it was under the control of the Spanish monarchy. Access to the legendary mines had not been secured, either in Benguela or in Brazil, creating a sense of stress in colonial officials, who hoped

---

[121] Heintze, *Fontes para a História de Angola*, 1, 93, and 2, 180, "Carta de Fernão de Sousa ao Governador," June 1, 1627. See also Delgado, *O Reino de Benguela*, 119; Felner, *Angola*, 352; Vansina, *Kingdoms of the Savanna*, 138; Heywood and Thornton, *Central Africans*, 118.

[122] Delgado, *O Reino de Benguela*, 120–3; T. J. Desch Obi, *Fighting for Honor: The History of African Martial Art Traditions in the Atlantic World* (Columbia: University of South Carolina Press, 2008), 47.

[123] By the end of the nineteenth century, Kambamba was remembered as a legendary female figure among the Chokwe. For more on Kambamba and the link with the Kinguri exodus and the Chokwe, see Heintze, "Translocal Kinship Relations in Central African Politics," 192–3; and Jan Vansina, "It Never Happened: Kinguri's Exodus and Its Consequences," *History in Africa* 25 (1998): 387–403.

that mineral wealth would bring Spanish domination to an end. Since the Iberian Union in 1580, Spanish traders had guaranteed access to mines in the viceroyalty of New Spain and Peru, enriching the public fund of the Spanish empire, whereas the Portuguese continued to face not only political failure but also economic crisis.

By the 1630s, the town was described as surrounded by fertile lands, with a salt mine nearby at the bay of São Francisco. Close to the fortress there was *pau de cacongo*, an aromatic wood employed in cooking utensils, such as spoons, and also worn by Ndombe in their necklaces.[124] The business in salt attracted traders from Huila in the southeast, at the margins of the Kunene River, who would come to acquire salt in exchange for ivory and ostrich plumes.[125] It was through these inland traders that colonial officials got information about the interior and continued to believe in the possibility of discovering silver and copper mines. In 1636, Nicolau de Lemos mentioned that "several metal mines" existed in the hinterland as a motive to gain control over land and rulers.[126] The expansion inland also was seen as an opportunity to establish an overland route to Luanda, from where troops could arrive more quickly. Winds and currents in the south Atlantic made it difficult to sail from Luanda into Benguela. Communication between the two Portuguese settlements in West Central Africa was exclusively nautical owing to the difficulties the Portuguese had in using overland routes through Kissama. Kissama remained outside of Portuguese control for most of the seventeenth century, which made Benguela very appealing to traders who were not willing to abide by the law and to European competitors who were unhappy with the Portuguese monopoly on the departure of slaves.[127] The conflicts in Kissama can be traced back to the beginning of the Paulo Dias expansion. After that, there were several attempts to control the region, and in 1593–4 a short-lived fortress was installed there. By 1625, the governor of Angola, Fernão de Sousa, explained the importance of Kissama

---

[124] Delgado, *O Reino de Benguela*, 97; *Benguela e seu Sertão*, 21. Battell described it as very esteemed by the Portuguese. See Ravenstein, *Strange Adventures*, 16.

[125] AHU, Angola, caixa 2, doc. 104, June 18, 1626; Cadornega, *História Geral*, 3, 172–3. For the importance of salt in this region, see Amaral, *O Rio Cuanza*, 36. For salt in other parts of Africa, see Paul E. Lovejoy, *Salt of the Desert Sun: A History of Salt Production and Trade in the Central Sudan* (Cambridge: Cambridge University Press, 1986).

[126] AHU, Angola, caixa 3, doc. 27, prior to February 1, 1636.

[127] Birmingham, *Trade and Conflict in Angola*, 140; Beatrix Heintze, "Historical Notes on the Kisama of Angola," *Journal of African History* 13, no. 3 (1972): 417–18. For the importance of nautical communication in the Portuguese domain, see Russell-Wood, "Pattern of Settlement," 170.

"as security for the city [of Luanda], control of the salt mines, and a route to the mines of Benguela."[128] Despite several attacks on Kissama, the Portuguese could not control that region, which allowed men on the spot in Benguela to act without oversight by officials stationed in Luanda. By 1695, the governor of Angola, Jacques de Magalhães, sent an expedition headed by Manuel de Magalhães Leitão to conquer Kissama, which resulted in the capture of "many people." The *soba* of Katala also was attacked along the way, which brought about several deaths. Despite these seventeenth-century raids, control over the Kissama region was achieved only in the late nineteenth century.[129] Reports from the first half of the seventeenth century clearly indicated the expansion of the trans-Atlantic slave trade in the region and the capture of a large number of people along the coast, many around Benguela itself. Yet the scholarship denies Benguela's role as an important slave port in the seventeenth century.[130]

Dutch Attack and Occupation

There is little information in the Portuguese sources about events during the 1640s, in part because the Dutch invaded and occupied Benguela from 1641 to 1648. A growing Atlantic power by the 1640s, Dutch merchants were briefly successful in displacing Portuguese traders from Atlantic commerce. Under Spanish control, Portuguese ports were targeted in the ongoing conflicts in Europe between the Netherlands and Spain. The attacks were motivated by the Dutch need to secure access to sources of African slaves to work on plantations in the northeast of Brazil and in the Caribbean, territories already seized by the Dutch. The ports of São Tomé, Luanda, and Benguela were desirable because Dutch merchants had previously imported slaves from those regions.[131] The Dutch invasion

---

[128] AHU, Angola, caixa 2, doc. 75, August 22, 1625. Felner, *Angola*, 367–9. Beatrix Heintze, *Asilo Ameaçado: Oportunidades e Consequências da Fuga de Escravos em Angola no Século XVII* (Luanda: Museu Nacional da Escravatura, 1995), 14–15.

[129] Elias Alexandre da Silva Corrêa, *História de Angola* (Lisbon: Ática, 1937), 324; Aguiar, *Administração Colonial*, 2, 31–3; René Pélissier, *História das Campanhas de Angola. Resistência e Revoltas 1845–1941* (Lisbon: Estampa, 1997), 1, 63.

[130] Curto, José C. "The Legal Portuguese Slave Trade from Benguela, Angola, 1730–1828: A Quantitative Re-appraisal," *África* 17, no. 1 (1993–94): 101–16; Eltis, "The Volume and Structure of the Trans-Atlantic Slave Trade," 17–46; and Heywood and Thornton, *Central Africans, Atlantic Creoles*, 116.

[131] Johannes Postma, *The Dutch in the Atlantic Slave Trade, 1600–1825* (New York: Cambridge University Press, 1990), 18; on the disputes between Portuguese and Dutch traders, see Maria Emilia Madeira Santos, *Problema da Segurança das Rotas e a Concorrência Luso-Holandesa antes de 1620* (Coimbra: Universidade de Coimbra,

of Benguela was a turning point in the way the Portuguese empire related to this Atlantic port. After the attack, the Portuguese Crown sent more troops and reinforced its commitment to the occupation, shifting from the improvisation that shaped its earlier presence to a firmer colonial effort. Moreover, the use of troops from the colony of Brazil to regain control of Benguela initiated a bilateral relationship that lasted until the 1850s. The importance of the South Atlantic link is expressed in the phrase, "without Angola, there is no Brazil."[132]

Lacking a strong military defense and isolated from Luanda, the residents of Benguela and their belongings were easy prey. Following the attack on Luanda and Brazilian ports, the Dutch consolidated their control of the slave trade by occupying Benguela on December 21, 1641.[133] After the attack, Captain Nicolau de Lemos of Benguela looked for refuge in the hinterland with the 90 soldiers (out the town's force of 260) still under his command. Other personnel, such as João Cardoso, a mixed-race soldier of the company of Benguela, and the *tendala* António Rodriguez, fled to the port of Kicombo, halfway between Luanda and Benguela.[134] Ironically, Governor Lemos, who weeks earlier had attacked neighbors who were searching for food, had to rely on them for protection against the Dutch forces, stressing the weakness of the colonial state. He died in the interior, apparently of starvation, according to his replacement, Jerônimo Rodriguez Calado. Calado reported that all the goods stored in the fortress intended to be exchanged for food and slaves were lost, indicating the success of the Dutch attacks. The Dutch were able to gain the support of the local population and African rulers who

---

1985), 121–59; and Robin Blackburn, *The Making of New World Slavery* (New York: Verso, 1998), 196–8.

[132] Alencastro, *O Trato dos Viventes*, 226; and Luiz Felipe de Alencastro, "Continental Drift: The Independence of Brazil (1822), Portugal and Africa," in *From Slave Trade to Empire: Europe and the Colonization of Black Africa, 1780–1880s*, ed. Olivier Pétré-Grenouilleau (New York: Routledge, 2004), 102. For more on the role of the Salvador de Sá army, see Ronaldo Vainfas, "Guerra Declarada e Paz fingida na Restauração Portuguesa," *Tempo* 14, no. 27 (2009): 82–100.

[133] AHU, Angola, caixa 4, doc. 20, March 1, 1643. See also Lima, *Ensaios sobre a statistica das possessões portuguezas*, 3, xxvi. For more on the Dutch presence in West Central Africa, see Alencastro, *O Trato dos Viventes*, 188–246; Klaas Ratelband, *Os Holandeses no Brasil e na costa africana: Angola, Kongo e São Tomé, 1600–1650* (Lisbon: Vega, 2003), 109; and Delgado, *O Reino de Benguela*, 141; and Felner, *Angola*, 356–7; and Heywood and Thornton, *Central Africans, Atlantic Creoles*, 35–44.

[134] AHU, Angola, caixa 4, doc. 57, September 13, 1645; and AHU, Angola, caixa 4, doc. 58, December 4, 1645.

resisted Portuguese control. Portuguese officials claimed that unlike the Portuguese, the Dutch offered

Good treatment and peace so people could live on their lands, with their culture.... The Portuguese, however, harassed and stole from the neighbors as if people were not under the protection and assistance of the [Portuguese] majesty.[135]

The troops only returned to Benguela after a peace agreement was signed between the Netherlands and Portugal in September 1642. According to the peace agreement, from the coast to 14.5 km inland remained under Dutch control. Beyond that, the land was under Portuguese jurisdiction. Thus the agreement did not restore Benguela to Portuguese control. Until 1648, Benguela was a Dutch territory, although some soldiers changed sides and joined the Portuguese later on.[136] If slave exports were not important in Benguela by the 1640s, how can we explain the Dutch invasion and occupation? The number of slaves shipped from Benguela had to be significant to attract interlopers and justify a Dutch attack. Indeed, slaves were shipped from Benguela even if the official documents are silent about this issue. Benguela slaves were found in a variety of locations in the Americas before the 1640s, a point I will explore further in Chapter 3. Although officially trade from Benguela to the Americas only began in the early eighteenth century, the Dutch presence in the 1640s indicates how Benguela was integrated in the Atlantic economy in the seventeenth century, even if this commerce was illegal and Portuguese colonial documents were silent about it. The quantitative approach based on the study of official documents concerning slave exports masks the fact that contraband was a feature of the early trans-Atlantic slave trade. Thus estimates on the volume of the slave trade for the sixteenth and seventeenth centuries were likely lower than the number of people actually enslaved.[137]

The Portuguese Crown regained control of Benguela in 1648, when the troops of Salvador Correia de Sá arrived from Brazil. After they

[135] AHU, Angola, caixa 5, doc. 108, April 5, 1653. A similar situation happened in Luanda. See Miller, *Kings and Kinsmen*, 203.

[136] Delgado, *O Reino de Benguela*, 142–3. See also David Birmingham, *Portugal and Africa* (New York: Palgrave Macmillan, 1999), 69–70.

[137] Other scholars have raised this issue as well: Green, *The Rise of the Trans-Atlantic Slave Trade*, 209–225; Linda A. Newson and Susie Minchin, *From Capture to Sale* (Leiden: Brill, 2007); Ilídio do Amaral, *O Reino do Congo, Os Mbundu (ou Ambundos), O Reino dos "Ngola" (ou De Angola) e a Presença Portuguesa de Finais do Século XV a Meados do Século XVI* (Lisbon: Ministério da Ciência e da Tecnologia, Instituto de Investigação Científica Tropic, 1996), 67–70.

established control of Luanda, they resumed control of the port of Benguela. The expedition to Angola of Governor Correia de Sá of Rio de Janeiro initiated a close relationship between Brazil and Portugal's West Central African territories. Called *brasileiros* or *americanos* to mark them from the Portuguese, some of the people born in Brazil remained in Benguela after the Dutch were expelled, forging interconnections between Benguela and Brazil that remained strong until the abolition of the trans-Atlantic slave trade.[138] The South Atlantic system was in many ways built by these actors, who bypassed Portuguese metropolitan control and established connections across the ocean.

The Colonization Effort

The second half of the seventeenth century was a period of colonizing effort in Benguela. After the Dutch takeover, it became clear that a larger Portuguese military force was necessarily to avoid external threats. More power had to be exercised over the local population, probably based on ongoing debates in Portugal related to the occupation of interior of Brazil, the control over the Amerindian population, and the expansion of sugar industry.[139] The Portuguese efforts to maintain a colony in Benguela should not be disassociated from events taking place across the Atlantic and in other parts of the Portuguese overseas empire. The Joint Iberian Crown came to an end with the enthronement of Dom João IV in 1640, which changed the direction of the Portuguese empire and its relationship with its overseas territories. It was only after 1648 that colonial agents put into practice the ideas presented in the royal charter given to Manoel Cerveira Pereira in 1615: "[C]onquer the Kingdom of Benguela … and plant the seed of the Catholic faith, as my solemnly obligation, and

---

[138] Alencastro, *O Trato dos Viventes*, 270–87; Roquinaldo Ferreira, "O Brasil e a arte da guerra em Angola (sécs. XVII e XVIII)," *Estudos Historicos* 1, no. 39 (2007): 3–23; and Mariana P. Candido, "South Atlantic Exchanges: The Role of Brazilian-Born Agents in Benguela, 1650–1850," *Luso-Brazilian Review* (forthcoming). For a later period, see Mariana P. Candido, "Trans-Atlantic Links: The Benguela-Bahia Connections, 1700–1850," in *Slaving Paths*, ed. Ana Lucia Araujo (Amherst, NY: Cambria Press, 2011), 239–72.

[139] Heintze, *Angola nos séculos XVI e XVII. Estudo sobre Fontes, Métodos e História*; Rafael Chambouleyron, "Portuguese Colonization of the Amazon Region, 1640–1706," PhD dissertation, Cambridge University, 2006; Rafael Chambouleyron, "Plantações, sesmarias e vilas. Uma reflexão sobra a ocupação da Amazônia seiscentista," *Nuevo Mundo Mundos Nuevos* (2006); available at http://nuevomundo.revues.org/2260; Walter Hawthorne, *From Africa to Brazil: Culture, Identity, and an Atlantic Slave Trade, 1600–1830* (New York: Cambridge University Press, 2010).

explore industry that can bring revenue and profits to my own treasury and of my subjects."[140] *Colonialism* is defined here as the effort to exert political control and economic expropriation (of labor and raw material) to the benefit of the metropolis. It is also the effort to deny the right of any other state to trade and expropriate wealth from the colony.[141]

By the end of the Dutch occupation in 1648, the fortress of Benguela was in ruins, with fewer than 100 soldiers, most of whom were *filhos da terra* ("sons of the land"), and only eight weapons. The Dutch had seized artillery, ammunition, and slaves.[142] The first home of the Catholic Church was probably destroyed because the new priest, Manuel Barriga, was in charge of constructing a new church. Salvador de Sá, occupying the position of governor of Angola, nominated new officials, including a Crown judge, a superintendent of the treasury, a secretary, a tax collector, a surgeon, and a barber to attend to the settlement of Benguela. Paulo Pereira, a former member of the Henrique Dias Regiment in Pernambuco, Brazil, was nominated sergeant of the *guerra preta*, the black troops in charge of patrolling the port and protecting colonial interests. Salvador de Sá also sent married couples and other new arrivals from Brazil to settle in Benguela in order to expand the population.[143] Some attempts were made to shift the location of the settlement to Catumbela, a few kilometers further north and considered to be healthier. However, that change never happened. The village remained without a governor until May 1652, when António de Abreu Selema received orders to travel from Lisbon to Benguela. By 1666, 200 white inhabitants and "a great number of blacks" lived in the town.[144] After the Dutch invasion, the Portuguese Crown made an effort to occupy the space and claim it as a colony. This included occupation of the space and confrontation with the

---

[140] AHU, Angola, caixa 1, doc. 33, February 14, 1615. For more on the changes in the Portuguese empire in the 1640s, see Subrahmanyam, *Improvising Empire*, 224–5; António Jose Chrystello Tavares, *Marcos Fundamentais da Presença Portuguesa no Daomé* (Lisbon: Universitaria Editora, 1999), 22–3.

[141] Wallerstein, *World-Systems Analysis*, 56.

[142] AHU, Angola, caixa 5, doc. 39, March 11, 1650; and AHU, Angola, caixa 5, doc. 141, March 9, 1654.

[143] "Patente do Sargento-Mor Paulo Pereira (30 de Setembro de 1648)," *Arquivos de Angola* 9, no 35 (1952), 193–4. For more on the Henrique Dias regiment, see Mattos, "Black Troops," 6–20. For the other nominations, see Delgado, *O Reino de Benguela*, 177–9; and "Do Sirurgião Mor do Reino de Benguela, Bernando Pinto (16 de Dezembro de 1649)," *Arquivos de Angola* 9, no. 35 (1952): 11–12.

[144] AHU, Angola, caixa 5, doc. 55, May 19, 1651; and AHU, Angola, caixa 5, doc. 96, May 6, 1652. See also Bolota, *Benguela, Mãe das Cidades*, 26; and Aguiar, *Administração Colonial Portuguesa*, 1, 216.

local population to secure the spread of Catholicism and to protect the settlement in the port. Benguela was seen as a "kingdom with many commercial opportunities."[145]

The relationship with neighboring African rulers continued to be marked by distrust and fear. Interactions with the ruler of Kakonda were particularly difficult and will be analyzed further in Chapter 5. In 1672, the Captain of Benguela, Manuel Rodriguez de Couto, notified Lisbon that the *jaga* of Kakonda had gathered troops and weapons and, in alliance with his neighbors, had disrupted commerce. The King authorized an attack; however, it never happened due to the sudden death of the captain. Without sufficient porters and soldiers, the attack on Kakonda was canceled. Nonetheless, the governor of Angola notified the King that Captain Manuel Rodriguez de Couto and residents of Benguela had personal interests in fomenting conflict because they planned to capture people and sell them in the trans-Atlantic slave trade.[146] It becomes clear that although the end of the seventeenth century was a moment of reconfiguration of the colony and its role in the Portuguese empire, colonial authorities were combining their interest in the copper mines in Benguela's interior with raiding activities. To ensure control of the port and internal trade, the Portuguese Crown supported territorial occupation as part of the expansion policy. The wars of "conquest" to expand territorial control inland disguised the additional Portuguese desire to capture people and enslave them. The presence of Portuguese officials contributed to the development of trade because they exported sought-after natural resources to Lisbon, such as ivory tusks and ostrich plumes. Officially, colonial administrators were in Benguela to enforce Crown monopoly over exports, but European interlopers visited the port and, in some cases, acted in connivance with authorities. By the 1670s, there was more ivory and slaves than traders could handle or Portuguese authorities could export.[147]

An order from the governor of the Kingdom of Angola, issued on February 12, 1676, declared that the governor had "the duty to know who is a subject or not of the Portuguese Crown. And their vassals should not allow the presence of runaway slaves in their territories, having the obligation to turn them in to Portuguese authorities."[148] Cordial, rather

---

[145] AHU, Angola, caixa 8, doc. 69, November 15, 1664.

[146] AHU, Angola, caixa 11, doc. 4, March 7, 1674. For more on the conflictive relations between Benguela and the *jaga* of Kakonda, see Miller, *Kings and Kinsmen*, 213.

[147] AHU, cod. 544, fl. 10v.–11, February 12, 1676. See also Amaral, *O Reino do Congo*, 86–8.

[148] AHU, cod. 544, fl. 3–3v., February 12, 1676.

than conflicting, relationships with neighboring rulers had to prevail. Vassalage treaties resulted in the collection of significant amounts of tax revenues for the Crown. In 1685, for example, the treasury collected 120 million reis with the sale of the slaves that the *soba* of Libolo had sent to the governor of Benguela.[149] The arrival of slave coffles from Libolo helped to consolidate the slave trade as the most important activity in Benguela by the 1680s. The establishment of the fortress of Caconda on the land of the *Soba* Bongo, a dependent of the *jaga* of Kakonda located 170 to 180 km inland from Benguela, was a Portuguese effort to regulate the movement of caravans and to expand control inland. On the banks of the Kupololo at a mosquito-free altitude, the fortress Nossa Senhora da Conceição of Caconda was well connected to preexisting trade routes and was considered to be a safe environment. The colonial presence away from the coast demonstrated the Portuguese effort to establish a presence in the hinterland despite the continuous threats of European interlopers and hinterland *sobas*.[150] Bureaucracy expanded, even though the number of colonial officials was small. The captain-major and other officials such as the major-lieutenant, the secretary, tax collectors, and captains of the fortress and of the artillery received a regular salary. However, the infantry, composed of 102 men, was not paid regularly.[151]

The defense of the port was then in the hands of only a few men who patrolled the coast and the borders of the settlement, providing security to the residents, without necessarily receiving payment. This led to a series of irregularities that will be explored further in Chapter 3, intimately linked the expansion of violence with the slave trade, tax evasion, and trade in contraband. The military force was not strong enough to prevent the arrival of European interlopers. Even after their expulsion, Dutch merchants continued to sail along the coast, looking for an opportunity to disembark and trade. In 1658, an English ship was caught smuggling, and in 1659, Dutch vessels were seen at Benguela Bay.[152] On March 28, 1677, a Dutch cutter (*pataxo*) arrived in Benguela with the official excuse of looking for two ships that had left the Cape of Good

---

[149] AHU, cod. 545, fl. 33v., August 15, 1685.

[150] AHU, Angola, caixa 13, doc. 51, February 7, 1688. See also Francisco Travassos Valdez, *Six Years of a Traveller's Life in Western Africa* (London: Hurst and Blackett, 1861), 324. See also Vansina, *Kingdoms of the Savanna*, 199; Miller, *Way of Death*, 150–1. For the role of mosquitoes in influencing political and military decisions, see John Robert McNeill, *Mosquito Empires: Ecology and War in the Greater Caribbean, 1620–1914* (New York: Cambridge University Press, 2010).

[151] AHU, Angola, caixa 12, doc. 161, November 20, 1684.

[152] Delgado, *O Reino de Benguela*, 188–9.

Hope and had never returned. The crew bought water, wood, cattle, and chickens from local residents. Days later they were seen negotiating with people south of Benguela.[153] In 1683, two English ships visited Benguela to acquire ivory and slaves, apparently with the support of the authorities. The superintendent of the treasury of Angola denounced the involvement of Benguela residents and authorities with English traders, who challenged the Portuguese monopoly over trade. These cases show the tensions that existed within the empire regarding operation, policies, and goals.[154] It also reveals the constant trade in contraband that characterized much of the economic activity in town for most of the seventeenth century. By the end of the century, the flow of slaves arriving in Benguela had further increased, attracting the attention of other European traders, who tried to bypass Portuguese control. The presence of colonial troops fueled conflicts inland, such as the uprising of the ruler of Kakonda in the 1670s and the attacks by the rulers of Sokoval and Katira in the 1680s and 1690s. The rulers who threatened Portuguese control were labeled as *jagas* in the official documents.[155] The secretary of the Royal Treasury, Vicente Borges Pinheiro, declared

In the hinterland of Benguela there are many *Jagas* and very powerful sobas, with whom our residents trade. Few are vassals of the Majesty, since we had enough power to conquer and maintain control with our weapons. In consequence, many times our *pombeiros* [itinerant traders] are robbed and killed while traveling inland.[156]

These conflicts generated large numbers of captives, which inevitably attracted more merchants. In 1698, a Dutch ship landed in Benguela with four French traders on board, who were well received by local traders.[157] French and English merchants were also well received by African traders because they offered firearms and gunpowder at lower prices, which inevitably fueled violence inland.[158] The Capuchin Antonio Zucchelli,

---

[153] AHU, Angola, caixa 11, doc. 86, July 12, 1677.

[154] AHU, Angola, caixa 12, doc. 116, November 22, 1683.

[155] AHU, Angola, caixa 15, doc. 92, December 12, 1698.

[156] AHU, Angola, caixa 12, doc. 161, November 20, 1684. *Pombeiros* were itinerant traders who carried on business on behalf of coastal traders. Some of them were trusted slaves. See Jan Vansina, "Long-Distance Trade-Routes in Central Africa," *Journal of African History* 3, no. 3 (1962): 378; and Beatrix Heintze, *Pioneiros Africanos: caravanas de carregadores na África Centro-Ocidental: entre 1850 e 1890* (Lisbon: Caminho, 2004), chap. 4.

[157] Delgado, *O Reino de Benguela*, 189–190. See also Birmingham, *The Portuguese Conquest of Angola*, 43.

[158] Birmingham, *Portuguese Conquest of Angola*, 47–8. See also R. A. Kea. "Firearms and Warfare on the Gold and Slave Coasts from the Sixteenth to the Nineteenth Centuries," *Journal of African History* 12, no. 2 (1971): 185–213.

who visited Benguela in 1698, stated that ships reached the port to buy slaves, yet captains and crews remained on board, afraid of the contaminated water and fruit.[159] Evidence suggests that merchants who were established in Benguela joined commercial operations with European traders from competing states. Portuguese, English, Dutch, and French merchants cooperated in business, bypassing national boundaries and royal monopolies. In the end, the opportunity to make a profit was more important than state allegiance to the merchants involved in Atlantic commerce in the seventeenth century.[160] Their international commercial alliances challenged Crown attempts to monopolize the trade. For the Portuguese Crown, foreign traders were pirates, and their presence was a clear violation of Portuguese authority. Foreign incursions on the coast of Benguela were considered illegal slave departures because no taxes were collected, increasing the difficulty of establishing an accurate estimate of the number of people exported from the port. Conflicts between Portuguese and other European forces have to be understood in the context of European disputes but also of commercial alliances along the entire coast of Africa, such as had occurred in Elmina in a conflict involving Portuguese, Dutch, French, and English traders. In Benguela, however, the Portuguese managed to remain officially in control, even if contraband and illegal exports prevailed.

In 1705, a new attack threatened the Portuguese colony. A French fleet arrived in Benguela and destroyed the village, probably looking for slaves and minerals. Considering that Brazilian traders used gold to acquire slaves in West Africa, French merchants were probably hoping to find Brazilian gold in Benguela as well. Besides Benguela, the French attacked the ports of Principe and São Tomé and, eventually, Rio de Janeiro, seeking to guarantee access to the gold from Minas Gerais.[161] Neighboring

---

[159] Antonio Zucchelli, *Relazioni del Viaggio e Missione di Congo nell'Etiopia inferiore Occidentale* (Venice: Bartolomeo Giavarina, 1712), 91.

[160] For other examples in the Atlantic world, see Daviken Studnicki-Gizbert, "La 'Nation' Portugaise. Réseaux Marchands dans l'espace Atlantique à l'époque Moderne," *Annales. Histoire, Sciences Sociales* 58, no. 3 (2003): 627–48; Christopher Ebert, *Between Empires: Brazilian Sugar in the Early Atlantic Economy, 1550–1630* (Leiden: Brill, 2008); Francesca Trivellato, "Juifs de Livourne, Italiens de Lisbonne, Hindous de Goa: Reseaux Marchands et Echanges Interculturels a l'epoque Modern," *Annales. Histoire, Sciences Sociales* 58, no. 3 (2003): 581–603; and David Wheat, "Afro-Portuguese Maritime World and the Foundations of Spanish Caribbean Society, 1570–1640," PhD dissertation, Vanderbilt University, 2009, 31–4.

[161] On the French attacks in Rio de Janeiro, see Russell-Wood, *A World on the Move*, 24–5. For the use of Brazilian gold to acquire slaves in West Africa in the early eighteenth century, see Boxer, "Brazilian Gold," 461; Mariza de Carvalho Soares, "Indícios para

African rulers, such as the *soba* of Mulundo from Dombe, took advantage of the chaos after the French attack and raided Benguela, invading houses and capturing slaves and cattle. Residents and colonial troops were trapped between the French and Mulundo forces. The only solution was to request asylum from the *soba* of Peringue, an old ally of Benguela residents, now located further inland.[162] Mulundo and the French joined forces to prevent resistance or the return of the Portuguese with Peringue forces. Benguela, by early 1700s, was still a very dangerous place for both foreigners and Africans, who could be seized in any raid. Its participation in the Atlantic economy resulted in attacks by European forces as conflicts encroached into Benguela, as with the Dutch and French assaults. Constant warfare, political instability, and weak control by Portuguese forces threatened the existence of the port, yet it was this same violence that made the slave trade a profitable business. The ongoing cycles of conflict explain the reasons behind the requests of African authorities to become allies of the Portuguese. By the end of the seventeenth century, the ruler Ngola Jimbo, close to the fortress of Caconda, declared vassalage to the Portuguese Crown in a ceremony in which local rites of power transfer were celebrated alongside his baptism.[163] Creolization prevailed in Benguela in the seventeenth century.

The Population of Benguela until about 1710

For most of the seventeenth century, Benguela was a small village, with few residents, most of them local Ndombe people. By the mid–seventeenth century, the expansion of the slave trade and the colonial enterprise

o traçado das Rotas Terrestres de Escravos na Baía do Benim, século XVIII," in *Rotas Atlânticas da Diáspora Africana: da Baía do Benim ao Rio de Janeiro* (Niterói: Eduff, 2007); Kenneth G. Kelly, "Change and Continuity in Coastal Benin," in *West Africa during the Atlantic Slave Trade: Archaelogical Perspectives*, ed. Christopher DeCorse (New York: Leicester University Press, 2001), 87. I am very grateful to Mariza de Carvalho Soares for bringing the trade in Brazilian gold in West Africa to my attention. For more on the interaction of smugglers of gold from Brazil and French traders, see Harms, *The Diligent*, 238.

[162] AHU, Angola, caixa 16, doc. 27, July, 1705; and AHU, Angola, caixa 18, doc. 14, June and July 1705; Delgado, *O Reino de Benguela*, 241. Cadornega, however, does not mention *Peringue* in his list of *sobas* of Benguela in 1681. According to him, Kasindi was the *soba* of Benguela. See Cadornega, *História Geral*, 250.

[163] AHU, Angola, caixa 15, doc. 92, December 12, 1698. See also Castro Soromenho, *A Maravilhosa Viagem*, 23. At the end of the nineteenth century, Hermenegildo Capelo and Roberto Ivens refer to a ruler of Njimbo, close to the River Kwango, although too far from the coast, miles away from Benguela. See Hermenegildo Capelo and Roberto Ivens, *De Benguella às terras de Iacca* (Lisbon: Imprensa Nacional, 1881), 2, 124.

resulted in the arrival of more merchants, military and administrative personal, and clergy. The conquest and initial settlement of Benguela were possible only because the Portuguese Crown made ample use of convicts, known as *degredados*, in its overseas territories.[164] In this section I will discuss the makeup of the population of Benguela and its link with the Atlantic world. No maps, censuses, or parish records are available for this period, which makes it very difficult to reconstruct the social life in the Atlantic port. It is through colonial reports, official documents, and rare accounts left by observers that I am able to get an insight into how people lived. Most of the information is limited to the European population, whose reports include constant complaints about their living conditions, disease, and the climate. The danger is to assume that tropical diseases affected every inhabitant in the same way and continue the trope of Africa as a dangerous place.[165] Joseph Miller has claimed that "the slave trade appears in some ways less a cause of depopulation than a consequence of it when viewed in terms of droughts and demographic changes in West Central Africa."[166] However, for the local population, the threat was the colonial presence, not because of disease or drought, but because of the widespread use of firearms, the expansion of violence, the destruction of agricultural land by raiders, and their possible capture and sale to trans-Atlantic slave traders. Famine that affected the Ndombe and others cannot be disassociated from the actions of the Portuguese agents and the pressures of the trans-Atlantic slave trade. Diseases, especially tropical diseases, did not affect all inhabitants of Benguela in the same way. The diseases that were most threatening to Europeans were malaria and yellow fever, usually referred to simply as "fevers" in the sources, and gastrointestinal infections owing to water and food contamination. An analysis of the population also reveals the incoherence and contradictions of colonialism. Or, as Frederick Cooper has stressed, "[C]olonialism simply does not have a single, transhistorical 'essence,' neither political nor material, social nor cultural. Rather, its form and

---

[164] Felner, *Angola*, 333. See also Coates, *Convicts and Orphans*, 65–9, and 76–93. Russell-Wood, *World on the Move*, 106–7; Geraldo Pieroni, *Os Excluídos do Reino* (Brasília: Editora Universidade de Brasília, 2000). For the case of convicts in Angola, see Miller, *Way of Death*, 247–60; Ferreira, "O Brasil e a Arte da Guerra," 3–21; and Candido, "Trans-Atlantic Links," 239–72.

[165] Curtin, *Disease and Empire*. Philip D. Curtin, *The Image of Africa: British Ideas and Action, 1780–1850* (Madison: University of Wisconsin Press, 1973); and Joseph C. Miller, "The Significance of Drought, Disease and Famine in the Agriculturally Marginal Zones of West-Central Africa," *Journal of African History* 23, no. 1 (1982): 17–61.

[166] Miller, "The Significance of Drought, Disease and Famine," 30.

substance are decided in the context of its making. And its making is in serious part a product of struggles among dominant ideologies and their perpetrators."[167]

With very few permanent constructions, Benguela was a small village for most of the seventeenth century. Although urban centers predated the arrival of the Portuguese in West Central Africa, Benguela was a market center but was not a large community before the fifteenth century. More archeological research has to be done to estimate the size of the early settlement. As in other places along the coast of Africa, the Portuguese initiated colonialism with the construction of a fortress. They eventually expanded beyond the fortress to guarantee territorial occupation, similar to what happened in other Atlantic ports.[168] The initial settlement at Benguela was composed of 130 men, including Portuguese and African troops from Luanda. One year later, the population was reduced to ninety people, among them only ten Portuguese men. No estimates are available for the free local population who moved to the lands surrounding the fortress, although those numbers certainly shifted depending on the allegiance agreements and the mood of the authority in power. In the 1630s, ninety-four men defended the village, some of them very sick, which prevented them from performing their duties.[169] By the time of the arrival of the Dutch, 24 years after the foundation, the number of Portuguese troops was around seventy to eighty men. An undeclared number of black soldiers complemented the defense of the port, even though their numbers were not enough to prevent the Dutch invasion.[170] The population who lived in Benguela had to face the menace of neighboring African rulers, European powers on the coast, and the environment. Tropical diseases

---

[167] Frederick Cooper, "Images of Empire, Contests of Conscience. Models of Colonial Domination in South Africa," in *Tensions of Empire: Colonial Cultures in a Bourgeois World*, ed. Frederick Cooper and Ann Laura Stoler (Berkeley: University of California Press, 1997), 192.

[168] Russell-Wood, "Patterns of Settlement," 183; and António Manuel Hespanha and Catarina Madeira Santos, "Os Poderes num Império Oceânico," in *História de Portugal, O Antigo Regime*, vol. 4, ed. António Manuel Hespanha (Lisbon: Estampa, 1993), 401. For similar experiences on the coast of Africa, including the establishment of an African settlement near Portuguese fortresses, see Feinberg, *Africans and Europeans*, 27–9; and Christopher R. DeCorse, *An Archaeology of Elmina, Africans and Europeans on the Gold Coast, 1400–1900* (Washington, DC: Smithsonian Institution Press, 2001); and Ivana Elbl, "Cross-Cultural Trade and Diplomacy: Portuguese Relations with West Africa, 1441–1521," *Journal of World History* 3, no. 2 (1992): 176–80.

[169] Heintze, *Fontes Para a História de Angola*, 1, 184, "Descrição dos Portos de Luanda e Benguela," January 8, 1618.

[170] Delgado, *O Reino de Benguela*, 160–1.

affected the ability of the Portuguese population to increase, yet it would be a mistake to assume that the local population died at the same rate. Several officers reported diseases and unhealthy conditions due to the climate. Benguela, however, must have offered some advantages because in 1650 André da Fonseca Gomes requested that the Overseas Council name him as Captain of Benguela. Among other obligations, he was in charge of renovation of the fortress. He was clearly interested in the position, although he recognized that very few people wanted to be in Benguela. In order to attract possible candidates to other colonial positions, he offered his daughter in marriage. The prospective son-in-law also would receive the noble title of *Hábito de Cristo*, associated with social prestige, and 50,000 réis. It is not clear if anyone accepted.[171] In 1653, the newly appointed governor, Rodrigo de Miranda Henriques, was not even able to inaugurate his position; he felt sick just after arriving and died of "fevers" on February 13.[172] In Benguela, the microbes that transmitted tropical diseases confined European officials to the settlements along the coast and limited Portuguese activity in general to regions close to the sea. The sudden deaths of recently arrived Europeans showed their vulnerability to the new environment where they did not have immunity.[173]

By the 1680s, twenty Portuguese residents lived in town with their families and slaves. Life in Benguela was characterized by open drains, animals in the streets, shallow interments in the cemeteries, and a variety of diseases that assailed people who were already malnourished.[174] Lack of doctors contributed to the high mortality, and most likely local treatments added to the risk. By 1674, authorities in Benguela started requesting a hospital to treat soldiers, suggesting that the taxes paid by residents

---

[171] AHU, Angola, caixa 5, doc. 39, May 11, 1650. *Hábito de Cristo*, or the Order of Christ, was one of the most important titles in the Portuguese nobility. See Fernanda de Olival, *As Ordens Militares e o Estado Moderno: Honra, Mercê e Venalidade em Portugal (1641–1789)* (Lisbon: Estar, 2001), 237; and from the same author, "Mercado de Hábitos e Serviços em Portugal (séculos XVII–XVIII)," *Análise Social* 38, no. 168 (2003): 743–69. For the Order of Christ as an institution in the Portuguese empire, see Isabel dos Guimarães Sá, "Ecclesiastical Structures and Religious Action," in *Portuguese Oceanic Expansion, 1400–1800*, ed. Francisco Bethencourt and Diogo Ramada Curto (Cambridge: Cambridge University Press, 2007), 255–82; and Evaldo Cabral de Mello, *O Nome e o Sangue. Uma parábolda genealógica no Pernambuco Colonial* (São Paulo: Companhia de Bolso, 2009), 18–19.

[172] AHU, Angola, caixa 5, doc. 108, April 5, 1653.

[173] See McNeill, *Mosquito Empire*, 15–62; and Miller, "The Significance of Drought, Disease and Famine," 24.

[174] AHU, Angola, caixa 1, doc. 93, November 20, 1618; and Delgado, *O Reino de Benguela*, 235–7.

should go for infrastructure improvement. By that time, the church and fortress were in ruins.[175] In 1698, the Capuchin Antonio Zucchelli still described the place as malign and deadly, where even the fruits expelled poison into the air. According to him, the "air of Benguela is exceedingly unhealthy, the Portuguese who reside there look more like ghosts than men." Zucchelli also reported that the heat was extreme, with high humidity, and the quality of the water was terrible.[176] The Portuguese struggled to maintain political control over a territory where their agents were under threat of tropical diseases. Unlike in the Americas, where the contact of Europeans with Amerindian population resulted in the spread of smallpox, measles, and other diseases previously unknown in the New World, along the coast of Africa, the presence of malaria and yellow fever worked in favor of the native population.

Benguela was founded as an administrative and commercial space, yet it also became a site for social interaction between officers and the indigenous population. Early explorers, though primarily Catholic, included Jews and Muslims. Cerveira Pereira denounced the presence of New Christians and people of "very low commitment" to Catholicism.[177] The majority of the Portuguese population was composed of men, creating a demographic imbalance among the white population. The lack of European women created a series of problems, including violence against the few who lived in Benguela when they became the subject of disputes among Portuguese officers. One of the soldiers under Cerveira Pereira's command, for example, invaded the house of one of the officials and raped his young daughter, who was *ainda donzela* ("still a virgin"). The assaulter was an exiled convict from Portugal, who had been sentenced to serve as a soldier in Benguela.[178] Although cases of sexual violence were probably common, colonial documents are silent regarding violence against local Ndombe women. The concern reflected in the official documents only

[175] AHU, Angola, caixa 11, doc. 29, October 6, 1674 and doc. 31, October 16, 1674. See also AHU, cod. 545, fl. 7v, October 16, 1674. See also, Delgado, *O Reino de Benguela*, 193. For the danger of doctors, see McNeill, *Mosquito Empires*, 63–87.

[176] Zucchelli, *Relazioni del Viaggio*, 91–2.

[177] AHU, Angola, caixa 1, doc. 103, January 24, 1619. For the use of New Christians in the Portuguese empire, see Blackburn, *The Making of New World Slavery*, 115. Birmingham notes that persecuted groups, including Jews and Gypsies, were sent to Angola in the earlier periods of colonization, and some of them engaged in relationships with African women. See Birmingham, *Central Africa to 1870*, 81; and Timothy J. Coates, *Convicts and Orphans: Forced and State-Sponsored Colonizers in the Portuguese Empire, 1550–1755* (Stanford, CA: Stanford University Press, 2001), 45–6.

[178] Delgado, *O Reino de Benguela*, 83. For more on the gender imbalance in the Portuguese expansion, see Elbl, "Men without Wives."

refers to consensual relationships and cohabitation of Portuguese men and local women. In order to contain concubinage, Governor Cerveira Pereira requested a priest, whose job was, among other things, to control the population. According to Pereira, the lack of Church personnel drove Portuguese men to live with African women outside of marriage, in defiance of Christian principles.[179] Official documents do not engage with European men's perception of life overseas. For some, it was an excuse to engage in sexual encounters with different women. For European men, the tropics allowed an unusual experience of sexual freedom, in part because African women were considered available and their bodies accessible to European men.[180] Yet officials preferred to frame such practices as resulting from a lack of Catholic supervision rather than violence inherent to the process of territorial occupation and colonization.

Consensual relationships probably took place as well, and from these relationships, a new group emerged. Known as *filhos da terra*, the locally born descendants of European men and local women were classified as white and Portuguese regardless of their skin color and birthplace. Inhabiting the port, the *filhos da terra* were key agents in the expansion of colonialism. Locally born, they had acquired immunity to tropical diseases and were raised as members of both Portuguese colonial and local African communities. Fluent in Portuguese and local languages, they acted as colonial officers, traders, and translators, in sum, as cultural brokers unifying the areas known to the Portuguese as the interior, thanks to the connections of their mothers and relatives on the maternal side. Many were baptized, and some could read and write and dressed in European fashion, wearing pants and shoes. Their emergence reveals how Portuguese colonialism and the trans-Atlantic slave trade have affected

---

[179] AHU, Angola, caixa 1, 87, July 2, 1618.

[180] For the interpretation that Portuguese men had relationships with local women because of the lack of white women, see Ivana Elbl, "'Men without Wives': Sexual Arrangements in the Early Portuguese Expansion in West Africa," in *Desire and Discipline: Sex and Sexuality in Premodern West*, ed. Jacqueline Murray and Konrad Eisenbichler (University of Toronto Press, 1996), 61–87. For the idea that Portuguese men were also motivated by the sexual opportunities that imperial expansion offered, see Ronald Hyam, *Empire and Sexuality. The British Experience* (Manchester: Manchester University Press, 1992); Anne McClintock, *Imperial Leather: Race, Gender and Sexuality in the Colonial Context* (London: Routledge, 1995); Jennifer L. Morgan, "'Some Could Suckle over Their Shoulder': Male Travelers, Female Bodies, and the Gendering of Racial Ideology, 1500–1700," *William and Mary Quarterly* 54, no. 1 (1997): 167–92. See also Selma Pantoja, "Women's Work in the Fairs and Markets of Luanda," in *Women in the Portuguese Colonial Empire: The Theater of Shadows*, ed. Clara Sarmento (Newcastle-upon-Tyne, UK: Cambridge Scholars Publishing, 2008), 91.

societies living around Benguela, leading to the creation of new social groups that shared values and codes with Portuguese colonialists and local Ndombe. The *filhos da terra* also transformed the colonial state, influencing how people took care of their health and how ceremonies were performed, including vassalage. As time passed, they developed into a merchant elite, autonomous from the *sobados* inland and associated with the Atlantic-based commerce.[181] These were intense two-way cultural exchanges that led to the formation of an intermediary group that identified themselves as Portuguese or white.

Another group that played a major role in the conquest and establishment of a colony in the seventeenth century was the *degredados*, or convicts, who also played key role in processes of cultural exchange and accommodation.[182] Similar to what had happened in Cape Verde and the Upper Guinea coast with the case of New Christians, Portuguese expansion relied on the presence of many subalterns, individuals who were not welcomed in Portugal but who assumed the role of colonial agents overseas and shaped the imagination of the "empire." Most of the Portuguese exiles had committed crimes against people or property, yet in Benguela they collected taxes, patrolled the port, and commanded attacks on *sobas* who resisted Portuguese expansion. Even criminals from Luanda served their sentences in Benguela, where they increased the degree of contact between Europeans and local populations. In 1673, three residents of Luanda were condemned to exile in Benguela for evading the treasury and using royal funds to acquire textiles. Lieutenant Roque Vieira de Lima, Captain Paulo Valente, and Captain Diogo Vaz Camelo used Crown funds for personal profit, buying and selling slaves. They were sentenced to serve 10 years in Benguela, where they would probably have more freedom to evade the state and engage in illegal activities than in Luanda, showing the limitations of their punishment.[183] Convicts from

---

[181] Beatrix Heintze, "A Lusofonia no Interior da África Central na era Pré-colonial. Um Contributo para a sua História e Compreensão na Actualidade," *Cadernos de Estudos Africanos* 6–7 (2006), 184–5. For more, see Metcalf, *Go-Betweens and the Colonization of Brazil, 1500–1600*, 57–9.

[182] Felner, *Angola*, 333. See also Charles Boxer, *The Portuguese Seaborne Empire, 1415–1825* (London: Hutchinson, 1969), 312; Coates, *Convicts and Orphans*, 65–9, 76–93; Russell-Wood, *World on the Move*, 106–7; and Geraldo Pieroni, *Os Excluídos do Reino* (Editora Universidade de Brasília, 2000). For the case of convicts in Angola, see Miller, *Way of Death*, 247–60. For the role of Brazilian-born convicts, see Ferreira, "O Brasil e a Arte da Guerra em Angola," 3–21; Candido, "Trans-Atlantic Links," 251–4.

[183] AHU, Angola, caixa 10, doc. 115, May 27, 1673. For more on the role of subalterns in the establishment of commercial and political alliances in Western Africa, see Green, *The Rise of the Trans-Atlantic Slave Trade*, 166–70.

Portugal were not warmly welcomed in Angola. Afraid of their presence, residents of Luanda suggested that the governor send "dangerous male *degredados*" to Benguela. Women, however, could stay in Luanda in order to marry Portuguese soldiers, which certainly contributed to increase the gender imbalance among the white population in Benguela.[184] As seen before, lack of European women and miscegenation were initially perceived as social problems. Colonial authorities made repeated requests to stimulate the migration of white women to contain the increase in the mixed population, the *filhos da terra*. In the late 1620s, Governor Lopo Soares requested that the governor of Angola send him "women, who could marry the soldiers and populate the land."[185] For Lopo Soares, *women* meant white women, not black women, even if the white women were *degredadas* from other parts of the overseas empire. In the eighteenth century, however, the Crown shifted its approach and began to encourage marriage between Europeans and African women, as will be explored in Chapter 2. Yet it becomes clear that racial bias was present in the seventeenth-century Portuguese world. In the eyes of the authorities, it was better to receive a white criminal than a free black person to populate Benguela.

Among the convicts, those born in the colony of Brazil were welcome. Identified as *americanos*, *brasiliences*, or *brasileiros* in the colonial documents to differentiate them from Portuguese-born individuals and the locally born *filhos da terra*, *brasileiros* were seen as already adjusted to the tropical environment and fit to rule in hot temperatures. They were sent to Benguela to serve the troops and replenish the population lost to conflict and epidemics. This practice, initiated in the seventeenth century, gained strength in the 1700s and consolidated the links across the South Atlantic. Alongside *filhos da terra*, *brasileiros* gained a reputation as being less susceptible to tropical diseases and started to occupy positions in the administration.[186] Born and raised in slave societies, many probably brought ideas from Brazil regarding slavery, racial hierarchy, and the treatment of the indigenous population, strengthening the link between the two colonies.

Portuguese, *brasileiros*, and *filhos da terra* faced a constant lack of food, which certainly led to the physical debilitation of Benguela residents and

---

[184] AHU, Angola, caixa 8, doc. 55, October 22, 1664.

[185] Felner, *Angola*, 353. For the importance of orphans and female convicts in the Portuguese empire, see Coates, *Convicts and Orphans*, 149–54; Elbl, "Men without Wives," 64–5.

[186] Mattos, "'Black Troops' and Hierarchies of Color," 6–29.

made them more vulnerable to disease. On different occasions, authorities reported that they had to rely on Ndombe neighbors to provide food staples. In Brazil, colonial settlers implemented cultivation around the initial settlement, but in Benguela, the focus was on trade rather than food production. The concentrated effort to organize raids and expeditions to find minerals led Benguela residents to rely on the local population to feed them. The local Ndombe had an advantage because they were more knowledgeable about the soil, crop use, and patterns of precipitation, which gave them an advantage in agricultural production. Women cultivated *masa mbala* or *massambala* ("sorghum"), *masango* ("millet"), cabbage, beans, and pumpkins. Later, crops such as maize, peanuts, and manioc were introduced from the Americas. Palm oil also was extracted and used in the preparation of dishes such as *moamba*, which is still consumed in Angola. Fish, meat, and milk and its by-products also were sold around the fortress. The sudden demand for local crops probably favored the accumulation of wealth in the hands of food producers, most of them women, showing once again how the Atlantic world transformed African societies. Eventually, some of these women became wealthy, as seen in their control over dependents, which I will explore further in Chapter 2.[187] The Portuguese vulnerability to tropical diseases allowed Ndombe men and women to profit from the situation and sell their products to the residents of Benguela. On several occasions, however, Portuguese forces turned to violence rather than trade. Inevitably, raids led to the destruction of fields and crops and therefore increased hunger, indicating how famine was linked directly to the expansion of the trans-Atlantic slave trade rather than an isolated and independent phenomenon, as Joseph Miller argued earlier.[188] Manioc flour also was processed in town, although probably not in sufficient quantity to feed the town's population. Residents had to

---

[187] For the local food produced, see Zucchelli, *Relazioni del viaggio*, 91–4; Elias Alexandre da Silva Corrêa, *História de Angola* (Lisbon: Atica, 1937), 130–40; and Valdez, *Six Years of a Traveller's Life in Western Africa*. Cadornega described the uses of palm oil and how it was cooked with meat, calling the dish *moamba*; see Cadornega, *História Geral*, 3, 358; Alvin W. Urquhart, *Patterns of Settlement and Subsistence in Southwestern Angola* (Washington, DC: National Academies, 1963), 90–4; Miller, *Way of Death*, 18–20; Adriano Parreira, *Economia e Sociedade em Angola na Época da Rainha Jinga (século XVII)* (Lisbon: Editorial Estampa, 1990), 43–8. For how colonial settlement could offer local women a chance to accumulate wealth, see Elizabeth Schmidt, "Farmers, Hunters, and Gold-Washers: A Reevaluation of Women's Roles in Precolonial and Colonial Zimbabwe," *African Economic History* 17 (1988): 58–9. For the case of Brazil, see Russell-Wood, "Patterns of Settlement," 184.

[188] Miller, "The Significance of Drought, Disease and Famine," 28–31.

import manioc flour from Luanda. In 1664, Simão Van Dunem sent 300 *exeques* of manioc flour to Benguela to assist the troops.[189]

The church, fortress, and other buildings were under constant renovation, employing a large number of skilled workers and attracting more people to settle close to the coast. The unstable white population, a large number of slaves, contentious African rulers, and the presence of convicts were cause for continual distress and disputes among authorities. After the restoration of Benguela to Portuguese control when Dutch rule was ended, the links between Brazil and Benguela increased, initiating a strong collaboration in the South Atlantic. Many of the administrators had spent time in the colony of Brazil before crossing the Atlantic. João Pereira do Lago, a sergeant in Benguela in 1688, had previously served in Bahia for 5 years.[190] Angelo da Cruz served in Luanda, Rio de Janeiro, and Mazagan in 1687, where "he killed many moors," before arriving in Benguela.[191] The captain-major of Benguela in 1701 had fought in the battle of Guararapes in Pernambuco and in the attack organized by the governor of Angola against the *jaga* of Kakonda.[192] Manoel de Nojosa, appointed captain-major, the highest authority in Benguela in 1685, was originally from Brazil. He had first arrived in Angola with the Brazilian troops who came from Pernambuco to expel the Dutch. He then returned to Pernambuco and served in Bahia, where in 1670 he took part in several expeditions against the Quilombo of Palmares, one of the most emblematic runway slave communities in Brazil in the seventeenth century.[193] The expansion of colonialism and increasing slave departures, which will be analyzed in greater detail in Chapters 2 and 3, respectively, accelerated the exchange of authorities and merchants between West Central Africa and Brazil. Rather than a triangular trade that characterized other parts of the Atlantic, in Benguela the trade developed in a bilateral form with Brazil.[194]

---

[189] AHU, Angola, caixa 8, doc. 45, September 23, 1664. The Capuchin Zucchelli mentioned manioc flour consumption; see his *Relazioni del viaggio*, 95. For the link between raids and hunger in the eighteenth and nineteenth centuries, see Jill R. Dias, "Famine and Disease in the History of Angola c. 1830–1930," *Journal of African History* 22, no. 3 (1981): 349–78; and Miller, "The Significance of Drought, Disease and Famine."

[190] AHU, Angola, caixa 13, doc. 74, March 31, 1688.

[191] AHU, Angola, caixa 14, doc. 27, July 18, 1690.

[192] AHU, Angola, caixa 16, doc. 18, March 5, 1701.

[193] AHU, Angola, caixa 13, doc. 3, January 26, 1685.

[194] For the "the myth of the triangular trade" in the South Atlantic, see Herbert Klein, *The Atlantic Slave Trade: New Approaches to the Americas* (New York: Cambridge University Press, 1999), 96–102; and José C. Curto, *Enslaving Spirits: The Portuguese-Brazilian Alcohol Trade at Luanda and Its Hinterland, c. 1550–1830* (Leiden: Brill, 2004). See

Conclusion

Founded in the early seventeenth century, Benguela gained a reputation as a white man's grave. Tropical diseases affected the ability of the Portuguese to move beyond the coast during the first century of colonialism. Yet Portuguese agents arrived in town and initiated settlement along the coast. The rush to secure access to gold, silver, and copper mines lured the Portuguese to establish a fortress at Benguela despite territorial disputes with African rulers and attacks by European fleets. During its first decades, Benguela was a settlement shaped by war, raids, and insecurity. It was a space of permanent negotiation owing to the fragility of the Portuguese presence. The Portuguese constantly relied on African allies to feed and protect them, sometimes even from the attack of other European forces. Local rulers allied with the Portuguese when it was convenient and signed diplomatic treaties that secured protection and trade relationships. Yet they were willing to break these agreements if they were dissatisfied with events. Owing to vassalage treaties, some rulers became partners in the Portuguese colonial enterprise, offering troops, slaves, and food.

The history of Benguela in the seventeenth century has to be placed in an Atlantic perspective because many events across the ocean influenced the decisions of colonial authorities and had repercussions in Benguela. Portuguese efforts to secure access to copper and to have an advantage in the Indian Ocean markets led to the trade of slaves from West Central Africa to the Americas. The participation of Portuguese traders in the early slave trade to the Americas created pressure for more captives, which resulted in cycles of warfare around Benguela. Colonial officials organized expeditions against densely populated territories, seizing people under the guise of "just wars" and conquest expeditions. Large number of captives called the attention of European merchants in search of new markets. From time to time, European forces challenged the Portuguese presence in Benguela. They attacked the fortress and captured free people, slaves, cattle, and weapons. In 1641, Dutch forces occupied Benguela and expelled Portuguese traders and bureaucrats, challenging Portuguese control over the South Atlantic. Decades later, French merchants attacked Benguela. Both attacks were short-lived, yet they created increased instability. African rulers took advantage of moments of uncertain control to

also Alencastro, "Continental Drift," 100–4. For the idea of a triangular trade as a model for Atlantic commerce, see Blackburn, *The Making of New World Slavery*, 542; and Eric Williams, *Capitalism and Slavery* (Chapel Hill: University of North Carolina Press, 1994), 51–84.

renegotiate the terms of their vassalage to and dependence on Portuguese forces. These vassalage treaties also indicate the extensive use of the indirect-rule model of colonialism, where local authorities were in charge of tax collection and troop organization. Thus Benguela in the seventeenth century was already a colony, with a bureaucracy in place and authorities and policies that emphasized territorial occupation and exploration.

Africans and Europeans who lived in Benguela were actively involved in Atlantic commerce, and these commercial exchanges accelerated cultural and social developments. Trade predated the arrival of Europeans, yet the establishment of a fortress on the coast shifted routes and created a new market for products such as ivory tusks and domestic slaves. The Portuguese tried to dominate the existing routes, yet their actions were limited to the region very close to the coast, allowing preexisting commercial networks to remain active. Colonialism and the expansion of the slave trade imposed new practices, such as baptism, and altered the diet, with the adoption of manioc. Interaction with the local population also altered vassalage ceremonies, showing how creolization was a two-way process. Contact with the African population around Benguela created a series of naming practices, similar to what the Portuguese had already experienced north of the Kwanza River and across the Atlantic Ocean. Indigenous populations were seen as scary people who threatened the social order and the Catholic way of life. People were labeled as cannibals to justify enslavement and land appropriation. Those who recognized Portuguese power were seen as allies. Those who resisted and challenged Portuguese control were seen as uncivilized, leading to the use of the term *jaga*, which had repercussions in the historiography of the seventeenth century in West Central Africa. The nomenclature given to the population around Benguela shaped the way they interacted with the colonial state in subsequent centuries.

S. FILIPPE DE BENGUELLA

IMAGE 2. São Felipe de Benguela. (*Source:* AHU, Iconografia 001, doc. 317.)

2

The Rise of an Atlantic Port, 1710–1850

After the insecurity that characterized Benguela's history in the seventeenth century when European and African forces disputed control over land and people, the period between 1710 and 1850 was a time of greater stability for the Portuguese settlement at the expense of Ndombe and neighboring populations in part due to the expansion of the trans-Atlantic slave trade. During the eighteenth century, more people were shipped from the port of Benguela, and the slave trade became the major economic activity in town. Benguela's residents, both locally and foreign born, were fully integrated into the Atlantic economy. The interactions with neighboring states also changed as a result of the growing Atlantic commerce. Although the local population along the coast continued to challenge the Portuguese presence, the colonial settlement was able to impose itself because its neighbors had diffuse political structures characterized by fragmentation. Only in the escarpments of the central highlands did the Portuguese encounter strong centralized states that slowed their penetration. The fortress of Caconda, initially located 180 km inland, received special attention in the Portuguese efforts to expand the colonial outpost. Traders did not necessarily recognize the Portuguese monopoly over commerce and found ways to evade the Crown and escape colonial control. With varying perceptions of the Portuguese role in Benguela, African rulers struggled to maintain their sovereignty. The Portuguese Crown sponsored attacks on populations living not far from the coast, which led to the displacement and relocation of *sobas* and their subjects. Yet the Portuguese presence was not strong or impressive in the interior or even along the coast. With garrisons reduced to a few men and under constant threat by European and African powers, Portuguese administrators were incapable of controlling most of the trade routes that crossed the Benguela hinterland. More concerned with their own endurance and profit on the littoral, colonial agents negotiated their survival with neighboring rulers.

This chapter discusses the events in Benguela in the eighteenth century, after the French invasion of 1705, and the first half of the nineteenth century. As in Chapter 1, the main stage is the port of Benguela, the center of Portuguese colonialism and slave exports south of the Kwanza River. This chapter also follows the Portuguese advance into the interior and shows how that expansion affected life in the port of Benguela. Initially, the Portuguese focused on the nearby escarpments of the central plateau, where the first fortress of Caconda was founded. Other factors under discussion include the geopolitics around Benguela, its impact on life in the colonial port, and the spread of enlightenment ideas in the mid–eighteenth century, including the tightened control over overseas territories. The last two sections of the chapter consider the social history of the port, discussing the spread of slave labor and the establishment of a slave society, and the formation of a Luso-African community, related to expansion of the slave trade. Events happening elsewhere in the African continent motivated Portuguese efforts in Benguela, which accelerated cultural exchanges to facilitate slave exports. Creolization and the slave trade were intimately related. Ndombe and other African actors helped to shape this new culture, which in many ways still prevails in Benguela and Luanda with their large numbers of residents who speak only Portuguese and have no knowledge of other Angolan languages, maintain a deep connection to Catholicism, and have adopted a model that celebrates *mestiçagem* ("miscegenation") and *crioulização* ("creolization") as national values despite the exclusion of other sectors of society. Contemporary Angolans are inheritors of a system that dates back to the early eighteenth century, and even earlier, that reshaped the region's communities and institutions and accelerated cultural change. The prevalence of these features in early twentieth-century Angola demonstrates the long-lasting effects of the trans-Atlantic slave trade on this region.[1]

---

[1] For the trans-Atlantic slave trade as a force of change, see Linda M. Heywood and John K. Thornton, *Central Africans, Atlantic Creoles, and the Making of the Foundation of the Americas, 1585–1660* (New York: Cambridge University Press, 2007), 49–106; Toby Green, *The Rise of the Trans-Atlantic Slave Trade in Western Africa, 1300–1589* (Cambridge: Cambridge University Press, 2011), 260–77; Walter Hawthorne, *From Africa to Brazil: Culture, Identity, and an Atlantic Slave Trade, 1600–1830* (Cambridge:

The first decades of the eighteenth century opened up new trade opportunities as more African rulers declared vassalage to the Portuguese Crown. In search of wealth, Portuguese traders started to arrive in Benguela. The colonial town was originally established as a fortress, where the administrators and soldiers had a strong commercial agenda in the name of the Portuguese Crown. The settlement by the beginning of the eighteenth century included slaves and free Africans, who participated in the transformation of this port town from a small village to one of the most important slave ports in the South Atlantic. During the eighteenth century, a colonial town slowly emerged with the arrival of more authorities and the bureaucratic apparatus that characterized the Portuguese empire. By the end of the century, the Santa Casa da Misericórdia hospital and a municipal chamber were installed, although with limited operations and resources. More colonial authorities were nominated to enforce Portuguese control, including judges and the administrator of the treasury. By the end of the century, Benguela was a port cloaked in colonial laws, similar to those implemented in Brazil.[2] The eighteenth and early nineteenth centuries also witnessed the consolidation of violence to enforce the Portuguese presence and the Atlantic trade. In the seventeenth century and first part of the eighteenth century this violence was random, reflecting the weakness of the colonial state, but it became endemic in the second half of the eighteenth century. By then, the importance of Benguela to the Crown required the deployment of armies to protect

Cambridge University Press, 2010); Paul E. Lovejoy, *Transformations in Slavery: A History of Slavery in Africa* (Cambridge: Cambridge University Press, 2000). For the idea of *crioulização* and the lasting impact of creolization in Angola, see Mário António, *Luanda, Ilha Crioula* (Lisbon: Agência-Geral do Ultramar, 1969); Jill R. Dias, "Uma Questão de Identidade: Respostas Intelectuais às Transformações Econômicas no Seio da Elite Crioula da Angola Portuguesa entre 1870 e 1930," *Revista Internacional de Estudos Africanos* 1 (1984): 61–94; Roquinaldo Ferreira, "Ilhas Crioulas: O Significado Plural da Mestiçagem Cultural na África Atlântica," *Revista de História* 155, no. 2 (2006): 17–41; Marcelo Bittencourt, *Dos Jornais às Armas: Trajectórias da Contestação Angolana* (Lisbon: Vega Editora, 1999); Jacopo Corrado, *The Creole Elite and the Rise of Angolan Protonationalism: 1870–1920* (Amherst, NY: Cambria Press, 2008).

[2] António Manuel Hespanha and Catarina Madeira Santos, "Os Poderes num Império Oceânico," in *História de Portugal, O Antigo Regime*, vol. 4, ed. António Manuel Hespanha (Lisbon: Estampa, 1993), 401; and A. J. R Russell-Wood, *A World on the Move: The Portuguese in Africa, Asia, and America, 1415–1808* (Manchester, UK: Carcanet, 1992), 104–6; Ralph Delgado, *O Reino de Benguela: Do Descobrimento a Criação do Governo Subalterno* ([S.l: s.n.], 1945), 383–4. For the *Misericórdia*, see António Brásio, "As Misericórdias de Angola," *Studia* 4 (1959): 106–49; A. J. R Russell-Wood, *Fidalgos and Philanthropists. The Santa Casa da Misericórdia of Bahia, 1550–1755* (Berkeley: University of California Press, 1968), 35–7.

it from the neighboring rulers and possible European competitors. The new town and the interior fortress of Caconda revealed the ambitions of administrators and military personnel, who were more focused on extracting resources and human beings than on establishing an urban center, despite Lisbon's efforts to expand colonialism and settlement. The events in Benguela in the eighteenth and nineteenth centuries revealed the disputes between authorities in the metropolis and men on the spot regarding imperial policies.

In a town infamous for its unhealthy environment, the population of Benguela maintained itself through an influx of people from Angola and Benguela's interior and from Brazil and Portugal. The strategy of using convicts to populate Benguela, initiated in the seventeenth century, was consolidated in the eighteenth century. Convicts from Portugal and Brazil were shipped to Benguela to replenish the European population lost to conflict and epidemics.[3] Though considered criminals elsewhere, they became the face of the Portuguese colonial state and were employed in the military forces and official colonial positions. Whites were saved from hard labor, showing the importance of skin color in defining roles in the Portuguese empire. Governors constantly requested more people, especially convicts from Brazil, although they also complained about their highly disruptive behavior.[4]

From the beginning, Africans were the majority of the population, with deep roots in the territory that became the Portuguese colony. Some of them were Ndombe, whereas others came from a variety of other groups, which resulted in continuous interactions among people from different backgrounds, both local and foreign. As Africans lived and labored in this colonial milieu, they acquired cultural insights that allowed them to navigate within the Portuguese world. They also changed institutions, such as the case of vassalage explored in Chapter 1, and influenced how Portuguese colonial officials lived, worshiped, and dealt with the world they faced. With knowledge of Portuguese, Umbundu, and other

---

[3] Arquivo Histórico Ultramarino (AHU), caixa 22, doc. 17, May 16, 1724; AHU, caixa 24, doc. 29, February 26, 1728; AHU, caixa 23, doc. 97, April 3, 1727. See also Timothy J. Coates, *Convicts and Orphans: Forced and State-Sponsored Colonizers in the Portuguese Empire, 1550–1755* (Stanford, CA: Stanford University Press, 2001); Selma Pantoja, "Inquisição, Degredo e Mestiçagem em Angola no século XVII," *Revista Lusófona de Ciência das Religiões* 3, nos. 5–6 (2004): 117–36.

[4] A. J. R. Russell-Wood, "Patterns of Settlement in the Portuguese Empire," in *Portuguese Oceanic Expansion, 1400–1800*, ed. Francisco Bethencourt and Diogo Ramada Curto (Cambridge: Cambridge University Press, 2007), 174–5; Russell-Wood, *A World on the Move*, 64–75; and Green, *The Rise of the Trans-Atlantic Slave Trade*, 167–70.

languages, deeply involved in the trans-Atlantic slave trade, and aware of their rights as subjects of the Portuguese Crown, Africans played a decisive role in the rise of Benguela. Savvy in the local environment, internal trade routes, and languages, Africans transformed the Portuguese colony of Benguela into a Luso-African town where African and Portuguese culture intersected, showing that creolization also affected Europeans who lived in the port town.[5] Mixed marriages, seen as a problem by the colonial administration in the seventeenth century, became the rule. Africans seized the opportunity to apprehend cultural practices and spaces of power and give a new meaning to the changes taking place in the period. For people living outside the town, Portuguese legislation was extended to them in the form of the vassal treaties. For their allegiance, though sometimes very superficial, *sobas* could impose terms of trade, request rights and gifts, and rely on Portuguese cooperation. Conflicts emerged with consequences for Portuguese conquests and African rulers' ability to remain in power and protect their subjects. The town of Benguela was the locus of conflict and negotiation, with its population involved in different political systems with multiple allegiances. While African ambassadors were received and treated as partners, European competitors refused to recognize the Portuguese monopoly over trade. African rulers could voice their discontent to Portuguese agents through intermediaries or written letters.[6] Colonial structures were seen as spaces to litigate rights by rulers and subjects alike. Foreign merchants married local women to solidify commercial interests, removing themselves from Crown and Catholic Church control, and adopted local practices and declared obedience to

---

[5] Linda M. Heywood, "Portuguese into African: The Eighteenth Century Central African Background to Atlantic Creole Culture," in *Central Africans and Cultural Transformations in the American Diaspora*, ed. Linda Heywood (New York: Cambridge University Press, 2002), 91–114; Linda M. Heywood and John K. Thornton, *Central Africans, Atlantic Creoles*; Kalle Kananoja, "Healers, Idolaters, and Good Christians: A Case Study of Creolization and Popular Religion in Mid-Eighteenth Century Angola," *International Journal of African Historical Studies* 43, no. 3 (2010): 443–65; Ferreira, "Ilhas Crioulas: O Significado Plural da Mestiçagem Cultural na África Atlântica," 17–41.

[6] Catarina Madeira Santos, "Écrire le pouvoir en Angola. Les Archives Ndembu (XVIIe–XXe siècles)," *Annales, Histoire Sciences Sociales* 64, no. 4 (2009): 767–95. For the importance of marriage and lineage unions in forging new links and accelerating cultural exchange and creolization in the end, see Green, *The Rise of the Trans-Atlantic Slave Trade*, 266–77; Beatrix Heintze, "Translocal Kinship Relations in Central African Politics of the 19th Century," in *Translocality. The Study of Globalising Processes from a Southern Perspective*, ed. Ulrike Freitag and Achim von Oppen (Leiden: Brill, 2010), 179–204; Beatrix Heintze, "A Lusofonia no Interior da África Central na era pré-colonial. Um contributo para a sua história e Compreensão na Actualidade," *Cadernos de Estudos Africanos* 6–7 (2005): 179–207.

sobas. They "Africanized themselves," as Portuguese colonial officers feared, or simply embraced creolization, as many local actors did as well. African women also played important roles in the transformation of this small village into a Luso-African port that was a major point of embarkation of slaves into the Atlantic slave trade. Fully integrated in the Atlantic economy, the society that emerged in Benguela during the eighteenth and early nineteenth centuries was similar to that of other African ports along the littoral, such as Ouidah, St. Louis, and Elmina. Yet this was a village with strong links to the interior of Benguela, from which food, cattle, captives, and ivory descended to the coast.

The Port and Its Surroundings in the First Half of the Eighteenth Century

Known as the *human abattoir*, Benguela was not a desirable place to live in the Portuguese empire. It acquired a reputation as a white man's grave, and exile there was seen as a death sentence, as explored in Chapter 1. In 1717, the governor of Angola, Paulo Caetano de Albuquerque, described Benguela as being in a "miserable condition, with soldiers reduced to thirty men due to diseases, lack of medication and care."[7] In the early eighteenth century, the settlement had very few people, and most of them were colonial officials who combined their political activities with commerce. The drought of the 1710s affected agriculture, but it is difficult to evaluate the demographic effect because it is not clear how many people lived in town at that time. Droughts also affected inland areas, yet historical evidence tends to emphasize the Portuguese perception of the place, and local inhabitants certainly had a different understanding of the environment. The Ndombe lived along the Bay of Benguela; thus, for them and other pastoralist groups, the place was a suitable environment. The small population along the coast also favored the mobility of pastoralists, who could migrate and resettle in more convenient locations when faced with drought, something that Portuguese colonialists could not do. After the French attacks of the previous decade, colonial administrators had to renegotiate the terms of the relationships they had established with neighboring African rulers. Environmental crises, such as the droughts of the 1710s, increased instability and competition for resources. The settlement, however, expanded after the 1710s despite its limitations and vulnerability.

---

[7] Delgado, *O Reino de Benguela*, 374, 379.

The administration of Benguela attempted to maintain tight control over trade and the population around the settlement. The distance from Luanda favored the concentration of power in the hands of a few colonial officials who had administrative and judicial authority and took most decisions without consulting the governor of Angola and the Lisbon administration. Due to its location, officers ruled Benguela as if it were a state within the Portuguese empire. Officials had autonomy to wage war and organize raids. They also could sign treaties with neighboring African authorities. The large number of states, some of which were in direct competition and opposed the Portuguese presence on the coast, made it difficult to consolidate diplomatic relationships.[8] While there were states along the coast, such as Kitumbela in the Catumbela and Kizamba in the Bay of São Francisco, the larger and stronger ones were inland in part because they were located far away from the Portuguese.

From 1720 onward, several conflicts were organized by the men on the spot in the name of colonial expansion. In 1729, the new captain of Benguela, Álvaro de Barros e Silva, organized attacks on the states of Bembe, Luceque, and Kalukembe and brought eight *sobas* under vassalage treaties with the Portuguese. All these states had a head of state and some level of bureaucracy in place. Some of them controlled a large number of subjects and relied on professional armies. Attacks on these states had repercussions for the interior and coastal regions. Captives of war were enslaved and sold to trans-Atlantic traders, showing how colonial expansion was linked to the slave trade. In fact, the Atlantic economy played an important role in escalating conflicts in Benguela's hinterland. The *soba* of Kiambela fought against Captain Barros e Silva and resisted the wars of conquests of the 1720s; he led his armies with rifles, demonstrating their participation in long-distance trade and the importance of shotguns in Benguela's interior by the early eighteenth century.[9] The *soba* of Kiambela, who had survived previous attacks, managed to escape, but

---

[8] The same situation happened in West Africa; see Feinberg, *Africans and Europeans in West Africa*, 10–12; J. K. Fynn, *Asante and its Neighbors, 1700–1807* (London: Longman, 1971).

[9] AHU, caixa 24, doc. 115, September 19, 1729. On weapons in the Benguela highlands, see Joseph C. Miller, *Way of Death: Merchant Capitalism and the Angolan Slave Trade, 1730–1830* (Madison: University of Wisconsin Press, 1988), 119. For the limited technological superiority of Portuguese guns in the early eighteenth century, see John K. Thornton, *Warfare in Atlantic Africa, 1500–1800* (London: Routledge, 1999); Allen F. Isaacman discusses how firearms helped to consolidate control along the Zambezi in *Mozambique: From Colonialism to Revolution, 1900–1982* (Boulder, CO: Westview Press, 1983), 18–20. For the fiscal systems of states in the central plateau of Angola, see Linda Heywood and John Thornton, "African Fiscal Systems as Sources for Demographic History: The Case of Central Angola, 1799–1920," *Journal of African History* 29, no. 2 (1988): 216–18.

Captain Barros e Silva and his soldiers apprehended many of his subjects, including one of his sisters. The captain ordered several villages and cultivated fields to be burned, indicating how environmental crises and famines were, on many occasions, human made. This *soba* had an adversarial past with Captains Barros e Silva and other soldiers from Benguela because he had captured Portuguese subjects in previous decades. On several occasions, Governor Paulo Caetano de Albuquerque of Angola declared that the Benguela soldiers were more concerned with making their own profits than with defending the colonial settlement. The attack on Kiambela shows how soldiers mixed both activities, conquering land in the name of the Portuguese Crown and taking people into custody, who later could be sold for personal profit.[10]

Despite several accounts that emphasize Portuguese conquests in the early eighteenth century, it is apparent that the colonial power was weak and that the town and its residents were under constant fear of invasion. In the 1730s, Captain Henrique de Figuereiro coerced residents and their slaves to build four new ramparts and defensive walls in the fortress.[11] Some of the construction workers were likely recently arrived convicts from Luanda, part of a group of more than 100 people. These *degredados* were convicted of robbing traders and colonial officials in the interior of Angola and were ordered into exile in Benguela by Governor Paulo Caetano de Albuquerque. Condemned for illicit activities in Luanda's hinterland, in Benguela these men became the face of the Portuguese state and the vehicle through which the colonial state harassed local rulers and their subjects.

By 1748, authorities stated that the fortress was in crumbling condition and that they lacked ammunition and military carts. The situation did not change in the next decade because captains continued to complain about buildings collapsing and deficient weapons and ammunition. The town was a combination of wattle-and-daub and adobe houses mostly covered with thatched roofs.[12] New construction started to appear, such as the

---

[10] AHU, caixa 24, doc. 115, September 19, 1729. Delgado also describes this conflict; see *Reino de Benguela*, 262–4. For Albuquerque's denunciation of soldiers' behavior, see AHU, caixa 22, doc. 54, January 8, 1725. For similar patterns in other parts of the Portuguese empire, see Russell-Wood, *A World on the Move*, 95–7. For a different interpretation of famines, see Joseph C. Miller, "The Significance of Drought, Disease and Famine in the Agriculturally Marginal Zones of West-Central Africa," *Journal of African History* 23, no. 1 (1982): 30–1.

[11] AHU, caixa 27, doc. 115, June 12, 1734; AHU, caixa 29, doc. 6, January 12, 1736; AHU, caixa 24, doc. 29, February 26, 1728.

[12] AHU, Angola, caixa 36, doc. 7, March 16, 1748, and AHU, Angola, caixa 39, doc. 32, June 18, 1754. See also Miller, *Way of Death*, 238.

foundations of the Nossa Senhora do Pópulo Church. The church was the central point of European life in town, home to many celebrations, including marriages and baptisms. Local Ndombe and other Africans also participated in gatherings and services at the church and also were baptized and married there. Military troops, for example, attended a mass there before departing on expeditions inland.[13] Beyond the waterfront and a central square, where the Nossa Senhora do Pópulo still stands, swamps and scrublands favored wild animals wandering during the night. Unburied bodies also attracted carnivorous beasts, which helped to perpetuate Benguela's infamy as a dangerous place.[14]

Facing problems in the settlement, authorities also had to deal with changes in the areas around Benguela. The pressure to acquire captives and territorial control led to instability in the hinterland and favored the emergence of new leaders who would align with the Portuguese. The 1730s was a period when Portuguese administrations recognized new local rulers. Colonial documents refer to a multiplicity of polities around Benguela that disappeared from the records later on, although the reason is not clear. Chiefdoms such as Malanka, Kakoko, and Zamba challenged Portuguese authority in the 1730s, yet they seem to have disappeared in the next decades, suggesting that the pressure of the trans-Atlantic slave trade led to the collapse of old chiefdoms and subsequent political reorganization. In a request for nomination to the position of captain of the fortress of Caconda, Belchior Raposo Pimentel listed several conflicts he participated in the 1730s outside Benguela, including the attack on the *soba* of Kapiango, which resulted in many captives.[15] The next decades continued the emergence of new yet ephemeral leaders who split from chiefdoms and relocated to abandoned lands and created a new polity or joined older ones. The small demographic concentration and political decentralization between the littoral and the central plateau favored mobility and political reconfiguration in the wake of slaving advances.

---

[13] AHU, Angola, caixa 40, doc. 72, January 22, 1756; AHU, Angola, caixa 40A, doc. 130, April 20, 1756. See also AHU, Angola, caixa 43, doc. 106, prior to October 23, 1760; Instituto Histórico Geográfico Brasileiro (IHGB), DL 06,01.05, "Relatório feito pelo comandante Domingos da Fonseca Negrão quando, por ordem de d. António Alvares da Cunha, governador de Angola, comandou os oficiais e soldados no interior de Benguela contra os revoltosos da Coroa Portuguesa," 1755.

[14] Delgado, *Reino de Benguela*, 369–70.

[15] Arquivo Nacional da Torre do Tombo (ANTT), Registro Geral das Mercês, D. Joao V, L. 30, fl. 90, "Belchior Raposo Pimentel," November 17, 1740. For accounts of small African polities, see AHU, Angola, caixa 29, doc. 68, November 7, 1736.

By the 1750s, the inland political rearrangements reverberated in Benguela. The *soba* of Kabunda rose in arms and represented a threat to the continuation of slave trading from the port. His forces attacked local rulers who were vassals of the Portuguese Crown and traders traveling from the Portuguese fortress of Caconda to the coast. Benguela troops were employed to halt Kabunda's attempt to expand his dominion. Domingos da Fonseca Negrão, captain of the infantry of Angola, was sent to Benguela to lead the troops. Aware of the limitations of the Benguela troops, Negrão requested *guerra preta* ("black troops") from the *sobas* of Mulundo and Peringue, vassals since the early seventeenth century, as seen in Chapter 1. After marching for three days, most of his men had deserted. The *soba* of Guindagongo, located along the way, was forced to provide 100 men to help the Portuguese troops.[16]

The raids can be considered a success from the colonial perspective: Kabunda was defeated, and around six hundred people were captured. Yet the colonial focus on warfare and territorial expansion created a series of problems. Insecurity was a factor that undermined any attempt by residents in the town to develop urban sanitation, expand agriculture, or make other improvements that would help to boost the colonial settlement. Lisbon administrators blamed whites who lived in the hinterland for the insecurity in the 1750s, denying their own involvement as agents of violence who encouraged enslaving people to support the growing business of slave exports.[17] According to Elias Alexandre da Silva Corrêa, who lived in Angola at the end of the eighteenth century, numerous conflicts south of the Kwanza in this period were the result of "the incompatibility between whites and blacks." He continued, "Although philosophy claims that color has no effect on character, experience shows us that the habits, thinking abilities, and skills are the opposite."[18] By the end of the eighteenth century, Portuguese agents continued to define their presence in Benguela as civilization versus barbarism. Under this colonial approach, Africans were seen as naturally subordinate to Portuguese power, which enforced more vassal treaties, pushed violence inland, and resulted in

---

[16] AHU, Angola, caixa 40, doc. 72, January 22, 1756; AHU, Angola, caixa 40A, doc. 130, April 20, 1756. See also AHU, Angola, caixa 43, doc. 106, prior to October 23, 1760; IHGB, DL 06,01.05, "Relatório feito pelo comandante Domingos da Fonseca Negrão quando, por ordem de d. António Alvares da Cunha, governador de Angola, comandou os oficiais e soldados no interior de Benguela contra os revoltosos da Coroa Portuguesa," 1755.

[17] AHU, caixa 42, doc. 65, May 22, 1759. See also Delgado, *Reino de Benguela*, 246–7.

[18] Elias Alexandre da Silva Corrêa, *História de Angola* (Lisbon: Editorial Ática, 1937), 1, 366.

larger numbers of captives. Minor rulers who were disenchanted with the control of the *sobas* and groups dissatisfied with a chiefdom's policies signed treaties with the Portuguese as a way to achieve independence from their sovereigns. Subordinated rulers offered the Portuguese access to trade routes and slaves in return for protection and imported goods. Allegiances shifted from African *sobas* and chiefs to Portuguese overlords, although those involved had different interpretations about the limits and extent of this loyalty.

Between 1730 and 1750, the rulers of Kakonda, Kabiunda, and Kabunda became vassals of the Portuguese. Yet they resisted every attempt to have their territories occupied by Portuguese forces, resulting in several "rebellions of vassal *sobas*," as described in the Portuguese colonial documentation.[19] Conflicts inland generated more captives, which inevitably resulted in the arrival of more trans-Atlantic slave traders and troops to organize and control slave departures. Conflicts, however, did not last long. Defeated forces were seized and sold to traders going to the littoral, or they joined stronger leaders as dependents or slaves. Old *sobas* and their people disappeared from the historical record, suggesting their annihilation. The political disputes in and around Benguela in the eighteenth century indicate how the trans-Atlantic slave trade altered political organization, led to cycles of violence, and transformed societies. The historiography, however, minimizes its effects in West Central Africa in general. Joseph Miller suggests that disease and drought had more devastating effects than the slave trade, and John Thornton claims that women were able to reproduce fast enough to recuperate from the demographic loss.[20] Yet examples from Benguela reveal that the impact of the trans-Atlantic

[19] For the different meanings of vassalage, see Rosa Cruz e Silva, "The Saga of Kakonda and Kilengues: Relations between Benguela and Its Interior, 1791–1796," in *Enslaving Connections: Changing Cultures of Africa and Brazil during the Era of Slavery*, ed. José C. Curto and Paul E. Lovejoy (Amherst, NY: Humanity Books, 2004), 245–8; Catarina Madeira Santos, "Escrever o Poder. Os autos de Vassalagem e a Vulgarização da Escrita entre as Elites Africanas Ndembu," *Revista de História* 155, no. 2 (2006): 81–95. For *sobas*' shifting political allegiances, see John Thornton, "The African Experience of the '20s and Odd Negroes' Arriving in Virginia in 1619," *William and Mary Quarterly* 55, no. 3, Third Series (1998): 425. For the revolts, see AHU, Angola, caixa 30, doc 1, January 8, 1737, and doc. 4, January 15, 1737; AHU, Angola, caixa 34, doc. 3, January 17, 1744; and doc. 35, August 3, 1744. For the lure of imported commodities and resulting political rearrangements, see Miller, *Way of Death*, 105, 117–19.

[20] For studies on the role of the trans-Atlantic slave trade in West Central Africa, see John Thornton, "The Slave Trade in Eighteenth Century Angola: Effects of Demographic Structure," *Canadian Journal of African Studies* 14, no. 3 (1980): 417–27; Joseph C. Miller, *Way of Death: Merchant Capitalism and the Angolan Slave Trade, 1730–1830* (Madison: University of Wisconsin Press, 1988). Miller, "The Significance of Drought,

slave trade went beyond demographics, altering the political and social institutions that organized people's lives. Long periods of warfare were avoided because they debilitated states and threatened long-distance trade, but violence prevailed. The first half of the eighteenth century was a period of constant low-level fighting and political reorganization. Rulers in the region around Benguela who survived that period had a strong connection with the Atlantic economy and managed to recruit refugees, who could be used as soldiers or concubines and even be sold as slaves later on. Dependents were incorporated into existing political entities by the *sobas* and colonial agents, thereby increasing their power and coercion over free impoverished subjects, who had their labor expropriated in military and agricultural efforts. Refugees also were employed as porters in commercial caravans. Thus the old aristocracy of Benguela, Kitumbela, and Peringue, among other chiefdoms that had played an important role in the first century of Portuguese settlement, were replaced by new elites loyal to the Portuguese, in a similar pattern to what happened in Kongo and Kasanje.[21] The political turmoil that characterized the first half of the eighteenth century affected everyone's life. Security and protection against wars and kidnappings were debated among Africans and European settlers, and new colonial institutions were put in place to protect allies of the Portuguese Crown. The Atlantic commerce had devastating long-term effects on the African societies located around Benguela.

New Bureaucracy and Population Changes

From 1760 to 1850, the metropolitan government attempted to exercise stronger control, which included regulating many personal aspects of life in the southern Portuguese possession. More officials were sent to Benguela, and more buildings appeared, emphasizing Portuguese control. During the rule of Sousa Coutinho as governor of Angola (1764–72), the population of Benguela was targeted in his attempt to impose a new moral lifestyle. Sousa Coutinho supported the renovation of the Nossa Senhora do Pópulo Church and publicized the importance of Catholic burials.[22] He also attempted to introduce mandatory marriage for all residents in order to impose order, a measure that was not successful. According to him, the "residents were in continuous disorder, running

Disease and Famine," 17–60; and Daniel B. Domingues da Silva, "Crossroads: Slave Frontiers of Angola, c. 1780–1867," PhD dissertation, Emory University, 2011.
[21] Miller, *Way of Death*, 128–33.
[22] Linda Heywood, "Portuguese into African," 99; and Delgado, *Reino de Benguela*, 281.

away to the hinterland and seeking refuge among African states.... Africans respected them since they wore shoes, allowing the disarray and bad behavior of white traders."[23] The governor's account revealed how the trans-Atlantic slave trade also created new styles of dress, with itinerant traders, the *pombeiros*, wearing shoes to assert their connection to the Atlantic world.[24]

In the second half of the eighteenth century, a new hospital of Santa Casa da Misericórida was created, primarily to serve the military component of the town, because the old hospital building was deteriorating and did not have any doctors or medications available. The shortage of supplies was not a new situation because the men on the spot had complained about the lack of doctors and medicines from the clinic's establishment.[25] Africans were employed in the hospital, such as Manoel Jorge, who served as *mestre*, a skilled worker, in the hospital of Benguela at the end of the eighteenth century.[26] Another example was Silvana, a slave who belonged to Luanda resident Francisca da Silveira Pacheco; Silvana worked at the hospital in the early nineteenth century.[27]

Efforts to maintain tight colonial control over Benguela were constantly threatened by neighboring African rulers. Several rulers rebelled and attacked Portuguese agents. In 1764, Captain Francisco Xavier de

---

[23] ANTT, Conde de Linhares, L. 99, vol. 1, fl. 3–5, June 10, 1764; and Delgado, *Reino de Benguela*, 283–4.

[24] For more on *pombeiros*, see Jan Vansina, "Long-Distance Trade-Routes in Central Africa," *Journal of African History* 3, no. 3 (1962): 378; and Beatrix Heintze, *Pioneiros Africanos: Caravanas de Carregadores na África Centro-Ocidental: Entre 1850 e 1890* (Lisbon: Caminho, 2004), chap. 4.

[25] Feo Cardoso de Castello e Branco e Torres, *Memórias Contendo a Biographia do Vice Almirante Luiz da Motta Feo e Torres* (Paris: Fantin Livreiro, 1825), 263; AHU, Angola, caixa 36, doc. 7, March 16, 1748; AHU, Angola, caixa 78, doc. 16, January 23, 1793; AHU, Angola, caixa 82, doc. s/n, June 15, 1795; AHU, Angola, caixa 88, doc. 46, March 28, 1798; AHU, Angola, caixa 103, doc. 55, March 23, 1802; AHU, Angola, caixa 120, doc. 31, June 15, 1809; AHU, Angola, Correspondência dos Governadores, pasta 1, March 23, 1835; AHU, Angola, cod. 472, fl. 127v., November 18, 1761; Arquivo Histórico Nacional de Angola (AHNA), cod. 446, fl. 57, January 15, 1816; AHU, Angola, caixa 78, doc. 13, November 24, 1792; AHU, Angola, caixa 85, doc. 24, January 1797; AHU, Angola, caixa 89, doc. 86, December 1798; AHU, Angola, caixa 105, doc. 44; AHNA, cod. 441, fl. 2v., July 27, 1796; AHNA, cod. 442, fl. 205, April 14, 1802; AHNA, cod. 442, fl. 106v., July 22, 1802; AHNA, cod. 446, fl. 9, September 21, 1814; AHNA, cod. 447, fl. 104v., February 8, 1820; and AHNA, cod. 449, fl. 4v., June 29, 1824.

[26] Arquivo do Arçobispado de Luanda (AAL), Batismo de Benguela, 1794–1806, fl. 46, May 23, 1796.

[27] AHNA, cod. 507, fl. 55, February 18, 1815. For more cases of slaves used in the hospital, see Francisco Tavares de Almeida, *Memória Justificativa do ex-Governador de Benguela* (Lisbon: Revista Universal, 1852), 19.

Mendonça notified the governor of Angola, Sousa Coutinho, that he had sent troops to punish the heathens of Benguela, "the bravest and most fearful people who lived in the hinterland."[28] Traders and their *pombeiros* had been captured and killed while en route, which demanded a quick and compelling response from the coastal authorities. These conflicts, officially based on territorial disputes and colonial control, had a clear goal, which was to capture people who could be sold to trans-Atlantic slave traders stationed in the port of Benguela. Decades later, in the 1790s, the expansion of the slave trade led to more conflicts around the fortresses of Caconda and Quilengues.[29] Conflicts in this region continued in the 1810s, when traders complained to the governor that nonvassal Africans incessantly robbed caravans.[30] If there was a constant factor in Benguela since its foundation in the 1617, it was the vulnerability of the Portuguese settlement and the continuous efforts made by neighboring rulers to overpower foreign merchants.

In the 1760s, António de Vasconcelos, governor of Angola, described Benguela as "miserable village" with few residents and fewer buildings.[31] The exiled Manoel Pires das Quintas, for example, died after just four months in Benguela. He was condemned to 5 years of exile in Benguela but died shortly after his arrival.[32] Reports of unsanitary conditions were regular and continued until the mid–nineteenth century. In the 1820s, the English traveler George Tams described his arrival in Benguela. According to him, "a death-like silence and solitude pervaded the town, and produced an anxious and ungenial impression."[33] In the 1840s, José Joaquim Lopes de Lima stated that living in Benguela was "a continual battle with disease and death.... there are no white women, nor could there be any considering the certain death, especially if they are still of child-bearing age."[34] In 1845, Benguela was described in the *Encyclopedia Americana* as

---

[28] ANTT, Conde de Linhares, L. 90, I, fl. 34v.–37, September 23, 1764; and ANTT, Condes de Linhares, mc 45, doc. 1, November 26, 1772.

[29] Silva, "Saga of Kakonda and Kilengues," 244–5.

[30] AHNA, cod. 442, fl. 153v., January 18, 1800; and AHNA, cod. 323, fl. 65v., September 28, 1812.

[31] AHU, Angola, caixa 45, doc. 58, June 28, 1762.

[32] ANTT, Conde Linhares, L. 50, vol. 1, fl. 2, May 21, 1764; and ANTT, Conde de Linhares, L. 90, vol. 1, fl. 34, September 23, 1764.

[33] George Tams, *Visit to the Portuguese Possessions in South-Western Africa* (London: T. C. Newby, 1845), 2, 77.

[34] Lopes de Lima in Gerald J Bender, *Angola Under the Portuguese: The Myth and the Reality* (London: Heinemann, 1978), 65.

a country in Africa.... One of the principal [products] is manioc; divers sorts of palms are found, dates grow in great abundance; the vines naturally from alleys and arbors; cassia and tamarinds also flourish; and from the humidity of the soil, there are two fruit seasons in the year. The air of the country is exceedingly unwholesome.[35]

Foreigners stationed in Benguela were hard hit by the high mortality rates, but it is not clear how diseases affected the local population.[36] It seems that mortality among slaves was related more to their poor diet and unhygienic conditions than to tropical diseases. Accounts reporting on yellow fever or smallpox episodes do not mention death rates of the African population. Sources refer mainly to the effects of diseases, the rainy season, and famine on the white settler population.[37] While evidence suggests high mortality for Europeans, scholars should be wary that the local population was not affected at the same level. As stated in Chapter 1, for the Ndombe and other local groups, colonial officers and slave raids were more threatening than tropical diseases. Despite its reputation, the settlement attracted more traders from the interior and across the Atlantic in the second half of the eighteenth century, showing that economic profit was more attractive than any fear of the environment.

Colonialism expanded in Benguela with the creation of new administrative and judicial positions, including a secretary who would keep track of correspondence, which explains the sudden increase in the number of colonial documents available for this period. As a result of new fiscal reforms introduced in Lisbon, new treasury positions were created in Benguela. In 1767, Pedro Nolasco Ferreira, born in Bahia, was appointed

[35] *Encyclopaedia Americana: A Popular Dictionary of Arts, Sciences Literature, History, Politics and Biography, Brought Down to the Present Time* (Philadelphia: Lea & Blanchard, 1844), 2, 56–7.

[36] On the mortality of the European population, see AHU, Angola, caixa 45, doc. 94, September 18, 1862; AHU, caixa 82, doc. 62, December 2, 1795; AHU, Angola, caixa 122 doc 75, July 15, 1811; AHU, pasta 10A, doc. March 18, 1846, and Pasta 10B, July 1, 1846; Miller, "Significance of Drought, Disease, and Famine," 29–31; and Miller, *Way of Death*, 284–311. See also Jill R. Dias, "Famine and Disease in the History of Angola c. 1830–1930," *Journal of African History* 22, no 3 (1981): 349–78; and Philip D. Curtin, *Disease and Empire* (Cambridge: Cambridge University Press, 1998). On the different mortality rates of foreigners and the native population, see John Robert McNeill, *Mosquito Empires: Ecology and War in the Greater Caribbean, 1620–1914* (New York: Cambridge University Press, 2010).

[37] Biblioteca Municipal Pública do Porto (BMPP), cod. 1369, "Direção para previnir e remediar as doenças desse vastíssimo países de Angola e Benguela, sujeitos a grande monarquia portuguesa e famosíssimo teatro das heróicas ações e incomparavel governo do Ill. Sr. D. Francisco de Inocêncio e Sousa, seu atual governador e capitão general," fl. 303, August 14, 1770; Biblioteca da Ajuda (BA), 54-XIII-32(8), February 8, 1856.

Crown judge and treasury superintendent, in charge of warehouses in Benguela.[38] The introduction of this position was part of a metropolitan attempt to make the Portuguese presence more visible and to limit illegal activities by men on the spot. In 1769, instructions were sent to appoint a *juiz de fora*, a judge who would preside over cases from complaints about food monopolies to inheritance disputes. Pedro Nolasco Ferreira, who had acted as Crown judge and treasury superintendent, assumed the position of *juiz de fora* in 1771. He presided over the town council, supervised local authorities (including African intermediaries), and ensured respect for judicial proceedings throughout the province.[39] Between 1776 and 1825, eleven judges were sent to Benguela, spending an average of 4.45 years in office. In places such as Benguela, with more than sixty residents, *juizes de fora* had to hold a public audience twice a week. Short-term appointments were preferred in order to prevent the involvement of judges in local networks of interest.[40] Inevitably, *juizes de fora* with judicial and administrative jurisdiction clashed with other colonial authorities and local merchants. The creation of the municipal council and the appointment of a secretary resulted in an improved exchange of correspondence between Benguela and Angolan authorities. Other officials in town were the chief justice (*ouvidor*), a customs receiver who oversaw imports and exports (*almoxarife*), a secretary who was in charge of notaries and official correspondence, and a surgeon. New positions were created for an individual to supervise the collection of taxes from salt production, called the *captain of the Salinas*, and for a barber to help the surgeon by performing minor surgeries, including dental care.[41]

[38] Delgado, *Reino de Benguela*, 334–5.
[39] ANTT, Conde de Linhares, L. 50, vol. 2, fl. 280–1v., after May 6, 1768; AHNA, cod. 292, fl. 214v.–216, September 16, 1805. "Instruções para o Novo Governador de Benguela." In *Textos para a História da África Austral (século XVIII)*, ed. Maria Emília Madeira dos Santos (Lisbon: Publicações Alfa, 1989), 39–40; Lauren Benton, "The Legal Regime of the South Atlantic World, 1400–1750," *Journal of World History* 11, no. 1 (2000): 34; and Maria Fernanda Bicalho, "As Câmaras Municipais no Império Português: o exemplo do Rio de Janeiro," *Revista Brasileira da História* 18, no. 36 (1998): 251–80.
[40] José Subtil, "Os Ministros do Rei no Poder Local, Ilhas e Ultramar (1772–1826)," *Penélope* 27 (2002), 52; *Ordenações Filipinas*, livro I, 135.
[41] ANTT, Conde de Linhares, Mc 52, doc. 95, April 27, 1771. See also Delgado, *Reino de Benguela*, 383. For the disputes between governors and judges, see José C. Curto, "Struggling Against Enslavement: The Case of José Manuel in Benguela, 1816–20," *Canadian Journal of African Studies* 39, no. 1, (2005): 99–100. I am very thankful to Mariza de Carvalho Soares for her insights on barbers. See her "A Biografia de Ignácio Montes: o Escravo que virou Rei," in *Retratos do Império: Trajetórias Individuais no Mundo Português nos séculos XVI a XIX*, ed. R. Vainfas, R. Santos, and G. Neves

By the 1760s, only four houses had red-clay-shingled roofs, and most of the population lived in the areas known as *senzalas*, around the colonial center, where most homes were made of mud and straw. *Senzalas*, a term that probably came from the interior of Luanda, crossed the Atlantic to designate slave quarters on plantations in Brazil.[42] In Benguela, free people, alongside their dependents and slaves, lived in the *senzalas*, which were surrounded by yards and farmlands where they raised livestock and cultivated vegetables. Free and forced laborers cultivated crops introduced from Brazil, such as corn and manioc, as well as local staples such as beans, sorghum, millet, and pumpkins. These products were consumed locally and sold in the streets of Benguela or used to supply the ships anchored in the port.[43] Crops from the New World enriched the diet and increased food production, altering social and economic practices. In 1762, a *terreiro público* ("public market") was opened to regulate vendors and the price of basic staples such as manioc flour.[44] Free and enslaved women, known as *quitandeiras*, were encouraged to sell their products there in an attempt by the colonial administration to regulate their activities and extend state control. Street vendors protested the locality chosen by the government, which led to several changes in the siting of the public market.[45] This measure did not

(Niterói: Eduff, 2006), 47–68; and Tania Salgado Pimenta, "Barbeiros-Sangradores e Curandeiros no Brasil (1808–28)," *História, Ciências e Saúde* 2 (1998): 353–4.

[42] AHU, Angola, caixa 45, doc. 58, June 28, 1762. See also Jan Vansina, "Ambaca Society and the Slave Trade, c. 1760–1845," *Journal of African History* 46 (2005): 8.

[43] AHU, Angola, caixa 45, doc. 58, June 28, 1762; IHGB, DL32,02.03, fl. 18–32, November 20, 1797; Ralph Delgado, *Ao Sul do Cuanza (Ocupação e Aproveitamento do Antigo Reino de Benguela* (Lisbon: na, 1945), 1, 71–5; "Relatório do Governo de D. Miguel António de Mello," 552–3; Silva Correa, *História de Angola*, 1, 80; Selma Pantoja, "A Dimensão Atlântica das Quitandeiras," in *Diálogos Oceânicos. Minas Gerais e as Novas Abordagens para uma História do Império Ultramarino Português*, ed. Júnia F. Furtado (Belo Horizonte: UFMG, 2001), 45–68; and José Carlos Venâncio, *A Economia de Luanda e Hinterland no século XVIII: um estudo de Sociologia Histórica* (Lisbon: Estampa, 1996), 63–70.

[44] AHU, Angola, caixa 45, doc. 23, April 23, 1762. For more on the significance of manioc adoption in West Central Africa, see R. Harms, "Fish and Cassava: The Changing Equation," *African Economic History* 7 (1979): 113–16; Jan Vansina, "Histoire du manioc en Afrique centrale avant 1850," *Paideuma* 43 (1997): 255–79; and Miller, *Way of Death*, 20–2. Recent research has explored the trade in manioc flour between Rio de Janeiro and West Central Africa. See Mariza de Carvalho Soares, "O Vinho e a Farinha, 'Zonas de Sombra' na Economia Atlântica no século XVIII," *Populaçaõ e Sociedade*, 16 (2008): 215–32; and Nielson Bezerra, "Mosaicos da Escravidão: Identidades Africanas e Conexões Atlânticas no Recôncavo da Guanabara (1780–1840)," PhD dissertation, Universidade Federal Fluminense, 2010.

[45] See Delgado, *Ao sul do Cuanza*, 1, 71–5; "Relatório do Governo de D. Miguel António de Mello," 552–3; Silva Correa, *História de Angola*, 1, 80. For a similar case in a different

bring an end to the sale of food and other goods in the streets because slaves and free people continued their practice of wandering the streets to sell their goods.

Before 1779, the highest authority in town was the *capitão-mor* ("captain-major") appointed by the governor of Angola and approved by the Conselho Ultramarino in Lisbon. Among other responsibilities, the captain-major ruled over the town, dispatched slave ships, and controlled the sale of food to slave traders, activities that allowed him to gain enormous power.[46] In 1779, António José Pimental de Castro e Mesquita was appointed the first eighteenth-century governor of the town. Unlike his predecessors, he was named governor, not captain-major, but continued to be subordinate to the governor of Angola. Sousa Coutinho, governor of Angola, tried to maintain control over business and other activities in Benguela. Nonetheless, the town's location, its relative isolation, and the corruption of colonial men on the spot made control more desired than a reality. The second governor, Pedro José Correia de Quevedo Homem e Magalhães, assumed power in 1784, and his government was characterized by conflicts with the governor of Angola, the local bureaucracy, and Benguela-based merchants. After his death, an interim government was in place for two months until José Maria Doutel de Almeida Machado Vasconcelos arrived from Brazil in 1788, reinforcing South Atlantic bilateral connections.[47]

With the intensification of metropolitan efforts to maintain control, more authorities arrived in town from different parts of the Portuguese empire, but most came from Brazil. The town became a space of colonial power and a place where cultures and languages coexisted in an ongoing process of creolization. The landscape of the town also changed. New residents built more houses to accommodate recently arrived traders, and the houses had larger yards, where the population cultivated lettuce, grapes, cabbage, and pomegranates. By the 1790s, Benguela was a town with 15 two-story houses, 69 *térreas de telhas* ("one-story shingled-roof houses"), 33 houses with straw roofs, surrounded by 100 *senzalas*, and

---

context, see Karen B. Graubart, "Indecent Living: Indigenous Women and the Politics of Representation in Early Colonial Peru," *Colonial Latin American Review* 9, no. 2 (2000): 226; for more on *quitandeiras*, see Pantoja, "A Dimensão Atlântica das Quitandeiras," 45–68.

[46] ANTT, Conde de Linhares, Mc 42, doc. 2, February 3, 1775. See also Delgado, *Reino de Benguela*, 383; and Miller, *Way of Death*, 264–8.

[47] Ralph Delgado, *A Famosa e Historica Benguela, Catálogo dos Governadores (1779 a 1940)* (Lisbon: Cosmos, 1944), 17; and Delgado, *Reino de Benguela*, 381.

more than 1,000 mud and straw huts.[48] Several taverns attended to travelers, residents, and authorities stationed in Benguela, who gathered around bar tables to socialize and drink *cachaça*, the Brazilian sugar-cane alcohol. Considered low-life places of gambling and criminal activity, bars were sometimes owned by local women who tapped into a lucrative business. Dona Aguida Gonçalves, for example, was a 45-year-old woman who owned a bar on the first floor of her multistory house, where she probably employed her two male and ten female slaves.[49] Widow of the trader José Rodriges Horta in 1784, in the following year she had another partner, Nuno Joaquim Pereira e Silva. Nuno Joaquim Pereira e Silva also was the father of her daughter, Joana Pereira da Silva, whom both had baptized in 1785. Nuno Joaquim Pereira e Silva died after 1785, and 13 years later, dona Aguida was an important business woman in Benguela.[50] Dona Aguida Gonçalves represented the active role of local women in local commerce, a topic I will treat with more attention in the last section of this chapter.

Despite the influx of people from the interior and from across the Atlantic, Benguela was still a small town at the end of the eighteenth century. According to the first population census commissioned in 1796 by Governor Alexandre José Botelho de Vasconcelos, the number of residents and their dependents was 1,489. Most of the population, accounting for 1,123 residents, were slaves. The number of free people was 366. The tabulation excluded the free and enslaved population living in the neighboring *senzalas*, the residential areas around Benguela.[51] The large number of slaves in town raises questions about security. Social control was

---

[48] Biblioteca Nacional do Rio de Janeiro (BNRJ), 28, 29, "Noticias da cidade de São Felipe de Benguela e Costumes dos Gentios Habitantes naquele Sertão, 1797"; and AHU, Angola, caixa 90, doc. 1, January 3, 1799; and Delgado, *Reino de Benguela*, 381.

[49] IHGB, DL32,02.02, fl 8v.–9, November 20, 1797. AHU, Angola, caixa 42, doc. 88, October 30, 1759; and José C. Curto, *Enslaving Spirits: The Portuguese-Brazilian Alcohol Trade at Luanda and its Hinterland, c. 1550–1830* (Leiden: Brill Academic Publishers, 2004).

[50] Arquivo do Arçobispado de Luanda (AAL), Benguela, Livro de Batismo, 1794–1814, fl. 138 and 138v., December 9, 1800; and Livro de Óbitos, 1770–1796, fl. 126v., March 29, 1784.

[51] AHNA, cod. 441, fl. 19, "Mapa das pessoas livres e escravos, e casas de sobrado, térreas, de telha e de palha, de que se compõem a cidade de Benguela em 15 de junho de 1796." A copy of this census is also available at ANTT, Ministério do Reino, Mc 604, caixa 707. June 15, 1796. Another copy is at AHU, Angola, caixa 83, doc. 66, June 15, 1796. This was also printed in Delgado, *Reino de Benguela*, 381. For a detailed demographic analysis of Benguela in 1780–1850, see Mariana P. Candido, *Fronteras de Esclavización: Esclavitud, Comercio e Identidad en Benguela, 1780–1850* (Mexico City: El Colegio de Mexico Press, 2011), 75–113.

maintained through the constant use of violence to prevent uprisings and maintain order. Colonial armies were in charge of imposing order not only in the territories around Benguela, keeping neighboring rulers at bay, but also within the colonial center, among free people and slaves. Power and violence, as understood by Pierre Bourdieu, were employed daily through different mechanisms and as a result of the economic structure of the society based on the expansion of slave raids. The expansion of violence could only exist in a context where that same violence was seen as acceptable and necessary by the actors involved. Slave masters relied on the state and its police force to punish wrong-doers and prevent conflict. Local laws supported the unequal use of violence, as seen in the ban on black people being allowed to carry a weapon. Power and violence were inherent in the colonial state, and their use justified and legitimized slavery, colonialism, and social hierarchies, altering societies dramatically as violence became a central feature. As in other slave societies, the use of violence, or simply the threat it represented, helped to maintain power relationships where colonial officials and masters terrorized dependents, free and slave, who relied on wealthier and more powerful people for their own survival. Authority and power represented not only economic power but also the symbolic power it generated, as defined by Pierre Bourdieu.[52] Violence became the key feature of the slave system and consolidated it as an institution. It defined social interactions in town, between Europeans and local Ndombe; between African states, slave masters and slaves; and between whites and blacks, men and women, and Luso-Africans and people not integrated into the Atlantic economy. Violence shaped all aspects of political and social life, transforming economies and societies.[53] No quantitative analysis can recognize the prevailing force of violence and its devastating effects on West Central African societies.

By 1798, the population of Benguela was counted at 3,023, the most residents ever recorded, without a clear explanation of why the number had doubled in less than 2 years.[54] Demographic data were collected

---

[52] Orlando Patterson, *Slavery and Social Death: A Comparative Study* (Boston: Harvard University Press, 1982), 36–7; Pierre Bourdieu, *Outline of a Theory of Practice* (Cambridge: Cambridge University Press, 2004), 94–6, 165–72, 227–31.

[53] Patterson, *Slavery and Social Death*, 243–7; Paul E. Lovejoy, *Transformations in Slavery* (Cambridge: Cambridge University Press, 2000), 1–12; Boubacar Barry, *Senegambia and the Atlantic Slave Trade* (Cambridge: Cambridge University Press, 1998), 81–93; Green, *The Rise of the Trans-Atlantic Slave Trade*, 231–59.

[54] AHU, Angola, caixa 89, doc. 88. January 1, 1799; "Mapa da Cidade de Benguela e suas mais próximas Vizinhanças, Relativo ao Estado dessa no ano Passado de 1798 e ao que mais Fica no Primeiro de Janeiro Corrente, feito segundo as Ordens e Modelos dado pelo

with regularity in the first half of the nineteenth century in part because colonial administrators wanted to know how many individuals were available for defensive purposes and tax collection.[55] Although the data are incomplete, they indicate that the population of Benguela was relatively small and never exceeded 3,000 people, excluding slaves in transit.[56] It is not clear how drought and disease affected the small population, although elsewhere such events brought about demographic reconfiguration.[57] As mentioned earlier, in Benguela, the impact of diseases recorded in Portuguese colonial sources mainly referred to Europeans and other recently arrived immigrants, a relatively small percentage of the total population. On April 14, 1802, for example, Doctor Jacinto José da Costa arrived in Benguela to assume a position at the town's hospital. He died three months later.[58] It is not clear how the several episodes of drought affected the Ndombe and neighboring populations.

By the turn of the century, most of the population who lived in and around Benguela continued to be composed of Ndombe. Some lived under the rule of the *soba* of Kizamba, also known as Dombe Grande da Kizamba, located around 55 km south of the colonial port, whereas others were within the urban limits of Benguela. In the region of Dombe Grande da Kizamba, much of the milk, butter, and yogurt the rural residents produced was sold in Benguela.[59] The close contact with the population living around the town facilitated trade, cultural exchange, and inevitably, the spread of disease. While malaria and yellow fever were not

Illm.o e Exm.o Snr. D. Miguel Ant.o de Mello, Governor e Cap.am gen.al do Reino de Angola e Suas Conquistas."

[55] ANTT, Ministério do Reino, Mc 600, caixa 703, Francisco de Sousa Coutinho to Marquês de Pombal, May 5, 1772; and ANTT, Ministério do Reino, Mc 600, caixa 703, Francisco de Sousa Coutinho, "Carta circular a todos os Capitães-Mores," May 4, 1772. See also AHNA, cod. 80, fl. 15v–16, December 5, 1771. See also Benedict Anderson, *Imagined Communities* (London: Verso, 1983), 163–84; Richard Lawton, "Introduction," in *The Census and Social Structure. An Interpretative Guide to Nineteenth Century Censuses for England and Wales* (London: Frank Cass, 1978); Sonia Corcuera de Mancera, *Voces y Silencios en la Historia. Siglos XIX e XX* (Mexico: Fondo de Cultura Económica, 1997), 134–5.

[56] AHU, Angola, caixa 73, doc. 44, October 12, 1788; AHU, Angola, caixa 122, doc. 36.

[57] AHU, Angola, caixa 113, doc. 26, August 12, 1805. See also Miller, "Significance of Drought, Disease and Famine;" 349–78; and Dias, "Famine and Disease."

[58] AHNA, cod. 442, fl. 205, April 14, 1802; AHNA, cod. 442, fl. 106v., July 22, 1802. For more on the effects of disease on foreigners, see AHNA, cod. 444, fl. 27–27v., July 7, 1796; and AHU, Correspondência dos Governadores, pasta 3, April 18, 1838. Boletim Geral do Governo da Provincia de Angola (BGGPA), 241, May 11, 1850.

[59] Paulo Martins Pinheiro de Lacerda, "Notícia da Cidade de S. Felippe de Benguella e dos Costumes dos Gentios Habitantes daquele Sertão," *Annaes do Conselho Ultramarino* 12 (1845), 486–7.

as deadly for the population that had immunity, smallpox and measles killed a large number of Africans. In the 1810s, when a smallpox epidemic threatened the coastal population, bonfires were lit in town to contain the spread of the disease. Even the local doctor, Elias António Botapouco, fell sick and went to Luanda for treatment, after losing his wife, dona Guiomar Antónia de Carvalho, and their son, José, to the epidemic.[60]

The Napoleonic Wars that led to the Portuguese Crown's exile to Brazil consolidated bilateral connections in the South Atlantic. Rio de Janeiro, suddenly promoted to the capital of the Portuguese empire, was closer to Benguela than Lisbon. The demand for slave labor intensified the exports from Benguela and the arrival of Brazilian traders. From 1808 until 1850, the strong links between Benguela and Rio de Janeiro's commercial elite increased in part due to political instability in Portugal.[61] While the Crown was struggling with pressure from Portuguese liberal sectors to return to Europe, residents, merchants, and administrators in Benguela saw a possibility of joining the new empire in Brazil. Dissatisfied with British pressure to bring the slave trade to an end, traders hoped the new independent state would maintain slave imports.[62] A Brazilian party was created, but its members suffered persecution by the Benguela authorities

---

[60] AHNA, cod. 446, fl. 37v., May 12, 1812; AHNA, cod. 446, fl. 43, July 13, 1815. For the burial records of his wife and son, see Arquivo do Arçobispado de Luanda, Benguela, Óbitos, 1797–1810, fl. 66, February 8, 1810 and March 6, 1810. For the danger of diseases and how they affected demography, see Miller, "The Significance of Drought," 17–61; Dias, "Famine and Disease," 349–78; Robert W. Harms, *River of Wealth, River of Sorrow: The Central Zaire Basin in the Era of the Slave and Ivory Trade, 1500–1891* (New Haven: Yale University Press, 1981), 231–2; and McNeill, *Mosquito Empires.*

[61] Mariana P. Candido, "Trans-Atlantic Links: The Benguela-Bahia Connections, 1750–1850," in *Slaving Paths*, ed. Ana Lúcia Araújo (Amherst, NY: Cambria Press, 2011), 239–72; and Roquinaldo Ferreira, "Atlantic Microhistories," in *Cultures of the Lusophone Black Atlantic*, ed. Nancy P. Naro, Roger Sansi-Roca, and David H. Treece (New York: Palgrave Macmillan, 2007), 112–3. For a review of the history of Portugal in the nineteenth century, see Paulo Jorges Fernandes, Filipe Roberto de Meneses, and Manoel Baiôa, "The Political History of Nineteenth Century Portugal," *E-Journal of Portuguese History* 1, no. 1 (2003); available at www.brown.edu/Departments/Portuguese_Brazilian_Studies/ejph/.

[62] Leslie Bethell, *The Abolition of the Brazilian Slave Trade, 1807–1869* (Cambridge: Cambridge University Press, 1970), 88–9; also see Valentim Alexandre, "O Liberalismo Português e as Colónias de África (1820–39)," *Análise Social* 16, nos. 61–62 (1980): 323–5. For more on the impact of Brazilian independence in Angola, see Luiz Felipe de Alencastro, *O Trato dos Viventes* (São Paulo: Companhia das Letras, 2000); João Pedro Marques, *Os Sons do Silêncio: O Portugal de Oitocentos e a Abolição do Tráfico de Escravos* (Lisbon: Imprensa da Ciências Sociais, 1999), 116–7; and Manuel dos Anjos da Silva Rebelo, *Relações entre Angola e Brasil (1808–1830)* (Lisbon: Agência-Geral do Ultramar, 1970), 235–60.

who remained loyal to the Portuguese Crown. Justiniano José dos Reis, a Rio de Janeiro slave trader based in Benguela, was one of the leaders of the Brazilian party, alongside António Lopes Anjos, who exercised the position of captain of the *ordenanças, juiz pela ordenação, provedor e presidente* of the Municipal Council of Benguela and interim governor of Benguela in late 1823.[63] Some of the Brazilians who were persecuted by authorities in Benguela returned to Brazil and published pamphlets recounting their versions of the events there.[64] Despite the turbulence, it does not seem to have created a wave of migration and abandonment of the port in the early 1820s. The town was peaceful, and trade continued to operate normally despite the drought that affected the region. Douville estimated that around 2,000 people lived in Benguela when he was there in the late 1820s.[65] The Liberal Wars that shook Portugal between 1826 and 1834 provoked instability. While struggling with internal problems, the Crown inevitably relaxed its control of the overseas territories. Fearing that economic collapse would result from British pressure to bring the slave trade to an end, some merchants left Benguela in the late 1820s and early 1830s. Manoel Joaquim Pinto de Almeida and Joaquim da Silva Caldas, two traders residing in Benguela, relocated to Portugal to try new economic activities with the anticipated end of the trans-Atlantic slave trade.[66]

The December 10, 1836, decree officially abolished the slave trade in the Portuguese colonies, yet slaves continued to be exported for another 15 years. The metropolitan government made efforts to shift the focus of the economy from slave exporting to agriculture, but the men on the spot were too invested in the commerce in human beings to give up easily. As a result, traders in collusion with colonial authorities installed *baracoons*, or holding cells, along the Benguela coast to tap into the

---

[63] Delgado, *Famosa e Histórica Benguela*, 52, 72–127; Rebelo, *Relações entre Angola e Brasil*, 261; Manolo Florentino, *Em Costas Negras: Uma História do Tráfico Atlântico de Escravos entre a Africa e o Rio de Janeiro, Séculos XVIII e XIX* (São Paulo: Companhia das Letras, 2000), 133.

[64] Joaquim Lopes dos Santos, *Memória da Violência Praticada pelo governador de Benguela, João António Pusich, contra o alferes Joaquim Lopes dos Santos* (Rio de Janeiro: Na Imprensa Nacional, 1824). For more on the efforts of Benguela-based merchants to join the newly independent Brazil, see Mariana P. Candido, "South Atlantic Exchanges: the Role of Brazilian-Born Agents in Benguela, 1650–1850," *Luso-Brazilian Review* (forthcoming).

[65] J. B. Douville, *Voyage au Congo et dans l'interieur de l'Afrique Equinoxiale, fait dans les années 1828, 1829, 1830* (Paris: Jules Renouard, 1832), 1, 13. See also AHNA, cod. 449, fl. 55, September 22, 1825; and AHNA, cod. 508, fl. 89v., February 23, 1827.

[66] See AHNA, cod. 449, fl. 178, November 24, 1829.

illegal trade.[67] Besides the attraction of reaping profits, the merchants avoided the town in order to escape droughts and smallpox that struck Benguela and the surrounding region. Neighboring peoples affected by crop destruction and hunger pressured their *sobas* to invade the town and take advantage of the moment of economic reorganization.[68] George Tams, who visited Benguela in 1841, thought that the town had 3,000 inhabitants, one-third of them being mixed-race or white. He counted fewer than 300 whites, noting that diseases were particularly deadly among white troops.[69]

In 1840s, Benguela had "fifty houses neatly built in the Old Portuguese style, tiled and whitewashed, but composed chiefly of mud."[70] Despite its abolition in 1836, the slave trade was still vibrant and involved most of the residents, including the governor, despite the British patrols along the coast. Wax, ivory, and copper continued to be exported as well. In 1850, the *Almanak Statístico da Província de Angola* recorded 2,634 people living in Benguela.[71] Thus, unlike other African ports that saw their populations increase in the nineteenth century as a result of plans to export raw materials as legitimate trade, the population of Benguela varied but remained small. Lagos, for example, had 5,000 inhabitants in the 1790s, and by 1850, the population jumped to 20,000 and then to 25,000 in 1866 in part because of the British shift to palm oil exports. Ouidah, another West African port, had a population around 8,000 in 1722, but in the 1850s its size was estimated at between 18,000 and 20,000.[72] Luanda, in contrast to Benguela, expanded from 5,605 in 1844 to 12,565 in 1850, with the closure of the Brazilian market for slave imports.[73] Coastal societies, such as the colony of Benguela, imported

---

[67] AHU, Angola, L. 679, fl. 33, July 1840; Boletim Geral do Governo da Província de Angola (BGGPA), 63, November 21, 1846, fl. 2; BGGPA, n. 126, February 5, 1848, fl. 2; and BGGPA, n. 138, May 13, 1848. John Purdy, *The New Sailing Directory for the Ethiopic or Southern Atlantic Ocean* (London: R. H. Laurie, 1844), 619.

[68] AHNA, cod. 452, fl. 11v., March 15, 1841; AHNA, cod. 221, fl. 65, February 22, 1841; BGGPA, n. 82, April 3, 1847, fl. 1; BGGPA, n. 84, April 17, 1847, fl. 1; and AHNA, Cod. 455, fl. 267v., December 1, 1846.

[69] George Tams, *Visita as Possessões Portuguesas na costa occidental d'Africa* (Porto: Tipografia do Calvario, 1850), 1, 111.

[70] Purdy, *New Sailing Directory*, 414–5, 618.

[71] *Almanak Statistico da Provincia de Angola e suas dependencies para o ano de 1852* (Luanda: Imprensa do Governo, 1851), 9. For the date of the census, see the discussion in José Curto, "The Anatomy of a Demographic Explosion: Luanda, 1844–1850," *International Journal of African Historical Studies* 32 (1999): 385.

[72] Robin Law, *Ouidah, The Social History of a West African Slaving "Port,"* 1727–1892 (Athens: Ohio University Press, 2004), 73–4.

[73] Curto, "Anatomy of a Demographic," 402.

captives from territories inland, yet it continued to enslave people along the coast. Thus, unlike regions where there was a population increase along port towns, in Benguela, the population decreased in part because local traders and neighboring rulers continued to enslave people living in and around Benguela. While other coastal societies such as the Fante saw a demographic increase in part because coastal polities unified with the common goal of targeting populations inland and protecting themselves from enslavement, traders based in Benguela did not shift their focus.[74] Rather than importing slaves from inland, who would eventually be exported but also incorporated into the urban population, their operations continue to target vulnerable people living within the colonial center as well as in its immediate interior.

While North America and Europe faced industrialization and urbanization, populations in many African ports grew in response to the demands of the North Atlantic economies that depended on the development of plantation economies and the shipment of raw materials. Benguela's population remained small in part because it was integrated into the South Atlantic world, where the slave trade only came to an end in 1850 with the cessation of Brazilian imports. It was only after 1850 that plantations and legitimate trade exports became the main economic activity and led to migration of free and coerced labor to the coastal plantations.[75] Before 1850, a large number of slaves also lived in town, performing a variety of tasks and productive roles, but the focus of the economy was not on the export of raw materials but rather on human beings. Thus, before its decline in the Atlantic economy, Benguela was already a slave society, where slave labor was the foundation of the economic and social order.

Development of a Slave Society

During the eighteenth and early nineteenth centuries, slavery and the slave trade became vital to life in Benguela. The town's central economic function was the slave trade. Slave labor also was employed locally, performing different kinds of economic activities. As soon as vessels docked in Benguela, slaves unloaded the ships and carried passengers to the decks. Porters also transported luggage and other belongings of administrators

---

[74] Rebecca Shumway, *The Fante and the Transatlantic Slave Trade* (Rochester, NY: University Rochester Press, 2011), 88–132.

[75] W. G. Clarence-Smith, *Slaves, Peasants, and Capitalists in Southern Angola, 1840–1926* (Cambridge: Cambridge University Press, 1979); and Aida Freudenthal. *Arimos e Fazendas. A Transição agrária em Angola* (Luanda: Chá de Caxinde, 2005).

and priests around town and in expeditions to the interior.[76] Slaves worked in the *arimos*, the farms of local residents, and in the salt mines.[77] Residents were committed to slavery and the slave trade, sometimes ignoring Crown prohibitions regarding the trade. The priest João Teixeira de Carvalho, stationed in Benguela in the 1720s, owned slaves and negotiated for them with foreign traders. Accused of smuggling, evading Crown demands, and keeping concubines, Carvalho was arrested. Paulo Caetano de Albuquerque, governor of Angola, called him "the most scandalous clergyman of the Portuguese empire."[78] Slavery was the dominant labor system and influenced every social relationship in town. By the end of the eighteenth century, people who lived in Benguela, as well as other places controlled by the Portuguese, were classified as either free or slave or as white, black, or mulatto in a clear demonstration that slavery shaped the social, political, and economic order. Benguela became a slave society, similar to others around the Atlantic, and the trans-Atlantic slave trade contributed to it.[79]

Despite Portuguese presence and colonialism, Benguela was an African town, where the large population of slaves influenced cultural practices. The African presence dominated the town, which resulted in complaints made by the Portuguese authorities, who expressed fearful concerns. Captains and governors reported that Portuguese residents "Africanized themselves." Sousa Coutinho claimed that "some white men forget the respect and fidelity to the sainted religion [of Christianity].... [They are] in a Christian capital, conquered for God Almighty."[80] The adoption of African practices and commercial allegiance to local rulers were seen with apprehension by administrators,

---

[76] AHNA, cod. 517, fl. 56v., January 7, 1796; Torres, *Memórias Contendo a Biographia*, 303.

[77] AHU, Angola, caixa 53, doc. 1, January 10, 1769; and AHU, caixa 62, doc. 42, May 22, 1779. For slave labor in the *arimos*, see David Birmingham, *Central Africa to 1870* (Cambridge: Cambridge University Press, 1981), 82–3; and Freudenthal, *Arimos*, 133–4, 143. For the salt mines in Benguela, see Miller, *Way of Death*, 143–4.

[78] Delgado, *Reino de Benguela*, 246.

[79] For the definition of a slave society, see Ira Berlin, "Time, Space, and the Evolution of Afro-American Society on British Mainland North America," *American Historical Review* 85, no. 1 (1980): 53–4; and Paul E. Lovejoy, *Transformations in Slavery: A History of Slavery in Africa* (Cambridge: Cambridge University Press, 2000), 1–5. For the expansion of slavery in Benguela and its interior after 1830, see Mariana P. Candido, "Trade, Slavery and Migration in the Interior of Benguela: The Case of the Caconda, 1830–1870," in *Angola on the Move: Transport Routes, Communications, and History*, ed. Beatrix Heintze and Achim von Oppen (Frankfurt am Main: Lembeck, 2008), 63–84.

[80] AHU, Angola, caixa 53, doc. 1, January 10, 1769.

who feared Africanization and observed that cultural exchanges were almost inevitable in such close interactions. European men assimilated to certain aspects of the local culture, as with the Portuguese authorities who relied on African healers to cure illnesses. In 1722, for example, Captain António de Freitas, a black, locally born Portuguese official, followed the advice of a Mbundu spiritual medium to cure a sore leg. A healing ritual was performed, which included the sacrifice of a cow and music and dancing in which Captain Freitas and his extended family and slaves participated. The expertise of the *feiticeiro* might have not been enough because Freitas died four months later, probably as a consequence of his leg infection.[81] The imposition of colonization and the Catholic Church did not prevent residents of Benguela from maintaining a religion where ancestors were respected and worshiped alongside territorial spirits. African cosmology and religious practices remained strong in Benguela in part because they offered explanations and solutions to everyday problems that Catholic priests and officials could not address. In fact, by the end of the eighteenth century, the Brazilian-born doctor José Pinto de Azeredo noticed that many whites embraced local practices and consulted healers.[82] As Linda Heywood and John Thornton, Roquinaldo Ferreira, Toby Green, and Kalle Kananoja and others have shown, creolization affected Portuguese and African peoples, integrating certain elements of each other's cultures, reinforced by their constant interaction in a process that Walter Hawthorne described as an example of "African cultural creativity under oppression."[83]

In this Atlantic port, slaves were everywhere, acting as domestic help, servants, and sailors. In the *senzalas* and *arimos*, slaves worked in the fields cultivating cabbage, grapes, pomegranates, and lettuce. These crops

---

[81] ANTT, Tribunal do Santo Ofício, n. 92, fl. 235–85; this case is also analyzed in Selma Pantoja, "Inquisição, Degredo e Mestiçagem em Angola no Século XVIII," *Revista Lusófona de Ciências das Religiões* 3 (2004): 124–8; and Kananoja mentions it in his "Healers, Idolaters, and Good Christians," 448. For more examples of Portuguese colonial officials who embraced African healing practices, see James H. Sweet, *Recreating Africa: Culture, Kinship, and Religion in the African-Portuguese World, 1441–1770* (Chapel Hill: University of North Carolina Press, 2003)

[82] Kananoja, "Healers, Idolaters, and Good Christians," 461–2.

[83] Hawthorne, *From Africa to Brazil*, 13. See also Linda M. Heywood, "Portuguese into African"; Linda M. Heywood and John K. Thornton, *Central Africans, Atlantic Creoles*; Ferreira, "Ilhas Crioulas: O Significado Plural da Mestiçagem Cultural na África Atlântica"; Green, *The Rise of the Trans-Atlantic Slave Trade*; Kananoja, "Healers, Idolaters, and Good Christians."

also were cultivated in the farms along the Catumbela River and sold in the *terreiro público*.[84] Slaves also were used in public works and as soldiers and served as porters for the transportation of weapons, gunpowder, food, and military supplies on expeditions. In some cases slaves belonged to the administration, yet residents were compelled to provide their own slaves for expeditions.[85] On the streets of Benguela, shoemakers, carpenters, blacksmiths, masons, and caulkers worked side by side with slave traders in the incipient urban center. The workforce produced lime, tiles, and bricks that were later exported to Luanda.[86] Slave and free workers gathered in the Rua da Direita or in the Rua da Igreja à Fortaleza, which connected the Nossa Senhora do Pópulo Church to the fortress, offering services for residents and travelers. Some of the skilled work was performed by immigrants coming from Brazil. António Botelho da Cruz, a black shoemaker from Rio de Janeiro, and the free mixed-race carpenters João Coelho and João da Matta sold their labor in the streets.[87] Most of the work, however, was performed by slaves.

By the end of the eighteenth century, slaves represented three-quarters of Benguela's population.[88] As in other African ports, such as Lagos, Cape Town, and Ouidah, slaves worked side by side with poor free people and

---

[84] Lacerda, "Notícia da Cidade de S. Felippe de Benguella," 486.

[85] AHNA, cod. 441, fl. 5, July 27, 1796. See also Douville, *Voyage au Congo*, 2, 117. For the use of slaves in the military, see AHU, Angola, caixa 88, doc. 8, June 10, 1798. See also AHNA, cod. 510, fl. 9v., May 20, 1847; Torres, *Memórias Contendo a Biographia*, 344; and Douville, *Voyage au Congo et dans l'interieur de l'Afrique Equinoxiale*, 1, 18. For slave soldiers in the Portuguese empire, see A. J. R. Russell-Wood, *The Black Man in Slavery and Freedom in Colonial Brazil* (New York: St. Martin's Press, 1982); and Silvia H. Lara, "Do Singular ao Plural. Palmares, Capitães do Mato e o Governo dos Escravos," in *Liberdade por um fio, História dos Quilombos no Brasil*, ed. João José Reis and Flávio Gomes dos Santos (São Paulo: Companhia das Letras, 1996), 81–109. Slaves were employed as auxiliary forces in other African societies; see Mohammed Ennaji, *Serving the Master: Slavery and Society in Nineteenth Century Morocco*, trans. Seth Graebner (New York: St. Martin's Press, 1998); Sean Stilwell, *Paradoxes of Power: The Kano "Mamluks" and Male Royal Slavery in the Sokoto Caliphate, 1804–1903* (Portsmouth, NH: Heinemann, 2004).

[86] IHGB, DL32,02.02 and IHGB DL32,02.03, November 20, 1797. AHU, Angola, caixa 103, doc. 11, January 19, 1801; AHU, Angola, caixa 106, doc. 42, August 6, 1803; AHU, Angola, Correspondência dos Governadores, pasta 8B, July 10, 1845; AHU, Angola, Correspondência dos Governadores, pasta 16, doc. "Mapa dos rendimentos da Alfândega de Benguela nos anos de 1848 e 1849"; AHU, cod. 1632, fl. 136, October 12, 1796; Benguela Governor Martinho de Melo e Castro complained about sending 2,000 slaves to Luanda annually; see AHNA, cod. 440, fl. 14v.–15.

[87] IHGB, DL32,02.02, fls. 11 and 13.

[88] AHU, Angola, caixa 89, doc. 88, 1798.

provided food to temporary and permanent residents.[89] Although male slaves worked at domestic tasks under slavery, most domestic laborers were women. Slave women cleaned, washed, and cooked. They also fanned their owners' residences with portable fans night and day to cool rooms and chase mosquitoes away.[90] Slave women also were in charge of maintaining fires indoors and outdoors to ward off mosquitoes and animals.[91] They acted as nurses and also met the sexual demands of their slave masters.[92] Children also were used as domestic help. In 1800, Brazilian-born Governor Félix Xavier Pinheiro de Lacerda had four children employed as domestic servants, in addition to other slaves.[93] Residents displayed slaves as evidence of social prestige and wealth. In sum, the acquisition of dependents, whether free or enslaved, reinforced the economic position of traders and urban residents, who could put those people to work in fields and domestic spaces. In a town where no animal transportation existed, slaves carried people in palanquins in a similar fashion to Brazil.[94] As mentioned earlier, slaves were important in the port not only because

[89] See Selma Pantoja, "As Fontes Escritas do Século XVII e o Estudo da Representação do Feminino em Luanda," in *Construindo o passado Angolano: As fontes e a sua interpretação. Actas do II Seminário internacional sobre a história de Angola* (Lisbon: Comissão Nacional para as Comemorações dos Descobrimentos Portugueses, 2000), 583–96. Silva Corrêa also described women selling fish in Luanda; see Silva Corrêa, *História de Angola*, vol. 1, 80. For the importance of slave labor in other Atlantic ports, see Kristin Mann, *Slavery and the Birth of an African City: Lagos, 1760–1900* (Bloomington: Indiana University Press, 2007); Law, *Ouidah*; Wayne Dooling, *Slavery, Emancipation and Colonial Rule in South Africa* (Athens: Ohio University Press, 2007).

[90] Tams, *Visita às Possessões Portuguesas*, 1, 125.

[91] Arquivo Histórico Militar (AHM), 2-2-3-d. 14, "Descrição da Catumbela," 1847, fl. 5.

[92] Magyar, *Reisen in Sud-Afrika*, chap. 1, "Estadia em Benguela," 10; Miguel António de Mello, "Relatório do Governador Miguel Antonuo de Mello," *Arquivos de Angola* 26, nos. 103–106 (1969), 59–60. For similarities in Luanda, see José C. Curto, "As if from a Free Womb: Baptism Manumissions in the Conceição Parish, Luanda, 1778–1807," *Portuguese Studies Review* 10, no. 1 (2002), 33–4; Miller, *Way of Death*, 291–2.

[93] ANTT, FF, JU, África, Mc. 12, n. 9, July 28, 1800.

[94] Mello, "Relatório do Governo," 550; Miller, *Way of Death*, 191–2, 293; Mary Karasch, *A Vida dos Escravos no Rio de Janeiro, 1808–1850* (São Paulo: Companhia das Letras, 2000), 265–6; Mary Karasch, "From Porterage to Proprietorship. African Occupations in Rio de Janeiro, 1880–1850," in *Race and Slavery in the Western Hemisphere: Quantitative Studies*, ed. Stanley Engerman and Eugene Genovese (Princeton, NJ: Princeton University Press, 1975), 377–9. For more on portage and prestige, see Magyar, *Reisen in Sud-Afrika*, chap. 1, "Estadia em Benguela," 22, and chap. 2, "Partida para o Interior de África," 1. For reactions, see António de Saldanha Gama, *Memoria sobre as colonias de Portugal situadas na costa occidental d'Africa* (Paris: Casimir, 1839), 75. For more on the idea of wealth on people, see Vansina, *Paths in the Rainforests*, 207; Joseph C. Miller, *Way of Death: Merchant Capitalism and the Angolan Slave Trade, 1730–1830* (Madison: University of Wisconsin Press, 1988), 45–59.

they unloaded cargo but also because they transported passengers to the beach. The movement of a passenger to or from a boat required the labor of four slaves to prevent the passenger from getting his or her clothes wet.[95] Porters also provided transportation inside the town and carried all sorts of products, including toilet waste.[96]

Male slaves who were employed in skilled positions could enjoy some social status and easier access to wealth accumulation. The monetary compensation that skilled slaves received allowed them to save for manumission, although some were also freed by slaveholders on their deathbed. This outcome was seen in the case of Manoel, a baker who belonged to Captain José de Sousa, resident of Benguela for some years. Captain Sousa died in 1785 and freed Manoel on his deathbed, claiming that "he always brought profit and helped me make money."[97] Another of his slaves, Carlos António, however, had to provide ten dobras to get his manumission letter because "he had made money working for him," although his specific tasks are not known. Captain José de Sousa divided part of his personal clothes among the slaves he freed.[98] In skilled positions, slaves could receive small sums of money and had a chance to accumulate some wealth, as is evident on the case of Carlos António. In another example from 1811, Francisco, dona Maria Domingos de Barros' slave, received a small salary for his work in the royal iron workshop.[99] Slaves who showed devotion and loyalty to their masters were perceived as good and virtuous and had a chance to be freed, as the case of Manoel demonstrates.[100] Skilled slaves could expand their social network, especially in a small town such as Benguela. Sometimes they were the only people in town who could perform a specific task. António Pascoal, slave of dona

---

[95] Torres, *Memórias Contendo a Biographia*, 364.

[96] Magyar, *Reisen in Sud-Afrika*, chap. 1, "Estadia em Benguela," 23. For comparisons with Luanda, see Miller, *Way of Death*, 252–3, 268–73.

[97] For cases of skilled slaves manumitted by slaveholders, see ANTT, FF, JU, África, Mc. 2, n. 3A; ANTT, FF, JU, África, Mc. 2, n. 3B; ANTT, FF, JU, África, Mc. 21, n. 12; ANTT, FF, JU, África, Mc. 22, n. 5. See also Magyar's comments on slave workshops in Benguela, *Reisen in Sud-Afrika*, chap. 1, "Estadia em Benguela," 10. For more information on skilled workers in Benguela, see *Almanak Statistico*, 49; and Tito Omboni, *Viaggi Nell'Africa Occidentale: Gia Medico di Consiglio Nel Regno d'Angola e Sue Dipendenze Membro Della R. Accademia Peloritana di Messina* (Milan: Civelli, 1846), 60–81.

[98] ANTT, FF, JU, África, Mc. 2, n. 3B, 1791; and ANTT, FF, JU, África, Mc. 21, doc. 12, 1791.

[99] AHNA, cod. 445, fl. 123v., February 1, 1812.

[100] In Muslim societies, freeing a slave was seen as a pious act. See Ennaji, *Serving the Master*, 53–4; Yacine Daddi Addoun, "Abolition de l'esclavage en Algérie, 1816–1871," PhD dissertation, York University, 2010.

Inês, for example, was the only blacksmith in town in 1796, and as such, he received the support of Benguela's governor to establish a workshop. Probably because of his skill, he had a slave himself, António Felipe, who was his apprentice.[101] Slave owners trained their slaves to fill in certain positions, aware that the slave's work would increase the owner's wealth. Some recognized this situation, as in the case seen above where Captain Sousa acknowledged the importance to his own wealth of the work of the baker Manoel. Others tried to tap into existing occupations. In 1794, the governor of Benguela recognized that there were no experienced sailors in town who could be used by slave ship captains.[102] A few years later, the merchant António de Carvalho trained one of his young slaves, João, to work as a sailor with Captain José da Silva Teixeira, thus filling a demand for a specific kind of labor.[103]

By 1805, 616 male slaves and 502 female slaves provided most of the workforce in town. A cemetery was created to bury non-Christian local slaves and captives who died before being sold to trans-Atlantic slavers.[104] External events changed the shape of life in Benguela, particularly notable in the growing size of the slave population. The abolition of the British slave trade in 1807 and the efforts to impose abolition north of the equator after 1815 probably were factors in the population increase. The proportion of slaves among the population jumped from 45 percent in 1811 to 59 percent in 1813 and then remained stable over the next decades. Some of the slaves had been born in Benguela's households and were accustomed to Portuguese culture. They probably spoke some Portuguese and attended the local church, actively participating in the creation of a Luso-African culture.[105] In 1811, the governor of Benguela, António Rebello de Andrade Vasconcelos e Souza, had at least two young *ladino* girls working as domestic slaves.[106] *Ladinos* or *crioulos* were locally born slaves who had culturally adjusted to Lusophone culture. Slaves who lived in town established their own families, thus increasing the number of locally born slaves, although they did not marry in the Nossa Senhora do Pópulo. The local slave population lived in concubinage, or *casados pela lei da natureza*, in the *senzalas*

---

[101] AHNA, cod. 442, fl. 21, October 31, 1796.
[102] AHU, Angola, cod. 1630, fl. 76, February 14, 1794.
[103] ANTT, FF, JU, África, Mc. 22, n. 5, 1803.
[104] Delgado, *A Famosa e Histórica Benguela*, 42.
[105] Heywood, "Portuguese into African," 95.
[106] AHNA, cod. 323, fl. 28–29, August 19, 1811; and AHNA, cod. 323, fl. 30–31, August 20, 1811.

around Benguela.[107] Teresa, a slave belonging to dona Luzia da Silva, and Mateus, a slave of Salvador Barbosa, baptized their son, Pedro, in December 1810.[108] Although they were not married in the Catholic Church, it was important for them to baptize Pedro, probably because naming powerful people as godparents was a method of expanding their circle of protection. Another couple, Felícia, a slave of dona Teresa Rodriguez de Assunção, and José, a slave belonging to the captain of Benguela, Luis José Dias Sobral, registered their daughter, Teresa, as a free child, indicating that Teresa's godmother, Felicia's owner, had freed the newborn. These two cases illustrate how local slaves formed families, challenging the idea of social death. While Pedro was born in bondage, becoming another slave in Benguela, Teresa was manumitted as if "from a free womb."[109] These examples and others demonstrate how slavery was not social annihilation but rather a process of negotiation, adaptation, invention, and transformation. Enslaved people tried to find meanings and solutions for the situations where they found themselves, searching for protection and ways to create their own world and guarantee social integration for themselves and their descendants.[110]

The evidence of births and baptisms in Benguela demonstrates the local reproduction of slaves; however, the majority of additions to the slave population came from regions around Benguela, contributing to the establishment of that urban multicultural society. Some of the slave women who were documented in baptism records in Benguela between 1794 and 1814 were originally from Kakonda, Mbailundu, Kiaca, Wambu, and Ndombe; consequently, they did not necessarily speak the

---

[107] Delgado, *A Famosa e Histórica Benguela*, 62. Among the marriages registered in the *Nossa Senhora do Pópulo* between 1806 and 1853, no slave married. See AAL, Benguela, Casamento 1806–1853.

[108] AAL, Benguela, Livro de Batismo 1794–1814, fl. 293, December 11, 1810.

[109] AAL, Benguela, Livro de Batismo, 1794–1814, fl. 303v., September 30, 1811. For slavery and manumission in Angola, see Curto, "As if from Free Womb."

[110] For the idea of social death, see Patterson, *Slavery and Social Death*. For studies that emphasize creation under slavery, see, among others, Audra Diptee, *From Africa to Jamaica: The Making of an Atlantic Slave Society, 1775–1807* (Gainesville: University Press of Florida, 2010); Hawthorne, *From Africa to Brazil*; Mariza de Carvalho Soares, *Devotos da Cor: Identidade Étnica, Religiosidade e Escravidão no Rio de Janeiro, século XVIII* (Rio de Janeiro: Civilização Brasileira, 2000); Jane Landers, *Atlantic Creoles in the Age of Revolutions* (Boston: Harvard University Press, 2010); David Wheat, "Afro-Portuguese Maritime World and the Foundations of Spanish Caribbean Society, 1570–1640," Ph.D. dissertation, Vanderbilt University, 2009; Karen B. Graubart, "'So Color de una Confradía': Catholic Confraternities and the Development of Afro-Peruvian Ethnicities in Early Colonial Peru," *Slavery & Abolition* (2012): 1–22.

same language nor share the same political allegiances. Language use was altered by the numbers of migrants. Benguela inhabitants spoke in their own languages, and over time, both Umbundu and Portuguese became *linguas francas.*[111]

In 1816, according to Governor João Joaquim Marquês da Graça, the town was expanding, with caravans bringing slaves, wax, and ivory on a regular basis.[112] Slaves continued to arrive in town in part to be sent to the Americas but also to meet the demand of Benguela's residents. Recruitment of slave labor increased in the 1820s. By 1826, 566 male slaves and 663 female slaves lived in Benguela. George Tams, a physician who visited Benguela sometime between 1841 and 1842, described Benguela as "beautiful and romantic village," filled with mud houses and huts, but he was incapable of acknowledging that the town had been a site of violence for over 200 years. By not mentioning the prevalence of violence, he suppressed the power struggle imbedded in the port and accepted the violence as legitimate and even admirable. While Europeans lived in multistoried houses surrounded by high walls, slaves were kept in closed compounds under tight control. Tams witnessed slaves paving and cleaning streets around the town's squares, working to keep the urban center "beautiful and romantic," as he observed, revealing how slavery was intertwined with notions of beauty and order, and violence was tolerated and justified in the eyes of Europeans, both residents and visitors.[113] The closure of the Brazilian market in 1850 might have resulted in an increase in the slave population. In the 1850 census, 984 male slaves and 843 female slaves lived in Benguela and were probably employed in new plantations along the coast. The end of the Brazilian slave trade forced

---

[111] See the 2,035 baptism records available at the AAL, Benguela, Batizado, 1794–1814. Tams, *Visita as Possessões,* vol. 1, 156–7. See also Jan Vansina, "Portuguese vs. Kimbundu: Language Use in the Colony of Angola (1575– c. 1845)," *Bulletin des Séances, Mededelingen der Zittingen* 47 (2001–3): 267–81, see 271; Maria Emilia Madeira Santos, "Abolição do tráfico de Escravos e Reconversão da Economia de Angola: um confronto participado por brasileiros," *Studia* 52 (1994): 221–44. For the fear of Africanization, see Catarina Madeira Santos, "Luanda: A Colonial City between Africa and the Atlantic, Seventeenth and Eighteenth Centuries," in *Portuguese Colonial Cities in the Early Modern World,* ed. Liam Matthew Brockey (New York: Ashgate, 2010), 263–4.

[112] AHNA, cod. 446, fl. 71–71v., March 30, 1816.

[113] Tams, *Visita as Possesões Portuguesas,* vol. 1, 101–5. Pierre Bourdieu classified as *meconnaissance* this misrecognition and misrepresentation of acts of violence, which results in its acceptance and legitimization. See his *Outline of a Theory of Practice,* 5. For more on how slavery allowed societies to flourish and changed notions of art and leisure, see Green, *The Rise of the Trans-Atlantic Slave Trade,* 3–4; and Simon Gikandi, *Slavery and the Culture of Taste* (Princeton, NJ: Princeton University Press, 2011).

the shift in Benguela's economy and increased the local use of slaves who previously would have been exported.[114]

Formation of a Luso-African Society

Proximity, ocean currents, and historical links connected Benguela to Brazil. Links with Brazil and Brazilian traders were so strong that a nineteenth-century sailing directory described Benguela as being inhabited "chiefly by Brazilians."[115] Populations that lived in the littoral or inland became part of the wider Atlantic world that maintained strong ties with the only Portuguese colony in the Americas. People from the interior migrated to the coast and settled in the port, looking for economic opportunities and a chance to profit from the trade. Foreign traders, some of them from other African ports in West Africa, also moved into Benguela, attracted by the large number of captives available and the possibilities of enrichment. Although they arrived alone, they created new social networks and engaged in relationships with local women, who enjoyed and were subjected to the attentions of foreign men. The colonial historian Ralph Delgado claimed that African women were treated as queens, neglecting the fact that many African women were objects of violence, including sexual abuse, by European men.[116] The society that emerged in Benguela was a Luso-African society, where local women played an active role in the economy and life at the port. Although I use the term *creolization* to describe the process of cultural amalgamation that happened in Benguela, I will refer to the individuals, regardless of their place of birth, as *Luso-Africans* and not Creoles. *Crioulo* was a term employed in Benguela, as well as in most of the Portuguese empire, to designate locally born slaves. Nowadays the term is loaded with negative

---

[114] W. G. Clarence-Smith, *The Third Portuguese Empire, 1825–1975* (Manchester University Press, 1985), 61–77; Candido, "Trade, Slavery and Migration in the Interior of Benguela, 63–84.

[115] John Purdy, *The Sailing Directory for the Ethiopic or Southern Atlantic Ocean*, 414.

[116] Delgado, *Reino de Benguela*, 375. For the idea that sexual violence was central in slave societies, see Hilary Beckles, *Natural Rebels: A Social History of Enslaved Black Women in Barbados* (New Brunswick, NJ: Rutgers University Press, 1989), 60. For the link between European expansion and sexual violence with non-European women, see Ronald Hyam, *Empire and Sexuality: The British Experience* (Manchester University Press, 1992), esp. chap. 4. Anne McClintock, *Imperial Leather: Race, Gender and Sexuality in the Colonial Context.* (New York: Routledge, 1995); and Ivana Elbl, "Men without Wives: Sexual Arrangements in the Early Portuguese Expansion in West Africa," in *Desire and Discipline: Sex and Sexuality in Postmodern West*, ed. Jacqueline Murray and Konrad Eisenbichler (University of Toronto Press, 1996), 61–87.

meanings in Angola.[117] Historically, the term was associated with slave status; thus I decided to use *Luso-African*, a clearer concept that has been used for decades by other scholars and which has been applied to free and enslaved Africans as well as Portuguese and Brazilian actors.[118] Yet, as seen earlier in this book, *creolization* is a term commonly used to explain the process of amalgamation of different cultures and backgrounds into something new, including religious syncretism, altered naming patterns, new clothing and housing practices, and the adoption of crops from the New World, among other things.[119] However, there is a risk that *creolization* will be understood as synonymous with *acculturation*, as seen in European cultures, as James Sweet has warned. I employ *creolization* here in order to emphasize cultural adaptation in Africa and to stress dialogue and exchange, not the dominance of European values.[120] Many European institutions incorporated local characteristics, such as the case

[117] I am influenced by the studies of Kamau Brathwaite, *The Development of Creole Society in Jamaica, 1770–1820* (Oxford, UK: Clarendon Press, 1971); and Carolyn Allen, "Creole: The Problems of Definition," in *Questioning Creole. Creolisation Discourses in Caribbean Culture*, ed. Verene Shepard and Glen L. Richards (Kingston: Ian Randle, 2002). See also Paul Lovejoy and David Trotman, "Enslaved Africans and their Expectations of Slave Life in the Americas: Toward a Reconsideration of Models of 'Creolisation,'" in *Questioning Creole: Creolisation Discourses in Caribbean Culture*, ed. Verene Shepard and Glen L. Richards (Kingston: Ian Randle, 2002). For the problems of using the term *creole* in Angola, see Maria da Conceição Neto, "Ideologias, Contradições e Mistificações da Colonização de Angola no Século XX," *Lusotopie* (1997): 327–59; and Beatriz Heintze, "Hidden Transfers: Luso-Africans as European Explorers' Experts in 19th Century West Central Africa," in *The Power of Doubt: Essays in Honor of David Henige*, ed. Paul Landau (Madison: University of Wisconsin Press, 2011), 19–40.

[118] Miller, *Way of Death*, 246; Beatrix Heintze, "A Lusofonia no Interior da África Central na era pré-colonial. Um contributo para a sua história e Compreensão na Actualidade," *Cadernos de Estudos Africanos* 6–7 (2005), 179–207.

[119] Linda M. Heywood and John Kelly Thornton, *Central Africans, Atlantic Creoles, and the Making of the Foundation of the Americas, 1585–1660* (New York: Cambridge University Press, 2007); Linda M. Heywood, "Portuguese into African: The Eighteenth Century Central African Background to Atlantic Creole Culture," 91–113; James H. Sweet, *Recreating Africa: Culture, Kinship, and Religion in the African-Portuguese World, 1441–1770* (Chapel Hill: University of North Carolina Press, 2003); Kananoja, "Healers, Idolaters, and Good Christians."

[120] James H. Sweet, *Domingos Álvares, African Healing, and the Intellectual History of the Atlantic World* (Chapel Hill: University of North Carolina Press, 2011), 5; Hawthorne, *From Africa to Brazil*; Green, *The Rise of the Trans-Atlantic Slave Trade*; Kananoja, "Healers, Idolaters, and Good Christians." Additional studies influencing my work include Paul E. Lovejoy and David Vincent Trotman (eds.), "Ethnic Designations of the Slave Trade and the Reconstructions of the History of Trans-Atlantic Slavery," in *Trans-Atlantic Dimensions of Ethnicity in the African Diaspora* (London: Continuum, 2003), 9–42.

IMAGE 3. Nossa Senhora do Pópulo, Benguela. (Photo by Mariana P. Candido.)

of the vassalage ceremonies that adopted aspects of *undar*. In Benguela, Europeans embraced institutions from West Central Africa, lived under African rulers, consulted healers, used Umbundu terms in their reports, and had many wives, in a public display of "Africanization," just as the colonial state feared. Moreover, the term *creolization* conveys the sense of a culture in constant transformation as a result of its close interaction with the Atlantic world.

People migrated from the interior to the coast, and vice versa; they learned new languages, changed political affiliations, and met people who prayed to different gods and ancestors, and they had to be affected by these encounters. Culture, languages, and ideas were in permanent interaction, influenced by the Portuguese colonial power but most of all by the local African population, free and enslaved and numerically dominant. People born in the colony of Brazil, already creolized in many ways, also contributed to these exchanges. The emphasis is on Africans' roles as active transformers of Lusophone cultural traits, not on Westernization. In my interpretation, creolization also affected European and Brazilian men who lived in Benguela and its interior and who contributed to an amalgamation of different cultures to give shape to a Luso-African identity.[121] It goes beyond assessing the influence of Africans in the Americas or the Westernization of Africans. Benguela was as creolized as any place in the Americas as a result of historical changes that predated the trans-Atlantic slave trade but which were inevitably accelerated by that trade.[122] In sum, economic and political factors accelerated social change, such as the constitution of new family structures and the reorganization of social networks, reinforcing the creation of a Luso-African society.

The prolonged practice of accepting convicts from other parts of the Portuguese empire bolstered Atlantic links between Brazil and Benguela. Authorities in Lisbon believed that people born in Brazil were already adjusted to the tropical environment and hot temperatures and that their mortality rates would be lower than officers coming directly from Portugal.[123] Felipe Nunes and António Freira, both from Bahia, were condemned to exile for committing homicide and robbery, respectively.[124] It is not clear what roles they played in Benguela, but they were incorporated in the colonial administration, probably as soldiers in charge of

---

[121] I follow particularly the lead of the works of James Sweet, Linda Heywood, and Paul Lovejoy. See Heywood, "Portuguese into African," 91–5; Paul Lovejoy, "The African Diaspora: Revisionist Interpretations of Ethnicity, Culture and Religion under Slavery," *Studies in the World History of Slavery, Abolition and Emancipation* 2, no. 1 (1997): 4–6, Sweet, *Domingos Álvares*, 4–6. See also Roquinaldo Amaral Ferreira, "Atlantic Microhistories: Mobility, Personal Ties, and Slaving in the Black Atlantic World (Angola and Brazil)," in *Cultures of the Lusophone Black Atlantic*, ed. Nancy Prisci Naro, Ro Sansi-Roca, and D. Treece (New York: Palgrave Macmillan, 2007), 101–6; and Kananoja, "Healers, Idolaters, and Good Christians," 444–6. For more on the development of new identities in the context of the trans-Atlantic slave trade, see Peter Mark, *"Portuguese" Style and Luso-African Identity: Precolonial Senegambia, Sixteenth-Nineteenth Centuries* (Bloomington: Indiana University Press, 2002); Heintze, "A Lusofonia no interior da África Central," 179–207; and Beatrix Heintze, *Pioneiros Africanos: Caravanas de Carregadores na África Centro-Ocidental: entre 1850 e 1890* (Lisbon: Caminho, 2004).

[122] A growing number of studies explore cultural transformations in the context of the trans-Atlantic slave trade and its significance for Africans. See Lovejoy and Trotman, "Ethnic Designations of the Slave Trade," 9–42; Heywood, "Portuguese into African," 91–114; Landers, *Atlantic Creoles*; Ira Berlin, "From Creole to African: Atlantic Creoles and the Origins of African-American Society in Mainland North America," *The William and Mary Quarterly* 53, no. 2, Third Series (April 1996): 251–88; Ira Berlin, *Generations of Captivity: A History of African-American Slaves* (Cambridge, MA: Belknap Press of Harvard University Press, 2003), 24–36.

[123] AHU, cod. 546, fl. 92, September 16, 1735; See also Ferreira, "A Arte da Guerra em Angola," 4–5.

[124] Maria Eugénia Martins Vieira, "Registro de Cartas de Guia de Degredados para Angola (1712–1757), Análise de um Códice do Arquivo da Câmara Municipal de Luanda," BA major research paper, Universidade de Lisboa, 1966, 120–2.

protecting the port and punishing runaway slaves and *sobas* who resisted Portuguese advances. Most of the individuals born in Brazil worked in the administration or were military personnel, at the same time subjects and part of the colonial forces. In 1725, the Bahian-born Miguel de Melo arrived at the fortress of Caconda, in the hinterland of Benguela, as a captain. He moved to Caconda without his family, who continued in Bahia, maintaining family relationships across the Atlantic.[125] Political criminals who were considered to be a threat to the colonial project in Brazil also were exiled to Benguela. Colonel João da Cunha Vasconcelos, for example, was condemned to exile in Benguela around 1742 for taking part in a conspiracy in the hinterland of Bahia.[126] A few decades later, another man from Bahia was accused of conspiracy against the Portuguese Crown. Pedro Leão de Aguilar Pantoja was condemned to 10 years in exile in Benguela after his property was confiscated, and he had to walk around the streets of Salvador with a rope around his neck in a public spectacle of social condemnation and humiliation.[127] In 1792, five men condemned for treason in the failed 1788–9 Inconfidência Mineira, or Conspiracy of Minas Gerais, in Brazil, were sent to Benguela.[128]

Feared in the colony of Brazil, political and criminal exiles became the face of Portuguese colonialism in Benguela. For some, exile in Benguela brought economic prosperity, especially if they were successful in their slaving activities. Coming from a slave society themselves, Brazilian-born individuals played key positions in the administration, subjugating local rulers, capturing people, and participating in the spread of violence. Subjects of the Portuguese Crown, in Benguela they became an auxiliary force of colonialism. By the early eighteenth century, 40 percent of the troops available in Luanda were composed of Brazilian soldiers.[129] For most colonial officials, an administrative position in Benguela offered an opportunity to increase their capital, especially by taking part in raids where they captured people destined for the slave trade. Brazilian-born officials established alliances with Brazilian-based merchants to facilitate trade. José Vieira Dias, for example, was a military commander in Benguela who was also involved in slave trading in the 1760s and maintained links with Atlantic slavers.[130]

[125] AHU, Angola, caixa 22, doc. 25, July 19, 1724; and AHU, cod. 546, fl. 4v.–5, July 23, 1726.

[126] AHU, Bahia, caixa 72, doc. 6086, May 29, 1742.

[127] Luiz Gonzaga, *Inconfidência Baiana* (São Paulo: Editora Schoba, 2009), 247.

[128] AHU, Angola, cod. 1629. fl. 73v., October 14, 1792; and IHGB, DL86,07.08, May 29, 1792.

[129] Ferreira, "A Arte da Guerra em Angola," 5.

[130] AHU, Angola, caixa 63, doc. 58.

Two decades later, the trader Joaquim José de Andrade e Silva Meneses, from Bahia, also held the position of captain of the Benguelan army, demonstrating the connection between the ports of Benguela and Salvador, in Bahia.[131] In some cases, families maintained the South Atlantic link. Before 1799, António de Sousa Vale, born in Porto, Portugal, was a lieutenant in Benguela, and his father, also named António de Sousa Vale, had been a slave trader between Benguela and Rio de Janeiro, illustrating how families functioned in the trans-Atlantic slave trade.[132]

Between 1798 and 1832, Brazilians living in Benguela included the itinerant trader José de Assunção e Mello, who traveled twice to the Lovar to acquire slaves.[133] Three men from Bahia, Valentim Muniz de Siqueira, João Nunes, and João Coelho, owned bars in the port of Benguela. Taverns were spaces of business and social networking where merchants, colonial officers, and residents congregated over drinks to exchange news, negotiate, and chat.[134] They probably drank *cachaça*, which had been traded in the region of Benguela by Brazilian slavers since the late seventeenth century.[135] The Atlantic economy united elites from both shores of the ocean, giving shape to a community with strong links with the Atlantic world but also with the interior. Coastal traders engaged in commerce with the states located inland. However, Brazil was the place where many invested and sent their children to be educated. The Portuguese trader Francisco Xavier do Reis, for example, had properties in Bahia. Reis had a female slave named Mariana Benguela, "whom I freed of my own free will, as if she was born free, and with whom I had a daughter, named Martinha, who was born after I left for Benguela."[136] Merchants in Benguela sent their children to Rio de Janeiro to receive a formal education, and regular business connections were reinforced accordingly. José Rodrigues Magalhães, a trader in Benguela at the end of eighteenth century, sent

---

[131] AHU, Angola, caixa 89, doc. 67, December 21, 1798. The link between Benguela and Bahia is often overlooked. See Candido, "Trans-Atlantic Links," 242–6.

[132] ANTT, FF, JU, Africa, Mc. 1, no. 3, caixa 2. For more on family networks, see Cátia Antunes and Filipa Ribeiro Da Silva, "Cross-Cultural Entrepreneurship in the Atlantic: Africans, Dutch and Sephardic Jews in Western Africa, 1580–1674," *Itinerario* 35, no. 1 (2011): 49–76.

[133] IHGB, DL32,02.01, "Relação dos sobas potentados, souvetas seus vassalos e sobas agregados pelos nomes das suas terras, que tem na capitania de Benguela," 1978, fl. 5v.–6. See also Francisco José de Lacerda e Almeida, *Lacerda's Journey to Cazembe in 1798* (London: John Murray, 1873), 24.

[134] IHGB, DL32,02.02, November 29, 1797, fl. 7–17v. For more on taverns, see Curto, *Enslaving Spirits*, 178.

[135] Alencastro, *Trato dos Viventes*, 319.

[136] ANTT, Feitos Findos, África, Mc. 24, n. 17, December 4, 1789.

at least one of his sons to Rio for education. He was the father of four sons and four daughters. Although it is not clear if all his sons had the opportunity to study, at least one, Lourenço, was in Rio in 1797 attending school when he was 9 years old.[137] Sending children to study in Brazil or Portugal was necessary because the Portuguese administration introduced primary schools to its African colonies only in 1845, and in most cases, including Benguela, there was no school until after 1850.[138] Raised in a slave society with strong racial and social hierarchies, eventually these children went back to Benguela, where they occupied positions in the colonial state.

In this Atlantic port, residents lived a religiously syncretic lifestyle, combining Catholic baptism with *entambe* (a week long burial ceremony celebrating the deceased) and Catholic weddings with polygamy.[139] The daily contact between foreigners and the Ndombe and other local populations led to the formation of a heterogeneous population that adopted elements of each other's cultures. The bond they shared was their involvement, directly or not, in the Atlantic commercial networks and in slaving activities. As with the *lançados* in Senegambia, traders who resided in Benguela became important actors in the spread of Portuguese culture and language and the expansion of the colony inland. Even the *degredados*, who were exiled in the port town, maintained links with the colonial state, which acted as their protector.[140] The contacts between foreign men and African women attracted the attention of metropolitan

---

[137] IHGB, DL32,02.02, fl. 7v.–8.

[138] Alexandre and Dias, *O Império Africano*, 160; René Pélissier, *História das Campanhas de Angola. Resistência e Revoltas 1845–1941* (Lisbon: Estampa, 1997), 1, 62.

[139] *Entambe* was a wake where family and friends gathered and played drums and danced. See AHU, Angola, caixa 53, doc. 1, January 10, 1769; and Silva Corrêa, *História De Angola*, 1, 88–9. Several reports indicate syncretism of religious and cultural practices. See AHU, Angola, caixa 62, doc. 42, May 22, 1779; see also John K. Thornton, "The Development of an African Catholic Church in the Kingdom of Kongo, 1491–1750," *Journal of African History* 25, no. 2 (1984): 147–67; and Kananoja, "Healers, Idolaters, and Good Christians." For a similar history on the Gold Coast, see Feinberg, *Africans and Europeans*, 29.

[140] Hespanha and Santos, "Os Poderes num Império Oceânico," 407; For the *lançados*, see Mark, *"Portuguese" Style and Luso-African Identity*, 13–27; Walter Hawthorne, "Strategies of the Decentralized: Defending Communities from Slave Raiders in Coastal Guinea-Bissau, 1450–1815," in *Fighting the Slave Trade: West African Strategies*, ed. Silviane Diouf (Athens: Ohio University Press, 2003), 163–4; Boubacar Barry, *Senegambia and the Atlantic Slave Trade* (Cambridge: Cambridge University Press, 1998), 41–4; Philip D. Curtin, *Economic Change in Precolonial Africa; Senegambia in the Era of the Slave Trade* (Madison: University of Wisconsin Press, 1974), 95–100; Green, *The Rise of the Trans-Atlantic Slave Trade*.

and Luanda-based administrators, who condemned it as part of the ongoing fear of Africanization. Men on the spot, colonial official or not, targeted the daughters of the local political and economic elite in search of a partnership with a family that would solidify their commercial enterprises.[141] African women who lived with foreign men also profited from these relationships, although colonial officials accused them of prostitution in a clear attempt to lower their social image and prestige. For those women, marriage offered a chance to accumulate wealth and, eventually, benefit from social mobility. Through their contacts with foreign traders, they had access to imported goods and displayed their wealth in their possessions and property. Dressed in a European fashion and wearing jewelry, powerful local women walked around surrounded by slaves and dependents, as did women in Luanda, Rio de Janeiro, or Cacheu.[142]

Although a legislative corpus was not formulated, as happened in the French, Spanish, and British empires, a series of social regulations created barriers between whites and the "others," the black population. The administration in Lisbon expected lower-rank officials to marry local women in order to maintain stronger links to the region. Poor whites were asked to integrate blacks into their social and sexual spheres, and soldiers who had families in Angola had to request government approval to abandon the territory.[143] Nevertheless, higher-ranked officials were asked to bring their families and live a "decent" lifestyle, where Christian

---

[141] Charles Boxer, *Race Relations in the Portuguese Colonial Empire, 1415–1825* (Oxford University Press, 1963), 19–20; Vansina, "Ambaca," 8; Selma Pantoja, "Três Leituras e Duas Cidades: Luanda e Rio de Janeiro nos Setencentos," in *Angola e Brasil nas Rotas do Atlântico Sul*, ed. Selma Pantoja and José Flávio Sombra Saraiva (Rio de Janeiro: Bertrand Brasil, 1999), 99–126.

[142] See Delgado, *Reino de Benguela*, 375. For similar behavior in Luanda and other African ports, see Selma Pantoja, "Women's Work in the Fairs and Markets of Luanda," in *Women in the Portuguese Colonial Empire: the Theater of Shadows*, ed. Clara Sarmento (Newcastle Upon Tyne: Cambridge Scholars Publishing, 2008), 81–93; Selma Pantoja, "Encontros nas Terras de Além-Mar: os Espaços Urbanos do Rio de Janeiro, Luanda e Ilha de Moçambique na era da Ilustração," PhD dissertation, Universidade de São Paulo, 1994; and Philip J. Havik, "Women and Trade in the Guinea Bissau Region: The Role of African and Luso-African Women in Trade Networks from the Early 16th to the Mid-19th Century," *Studia* 52 (1994): 83–120. For examples in Brazil, see Silvia H. Lara, "The Signs of Color: Women's Dress and Racial Relations in Salvador and Rio de Janeiro, ca. 1750–1815," *Colonial Latin American Review* 6, no. 2 (1997): 205–24; Mary Karasch, "As Mulheres Livres de Cor no Brasil, 1779–1832," *Revista da Sociedade Brasileira de Pesquisa Histórica* 15 (1998): 3–20.

[143] AHU, Angola, caixa 26, doc. 38, October 9, 1717. See A. J. R. Russell-Wood, "Iberian Expansion and the Issue of Black Slavery: Changing Portuguese Attitudes, 1440–1770," *American Historical Review* 83, no. 1 (1978): 16–42.

values were respected and displayed. This situation was the case for Judge Alberto António Pereira, who brought his wife, dona Maria José da Silveira Sousa, to Benguela. It is not clear how long the couple lived there. In 1799, they baptized their son, Luís. To celebrate Luís' baptism, the bishop of Angola, Dom Luís de Brito, was named as his godfather, and dona Maria Vicencia Xavier, wife of the *ouvidor* (the Crown judge) Félix Correia de Araújo, was named as his godmother.[144] However, such cases are an exception in the baptismal records, where most children were registered as *natural*, that is, in the state of nature, not from a married couple. Metropolitan administrators tried to control the behavior of European men and threatened to sentence those who did not follow a "religious, justifiable, and industrial way of life" to prison.[145] However, men on the spot and local women continued to mingle despite metropolitan attempts at social control.

Foreign men and local women formed families and raised Luso-African children who were considered to be Portuguese. As a result of the large black population, the high mortality among Europeans, and the miscegenation that was common in Benguela, the Portuguese overseas council turned a blind eye to the practice of concubinage and supported the employment of *filhos da terra*, descendents of locally born Portuguese, in colonial administrative positions. In Brazil, however, restrictions were put in place to prevent African descendents from filling certain positions in the administration.[146] In Benguela, the descendants of European or Brazilian men and local women occupied key positions in the administration in part because administrators believed that they had a natural resistance to the weather and local diseases, as already explained in Chapter 1.[147] In 1732, Belchior Raposo Pimentel, born in Luanda, a *filho da terra*, occupied the position of probate judge in Benguela. In 1740 he was nominated captain of the fortress of Benguela, although more details of his

---

[144] AAL, Benguela, Batismos, 1794–1814, fl. 107v., April 17, 1799.

[145] "Não estivessem sujeitos a viver unidos em sociedade em religião, em justiça, e em indústria, será imediatamente preso e remetido para esta capital," *Arquivo de Angola* 1, no. 1 (1936), 178. See also AHU, Angola, caixa 43, docs. 111, November 20, 1760.

[146] For the recruitment of *filhos da terra* in Angola, see Santos, "Luanda," 260. For the experience in Brazil, see Muriel Nazzari, "Concubinage in Colonial Brazil: The Inequalities of Race, Class and Gender," *Journal of Family History* 21 (1996): 107–21, See also Charles R. Boxer, *The Golden Age of Brazil, 1695–1750* (Berkeley: University of California Press, 1962), 166. For specific cases, see Cadornega, *História Geral*, vol. 2, 18, 180.

[147] AHU, caixa 27, doc. 42, June 20, 1733. See also Candido, *Fronteras de la Esclavización*, 134; and Santos, "Luanda: A Colonial City," 263.

life, such as skin color and marital status, are not available.[148] Locally born descendants of Europeans were classified as Portuguese regardless of their skin color. Being perceived as a Portuguese or white was a crucial factor in determining who was vulnerable to being coerced into the trans-Atlantic slave trade, as will be seen in Chapter 4. For local women, marriage with a foreigner provided instant access to the Atlantic world and its commodities.

Portuguese settlers in different parts of Africa used marriage and long-term relationships with local women to advance commercial alliances. Unions with local African women were a reality for many of the Europeans residing in Benguela. By the early 1620s, Governor Lopo Soares had already reported that a soldier from Brazil went to the hinterland and, after meeting some women, never returned, "enchanted" by them.[149] Concubinage was widespread and did not necessarily mean that a man was involved with more than one woman. On very few occasions, colonial documents indicate cases where women had more than one partner, such as the case of Mariana Fernandes, who was married to an administrator of the royal contract, André Ferreira Gil. She also maintained an affair for years with the priest stationed in Benguela, João Teixeira de Carvalho, described as "a mulatto of the Hebrew race" who lived in concubinage in Benguela.[150] In 1726, in a jealous attack, the priest Carvalho gathered eight of his slaves and invaded the house where the administrator lived with Mariana. The priest stabbed Ferreira Gil several times. Scared, Mariana Fernandes escaped through the window.[151] Another case of female polygamy is a woman identified only as the sister-in-law of the trader Alexandre José Gonçalves, who was accused of having an affair with one of his slaves.[152] In both cases, these women disrupted the social order by maintaining relationships with more than one man, in some cases even crossing racial barriers in a society highly stratified in terms of status and skin color. However, the colonial documents tend to be silent regarding the matrimonial arrangements of white Portuguese women.

---

[148] AHU, caixa 27, doc. 21, prior to February 12, 1733; AHU, caixa 32, doc. 12, May 23, 1740.
[149] Delgado, *Reino de Benguela*, 123; Alfredo de Albuquerque Felner, *Angola: Apontamentos sobre a Colonização dos Planaltos e Litoral do Sul de Angola* (Lisbon: Agência do Ultramar, 1940), 359.
[150] Heywood, "Portuguese into African," 94.
[151] AHU, cod. 546, fl. 8v., November 5, 1726.
[152] AHNA, cod. 446, fl. 61v.–64, February 24, 1816.

Relationships between foreign men and African women were more common and often resulted in the offspring. Although several cases indicate that the unions were voluntary, slave owners also lived in concubinage with slave women. In some cases, these sexual relationships aimed to expand the number of slaves.[153] However, in other cases, slave owners and slave women maintained long relationships that led to the establishment of families. Some of these slave women could be freed on the death of their master, such as the case of Vitória and Francisca. Vitória and Francisca served as domestic slaves in the household of the merchant António José de Barros, although it is not clear for how long. Barros fathered children with these women. With Vitória he had two daughters, Rita and Rosa. Francisca also had a daughter with him, named Joana. Barros freed his children on their baptism but maintained their mothers in bondage until his death.[154] The growing mixed population concerned the authorities, who feared that whites eventually would be Africanized, which would represent failure of the colonial enterprise. The relationships fostered a process of cultural mixing, or creolization, that also was seen in Luanda.[155]

Despite its small size, the population of Benguela was cosmopolitan. Residents arrived from the Portuguese cities of Lisbon, Braga, and Porto; the Brazilian ports of Salvador and Rio de Janeiro; and other parts of the African continent such as Luanda and the Costa da Mina in West Africa.[156] In the 1780s, some of the foreign residents in Benguela were Felipe da Silva and João José Pinto from Bahia, Fortunato José da Cruz from Rio de Janeiro, Matias Ferreira from the Madeira archipelago, and António do Rosário from Ouidah.[157] Yet very few Portuguese women immigrated to Benguela or to Angola in general. The number of white women ranged from two to nine in Benguela, although it is not clear whether they were European or not. In 1797, for example, authorities listed nine white

---

[153] AHU, caixa 42, doc. 65, May 22, 1759.

[154] ANTT, FF, JU, África, Mc. 2, n. 3 A, 1800.

[155] On the fear of Africanization of the white population, see the report of Francisco Inocêncio de Sousa Coutinho, IHGB, DL81,02.14, fl. 46–7, November 13, 1769. For more on the adoption of local languages by the Portuguese, see Heintze, "A Lusofonia no interior da África Central," 179–207. For more on creolization, see António, *Luanda, Ilha Crioula*; and Ferreira, "'Ilhas Crioulas," 17–41; Heywood, "Portuguese into African;" Green, *The Rise of the Trans-Atlantic Slave Trade*, 260–77.

[156] The Portuguese term *Costa da Mina* refers to the Windward Coast, Gold Coast, Bight of Benin, and Bight of Biafra. See Luís Viana Filho, *O Negro na Bahia* (São Paulo: Martins, 1976), 26.

[157] AHU, Angola, caixa 63, doc. 2, January 7, 1780.

women residing in Benguela. Between 1800 and 1808, their number was five or six. In 1809, only two white women remained, and there was only one listed as a resident of Benguela in 1816. In 1826, two white women lived in town. By 1850, their number had increased to seven.[158] The absence of European women worked against the establishment of a white elite in control of the colonial state, as happened in other colonial contexts in the Americas and Southern Africa.[159] This led to the emergence of a Luso-African elite, descendants of Portuguese and other foreigners and local women, who were perceived and socially classified as Portuguese and enjoyed many privileges.

In African societies, marriage was one of the ways to incorporate strangers. Some Portuguese men chose this route and adopted family arrangements influenced by local practices. In 1797, a merchant named Manuel Francisco da Silva lived in the territory of Fende under the protection of the ruler. Fende was located close to Caconda, although not under the jurisdiction of the Portuguese fortress. He married into the extended family of Fende's *soba*, which certainly allowed him to be embraced as a relative.[160] Daughters of important rulers were very attractive marriage partners. This type of bond was the case for the Portuguese trader António de Carvalho, who, by the end of the eighteenth century, had had a long union with the daughter of Kamlocoxo, who was subordinated to the *soba* of Ngalangue. Carvalho had two children with her, Mariana and Agostinho.[161] He also maintained relationships with at least two women in Benguela, Bibiana, a free black woman, and Beba, one of his slaves. A union with the daughter of the *soba* was a common way to establish a favorable business relationship. António de Carvalho, through marriage, became a relative of Kamlocoxo and, as such, enjoyed certain privileges. In different societies, including the Portuguese, exchange of women was a way to consolidate diplomatic and commercial ties between foreign merchants and local political elites.[162] Common in the Atlantic world, alliances

---

[158] For a discussion on the demographics of Benguela and the number of white women listed in censuses, see Candido, *Fronteras de la Esclavización*, 94.

[159] See Leonard Guelke, 'The Anatomy of a Colonial Settler Population: Cape Colony, 1657–1750," in *Families in the Expansion of Europe, 1500–1800*, ed. Maria Beatriz Nizza da Silva (Aldershot, UK: Ashgate, 1998), 293–313.

[160] IHGB DL31,05, "Relação feita por João da Costa Frade, do Presídio de Caconda em Benguela, sobre moradores, escravos, forros, mantimentos e gados existentes no presídio," fl. 10, December 31, 1797.

[161] ANTT, Feitos Findos, JU, África, Mc. 22, doc. 5, 1803.

[162] See Claude Meillassoux, *Mujeres, Graneros y Capitales: Economía Doméstica Y Capitalismo* (Mexico: Siglo XXI, 1977); Elizabeth Schmidt, *Peasants, Traders and Wives:*

between foreign traders and local elites continued to exist until the mid–nineteenth century. Powerful families guaranteed the maintenance of their social position and economic privilege through marriage, which unified assets and increased symbolic power.[163] In 1849, to maintain a loyal relationship with the Hungarian trader László Magyar, the ruler of Viye, Olosoma Kanyangula, married his daughter to the foreigner. This relationship facilitated Magyar's contacts and enhanced his position among Viye nobles.[164] Another trader, Silva Porto, also sought an alliance with the ruler of Viye. He married Luzia Massak, great-great-granddaughter of the *soba* of Viye, and they had a daughter.[165]

Trade alliances offered opportunities to local women, who became commercial partners. They facilitated communication and transportation, connecting distant communities. Business-oriented unions were common along the coast of Africa and gave origin to mixed populations in Luanda, Saint Louis, Cacheu, Bissau, and the Zambezi valley.[166] As part of the ongoing relationships, local women displayed external signs of Lusophone culture, such as the use of the Portuguese language,

---

Shona Women in the History of Zimbabwe 1870–1939 (Portsmouth, NH: Heineman, 1992). For the exchange of wives in Portugal as a way to unify power, see the marriage of Joana, sister of Afonso V of Portugal, to Enrique IV of Castile in 1455. Bailey W. Diffie, *Foundations of the Portuguese Empire, 1415–1580, Europe and the World in the Age of Expansion* (Minneapolis: University of Minnesota Press, 1977), 148.

[163] Pamela Scully, "Malintizin, Pocahontas, and Krotoa: Indigenous Women and Myth Models of the Atlantic World," *Journal of Colonialism and Colonial History* 6, no. 3 (2005); Elbl, "Men without Wives," 61–86; Hilary Jones, "From Marriage à la Mode to Weddings at Town Hall: Marriage, Colonialism, and Mixed-Race Society in Nineteenth-Century Senegal," *International Journal of African Historical Studies* 38, no. 1 (2005): 35–6. See also Bourdieu, *Outline of a Theory of Practice*, 159–97; and Pierre Bourdieu, *Pascalian Meditations* (Stanford, CA: Stanford University Press, 2000), 164–202; Miller, *Way of Death*, 43–7.

[164] Heywood, *Contested Power*, 19. See also Linda Heywood and John Thornton, "African Fiscal Systems as Sources for Demographic History: The Case of Central Angola, 1799–1920," *Journal of African History* 29, no. 2 (1988), 214.

[165] Contança do Nascimento da Rosa Ferreira de Ceita Miguel, "A Vida e a Obra do Portuense Silva Porto no reino Ovimbundu-Bié," MA thesis, Universidade do Porto, 2001, 71.

[166] Miller, *Way of Death*, 246–50; Searing, *West African Slavery and Atlantic Commerce*, 97–106; Philip J. Havik, *Silences and Soundbites: The Gendered Dynamics of Trade and Brokerage in the Pre-Colonial Guinea Bissau Region* (Munster: Lit. Verlag, 2004); Havik, "Women and Trade," 96; Allen Issacman, *Mozambique: The Africanization of a European Institution: The Zambezi Prazos, 1750–1902* (Madison: University of Wisconsin Press, 1972); José Capela, *Donas, Senhores e Escravos* (Porto: Afrontamento, 1995); Eugénia Rodrigues, "Portugueses e Africanos nos Rios de Sena. Os Prazos da Coroa nos séculos XVII e XVIII," PhD dissertation, Universidade Nova de Lisboa, 2002.

affiliation with Christianity, and allegiance to Portuguese authority, either nominally or avowedly. As a result of their involvement with Portuguese and Brazilian men, the local women acquired wealth and became known as *donas*. Donas controlled a large number of dependents and had compounds in town. In the 1770s, Governor Sousa Coutinho commented that many donas in Angola were widows five times over.[167] Widows or singles, local African women became involved in local businesses and invested in the slave trade after the deaths of foreign husbands.

Wives were vital to the organization of the trade between Benguela and inland markets. Some of the donas, such as Aguida Gonçalves da Silva, controlled and directed the work of slaves. In her fields, slaves cultivated crops that were sold in the local market. They also had other businesses, such as taverns.[168] Benguela houses became the sites of small industries, where free people and slaves worked side by side to increase production. In 1798, dona Catarina Pereira Lisboa, a single woman, lived in a one-story house in Benguela with relatives and nineteen slaves, including skilled coopers and sailors, two important skills in an Atlantic port.[169] Committed to slavery and the slave trade, these women consolidated their power and prestige by assembling a large number of dependents in their houses. Slaves of dona Catarina were baptized in the Nossa Senhora do Pópulo Church in 1794 and 1806, indicating that she was a slaveholder throughout the period.[170] Women became essential for the transmission of colonial and Western values to their descendants and dependents. They assumed the responsibility of reproducing social hierarchies, emphasizing their allegiance to the Catholic Church and Atlantic commerce.[171] As colonial intermediaries, their position in society was anchored on violence, including the institutionalized violence that justified and rationalized economic disparity and, ultimately, slavery.

---

[167] See AHU, Angola, caixa 54, doc. 20, March 15, 1770. For more on donas, see Vansina, "Ambaca," 8–9; Selma Pantoja, "Gênero e Comércio: as Traficantes de Escravos na Região de Angola," *Travessias* 4–5 (2004): 79–97; Charles Boxer, *A Mulher na Expansão Ultramarina Ibérica* (Lisbon: Horizonte, 1977), 29.

[168] IHGB, DL32,02.02, "Relação de Manuel José de Silveira Teixeira sobre os moradores da cidade de São Felipe de Benguela separados por raça, idade, emprego, título de habitação, ofícios mecânicos e quantos mestres e aprendizes existem," 1797, fl. 9.

[169] IHGB, DL32,02.02, fl. 9.

[170] AAL, Benguela, Livro de Batismos, 1794–1814, fl. 4v., and fl. 10v., December 9, 1794; fl. 227, March 29, 1806.

[171] Ann Laura Stoler, *Carnal Knowledge and Imperial Power: Race and the Intimate in Colonial Rule* (Berkeley: University of California Press, 2002), 112.

Marriage reinforced social connections. High-ranking administrators or powerful merchants were selected as witnesses so as to create a fictional kinship link that protected those involved. This practice seems to be the case for the Bahian trader Manoel Pereira Gonçalves, who married dona Marcelina Francisca dos Santos in 1809. Marcelina was born in Benguela, of unknown parents, and it is not clear if she was a rich dona or not. Pereira Gonçalves secured protection and cooperation from the highest authority in town, Governor Joaquim Vieira de Abreu e Paiva, by having him as a witness.[172] There is no indication of dona Marcelina's skin color, although she was a *filha da terra*. Another Brazilian, José de Andrade from Rio de Janeiro, married dona Rita Maria dos Remédio from Mbailundu in 1813. Mbailundu was a powerful state in the Benguela central highlands in the early nineteenth century.[173] Living in Benguela, dona Rita Maria probably had some knowledge of local languages and Portuguese, offering the trader Gonçalves the possibility of employing his wife as a translator. Dona Rita's parents were Rita, a black woman from Mbailundu, and Bernardino José, probably a trader in the highlands. These marriages fall in the pattern of business associations. In addition to a wife, foreign traders secured personal interpreters and close contacts with traders already established inland of Benguela. Finding an available partner in Benguela was a way to overcome loneliness and business isolation. Local women had social connections and helped foreigners establish relationships with local families and men on the spot in order to gain benefits in their trading operations.[174] Dona Marcelina and dona Rita Maria, like many other African women, provided companionship, expert care in case of a tropical disease, and local social networks. They also owned a house and slaves and had a structure in place to accommodate a recently arrived trader. If the benefits that male traders obtained from the liaison are clear, we should not assume that women were duped in these contracts. They enjoyed the prestige of being connected to wealthy traders and shared the fortunes and misfortunes of their spouses. Local women who married foreign traders were in the unique position of being an intermediary, building on the existing commercial networks to establish themselves as traders

---

[172] AAL, Benguela, Casamento, 1806–1853, April 19, 1809, fl. 4v.

[173] Heywood, *Contested Power*, 28; Miller, *Way of Death*, 28–30. I will explore the role of Mbailundu and its importance in the interior of Benguela in Chapter 5.

[174] Susan Migden Socolow, "Marriage, Birth and Inheritance: The Merchants of 18th Century Buenos Aires," *Hispanic American Historical Review* 60, no. 3 (1980), 387–406.

on their own.[175] They also could inherit the trade goods in the case of foreigners who died while in Benguela.

In the nineteenth century, merchants from northern regions headed south as a result of British antislavery patrols off the coast of West Africa. Traders such as Francisco Teixeira, originally from Costa da Mina, settled and married in Benguela in 1808. Teixeira married Juliana Maria de Assunção, a woman from the hinterland.[176] Marcos Vaz da Conceição, from São Tomé, married dona Cristiana das Neves from the fortress of Quilengues. Dona Cristina das Neves was a widow, baptized, and previously married in the Portuguese fortress of Quilengues, although the names of her parents are not listed.[177] The arrival of people from other parts of Africa shows how Benguela continued to be a viable port for traders facing constraints as a result of British pressure to bring the slave trade to an end. While the Brazilian market continued to expand in the nineteenth century, Benguela was a major destination for slave traders. It was isolated and surrounded by beaches that could be used to bypass British patrols. Men on the spot who were involved in the slave trade were trying to make a profit while it lasted.[178]

The absence of European women put pressure on Benguela families to socialize their children to recognize their place in a society shaped by racial and status hierarchies. Facing a shortage of European men to play administrative roles, Lisbon capitulated in its policy to emphasize European origin and shifted to an approach that focused on officials belonging to the Lusophone world: speaking Portuguese and being Catholic. African women were in charge of raising their children as Portuguese subjects and transmitting colonial and Western values, demonstrating once again how the trans-Atlantic slave trade altered institutions and society. Seen as a threat to the colonial power in the mid–eighteenth century, the donas became central to the colonial order and its hierarchies. Their role as keepers of colonial values was pushed into the domestic sphere, where they could prevent children and slaves from speaking Umbundu.

---

[175] Pantoja, "Três Leituras," 99–126.
[176] AAL, Benguela, Casamento, 1806–1853, 2v., April 3, 1806.
[177] AAL, Benguela, Casamento, 1806–1853, 16v., May 4, 1818.
[178] AHU, Angola, cod. 542. fl. 77v.; AHU, Angola, caixa 60, doc. 22; AHU, Angola, caixa 65, doc. 17; AHU, Angola, caixa 70, doc. 12; also see Roquinaldo Amaral Ferreira, "Transforming Atlantic Slaving: Trade, Warfare and Territorial Control in Angola, 1650–1800," PhD dissertation, University of California, Los Angeles, 2003, 256; Curto, *Enslaving Spirits*, 94; and Herbert Klein, "The Trade in African Slaves to Rio de Janeiro, 1795–1811: Estimates of Mortality and Patterns of Voyages," *Journal of African History* 10, no. 4 (1969): 533–49. See also Curto, "Struggling against Enslavement," 113–14.

Heads of households should follow what was done in Brazil, "where Blacks and slaves are forced to speak the royal language [Portuguese] and leave [Umbundu] to be used in the interior where it is necessary to communicate with blacks."[179] Despite state efforts, the Portuguese language was restricted to a very few Portuguese and Brazilian traders and to some Africans who interacted with them. In Benguela, as in Luanda, African languages "gradually came to be as essential in the administration, the army, and the church as it was for inland commerce."[180] Local languages were so commonly used that Sousa Coutinho, governor of Angola, stated the importance of employing an interpreter of Umbundu with enough knowledge of local cultures to arbitrate freedom suits and other trials.[181] In 1800, Governor Vasconcelos reported that most of the population of Benguela did not speak Portuguese and were unable to attend mass.[182] By imposing the burden of keeping Portuguese alive in the domestic arena, Portuguese authorities denied the heterogeneous reality of African women, who worked in various spaces and capacities to maintain themselves and their families. As the people with the responsibility to pass on colonial values, they were seen solely as wives and mothers rather than as traders, business women, or agricultural producers. And their economic role before the twentieth century is often neglected.

The colonial tension over Umbundu use in Benguela also reveals that creolization in Benguela was not a one-way path. Benguela residents, including Portuguese men, adjusted to the local culture, spoke Umbundu and Portuguese as a *lingua franca*, employed it in official documents, consulted healers to cure illnesses, and married multiple partners. Authorities reported what they considered to be a decadent lifestyle, where local culture dominated the colonial space, and Portuguese and other foreigners lived like the natives. Population mixing was almost inevitable in a town with so few white women, and the demographically dominant presence of Africans was expected. To overcome the limited number of Portuguese, people were classified according to their family background. Thus the sons and daughters of foreign men and local women were classified as *filho da terra* ("locally born"), regardless of phenotype. The term *mulato*

---

[179] ANTT, Feitos Findos, Conde de Linhares, L. 1, fl. 68v.–70, January 9, 1765.

[180] Vansina, "Portuguese vs Kimbundu," 271.

[181] ANTT, Conde de Linhares, L. 50, vol. 2, fl. 280–281v., after May 6, 1768. Santos, "Luanda," 267. See also Vansina, "Portuguese vs. Kimbundu"; and Tavares and Santos, *Africæ monumenta: Arquivo Caculo Cacahenda*.

[182] Heywood, "Portuguese into African," 104.

referred to a range of people from poor mixed-race people to Westernized black Africans. The trader Silva Porto complained that in Benguela anyone who wore pants, regardless of their skin color and social condition, was perceived as white.[183] Social classification into white, mulato, and black categories was based on subjective ascriptions, including family, economic activity, place of residence, language skills, social behavior, and appearance (as characterized by hair style, clothing, and body language). The simple use of such terms as white, mulato, and black and the hierarchies associated with those categories emphasizes the impact of the trans-Atlantic slave trade and the Atlantic world on local societies. It provoked violence and enslavement, but it also transformed the lives of those continuing to live free, imposing new patterns of classification and social hierarchies. Black Africans living in town who spoke Portuguese and were Catholics could be perceived as white or mixed-race, and that categorization was vital to protect them from enslavement, which will be analyzed in Chapter 4. In a small town of fewer than 3,000 inhabitants, everyone was aware of the family history of residents. Ascendancy was vital.

Conclusion

During the eighteenth and early nineteenth centuries, the population of Benguela faced several changes. After the threat of foreign invasions that characterized the period before 1710, colonial administrators could focus their attention on protecting its residents from constant attacks from African neighbors. The adversarial nature of relationships with local rulers continued in the eighteenth century and first half of the nineteenth century in part because they had different understandings of vassalage treaties and each other's roles. The regular arrival of people from different areas forced the population of Benguela to adjust to newcomers, and at the same time, the immigrants adapted themselves to the town. Europeans and Brazilian foreigners mixed with local Portuguese and Umbundu and maintained long relationships with African women. Some married in the Nossa Senhora do Pópulo Church, whereas the majority followed customary wedding practices. Although living in a Catholic town, administrators were known to consult African healers to cure illnesses. With a population shaped by its geographic mobility, Benguela

---

[183] Maria Emilia Madeira Santos (ed.), *Viagens e Apontamentos de um Portuense em África* (Coimbra: Biblioteca Geral, 1986), 37.

witnessed a great mix of languages and cultures. Sometimes these interactions of cultures and different lifestyles clashed. However, due to the
demographic majority of the African population, foreigners more often
adjusted to local norms. In the same way, slaves who stayed in Benguela
adjusted to the society that had formed in the context of the external slave
trade. Thus the creolization process in Benguela happened among the
foreign trader community and free and enslaved Africans in a two-way
process involving negotiation, adaptation, and transformation.

Colonialism expanded in the eighteenth century. More soldiers and
officers were dispatched to Benguela. Many were *degredados*, and most
maintained strong connections with Brazil. Born there or not, Benguela
merchants helped to maintain the bilateral connections established in the
seventeenth century. From 1719 to 1850, Brazil-born traders exercised
more pressure, and the colony in the Americas became a model to be
copied. As with Brazil, Benguela was a slave society. Slaves performed
productive tasks and consolidated the prestige of their masters. Foreign
and local residents made a living from the trade in human beings. The
trans-Atlantic slave trade introduced Atlantic traders as attractive prospective partners for local women. Mixed marriages became the rule, and
African women seized the opportunity to apprehend cultural practices
and spaces of power. They associated themselves with foreign men and
became intermediaries between different cultures, which allowed them
to play major economic roles in the town and control crucial economic
activities, such as food production. Business partners, commercial agents,
and tavern owners, the donas embraced colonial power and Portuguese
culture and gave origin to a new generation of Luso-Africans, who had
strong links to slaving operations in the interior, as will be explored in
Chapter 3.

The impact of the trans-Atlantic slave trade was dramatic, as many
examples explored in this chapter have revealed. First, it led to political
disturbances around the port town and the emergence of new states at the
expense of smaller and weaker chiefdoms and states. Second, it resulted
in shifts in agriculture and the adoption of new crops imported from
the Americas, such as tobacco, corn, and manioc, which altered local
diets. Third, it provoked the expansion of Catholicism, in many ways
syncretic, which imposed new naming and marriage practices. Fourth, it
led to the emergence of a Luso-African society shaped by creolization and
intimately linked to the trans-Atlantic slave trade. Africans who lived and
labored in this colonial milieu acquired the cultural insight to navigate

in the Portuguese world. With knowledge of Portuguese and Umbundu, deeply involved in the trans-Atlantic slave trade, and aware of legal and Catholic rights, Africans played a decisive role in the rise of Benguela. Well informed on the local environment, trade organization, languages, and cultures, Africans transformed the Portuguese colony of Benguela into a Luso-African town where African and Portuguese cultures were in constant interaction. Ndombe and other Africans living in the urban port played important roles in the transformation of Benguela from a small village to a major point of embarkation of slaves into the trans-Atlantic slave trade. The end of the trans-Atlantic slave trade, however, did not change the size of the population of Benguela. Unlike other Africans ports that witnessed population expansion in the nineteenth century, Benguela remained a small town.

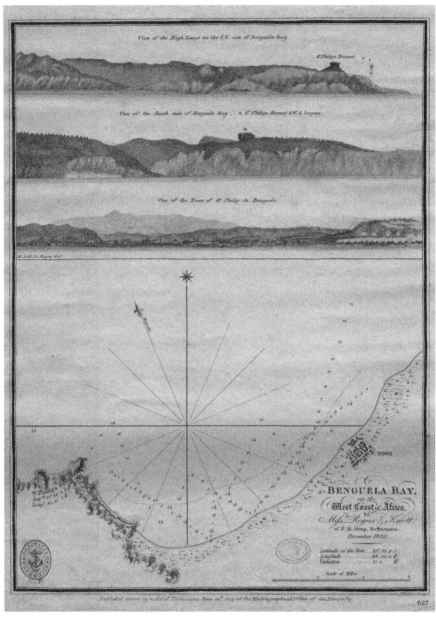

IMAGE 4. Benguela Bay. (*Source:* AHU, Cartografia 001, doc. 268.)

3

Benguela and the South Atlantic World

As seen in Chapter 1, Benguela attracted the attention of Portuguese administrators even before its foundation in 1617. With reports of mines in the interior, the arrival of caravans in Luanda bringing slaves, animal skins, bird plumes, and ivory, Benguela acquired a reputation as a land of abundance. Natural resources, such as turtle shells, bird feathers, and ostrich eggs, decorated palaces and ballrooms in Europe, where they continue to impress museum visitors. Yet it was the commerce in human beings that transformed the political, economic, and social life of this region and inserted its population, even those located far inland, into the South Atlantic economy. Sugar-cane alcohol produced in Brazil known as *cachaça*, *gerebita*, or *aguardente*; Portuguese wine; and Asian textiles, beads, gunpowder, cloth items, and paper circulated in the central highlands in the interior of Benguela. Thus even people who lived hundreds of miles from the coast were integrated into and affected by the Atlantic economy because they consumed, or aspired to own, commodities introduced by slave traders and Portuguese authorities. The only way they could acquire wool and silk textiles, bottles of spirits and wines, or fedoras and handkerchiefs was if they sold slaves in exchange for the desired items. The Atlantic market changed forever how African rulers and their subjects understood war, justice, and protection.

For decades, scholars have debated the effects of the trans-Atlantic slave trade on African societies. Since the early 1960s, Walter Rodney, J. D. Fage, and Philip Curtin engaged in a debate over its consequences on the continent.[1] Later, Paul Lovejoy, David Eltis, and Joseph Inikori

[1] Walter Rodney, *West Africa and the Atlantic Slave-Trade* (Nairobi: East African Publication House, 1967), and *How Europe Underdeveloped Africa* (Washington,

continued to debate the size and effects of the international trade.[2] In addition to demographics, scholars also explored how the international market affected the institution of slavery itself, which resulted in the expansion of slavery within Africa.[3] Specialists on West Central Africa analyzed the political and economic changes imposed by the trans-Atlantic slave trade on Loango, Kongo, and Angola and its hinterland, including its relationship to the local economic and political elite.[4] In the 1980s, in an influential article, John Thornton claimed that the trans-Atlantic slave trade did not have a significant demographic impact in Angola because women's ability to reproduce allowed the population to recuperate those who were lost to the slave trade. That controversial argument was supported by Joseph Miller, who argued that famine and drought

---

DC: Howard University Press, 1974); John D. Fage, "Slavery and the Slave Trade in the Context of African History," *Journal of African History* 10, no. 3 (1969): 393–404; and Philip Curtin, *Economic Change in Pre-Colonial Africa: Senegambia in the Era of the Slave Trade* (Madison: University of Wisconsin Press, 1975).

[2] Paul Lovejoy, *Transformations in Slavery: A History of Slavery in Africa* (New York: Cambridge University Press, 2000); and "The Impact of the Atlantic Slave Trade on Africa: A Review of the Literature," *Journal of African History* 30 (1989): 1–30; David Eltis, "Fluctuations in the Age and Sex Ratios of Slaves in the Nineteenth Century Transatlantic Slave Traffic," *Slavery and Abolition* 7, no. 3 (1986): 257–72; Joseph Inikori, *Forced Migrations: The Impact of the Export Slave Trade on African Societies* (London: Holmes and Meier, 1982); and Patrick Manning, *Slavery, Colonialism and Economic Growth in Dahomey, 1640–1960* (Cambridge University Press, 1982).

[3] Among many studies, see Lovejoy, *Transformations*; Martin A. Klein, *Slavery and Colonial Rule in French West Africa* (Cambridge University Press, 1998); Frederick Cooper, *Plantation Slavery on the East Coast of Africa* (Portsmouth, NH: Heinemann, 1997); Allan Isaacman and Barbara Isaacman, *Slavery and Beyond: The Making of Men and Chikunda Ethnic Identities in the Unstable World of South-Central Africa, 1750–1920* (Portsmouth, NH: Heinemann, 2004); James F. Searing, *West African Slavery and Atlantic Commerce. The Senegal River Valley, 1700–1860* (New York: Cambridge University Press, 2003).

[4] Phyllis Martin, *The External Trade of the Loango Coast, 1576–1870: The Effects of Changing Commercial Relations on the Vili Kingdom of Loango* (Oxford, UK: Clarendon Press, 1972); David Birmingham, *Trade and Conflict in Angola: The Mbundu and Their Neighbours Under the Influence of the Portuguese, 1483–1790* (Oxford, UK: Clarendon Press, 1966); for Kongo, see Phyllis Martin, *The External Trade of the Loango Coast, 1576–1870: The Effects of Changing Commercial Relations on the Vili Kingdom of Loango* (Oxford, UK: Clarendon Press, 1972); David Birmingham, *Trade and Conflict in Angola: The Mbundu and Their Neighbours Under the Influence of the Portuguese, 1483–1790* (Oxford, UK: Clarendon Press, 1966); Douglas L. Wheeler, "Nineteenth-Century African Protest in Angola: Prince Nicolas of Kongo (1830?–1860)," *African Historical Studies* 1, no. 1 (1968): 40–59; John K. Thornton, *The Kingdom of Kongo: Civil War and Transition, 1641–1718* (Madison: University of Wisconsin Press, 1983); Anne Hilton, *Kingdom of Kongo* (Oxford, UK: Clarendon Press, 1985); and Linda Heywood, "Slavery and its Transformation in the Kingdom of Kongo: 1491–1800," *Journal of African History* 50 (2009): 1–22.

had provoked more constraints on the population of West Central Africa than the trans-Atlantic slave trade.[5] Patrick Manning criticized Miller's arguments, emphasizing how slave raids and warfare favored the destruction of crops, leading to food crises and famine, at the same time that droughts forced people into economic constraints that pushed them into offering themselves and relatives into bondage.[6] In sum, Manning argued that environmentally related crises did not happen in a vacuum but that they exacerbated other political and social struggles that communities were facing. In subsequent decades, Jill Dias, Beatrix Heintze, Isabel de Castro Henriques, José Curto, and Roquinaldo Ferreira added to the debate, examining the effects of the trans-Atlantic slave trade on Luanda and its interior in studies that explored the links between warfare, expansion of the slave trade, and political transformations.[7] Phyllis Martin, Curto, and Ferreira analyzed how imported textiles and alcohol altered patterns of consumption and patterns of power and politics in Loango and Luanda.[8] The last decade also has seen the publication of studies that have explored new patterns of credit, processes of enslavement,

---

[5] John Thornton, "The Slave Trade in Eighteenth Century Angola: Effects of Demographic Structure," *Canadian Journal of African Studies* 14, no. 3 (1980): 417–27; Joseph C. Miller, "The Significance of Drought, Disease and Famine in the Agriculturally Marginal Zones of West-Central Africa," *Journal of African History* 23, no. 1 (1982): 17–61; Joseph C. Miller, *Way of Death: Merchant Capitalism and the Angolan Slave Trade, 1730–1830* (Madison: University of Wisconsin Press, 1988).

[6] Patrick Manning, *Slavery and African Life: Occidental, Oriental, and African Slave Trades* (Cambridge University Press, 1990), 56–7.

[7] Jill R. Dias, "Changing Patterns of Power in the Luanda Hinterland. The Impact of Trade and Colonisation on the Mbundu ca. 1845–1920," *Paideuma* 32 (1986): 285–318; Beatrix Heintze, *Angola nos Séculos XVI e XVII: Estudos sobre Fontes, Métodos e História* (Luanda: Kilombelombe, 2007); José C. Curto, "Un Butin Illégitime: Razzias d'esclaves et relations luso-africaines dans la région des fleuves Kwanza et Kwango en 1805," in *Déraison, Esclavage et Droit: Les Fondements Idéologiques et Juridiques de la Traite Négrière et de l'Esclavage*, ed. Isabel de Castro Henriques and Louis Sala-Molins (Paris: Unesco, 2002), 315–27; Roquinaldo Amaral Ferreira, "Transforming Atlantic Slaving: Trade, Warfare and Territorial Control in Angola, 1650–1800," PhD dissertation, UCLA, Los Angeles, 2004; Isabel de Castro Henriques, *Percursos da Modernidade em Angola: Dinâmicas Comerciais e Transformações Sociais no Século XIX* (Lisbon: Instituto de Investigação Científica Tropical, 1997).

[8] Phyllis M. Martin, "Power, Cloth and Currency on the Loango Coast," *African Economic History* 15 (1986): 1–12; Roquinaldo Ferreira, "Dinâmica do comércio intracolonial: Gerebitas, panos asiáticos e guerra no tráfico angolanos de escravos, século XVIII," in *O Antigo Regime nos Trópicos: A Dinâmica Imperial Portuguesa, Séculos XVI-XVIII*, ed. João Luís Ribe Fragoso, Maria de Fátima Gouvêa, and Maria Fernanda Bicalho (Rio de Janeiro: Civilização Brasileira, 2001), 339–78; José Curto, *Enslaving Spirits: The Portuguese-Brazilian Alcohol Trade at Luanda and Its Hinterland, C. 1550–1830* (Leiden: Brill, 2004).

and changes in culture and economy in specific locations, increasing our knowledge of how the trans-Atlantic slave trade transformed economic, political, and social life.[9] Most of the studies of slavery in Africa, with very few exceptions, have ignored its development in Benguela and its interior.[10] Specialists on the slave trade recognized the importance of Benguela and West Central Africa in general, but they tended to see the slave trade there only developing by the end of the eighteenth century.[11] Yet, in a study published in the 1980s, David Birmingham claimed that a slave market was operating in the port around 1615, although most of

---

[9] Jan Vansina, "Ambaca Society and the Slave Trade c. 1760–1845," *Journal of African History* 46, no. 1 (2005): 1–27; Ana Paula Tavares and Catarina Madeira Santos, "Uma Leitura Africana das Estratégias Políticas e Jurídicas. Textos dos e para os Dembos," in *Africae Monumenta. A Apropriação da Escrita pelos Africanos,* ed. Ana Paula Tavares and Catarina Madeira Santos (Lisbon: Instituto de Investigação Científica Tropical, 2002), 243–60; Kalle Kananoja, "Healers, Idolaters, and Good Christians: A Case Study of Creolization and Popular Religion in Mid-Eighteenth Century Angola," *International Journal of African Historical Studies* 43, no. 3 (2010): 443–65; Rosa da Cruz Silva, "Saga of Kakonda and Kilengues: Relations between Benguela and Its Interior, 1791–1796," in *Enslaving Connections: Changing Cultures of Africa and Brazil During the Era of Slavery,* ed. José C. Curto and Paul E. Lovejoy (Amherst, NY: Humanity Books, 2003), 245–259; José C. Curto, "Struggling against Enslavement: The Case of José Manuel in Benguela, 1816–20," *Canadian Journal of African Studies* 39, no. 1 (2005): 96–122; Mariana P. Candido, "Slave Trade and New Identities in Benguela, 1700–1860," *Portuguese Studies Review* 19, no. 1–2 (2011): 59–75; Roquinaldo Ferreira, "O Brasil e a arte da guerra em Angola (séculos XVII e XVIII)," *Estudos Historicos* 39 (2007): 3–23; Selma Pantoja, "Inquisição, Degredo e Mestiçagem em Angola no século XVII," *Revista Lusófona de Ciência das Religiões* 3, nos. 5–6 (2004): 117–36; Estevam Costa Thompson, "Negreiros nos Mares do Sul. Famílias Traficantes nas rotas entre Angola e Brasil em fins do século XVIII," PhD dissertation, Universidade de Brasília, 2006.

[10] There are some exceptions, such as José C. Curto, "Luso-Brazilian Alcohol and the Legal Slave Trade at Benguela and its Hinterland, c. 1617–1830," in *Négoce Blanc en Afrique Noire: L'évolution du Commerce à Longue Distance en Afrique Noire du 18e au 20e Siècles,* ed. H. Bonin and M. Cahen (Paris: Publications de la Société Française d'Histoire d'Outre-mer, 2001); Roquinaldo Ferreira, "Atlantic Microhistories: Mobility, Personal Ties, and Slaving in the Black Atlantic World (Angola and Brazil)," in *Cultures of the Lusophone Black Atlantic,* ed. Nancy Priscilla Naro, Roger Sansi-Roca, and David H. Treece (New York: Palgrave, 2007), 99–128; Mariana P. Candido, "African Freedom Suits and Portuguese Vassal Status: Legal Mechanisms for Fighting Enslavement in Benguela, Angola, 1800–1830," *Slavery & Abolition* 32 (2011): 447–59; Mariana P. Candido, *Fronteras de Esclavización: Esclavitud, Comercio e Identidad en Benguela, 1780–1850* (Mexico City: El Colegio de Mexico Press, 2011).

[11] Philip Curtin, *The Atlantic Slave Trade: A Census* (Madison: University of Wisconsin Press, 1969), 205–10; Herbert Klein, "The Portuguese Slave Trade from Angola in the Eighteenth Century," *Journal of Economic History* 32, no. 4 (1972): 895; Lovejoy, *Transformations in Slavery,* 51, 53, 146; José C. Curto, "The Legal Portuguese Slave Trade from Benguela, Angola, 1730–1828: A Quantitative Re-appraisal," *África* 17, no. 1 (1993–1994): 101–16.

the ensuing studies emphasized that Benguela was not integrated in the Atlantic slave trade until the end of the eighteenth century.[12]

This book dialogued with these earlier contributions and in many ways benefited from them, reassessing the role of Benguela in the Atlantic commerce and the effects the trans-Atlantic trade imposed on societies on the coast and in the interior. As Toby Green and António Mendes have shown for Western Africa, figures for the sixteenth- and seventeenth-century Atlantic slave trade are inconclusive, particularly because of the existence of contraband and the unreliable official figures.[13] The same applies to Benguela, demonstrating that the number of West Central Africans exported from this area was certainly higher than the numbers presented at the online *Trans-Atlantic Slave Trade Database*.[14] Quantitative efforts to capture the size of the trans-Atlantic slave trade also must acknowledge the fact that bureaucratic efforts to quantify and tax people were imperfect and that the emphasis on numbers obliterated the social and cultural implications of the massive displacements of Africans during the era of the trans-Atlantic slave trade.

An important aspect in the expansion of the slave trade in this region was the direct involvement of Portuguese officials in raids, warfare, and other processes of capture. Unlike other parts of the African continent, where Europeans were limited to the coast and failed to conquer territory, in West Central Africa the Portuguese had established the colony of Luanda in 1576 and Benguela in 1617. Portuguese traders and administrators were quite successful in establishing a foothold in African territories, where they actively participated in the enslavement of Africans. In West Central Africa, slave raids were disguised as territorial conquest to implement and guarantee colonialism.[15] For the past

---

[12] David Birmingham, *Central Angola to 1870: Zambezia, Zaire, and the South Atlantic* (Cambridge University Press, 1981), 1, 134.

[13] Toby Green, *The Rise of the Trans-Atlantic Slave Trade in Western Africa, 1300–1589* (New York: Cambridge University Press, 2011), 214–6; and António de Almeida Mendes, "The Foundations of the System: A Reassessment on the Slave Trade to the Americas in the Sixteenth and Seventeenth Centuries," in *Extending the Frontiers: Essays on the New Transatlantic Slave Trade Database*, ed. David Eltis and David Richardson (New Haven: Yale University Press, 2008), 63–94. For other criticism of the quantitative approach and its denial of social effects, see Walter Hawthorne, *From Africa to Brazil: Culture, Identity, and an Atlantic Slave Trade, 1600–1830* (Cambridge University Press, 2010); Gwendolyn Midlo Hall, "Africa and Africans in the African Diaspora: The Uses of Relational Databases," *American Historical Review* 115, no. 1 (February 1, 2010): 136–50.

[14] http://slavevoyages.org/tast/index.faces.

[15] For references on how the slave trade operated elsewhere, see James F. Searing, *West African Slavery and Atlantic Commerce: The Senegal River Valley, 1700–1860* (Cambridge

four decades historians have emphasized the participation of African rulers and merchants in the slave trade, and in this process, the role of Portuguese officers in kidnapping and other violent strategies to reduce Africans to bondage has been almost forgotten. As they had already done in the Senegambia in the fifteenth century, Portuguese officials and traders, the men on the spot, made extensive use of kidnapping in Benguela throughout the era of the trans-Atlantic slave trade.[16] Yet this is almost forgotten. In 2009, the public contest, *Maravilhas de Origem Portuguesa no Mundo*, elected seven architectural wonders of Portuguese origin in the world. All of them were directly linked to the trans-Atlantic slave trade and colonialism, although there was no mention of the violence these historic buildings represented.[17] This approach was not an isolated event. In November 2011, Angolan economist Jonuel Gonçalves gave an interview to publicize his book, *A Economia ao Longo da História de Angola*, in which he minimized the participation of the Portuguese in the slave trade and blamed African leaders for the "extractive exploitation of human beings."[18] Concerned about how the history of Portuguese

---

University Press, 1993), 27–58; Paul E. Lovejoy, *Transformations in Slavery: A History of Slavery in Africa* (New York: Cambridge University Press, 2000), 68–90; and Robin Law, *Ouidah: The Social History of a West African Slaving "port" 1727–1892* (Athens: Ohio University Press, 2004), 126–38. For one of the few studies that explores the association between territorial conquest and slave raids in West Central Africa, see José C. Curto, "Un Butin Illégitime."

[16] For studies exploring the participation of African rulers, see John K. Thornton, *Africa and Africans in the Making of the Atlantic World, 1400–1800* (Cambridge University Press, 1998); Harvey M. Feinberg, *Africans and Europeans in West Africa: Elminans and Dutchmen on the Gold Coast during the Eighteenth Century* (Philadelphia: American Philosophical Society, 1989); Joseph C. Miller, "Angola Central e Sul por volta de 1840," *Estudos Afro-Asiáticos* 32 (1997): 7–54; Herbert S. Klein, "The Portuguese Slave Trade From Angola in the Eighteenth Century," *Journal of Economic History* 32, no. 4 (1972): 894–918; Paul E. Lovejoy, *Transformations in Slavery: A History of Slavery in Africa*, African Studies Series 36 (Cambridge University Press, 1983); Robin Law, *The Oyo Empire, C.1600–C.1836: A West African Imperialism in the Era of the Atlantic Slave Trade* (Oxford, UK: Clarendon Press, 1977); Johannes Postma, *The Dutch in the Atlantic Slave Trade, 1600–1815* (Cambridge University Press, 1990); David Eltis, *The Rise of African Slavery in the Americas* (New York: Cambridge University Press, 2000); Boubacar Barry, *Senegambia and the Atlantic Slave Trade* (Cambridge University Press, 1998).

[17] See www.7maravilhas.sapo.pt/o-que-ja-fizemos/7-maravilhas-de-origem-portuguesa-no-mundo. For the repercussion among scholars, see the "Carta Aberta, o Concurso 'As 7 Maravilhas Portuguesas no Mundo,' Ignora a História da Escravidão e do Tráfico Atlântico," *Lusotopie* 16, no. 2 (2009), xiii–xvii. I am very grateful to Ana Lucia Araujo, who reminded me that *Lusotopie* published the online petition.

[18] Jonuel Gonçalves, *A Economia ao Longo da História de Angola* (Luanda: União dos Escritores Angolanos, 2011). See www.voanews.com/portuguese/

interaction with Africans during the era of trans-Atlantic slave trade has been understood, my goal is to emphasize the participation of Portuguese colonial authorities, many of them born in the colony of Brazil, in the process of capture and enslavement of Africans.[19] Colonial documents, produced by Portuguese agents, revealed their participation in raids and their role in organizing wars and denounced their involvement in kidnapping. In this study, Europeans and their descendants also were motors of violence along the coast and inland, which accelerated political reorganization, migration, and enslavement.

After the discussion in earlier chapters of the foundation, development, and emergence of Benguela in the period between 1600 and 1850, this chapter focuses on the integration of Benguela into a South Atlantic world. Currents and winds favored expansion of the port in the land of the Ndombe in the seventeenth century. Portuguese and African traders provided the labor force that miners and planters in the Americas needed in the form of cheap slave labor. Despite the lack of ship export data for seventeenth-century Benguela, documents available in the African diaspora reveal the importance of the early slave trade, challenging the estimates available by the *Trans-Atlantic Slave Trade Database* project. Moreover, this chapter reveals how the scholarship has minimized the effects of the trans-Atlantic slave trade in West Central Africa, a topic that has already been explored in earlier chapters but which will also be analyzed here. This chapter discusses the size of the slave exports and also how this trade changed in 200 years.[20] It also joins the efforts of Peter Beattie to "re-Capricornize the Atlantic," emphasizing the importance of the bilateral connections in the South Atlantic in our effort to understand the trends and paradigms in Atlantic history.[21]

---

news/11_10_2011_aangolaeconomichistory_voanews-133632303.html; accessed November 13, 2011.

[19] A few studies have emphasized the participation of Portuguese colonial officials in raids and enslavement; among them, see Walter Rodney, *History of the Upper Guinea Coast: 1545–1800* (New York: Monthly Review Press, 1980); Silva, "Saga of Kakonda and Kilengues: Relations between Benguela and Its Interior, 1791–1796"; José C. Curto, "Struggling against Enslavement"; Candido, "African Freedom Suits and Portuguese Vassal Status"; Candido, *Fronteras de Esclavización: Esclavitud, Comercio e Identidad en Benguela, 1780–1850*; Toby Green, *The Rise of the Trans-Atlantic Slave Trade in Western Africa, 1300–1589* (Cambridge University Press, 2011), 116–7.

[20] John Thornton, "The Slave Trade in Eighteenth Century Angola: Effects of Demographic Structure," *Canadian Journal of African Studies* 14, no. 3 (1980): 417–27; Joseph C. Miller, *Way of Death*.

[21] Peter Beattie, "ReCapricorning' the Atlantic," *Luso-Brazilian Review* 45, no. 1 (2008), 1–2.

The analysis centers on the importance of Benguela in the Atlantic world by exploring the organization of the slave trade in Benguela and the roles of Portuguese agents in slaving activities and the commercial networks in the interior.

Benguela and the Trans-Atlantic Slave Trade

The foundation of Benguela, as seen in Chapter 1, was intimately related to the idea that slaves, as well as ivory and minerals, could be exported from there. As early as the late sixteenth century, explorers reported shipping slaves from Benguela-Velha.[22] By 1611, King Felipe II of Portugal recognized that vessels packed with slaves could be sent from Benguela-Velha to ports of Brazil.[23] Following the advice of the King, and aware of the potential economic advantages it would bring to the Crown and those involved, the first governor of Benguela, Manoel Cerveira Pereira, sent slaves to Luanda in 1618.[24] Thus it is clear that slaves were forcibly taken from Benguela by the seventeenth century, even if no shipping data are available to calculate their numbers. In the 1680s, António Cadornega stated that there was "lots of business in *peças* [slaves] and ivory," although he did not present any estimates.[25] Another seventeenth-century observer, the Capuchin Antonio Zucchelli, reported that captains of different ships visited Benguela in 1698 and bought slaves.[26] Despite this evidence of slave commerce, no estimates are available in part because most of the slaves were sent to the port of Luanda in Angola, where taxes were collected, and only then sent to the Americas. The internal trade between Benguela and Luanda was diluted in the Portuguese documents, leading scholars to believe that it did not exist. The lack of tax records, however, did not mean absence of trade. In addition to the trade to the port of Luanda, a certain level of smuggling must have existed. During the seventeenth century, any ship sailing from Benguela to ports on the Western side of the Atlantic

---

[22] "Benguela e seu Sertão, 1617–1622," in *Mémorias do Ultramar: Viagens, Explorações e Conquistas dos Portugueses*, ed. Luciano Cordeiro (Lisbon: Impressa Nacional, 1881), 7.

[23] António Brásio, *Monumenta Missionária Africana* (Lisbon: Agência do Ultramar, 1953), 6, 32–3.

[24] Adriano Parreira, "A Primeira 'Conquista' de Benguela (Século XVII)," *História*, 28 (1990), 67.

[25] António de Oliveira Cadornega, *História Geral das Guerras Angolanas* (Lisbon: Agência Geral do Ultramar, 1972), 3, 171.

[26] Antonio Zucchelli, *Relazioni del Viaggio e Missione di Congo nell'Etiopia Inferiore Occidentale* (Venice: Bartolomeo Giavarina, 1712), 91.

most likely would have been engaged in illegal activities and evading the Portuguese Crown, which further explains the lack of sources.[27] We might not know the numbers, yet slaves were shipped from Benguela beginning in the early seventeenth century.

Benguela participated in the trans-Atlantic slave trade because of its location and the ability of traders to ship large numbers of people quickly. Ralph Delgado noticed that slave traders were already organized in town by the late seventeenth century.[28] The specificity of winds and ocean currents in that zone of the South Atlantic forced ships' captains to sail south along the Angolan coast before heading north.[29] In 1764, in a diary written during the journey on his way to assume the role of governor of Angola, Francisco de Sousa Coutinho reported the difficulties of sailing along the West Central African coast from north to south. After a mistake made by the pilot, the ship missed the entrance of Cattle Bay and struggled to come back to Benguela. "In this region that water runs towards the north, making it difficult and painful to go against the current."[30] After five days of failed attempts to land in Benguela, the crew faced hunger and thirst during the unexpectedly longer trip. Sousa Coutinho ordered the pilot to change direction and sail toward Luanda, which took another four days. Thus, due to its oceanographic condition, ships coming from Portugal, Brazil, and Asia usually stopped in Benguela before heading to the northern ports of Luanda, Ambriz, and Loango. Despite the difficulty in sailing south, trade between Luanda and Benguela continued to be exclusively maritime based owing to the difficulties the Portuguese had in using the overland route through the region of Kissama. Portuguese traders could not travel overland to the highlands behind Benguela because of ongoing conflicts and the hostility of the people of Kissama, who blocked the route.[31] Even as late as 1791, the governor of Angola, Manoel de

---

[27] For more on this topic and an indication of the French purchase of slaves in Benguela and other West Central African ports, see David Geggus, "The French Slave Trade: An Overview," *William and Mary Quarterly* 58, no. 1 (2001): 119–38. On the prevalence of evasion and contraband on the early transatlantic slave trade, see Green, *The Rise of the Trans-Atlantic Slave Trade*, 214–6; and Mendes, "The Foundations of the System," 63–94.

[28] Ralph Delgado, *O Reino de Benguela. Do Descobrimento à Criação do Governo Subalterno* (Lisbon: Imprensa Beleza, 1945), 186–200.

[29] Frédéric Mauro, *Portugal, o Brasil e o Atlântico* (Lisbon: Estampa, 1997), 48–9.

[30] Arquivos Nacionais da Torre do Tombo (ANTT), Conde de Linhares, Mc. 91, doc. 110, "Jornal da Viagem da Nau em que seguiu para o Governo de Angola D. Francisco de Sousa Coutinho" [Undated but probably 1764].

[31] David Birmingham, *Trade and Conflict in Angola* (Oxford University Press, 1966). 140; Beatrix Heintze, "Historical Notes on the Kisama of Angola," *Journal of African History* 13, no. 3 (1972): 417–18.

Almeida e Vasconcelos, mentioned that "it would be very fruitful to establish overland communication with Kissama, although these people mistrust [the Portuguese]."[32] Only African traders could cross the region and use it as a route to Luanda. The solution was to use the sea to access the southern region, which favored the emergence of Benguela as a port located relatively far away from authorities in Luanda.

Although we do not know the number of people shipped from the port in the seventeenth century, current estimates on the size of the slave trade can be found in the *Trans-Atlantic Slave Trade Database*, published in 1998 and updated and made available online in 2007. According to the database, at least 342,000 people left Benguela between 1699 and 1867, but if we add to this number estimates from the unidentified voyages from West Central African ports, the number jump to 679,000, higher than the departures from the ports of Cabinda, Elmina, and Calabar, for example.[33] The database, however, does not provide information on the slaves who embarked before 1699 because no ship records or export data have been located indicating precise numbers. Yet evidence from archives in the Americas reveals the existence of Benguela slaves in Cuba, Peru, and Colombia before the 1700, indicating that illegal slave trading was operating from the port of Benguela and that the number of slaves exported from the port is higher than the editors of the *Trans-Atlantic Slave Trade Database* acknowledge. From the data available, we can conclude that the Benguela slave trade in the South Atlantic was only exceeded by exports from Luanda, which was by far the largest port on the African coast from which more than 1.5 million African slaves were sent to the Americas. Benguela was the second largest port in West Central Africa, larger than Ambriz, Cabinda, and Loango, and the third largest place of embarkation of African slaves in the overall trans-Atlantic commerce after Luanda and Ouidah.

Besides the force of the ocean currents, the shorter distance between Benguela and ports in the Americas made it an attractive place for trade.

---

[32] Arquivo Histórico Ultramarino (AHU), Angola, cod. 1627, fl. 63, April 5, 1791. See also AHU, Angola, caixa 70, doc. 5, February 24, 1785.

[33] For the calculation on the estimates, see David Eltis and David Richardson, "A New Assessment of the Transatlantic Slave Trade," in *Extending the Frontiers: Essays on the New Transatlantic Slave Trade Database* (New Haven: Yale University Press, 2008), 1–60; I am also grateful to Daniel B. Domingues da Silva, who helped me to calculate estimates from Benguela. For more on estimates on slave exports from West Central Africa, see his "The Coastal Origins of Slaves Leaving Angola," paper presented at the 124th Annual Meeting of the American Historical Association, San Diego, CA, 2010. These numbers are presented in David Eltis and David Richardson, *Atlas of the Transatlantic Slave Trade* (New Haven: Yale University Press, 2010).

In the first half of the eighteenth century, slave ships took forty-five days to sail from Benguela to Salvador, and after 1750, that dropped to forty-one days on average. For Rio, captains spent an average of fifty days after the 1750s, and data are not available for the earlier period. The official mortality was less than 10 percent.[34] Schooners employed in the South Atlantic also were faster and required a smaller crew than the galleons employed by Portuguese traders.[35] In sum, the slave voyage between Benguela and Rio de Janeiro, as well as between Benguela and Salvador, was shorter and more profitable for traders based in Brazil than for the owners of ships originating in Portugal. These factors explain the development of a South Atlantic slave route and the establishment of bilateral trade between the Portuguese colonies and South America that excluded, for most part, the metropolis. The Portuguese Crown taxed and supervised the trade, but commodities produced in Portugal slowly lost space in the cargo holds to goods produced in Brazil.[36] In addition to slaves, traders based in Benguela sent commodities such as copper rings, salt, nzimbu shells, and ivory to Luanda.[37] The trade was vibrant and continuous despite external threats. In the seventeenth century and first half of the eighteenth century, merchants and authorities in Benguela sent to Luanda wild animals, such as zebras, lions, and even birds. Animal skins also were shipped to Portugal. In the late eighteenth to the early nineteenth centuries, the commerce with Luanda also included whitewash, tiles, bricks, and wax.[38] In exchange, Benguela traders imported Asian

[34] Transatlantic Slave Trade Database, www.slavevoyages.org/tast/database/search.faces; and Eltis and Richardson, *Atlas*, 151.

[35] Miller, *Way of Death*, 368.

[36] Klein, "The Portuguese Slave Trade," 538–40; Manolo Florentino, *Em Costas Negras. Uma História do Tráfico de Escravos entre a África e o Rio de Janeiro* (São Paulo: Companhia das Letras, 1997), 78–82; and Joseph Miller, "The Numbers, Origins, and Destinations of Slaves in the Eighteenth Century Angolan Slave Trade," in *The Atlantic Slave Trade: Effects on Economies, Societies, and People in Africa, the Americas, and Europe*, ed. Joseph Inikori and Stanley L. Engerman (Durham, NC: Duke University Press, 1992), 100.

[37] Instituto Histórico Geográfico Brasileiro (IHGB), DL. 86,03, 1770, "Ofício sobre a extinção do contarto dos escravos e administraçõ régias destes direitos"; and Cadornega, *História Geral*, 3, 32. See also José Carlos Venâncio, *A Economia de Luanda e Hinterland no Século XVII. Um Estudo de Sociologia Histórica* (Lisbon: Estampa, 1996), 132; Roquinaldo A. Ferreira, "Transforming Atlantic Slaving: Trade, Warfare and Territorial Control in Angola, 1650–1800," PhD dissertation, University of California, Los Angeles, 2003, 72; Miller, *Way of Death*, 181. On ivory and salt, see Maria Luisa Esteves, "Para o Estudo do Tráfico de Escravos de Angola (1640–1668)," *Studia* 50 (1991): 90–1.

[38] For requests for animals, see the various petitions to the inland captains to catch zebras, lions, and birds to be sent to the royal authorities during the terms of Francisco de

textiles, beads, gunpowder, and other commodities used in internal trade. Manioc flour came mainly from Brazil and complemented the diet of the local population.[39]

The Early Trade

As seen earlier, the presence of foreign ships along the coast of Benguela in the seventeenth century indicates that this port was known by slave traders as a possible destination. The Portuguese wars of conquest and a series of conflicts between African political entities explored in Chapter 1 led to the accumulation of war prisoners who could be easily sold to slavers. Raids along the coast of Benguela resulted in "very great number of people, men, women and children, who were taken captive or slain."[40] Slavery and slaving practices predated the arrival of the Portuguese, as was true in many other African societies. The Portuguese, however, tapped the market to export captives of war, creating a demand for more slaves and transforming the commerce and slavery in the process. As a result, violence spread, provoking the collapse of old chiefdoms, as seen in Chapter 2, and favoring the consolidation of stronger military states, as

Sousa Coutinho listed in ANTT, Conde de Linhares, L. 50, vol. 1, fl. 3, and L. 99, fl. 56. Cadornega also mentions the export of animal skins in *Historia das Guerras Angolas*, 3, 171. For requests for African wild animals, see AHU, Angola, caixa 103, doc. 11, January 19, 1801; AHU, Angola, caixa 106, doc. 42, August 6, 1803; AHU, Angola, caixa 107, doc. 30; AHU, Angola, caixa 118, doc. 21, February 12, 1807; AHU, Angola, caixa 120, doc. 1; AHU, Angola, caixa 121, doc. 32; AHU, Angola, caixa 124, doc. 2; AHU, Angola, caixa 127, doc. 1; AHU, Angola, caixa 128, doc. 31; AHU, Angola, caixa 131, doc. 45; AHU, Angola, caixa 137, doc. 72; AHU, Angola, caixa 153, doc. 29; AHU, Angola, caixa 167, doc. 33; AHU, Angola, Correspondência dos Governadores, pasta 8B, July 10, 1845; AHU, Angola, Correspondência dos Governadores, pasta 16, doc. "Mapa dos rendimentos da Alfândega de Benguela nos anos de 1848 e 1849"; AHU, cod. 1632, fl. 136, October 12, 1796. Governor Martinho de Melo e Castro of Benguela complained about sending 2,000 slaves to Luanda annually; see AHNA, cod. 440, fl. 14v.–15; and AHNA, cod. 441, fl. 85, "Mapa do que se exportou em Benguela em 1798."

[39] AHU, Angola, caixa 8, doc. 45, September 23, 1664; AHU, Angola, caixa 79, doc. 12, July 20, 1793; AHU, Angola, caixa 79, doc. 17, August 7, 1793; and Venâncio, *A Economia de Luanda*, 131. Manioc flour continued to be imported in the late 1850s. See Biblioteca da Sociedade de Geografia de Lisboa (BSGL), res. 2, Mc. 6, doc. 8–8, "Carta de José Rodrigues Coelho do Amaral, sobre a carestia de alimentos e o clima de Luanda," 1857. For more on the trade on manioc between Brazil and African ports, see Nielson Bezerra, "Mosaicos da Escravidão: Identidades Africanas e Conexões Atlânticas no Recôncavo da Guanabara (1780–1840)," PhD dissertation, Universidade Federal Fluminense, 2010, chap. 4.

[40] E. G. Ravenstein, *The Strange Adventures of Andrew Battell in Angola and Adjoining Regions* (London: Hakluyt Society), 21.

will be explored in Chapter 5. Notions of war and law changed, resulting in expanding slavery. The value of human life decreased as communities tried to meet the demands of the Atlantic trade, a process of transformation that began in the seventeenth century, during the early phase of the trade.

During the sixteenth century, the discovery of silver mines in the Spanish colonies in the New World led to the employment of African slave labor in the Americas. The unification of the Iberian Crowns (1580–1621) facilitated the activities of Portuguese traders in the slave trade to the Spanish colonies. The Asiento of 1594 gave Portuguese traders a monopoly in providing slaves to the Spanish territories in the New World. Payment was made mainly with silver.[41] Thus, under Spanish control, Portuguese merchants had access to silver from the Americas, which was used to acquire spices in Asia and slaves in Africa, connecting different parts of the empire. Benguela was certainly one of the slave ports in the early trade. In the seventeenth century, before the Dutch occupation, Cadornega reported that Benguela had a *feitoria* ("trading post") and royal officials who shipped *peças* ("slaves") to São Paulo de Assumpção (Luanda). Taxes remained in Benguela and were used to pay and feed the infantry and other soldiers.[42]

The slave trade was initially based on captives acquired in conflicts with neighboring *sobas*, as described in Chapter 1. Between 1595 and 1640, Portuguese merchants in West Central Africa transported between 250,000 and 300,000 African slaves into the ports of Buenos Aires and Cartagena in Spanish America. From there they were sent to the mines of Peru.[43] Some of those slaves were probably seized in the early conflicts close to the coast. Military expeditions around Benguela could result in the acquisition of more than 1,000 slaves, as well as cows and sheep.[44] Captives were quickly sold to trans-Atlantic traders and placed

[41] Joseph C. Miller, "Central Africa during the Era of the Slave Trade," in *Central Africans and Cultural Transformations in the American Diaspora*, ed. Linda Heywood (New York: Cambridge University Press, 2001), 21–69; Stuart B. Schwartz, "Prata, Açúcar e Escravos: de como o Império Restaurou Portugal," *Tempo* 12, no. 24 (2008): 201–23; Luiz Felipe de Alencastro, "The Apprenticeship of Colonization," in *Slavery and the Rise of the Atlantic System*, ed. Barbara L. Solow (Cambridge University Press, 1991), 154.

[42] Cadornega, *História das Guerras Angolas*, vol. 3, 169.

[43] John Elliot, *Empires of the Atlantic World: Britain and Spain in the America, 1492–1830* (New Haven: Yale University Press, 2006), 100.

[44] Curto, "Luso-Brazilian Alcohol," 353; Parreira, "A Primeira Conquista de Benguela," 67; and Luciano Cordeiro, *Viagens e Explorações e Conquistas dos Portuguezes* (Lisbon: Imprensa Nacional, 1881), 10–12.

on board Portuguese vessels, which carried them to the Americas. There they were exchanged for silver and further transported to different parts of the Spanish empire. In 1615, at least two slaves identified as Benguelas were in Lima, Peru, and in 1618–20, some were in Havana, Cuba.[45] By the 1630s, Spanish settlers and explorers in Vera Cruz, Potosí, and Buenos Aires relied on the importation of more African slaves supplied by Portuguese traders.[46] The Portuguese settlement and early exploitation of Benguela shows how the Portuguese and Spanish empires were connected in the sixteenth century not only because of the Joint Crowns but also because of the slave trade. The demand for African slaves in the mining industries in the Spanish colonies and the ability of the Portuguese to acquire and transport them across the Atlantic at attractive prices placed the Portuguese as the major slave traders to the Americas. Besides the market in the Spanish Americas, growth of the sugar industry in Bahia and Pernambuco after 1570 also led to an increased demand for African slaves to replace Amerindian slave labor in Brazil.[47]

The early slave trade did not leave many traces in Portuguese records in Benguela owing to its illegality. Nonetheless, some documents indicate that the trade was active. In 1652, for example, Baltasar Van Dunen, probably a Dutch settler who remained in Benguela, acquired royal permission to trade in slaves from Benguela for 3 years. The license indicates that slaves were embarked at the port.[48] Moreover, in 1666, King Afonso

---

[45] For slaves in Peru who were identified as Benguela, see Frederick P. Bowser, *The African Slave in Colonial Peru* (Stanford, CA: Stanford University Press, 1974), 40–1; I am very grateful for Karen Graubart and David Wheat's insight on the seventeenth-century Spanish Americas. David Wheat kindly shared his research notes from the Cuban and Spanish archives with me. He has found some Africans identified as Benguela in different parts of the Spanish Americas in the seventeenth century. For references to Benguelas in Havana, see Archivo del Sagrado Catedral de San Cristobal de la Habana, Libro de Barajas: Matrimonios (1584–1622), fl. 179v., November 25, 1618; and Archivo General de las Indias, Contaduria, 1117–18, Caja de La Habana, Cuentas del mayordomo de esclavos del Rey, 1631–9.

[46] Schwartz, "Prata, Açúcar e escravos." See also R. Valladares, "El Brasil y las Índias espanolas durante la sublevacion (1640–68)," *Cuadernos de História Moderna* 14 (1993): 151–72; and Esteves, "Para o estudo do tráfico de escravos," 79–108. David Eltis also commented on this Portuguese dominance in his "The Volume and Structure of the Transatlantic Slave Trade: A Reassessment," *William and Mary Quarterly* 58, no. 1 (2001): 17–46.

[47] For the Portuguese monopoly of trade in the seventeenth century, see Linda A. Newson and Susie Minchin, *From Capture to Sale: The Portuguese Slave Trade to Spanish South America in the Early Seventeenth Century* (Leiden: Brill, 2007), 3–4. For the early trade to Brazil, see Stuart Schwartz, "'A Commonwealth within Itself': The Early Brazilian Sugar Industry, 1550–1670," *Revista de Indias* 65, no. 233 (2005): 112–13.

[48] Esteves, "Para o Estudo do Tráfico de Escravos," 85.

VI affirmed "that there were many captives in Benguela and many ivory tusks; however the trade could not expand due to the lack of wealthy residents who could sustain the commerce."[49] In addition, information from the African diaspora helps to explain the initial trade. Cuba seems to have emerged as an important destination for slaves sent from Benguela in the seventeenth century. On November 25, 1618, a woman identified as Isabel Benguela married António Angola in Havana,[50] which suggests that they had arrived in the early decades of the seventeenth century. In the 1630s, among royal slaves disembarked in Havana, there was a Juan and a Sebastian Benguela.[51] The existence of African slaves who identified themselves or were identified by others as Benguelas by the early seventeenth century challenges our understanding of the early trans-Atlantic slave trade.[52] If Benguela slaves were in Cuba and Peru by the seventeenth century and identified as such, not as Angola, were they shipped from the port of Benguela? Ferreira argues that in Luanda, slaves exported from Benguela became known as "Benguela slaves."[53] The fact that Benguela slaves were in the Americas by the early seventeenth century helps to explain the reasons behind the Dutch occupation of Benguela from 1641 to 1648. The Dutch went to Benguela with the knowledge that minerals and slaves had already been exported from there.

More research has to be done on those identified as Benguela in the Americas in order to be able to map the place and time of their origin in Africa. Yet slaves exported from Benguela were in different parts of the Americas in the seventeenth and early eighteenth centuries. On August 23, 1653, Francisco Benguela, who was around 20 years old, was sold to the soldier Ignácio de Losa in Havana. Captain Luís Beltran had brought him to Cuba on board of the ship *Nuestra Senhora del Rosario y el Santo Cristo de San Augustin*. A woman identified as Maria Ganguela, probably

---

[49] AHU, Angola, caixa 9, doc. 25, April 10, 1666.

[50] Arquivo del Sagrado Catedral de San Cristobal de La Habana, Libro de Barajas, Matrimonios (1548–1622), fl. 179v. See http://diglib.library.vanderbilt.edu/esss.pl. I am very grateful to David Wheat, who shared his own research on Cuba with me.

[51] See Arquivo General de las Indias, Contaduria 1117–18, Caja de la Habana, Cuentas del Mayordomo de Escravos del Rey, 1631, 1639. Again, thanks to David Wheat who provided this information to me.

[52] For a discussion of this issue, see Mariana P. Candido, "Trans-Atlantic Links: The Benguela-Bahia Connections, 1700–1850," in *Paths of the Atlantic Slave Trade: Interactions, Identities, and Images*, ed. Ana Lucia Araujo (Amherst, NY: Cambria Press, 2011), 239–42.

[53] Roquinaldo Ferreira, "Slaving and Resistance to Slaving in West Central Africa," in *The Cambridge World History of Slavery, AD 1420–AD 1804*, vol. 3, ed. David Eltis and Stanley L. Engerman (New York: Cambridge University Press, 2011), 116.

from Nganguela, a region in the interior of Benguela outside the control of Portuguese authorities in the seventeenth century, also had arrived on the same slave ship. Benguela and Ganguela should not be read as a particular ethnicity but rather as a place of provenance or origin.[54] In addition to these two cases, Alejandro de la Fuente located a further five slaves identified as Benguela in Havana in the seventeenth century.[55] Although few in number, especially when compared with the 233 Angolan slaves in Cuba at that time, these cases raise some questions regarding slave trade from Benguela. Roquinaldo Ferreira estimated that from the 1680s to the first decade of the eighteenth century, traders located in Benguela dispatched approximately 2,000 slaves annually to Luanda. If so, at least 40,000 slaves left Benguela in the last two decades of the seventeenth century. The numbers are so high that Ferreira estimates that approximately one-third of the slaves shipped from Luanda actually came from Benguela.[56] Yet, if they were grouped together in the *feitorias* in Luanda before being forcibly exported, it is not clear why they were identified as Benguela and not Angola once they reached Cuba or Peru.

If in the seventeenth century most people who left from Benguela ended up in Spanish colonies, by the eighteenth century they were heading to Brazil. Before 1703, a man called José Benguela lived in the parish of Nossa Senhora da Piedade in Bahia. His presence in Brazil in the early eighteenth century was recorded because he was accused of sodomy. With the Inquisition still powerful, José Benguela traveled to Évora, Portugal, to face a trial. In front of Inquisition judges he identified himself as a "black man, slave of João Carvalho de Barros, single, son of Manoel Luís and Maria; native of Benguela."[57] Thus, in a formal legal

---

[54] These cases were identified by Alejandro de la Fuente. See his "Introducción al Estudio de la Trata em Cuba, Siglos XVI y XVI," *Santiago* 61 (1986), 206–7. For the idea of place of provenance, see Mariza de Carvalho Soares, *Devotos da cor* (Rio de Janeiro: Civilização Brasileira, 2000), 95–100; and Mariza de C. Soares, "A Nação que se tem e a terra de onde se vem: Categorias de Inserção Social de Africanos no Império Português, Século XVIII," *Estudos Afro-Asiáticos* 26, no. 2 (2004): 303–30. See also James Sweet, "African Identity and Slave Resistance in the Portuguese Atlantic," in *The Atlantic World and Virginia, 1550–1624*, ed. Peter C. Mancall (Chapel Hill: University of North Carolina Press, 2007), 244–5; and Karen B. Graubart, "'So Color de una Confradía': Catholic Confraternities and the Development of Afro-Peruvian Ethnicities in Early Colonial Peru," *Slavery & Abolition* 10 (2012): 1–22.

[55] Alejandro de la Fuente, "Denominaciones Étnicas de los Esclavos Introducidos em Cuba, Siglos XVI y XVII," *Anales del Caribe* 6 (1986): 88, 95.

[56] Ferreira, "Transforming Atlantic Slaving," 85.

[57] ANTT, Tribunal do Santo Ofício, Inquisição de Lisboa, Process 6478, December 6, 1703.

venue, José clearly identified himself and his parents as originally from Benguela. He, rather than his owner or other officials, claimed Benguela as his identity and place of origin. This case, as well as the cases in Lima and Havana, shows that trans-Atlantic merchants were trading people in Benguela during the seventeenth and early eighteenth centuries, even before it was legal to dispatch slave ships without having to go to Luanda to pay taxes.[58] This example demonstrates how studies and records about Africans in the diaspora can illuminate our understanding of events in Africa, showing that despite the lack of documents, slaves were shipped from Benguela, probably illegally, in the seventeenth century.[59]

Besides court and slave sale records, parish registers reveal the presence of Benguelas in Rio de Janeiro in the second decade of the eighteenth century. Benguela slaves start showing up in Rio de Janeiro in 1719. In 1719, a Benguela woman baptized her daughter at the Church of Sé, in Rio de Janeiro.[60] By the 1730s, more Benguela slaves were in Rio, some of them even guaranteeing their burial at the main church in town, the Nossa Senhora da Candelária.[61] The discovery of gold mines in Minas Gerais created a new demand for African slave labor. In Mariana, Minas Gerais, Brazil, some people were also identified as Benguela by early eighteenth century. In 1723, of the 1,526 slaves in the parish of Nossa Senhora do Carmo, 106 of them were Benguela.[62] The existence of these Benguelas in the interior of Brazil in the first half of the eighteenth century supports the argument that Benguela was a major port of embarkation of

[58] On the need to go to Luanda to pay taxes, see Mariana Candido, "Merchants and the Business of the Slave Trade at Benguela, 1750–1850," *African Economic History* 35, no. 1 (2007): 1.

[59] Toby Green also made use of notarial documents from the Americas to shed some light on events in Western Africa. See Green, *The Rise of the Trans-Atlantic Slave Trade*.

[60] Arquivo da Cúria Metropolitana do Rio de Janeiro (ACMRJ), Livro de Batismo da Freguesia da Sé, Assento 44, 1SeBES. I would like to thank Mariza de Carvalho Soares for generously sharing her database of slave baptisms with me. For the importance of baptism to African slaves and their descendants in Brazil, see Soares, *Devotos da Cor,* 131–46; and Patricia Mulvey, "Slave Confraternities in Brazil: Their Role in Colonial Society," *The Americas* 39, no. 1 (1982): 39–40.

[61] Soares, *Devotos da Cor,* 147.

[62] Arquivo da Câmara Municipal de Mariana (ACMM), Impostos, Taxas e Multas, Lançamento dos Reais Quintos, 1723, cod. 166. I would like to thank Samila Xavier de Queiroz, who has helped me collect the data. For more on the links between the economies of Bahia and Minas Gerais, see Stuart B. Schwartz, "The Economy of the Portuguese Empire," in *Portuguese Oceanic Expansion, 1400–1800,* ed. Francisco Bethencourt and Diogo Ramada Curto (New York: Cambridge University Press, 2007), 35. See also Charles Boxer, *A Idade de Ouro do Brasil: Dores de Crescimento de uma Sociedade Colonial* (Rio de Janeiro: Nova Fronteira, 2000), 61. Higgins indicated that 1735–1750 were the

African slaves during those years. Lack of evidence of slave departures from Benguela before the 1720s suggests that Benguela was a center of smuggling before the Portuguese Crown regulated and legalized shipping from this port.

The importance of Benguela as a slave port is also reinforced by the presence of European interlopers. Since the mid–seventeenth century, West Central Africa attracted the attention of Dutch, French, and English traders. The Dutch invasion in the mid–seventeenth century is another indication of slave trade from Benguela. The Dutch occupied ports along the coast of Africa to control the supply of slaves to the Americas, which suggests that Benguela was already an important slaving area by the 1640s. By 1666, the lack of residents and traders in town affected the slave trade, although a substantial number of captives were available.[63] Conflicts with Luanda authorities increased during the late 1600s with larger numbers of slaves and the arrival of new traders. The Capuchin Antonio Zucchelli, who visited Benguela in 1698, stated that ships reached the port to buy slaves, yet captains and crews remained on board, afraid of the contaminated water and fruit.[64] However, he emphasized that the profits were attractive enough to compel merchants to sail to Benguela despite the dangers. In addition, by the seventeenth century, Portuguese raiding expeditions reinforced the idea that there was a market for those captives. The French attack in 1705 underscored how news of the wealth of Benguela traveled across the Atlantic. An illegal trade operated extensively along the Benguela coast, provoking concern among Portuguese authorities who protested against the non-payment of duties.[65]

Organization of the Slave Trade

The growing demand for African slave labor in the Americas forced the Portuguese Crown to negotiate contracts with private merchants. In 1711, the municipal council of Luanda reported that traders from Bahia and Rio de Janeiro requested more slaves from Angola and Benguela.[66]

years of gold mining boom in Sabará; Kathleen Higgins, *Licentious Liberty in a Brazilian Gold-Mining Region* (University Park: Pennsylvania State University Press, 1999), 26.

[63] AHU, Angola, caixa 9, doc. 25, April 10, 1666. Miller also argues that in the 1670s and 1680s, Portuguese forces raided and captured people in the central highlands. See Miller, "Central Africa during the Era of the Slave Trade," 49.

[64] Antonio Zucchelli, *Relazioni del Viaggio e Missione di Congo nell'Etiopia inferiore Occidentale* (Venice: Bartolomeo Giavarina, 1712), 91.

[65] Cadornega, *História Geral das Guerras Angolanas*, 2, 137, 163, 164.

[66] AHU, Angola, caixa, 19, doc. 21, September 26, 1711.

In January of 1716, the trader António Francisco de Oliveira, captain of the galley *Nossa Senhora da Monsarrata e Liberdade*, applied for an overseas council license to sail to Benguela and "do his business without the interference of the governor."[67] This document is the first known official request from a trader who was apparently responding to an increase in the demand for slaves in Brazil.[68] By 1722, Rio de Janeiro traders sent a ship to acquire slaves in Benguela. On board, they shipped 100 *pipas* (500-liter barrels) of *cachaça*, sugar-cane distilled alcohol produced in sugar mills in Brazil.[69] These expeditions were followed by other traders who intended to take advantage of the rising price of slaves in Brazil. António de Almeida e Souza, captain of the *curveta São Pedro and São Paulo*, asked for royal permission to sail to Benguela in 1725. In his appeal, Almeida e Souza declared that he intended to acquire slaves in Benguela and sail to Bahia without stopping at Luanda to pay taxes. He also requested the collaboration of the governor of Benguela in expediting his trip and negotiations.[70] A few months later, another trader from Bahia, José de Carvalho, followed the same procedure of sending his ship directly to Benguela.[71] The *Mesa do Bem Comun e dos Comerciantes*, the Portuguese board that issued overseas trade licenses before 1756, granted both traders permission to stay in Benguela for as many days as they needed to conduct business, initiating the direct slave trade between Benguela and the Brazilian ports.[72] By December 1733, Rio de Janeiro traders had started requesting permission to sail to Benguela. Manoel da Silva, master of the *curveta São Pedro e São Paulo*, was among the first merchants based in Rio de Janeiro to sail to Benguela.[73] In the 1730s and 1740s, several merchants sailed straight from Rio de Janeiro to Benguela to acquire slaves.[74] In 1755, the Portuguese government instituted the *Companhia Geral do Grão Pará e Maranhão and Pernambuco e Paraíba*,

[67] Ferreira, "Transforming Atlantic Slaving," 79.
[68] C. R. Boxer, *O Império Marítimo Português* (Rio de Janeiro: São Paulo, 2002), 167–73; Laura de Mello e Sousa, *Desclassificados do Ouro. A Pobreza Mineira no Século XVIII* (Rio de Janeiro: Graal, 1985).
[69] Curto, "Luso-Brazilian Alcohol," 356.
[70] AHU, Angola, caixa 22, doc. 58, January 25, 1725.
[71] AHU, Angola, caixa 22, doc. 64, March 20, 1725.
[72] AHU, Angola, caixa 22, doc. 158, prior to December 22, 1725.
[73] AHU, Brazil, Rio de Janeiro, caixa 28, doc. 102, December 23, 1733; and AHU, Brazil, Rio de Janeiro, caixa 31, doc. 20, prior to October 22, 1735. The ship *São Pedro e São Paulo* is in the *Transatlantic Slave Trade Database* (Voyage ID 8660).
[74] AHU, Brazil, Rio de Janeiro, caixa 30, doc. 8, prior to January 27, 1735; caixa 32, doc. 106, prior to December 17, 1736; caixa 33, doc. 2, prior to February 7, 1737; caixa 34, doc. 42, prior to April 15, 1738; caixa 45, doc. 48, prior to April 1, 1746; caixa 46, doc. 34, September 28, 1746. The *Transatlantic Slave Trade Database* only indicated three

trading companies to oversee the slave trade to Brazil.[75] The goal of the Portuguese Crown was to maintain tight control over the overseas trade and prevent smuggling and tax evasion.

Sailing slave ships from Benguela directly to Brazil was met with the resistance of traders in the Portuguese capital in Angola. Luanda residents complained about a sudden decrease in exports, which led to the ruin of local merchants. In the eyes of the governor of Angola, Benguela represented a major threat to the continuation of slaving departures from Luanda because very few of the itinerant merchants known as *pombeiros* were using it as a marketplace.[76] The conflicts in Kakonda in the 1730s, explored in Chapter 2, flooded Benguela with captives brought by itinerant traders.[77] From 1727 to 1734, Luanda traders complained that they advanced textiles and other items to their *pombeiros* as credit against the expected delivery of slaves. Rather than returning to Luanda, *pombeiros* brought the slaves they acquired in the interior to Benguela, where slavers offered better prices. The slaves who left from Benguela probably ended up in Rio de Janeiro or other places in Brazil.[78]

Since Benguela was a Portuguese colony where few officers lived, it was very attractive to merchants in search of ways to avoid fiscal control over their business by the Crown. Besides, slaves were sold for better prices than in Luanda or Loango. Between 1700 and 1750, at least 22,596 slaves were shipped from Benguela. To please Luanda

slave voyages between Benguela and Rio de Janeiro in the 1730s and 1740s. See www.slavevoyages.org/tast/database/search.faces, Voyages 8488, 8494, and 4786.

[75] António Carreira, *As Companhias Pombalinas de Grão Pará e Maranhão e Pernambuco e Paraíba* (Lisbon: Presença, 1983); and Maria Leonor Freire Costa, *Império e Grupos Mercantis: Entre o Oriente e o Atlântico (Séc. XVII)* (Lisbon: Livro Horizonte, 2002); Schwartz, "Prata, Açucar e Escravos," 206.

[76] AHU, Angola, caixa 23, doc. 104, April 17, 1727. See also Birmingham, *Trade and Conflict in Angola*, 140–1; and Miller, *Way of Death*, 222–5.

[77] Arquivo Histórico Nacional de Angola (AHNA), cod. 1, fl. 92v.–93, April 12, 1730.

[78] AHU, Angola, caixa 24, doc. 36, April 17, 1728; and AHU, Angola, caixa 27, doc. 159, December 22, 1734. On the better prices for Benguela slaves, see Birmingham, *Trade and Conflict*, 140–1; and Miller, *Way of Death*, 222–5. On credit operations, see Candido, "Merchants and the Business," 13–17; Robin Law, *Ouidah: The Social History of a West African Slaving "Port,"* 130–7; Paul E. Lovejoy and David Richardson, "Trust, Pawnship and Atlantic History: The Institutional Foundations of the Old Calabar Slave Trade," *American Historical Review* 102 (1999), 333–55. For Benguela slaves in Brazil in the 1740s and 1750s, see James Sweet, "Manumission in Rio de Janeiro, 1749–1754: An African Perspective," *Slavery and Abolition* 24 (2003): 54–70; Soares, *Devotos da Cor*, 147; and Sweet, *Recreating Africa: Culture, Kinship, and Religion in the African-Portuguese World, 1441–1770* (Chapel Hill: University of North Carolina Press, 2003), 32.

merchants, the overseas council issued a law in 1760 that prohibited ship captains from calling at the port of Benguela before disembarking in Luanda. This measure was supposed to prevent traders from loading their ships with slaves before reaching Luanda; however, captains continued to stop at Benguela, claiming that the winds forced them to do so, and in the process, they bought slaves there, to the annoyance of Luanda merchants.[79] Royal attempts to control trade at the same time that they allowed investment by private merchants resulted in a series of irregularities. Smuggling, tax evasion, and lack of law enforcement were some of the common infractions. D. José I, King of Portugal, introduced a reform on tax collection in Angola that required traders who had been previously exempt to pay export duties on their goods. It also changed the system of the slave tax from *peça da india* to *cabeça* ("head") collection. Before 1760, slaves were taxed based on their age and height. A young adult male was a *peça*. Two slaves in their thirties were considered to be a *peça*, as well as children from 4 to 8 years of age. Infants were not counted.[80] From 1760 onward, the Portuguese decided to simplify the collection according to three age groups: Adults were a *cabeça*; standing children were *crias de pé*, who paid half taxes; and infants were called *crias de peito* and were shipped without paying taxes if in the company of their mothers.[81] Despite attempts to control the trade, merchants and *feitores do contrato* (in charge of supervising slave departures) continued to ship more people than they had paid taxes for.

In the late 1760s, Governor Sousa Coutinho of Angola appointed three inspectors to combat fraud and tax evasion, who also acted in Benguela. The new measures included the construction of a fort at Novo Redondo (Sumbe, nowadays) in 1769, halfway between Luanda and Benguela,

---

[79] AHNA, cod. 81, fl. 121–122v., January 31, 1779. See Candido, "Merchants and the Business," 10; Ferreira, "Transforming Atlantic Slaving," 75–7; and Curto, *Enslaving Spirits*, 94; Joseph Miller, "The Paradoxes of Impoverishment in the Atlantic Zone," in *History of Central Africa*, ed. David Birmingham and Phyllis Martin (London: Longman, 1983), I, 260–2.

[80] "Alvará porque Vossa Magestade ha por bem regular o despacho das mercadorias, que pertencem à Casa da Índia, na forma acima Declarada" (July 27, 1767), in *Coleção das Leyes, Decretos e Alvarás que comprehende o feliz Reinado del Rey Fidelisimo D. José I Nosso Senhor desde o ano de 1761 ate o de 1769* (Lisbon: Officina de António Rodrigues Galhardo, 1776). See also Esteves, "Para o Estudo do Tráfico de Escravos de Angola," 88.

[81] Klein, "The Portuguese Slave Trade," 903–6; see also Silva, "The Coastal Origins of Slaves Leaving Angola."

to monitor foreign ships and intercept illegal trade.[82] The metropolitan government wanted to prevent the internationalization of trade that characterized the ports of Loango and Cabinda to the north of the Congo River. However, these actions were not successful. In the decades from the 1760s to the 1780s, English and French traders continued to buy slaves in the region around Benguela.[83] In November 1785, Navy Lieutenant António José Valente reported

This town [Benguela] looks more French than Portuguese. From July 8 to August 4, four different French vessels anchored in the Benguela harbor. As soon as they arrived, the crew landed and the officers visited the governor in his house; the town then was under the influence of the officials and their sailors who walked freely across the town, day and night, as comfortable as our Portuguese men. The first of the four ships stayed anchored for seventeen days, and embarked more than 700 slaves, and lots of ivory.[84]

By the end of the eighteenth century, Portuguese authorities protested and denounced the attempts of trans-Atlantic slavers to evade taxation.[85]

[82] AHU, Angola, caixa 59, doc. 29, May 16, 1769; AHU, Angola, caixa 59, doc. 44, August 1, 1769; AHU, Angola, caixa 59, doc. 57, September 6, 1769; AHU, Angola, caixa 59, doc. 73, November 28, 1769; AHU, Angola, caixa 61, doc. 14, May 14, 1776; AHU, Angola, caixa 61, doc. 18, June 17, 1776; and AHU, Angola, caixa 123, doc. 67, December 22, 1811. See also J. C. Feo Cardoso de Castello e Branco e Torres, *Memórias Contendo a Biographia do Vice Almirante Luiz da Motta Feo e Torres* (Paris: Fantin Livreiro, 1825), 263; and José Joaquim Lopes de Lima, *Ensaios sobre a statistica d'Angola e Benguella e suas dependencies na costa Occidental d'Africa ao sul do Equador* (Lisbon: Imprensa Nacional, 1844), xxxiv–xxxvi.
[83] Miller, "Central Africa during the Era of the Slave Trade," 29. For Loango and Cabinda, see Susan Herlin, "Brazil and the Commercialization of Kongo," in *Enslaving Connections: Changing Cultures of Africa and Brazil During the Era of Slavery*, ed. José Curto and Paul Lovejoy (Amherst, NY: Humanity Books, 2004); Phyllis Martin, *The External Trade of the Loango Coast, 1576–1870* (Oxford, UK: Clarendon Press, 1972); and Roquinaldo Ferreira, "Dos Sertões ao Atlântico: Tráfico Ilegal de Escravos e Comércio Lícito em Angola, 1830–1860," MA thesis, Universidade Federal do Rio de Janeiro, 1996.
[84] AHU, Angola, caixa 70, doc. 56, November 11, 1785.
[85] AHU, Angola, caixa 53, doc. 76, October 30, 1769; AHU, Angola, caixa 59, doc. 29, May 16, 1769; AHU, Angola, caixa 70, doc. 56, November 11, 1785; AHU, Angola, caixa 73, doc. 44, October 12, 1788; AHU, Angola, caixa 75, doc. 35, August 15, 1790; AHU, Angola, cod. 552, fl. 138, October 16, 1820; AHU, Angola, cod. 1627, April 15, 1791; AHU, Angola, cod. 1628, fl. 103, November 17, 1791; AHU, Angola, cod. 1630, fl. 44v., November 20, 1793; AHU, cod. 1631, fl. 63v., March 18, 1795; Erário Régio, L. 4197, fl. 19, January 10, 1800; AHNA, cod. 446, fl. 100, October 23, 1816; Elias Alexandre da Silva Corrêa, *Historia de Angola* (Lisbon: Ática, 1937), I, 276; IHGB, doc. DL347,30.01. January 9, 1800, "Comerciantes de Benguela reclamando da presença de navios franceses"; ANTT, Ministério do Reino, Mc. 605, caixa 708, December 1791; and Cadornega, *História Geral das Guerras Angolanas*, 2, 137, 163, 164.

The volume of the slave trade grew exponentially during the eighteenth century in part because of the demand in the Americas but also owing to the political instability in the Benguela hinterland. Between 1751 and 1800, at least 305,057 slaves left the port of Benguela, and most of them landed in Rio de Janeiro and Bahia.[86] The expansion of the sugar industry in Bahia and Cuba also accelerated demand along the West Central African coast for slaves to ship to new regions of the Americas.[87] The decline of gold exports in Minas Gerais by the second half of the eighteenth century was compensated by the Cuban market and expansion of the cocoa and sugar industries in Bahia, as well as rice and cotton production in Maranhão.[88] Slavers also searched for markets where slaves could be acquired at a lower cost, and Benguela was one of them.[89] The violence in the interior of Benguela reached incredible levels and generated a large number of captives. Besides the slaves forcibly shipped through the port, traders continued to send slaves to Luanda in the early nineteenth century, even though Benguela merchants were also exporting directly to Brazil. Although it is very difficult to quantify and explore the extent of smuggling, it operated in Benguela under the support of Portuguese authorities who were involved in illegal activities. Increased transactions with foreign traders disrupted the flow of business for Brazilian and Portuguese merchants and, most important of all, threatened the colonial order and made local residents vulnerable to the growing violence.

Few trans-Atlantic slavers had enough capital to enter the business alone, and many searched for partners established in Benguela. Estimates from the middle of the eighteenth to the early nineteenth centuries identify only a dozen or so large traders, although there were smaller merchants who handled a few slaves a time.[90] In the 1780s, traders in

---

[86] *Transatlantic Slave Trade Database*, www.slavevoyages.org/tast/database/search.faces.

[87] Manuel Moreno Fraginals, *The Sugarmill: the Socioeconomic Complex of Sugar in Cuba, 1760–1860* (New York: Cambridge University Press, 1976), 25; Sherry Johnson, *The Social Transformation of Eighteenth Century Cuba* (Gainesville: University Press of Florida, 2001); Laird W. Bergad, *The Comparative Histories of Slavery in Brazil, Cuba and the United States* (New York: Cambridge University Press, 2007)

[88] Herbert Klein and Francisco de la Luna, *Slavery in Brazil* (New York: Cambridge University Press, 2010), 65–73; Walter Hawthorne, "From 'Black Rice' to 'Brown': Rethinking the History of Risiculture in the Seventeenth and Eighteenth Century Atlantic," *American Historical Review* 115, no. 1 (2010): 157–8; Judith Carney, "With Grains in Her Hair': Rice in Colonial Brazil," *Slavery and Abolition* 25, no. 1 (2004): 1–27; Stuart Schwartz, *Sugar Plantations in the Formation of Brazilian Society: Bahia, 1550–1835* (New York: Cambridge University Press, 1986), 415–38.

[89] Curto, "Luso-Brazilian Alcohol," 356.

[90] Candido, "Merchants and the Business of the Slave Trade," 4.

Benguela operated through three or four large firms that maintained close ties with merchants in Rio de Janeiro.[91] By the end of eighteenth century, Brazilians who lived in town facilitated the trans-Atlantic connections, such as soldier and trader Hipólito Ferreira da Silva, born in Rio de Janeiro, and Crispim de Silveira e Souza, originally from Bahia. People born in the colony of Brazil also acted on behalf of traders. Some of the bar owners identified in Chapter 2, such as Valentim Muniz de Siqueira and João Nunes, participated in the slave trade. Besides acting as a bar owner, João Nunes also was enlisted as an *Henrique* soldier, an all-black regiment in the Lusophone South Atlantic World that was directly involved in wars of conquest that enslaved many people.[92] Nunes combined his role as an alcohol merchant with his position in the colonial forces. Other *brasileiros* also were located near Benguela, facilitating communication between that port and other markets. In 1797, authorities noted that there was a Brazilian trader, Manoel Isidoro dos Santos, in Novo Redondo, a small port town to the north of Benguela, probably enjoying its isolation and lack of colonial control.[93] In the fortress of Caconda, José da Assunção de Mello conducted caravans to the interior in the late eighteenth century, searching for new markets.[94] With transfer of the Portuguese Crown to Rio de Janeiro, the link between Benguela and Brazilian merchants strengthened. After 1808, Brazilian goods dominated the import market in Benguela. Between 1811 and 1830, fourteen of the seventeen largest slave traders in Rio maintained business links with Benguela.[95] *Brasileiros* were everywhere, from high-ranking officials to political exiles, as seen in Chapter 2. The presence of such individuals reinforced connections with Brazilian ports and helped to consolidate the colony of Brazil as the model to be followed.

---

[91] Silva Corrêa, *História de Angola*, 1, 39.

[92] AHU, Angola, caixa 89, doc. 67, December 21, 1798. For more on the Henriques Regiment and its origins, see Hebe Matos, "'Black Troops' and Hierarchies of Color in the Portuguese Atlantic World: The Case of Henrique Dias and His Black Regiment," *Luso-Brazilian Review* 45, no. 1 (2008): 6–29.

[93] IHGB, DL31,09, fl. 14–14v., October 25, 1797, "Ofício de Fernando da Silva Correia, tenente regente, a d. Miguel António de Melo, [governador de Angola], comunicando o envio do mapa das pessoas de artilharia da Fortaleza de Novo Redondo, das imagens da igreja de Nossa Senhora da Conceição, pagamento dos sacerdotes, sobas, armamentos, dos moradores, batismos, casamentos e óbitos, prédios rústicos, gado e escravos existentes no Presídio Novo Redondo."

[94] IHGB, DL32,02.01, fl. 5v.–6, "Relação dos sobas potentados, souvetas seus vassalos e sobas agregados pelos nomes das suas terras, que tem na capitania de Benguela."

[95] Florentino, *Em Costas Negras*, 243.

The British ban on the slave trade in 1807 and the 1815 prohibition on slave trade north of the equator, rather than stopping the trade, accelerated international commerce in Benguela.[96] In the first two decades of the nineteenth century, an estimated 95,522 people were sent from Benguela.[97] Portuguese agents tried to limit the number of slaves loaded on each ship to avoid irregularities, including overly tight packing. New laws were issued to address the misconduct. On November 24, 1813, an edict was published to prevent trans-Atlantic traders from overloading ships, with the goal of lowering mortality among slaves. Ignoring the Lisbon legislation, on several occasions the governor of Benguela authorized more slaves to be loaded than was legal. On October 19, 1814, he allowed the captain of a slave ship to carry 541 slaves, although his license permitted only 327 slaves onboard. The governor claimed that in the port of Benguela there were 1,400 slaves at risk of dying from hunger or disease if left behind. Using the argument that the slave trade was saving lives, he allowed the captain to sail with a ship that carried 214 slaves over the legal limit.[98] Months later, the ship *Feliz Eugenia* received another special license to board 688 slaves, which again surpassed the limit. Slave traders were willing to smuggle slaves in order to increase their profit margin, in many cases acting in connivance with Benguela authorities, as the two previous cases illustrate.

After the 1826 British–Brazilian treaty that outlawed the slave trade to Brazil, slave merchants and local authorities had to reorganize their commercial activities. During the 1820s, an estimated 53,798 slaves were shipped from Benguela. In the next decade, 1831–40, the number of slaves exported reached 76,607. Thus British pressure to bring the slave trade to an end resulted in more slaves crossing the South Atlantic. Slave traders increased their profits and forcibly moved more people after 1826, despite the legislation banishing exports.[99] French traveler Douville visited Benguela in 1828 and reported a number of houses abandoned or closed.[100] Yet the slave trade seemed to have increased rather than declined in that period. In fact, in 1829, Governor Aurélio

---

[96] Leslie Bethell, *The Abolition of the Brazilian Slave Trade, 1807–1869* (Cambridge University Press, 1970), 13–14.

[97] See Silva, "The Coastal Origins of Slaves Leaving Angola."

[98] AHNA, cod. 446, fl. 11v.–12, October 19, 1814.

[99] AHNA, cod. 449, fl. 113, August 2, 1827; and Miller, "Numbers, Origins, and Destinations," 410–11.

[100] J. B. Douville, *Voyage au Congo et dans l'interieur de l'Afrique Equinoxiale, fait dans les annees 1828, 1829, 1830* (Paris: Jules Renouard, 1832), 1, 8.

de Oliveira warned that merchants would react negatively to the treaty between Britain and Brazil. He thought that news of the end of the slave trade could "provoke protest and uprisings." He feared that itinerant traders would be murdered. Inland rulers threatened to invade Benguela. Some suggested that "if your majesty is not interested in slaves anymore, you should leave these lands to other nations interested in buying slaves."[101]

Most of the merchants who had engaged in slaving activities prior to the abolition continued to trade in slaves.[102] Under British pressure, the Portuguese prohibited the slave trade from all their colonies in Africa in 1836. In the same year, the Portuguese government canceled the Crown monopoly on ivory exported from Angola in order to increase the diversification of exported goods.[103] Along with ivory, beeswax, gum-copal, orchilla weed (a lichen that produces a purple dye), and later rubber became important exports.[104] The development of this new trade led to the expansion of internal slavery because it required labor and porters to bring commodities to the coast. Merchants in Benguela continued to rely heavily on their *pombeiros* based in the fortresses in the interior, including Caconda.[105] Most of the slaves were acquired in the highlands through African traders connected to the rulers of local states. *Sobas* in the interior controlled markets and guaranteed control over commerce. Slaves acquired in the inland markets were lined up in a coffle and forced to walk the long journey to the coast. They carried the commodities acquired by the *pombeiros*, such as loads of beeswax, gum-copal, and even ivory tusks. Rulers also decided who could or could not enter a state

---

[101] AHU, Angola, caixa 164, doc. 75, December 1, 1829.

[102] AHNA, cod. 453, fl. 12, November 27, 1846; AHNA, cod. 455, fl. 265, November 17, 1846; AHNA, cod. 453, fl. 76v., April 1, 1850; AHNA, cod. 456, fl. 8, April 4, 1844; AHNA, cod. 456, fl. 119, November 26, 1844; AHNA, cod. 459, fl. 20–20v., December 3, 1853; and AHNA, cod. 511, fl. 7, April 24, 1850.

[103] According to Tito Omboni, who visited Benguela in 1835, the ivory trade was the second most profitable commercial activity after illegal slaving. T. Omboni, *Viaggi Nell'Africa Occidentale: Gia Medico di Consiglio Nel Regno d'Angola e Sue Dipendenze Membro Della R. Accademia Peloritana di Messina* (Milan: Civelli, 1846), 75.

[104] Lopes de Lima, *Ensaios sobre a statistica d'Angola e Benguella*, 50–2.

[105] Maria Emília Madeira Santos (ed.), *Viagens e Apontamentos de um Portuense em África* (Coimbra: Biblioteca Geral da Universidade de Coimbra, 1986), 48–51; Luiz Alfredo Keiling, *Quarenta Anos de Africa* (Braga: Edição das Missões de Angola e Congo, 1934), 9–10, 61, 107–8; Isabel Castro Henriques, *Percursos da Modernidade em Angola: Dinâmicas Comercias e Transformações Sociais no Século XIX* (Lisbon: Instituto de Investigação Científica Tropical, 1997), 363–84; and Valentim Alexandre and Jill Dias, *O Império Africano, 1825–1890* (Lisbon: Estampa, 1998), 398–408.

to trade in slaves, and they controlled prices and established the taxes that itinerant merchants had to pay.[106]

In 1840, the governor of Angola, Manuel Eleutério Malheiro, complained that traders had installed barracoons along the Benguela coast to engage in illegal trade.[107] Despite the efforts to diversify the economy and expand agriculture, it was difficult to convince "traders dedicated since the beginning of their careers to the [slave trade], which generated at least 50 percent profit, to adjust [to new activities], since a 6 percent profit does not seem too attractive."[108] In 1841, traveler George Tams reported that "all the slave-dealers in Benguela are Portuguese, with the exception of two or three Italians, and their iniquitous trade is so flourishing, that in the years 1838, nearly 20,000 slaves were exported."[109] Although illegal, slave traders operated with relative freedom in town. Slaves were kept in warehouses in town or within the compounds where traders lived. In 1846, twenty-three traders still operated in town, including two women, dona Mariana António de Carvalho and dona Joana Mendes.[110] African slaves continued to depart in growing numbers. In the 1840s, more than 105,000 slaves left the port of Benguela. Some ended up in the ships apprehended along the coast by British and Portuguese authorities. The slave trade only came to an end in 1850, when the Brazilian market closed, although illegal exports continued to operate until 1856.[111]

As in other parts of the African coast, slaves were exchanged for a series of imported goods from different parts of the world. Before 1650,

---

[106] IHGB, DL81,02.20, fl. 62–63, January 15, 1772; and Linda Heywood, *Contested Power in Angola, 1840 to the Present* (Rochester, NY: University of Rochester Press, 2000), 12.

[107] AHU, Angola, L. 679, fl. 33, July 1840; Boletim Geral do Governo da Provincia de Angola (BGGPA), 63, November 21, 1846, fl. 2; BGGPA, n. 126, February 5, 1848, fl. 2; and BGGPA, n. 138, May 13, 1848.

[108] AHU, Angola, Correspondência dos Governadores, pasta 2, April 8, 1836.

[109] George Tams, *Visit to the Portuguese Possessions in South-Western Africa* (London: T. C. Newby, 1845), 1, 97.

[110] AHNA, cod. 461, fl. 10–10v., September 12, 1846. For descriptions of warehouses, see Tams, 110.

[111] *Transatlantic Slave Trade Database*; and Domingues da Silva, "The Coastal Origins of Slaves Leaving Angola." See also AHU, Angola, Mc. 874, "Embarcações Apressadas nas águas territoriais, 1841–1848;" where a long list of slave ships embarked between 1841 and 1848 in Benguela is available; AHU, Angola, Mc. 768, August 1, 1857; AHU, Angola, Mc. 2760, also contains several cases of ships apprehended, a large number of them loaded in Benguela. See esp. AHU, Angola, Mc. 2760, doc. 82, November 21, 1855; AHU, Angola, Correspondência dos Governadores, pasta 16A, doc. "Oficios do Governador de Benguela," March 27, 1850; AHU, Angola, L. 679, fl. 71v., May 26, 1841; and AHU, Angola, L. 679, fl. 178, September 6, 1843.

contraband silver from the Spanish colonies in the Americas and manioc flour processed in Brazil dominated the exchange trade between Brazil and West Central Africa.[112] Later, alcohol, textiles, and gunpowder were among the items exchanged. José Curto has shown how Brazilian *cachaça* replaced Portuguese wine among the goods exchanged in West Central Africa and changed drinking habits. Despite the importance of alcohol in trading slaves in West Central Africa, the importation of alcohol never reached the same level as in Angola. Still, alcohol was an important trade commodity in Benguela and its hinterland, accounting for one-quarter of the slaves exported from the port.[113] Beads were of particular value in the interior. By the end of the eighteenth century, they were highly prized as indications of wealth and social position around Novo Redondo.[114] Beads and textiles were used to pay troops in Caconda, who exchanged them for slaves in the interior.[115] At the end of the eighteenth century, soldiers, who were not paid a regular salary, exchanged gunpowder and textiles in the interior for slaves, chickens, and agricultural products. If supplies from Brazil were not sufficient, coastal traders purchased gunpowder from English and French interlopers.[116] To bypass restrictions from the Portuguese administration, Benguela merchants smuggled gunpowder in barrels of manioc flour, pepper, and rice.[117] Gunpowder and weapons were essential to maintaining the levels of violence among African states, yet they were also used against Portuguese Crown interests in raids organized by colonial agents.

[112] Luis Felipe de Alencastro, "The Economic Network of Portugal's Atlantic World," in *Portuguese Oceanic Expansion*, ed. Francisco Bethencourt and Diogo Ramada Curto (New York: Cambridge University Press, 2007), 118–19.

[113] Curto, *Enslaving Spirits*, 57–9; Curto, "Luso-Brazilian Alcohol and the Legal Slave Trade at Benguela," 352; Alencastro, "Economic Network," 119.

[114] IHGB, DL31,09, "Ofício de Fernando da Silva Correia, tenente regente, a d. Miguel António de Melo, [governador de Angola], comunicando o envio do mapa das pessoas de artilharia da Fortaleza de Novo Redondo, das imagens da igreja de Nossa Senhora da Conceição, pagamento dos sacerdotes, sobas, armamentos, dos moradores, batismos, casamentos e óbitos, prédios rústicos, gado e escravos existentes no Presídio Novo Redondo," October 25, 1797.

[115] AHU, Angola, caixa 89, doc. 25, October 25, 1798.

[116] AHU, Angola, caixa 62, doc. 42, May 22, 1779; and AHU, Angola, caixa 76, doc. 8, February 3, 1791. In the Gold Coast, Dutch soldiers received regular salaries, although they were low. See Harvey M. Feinberg, *Africans and Europeans in West Africa: Elminans and Dutchmen on the Gold Coast during the Eighteenth Century* (Philadelphia: American Philosophical Society, 1989), 39–40.

[117] AHU, Angola, caixa 62, doc. 88, November 12, 1779; AHU, Angola, caixa 63, doc. 3A, January 12, 1780; AHU, Angola, caixa 63, doc. 7, February 22, 1780; and AHU, Angola, caixa 71, doc. 60, November 15, 1786.

Trade Network in the Central Highlands

Beginning in the first half of the seventeenth century, Portuguese authorities tried to control the slave trade coming from the Benguela highlands. The fortress of Caconda was established in the 1680s, 180 km inland, and by the mid–eighteenth century it was transferred to a safer location in the region of Katala, another 40 km further inland.[118] The new Portuguese fortress of Caconda, now located 220 km inland, connected Benguela to the inland states of Ngalange, Mbailundu, and Viye, among others.[119] By the end of the eighteenth century, there were seventeen white, fifty-four mixed-race, and forty-four black residents in Caconda. The small number of European settlers demonstrated the weakness of the Portuguese territorial "conquest." Most of them engaged in trade and exercised official positions, such as António José Rodrigues, a white trader who lived in a compound with his son and 300 dependents, including nineteen slave men, twenty-nine slave women, and thirty-two slave children. Rodrigues was clearly an important trader, who also was responsible for producing food crops and raising cattle.[120] Other traders lived around the fortresses, such as Pedro Joaquim Ignácio, who lived in the territory of Kamburo. Francisco António da Glórias lived under the control of the *soba* of Kitata, and Jorge do Porto Ribeiro lived in Kalukembe. These traders opted to live apart from the colonial settlement, living among the "heathens without respecting the law and regulations."[121]

In the territory of Mbailundu, a Portuguese colonial official was appointed to regulate trade and provide direct communication between the governor in Benguela and the ruler of Mbailundu. In 1797, he made an inventory of the traders who lived under the *soba*'s control. Manoel José da Costa Arouca, Francisco José Cordeiro, and Manoel A. Sá were the only white traders established in Mbailundu at that time, and they probably already had established families because Arouca was listed with two children and Cordeiro with one. There is no mention of the names

[118] Biblioteca Nacional-Lisboa (BNL), cod. 8553, fl. 92–92v., August 14, 1768.
[119] Balsemão, "Concelho de Caconda," 48; João Francisco, "Explorações do sertão de Benguela. Derrota que fez o tenente de artilharia João Francisco Garcia," *Annaes Marítimos e Colonias* 4a série 6 (1844), 252; Deolinda Barrocas and Maria de Jesus Sousa, "As populações do hinterland do Benguela e a passagem das caravanas comerciais (1846–1860)," in *II Reunião Internacional de História da África* (São Paulo/Rio de Janeiro: CEA/USP /SDG Marinha, 1997), 96–8. See also Candido, "Trade, Slavery and Migration in the Interior of Benguela," 70–5.
[120] IHGB, DL.31,05, fl. 3v.–4, "NotQicias do Presidio de Caconda em Benguela," 1797.
[121] IHGB DL31,05, fl. 10, December 31, 1797.

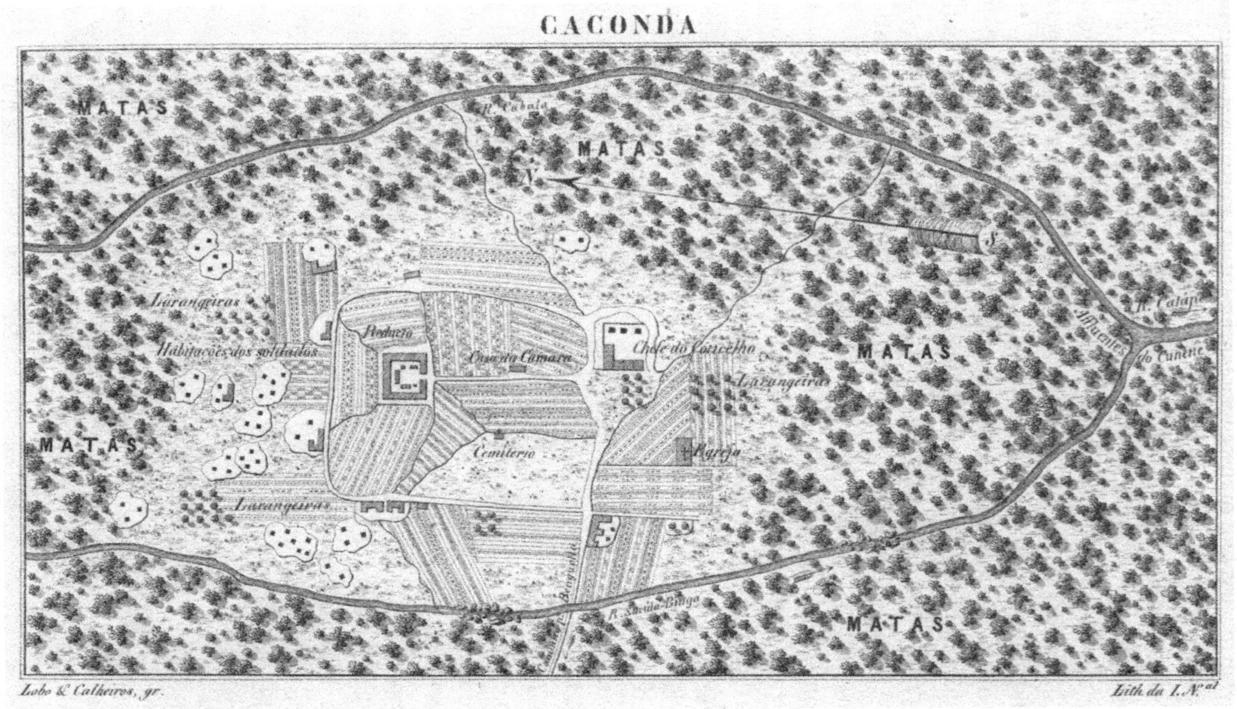

IMAGE 5. Caconda. (*Source:* AHU, Iconografia 001, doc. 267.)

of the mothers, yet their children were identified as *mulato*, indicating an African mother.[122] João da Costa Arouca was 10 years old, whereas Estevão José Cordeiro was 12 years old. Most of the other traders were listed as black or *mulato*.

African states traded in the highlands independently of the Portuguese fortress. The origin of the trade between the highland states was probably derived from the exchange of grains, salt, cattle, and other food products that predated the arrival of Europeans. Inland states had their own markets that could attract thousands of people from surrounding areas, and colonial officials were eager to have access to those markets. In 1771, Captain-Major José António Nogueira of Caconda reported that the *soba* of Humbe did not allow the entrance of itinerant traders into his market. Afraid of coastal traders, he forbade white merchants or their agents access to Humbe.[123] Later, Viye, Mbailundu, and Wambu prospered by exchanging textiles, alcohol, and other commodities obtained from coastal networks for slaves. In 1794, the *soba* of Mbailundu requested that *pombeiros* bring swords, textiles, hats, socks, shirts, flags, alcohol, paper, and stamps.[124] This list indicates the penetration of the Atlantic economy and the adoption of new ideas, including writing, as indicated by the paper request, and Western fashion, as shown by the request for shirts and hats. Other rulers also imported commodities and used them to show prestige and links to the Atlantic commerce. These examples indicate how the impact of the trans-Atlantic slave trade cannot simply be measured by the number of people exported from the continent. Its effects went beyond demographics, altering styles of dress, diet, and drinking habits and allowing for the introduction of new ideas and technologies. By 1797, the ruler of Viye was wearing cotton textiles wrapped around his waist with a leather belt. The textiles covered his pants. He also wore a shirt and a jacket, although he remained barefoot. His wife dressed in a loose dress made of cotton textiles, also cinched with a leather belt, although she was also barefoot.[125] Imported commodities changed highland fashion styles and drinking habits. By the early nineteenth century,

[122] IHGB, DL32,02.05, fl. 35, "Relação de António José Fernandes, capitão-mor, a Alexandre José Botelho de Vasconcelos, governador de Benguela, dos moradores e de seus filhos desta província (Bailundo)," 1798.

[123] IHGB, DL81,02.18, fl. 59–9v., June 22, 1771.

[124] AHU, cod. 1630, fl. 148, July 5, 1794; and AHU, cod. 1631, fl. 153, August 1, 1795.

[125] IHGB, DL29,17, "Notícia Geral dos Costumes da Província de Bihé, em Benguela, por Joao Napomuceno Correio, 1797," fl. 9, 1797. For the impact of imported textiles in Viye in the 1840s, see Heywood, "Production, Trade and Power," 36.

the explorer Edward Bowdich reported that African rulers in the areas around Benguela wrapped themselves in imported textiles. He also saw 120 military troops armed with muskets in the interior of Benguela.[126] In the 1820s, the *soba* of Viye controlled a market in his territory. He allowed the entrance of *pombeiros*, but he set prices, imposed taxes, and sold his own slaves. The market was in a square surrounded by houses and shops built by mixed-race traders, who exchanged imported goods for slaves who were held in storehouses.[127] Rulers also decided who could or could not enter their state to trade in slaves, and they controlled prices as well as the taxes that itinerant merchants had to pay.[128] In the 1860s, Silva Porto reported that the *soba* of Kipata kept requesting "*aguardente* to heal his throat. The old *soba* has [his throat] already burnt [by the firewater], and the alcohol does not affect him anymore. One day he will not wake up."[129] These reports indicate the fast adoption of imported goods and also reveal the political elites' dependence on luxury commodities imported from the Atlantic world. Inland rulers also competed to attract coastal traders and caravans, who generated more income and brought more imported goods. Slaves acquired in the inland markets were lined up in coffles and forced to walk the long distance to the coast. They carried any commodities acquired inland by the *pombeiros*, such as loads of beeswax, gum-copal, and even ivory tusks.[130]

The expansion of the trans-Atlantic slave trade and links to the Atlantic economy created a market for luxury goods, and rulers and traders displayed imported commodities to their subjects and their peers in order to solidify their power. Silva Porto described meeting a subordinate of the *soba* of Nganguela in 1858 who was dressed in a red baize textile (*pano de baeta*), a shirt and jacket of *chita* ("calico"), a headband of colorful beads, and a headdress of feathers. At his waist he carried a firearm and a sword.[131] It is clear that he was a ruler connected to long-distance trade and the luxury products introduced by Atlantic traders. Moreover, these examples reveal societies facing changes and adopting new ideas in order to adjust to the new order. Studies focused solely on demography tend to

---

[126] Thomas E. Bowdich, *Account of Discoveries of the Portuguese in the Interior of Angola and Mozambique* (Portland, ME: John Booth, 1824), 31–2.

[127] Douville, *Voyage au Congo et dans l'interieur de l'Afrique Equinoxiale*, 2, 121–2.

[128] Heywood, *Contested Power*, 12.

[129] Biblioteca da Sociedade de Geografica de Lisboa (BSGL), res. 2C6, vol. 2, May 12, 1861.

[130] IHGB, DL81,02.20, fl. 62–63, January 15, 1772.

[131] BSGL, res. 2C6, "Silva Porto, Apontamentos de um Portuense em África," vol. 2, Bié, October 25, 1860.

overlook these cultural and social changes and the violence they perpetrated in societies located miles away from the coast.

Portuguese Authorities and Their Participation in the Slave Trade

Unlike other places on the African continent, where European actions were limited to the coast, in West Central Africa, Portuguese traders and administrators were quite successful in establishing a foothold in African territory.[132] From the beginning of the Portuguese presence, they were involved in seizing Africans and enslaving them for a growing Atlantic market. On the expedition to conquer Benguela in early seventeenth century, Manoel Cerveira Pereira brought along António Pinto, an exiled man who had been condemned for his smuggling activities with the English. After the death of Cerveira Pereira, Pinto assumed the position of captain-major, the highest authority of the port.[133] Thus the colonization process in itself was guided by someone who had been involved in contraband. The isolation of Benguela favored the actions of individuals who sought speedy enrichment. The colonial policy of not paying regular salaries to lower-ranked military personal also contributed to the commercial activities of those in power. In 1626, the governor of Angola, Fernão Sousa, stated, "[T]he royal treasurer does not want to pay the salaries of officials.... The officials have to collect the funds necessary for their maintenance in Brazil," indicating their involvement in the slave trade. He added, "They cannot maintain themselves only with textiles," a reference to the use of textiles to pay the troops.[134] By the end of the eighteenth century, the situation had not changed. Elias Alexandre da Silva Corrêa mentioned that captains "did not receive any salary and had their greed [as slave traders] tolerated."[135]

Portuguese officials organized wars that resulted in the capture of large numbers of people. Yet most recent studies on the slave trade have focused on how slaves were generated in areas outside the control of European forces. In the process, scholars have underestimated the role of Portuguese agents – including many Brazilian-born individuals – in the processes of

---

[132] For references on how the slave trade operated elsewhere, see Searing, *West African Slavery*, 27–58; Lovejoy, *Transformations in Slavery*, 68–90; and Law, *Ouidah*, 126–38.
[133] AHU, Angola, caixa 2, doc. 104, June 18, 1626.
[134] AHU, Angola, caixa 2, doc. 103, July 16, 1626.
[135] Silva Corrêa, *História de Angola*, vol. 1, 25.

enslavement.[136] The emphasis on the involvement of some African elites in the Atlantic commerce, stressing African agency and participation in the global economy, has minimized the role of Portuguese agents in West Central Africa. And without the actions of Portuguese actors, including providing credit and bringing slave ships but also in organizing raids and promoting conflicts between autonomous rulers, slaving exports from Benguela certainly would have been lower. By the 1630s, under the command of Governor Lopo Soares Lasso, the Portuguese raided communities around Kilengues, on the edges of the central highlands, and by the 1650s, they were already at the Bembe area on the upper Catumbela River. These wars were not officially fought to acquire captives, but they were considered essential to maintaining Portuguese settlements and expanding internal trade networks.[137] Nonetheless, they generated a massive number of captives. Although the Portuguese sources are silent about slave departures from Benguela, Dutch ships were seen along the coast beginning in the mid-1620s, and slaves from Benguela were in Havana and Lima, as seen earlier in this chapter. A few years later, the Dutch occupied the town, signaling its importance to the trans-Atlantic slave trade.

[136] Daniel Domingues da Silva, for example, has claimed that "they [the Portuguese] had little control over these conflicts," when referring to nineteenth-century wars in the Benguela highlands. See Daniel B. Domingues da Silva, "Crossroads: Slave Frontiers of Angola, c. 1780–1867," PhD dissertation, Emory University, 2011, 113. For studies focused on slave-supply regions, see Sean Stilwell, *Paradoxes of Power: The Kano "Mamluks" and Male Royal Slavery in the Sokoto Caliphate, 1804–1903* (Portsmouth, NH: Heinemann, 2004); Paul E. Lovejoy, "Plantations in the Economy of the Sokoto Caliphate," *Journal of African History* 19, no. 3 (1978): 341–68; Martin A. Klein, "Social and Economic Factors in the Muslim Revolution in Senegambia," *Journal of African History* 13, no. 3 (1972): 419–41; Walter Hawthorne, *Planting Rice and Harvesting Slaves: Transformations Along the Guinea-Bissau Coast, 1400–1900* (Portsmouth, NH: Heinemann, 2003). For studies that explore the role of Portuguese officials in enslaving, see Curto, "Struggling against Enslavement"; José C. Curto, "Un Butin Illégitime: Razzias d'esclaves et relations luso-africaines dans la région des fleuves Kwanza et Kwango en 1805," in *Déraison, Esclavage et Droit: Les fondements idéologiques et juridiques de la traite négrière et de l'esclavage*, ed. Isabel de Castro Henriques and Louis Sala-Molins (Paris: Unesco, 2002), 315–27; José C. Curto, "The Story of Nbena, 1817–1820: Unlawful Enslavement and the Concept of 'Original Freedom' in Angola," in *Trans-Atlantic Dimensions of Ethnicity in the African Diaspora*, ed. Paul E. Lovejoy and David V. Trotman (London: Continuum, 2003), 44–64; Mariana P. Candido, "African Freedom Suits and Portuguese Vassal Status: Legal Mechanisms for Fighting Enslavement in Benguela, Angola, 1800–1830," *Slavery & Abolition* 32, no. 3 (2011): 447–59.

[137] Roquinaldo Ferreira, "O Brasil e a Arte da Guerra em Angola (sécs XVII e XVIII)," *Estudos Historicos* 39 (2007): 5; Delgado, *Reino de Benguela*, 120–3, 214–26; and Curto, "Luso-Brazilian Alcohol," 353–4.

Governors abused their power and imposed arbitrary taxes, such as demanding one slave for every ten traded in the markets. They also requested more slaves from the *sobas* than they were obliged to offer according to the vassal treaties. By 1652, the Crown judge (*ouvidor*) and treasury commissioner (*provedor da fazenda*) of Angola, Bento Teixeira Saldanha, complained about the behavior of captains and the governor who "use[s] any pretext to attack the heathens, with the only intention of capturing and later selling people." For Saldanha, the behavior of colonial officials was dubious because he believed that they should act as "the lords of the land, rather than run over the laws of nature."[138] To avoid problems such as this, in 1653, the treasury commissioner of Angola prohibited the travel of white men to the hinterland, expecting that Portuguese traders, including officials, would remain in Benguela waiting for slave coffles to come from the interior. Captains of fortresses in the interior were ordered to arrest any white men wandering in the hinterland. Bento Teixeira Saldanha stated that *sobas* in the interior of Benguela were in such a desperate situation that some were forced to trade away freeborn subjects and even wives under pressure from Benguela officials who were acting as traders.[139] It is difficult to determine the root of the problem. In several instances, soldiers complained about the lack of payment. In 1664, for example, António Jorge de Góes, captain-major of Benguela, declared that he had not received his salary for four months and did not have the means to maintain himself in the port. A few months later, in April 1665, he complained once again about the lack of payment.[140] In such cases, officials turned to raiding operations as a way to overcome their lack of money. Taking prisoners to be enslaved was one of the goals of raids organized in and around Benguela. Soldiers divided captives and later sold them, compensating the lack of a regular salary and participating directly in the capture of people and their enslavement.[141]

Authorities in Luanda recognized that some wars were motivated by personal interest and not for the gain of the colonial enterprise. In the 1680s, Luis Lobo da Silva organized an expedition to punish the *jaga*

---

[138] AHU, Angola, caixa 5, doc. 101, December 14, 1652. See also Esteves, "Para o Estudo do Tráfico de Escravos," 80.

[139] AHU, Angola, caixa 5, doc. 108, April 5, 1653. See also, Esteves, "Tráfico de Escravos de Angola," 81–2.

[140] AHU, Angola, caixa 8, doc. 50, October 14, 1664; and caixa 8, doc. 97, April 14, 1665.

[141] Mattos, "Black Troops," 13; and José C. Curto, "Experiences of Enslavement in West Central Africa," *Histoire Sociale/Social History* 41, no. 82 (2008): 395.

of Kakonda, who had attacked the Portuguese fortress.[142] Decades later, probably motivated by expansion of the slave trade in Benguela, the captain of Caconda, and the governor of Benguela, Manoel Simão, joined forces and assaulted the populations around the Benguela and Caconda fortresses. They justified their actions stating that the Ndombe and Kakonda represented a threat to regional security. By then the ruler of Kakonda had been replaced and subjected to Portuguese control. He and his subjects were vassals of the Portuguese, and therefore, they were people who should be protected and not attacked. The governor of Angola and the war council did not accept their explanation and accused them of causing the uprising.[143] The situation continued to be adversarial around Benguela during the 1720s, probably related to the arrival of Brazilian traders along the coast. The officer António Vieira Guimarães was convicted and sentenced to prison in December of 1727 for his involvement in and provocation of the revolt among the Kakonda and Ndombe. Yet, despite his conviction, Francisco de Sousa da Fonseca, captain of Benguela, organized more raids in 1729. Later, he was removed from office, arrested, and sent to Lisbon in consequence of his open involvement in capture of slaves and their export.[144]

Men on the spot in Benguela made use of violence and promoted local disputes to obtain slaves in the interior, which led to ongoing disputes between Angola and Benguela authorities throughout the slave-trade era.[145] Thus, in 1755, Captain Manoel Pires Jucele sent troops to Kizemba, where they destroyed villages, murdered people, took captives, stole goods, and burned houses.[146] Thus, unlike in West Africa, where Europeans remained on the coast, in Benguela's interior, Portuguese officials were among the

---

[142] AHU, cod. 545, fl. 36v. and fl. 43, March 14, 1688. See also Cruz e Silva, "The Saga of Kakonda and Kilengues," 245–59; Curto, "Un butin illégitime," 315–27; Curto, "A Restituição dos 10.000 Súditos Ndongo," 191–4; John K. Thornton, "The Art of War in Angola, 1575–1680," *Comparative Studies in Society and History* 30 (1988): 360–78.

[143] AHU, caixa 21, doc. 51, September 2, 1721

[144] Pascoal Leite de Aguair, *Administração Colonial Portuguesa no Congo, em Angola e em Benguela* (Lisbon: Sociedade Histórica da Independência de Portugal, 2006), 1, 125.

[145] Silva Corrêa, *Historia de Angola*, 1, 36; see also Ana Paula Tavares and Catarina Madeira Santos, "Uma Leitura Africana das Estratégias Políticas e Jurídicas. Textos dos e para os Dembos," in *Africae Monumenta. A Apropriação da Escrita pelos Africanos* (Lisbon: IICT, 2002), 510–34; Curto, "Experiences of Enslavement in West Central Africa," 381–415; and José C. Curto "The Story of Nbena, 1817–1820: Unlawful Enslavement and the Concept of 'Original Freedom' in Angola," in *Trans-Atlantic Dimensions of Ethnicity in the African Diaspora*, ed. Paul E. Lovejoy and David V. Trotman (London: Continuum, 2003), 43–64.

[146] AHU, Angola, caixa 40, doc. 61, before September 27, 1755.

driving forces behind the enslavement of Africans. In situations such as those described earlier, survivors of these attacks were forced to look for protection from other African rulers or Portuguese officials. To administrate irregularities, Governor Francisco Inocêncio de Sousa Coutinho issued a series of decrees in 1765 regulating the duties of captains in the interior. The regulations stated that captains and other authorities in the hinterland had a commitment to maintain peace and protect vassals of the Portuguese Crown. It was the duty of the governors to control the slave trade by maintaining peace and assuring that no illegal slave embarkation occurred. The governors' actions were perceived as fundamental to facilitate trade. Yet, more interested in assuring their own profits from the slave trade, they participated in and even organized punitive wars and raids to gather slaves who could be sold.[147] Distance from Portuguese authorities and the difficulties of transportation, combined with the lack of a strong military presence, allowed officers to act without any serious threat of interference from Luanda.

The organization of the *guerras pretas* ("black troops") in the 1700s was a feature of the Portuguese presence in West Central Africa that intertwined the public and private interests of Portuguese authorities. Under the leadership of colonial officials, these troops, composed mainly of soldiers provided by the *sobas*, favored the expansion of warfare and enslavement.[148] Punitive wars became a strategy by which colonial officials engaged directly in slaving activities. In the name of protection and geopolitics, they raided autonomous states, capturing a large number of people, shared the war booty, and sold the captives to slavers in the port. In 1779, the governor of Angola, Don António de Lencastre, approved the request of the captain of Caconda to retaliate for an attack on the

---

[147] AHNA, cod. 443, fl. 117, February 17, 1803; and Douville, *Voyage au Congo et dans l'interieur de l'Afrique*, 1, 16. See also Carlos Couto, "Regimento de Governo Subalterno de Benguela," *Studia* 45 (1981), 288–9; Couto, *Os Capitães-Mores em Angola* (Lisbon: Instituto de Investigação Científica e Tropical, 1972), 323–33; Silva, "Saga of Kakonda and Kilengues," 245–6; Boxer, *O Império Marítimo Português* (São Paulo: Companhia das Letras, 2002), 338; Ferreira, "Transforming Atlantic Slaving," 75–7; and Curto, *Enslaving Spirits*, 94.

[148] Mattos, "Black Troops," 6–29; See also Ferreira, "O Brasil e a Arte da Guerra," 4; Raimundo José da Cunha Matos, *Compêndio Histórico das Possessões de Portugal na África* (Rio de Janeiro: Arquivo Histórico Nacional, 1963), 271; Alberto Costa e Silva, *Manilha e o Libambo: A África e a Escravidão, de 1500–1700* (Rio de Janeiro: Nova Fronteira, 2002), 441; and Linda Heywood, "Portuguese into African: The Eighteenth-Century Central African Background to Atlantic Creole Cultures," in *Central Africans and Cultural Transformations in the American Diaspora* (Cambridge University Press, 2002), 106.

sobado of Fende and advised him to safeguard the "royal fifth."[149] The collection of the royal fifth also opened space for irregularities. Captains and leaders of punitive expeditions were in charge of collecting royal duties, one-fifth of everything apprehended. Commodities and slaves were sold in the market and the income sent to the Crown. Authorities coveted the captives and reported only those considered less valuable by trans-Atlantic standards as part of the royal fifth. Usually people with physical disabilities and very young children were designated as part of the royal tax, and soldiers and captains seized the most valuable captives for their own profit. In an inventory from 1738, women and children composed most of the royal fifth. Of the seventy-seven people listed, there were twelve men, including an old man with an injured leg and another with a wounded eye. Young, healthy women and especially young men, highly valued by slave traders along the coast, appear to have remained in the hands of the soldiers engaged in the war. [150] Captives consigned to the royal fifth generated income for the Crown. In 1756, two different groups of 132 and 34 slaves were sent to Benguela within days of each other as the royal fifth. In 1760, another 166 slaves were sent as the royal fifth to Benguela. In both cases, women composed the majority of these allotments, although their ages are not known.[151] These examples, along with others, highlight the role of Portuguese authorities in raids and the capture of Africans around Benguela.

By the end of eighteenth century, several reports indicate a heightening of violence, probably linked to the increasing volume of slaves exported from Benguela. In 1791, the governor of Angola, Martinho de Melo e Castro, stressed his discontent with the behavior of captains assigned to the fortresses in the interior. According to him,

Why send troops to fight in the interior, if the commander [of fortresses], and following his example, all of his subordinates are simply thieves, who intend to destroy [the African rulers], punishing the poorest and privileging the wealthiest, although the last were the rebels and the first were the faithful vassals.[152]

Martinho de Melo e Castro's remarks were based on events that took place in the hinterland of Benguela months earlier. Captains of *presídios*

---

[149] AHNA, cod. 81, fl. 118–120, January 30, 1779.
[150] AHU, caixa 30, doc. 90, April 29, 1738. This inventory is reproduced in Miller, *Way of Death*, xii–xiii.
[151] AHU, Angola, caixa 40A, doc. 130, April 20, 1756; and AHU, Angola, caixa 43, doc. 106, October 23, 1760. For the interest of authorities in the royal fifth, see AHU, Angola, caixa 70, doc. 7, March 15, 1785.
[152] AHNA, cod. 440, fl. 7v., June 21, 1791.

in the interior engaged in disputes with the *sobas* of Kiaka, Ganda, and Bongo in 1791 that led to attacks and the subsequent enslavement of their subjects.[153] In 1795, Portuguese forces attacked the *soba* of Sokoval, located near the fortress of Caconda[154] and, in the next year, raided the people located at Kakombo, under the protection of the *soba* of Sokoval.[155] African rulers reported the actions of Portuguese captains whom they perceived as abusive. The *soba* of Sokoval, for example, reported to the governor of Benguela, Alexandre Botelho de Vasconcelos, that the captain-major of Quilengues, Joaquim Vieira de Andrade, had "threatened the peace of the interior" when he attacked his subordinate ruler, the *soba* of Kakombo. The *soba* of Kakombo in fact requested that Vasconcelos assign new land to his people because he feared the actions of Captain Andrade.[156] The irregularities of Andrade's actions were limited not only to the raid, but he also defrauded the Crown. Although Captain Andrade had kidnapped more than thirty people from the *soba* of Kakombo, he dispatched only three slaves as the royal fifth, instead of the six that he was required to send.[157] The actions of Benguela authorities demonstrate their involvement in the slaving operations and in the expansion of violence and abuse. Violence and the resulting insecurity were effective mechanisms for increasing the number of captives in other parts of the continent.[158] Benguela was not an exception, and its high level of insecurity and the corruption of Portuguese officials were reflected in the large number of captives available. The trans-Atlantic slave trade in Benguela knew its highest point in the 1790s, when 91,397 slaves left through the port.[159]

Portuguese authorities in Angola discussed strategies to prevent the involvement of colonial officials in slaving actions in the hinterland of

[153] AHU, cod. 1628, fl. 6ov., August 16, 1791.
[154] AHNA, cod. 441, fl. 15, July 27, 1796.
[155] AHNA, cod. 443, fl. 8, September 22, 1796.
[156] AHNA, cod. 443, fl. 7–7v, September 22, 1796. See also Cruz e Silva, "Saga of Kakonda and Kilengues," 254.
[157] AHNA, cod. 443, fl. 8. September 22, 1796.
[158] For some examples from other parts of Angola, see Beatrix Heintze, "Angola nas Garras do Tráfico de Escravos: As Guerras Angolanas do Ndongo (1611–1630)," *Revista Internacional de Estudos Africanos* 1 (1984): 11–59; Miller, *Way of Death:* 105–39; Joseph C. Miller, "Angola Central e Sul por Volta de 1840," *Estudos Afro-Asiáticos* 32 (1997): 7–54; Thornton, *Africa and Africans in the Making of the Atlantic World*, 98–125; Jan Vansina, "Ambaca Society and the Slave Trade c. 1760–1845," *Journal of African History* 46 (2005): 1–27.
[159] *Transatlantic Slave Trade Database*; and Domingues da Silva, "The Coastal Origins of Slaves Leaving Angola."

Benguela. Dom António de Lencastre (1772–9) and Dom Miguel António de Melo (1797–1802) stressed that wars and attacks on African populations in the interior of Benguela would diminish if the captains and the black troops in the interior were not entitled to share the booty acquired in the assaults, including people and cattle. According to the governor, Portuguese troops promoted such attacks with the specific intention of profiting from them, provoking African rulers to retaliate, and perpetuating an endless cycle of violence.[160] To avoid such situations, the governor of Angola proclaimed an edict in 1799 prohibiting the involvement of administrative authorities in the slave trade, attempting to delimit the duties and tasks of both governors and their direct subordinates. The regulations were strict on how governors and Portuguese authorities should protect the trade and set limits in the involvement in trading activities, reinstating prohibitions that had existed since the early seventeenth century and demonstrating the fragility of Portuguese power in Benguela. Despite such occasional prohibitions, conditions were such that traders could benefit from the commerce without much interference from the government of Angola.[161]

The accusations between the governors of Angola and Benguela also reflected the way authorities referred to the officials located in the fortresses inland. When they faced accusations of misconduct, the governors of Benguela referred to the captains in the hinterland *presídios* as individuals of bad character who inflicted hostilities on both traders and the African population.[162] The men on the spot denied their involvement and blamed their subordinates for the raids. At least one captain was threatened with removal from office in 1797,[163] whereas two others were forcibly relieved of their duties in 1818 and 1828, respectively.[164] By the end

[160] D. Miguel António de Mello, "Relatório do Governador de Angola D. Miguel António de Melo," *Boletim da Sociedade de Geografia de Lisboa*, 5a series, no. 8 (1885), 554.

[161] The first regulations were sent to Governor Alexandre Botelho de Vasconcelos in 1799, when Benguela was subject to the orders of the governor of Angola. AHU, Angola, caixa 93A, doc. 11, November 6, 1799; the Queen of Portugal, however, revoked the regulation in August 1798. See Couto, "Regimento de Governo," 291. See also Ferreira, "Transforming Atlantic Slaving," 75–7; and Curto, *Enslaving Spirits*, 94.

[162] AHNA, cód. 441, fl. 24v., February 28, 1796; AHNA, cod.442, fl. 34v., April 25, 1797; AHU, Angola, caixa 125, doc. 67, August 31, 1812; AHNA, cod. 446, fl. 96, October 7, 1816; and AHNA, cod. 447, fl. 136v., July 8, 1820.

[163] This was the case of Captain João da Costa Frade; see AHNA, cod.443, fl. 19, August 14, 1797.

[164] These were, respectively, Interim Commander António Ezequiel de Carvalho and Lieutenant Colonel Domingos Pereira Dinis; AHNA, cod. 447, fl. 45, January 9, 1819; and AHNA, cod. 508, fl. 134, August 23, 1828.

of 1809, Viscount João Rodrigues de Sá e Melo of Anadia, secretary of the navy and overseas departments, complained of the scandalous behavior of the captains and regents of the fortress *presídios* against *sobas* allied with the Portuguese state, "including arresting them to obtain profit for their release."[165]

Governors sometimes tried to settle disputes without deploying troops.[166] In 1812, Francisco de Moraes, an auxiliary in the fort of Catumbela, asked Governor Leiria in Benguela for authorization to raid in the territory of the *soba* of Lumbo.[167] The reasons for his request are not clear. Weeks later, the trader Manoel Oliveira, who had been robbed by people from Ngalange, asked the governor for permission to seize people in retribution for his loss.[168] According to his report, subjects of the *soba* of Ngalange had stolen the textiles that he intended to trade in the interior. In both cases, Governor João Leiria refused to sanction any action that would result in the enslavement of free people. He considered that some merchants had committed theft and that certain regents had perpetrated injustices, thereby provoking the *soba* of Ngalange to "rebel." Instead of sanctioning the raids, the governor reproached the regent of Caconda and censured the violence that had been committed, unaware or preferring not to acknowledge that violence was inherent to the Portuguese presence in the region and the continuation of the trans-Atlantic slave trade.[169] Although unusual, this incident does indicate that occasionally there was concern for law and order that might actually have inhibited the slaving, yet it also reveals that violence was so widespread that the men on the spot, the colonial agents, were incapable of controling it.

Attacks on important African *sobados* were carefully planned and demanded the participation of several authorities. In theory, these wars targeted rulers involved in social disruption, such as those who did not pay tribute or those who did not respect Portuguese authorities. Nonetheless, it is clear that potential profits, often short term, also stimulated Portuguese officials. In 1814, for example, the captain of Caconda

---

[165] AHU, Angola, cod. 551, fl. 45–48v., January 30, 1810.
[166] The governor tried to send gifts or official representatives to solve conflicts. Examples of these can be seen in AHNA, cod. 507, fl. 36v.–37, May 24, 1814; AHNA, cod. 510, fl. 31v., September 24, 1847, and fl. 82v., May 1, 1848.
[167] AHNA, cod. 440, fl. 22v., requisition n. 14, July 15, 1812.
[168] AHNA, cod. 440, fl. 27v., requisition n. 76, August 7, 1812.
[169] AHNA, cod. 507, fl. 9v.–10, September 28, 1812; George Tams, *Visita as Possessões Portuguesas na costa occidental d'Africa* (Porto: Tipografia do Calvario, 1850), 1, 103.

organized a punitive war against the *sobas* of Viye, Mbailundu, Wambu, and Ngalange, the most important suppliers of slaves.[170] The governors of Angola and Benguela approved this action because it would generate the royal fifth. For other officials and traders, the possibility of seizing people almost guaranteed high profits from their sale, and they did not hesitate in employing the colonial army. The perpetrators of raids even evaded paying the fifth and thereby increased their gains. People often acted outside the law without moral restraint or even punishment. In 1817, after reports of instability in the *sobado* of Mbailundu, Captain José Velasco Galiano forwarded only two boys and three women with two babies as the royal fifth, even though it is probable that Portuguese forces had captured more than thirty people during the raid on Mbailundu.[171]

Before 1820, there are several reports of the involvement of Portuguese officials in the slave trade. Thereafter, however, documents concerning their involvement are scarce. The silence may well have arisen as a result of the reorganization of the slave trade in anticipation of legal termination of the trade in 1830. Several reports indicate that high-ranking authorities in Benguela acted in connivance with smugglers operating along the coast.[172] The development and expansion of the trans-Atlantic slave trade in this region were directly linked to the actions of greedy and corrupt officials. Collaborating authorities replaced those who had initially tried to prevent illegal commerce.[173] News of the impending end of the trade spread throughout the Benguela hinterland by 1827.[174] Portuguese agents and Brazilian traders continued to participate actively in the commerce despite the prohibitions for either direct or indirect involvement in the slave trade of governors, regents, judges, and other high-ranking officers. In Benguela, authorities were afraid that the neighboring *sobas* would organize a revolt and kill traders.[175] Inevitably, the situation led to conflicts between the metropolitan authorities, the Luanda-based governor,

---

[170] AHNA, cod. 446, fl. 2–5, August 24, 1814.

[171] AHNA, cod. 446, fl. 10, January 31, 1817.

[172] AHNA, cod. 440, fl. 1–2, July 14, 1791; AHU, cod. 551, fl. 45–53, January 30, 1810; and AHU, Angola, Correspondência dos Governadores, pasta 2, April 8, 1836; John Purdy, *The New Sailing Directory for the Ethiopic or Southern Atlantic Ocean* (London: R. H. Laurie, 1844), 414–15, 618–19; Tams, *Visita as Possessões Portuguesas*, 1, 111. See also Ferreira, "Dos Sertões ao Atlântico," 165; and David Eltis, *Economic Growth and the Ending of the Transatlantic Slave Trade* (New York: Oxford University Press, 1987), 253.

[173] *Almanak Statistico da Provincia de Angola e suas dependencies para o ano de 1852* (Luanda: Imprensa do Governo, 1851), xxi.

[174] AHNA, cod. 508, fl. 111–111v., September 2, 1827.

[175] AHU, Angola, caixa 164, doc. 75, December 1, 1829.

and the men on the spot in Benguela, including the governor, captains, local magistrates, and soldiers, as well as traders and African rulers. The Benguela governor also had to deal with private interests, as happened to the Governor António Manoel de Noronha, who was sent back to Lisbon in 1839 as a consequence of his opposition to continuation of the slave trade.[176]

Tribute and Conflicts with African Rulers

At Luanda and at strategic locations inland, Portuguese authorities established public markets to regulate trade, promote fair practices, and restrict the activities of the *pombeiros*, who were thought to be disruptive and disrespectful of Portuguese legal restrictions.[177] By contrast, in the region around Benguela, the *feiras* were in territories controlled by African rulers, and Luso-African traders circulated freely, interacted with the local authorities, and even engaged in slave raids in the interior.[178] Traders at Benguela who were dissatisfied with the local Portuguese authorities complained to the governor of Angola, whereas the governor of Benguela frequently insisted that the traders themselves were at the root of the insecurity that damaged trade, with different actors pushing the blame onto someone else.[179] In some parts of the hinterland, people fled whenever caravans from Benguela were sighted for fear of possible raids or traders ready to kidnap them.[180] Private merchants could form caravans, whether they were Portuguese or not, but Portuguese officials were legally prohibited from either direct or indirect involvement in the slave trade. This restriction applied to governors, regents, judges, and military officers.[181] Instructions sent to officers stationed in the interior

---

[176] Lopes de Lima, *Ensaios sobre a Statistica*, 133; and *Almanak Statistico*, 21.

[177] AHU, caixa 95, doc. 9, March 10, 1800; see also Joseph Miller. "Some Aspects of the Commercial Organization of Slaving at Luanda, Angola – 1760–1830," in *The Uncommon Market: Essays in the Economic History of the Atlantic Slave Trade*, ed. Henry Gemery and Jan Hogendorn (New York: Academic Press, 1979), 77–106; Herbert Klein also stresses the mobility of Luso-African traders in the Benguela region; see Klein, *Atlantic Slave Trade*, 65–6.

[178] AHU, caixa 36, doc. 6, March 16, 1748; and AHNA, cod. 82, fl. 61v., July 17, 1787; see also Heywood, *Contested Power in Angola*, 12; and Curto, "Un butin illégitime."

[179] AHU, caixa 124, doc. 53; for another report blaming *pombeiros* for disturbing commerce, see AHU, caixa 129, doc. 47, October 5, 1814.

[180] Arquivo Histórico Militar (AHM), 2-2-1-7, "Cópia do exército que o senhor general dirigiu castigar o rebelde Marques de Mussulo e seus sequezes que foram invasores dos dominios da sua magestade," 1790–1791. See also Affonso de E. Taunay, *Subsídios para a história do Tráfico aAricano no Brasil* (São Paulo: Imprensa Oficial do Estado, 1941), 212.

[181] AHU, cod. 551, fl. 45–53, January 30, 1810.

of Benguela stressed the importance of maintaining cordial relations with the *sobas* so that commerce would not suffer from diplomatic blunders, denying the inherent violence of territorial conquest.[182] More interested in ensuring their own profits from the slave trade, Portuguese officials stationed in Benguela acted in order to maximize their profits, including creating new taxes and obligations not approved by Lisbon authorities. They also disguised these new obligations to avoid reprehension and punishment.

The Portuguese authorities profited from the trade by imposing heavy taxation on African rulers and by requesting gifts. *Sobas* had to send slaves and cattle to the authorities disguised as personal gifts, in addition to the regular payment of taxes and tribute. The gift exchange was a common way to avoid conflict with the metropolitan administration, which prohibited the involvement of colonial officials in the slave trade, and to gain some political and economic advantage. Governors were not the only ones to receive gifts. Captains, regents, and soldiers in the *presídios* also had access to presents from *sobas*, a practice that recalls gift exchanges during the ancient regime. The regent of Caconda, for example, received seven slaves from the *soba* of Ngalange in 1763.[183] In 1770, the *soba* of Humbe sent gifts to the governor of Benguela with his traders who were moving a slave coffle to port. The *pombeiros* from Humbe who arrived at Benguela felt obliged to offer gifts to authorities in order to conduct business in peace, indicating these were not "true gifts," as defined by Pierre Bourdieu, but a disguised tribute imposed on Humbe *pombeiros*.[184] True gifts are those offered without the perspective of a counteroffer, and as many cases indicated, this situation was apparently not the case between Portuguese and rulers in West Central Africa. In the Kingdom of Kongo in the sixteenth century, for example, the King of Kongo offered slaves as gifts to the King and Queen of Portugal, to a Portuguese envoy, and even to relatives of a major land grantee from São Tomé and in exchange

---

[182] AHNA, cod. 81, fl. 14v.–15, July 2, 1777; AHU, cod. 448, fl. 31v., January 11, 1823; and AHU, cod. 449, fl. 23v., January 28, 1825. See also Couto, "Regimento do Governo," 284–94.

[183] AHU, Angola, caixa 46, doc. 31, May 30, 1763. On the exchange of gifts between Portuguese and African authorities as a practice in the ancient regime, see Silvia H. Lara, "Palmares, Cuacu e as Perspectivas de Liberdade," in *Trabalho Livre, Trabalho Escravo*, ed. Douglas Cole Libby and Júnia Ferreira Furtado (São Paulo: Annablume, 2006), 361–81.

[184] Biblioteca Nacional do Rio de Janeiro (BNRJ), I-28, 28, 28, "Informação que dá João Pilarta da Silva ao capitão mor de Benguela José Viera de Araújo da viagem que fez por terra a Cabo Negro em companhia de José dos Santos no Ano de 1770."

received priests, masons, and clothing.[185] John Thornton, however, does not regard these transactions as a disguised trade or even as a form of coercive engagement but rather as a simple generous gift offering. Yet gift exchange is an important feature of kinship-based systems, where the temporal aspect is crucial in the process of exchange. According to Pierre Bourdieu, gifts cannot be returned immediately, as seems to have happened in Kongo and the Benguela interior. The lapse of time between gift offering and reciprocation reinforced the power relationship between the donor and the recipient and maintained their connection over time.[186] Obligation and lapse of time had to be observed; otherwise, it was not a gift exchange but was simply trade. Through these offerings, colonial authorities had regular access to captives without having to engage directly in raids. Captives offered as gifts were sold in the market in Benguela to any interested buyer. The money acquired in these transactions stayed in the hands of the colonial officials because it was not officially declared as tribute. Probably for the ruler who provided slaves there was not a clear difference between gifts and tribute, and for this reason, I grouped both in this section.

Another source of slaves was through the payment of tribute, although in such situations the money nominally belonged to the Portuguese Crown and not to individuals. Tribute payment usually included slaves. In 1744, an unnamed *soba* dispatched fifty-two adult slaves, eleven children, and five infants plus cattle to the governor of Benguela as tribute.[187] The necessity of offering gifts and paying tribute inevitably provoked violence in the interior. African *sobas* had to engage in wars, raids, or kidnapping to obtain captives. Yet, as gifts, the slaves sent by *sobas* to the authorities in Benguela were appropriated for personal gain. In 1794, for example, the *soba* of Mbailundu sent thirteen slaves and twelve heads of cattle to the governor of Benguela. One woman and two of the animals perished during the journey, but the governor readily accepted the gifts, expressing his satisfaction with the good condition of the slaves. In return, the governor forwarded textiles, swords, seven hats, socks, shirts, flags, alcohol, paper, stamps, guns, and gunpowder to the *soba*.[188] These gifts, in turn,

[185] John K. Thornton, "African Political Ethics and the Slave Trade," in *Abolitionism and Imperialism in Britain, Africa, and the Atlantic*, ed. Derek R. Peterson (Athens: Ohio University Press, 2010), 41–3.

[186] Bourdieu, *Pascalian Meditations*, 191–6.

[187] AHU, caixa 34, doc. 45, December 9, 1744.

[188] AHU, Angola, cod. 1630, fl. 148, July 5, 1794; and AHU, Angola, cod. 1631, fl. 153, August 1, 1795.

prompted the *soba* of Mbailundu to send another thirty slaves toward the end of 1794.[189] Disguised as reciprocal gifts, this exchange in fact was a trade in slaves, an activity the governor was not allowed to engage in; such subterfuge had been practiced since the beginning of the Portuguese presence in West Central Africa.

The practice of *sobas* sending slaves as tribute was an operation that blended public and private interests in a sometimes shadowy way. In most cases, soldiers accompanied the slave coffles that took the royal fifth to Benguela, and sometimes merchants made use of soldiers to conduct slaves to the coast. Traders protested official involvement in the slave trade, especially their assistance in moving captives to the coast.[190] In 1796, for example, Captain Regilde of the fortress of Caconda sent two soldiers and a trader with fifty slaves, including children and infants, for sale in Benguela. One slave died during the journey, but the remaining forty-nine were put up for sale. However, no one in Benguela showed interest in buying them because they were weak. Eventually, the governor of Benguela ordered the slaves put on the *Galizia* for Luanda to be sold there.[191]

Portuguese authorities participated actively in slaving operations in the interior of Benguela. Punitive wars and the payment of tribute were opportunities for soldiers, captains, and governors to profit from the slave trade. Through these actions, they complemented their salaries or generated an income because low-ranking officials did not receive regular pay. Blending official activities with private interests, administrators and soldiers had an advantage over traders stationed on the coast because they acted on behalf of the colonial state and could recruit soldiers to protect their caravans.

Conclusion

Location made Benguela an important slave port. Slaves, minerals, and other commodities attracted traders from different parts of the Portuguese empire, who, with the know-how of local Africans, transformed it from a small port to one of the most important places of embarkation of slaves on the coast of Africa. Foreign merchants and colonial

---

[189] AHU, Angola, cod. 1631, fl. 235v., December 14, 1795.

[190] See, for example, the case of António Pires Lousada, captain of Quilengues, AHNA, cod. 442, fl. 143, October 19, 1800.

[191] AHNA, cod. 442, fl. 13, August 11, 1796; AHNA, cod. 443, fl. 4v., August 15, 1796; and AHU, Angola, cod. 1632, fl. 136, October 12, 1796.

authorities stationed there provided the credit for itinerant traders who connected the coast to the hinterland markets. Along the coast and inland, Luso-African traders and rulers organized *feiras* and caravans that brought slaves from the highlands to the coast. The same traders carried imported commodities to the interior. While slaves, ivory, wax, animal skins, and plumes left through the port of Benguela, textiles, gunpowder, weapons, clothes, and paper were imported. These goods were consumed in the town of Benguela and in the inland states. Diet and fashion changed as new imported foods and Asian textiles were incorporated into local lifestyles, stressing the social impact of the Atlantic commerce. In addition to the negative impact of the demographic drain, the trans-Atlantic slave trade led to the adoption of new values, which resulted in dependency on imported goods. By the mid–nineteenth century, commodities that were produced elsewhere were consumed in regions more than 300 km inland, revealing the prevailing force of the trans-Atlantic slave trade.

From 1700 to 1850, an estimated 679,000 African slaves left from this coastal town. The actual number is certainly higher, considering that slave departure estimates before 1700 are not available and evasion and illegal slaving were widespread in Benguela and its interior. We might not be able to quantify the number of people who left Benguela before 1699, but their existence in the Americas challenges the current estimates of the slave trade. The presence of European vessels on the littoral of Benguela and of Benguela slaves in the Americas in the seventeenth century indicate that Benguela was integrated into the Atlantic economy earlier than previously recognized. Besides the slaves who left from the port, an unknown number of slaves were retained in Benguela, as seen in Chapter 2, and in its immediate interior.

The trans-Atlantic slave trade consolidated links between Brazil and Benguela. A bilateral trade developed in the South Atlantic, although the metropolis exercised control over the trade through the collection of taxes. Links between Brazil and Benguela went beyond the slave trade, as seen in Chapter 2. People born in Brazil were sent to Benguela as colonial agents, administrators, and soldiers. They became dynamic auxiliary agents of the Portuguese empire and enjoyed many privileges. Alongside their Portuguese peers, they provoked conflicts and instability around Benguela, which resulted in a large number of war captives. Administrators and military personnel participated actively in raids and wars, blending official and private business. Cases explored in this chapter show how captains, governors, and soldiers became a source of conflict and violence in the interior of Benguela. Despite their mandate to promote peaceful relationships, they invaded neighboring vassal *sobas*, raided different communities, and enslaved a large number of people. Differently from West Africa, where trans-Atlantic slavers did not go inland, in Benguela, colonial agents not only organized the trade in slaves but also captured free Africans and enslaved them. They also evaded the Crown, appropriating the royal fifth and other forms of tribute, and received gifts from local rulers, becoming central agents of the spread of violence and the expansion of the trans-Atlantic slave trade.

From the early seventeenth century, officials organized trade routes that resulted in the dispersal of people from the coast and interior of Benguela throughout the African diaspora. We might never know the number of all those who left from Benguela, yet their presence in the Americas revealed the importance of Benguela in the Atlantic world. Some ended up in the Spanish colonies, although most entered the Americas through the ports of Salvador and Rio de Janeiro in Brazil. Located in Lima, Havana, and different cities in the provinces of Minas Gerais, Bahia, and Rio de Janeiro, they reveal the intricacies of the slave trade in the South Atlantic world and show how the lives of African slaves were recorded in a variety of colonial documents. The same trans-Atlantic slave trade connected people who lived miles from the coast to Atlantic trading networks. Daily activities and the lifestyle of populations located far from the coast changed, reflecting the widespread consumption of imported goods. New drinking patterns, food habits, and fashion styles became desirable and required more slaves to meet the demands in the Americas. Along the coast and in the interior, African rulers and their subjects, as well as Portuguese agents, engaged in more raids and warfare, generating more captives. The maintenance of violence for more than 200 years led to political instability and social change in and around Benguela. South Atlantic commerce only favored the colonizers and the merchant elite along the western shore of the ocean. African elites acquired disposable goods, whereas African slave labor generated wealth for the elites in the New and Old Worlds.

4

Mechanisms of Enslavement

In the early 1760s, a young woman named Juliana was enslaved in the interior of Benguela, probably around the colonial fortress of Quilengues.[1] Juliana was separated from her family and forced to walk to the fortress of Caconda. After arriving in Caconda, she was sold in the public market to the captain-major, the highest authority in the fortress. José dos Santos Pereira bought Juliana sometime before February of 1765. A few days later, Pereira received a visit from Xaucuri, ambassador of the *soba* of Kilengues. Xaucuri claimed that he knew Juliana, and as a friend of her family, he had brought a ransom on behalf of her relatives to rescue the young woman from enslavement. Captain Pereira agreed to free Juliana on the payment of two *peças da india*, that is, two young slaves or three or four male slaves over 30 years of age and ten cows, a price he recognized as higher than what he originally had paid for her. Xaucuri could only offer a male slave and the cattle and requested permission to travel to Kilengues and return with another slave. Captain-Major Pereira agreed and stated that unless Xaucuri could offer another slave, Juliana would spend the rest of her life as Pereira's servant. Xaucuri never returned, probably because his village and people had been devastated by a raid organized by the *soba* of Kibanda while he was in Caconda. The dramatic events in the interior of Benguela had the potential of sealing

---

[1] For more on Kilengues, see Rosa Cruz e Silva, "The Saga of Kakonda and Kilengues: Relations between Benguela and Its Interior, 1791–1796," in *Enslaving Connections: Changing Cultures of Africa and Brazil during the Era of Slavery*, ed. José C. Curto and Paul E. Lovejoy (Amherst, NY: Humanity Books), 245–59; and Jan Vansina, *How Societies Are Born: Governance in West Central Africa before 1600* (Charlottesville: University of Virginia Press, 2004), 197.

Juliana's destiny. Captain-Major Pereira, concerned that Xaucuri would never return, brought Juliana and four witnesses, all soldiers under his command, to the town's notary. There he declared Juliana would be a free woman after his death, although she was forced to serve him until then, unless her relatives were able to provide the remaining slaves. In the presence of the notary, Pereira wrote a manumission letter and gave it to Juliana. When the news reached Luanda, the governor of Angola, Francisco Inocêncio de Sousa Coutinho (1764–72), intervened. He ordered Juliana to be freed from captivity and claimed that freedom should not be granted with conditions. He stated that the young woman could not be simultaneously free and live as a slave, that such a situation was a "repugnant contradiction." Sousa Coutinho also understood that Captain-Major Pereira did not need the services of Juliana and only intended to profit from her sale.[2]

Juliana's story is a good starting point for the study on enslavement in the interior of Benguela. Although Juliana's status in Kilengues and the route to her enslavement are not clear, this case reveals the vulnerability of free people in Benguela and the surrounding region. According to Jan Vansina, in matrilineal societies such as Kilengues, "a person without lineage was a slave, a person with one was free." In Juliana's case, she seemed to be fully integrated in her lineage and community, which sent an envoy to rescue her. Vansina continues, "[P]ersons who lost the protection of their lineage by kidnapping or sale became slaves."[3] Despite Juliana's full status in her society, she ended up captured and sold as a slave, indicating that the institution of slavery itself had been affected by the trans-Atlantic slave trade and market demand, bringing violence toward individuals who should have been protected rather than vulnerable. In sum, as a result of expansion of the trans-Atlantic slave trade, the clear line dividing free people from slaves became blurred.

John Thornton, Jan Vansina, and Roquinaldo Ferreira have shown that African rulers in West Central Africa were involved in the slave trade, selling captives to *pombeiros* traveling to the coast, yet legal limits had to be imposed to protect subjects and enforce codes establishing who could or could not be enslaved.[4] As Juliana's case shows, expansion

---

[2] Arquivo Nacionais da Torre do Tombo (ANTT), Conde Linhares, L. 90, vol. 1, fl. 142v.–143v., June 21, 1765.

[3] Jan Vansina, "Ambaca Society and the Slave Trade, c. 1760–1845," *Journal of African History* 46, no. 1 (2005): 6.

[4] Vansina, "Ambaca Society and the Slave Trade"; John K. Thornton, "African Political Ethics and the Slave Trade," in *Abolitionism and Imperialism in Britain, Africa, and the Atlantic,* ed. Derek R. Peterson (Athens: Ohio University Press, 2010), 38–62; Roquinaldo

of the trans-Atlantic slave trade disrupted orders and provoked disputes between rulers and political elites over the limits of states' involvement in the slave trade. It also raised tensions among Portuguese colonial authorities and conflicts over the use of Portuguese legislation to define freedom or enslavement. We do not have Juliana's account, but we can assume that she felt a deep sense of loss when she was removed from her community and separated from her family and friends. As a free person in Kilengues, she probably was familiar with the use of slaves and perhaps witnessed the sale of captives and slave coffles crossing her village. Her case demonstrates that freedom was not a permanent status because any free person could be seized and enslaved. Enslavement, however, could be questioned, and sometimes freedom was regained.[5] Ransoming captives was a possibility if families could act quickly and find the lost relatives. We do not know the end of Juliana's story, but as we will see in this chapter, her enslavement was far from extraordinary, and her experience shows how rulers intervened on behalf of their subjects. Many Africans were similarly violently seized in regions not far from the coast. Their process of enslavement did not start at the littoral, but at the moment they were captured and forced to cut links with their communities. We now have estimates on how many human beings left the African continent and crossed the Atlantic to a life of servitude in the Americas. The numbers are far from complete and comprehensive, and they fail to tell us personal stories that demonstrate how individuals ended up enslaved. Africans, however, left testimonies about the circumstances of their capture. In this chapter I will explore the processes of enslavement in and around Benguela in an attempt to understand the plight of Africans, following Paul Lovejoy's call to examine African experiences in the context of the expanding slave trade.[6] This chapter investigates the locations where people were captured and enslaved. Many cases indicate that captives came from regions along or very close to the coast, under nominal Portuguese control or at least of a vassal state. This evidence reveals

Ferreira, "Slaving and Resistance to Slaving in West Central Africa," in *The Cambridge World History of Slavery. AD 1420–AD 1804*, vol. 3, ed. David Eltis and Stanley L Engerman (New York: Cambridge University Press, 2011), 111–30.

[5] Mariana Candido, "Enslaving Frontiers: Slavery, Trade and Identity in Benguela, 1780–1850" PhD dissertation, York University, Toronto, 2006; Ferreira, "Slaving and Resistance to Slaving in West Central Africa"; José C. Curto, "Struggling Against Enslavement: The Case of José Manuel in Benguela, 1816–20," *Canadian Journal of African Studies* 39, no. 1 (2005): 96–122.

[6] Paul Lovejoy, "Identifying Enslaved Africans in the African Diaspora," in *Identity in the Shadow of Slavery*, ed. Paul Lovejoy (London: Cassell Academic, 2000), 3–5.

that some of the slaves exported from the region of Benguela, even in the nineteenth century, came from villages and groups that maintained a long history of contact with the Atlantic world and the colonial forces. Some of them probably were exposed to the Portuguese language and Christianity before being exported from West Central Africa, facts that would have had a profound effect on how they understood slavery in the Americas.

This chapter analyzes cycles of violence and slave raiding and what those things meant for the expansion of slavery and for the geopolitics of the region. As a result of warfare and random violence, the nature of political and commercial power changed. The examples explored in this chapter indicate that people were captured and enslaved along the coast despite an emphasis in the scholarship on the gradual movement inland of the slaving frontier. Rather than cases of captives coming from distant lands in the interior of the continent, the colonial sources reveal that people continued to be captured and enslaved in locations very close to the coast even in the nineteenth century.[7] This forces a reassessment of the ideas of the slaving frontier, defined by Joseph Miller in *Way of Death* as "the moving frontier zone of slaving violence." Miller's conception recognized the insecurity left in the wake of this surging frontier, yet it insisted on its progressive movement away from the Atlantic shore, creating zones of stability. According to Miller,

[T]he slaving frontier zone was washed inland in the sixteenth century and surged east like a demographic wave bearing the sea-borne goods of the Europeans on its crest.... By the middle third of the nineteenth century, the wave had tumbled populations all the way to the center of the continent. There it rose to towering heights of chaos as its force combined with a similar demographic surge flooding the areas from the Indian Ocean. Behind it, toward the Atlantic to the west, the turbulence subsided into relatively still demographic pools where quiet-flowing currents of reproduction and debt carried off most of the people sent into slaving,

---

[7] For studies that explore the idea of the slaving frontier moving inland, see Joseph C. Miller, *Way of Death: Merchant Capitalism and the Angolan Slave Trade, 1730–1830* (Madison: University of Wisconsin Press, 1988), 140–69; David Birmingham, *Trade and Conflict in Angola: The Mbundu and Their Neighbours Under the Influence of the Portuguese, 1483–1790* (Oxford, UK: Clarendon Press, 1966); Dennis Cordell, "The Myth of Inevitability and Invincibility: Resistance to Slavery and the Slave Trade in Central Africa, 1850–1910," in *Fighting the Slave Trade: West African Strategies*, ed. Sylviane A. Diouf (Athens: Ohio University Press, 2003), 31–4; Paul Lovejoy and David Richardson, "'Pawns Will Live When Slaves Is Apt to Dye': Credit, Slaving and Pawnship at Old Calabar in the Era of the Slave Trade," Working Papers in Economic History 38, London School of Economics and Political Science, 1997, 1–34; Jan Vansina, *Kingdoms of the Savanna* (Madison: University of Wisconsin Press, 1966).

and where only eddies of periodic succession struggles and banditry from the distant sweeping tide continued to disturb the calm surface of politics.[8]

For most of the era of the trans-Atlantic slave trade, coastal societies, such as the colony of Benguela, imported captives from inland territories, yet traders based in Benguela also continue to enslave people along the coast. From the cases explored in this chapter it becomes clear that the interior of Benguela and the port itself were enmeshed in slave raids, from coastal and inland forces, that had profound repercussions on political and commercial organization. Continuous levels of violence had consequences for African states, their rulers, and their subjects. Even strong states and rulers could not continuously employ their armies in the process of capturing people while neglecting other fronts. Eventually, states moved into new mechanisms, such as collection of tribute from tributary states, although sporadically relying on warfare as a mechanism of capture.[9] Societies adapted to suit the demands of trade, adjusting to cycles of violence, warfare, and slave raids linked to the trans-Atlantic slave trade. This violence, however, affected the ability of states and societies to survive, and despite Jan Vansina's claim that until 1840 uniform and stable states were headed by rulers who succeeded their predecessor without much turmoil, the coast and the interior of Benguela were facing ongoing political reorganization since the early seventeenth century.[10] And the trans-Atlantic slave trade was responsible for the spread of violence and the subsequent collapse of old states and emergence of new ones. In the processes, societies were unprotected and vulnerable to slavers' forces.

Although numerous sources offer insights into the enslavement process and the thin line that separated freedom from slavery in West Central Africa, they represent a very small sample considering the large number of people exported from the region. The lack of a single centralized state

---

[8] Miller, *Way of Death*, 149.

[9] Looking at different data, Daniel Domingues da Silva came to similar conclusions, although he downplays the effects of Portuguese expansionist wars in the central highlands. See his, "Crossroads: Slave Frontiers of Angola, c. 1780–1867," PhD dissertation, Emory University, 2011, 112–16. For more on tributes of slaves, see Gladwyn Childs, *Umbundu Kinship and Character* (Oxford University Press, 1949), 168–9; Paul E. Lovejoy, *Transformations in Slavery: A History of Slavery in Africa* (Cambridge University Press, 2000), 87. For more on how the concept of slaving frontier does not apply to Benguela's hinterland, see Mariana P. Candido, *Fronteras de Esclavización: Esclavitud, Comercio e Identidad en Benguela, 1780–1850* (Mexico City: El Colegio de Mexico Press, 2011), 155–204.

[10] Vansina, *Kingdoms of the Savanna*, 280.

in the interior of Benguela, as in the case of Kongo, makes it difficult to generalize how the processes of enslavement occurred. Different states and chiefdoms employed different mechanisms to enslave outsiders and insiders. Before Benguela was founded in 1617, the Portuguese relied on acquiring captives from African rulers. Like the Imbangala north of the Kwanza River, the Ndombe and other groups sold captives of war to anyone willing to exchange imported commodities for them. Enslaved, the captives were then sent to Luanda and reexported from there.[11] After 1617, even with insecurities and the precarious condition of the fortress, Portuguese forces raided nearby villages, as seen in Chapter 3. The punitive raids that targeted "rebellious" rulers resulted in large numbers of captives and can be considered "war for slaves."[12]

Another important factor was raids perpetrated by autonomous warlords in the highlands, although there are few sources that provide stories of those captives. Raids and internal conflicts happened as a result of local pressures, including drought and disease, and external pressures, such as the demand for captives along the coast. Luso-African traders who were connected to the rulers of local states brought captives to the coast in slave coffles in the same way that *pombeiros*, itinerant traders acting on behalf of their coastal representation, introduced new captives to Benguela.[13] A system of reliable trade patterns developed. Rulers in the interior controlled markets and guaranteed control over commerce. The Portuguese tried to control commercial routes through the establishment of fortresses inland, such as Caconda and Quilengues. In autonomous regions in the interior, rulers and their political allies decided who could or could not enter a state to trade in slaves. They also controlled prices

---

[11] Joseph C. Miller, *Kings and Kinsmen: Early Mbundu States in Angola* (Oxford, UK: Clarendon Press, 1976), 180–1.

[12] Vansina, *Kingdoms of the Savanna*, 248.

[13] For the organization of the trade, see Mariana Candido, "Merchants and the Business of the Slave Trade at Benguela, 1750–1850," *African Economic History* 35, no. 1 (2007), 1–30. For raids in the seventeenth century, see Beatrix Heintze, "Angola nas Garras do Tráfico de Escravos: As Guerras Angolanas do Ndongo (1611–1630)," *Revista Internacional de Estudos Africanos* 1 (1984), 11–59; José C. Curto: "A restituição de 10.000 súbditos ndongo 'roubados' na Angola de meados do século XVII: uma análise preliminar," in *Escravatura e Transformações Culturais: África-Brasil-Caraíbas*, ed. Isabel C. Henriques (Lisbon: Editora Vulgata, 2002), 185–208; Curto, "Un Butin Illégitime: Razzias d'esclaves et relations luso-africaines dans la région des fleuves Kwanza et Kwango en 1805," in *Déraison, Esclavage et Droit: Les fondements idéologiques et juridiques de la traite négrière et de l'esclavage*, ed. Isabel C. Henriques and Louis Sala-Molins (Paris: Éditions UNESCO, 2002), 315–27; and John K. Thornton, "The African Experience of the '20s and Odd Negroes' Arriving in Virginia in 1619," *William and Mary Quarterly* 55 (1998), 421–34.

and taxes that itinerant merchants had to pay.[14] In sum, the mechanisms of enslavement were layered, targeting people from distant lands as well as those located along the coast and within Benguela. Hence the populations along the coast were not immune from raids. They were subjected to kidnapping, trickery, and occasional raids. Inhabitants of lands between the coast and the fortress of Caconda were enslaved mainly in warfare and raids organized by the colonial armies and/or competing rulers. Several cases indicate that Luso-Africans were particularly vulnerable to kidnapping when traveling between the coast and Caconda, as well as when going from the fortress to states located further inland. Inhabitants of the highlands beyond the fortress of Caconda could be enslaved through debt and judicial condemnation imposed by *sobas* and their councils, as well as in warfare. In contrast to the idea of an inland gradual progression of enslavement, violence moved not only eastward but also southward and northward and eventually even rebounded westward toward unprotected populations close to the coast, indicating the devastating impact of the trans-Atlantic slave trade and the spread of insecurity.[15] By looking at mechanisms of enslavement, as well as cycles of warfare provoked by Portuguese authorities, as explored in Chapter 3, it is possible to claim that expansion of the trans-Atlantic slave trade altered political organization and people's lives, as well as notions of legality and regard for human life. These changes reveal how the region was profoundly shaken by contact with the Atlantic world and the trans-Atlantic slave trade.

This chapter will explore the mechanisms through which people seized captives and transformed them into slaves in and around Benguela. The roles of European credit and demand were crucial in promoting competition and expanding violence toward smaller groups. Through the cases analyzed in this chapter, I will discuss the different strategies men on the spot employed to seize people, from warfare and raids to kidnapping,

[14] Linda Heywood, *Contested Power in Angola* (Rochester, NY: University of Rochester Press, 2000), 12.
[15] For other studies that have pointed out the enslavement of people from coastal areas, see José Curto, "Resistência à escravidão na África: O caso dos escravos fugitivos recapturados em Angola, 1846–1876," *Afro-Ásia* 33 (2005): 67–88; Walter Hawthorne, *From Africa to Brazil: Culture, Identity, and an Atlantic Slave Trade, 1600–1830* (New York: Cambridge University Press, 2010), 74–5; and Roquinaldo A. Ferreira, "Fontes para o estudo da escravidão em Angola: Luanda e Icolo e Bengo no pós-tráfico de escravos," in *Construindo o passado Angolano: As fontes e a sua interpretação. Actas do II Seminário internacional sobre a história de Angola* (Lisbon: Comissão Nacional para as Comemorações dos Descobrimentos Portugueses, 2000), 667–80; Silva, "Crossroads," 117–30; Candido, *Fronteras de Esclavización*.

trickery, and judicial condemnation. The intent is not to present an exhaustive list of episodes where people were captured, but to stress the different mechanisms available to generate the hundreds of thousands of slaves exported from Benguela, rescuing individual stories. The sources do not allow me to discuss which forms of enslavement – raids, judicial cases, or debt – constituted what proportion of slave exports from Benguela over time because there is no indication which slaves were exported and which remained enslaved in the urban port. They reveal, however, that moments of increasing Atlantic pressure for more slaves generated violence around the port, resulting in the enslavement of coastal people. Episodes of kidnappings and raids increased when slave ships needed to fill their holds quickly, threatening those nearby. Thus coastal people tended to be kidnapped and seized in raids.

The examples indicate how the authorities in the Portuguese colony relied on violence to impose force and guarantee a supply of captives who could be exported. Judicial cases, where litigants testified about how and when they were captured, allow us to understand capture on an individual level, moving away from a quantitative analysis, which prevails in the literature on the slave trade. Studies that focus on numbers rather than individual cases tend to conceal the fact that those numbers represent human beings who faced physical and mental violence. In some cases we have names, places of origin, and the outline of a life story, allowing us to see how specific communities dealt with the pressure of the trans-Atlantic slave trade. Raids around Benguela and in the interior were connected to demand at the coast, the advance of credit, and the pressure of men on the spot linked to the trans-Atlantic slave trade. Portuguese forces also fomented conflicts, as seen in Chapter 3. Through the analysis of specific cases, I will focus on the enslavement of individuals rather than large groups. Violence was endemic, and no black person was safe in Benguela or its interior. The legal suits of people seeking their freedom stress the vulnerability of the population that lived around the Portuguese settlement and show how the pressures of the international slave market spread instability, even for those who were supposed to be protected by the law. The enslavement of a significant number of people along the coast had repercussions on how we understand the African experience in the Americas. The capture of people who could understand Portuguese and lived in urban centers controlled by the Portuguese force us to reconsider the movement of the slaving frontier inland and the degree of exposure to Lusophone culture that slaves shared before their shipment from Benguela.

Warfare and Raids

Warfare was the main strategy to acquire slaves in the first century of Benguela's occupation and had profound repercussions for the political organization of this region. Reports of attacks and insecurity, as seen in Chapter 1, indicate that most of the people exported from Benguela in the seventeenth and early eighteenth centuries were enslaved in armed conflicts. Ferreira suggests the Portuguese eventually moved away from warfare, favoring trade and commerce. As we have seen in Chapter 3, however, the colonial army made full use of its military capability in raids and wars until the mid–nineteenth century. In Benguela and its interior, warfare coexisted with "more commercialized forms of slaving."[16] On most occasions, Portuguese officials participated actively in creating animosity between autonomous polities, or they directly intervened, organizing raids disguised as colonial expansion. The trade in the seventeenth and early eighteenth centuries left few records, including no descriptions from Africans concerning how and when they were captured. Judicial cases where people told their stories became common by the late eighteenth and early nineteenth centuries owing to expansion of the colonial administration in Benguela. Before that, the sources simply described warfare and raids where large numbers of people were seized, indicating that events in Benguela were similar to those happening elsewhere on the continent. Luis Candido Furtado, a Portuguese army officer who was on the Benguela coast in 1785, noted that only societies that engaged in warfare had slaves to sell; without violence, there could be no slaves.[17] Furtado certainly was correct in observing that warring groups targeted communities of outsiders who could be enslaved. Like their neighbors north of the Kwanza River, polities south of the Kwanza considered war enemies as legitimate objects of enslavement. Inevitably the incessant warfare throughout the region led to political, economic, and social instability that generated slaves. The resulting insecurity weakened the areas close to the coast by constantly depriving them of their reproductive

---

[16] Ferreira, "Slaving and Resistance to Slaving in West Central Africa," 118.

[17] Biblioteca Nacional (BNL), Lisbon, cod. 8094, "Luis Candido Cordeiro Pinheiro Furtado to Barão de Mossamedes [Governor of Angola]," September 22, 1785. For more on warfare and enslavement in the seventeenth century, see José C. Curto, "Luso-Brazilian Alcohol and the Legal Slave Trade at Benguela and its Hinterland, c. 1617–1830," in *Négoce Blanc en Afrique Noire: L'évolution du Commerce à Longue Distance en Afrique Noire du 18e au 20e Siècles*, ed. H. Bonin and M. Cahen (Paris: Publications de la Société Française D'histoire D'outre-mer, 2001), 354.

and productive capacities.[18] Portuguese colonial officials and local rulers employed defensive and strategic aims as the justifications behind wars. Although warfare was usually accepted as a legitimate mode of enslavement, the spread of conflict had repercussions that went beyond the battlefield, affecting production, reproduction, and eventually the political survival of those involved.

The Portuguese empire was based on a juridical discourse in which the concept of a "just war" and an acceptance of slavery were central in defining the limits of territorial conquest and determining which people were allowed to be conquered and which were to be protected by the colonial state. This concept was not foreign to most states and chiefdoms around Benguela because those rulers also protected their subjects. Any "defensive" war – that is, any war that was fought to guarantee trade control and protect territorial limits – was considered a just war by both the Portuguese and the local rulers. As was the case in the Mediterranean world, of which Portugal was part, seizure of people as slaves in raids was a persistent and ordinary feature of life from antiquity through the nineteenth century.[19] The Portuguese had previously used this technique to seize Muslims in continental Portugal as well as in North Africa. Thus people enslaved in conflicts could "legitimately be reduced to bondage."[20] Central to this

---

[18] For the role of warfare in generating captives north of the Kwanza, see Miller, *Kings and Kinsmen*; and Joseph Miller, "The Paradoxes of Impoverishment in the Atlantic Zone," in *History of Central Africa*, ed. David Birmingham and Phyllis Martin (London: Longman, 1983); John Thornton, *Warfare in Atlantic Africa, 1500–1800* (London: UCL Press, 1999); and John Thornton, *Africa and Africans in the Making of the Atlantic World, 1400–1800* (New York: Cambridge University Press, 1998). For other regions of the continent, see Philip Curtin, *Economic Change in Precolonial Africa: Senegambia in the Era of the Slave Trade* (Madison: University of Wisconsin Press, 1975); Herbert Klein, *The Atlantic Slave Trade* (New York: Cambridge University Press, 1999); Paul Lovejoy, *Transformations in Slavery: A History of Slavery in Africa* (New York: Cambridge University Press, 2000); Robin Law, "Slave-Raiders and Middlemen, Monopolists and Free Traders: The Supply of Slaves for the Atlantic Trade in Dahomey, c. 1715–1850," *Journal of African History* 30 (1989), 45–68; Boubacar Barry, *Senegambia and the Atlantic Slave Trade* (Cambridge University Press, 1998); Jean Bazin, "War and Servitude in Segou," *Economy and Society* 3 (1974), 107–44; Toby Green, *The Rise of the Trans-Atlantic Slave Trade in Western Africa, 1300–1589* (Cambridge University Press, 2011), 234–52; Hawthorne, *From Africa to Brazil*, 62–81.

[19] Lauren Benton, "Legal Regime of the South Atlantic World, 1400–1750: Jurisdictional Complexity as Institutional Order," *Journal of World History* 11, no. 1 (2000), 14. See also António Manuel Hespanha and Catarina Madeira Santos, "Os Poderes num Império Oceânico," in *História de Portugal, O Antigo Regime*, vol. 4, ed. António Manuel Hespanha (Lisbon: Estampa, 1993), 396–7.

[20] A. J. R. Russell-Wood, "Iberian Expansion and the Issue of Black Slavery: Changing Portuguese Attitudes, 1440–1770," *American Historical Review* 83, no. 1 (1978), 24; see also Mariza Soares, "Descobrindo a Guiné no Brasil Colonial," *Revista do Instituto*

interaction was the idea that the King of Portugal received one-fifth of any booty. Indeed, the idea of a "royal fifth" in itself demonstrates that in the Portuguese legal tradition there were legitimate reasons and a budgetary need for warfare, raids, and enslavement.

In 1670, the *Provedor da Fazenda,* or the superintendent of the royal treasury,[21] Andrade Colaço, stated that slaves of the coastal residents engaged in warfare in the interior. On their arrival in Benguela, the residents had to pay the royal fifth. Colaço claimed that payment of the royal fifth prevented coastal traders from profiting. Despite Colaço's report, it is difficult to believe that coastal traders made no profit. By the turn of the nineteenth century, Governor Miguel Antonio de Mello stated that it "was rare that one lost money in the slave trade," indicating its profitability.[22] Perhaps Colaço, as a public figure with a local trading network of his own, was interested in a larger margin of profit on behalf of traders. This example shows the direct link between the fiscal authorities, who were responsible for the collection of taxes, and merchant elites, who worked side by side with those men on the spot with whom they shared economic interests.

During the eighteenth and nineteenth centuries, Angolan authorities accused Benguela officials of being more interested in seizure than in being committed to maintaining order and security. In 1725, Captain José da Nóbrega organized an expedition against the *soba* of Kiambela. Located close to the fortress of Caconda, Kiambela had been a vassal of the Portuguese Crown for less than 3 years when the *soba* decided not to pay taxes, which was interpreted as insubordination and a cause for a "just war." In the attack, the *soba* and hundreds of his subjects were seized, and 130 captives were sent to Benguela as royal fifths. Witnesses,

---

Historico Geografico Brasileiro 161, no. 407 (2000), 80–1; Angela Domingues, "O Conceito de Guerra Justa e Resgate e os Ameríndios do Norte do Brasil," in *Brasil. Colonização e Escravidão,* ed. Maria Beatriz Nizza da Silva (Rio de Janeiro: Nova Fronteira, 1999), 46–9; and Hebe M. Mattos, "A Escravidão Moderna nos Quadros do Império Português: O Antigo Regime em perspectiva Atlântica', in *O Antigo Regime nos Trópicos: a dinâmica imperial portuguesa (séc. XVI–XVIII),* ed. João Fragoso, Maria Fernanda Bicalho, and Maria Fátima Gouveia (Rio de Janeiro: Civilização Brasileira, 2001), 146. For a discussion of Portuguese slaving activities in North Africa, see Yacine Daddi Addoun, "Abolition de l'esclavage en Algérie: 1816–1871," PhD dissertation, York University, 2010.

[21] *Provedor da Fazenda* was in charge of tax collection, public works, payment of personnel, administration of the port, and preventing trade in contraband. See Herbert Klein, "The Portuguese Slave Trade from Angola in the Eighteenth Century," *Journal of Economic History* 32, no. 4 (1972), 904.

[22] Vansina, *Kingdoms of the Savanna,* 185.

however, declared that Captain Nóbrega had captured more than 600 people, which was more than he declared to the Crown.[23] Kiambela was killed and replaced by a new leader, who, in 1729, organized another revolt. In 1728, the attack organized by Captain Nóbrega was subjected to a legal proceeding, which found that it was illegal and unjustified because it was motivated by personal interests and resulted in major disturbances in the interior. In the conflict, more than 10,500 *libata* ("huts with straw roofs") had been destroyed, and people faced starvation after fields were burned, indicating how raids and slaving provoked famine in Benguela's hinterland. The judge in Angola suggested that all the people captured should have their freedom restored, although he considered it to be impossible due to the length of time (more than 3 years) that had passed since the episode.[24] This case illustrates how local rulers signed vassalage treaties assuming that they could change the rules later on, whereas the Portuguese administrators viewed the agreement as set in stone. People in the interior, even those considered vassals, were vulnerable to the attacks of the men on the spot, even if the attack was later considered illegal. For those captured, killed, and displaced, the legal finding did not alter their suffering and losses. In this specific event, the *soba* of Kiambela was unable to defend his people and protect them against capture and enslavement. His subjects were vulnerable, regardless of social status, because even members of the royal family were captured.[25] Nóbrega was arrested and found guilty, although it is not clear what kind of punishment he received. The attacks resulted in a large number of captives, depopulation of the chiefdom, murder of the ruler, and the resettlement of many subjects as refugees under any authority willing to protect them. Moreover, this case reveals the massive enslavement of captives, in this case more than six hundred people apprehended, and the active role of European authorities, even though the idea of small-scale enslavement prevails in the scholarship. Joseph Miller had suggested, "For five hundred kilometers south of Benguela to the mouth of the Kunene, traders

---

[23] AHU, caixa 22, doc. 54, January 8, 1725. On this attack, see also Pascoal Leite de Aguiar, *Administração Colonial Portuguesa no Congo, em Angola e em Benguela* (Lisbon: Sociedade Histórica da Independência de Portugal, 2006), 2, 90–3.

[24] AHU, caixa 24, doc. 66, December 28, 1728. For Kiumbela's revolt in 1729, see Aguiar, *Administração Colonial Portuguesa*, 2, 122–3. For the link between the trans-Atlantic slave trade and famines, see Patrick Manning, *Slavery and African Life: Occidental, Oriental, and African Slave Trades* (Cambridge University Press, 1990), 56–7.

[25] For other cases in West Central Africa, see Linda Heywood, "Slavery and Its Transformation in the Kingdom of Kongo: 1491–1800," *Journal of African History* 50 (2009), 1–22.

gathered slaves only in small numbers for transfer to ships."[26] Yet there is evidence of several cases where large numbers of people were captured in the interior of Benguela.

After this episode, official permission from the governor was required before local sovereigns could be attacked. After a request was presented, colonial authorities in Luanda gathered and read the proposal of the war and its justification. A committee was organized to discuss the pros and cons, and a verdict was issued. For example, in 1736, the captain of Benguela, Álvaro de Barros e Silva, suggested attacking several *sobas* who were vassals of the Portuguese Crown and who lived adjacent to Benguela. According to the captain, these vassals "acted in an insulting and excessive way; [they also] killed and stole from whites who went to the hinterland."[27] The just cause of the war was decided by a committee composed of authorities based in Luanda, including the Crown judge (*ouvidor geral*), priests, and military personnel, among whom were the captain-major, a colonel, and a sergeant, as well as the municipal attorney and the administrator of slave export contracts. The committee read Barros e Silva's claim, including letters of support from Benguela residents and traders. After deliberation, most of the committee members agreed on the necessity of the punitive expedition, with the exception of the president of the chamber. By the time of the results of his petition, Barros e Silva was no longer the captain in Benguela, and his successor received Crown support to organize a punitive war. Wars were a way to guarantee captives and to incorporate vassals into the Portuguese empire; thus they tended to be supported by metropolitan and Angola-based authorities. Attacks on neighboring rulers who threatened the expansion of the colony also permitted Portuguese agents in Benguela to continue trading, even if those rulers were already vassals.[28]

Religious belief was a further factor in the history of war and slavery. Raiders could enslave anyone seized in "just wars," that is, in conflicts with non-Christians or people "without faith, king or law."[29] *Jagas*, by definition cannibals and considered to be lawless nomads, also were subjected to enslavement. Whether or not local authorities in West Central Africa had similar traditions that allowed them to enslave people from different religious traditions is not known. What is clear is that

---

[26] Miller, *Way of Death*, 17.
[27] AHU, caixa 29, doc. 88, December 21, 1736. For a discussion on how to proceed with legal wars, see the Carta Régia of July 13, 1703, in ANTT, Mç. 7, doc. 1.
[28] Hespanha and Santos, "Os Poderes num Império Oceanico," 396.
[29] Hespanha e Santos, "Os Poderes num Império Oceânico," 396.

throughout the era of the trans-Atlantic slave trade, both Portuguese and Africans agreed that there were legitimate ways of acquiring slaves: Warfare and raids in particular were morally accepted by both cultures involved, and colonial authorities and men on the spot benefited from them. As seen in Chapters 1 and 2, the concept of just war protected vassals of the Portuguese at the same time that it endangered anyone living outside the Portuguese enclaves along the coast. Concepts of "legitimate enslavement" and "original freedom" were employed to decide the fate of Africans.[30] While captives of a just war or criminals could be seen as legitimately enslaved, any African who claimed being a vassal of the Portuguese Crown or a Catholic was seen as originally free, as if both classifications were exclusive. Several raids in the seventeenth, eighteenth, and early nineteenth centuries targeted vassals of the Portuguese Crown, yet the captives remained enslaved, showing the incoherence of the legislation. Further, I assume that most of the residents in the interior of Benguela were free, although the Portuguese legislation only considered "originally free" those who lived under vassalage. Thus the idea of "original freedom" was restricted to just a few people in Benguela and its hinterland. Slavery was a legal condition in the Portuguese code, and non-Christians were subject to enslavement because they were positioned as vulnerable people outside the legal protection of the state.

In 1779, the captain of Caconda petitioned Angola for permission to organize a military offensive in retaliation against those who had invaded the *sobado* of Fende, a vassal of the Portuguese Crown.[31] Neither the identity of those who attacked Fende nor the number of people captured during the operation is known. The governor of Angola, Don António de Lencastre, nevertheless approved a punitive attack and stressed the religious threat, claiming that "it is necessary keep the *gentio*, the heathens, from getting into a comfortable situation."[32] The governor also reminded

---

[30] For cannibalism as a trope to define the *jagas*, see Beatrix Heintze, "Contra as Teorias Simplificadoras: O 'Canibalismo' na Antropologia e História da Angola," in *Portugal não é um País Pequeno. Contar o "Império" na Pós-Colonidade*, ed. Manuela Ribeiro Sanches (Lisbon: Cotovia, 2006), 223–32. For more on the concept of original freedom, see José C. Curto "The Story of Nbena, 1817–1820: Unlawful Enslavement and the Concept of 'Original Freedom' in Angola," in *Trans-Atlantic Dimensions of Ethnicity in the African Diaspora*, ed. Paul E. Lovejoy and David V. Trotman (London: Continuum, 2003), 43–64. For the new laws employed in the colonies, see Catarina Madeira Santos, "Entre deux droits: les Lumières en Angola (1750–v.1800)," *Annales – Histoire, Sciences Sociales* 60, no. 4 (2005), 817–48.

[31] Beatriz Heintze, "Luso-African Feudalism in Angola? The Vassal Treaties of the 16th to the 18th Century," *Separata da Revista Portuguesa de História* 18 (1980), 111–31.

[32] Arquivo Histórico Nacional de Angola (AHNA), cod. 81, fl. 118–20, January 30, 1779.

the captain of Caconda to collect the royal fifth. Indeed, under such a context, collection of the royal fifth indicated nothing less than a legitimate war that generated revenue for the state, despite the fact that the Crown and the overseas council forbade the involvement of authorities and soldiers in the trade. In a law of 1764, Sousa Coutinho declared, "[S]oldiers are not traders. *Degredados* or *filhos da terra* (exiled or locally born) cannot do business in the hinterland. Captains and commanders cannot issue authorization to subordinates to go inland, under any circumstances. I also forbid the envoy of authorities' *pombeiros* ["itinerant traders"] to carry on business beyond the public office."[33] Nonetheless, men on the spot were deeply involved not only in the trade but also in the slaving raids. Collection of the royal fifth could create problems and conflicts among officials. In a letter of 1764, Francisco Inocêncio da Sousa Coutinho gave instructions to the captain of Benguela, Apolinário Francisco de Carvalho, on how to collect the royal fifth:

You will apprehend the captives who correspond to the royal fifth, and sell them in the public market. The superintendent [*provedor*] will witness the sale and retain the money collected in the safe of the royal treasury. If this procedure is not possible, send the captives to [Luanda] and I will take care of the transaction.[34]

It is clear that slaves paid as part of a royal fifth were fundamental to the colonial budget, creating a cycle that depended on war to generate captives who then could be enslaved and sold to trans-Atlantic slave traders or in the public market. The result was an increased sense of insecurity and the further spread of warfare.[35] Corrupt authorities attacked vassals who should have been protected by the law, using justifications such as claiming insubordination, lack of tax payment, or any other reason to validate an attack, increasing political insecurity in the region.

Joaquim Vieira de Andrade, captain of the fortress of Quilengues, seized subjects of the *soba* of Sokoval in 1797, one of the most important rulers under Quilengues jurisdiction, an inland colonial fortress located some 180 km southeast of Benguela and 150 km southwest of Caconda.[36] Thus the captain of Quilengues organized a punitive expedition against people he was there to protect. According to the vassal treaties, the signatories

---

[33] ANTT, Conde de Linhares, L. 90, vol. 1, fl. 63–63v., September 16, 1764.
[34] ANTT, Conde de Linhares, L. 50, vol. 1, fl. 40–45v., August 21, 1764.
[35] Slavery, violence, warfare, and raids were intimately related. See Miller, *Way of Death*, 105–39, and "Angola Central e Sul por Volta de 1840," *Estudos Afro-Asiáticos* 32 (1997), 7–54; Thornton, *Africa and Africans*, 98–125.
[36] Vansina, *How Societies Are Born*, 122; Cruz e Silva, "The Saga of Kakonda and Kilengues," 246–8.

could not be enslaved because they were considered to have embraced the Christian faith. The treaty involved rights, not subjugation, yet Captain Andrade did not respect those rights with regard to the Sokoval ruler.[37] During the raid, Portuguese troops captured the *soba* of Sokoval and sent him to Benguela, where he was imprisoned in the local fortress. A more "collaborative" *soba* replaced him, in order to facilitate cooperation with the Portuguese colonial state and the actions of *pombeiros*. From the inventory of forty-five slaves sent as the royal fifth, nineteen were old women and three were old women with children. There also were seven girls, one very skinny; six old men, including one blind man; and three boys, one of whom was very thin and another who had wounds on his foot. Two girls of five and a half palms and one girl of six palms also were seized, as well as four young boys, one with a bloated belly. The captives sent as the royal fifth were in debilitated physical condition or were very young or very old and therefore with less commercial value in the eyes of trans-Atlantic slave traders.

From a probable total number of 225 people seized in the raids, the captain of Quilengues sent to Benguela only those in bad shape and considered "disposable." However, those people did not remain in captivity. After their imprisonment, the *soba* of Sokoval complained to the governor of Benguela that Captain Andrade and his forces had captured his relatives, tributaries, and slaves without any regard to individual background. Aware of the legal constraints, the governor ordered the release of all the captives and their return to Sokoval. Any resident of Quilengues or Benguela who had acquired captives resulting from this operation had to free them. Further, those shipped to Brazil had to be returned to Benguela.[38] Although Captain Andrade had to release all the slaves captured during this unjustified war, not much is known about the fate of those sold locally and those sent to Brazil because there was no indication that anyone returned.[39] Therefore, it is not possible to ascertain whether

[37] Beatrix Heintze, "Angolan Vassal Tributes of the 17th Century," *Revista de História Económica e Social* 6 (1980): 57–78; Heintze, "Luso-African Feudalism in Angola?"; and Ana Paula Tavares and Catarina Madeira Santos, "Uma Leitura Africana das Estratégias Políticas e Jurídicas. Textos dos e para os Dembos," in *Africae Monumenta. A Apropriação da Escrita pelos Africanos* (Lisbon: IICT, 2002), 531.

[38] AHNA, cod. 516, fl. 51–51v., "Relação dos escravos de Quilengues que trouxe o capitão Miguel António Simão." November 27, 1797; see also AHU, Angola, caixa 87, doc. 28, January 26, 1798; AHNA, cod. 443, fl. 18, June 21, 1797; AHU, Angola, caixa 87, doc. 42, March 22, 1798; AHU, Angola, caixa 87, doc. 73, April 30, 1798; AHU, Angola, caixa 87, doc. 80, April 30, 1798.

[39] AHNA, cod. 443, fl. 18, June 21, 1797.

those captured regained their freedom or if anyone actually did return from Brazil, indicating how the colonial bureaucracy protected the men on the spot. Even so, this case highlights the illogical aspects of colonialism, such as juridical recognition of the rights extended to *sobas* and at the same time their consideration as subjects. The colonial state created a legal framework where subjects could claim their own freedom as well as that of their dependents and other people considered to be illegally enslaved. As scholarship on slavery in the Americas has shown, Africans used legal courts to fight against their fate and protect dependents.[40] In the process, however, they accepted the legitimacy of slavery, of the concept of "original freedom," and of the inherent process of violence associated with expansion of the trans-Atlantic slave trade and colonialism. The violence of the law was accepted and legitimated in what Pierre Bourdieu called the most supreme form of violence, the symbolic one, entrenched in Benguela during the era of the trans-Atlantic slave trade.[41]

In the period of commercial pressure along the coast, such as occurred at the end of the eighteenth century, no one was safe from violent warlords. Ferreira argued that most of the slaves exported from Benguela were captured in wars in the interior "pitting Africans against each other."[42] In fact, during the seventeenth and eighteenth centuries, no one in Benguela's hinterland saw themselves as African or even as members of a common collective identity, a topic I will explore further in Chapter 5. Sometime during 1798, in a single military operation, marauding warriors captured around 600 people in Kalukembe, fewer than 195 km southeast of Benguela and around 41 km from the fortress of Caconda. Kalukembe was under the jurisdiction of Caconda. According to the governor of Benguela, revenge motivated this raid because the *soba* of Kalukembe had been cooperating with the Portuguese army, creating animosity in

---

[40] For some examples, see Alejandro de la Fuente, "Slaves and the Creation of Legal Rights in Cuba: Coartación and Papel," *Hispanic American Historical Review* 87, no. 4 (2007): 659–92; Rebecca J. Scott, "She ... Refuses to Deliver Up Herself as the Slave of Your Petition: Emigres, Enslavement, and the 1808 Louisiana Digest of the Civil Laws," *Tulane European and Civil Law Forum* 24 (2009): 115–36; Rebecca J. Scott, "Paper Thin: Freedom and Re-Enslavement in the Diaspora of the Haitian Revolution," *Law and History Review* 29, no. 4 (2011): 1061–87; Keila Grinberg, "Slavery, Manumission and the Law in Nineteenth-Century Brazil: Reflections on the Law of 1831 and the 'Principle of Liberty' on the Southern Frontier of the Brazilian Empire," *European Review of History: Revue Europeenne d'Histoire* 16, no. 3 (2009): 401–11; Keila Grinberg, *Liberata: "a lei da ambigüidade": as ações de liberdade da Corte de Apelação do Rio de Janeiro no século XIX* (Rio de Janeiro: Relume Dumará, 1994).
[41] Pierre Bourdieu, *Pascalian Meditations* (Stanford, CA: Stanford University Press, 2000).
[42] Ferreira, "Slaving and Resistance to Slaving in West Central Africa," 121.

the region.[43] In cases such as this, independent *sobas* joined forces to punish an African ruler who had assisted the Portuguese, an event seen as a threat to the geopolitics of the region. Raids generated local instability and contributed to the cycle of warfare by causing adverse reactions and punitive attacks by Portuguese troops.

Sobas who were raided eventually raided others as a way to generate captives who could be exchanged for weapons, alcohol, and other imported goods, indicating the pervasive effects of the trans-Atlantic slave trade.[44] Positions shifted according to military conditions and strategic associations and had effects on social and political institutions.[45] The *sobas* of Kalukembe and Sokoval are examples of rulers who raided other communities and were themselves raided shortly thereafter, demonstrating that alliances changed and no military power was able to keep people protected. Violence threatened those on the coast and inland. In 1799, the *soba* of Kalukembe, who had suffered a raid in the previous year, became a raider himself, seizing 200 Jau people from *soba* Dom Matheus. The raiders not only enslaved people but also seized cattle, gunpowder, textiles, and even chairs.[46] Portuguese authorities had a mandate to intervene on behalf of African vassals. In this particular case, the regent of Caconda arrested the *soba* of Kalukembe after his attack on the Jau, although no information is available on the fate of the people captured in these events.[47]

The trans-Atlantic demand for captives at the turn of the nineteenth century unleashed a new cycle of violence. Wars and raids were orchestrated and waged to generate captives and attend the slavers' demand. The *soba* of Sokoval, who had been raided and enslaved by the captain of Quilengues in 1797, himself raided hunter and gatherer Kwandu coastal groups in 1814. Since the Portuguese wanted to eliminate Kwandu and gain control of the territory in order to explore for sulfur, the governor of Benguela assisted Sokoval and provided soldiers, facilitating the

[43] AHNA, cod. 441, fl. 59, May 15, 1798; see also AHNA, cod. 442, fl. 59v., May 15, 1798; and AHU, caixa 88, doc. 3, May 15, 1798.

[44] Curto, "Un Butin Illégitime," 315–27. For examples from other parts of Africa, see Boubacar Barry, *Senegambia and the Atlantic Slave Trade*, 160; Elizabeth Eldredge and Fred Morton, *Slavery in South Africa: Captive Labor on the Dutch Frontier* (Boulder, CO: Westview Press, 1994), 93.

[45] Lovejoy, *Transformations in Slavery*; Thornton, *Africa and Africans*; Johannes M. Postman, *The Dutch in the Atlantic Slave Trade, 1600–1815* (Cambridge University Press, 1990), 1.

[46] AHNA, cod. 443, fl. 39, July 16, 1799.

[47] AHNA, cod. 443, fl. 60, May 13, 1800.

actions of a vassal *soba* against a nonvassal entity. The Kwandu were organized in small groups and, without a clear leader, were seen as a major holdup for the colonial expansion.[48] A few years later, in 1817, the *sobas* of Kitata and Kalukembe, vassals within the jurisdiction of Caconda, invaded some of the Ndombe territory in between the port of Benguela and Kalukembe, capturing people and cattle.[49] The Ndombe had been a vassal of the Portuguese since the 1620s, as seen in Chapter 1. They lived just outside of Benguela and along the coast under different chiefdoms. Any attack on them represented a threat to the residents along the coast. Owing to their proximity to and long relationship with the colonial state, the Ndombe were relatively familiar with the Portuguese. Kitata and Kalukembe raiders seized people who probably understood some Portuguese and had previous contact with the Atlantic world, and some of them probably were Luso-Africans. It is not clear where these people ended up enslaved, although probably some were brought to the market in Benguela to be sold to trans-Atlantic slave traders. Enslavement of the Ndombe in the early nineteenth century shows that the slaving frontier was not moving inland. Men on the spot and African rulers targeted vulnerable people, even if they were living just outside of Benguela in areas that were supposed to be protected by the Portuguese Crown. As this case demonstrates, the Ndombe and other groups living on the coast did not enjoy the "calm surface of politics" after the slaving began moving inland.[50] They continued to be targeted and captured by slavers.

Warfare generated a large number of women and children as captives. Seized in raids, they could be sold in public markets in the colonial port or in the interior, where there was a continuous high demand for female slaves.[51] They also could be incorporated into groups to perform productive tasks such as clearing land and cultivating crops. Women could be absorbed as dependents, but they also might be sold or even kidnapped

---

[48] AHU, caixa 129, doc. 47, October 5, 1814.

[49] AHNA, cod. 155, fl 5–6v., August 29, 1817. Cadornega mentioned that the Ndombe were loyal vassals to the Portuguese, who used to raid for slaves in this territory; see António de Oliveira Cadornega, *História Geral das Guerras Angolanas* (Lisbon: Agência Geral do Ultramar, 1972 [1680]), 3, 172. See also Curto, "Story of Nbena," 44.

[50] Miller, *Way of Death*, 149.

[51] See Roquinaldo A. Ferreira, "Transforming Atlantic Slaving: Trade, Warfare and Territorial Control in Angola, 1650–1800," PhD dissertation, University of California, Los Angeles, 2003, 177–8; and John K. Thornton, "The Art of War in Angola, 1575–1680," *Comparative Studies in Society and History* 30 (1988), 360–78. For the internal market for female slaves, see Claire Robertson and Martin Klein (eds.), *Women and Slavery in Africa* (Madison: University of Wisconsin Press, 1983), 3–25.

again. A list of people captured in a small raid in Catumbela in 1808 highlights the vulnerable situation of women and children. In this village north of Benguela, on the littoral, of eighty-four people seized, there were only nine men. The rest included twenty-six women and forty-nine children.[52] Women and children outnumbered the men by a ratio of nine to one. The number of children, including ten boys, eleven girls, and twenty-five younger children whose gender is not specified, corresponds to existing information on the age profile of the export trade from West Central Africa.[53]

The correspondence of the governors of Angola and Benguela with officials in the interior portrays the image of endemic raiding. No African leader could adequately defend his subjects and dependents under these conditions.[54] Even strong political entities, such as the *sobados* of Mbailundu and Ngalangue in the highlands, were constantly attacking and being attacked, indicating that military power was not enough to protect subjects. The alliances between *sobas* were temporary and responded to immediate necessities and motivations. In fact, the pressure of trans-Atlantic commerce reinforced competition and political fragmentation, pushing neighboring states to attack each other and increasing the demand for gunpowder and weapons from individuals and leaders in the interior who were trying to defend themselves. Societies adapted to the growing pressure of violence, as they have done in other historical moments. In January 1809, the *sobas* of Wambu, Kitete, and Kipeio raided the *presídio* of Caconda, an act of resistance against colonial power, the constant raids, demands for tribute, and in general, the violence associated with the Portuguese presence inland. In the attack, the forces of these *sobas* destroyed crops, stole cattle, and captured a large number of dependents, people who probably were baptized and had some understanding of Portuguese.[55] Yet these traits were not enough to protect

---

[52] AHNA, cod. 445, fl. 19–19v., June 10, 1808. For a case of a man kidnapped in the interior of Benguela, see Miller, *Way of Death*, 2–3.

[53] David Eltis and Stanley Engerman, "Was the Slave Trade Dominated by Men?" *Journal of Interdisciplinary History* 23, no. 2 (1992), 252; and Eltis, Behrendt, Richardson, and Klein, *The Transatlantic Slave Trade*.

[54] See the case of the *sobas* of Ngalangue, Sambo, and Kingolo, who joined forces in 1824; AHNA, cod. 508. fl. 14–14v., January 16, 1824. Also, the joint forces of five *sobas* of Nano attacked the *soba* of Sapa, who was collaborating with the Portuguese; AHU, caixa 121, doc. 68, August 28, 1810. For the adoption of warfare as a mechanism to enslave people, see, among others, José C. Curto, "Experiences of Enslavement in West Central Africa," *Social History* 41, no. 82 (2008), 3; and Miller, *Way of Death*, 105–39.

[55] AHNA, cod. 445, fl. 34–34v., January 27, 1809.

them. In fact, they could even be seen as the reason for their enslavement because Luso-Africans in Benguela, as with the *lançados* on the Upper Guinea coast, were particularly vulnerable. People who lived in the fortress of Caconda were exposed to some degree to a Portuguese culture because it was a colonial fort. Caconda's population could be considered Luso-African, in the sense that most of its residents had adjusted to both cultures, similar to the population who lived in Benguela. Supposedly protected by Portuguese legislation, those captured in Caconda were deeply connected to the trans-Atlantic slave trade, including a large number of merchants and colonial officials who had settled there. Moreover, some of these people had been baptized and married at the Nossa Senhora da Conceição Church, showing the creolization of the local population and their exposure to some Catholic practices. *Filhos da terra* or not, these were Luso-Africans who suddenly were enslaved and sold to Atlantic slavers.[56] In September, Caconda was raided again, the raiders almost reaching the fort itself on that occasion. In the process, they captured people and destroyed food supplies, once again indicating that periods of famine were human-made and a direct consequence of expansion of the trans-Atlantic slave trade.[57] By early 1811, the *soba* of Ngalangue directed another raid against Caconda, which resulted in far more devastation than before. Only two agricultural estates in the *presídio* escaped the raid, whereas the remaining inhabitants suffered great material losses, and most of them lost dependents.[58] Raided at least three times in less than 2 years, the inhabitants of Caconda faced economic hardship and had seen the capture of relatives, dependents, and friends, people like themselves who were seized, enslaved, and forced to march to the coast. They realized their vulnerability and witnessed the encroaching power of the trans-Atlantic slave trade, which from some perspectives they were responsible for once they engaged in slave trading. When the people captured in Caconda arrived in Brazil, they were recognized as "*crioulos*" or even "*crioulos* of Benguela."[59] Identified as seasoned slaves, the people

---

[56] Mariana Candido, "Trade, Slavery and Migration in the Interior of Benguela: The Case of the Caconda, 1830–1870," in *Angola on the Move: Transport Routes, Communications, and History*, ed. Beatrix Heintze and Achim von Oppen (Frankfurt: Otto Lemberck, 2008), 63–84; and Green, *The Rise of the Trans-Atlantic Slave Trade*, 248–51.

[57] AHNA, cod. 445, fl. 41., September 6, 1809.

[58] AHNA, cod. 445, fl. 88–88v., March 10, 1811; and AHU, caixa 123, doc. 15, March 10, 1811.

[59] See Arquivo Nacional do Rio de Janeiro (ANRJ), cod. 184, vol. 3, "Escravos Emancipados." See also Luis Raposo, *Marcas de Escravos. Listas de escravos emancipados vindos a bordo de navios negreiros (1839–1841)* (Rio de Janeiro: Arquivo Nacional, 1990).

captured in regions not far from the coast were somewhat conversant with the Portuguese Atlantic world.

During the late 1820s, Portuguese administrators described a period of particularly intense turbulence throughout the interior. The governor of Benguela and the captains of the inland *presídios* reported a series of wars that pitted *sobas* against other rulers, some attacking Portuguese-controlled territory and others expropriating goods from *pombeiros* almost at random.[60] On October 18, 1827, the interim governor of Benguela, Joaquim Aurélio de Oliveira, reported that subjects of the *sobas* of Kitata, Kiaka, Ika, Fundi, Bengo, and Kitete had attacked *pombeiros* along the road that led to the fort of Quilengues. Their action lasted approximately twenty days, during which they seized slaves and stole weapons and textiles.[61] Months later, on February 29, 1828, the same Aurélio de Oliveira reported to the governor of Angola, Nicolau de Abreu Castelo Branco, that the *soba* of Wambu had organized an offensive against the fort of Dombe Grande. The attempt by the captain of the *presídio* of Quilengues to enforce the payment of tribute had encouraged this *soba* to retaliate. Knowing that the Portuguese force at the fortress of Quilengues was ready for a possible attack, the *soba* of Wambu attacked Dombe Grande, a smaller and less-well-protected *presidio*, founded in the 1770s. Aurélio de Oliveira reported, "There is news that the *soba*'s attack was successful and he obtained a large number of slaves."[62] These slaves were probably captured from the five *sobas* who lived around the fortress of Dombe Grande, Muene Kalunga, on the littoral and Muene Mama, Kapembe, Muene Chela, and Muene Kizamba, who were located miles away from the port of Benguela. People who lived in Dombe Grande, 60 km south of Benguela, also were exposed to Portuguese culture and, if enslaved and sold to trans-Atlantic slave traders, arrived in the Americas with a strong repertoire of Lusophone cultural practices. *Presídios*, such as Dombe Grande and Caconda, often were the targets of powerful rulers' raids, who resented the presence of

---

[60] See especially the reports on AHNA, cod. 449, fl. 116v.–117, October 18, 1827; fl. 128, February 29, 1828; and fl. 147–147v., October 2, 1828. For the violence in this period, see Miller, "Angola Central," 38–9.

[61] AHNA, cod. 449, fl. 116v.–117, October 18, 1827.

[62] AHNA, cod. 449, fl. 128, February 29, 1828; and AHNA, cod. 449, fl. 147–147v., October 2, 1828. For more on the Dombe Grande, see Ralph Delgado, *Ao Sul do Cuanza* (Lisbon: Beleza, 1944), 183–5; and Maria Alexandra Aparício, "Política de Boa Vizinhança: os Chefes Locais e os Europeus em Meados do século XIX. O Caso do Dombe Grande," in *II Reunião Internacional História de Angola* (São Paulo: CEA-USP/SDG-Marinha/ CAPES, 1997), 109–16.

Portuguese colonialism, as seen in the actions of men on the spot, but who also desired weapons and ammunition, as well as the alcohol and textiles stored there.[63]

Characterized by a lack of soldiers and serving as *entrepôts* for *pombeiros* carrying their wares, these Portuguese military administrative sites were vulnerable in part because of the violence they represented. As late as 1836, for example, the *sobas* of Kalukembe, Luceque, Nguela, Lubando, and Kipungo invaded the *presídio* of Quilengues, during which they robbed a large number of residents, captured people, and destroyed crops.[64] Although no information exists on the number of people kidnapped, let alone their gender, it is easy to imagine that women and children predominated among those captured in these raids. Caught by surprise, those in vulnerable situations would have been the easiest targets. The population of the fortress was considered to be allied with the Portuguese in the colonial and trade enterprise and a target for *sobas* unhappy with colonial policies. People who lived within and around Portuguese fortresses inevitably negotiated their existence with colonial troops and vice versa. As Luso-Africans, they mediated the contact between foreigner traders and local populations beyond the control of Portuguese forces. They were active agents of creolization, and if enslaved, they would bring their know-how to the Americas.

All these accounts of warfare force us to rethink the concept of the slaving region as moving constantly inland, an assumption that armies had to go further inland to obtain more victims in what can be considered a moving slave frontier.[65] The examples explored here demonstrate that warfare happened in regions not far from the coast at relatively later

---

[63] AHNA, cod. 508, fl. 125., April 18, 1828; see also fl. 128, April 24, 1828; and fl. 149v., January 24, 1829; AHNA, cod. 509, fl. 60v.–61, January 17, 1830; and 146v.–149v., October 18, 1836; AHNA, cod. 510, fl. 97v.–98, September 6, 1848. See also instructions from Lisbon to the governor of Benguela to be vigilant and help the *presídios'* commanders to resist the *sobas'* attacks; AHU, cod. 543, fl. 12, July 2, 1830; AHU, caixa 30, doc. 6, January 29, 1737; AHU, sala 12, L. 679, fl. 158, April 18, 1843; AHU, caixa 83, doc. 16, January 22, 1796; AHU, caixa 84, doc. 29, September 24, 1796; AHU, caixa 93A, doc. 20, November 11, 1799; AHU, caixa 95, doc. 18, March 18, 1800; AHU, caixa 123, doc. 15, March 10, 1811; AHU, Angola, Correspondencia dos Governadores, pasta 5, October 5, 1839; AHU, Angola, Correspondencia dos Governadores, pasta 5B, December 24, 1842; and AHU, Angola, Correspondencia dos Governadores, pasta 6A, February 9, 1843. For more on the Dombe Grande, see Ralph Delgado, *Ao Sul do Cuanza* (Lisbon: Beleza, 1944), 183–5; and Mariana P Candido, "Slave Trade and New Identities in Benguela, 1700–1860," *Portuguese Studies Review* 19, no. 1–2 (2011): 59–75.
[64] AHNA, cod. 509. 146 v.–149v., October 18, 1836.
[65] Miller, *Way of Death*, 140–53.

dates. Several of the raids investigated here targeted populations that were already exposed to Portuguese culture and colonial code. We might not know how many people were enslaved in the areas around the colonial fortresses of Quilengues, Dombe Grande, or Caconda, but the existence of raids on communities fewer than 250 km from the coast shows that the slaving frontier had not moved inland by the nineteenth century. Slavers and raiders targeted unprotected people regardless of where they were. The Portuguese and African forces were not able to protect subjects or vassals and even people living within fortresses. Notions of identity, of being insiders or outsiders, and of allegiance to the Portuguese Crown also were fundamental in defining who could or could not be enslaved.[66]

Kidnapping and the Vulnerability of Free Blacks

The consolidation of Benguela as a colony led to urbanization and new administrative positions to ensure that people living in the overseas territories enjoyed some rights as Portuguese citizens. As a result, the bureaucracy put in place to benefit European subjects offered new rights and new legal spaces for local populations. The expansion of the trans-Atlantic slave trade and the heightened level of violence and insecurity made it impossible to protect people from enslavement. Free blacks in Benguela and Caconda were particularly vulnerable.[67] Recognizing the problem, by 1676, the Overseas Council, the *Conselho Ultramarino*, suggested the prohibition of white men, mixed-race, or blacks wearing pants and canes from traveling in the interior. The argument was that those men were responsible for capturing free people, regardless of their free status or position as vassals to the Portuguese.[68] In 1689, a royal decree recommended that suits for freedom, the *mucanos*, include the

[66] See John and Jean Comaroff, *Ethnography and the Historical Imagination* (Boulder, CO: Westview Press, 1992), especially chap. 2; and Frederik Barth, *Los grupos étnicos y sus fronteras* (Mexico: Fondo de Cultura Economica, 1976), 19–22, 36.

[67] For more examples, see Candido, "African Freedom Suits," 447–59; Roquinaldo Ferreira, "Atlantic Microhistories: Mobility, Personal Ties, and Slaving in the Black Atlantic World (Angola and Brazil)," in *Cultures of the Lusophone Black Atlantic*, ed. Nancy Priscilla Naro, Roger Sansi-Roca, and David H. Treece (New York: Palgrave, 2007), 99–128; Curto, "Experiences of Enslavement"; and several examples in James Sweet, *Recreating Africa. Culture, Kinship, and Religion in the African-Portuguese World, 1441–1770* (Chapel Hill: University of North Carolina Press, 2003). Free blacks also were vulnerable in the interior, although fewer sources reveal processes of capture and enslavement. For a reconstruction of a case from the interior of Benguela, see Miller, *Way of Death*, 2–3.

[68] AHU, cod. 544, fl. 9, February 12, 1676, fl. 7 and 7v.

presence of two priests to ensure that laws were being followed and that no person originally free was enslaved.[69] The *mucano* tribunal heard cases pertaining to civil and criminal law, originally in Mbundu states and later including other people, among them non-Kimbundu and others living in the hinterland of Benguela. A local institution, the tribunal was adopted by the colonial state to handle cases of "indigenous rights." In the process, the *mucano* institution was transformed as well, producing written documents rather than the oral agreements that previously had characterized the institution. In order to keep control and bring the tribunal under colonial authority, in 1698 the Overseas Council decided to place the captain-major in charge of the *mucanos* trials, requiring that the cases be registered in a book listing the presentation of the case, the witnesses, the defense, the sentence, and the appeal.[70] No *mucanos* book for Benguela has been found; while there are some cases and legal procedures registered in official correspondence, they are not necessarily recorded in a distinctive book. As in the case of the ceremonies of *undar* that became associated with the vassalage treaties (seen in Chapter 1), the adoption of the *mucano* institution by the colonial state reveals how creolization was a two-way phenomenon that affected all involved. It also reinforces my argument that the trans-Atlantic slave trade transformed institutions, including appropriating some for its own survival and continuation, provoking major readjustments in the societies of Benguela and its hinterland.

This section explores the vulnerability of free blacks who were accused of being slaves and had to prove otherwise. Freedom in Benguela had to be established by witnesses and protected by the court. Unlike other places where an African or people of African descent were not considered to be credible witnesses, in Benguela, Africans were the only witnesses available for most people.[71] As a way to overcome the enslavement of vassals and free black people, the Portuguese colonial administration introduced in 1769 the *inquisidor das liberdades* (the "interrogator of freedom") to "examine the slaves coming from the interior to be sold and embarked to Brazil, hoping that no free person is among the slaves."[72]

---

[69] ANTT, Mç. 7, doc. 1, "Carta Régia de 22 de Março de 1689."
[70] ANTT, Mç. 7, doc. 1 "Carta Régia de 15 de Março de 1698." For more on *mucanos*, see Catarina Madeira Santos, "Entre deux droits: les Lumières en Angola (1750–v.1800)," *Annales. Histoire, Sciences Sociales* 60, no. 4 (2007): 817–48; and Ferreira, "Slaving and Resistance to Slaving in West Central Africa," 128–30.
[71] Scott, "'She … Refuses to Deliver Up Herself," 121.
[72] ANTT, Conde de Linhares, Mç. 52, doc. 14, November 11, 1769.

Manoel Gonçalves, the first priest to occupy the position in Benguela, was in charge of baptisms and of inquiring into the conditions of enslavement of each captive. If no claim of original freedom was found, the priest baptized the person and then branded him or her with the royal mark, confirming his or her slave status. The creation of this position stresses the fact that the enslavement of free-born people must have been common in the eighteenth century.

After successful commercial exchanges in his state around 1789, the *soba* of Mbailundu offered the Luso-African trader António José da Costa porters to carry his goods to Benguela. On arrival, the *pombeiro* not only sold the ivory, beeswax, and slaves bought in Mbailundu, but he also sold the free porters to a coastal trader who shipped them to Luanda. Tricked, the free porters were enslaved while away from their community and the ruler who could protect them. The porters remained nameless in the documents but attracted the attention of the governor, who intervened because he feared the *soba*'s reaction. He secured the release of the porters and reprimanded the trader.[73] In the same year, another trader seized eight people from Mbailundu, justifying his actions by claiming that the *soba* owed him money. Other traders based in Benguela obtained the intervention of the governor of Angola to avoid upsetting commercial relations with the African *soba* of Mbailundu, who controlled the major highland markets for slaves, beeswax, and ivory.[74] In 1798, the governor of Benguela, Alexandre José Botelho, "suspected that the *pombeiros* [were] responsible for the violence against blacks in the interior."[75] And decades later, in 1845, Olosoma Riambulla requested that the governor of Angola free his porters, who had been kidnapped while trading in Pungo Ndongo.[76] As these cases demonstrate, it was relatively easy to seize free porters provided by rulers and sell them as if they had been

---

[73] AHU, Angola, caixa 74, doc. 15, April 21, 1789.

[74] AHU, Angola, caixa 74, doc. 49, November 10, 1789; and AHU, Angola, cod. 1630, fl. 148, July 5, 1794; and AHU, Angola, cod. 1631, fl. 153, August 1, 1795. For more on Mbailundu, see Heywood, *Contested Power*; Delgado, *Ao Sul do Cuanza: Ocupação e Aproveitamento do Antigo Reino de Benguela* (Lisbon: Imprensa Beleza, 1944); Jan Vansina, *Kingdoms of the Savanna: A History of Central African States until European Occupation* (Madison: University of Wisconsin Press, 1970), 198.

[75] AHNA, cod. 443, fl. 29, June 18, 1798. On trickery in other contexts, see Randy J. Sparks, "Two Princes of Calabar: An Atlantic Odyssey from Slavery to Freedom," *William and Mary Quarterly* 59, no. 3 (2002), 555–84.

[76] Linda Heywood, *Contested Power*, 20. For other cases of conflicts between traders, porters, and African rulers, see the conflicts in Kitata and Kaluquembe; AHNA, cod. 443, fl. 114v.–115, January 9, 1803; AHNA, cod. 442, fl. 223–223v., May 10, 1803.

bought in the interior. African rulers could appeal to the authorities on behalf of their subjects, but porters were in an extremely vulnerable position throughout the period, even though rulers recognized their obligation to protect them.

Rulers struggled to obtain slaves to pay for commodities and alliances with the Portuguese at the same time that they had to protect their own people. Kidnapping outsiders became a strategy to enslave people. Such was the case of a free *mulatto* woman who traveled to Mbailundu in 1811 to collect the debts of her deceased husband. Dona Leonor de Carvalho Fonseca traveled to Mbailundu in the company of her two daughters. The *soba* of Mbailundu, probably unhappy with her presence and the need to repay old debts, ordered her enslavement, which can be understood here as a political act, where, by enslaving a Luso-African, he disputed Portuguese notions of legal enslavement. A vassal of the Portuguese Crown by 1810s, the *soba* had agreed on protecting *pombeiros*, and his decision to enslave Dona Leonor should be read as a political dispute with the colonial forces over his obligations, such as paying tribute in the form of slaves. The three women then were sold to an itinerant trader who transported them to the town of Benguela. In Benguela, Dona Leonor was sold to the captain of the ship *Grão Penedo* and put on board, destined to be sold in Rio de Janeiro. Her two daughters remained in Benguela. The governor of Benguela, rather than protecting the widow of a Benguela trader, seized Dona Leonor's two daughters. In a small town of fewer than 3,000 people, it is difficult to imagine that the governor did not know one of the traders based under his jurisdiction. Probably more interested in his personal profit, he ignored the fact that Dona Leonor spoke Portuguese, lived in Benguela, and was a slave trader. Her daughters were put to work as domestic servants at his official house. On arrival in Luanda, Dona Leonor's story reached the governor of Angola, José de Oliveira Barbosa, probably through the freedom inquisitor.[77] She claimed that she was a vassal of the Portuguese Crown. As a vassal and a mixed-race person, probably implying that she was a locally born descendant of Portuguese, she could not be enslaved. Dona Leonor got the attention of the Luanda-based authorities, and the governor declared her free and ordered that she be returned to Benguela and reunited with her daughters.

[77] AHNA, Cod. 323, fl. 28v.–29, August 19, 1811; AHNA, cod. 323, fl. 30v.–31, August 20, 1811. For more on D. Leonor's case, see Candido, "African Freedom Suits."

Scholars have pointed to the use of judicial litigation as an example of African agency and resistance to enslavement.[78] José Curto and Roquinaldo Ferreira, for example, have identified cases where captives relied on relatives to challenge their enslavement. Curto and Ferreira failed to recognize, however, that despite their agency, litigants reinforced the role of Portuguese colonial officials as arbitrators of their fate. West Central Africans were compelled to accept that Portuguese agents could decide who was "legally" or "illegally" enslaved, revealing the compliance of all involved with the system and the notion of slavery as a legal institution. In the process of fighting for their freedom, litigants accepted and reinforced the legality of slavery. Victims of the expansion of the trans-Atlantic slave trade, through their resistance, contributed to legitimizing slavery.

Free black people, especially traders, were far from secure. Their economic activities did not protect them from enslavement, and neither did their ownership of valuable goods such as textiles and guns. They were not protected by their place of residence, as seen in the case of Dona Leonor and others. Luso-Africans living in or outside Portuguese control were not protected against capture. In fact, they were frequently attacked, demonstrating how rulers and Africans in the interior saw the traders' presence as linked to the Atlantic economy and therefore disruptive. In 1817, four *pombeiros* operating in the interior on behalf of a Benguela lieutenant had their bodies branded. When they finally managed to tell their stories to a priest, they explained that they were free black men sent to the interior with orders to buy slaves when they were captured by *gentio*, or heathens, who were probably threatened by the presence of coastal petty traders. The traders changed hands three times before arriving in Benguela, where they were about to be placed on a ship.[79]

The cases of the traders and Dona Leonor indicate how *pombeiros* and other petty traders were seen in Benguela's interior – as agents of the Atlantic economy, allies of coastal slave traders, and perpetrators of violence. Like the *lançados* of Upper Guinea, *pombeiros* and other Luso-Africans facilitated the expansion of creolization inland, adapting traits of different cultures. Yet they were seen also as agents of destabilization of preexisting economies and political structures. As a result,

---

[78] Curto, "Struggling Against Enslavement: The Case of José Manuel in Benguela, 1816–20"; Ferreira, "Slaving and Resistance to Slaving in West Central Africa."

[79] AHNA, cod. 446, fl. 112v.–113v., January 31, 1817; AHNA, cod. 446, fl. 136v., July 12, 1817; see also, AHU, Angola, caixa 132, doc. 30, January 31, 1817.

they were in a vulnerable situation, constantly attacked and enslaved, showing how the trans-Atlantic slave trade had a destructive effect even among those deeply engaged in and profiting from it.[80] These cases also reveal the ability of captives to contact the freedom inquisitor and, using Portuguese legislation, claim their original freedom. By arguing their vassal status and knowledge of Portuguese, they differentiated themselves from most Africans, who were also free but unable to use the legal code to protect themselves. Like Dona Leonor and her daughters; Juliana, the woman from Kilengues described in the beginning of the chapter; and other free Africans, although theoretically protected by Portuguese legislation, they were enslaved. They were removed from their society, enslaved, and put under a "relation of domination." Nonetheless, they were not socially dead.[81] For Orlando Patterson, slavery was social death because slaves had no rights and no honor and were cut off from their kin in what he calls "natal alienation." Yet the cases analyzed here show that enslavement in Benguela was strongly legalized by both Portuguese and African rulers. More important is the fact that captives did not see themselves as socially dead, as these cases demonstrate. They resisted throughout the process. Although we cannot recover the ways in which most people resisted, which might have included escaping from caravans, fighting back against their captors, or killing aggressors, the cases presented here show the use of Portuguese courts and their refusal to remain passive and accept their fate.

Along the coast, the pressure to supply the trans-Atlantic slave traders generated tension and perpetuated violence. To restore peace, new authorities arrived in Angola, committed to respecting the law. In 1812, João de Alvelos Leiria assumed the position of governor of Benguela. He declared that he would follow the regulations and ensure that no free person was enslaved.[82] His mandate was to release illegally enslaved people, and in this practice he had the support of the Benguela traders, who feared retaliation from African authorities.[83] A few months after

---

[80] For more on *lançados*, see Green, *The Rise of the Trans-Atlantic Slave Trade*, 248–51.

[81] Orlando Patterson, *Slavery and Social Death: A Comparative Study* (Cambridge, MA: Harvard University Press, 1982), 13. For a more recent interpretation of slavery as social death, see Stephanie Smallwood, *Saltwater Slavery. A Middle Passage from Africa to American Diaspora* (Cambridge, MA: Harvard University Press, 2007), 59–61. For an opposite perspective on the debate, see Lovejoy, "Identifying Enslaved Africans," 1–28.

[82] AHU, Angola, caixa 125, doc. 42, 5 October, 1812.

[83] It was part of the governor's duty to ensure that no free person was enslaved. See Carlos Couto, "Regimento de Governo Subalterno de Benguela," *Studia*, 45 (1981): 289; See AHU, Angola, caixa 125, doc. 22.

the inauguration of Leiria, a kidnapping case was brought to his attention. According to a free woman named Maria, soldiers had seized her daughter in Benguela.[84] Maria lived in the house of the traders Francisco José Bandeira and Dona Maria Gomes Moutinho. It is not clear whether she worked there or had some more intimate relationship with him, but a baptism record from 1812 offers some clues. In February 1812, a slave woman named Maria brought her daughter, Vitória, to receive the holy sacraments at the Nossa Senhora do Pópulo Church. Young Vitória was baptized as a free person, despite the fact that her mother, Maria, belonged to Dona Maria Gomes Moutinho. No one was named as the father of the girl, raising the possibility that the trader Francisco José Bandeira, Dona Moutinho's husband, was the father of Vitória. By mid-September 1812, the trader Bandeira had died. After his death, soldiers and Portuguese officers visited his house in order to make an inventory of his belongings, as was practiced at that time. During their activities, they apprehended Maria's daughter, possibly believing that she was one of Bandeira's slaves. They did not take into consideration that there were free people living as Bandeira's dependents. On appeal, the governor of Benguela restored the freedom of Vitória, Maria's daughter. Vitória's case demonstrates further that free people were vulnerable, even when living in the urban port under Portuguese authority, because they and their descendants could be mistaken as slaves, undermining their freedom. Maria could only secure her daughter's freedom through intervention of the governor, who recognized her rights as a free person. A corrupt official unwilling to help would have easily confirmed Maria's daughter's enslavement. Maria's social contacts, rather than her daughter's baptism and Christian name, were instrumental in protecting her daughter.

The first 20 years of the nineteenth century saw an increase in the number of slaves from Benguela, probably a result of the Anglo-Portuguese treaties restricting the slave trade to south of the equator.[85] External demand exacerbated the cycle of violence and increased the incidence of kidnappings taking place around Benguela. Unscrupulous people found many ways to enslave members of their own kin. In 1812, Katete, a free

---

[84] AHNA, cod. 440, fl. 54, requisition n. 144, September 19, 1812. For more on Francisco José Bandeira and Dona Maria Gomes Moutinho, see Arquivo do Arçobispado de Luanda, Benguela, Livro de Óbitos, fl. 104v., April 4, 1806.

[85] Between 1781 and 1800, 77,580 slaves were exported from Benguela. For the next two decades, the number jumped to 116,371. See *The Trans-Atlantic Slave Trade Database*, www.slavevoyages.org/tast/database/search.faces. For suppression of the trade, see Lovejoy, *Transformations in Slavery*, 252–75.

black man in Catumbela, requested the protection of the governor of Benguela. After seeing his mother sold by her relatives, Katete was afraid that he would suffer the same fate. Lacking the support of his community, he opted to seek Portuguese protection and avoided enslavement.[86] Cases like this reveal how the profits of the slave trade were so tempting that they obscured moral standards.[87] Kidnapping and trickery could overlap because people were susceptible to deception when they had confidence that a trusted person would not enslave them. Less lucky than Katete, who managed to avoid enslavement, was Albano, who was sold by his relatives to an itinerant trader. His situation was difficult because no one came to support his claim of "original freedom." Albano's request for freedom was denied in 1812, and he remained a slave in Benguela.[88] Albano's case shows the importance of friends and family in rescuing someone from enslavement. Like Katete, who was afraid of relatives who could enslave him, Albano could not rely on his next of kin and remained enslaved. As happened with Juliana, in the opening of this chapter, Albano was stripped of his freedom, a victim of the high demand for slave labor in Benguela. Yet, unlike Juliana, no one came to help him.

Other stories demonstrate how community members took advantage of people who trusted them, as with Nbena. In 1817, while traveling from the fortress of Catumbela to Benguela, Nbena met an old woman who belonged to António Leal do Sacramento, a lieutenant-colonel in the Benguela militia. For reasons that are not clear, Nbena followed the old woman to Sacramento's house. After their arrival, António Leal do Sacramento gave Nbena an axe and forced her to work on his land. Nbena was held in captivity despite the fact she was born a free Ndombe woman, nominally under Portuguese protection. After two days, Nbena escaped to her village. Months later, Sacramento learned that Nbena and her daughter were in Benguela and ordered their seizure. She was branded and sold to João de Oliveira Dias, the shipmaster of the *Astrea*. Nbena and her daughter were sent to Luanda, presumably for eventual transport to Brazil. However, the *soba* of Katumbela and several other witnesses testified to the governor of Benguela that Nbena was a free woman and that Sacramento had enslaved her illegally.[89] The governor ordered

---

[86] AHNA, cod. 440, fl. 29, requisition n. 91, August 17, 1812.

[87] See, among others, Curto, "The Story of Nbena"; and Sparks, "The Two Princes of Calabar."

[88] AHNA, cod. 440, fl. 30, requisition n. 107, August 25, 1812.

[89] Curto, "Story of Nbena, 1817–1820," has an interesting reconstruction and analysis of Nbena's case. For more on Nbena, see also AHNA, cod. 446, fl. 154v.–155v.,

her return to Benguela so that he could investigate the case, which took several months, during which time the governor held her in custody.

Nbena was not the only free person to suffer at Sacramento's hands. José Manoel, a free black soldier serving under Sacramento in the Henriques regiment, went inland to conduct business. On his journey, a *soba* captured him. The *soba* gave him the opportunity to regain his freedom if he paid a fine of forty-six pieces of cloth. José Manoel paid the fine and was set free, hoping that on returning to Benguela he would find someone willing to lend him the textiles. Knowing that Sacramento could afford the fine, José Manoel sought his help. Sacramento advanced the cloth and a bottle of *gerebita* on condition that José Manoel would serve him until the debt was liquidated. For more than 2 years, José Manoel served as a porter, carrying Sacramento on his palanquin. Then Sacramento considered selling José Manoel into slavery, as he had done with Nbena. José Manoel's relatives offered Sacramento forty-six pieces of cloth to regain their kin's freedom. However, Sacramento demanded two male slaves as compensation for José Manoel's freedom. José Manoel's relatives had no alternative but to recognize the increase in the redemption price. They offered a young slave woman to settle the debt. Sacramento took the slave but promised to release José only after he received the difference between the price of the young slave woman and the male slaves he had demanded. José Manoel eventually regained his freedom, but only after the governor of Benguela intervened.[90] Cases such as these illustrate the vulnerability of people in Benguela and its hinterland to men on the spot who abused their power and violently subjugated people. Captains could commit crimes, enslave entire families, and pawn people.[91] By the time that someone could complain about these actions, the captives could have disappeared into the international slave trade.

Colonial legislation available in Benguela should be read as the result of clashes between different sectors of the society. In Brazil, the Crown

---

December 11, 1817; AHNA, cod. 447, fl. 9v.–10v., July 7, 1818; AHNA, cod. 447, fl. 16–17, September 16, 1818; AHNA, cod. 447, fl. 25, November 3, 1818; and AHNA, cod. 447, fl. 30v.–34, October 12, 1818.

[90] AHNA, cod. 447, fl. 30v.–34, October 6, 1818; and AHNA, cod. 507, fl. 129v.–132v., January 18, 1819. For more on José Manoel's case, see José C. Curto, "Struggling Against Enslavement: The Case of José Manuel in Benguela, 1816–20," *Canadian Journal of African Studies* 39, no. 1 (2005), 96–122.

[91] For pawnship in West Central Africa, see Miller, *Way of Death*, 567; Jan Vansina, "Ambaca Society and the Slave Trade, c. 1760–1845," *Journal of African History* 46, no. 1 (2005), 14–20; and Curto, "Struggling Against Enslavement," 96–122.

tried not to interfere with the slave owner's power over his or her slaves,[92] whereas in Angola, authorities regulated who could or could not be enslaved. The laws represented an attempt to bring order during a period of social instability, when boundaries of freedom and enslavement were easily forgotten or ignored. Authorities also intervened and arbitrated conflicts between residents and men on the spot in order to guarantee order and the continuation of trade. In 1826, the Benguela trader Vicente de Barros purchased a captive in the interior and brought him with a group of slaves to be baptized in Benguela. During the collective ceremony, the enslaved man identified himself as Manoel Joaquim Pinto de Almeida, a black soldier who had deserted and subsequently been enslaved in the interior. The priest, who was ready to brand him with the royal stamp, paid attention to his story,[93] particularly because in 1796 the Queen of Portugal had ordered that if there was any doubt, the priest should not brand people claiming freedom. They were to be imprisoned until a further investigation could be concluded. Following the rules, the priest brought Vicente de Barros to see the governor of Benguela, João Victor Jorge. Situations such as this example show that even colonial officials were vulnerable to seizure when they were away from their community. Without committed people who could protect them, free blacks were subject to capture. In many cases it was the support of kin that brought about an individual's release. In other instances, relatives enslaved their own kin. Those who could claim to belong to the Portuguese empire had a better chance of avoiding the middle passage, and the category of being free born was an important source of protection. In order to safeguard people who were illegally enslaved, in 1828 the governor ordered the strict inspection of every ship leaving the coast.[94] Yet people continued to be captured and enslaved within Benguela and its immediate interior.

In January 1829, Francisca Joaquina Ignácia reported to the interim governor of Benguela, Joaquim Aurélio de Oliveira, that the captain of the militia had strangled a couple of people "originally free" and enslaved several others, including her sister. Ignácia accused the captain of following

---

[92] Silvia Lara, *Campos da Violencia: Escravos e Senhores na Capitania do Rio de Janeiro, 1750–1808* (São Paulo: Paz e Terra, 1988); and Grinberg, "Slavery, Manumission and the Law," 401–11.

[93] AHNA, cod. 508, fl. 74–74v., October 4, 1826.

[94] AHU, Angola, caixa 159, doc. 55, August 9, 1828. For the purchase of slaves directly from the *gentio*, see AHU, Angola, Correspondência dos Governadores, pasta 1B, September 12, 1837. For the litigation, see AHU, Angola, caixa 83, doc. 41, April 13, 1796. See also Heywood, "Slavery and its Transformation," 22.

customary law to justify enslaving people under any pretext, despite the fact that they lived under Portuguese jurisdiction. Oliveira supported Francisca Joaquina Ignácia's claim and notified the governor of Angola about the captain's behavior. The captain had enslaved people because of debt, legal under some African rulers around Benguela, but illegal in the eyes of the Portuguese Crown. Oliveira declared his commitment to locating Ignácia's sister. According to the letter of the governor, captains, including those born in Angola, had to abide by Portuguese law and could not subject people who committed "minor crimes to enslavement, even if they were blacks." This interesting case of Captain Oliveira employing customary law shows how plural legal systems coexisted in the first half of the nineteenth century in Benguela and its interior, blending local and colonial legal systems, as in the case of the Portuguese colonial state adopting the *mucanos* tribunal, explored earlier in the chapter. As this case exemplifies, "Atlantic traders [or in this case colonial authorities] had to respond to local patterns of culture, economics and politics in order to meet their commercial needs."[95] Men on the spot who were supposed to "respect Portuguese legislation" sometimes employed customary law if that offered an advantage, in a clear process of institution creolization, where the African legal system could be employed for the advantage of the Portuguese officer.[96] The behavior of the captain also violated the instructions of the Portuguese Crown that "punishment for capital crimes shall be either the death penalty or public work, for both blacks and whites."[97] There is no mention of enslavement. Ignacia's denunciation was vital to guaranteeing freedom for those enslaved by the captain of the militia. Rather than the "principle of liberty" that afforded freedom to slaves who stepped on free soil, people captured in Benguela used the principle of "original freedom," challenging the legality of their enslavement and the actions of perpetrators and relying on Portuguese or local notions of legality to recuperate their freedom.[98] In the process, slavery and the slave trade were internalized as the norm as well as legitimate.

---

[95] Green, *The Rise of the Trans-Atlantic Slave Trade*, 259.

[96] AHNA, cod. 449, fl. 160v.–161, January 27, 1829.

[97] "Instruções para o Novo Governador de Benguela," in *Textos para a História da África Austral (século XVIII)*, ed. Maria Emília Madeira dos Santos (Lisbon: Publicações Alfa, 1989), 52.

[98] For the principle of free soil see, among others, Sue Peabody, *"There Are No Slaves in France: "The Political Culture of Race and Slavery in the Ancien Régime"* (New York: Oxford University Press, 1996). For slaves' strategies using the legal system in Brazil, see Keila Grinberg, *Liberata – a lei da Ambiguade: as Ações de Liberdade da Corte de Apelação do Rio de Janeiro no século XIX* (Rio de Janeiro: Relume Dumará, 1994);

In the 1830s, a young woman from Caconda named Quitéria faced kidnapping by someone she trusted. Quitéria was a free woman working for Captain José Joaquim Domingues and his wife. In 1837, Maria de Barros reported that one of her protégés had been seized and sold as a slave. She denounced her husband, Captain Domingues, as the perpetrator. Domingues had not only physically abused Maria, but he had also sold Quitéria, a free woman who was under her protection, to trans-Atlantic slave traders stationed in Benguela. Quitéria and Maria were both from Caconda and probably shared other social or even kin connections. Quitéria's widowed mother had trusted Maria de Barros to support the young woman and teach her how to be a seamstress. After recovering from Domingues' attack, Maria de Barros ran to the port to find Quitéria, who had already been sold and branded. She was on board a slave vessel, but in last minute negotiations, Maria de Barros was able to ransom her with one of her domestic slaves.[99] After hearing Maria de Barros's report, the judge of Benguela ordered José Joaquim Domingues to be arrested. Captain Domingues was sentenced to house detention for six months. This case reveals how coastal people were vulnerable to kidnapping. Although free blacks could be enslaved in the wake of expansion of the trans-Atlantic slave trade, there were cases, including those of Quitéria, Juliana, Nbena, and others, where captive free blacks regained their freedom through ransoming. Ransoming, however, implied the enslavement of another person because a slave was given in exchange for release of the free-born individual. Thus, in itself, ransoming was not a strategy to combat slavery because it required that someone continue in slavery, also legitimizing it as an acceptable institution with codes to be followed and respected. The violence inherent in expansion of the trans-Atlantic slave trade transformed notions of legality and morality, which had a profound effect on the region.

The rising prices of slaves in the 1830s probably stimulated illegal actions. In 1837, the governor of Benguela, Justiniano José dos Reis, wrote to the judge of Benguela, José Dias de Sobral, requesting him to stop allowing traders to seize the subjects of African rulers. According to Reis, Luis Rodrigues Caparica had kidnapped one of the nephews of the *soba* of Kibanda and locked him up in his house, intending to keep the

Eduardo S. Pena, *Pajens da Casa Imperial: Jurisconsultos, Escravidão e a Lei de 1871* (Campinas: Unicamp, 2001); and Regina Xavier, *A Conquista da Liberdade: Libertos em Campinas na Segunda metade do Século XIX* (Campinas: Unicamp, 1997).

[99] AHNA, cod. 509, fl. 215v., March 17, 1837; and AHNA, cod. 450, fl. 49v.–50, February 20, 1837.

nephew until it was safe to sell him. After intervention by the governor, Caparica was forced to free the young man.[100] In the 1840s, a similar case occurred. *Soba* Joanes Gaspar, who was known for conflicting with the Portuguese, captured the son of the *soba* of Katumbela, Francisco Pedro de Moraes, and sold him to a slave trader from Benguela. In 1846, after the appeal of the *soba* of Katumbela, the governor of Benguela ordered the release of the son of Francisco Pedro de Moraes and provided him with a letter asserting his freedom.[101] In 1847, the *soba* of Viye asked Portuguese authorities to locate his son, Katiabala, who had been seized on a journey.[102] However, the governor of Benguela insisted that Katiabala was not in Benguela, even though his other son, Kaucia, had already escaped from António Joaquim de Carvalho's house, where the trader had pretended to be his "friendly" host.[103]

Portuguese officials, for strategic reasons and weak military power, had to respect the wishes of the *sobas*. Portuguese forces were limited in the interior, and they counted on the collaboration of the *sobas* to maintain a minimum level of security and protect the populations living in Portuguese colonial centers. Kidnapping a relative of a ruler was a threat to the maintenance of diplomatic and commercial links. It also revealed that not even members of the political elites, including long-time *sobado* allies, were safe during the era of the trans-Atlantic slave trade. Societies were immersed in insecurity and the waves of violence directly provoked by the pressures of Atlantic commerce and the actions of colonial agents. Slavery was widespread, and relatives of those who had been enslaved had to act quickly because cases of people being seized and shipped to Brazil were common. When arriving in Benguela, slave traders were not obliged to display slaves bought directly from the *gentio*, or non-Christian lands, to Portuguese authorities. They did have to declare slaves from the interior who had been bought through a third party. Merchants were not required to present captives for inspection if they had been bought from *sobas* or anyone else from the hinterland. Merchants could trade enslaved people who had been kidnapped or otherwise illegally acquired, and there was little oversight if African rulers were involved in the capture.

Free blacks were in a vulnerable position, and their peers realized the importance of saving people from captivity and sale into the trans-Atlantic

[100] AHNA, cod. 450, fl. 64–64v., July 19, 1837.
[101] AHNA, cod. 455, fl. 241v., October 28, 1846; AHNA, cod. 455, fl. 272, December 1, 1846; and AHNA, cod. 460, fl. 22v., October 28, 1846.
[102] AHNA, cod. 461, fl. 44v., October 22, 1847.
[103] AHNA, cod. 463, fl. 6v.–7, October 25, 1847.

slave trade. The circumstances of a person's enslavement were crucial to defining the legality of individual cases in the eyes of the Portuguese legal code. Through these accounts, we can glimpse the way that enslavement happened in the interior and along the coast. The cases of Luso-Africans who were enslaved demonstrated that urban people living in areas under Portuguese control, some very close to the coast, were targeted and vulnerable to capture despite Miller's idea that "centralized regimes of the old sort drew the slaving frontier to the center of the continent early in the nineteenth century."[104] As in the case of many Muslims who ended up in slavery in the Americas, Africans who were baptized in Benguela, Caconda, and other places under Portuguese control were not protected by religious affiliation.[105] Even traders in Benguela were in a vulnerable position because Luso-Africans who acted as slave traders could be caught and enslaved, showing the spread of violence and insecurity. Some captives called on kin networks to challenge the legality of their enslavement, and some also used the colonial judicial system and its complex procedure of defining slavery and determining who was liable to enslavement.[106] Ironically, in the process of protecting loved ones from bondage, litigants helped to legitimize the trans-Atlantic slave trade and the violence associated with it.

Judicial Mechanisms, Tribute, and Debt Enslavement

Besides warfare, raids, and kidnapping, other enslavement mechanisms existed in Benguela and its interior. African rulers had to find ways to continuously generate captives to feed the trans-Atlantic demands and the requests for gifts and tribute payments. Slaves could be generated locally through judicial mechanisms, taxation, and debt. Roquinaldo Ferreira claims that "a judicial system ... prone to producing slaves by non-violent means was an essential piece in the architecture of

---

[104] Miller, *Way of Death*, 146. For cases of urban people who were enslaved, see Philip D. Curtin, *Africa Remembered: Narratives by West Africans from the Era of the Slave Trade* (Long Grove, IL: Waveland Press, 1997); Paul E. Lovejoy, "The Urban Background of Enslaved Muslims in the Americas," *Slavery and Abolition* 26, no. 3 (2005), 349–76.

[105] Lovejoy, "The Urban Background"; Robin Law and Paul E. Lovejoy, *The Biography of Mohammah Gardo Baquaqua: His Passage from Slavery to Freedom in Africa and America* (Princeton, NJ: Markus Wiener, 2001); Thornton, *Africa and Africans*; Heywood and Thornton, *Central Africans, Atlantic Creoles*.

[106] On that topic, see Heywood, "Slavery in Kongo," 7. See also Benton, "Legal Regime of the South Atlantic," 47; Curto, "Struggling against Enslavement," 97; and Sparks, *The Two Princes of Calabar*.

enslavement."[107] Ferreira overlooks the fact that the law and violence are intertwined as part of a system that uses these means, that is, the judicial system, to legitimize its violence. The violence is so inherent to the system and the social order that it becomes invisible. Thus I understand judicial mechanisms, tribute, and debt enslavement as mechanisms of violence, as destructive to societies and individuals as warfare and kidnapping. Under extreme conditions, rulers abducted local free people to feed the Atlantic demand. As in Kongo and other African societies, people who lived in the Benguela plateau had strict legislation concerning who could be enslaved. Kongo subjects, for example, could not be sold to the Portuguese, and when they were, it resulted in major conflicts between Portuguese and the Manikongo.[108] The evolution and changes of legislation in the autonomous African states in the Benguela central highlands are not entirely clear. Reports and accounts are limited in time and space, and they provide a glimpse of a specific moment rather than a deep analysis on how legislation changed. To generate a consistent number of slaves to supply *pombeiros* as well as to pay tribute to the Portuguese officials, African authorities had to find mechanisms to get captives outside their own political boundaries rather than raiding neighbors and creating animosity, which would have interfered with their own political survival.

According to a 1797 report by João Nepomuceno Correia, political succession and raids in Viye were closely linked. Before a new ruler was enthroned, there was a period in which he engaged in kidnapping and raiding. Many took part in these violent actions, capturing as many people as possible and profiting from their sale. Nepomuceno Correia described such actions as a common practice that effectively constituted a state of "permitted" civil war that lasted for two or three days.[109] During military expeditions, anyone could kidnap free people and transform them into captives. After paying tribute to the *soba* in the form of slaves, raiders then could sell the captives to *pombeiros* or receive a ransom for them within the *sobado*.[110] It is striking that a ruler allowed internal raids without any control, unless he was attempting to eliminate opposition.

---

[107] Ferreira, "Slaving and Resistance to Slaving in West Central Africa," 113.

[108] For more on this topic, see John K. Thornton, *The Kingdom of Kongo: Civil War and Transition, 1641–1718* (Madison: University of Wisconsin Press, 1983); Anne Hilton, *The Kingdom of Kongo* (Oxford, UK: Clarendon, 1985); and Heywood, "Slavery in Kongo," 6–7.

[109] Instituto Historico Geografico Brasileiro (IGHB), DL29,17, "Notícia Geral dos Costumes do Bié," 1797, fl. 2v.

[110] IHGB, DL29,17, "Notícia Geral dos Costumes do Bié," 1797, fl. 5v.

It may be that Nepomuceno Correia's report failed to grasp what was actually going on during this period or that he was not able to differentiate between the groups involved because the people raided may well have been defined as "outsiders." Another report from the same time period does not mention internal raids but stresses that in some regions of the interior, including Wambu, Ngalangue, and Mbailundu, when a new *soba* was invested, he had to engage in external raids to seize people to secure access to imported commodities. After the raids, the *soba* exchanged the newly seized slaves for ammunition and textiles from *pombeiros*, which strengthened his military power and his prestige among subjects. Those raids allowed a ruler to pay for the cost of his official installation.[111] It is not clear if Juliana, the young woman discussed at the beginning of this chapter, was captured in a raid similar to those organized in and around Kilengues by its neighbors.

Sobas ruled by a set of customary laws that regulated the limits of the slave trade and slavery, imposing proper order to ensure that procedures were followed and subjects protected, even under the pressure to generate slaves locally. At the end of the eighteenth century, it was common in Viye for people to offer slaves to the ruler to settle problems. *Sovetas* ("tributaries") and *makotas* ("counselors") further provided slaves when seeking advancement. No *pombeiro* could engage in trade without paying a tax to the rulers. *Sobas* also could order the enslavement of subjects who defaulted on debts. If a person could not pay the annual tribute to the state, which usually corresponded to a portion of agricultural production or a share of the spoils of hunting, the ruler could force people into slavery. Since the *soba* was the administrator of the land, he could impose enslavement on an indebted person, as well as on that person's wives, offspring, brothers, and other dependents, including slaves. They would become slaves of the state and technically could not be sold outside the community. However, if state slaves were found to engage in treason, conspiracy, or witchcraft, the *soba* had the jurisdiction to sell them to any interested buyer.[112] As with judicial condemnation, if demand was high enough, *sobas* could sell their own people by using debt as an

---

[111] BNRJ, I-28,28,29, Paulo Martins Lacerda, "Notícia da Cidade de S. Filipe de Benguella e dos costumes dos gentios habitantes daquele sertão," November 10, 1797, published in *Annaes Maritimos e Coloniais* 12, no. 5 (1845): 488.

[112] For a description of the process by which *sobas* could enslave their own people, see IHGB, DL29,17, "Notícia Geral dos Costumes do Bié," 1797, fl. 6v.– 7v. John Thornton discusses the ethics guiding African rulers; see "African Political Ethics and the Slave Trade."

excuse. Other mechanisms included accusations of witchcraft or treason, as the case of Viye demonstrated.[113] Observers in the late eighteenth and mid–nineteenth centuries indicated that some judicial cases in Viye were fraudulent and hence thinly disguised mechanisms of deliberate enslavement, indicating how Atlantic demand altered legal systems and notions of morality.[114] These practices raise the question of how slavery became an institution used to punish outlaws and political enemies in the context of the expanding trans-Atlantic slave trade. Renegades and troublemakers also could be banished from society and sold into the trans-Atlantic slave trade, as seen in the cases of the soldiers of Kongo shipped to the Americas.[115] Rulers also could accept slaves as part of tribute payments. In the case of an individual subjected to taxation, the person could use a slave for payment. The captive need not have been a new slave *stricto senso* but a local slave transferred to the government. In the case of tributary states, rulers also could pay tribute in the form of slaves. In mid-nineteenth-century Viye it was common to offer slaves to the *soba* to settle a problem. Second-tier rulers and counselors also provided slaves when requesting a better political position.[116] The Portuguese accepted slaves as tribute, as in the case of the royal fifth, without questioning how individuals were captured and held in bondage. In fact, according to Portuguese law, these people were legally enslaved and therefore could be sold into the trans-Atlantic market or used locally. Displaced from their regions of origin, slaves such as these fulfilled any economic demand, whether for labor, trade, or tribute.[117]

Nineteenth-century accounts offer glimpses into the processes by which the ruler of Viye enslaved his own subjects. According to these reports, anyone accused of seducing one of the *soba*'s wives could be condemned to death and his relatives enslaved, and the "offended" party was entitled to sell the victims to outside *pombeiros*. Adultery certainly was taboo, especially among the elite. The mere accusation of infidelity with the wife of a *soba* could result in the death of the alleged lover and

[113] Heywood, "Slavery and its Transformation," 17.

[114] IHGB, DL29,17, "Notícia Geral dos Costumes do Bié," fl. 6; and Magyar, *Reisen in Sud-Afrika*, chap. 7, "A Nação dos Quimbundos e seus Costumes," 24–5. For more on the disruptive effect of the trans-Atlantic trade on local institutions, see Green, *The Rise of the Trans-Atlantic Slave Trade*, 248–59.

[115] See John Thornton, "African Dimensions of the Stono Rebellion," *American Historical Review*, 96, no. 4 (1991), 1103.

[116] IHGB, DL29,17, "Notícia Geral dos Costumes do Bié," fl. 6v.

[117] As in the case of the two "Benguela" males sent to Calumbo in 1787 as a tax payment; AHNA, cod. 82, fl. 81, October 11, 1787.

the enslavement of a whole set of his relatives. Accusations of seducing wives resulted in the payment of 200 pieces of cloth to compensate for the crime. If the accused could not afford the fine, he faced enslavement. One of the advisors (*sekulo*) of Viye accused Felipe, a slave serving in Silva Porto's caravan, of having an affair with one of his concubines. Later, Felipe was alleged to have had another affair, but this time with a concubine of a *sobeta*. In consequence of his slave's supposed crimes, Silva Porto received an edict to pay compensation for both. It cost him 120 and 130 pieces of cloth, respectively. After the second accusation, Felipe had to flee. He eventually found asylum with the ruler of Kipupire, to whom he offered himself as a slave.[118]

The Hungarian traveler László Magyar also reported cases of alleged female infidelity being punished with slavery. Supposedly, if an unfaithful wife denounced her lover, she did not receive punishment. However, the accused had to pay compensation to the betrayed husband. According to Magyar, if the man was from a wealthy family, his family members could be enslaved. It is not clear why slavery was related to wealth, but it is likely that it represented elevated demands for ransom.[119] Moreover, the relationship between crime and punishment by enslavement also changed. While in the mid–nineteenth century the Kimboas and Katumbelas did not condemn those accused of adultery, their relatives could be punished with enslavement. They also punished individuals who were accused of witchcraft with enslavement. Persons accused of adultery were executed, their belongings appropriated by those who suffered the loss and their relatives and dependents sold into slavery.[120] Most of the information on patterns of enslavement in African states in Benguela's hinterland comes from external observers who traveled through the region in the nineteenth century, mostly after the 1820s. Before then, there is little information on the mechanisms of enslavement in territories outside direct Portuguese control. In the late 1820s, while traveling in the highlands, the French traveler Jean Baptiste Douville observed a case of infidelity in

---

[118] Biblioteca da Sociedade de Geografia de Lisboa (BSGL), res 1-E-2, July 10, 1848, and August 17, 1851; for other cases, see also August 13, 1857, January 25, 1858, April 10, 1858, and December 13, 1860. Female infidelity was severely punished in other parts of the continent; see Marcia Wright, *Strategies of Slaves and Women: Life-Stories from East/Central Africa* (New York: Lilian Barber Press, 1993), 35.

[119] Magyar, *Reisen in Sud-Afrika*, chap. 7, "A Nação dos Quimbundos e seus Costumes," 18; see also chap. 8 on crime and punishment.

[120] AHM, 2-2-3-doc. 14, Arquivo Histórico Militar (AHM), 2-2-3-doc. 14, Francisco Xavier Lopes. "Descrição da Catumbela (Usos e costumes dos seus indígenas e construção do reduto de S. Pedro)," fl. 7–8.

which the ruler enslaved the seducer as well as another ten members of his family, who then could be sold outside their community.[121] Africans and Portuguese shared the same moral aversion to infidelity. In Portugal, legislation condemned infidelity with *degredo* ("overseas exile"), whereas in the central highland *sobados*, an "unfaithful" man, the "seducer," faced slavery and deportation. Local legislation banned him from social interaction, allowed his sale into slavery, and forced him into *degredo*.[122] However, laws in the central highlands guaranteed that condemned women were to be kept locally, probably because they could be incorporated into different lineages and put to work in agricultural fields. Viye legislation also punished murderers with enslavement. Individuals could be fined 300 pieces of cloth, four slaves, a cow, and a goat. As with adultery, the inability to pay fines could result in enslavement.[123]

It is important to highlight that travelers identified these judicial mechanisms only during the mid–nineteenth century. There is no evidence concerning earlier periods. The legal mechanisms for determining who was guilty, what crime they had committed, and which form of punishment was appropriate undoubtedly changed over time. For example, in 1845, Silva Porto publicly beat one of his slaves who tried to run away. Ten days following his punishment, the slave died. The *soba* of Viye demanded that Silva Porto be condemned for killing a person within his territory. In order to avoid a conflict with the ruler, Silva Porto paid a fine amounting to 1,553 pieces of cloth, one *ancoreta* (thirty-six liters) of alcohol, one barrel of gunpowder, one gun, and a cow.[124] While local political leaders valued textiles and alcohol for the social status they conveyed, they also appreciated gunpowder because it made hunting easier and also facilitated warfare and the capture of people.[125] This region was

---

[121] J. B. Douville, *Voyage au Congo et dans l'interieur de l'Afrique Equinoxiale, fait dans les années 1828, 1829, 1830*, vol. 1 (Paris: Jules Renouard, 1832), 259–60.

[122] For Portuguese legislation on infidelity and exile, see Geraldo Pieroni, *Os Excluídos do Reino* (Brasília: Editora UNB, 2000), especially chaps. 2 and 3. See also Timothy J. Coates, *Convicts and Orphans. Forced and State-Sponsored Colonizers in the Portuguese Empire, 1550–1755* (Stanford, CA: Stanford University Press, 2001).

[123] AHNA, cod. 462, fl. 31–32, November 4, 1847.

[124] SGL, res 1-E-2, May 7, 1845.

[125] Among the interesting reports about gunpowder dependency, see AHU, Angola, caixa 61, doc. 55, October, 1777; AHU, Angola, caixa 62, doc. 4, May 22, 1779; AHU, Angola, caixa 63, doc. 7, February 22, 1780; AHU, Angola, caixa 115, doc. 24, February 14, 1806; and AHU, Angola, caixa 129, doc. 23, August 5, 1814; for the authorities' concern with the number of guns available in the interior, see AHU, Angola, caixa 76, doc. 15; also AHU, Angola, cod. 549, "Instrução para Joseph Gonçalo Câmara," June 22, 1779. There are also attempts to inventory the number of guns available to the *gentio*.

characterized by chronic instability during the era of the trans-Atlantic slave trade. Insecurity of trade, constant warfare, kidnappings, the sale of relatives, and frequent clashes between vassal states were characteristic of the period as people sought to dominate access to imported goods.[126] Violence as a result of the region's involvement in the trans-Atlantic slave trade was widespread by the mid–nineteenth century. Travelers reported assaults on the roads. Silva Porto mentioned that raiding parties attacked his caravans several times along commercial routes. On one occasion, a large contingent of armed men forced him to pay tribute or suffer the consequences.[127]

Analysis of judicial mechanisms and debt enslavement reveal how states in the interior of Benguela generated captives to meet the growing Atlantic demand for African labor. Unable to maintain constant warfare targeting their neighbors, rulers had to manipulate the law and impose new taxation to guarantee large number of captives available to supply caravans and colonial officials. As this section reveals, the trans-Atlantic slave trade disrupted legal systems and led to a situation where even minor crimes were punishable with enslavement and sale. Its social impact on societies located in the Benguela highlands was dramatic.

Conclusion

This chapter explored the mechanisms of enslavement in and around Benguela in order to identify how and where people were enslaved. During the era of the trans-Atlantic slave trade, wars and raids in regions around Benguela threatened the freedom of people, provoking major political and social reorganization, which will be analyzed further in Chapter 5. Mechanisms had to be put in place to defend the rights of subjects of Portuguese and African forces alike, but violence was endemic, threatening even allies of the colonial state, as seen in the cases of Luso-Africans

---

See AHU, Angola, caixa 71, doc. 60, November 15, 1786. On the implications of gunpowder trade, see R. A. Kea, "Firearms and Warfare on the Gold and Slave Coasts from the Sixteenth to the Nineteenth Centuries," *Journal of African History* 12, no. 2 (1971), 185–213; and Thornton, "The Art of War in Angola," 360–78.

[126] AHU, caixa 64, doc. 59; see as well AHU, caixa 76, doc. 8, February 3, 1791; AHU, caixa 77, doc. 14, February 1, 1792.

[127] See BSGL, 1-E-2, Silva Porto, "Memorial dos Mucanos, 1841–1885." For more on traders killed in confrontations on the roads, see AHU, caixa 88, doc. 5, May 25, 1798. Magyar also commented on similar cases and highlighted the danger of meeting groups of armed men on the roads who were seeking to acquire captives, alcohol, and textiles; see Magyar, *Reisen in Sud-Afrika*, chap. 5, "Chegada ao Bié."

who were enslaved. Local states and chiefdoms, as well as the Portuguese colonial state, protected insiders, who sometimes could benefit from the coexistence of pluralistic juridical codes. For the people living around Benguela and its interior, Portuguese law was simply another set of legal requirements that limited actions and protected its subjects. The legal pluralism that existed in West Central Africa facilitated the appropriation of legal rights by African subjects, who blended *mucano* tribunals with Portuguese law, showing that creolization was not limited to the adoption of Western culture but also incorporation of African institutions into the colonial state.[128] This pluralism that allowed the coexistence of local and foreign law and the role of colonial officials as heads of *mucano* hearings also suggests how slavery became endemic during the era of the trans-Atlantic slave trade, when even people who were protected by the law and the colonial state could find themselves in shackles. Given the fact that they were enslaved in warfare, thousands of men and women who had lived their lives as free people were declared to be legal captives subject to sale and enslavement. The process of being captured and the declaration of their captors was enough to decide the fate of thousands of people. Very few people could challenge the system and prove the illegality of their enslavement.

The examples explored in this chapter show how some people were captured in areas close to the coast. People such as Dona Leonor, Nbena, Quitéria, Juliana, and José Manuel, who lived in Portuguese settlements, could be considered Luso-Africans. They displayed elements of Portuguese culture and integrated aspects of the Atlantic world into their lives. Some of them were fluent in Portuguese. By actively engaging in trading, they served as intermediaries between Portuguese and African merchants and also pushed violence inland. They probably attended the Catholic Church, dressed in European fashion, and in varying degrees displayed affiliation to an Atlantic world. Their position as cultural intermediaries brought them profits but also threatened their security, as the cases of enslaved Luso-Africans demonstrated. Rulers and merchants in the interior attacked and enslaved Luso-Africans, perhaps as a strategy to avoid debts already acquired. Yet the attacks on Luso-Africans revealed strategies of resistance to the trans-Atlantic slave trade, which

---

128 Hespanha and Santos, "Poderes de um Império Oceânico," 398–9; Benton, "The Legal Regime of the South Atlantic," 32; and Lauren Benton, *Law and Colonial Cultures: Legal Regimes in World History, 1400–1900* (New York: Cambridge University Press, 2002), 49–55.

in some cases involved seizing its agents and, ironically, enslaving them. Some of the people who were enslaved in the interior of Benguela, such as Katiabala and Kaucia from Viye, also were familiar with Portuguese culture, legislation, and habits because they were members of political elites, intimately associated with the colonial state and expansion of the trans-Atlantic slave trade. Indeed, they also were familiar with the trans-Atlantic slave trade and its dependence on human captives because they were members of states deeply involved in raids and the acquisition of imported goods. Some of these Luso-Africans regained their freedom through legal means, whereas most people captured in Benguela and its interior had a different fate. Luso-Africans living in Portuguese settlements believed that they could not be enslaved, forgetting that most of the people captured in warfare and raids were also free before capture. By defending their freedom, they indicated their difference from people living outside Portuguese-controlled regions and made slavery legitimated and something that happens to the "other," not to an ally of the colonial regime. They demonstrated knowledge of the Portuguese judicial system and the intricacies of the colonial state, revealing their acceptance of the system and the trans-Atlantic slave trade. Although they challenged their enslavement, Luso-Africans reinforced the power of the Portuguese and the influence of the slave trade, which altered societies and their institutions. By requesting Portuguese arbitration, captured Africans solidified the role of the colonial agents as responsible for their destinies. It also indicates how slavery and the trans-Atlantic slave trade were accepted and legitimized.

The different cases presented here suggest that the middle passage started in Africa and not only on the littoral. To claim that people were transformed into slaves at the coast, as Smallwood does, is to negate the existence of many Africans who remained enslaved on the African continent.[129] The case of Albano, analyzed earlier, shows that he was a slave in Benguela, and the treatment he suffered is no different from the treatment slaves in the Americas received. Many of the slaves in Benguela were subjected to physical and mental violence and removed from their communities, and their plight should not be denied.

Enslavement in Benguela and its hinterland challenges the idea of a single enslaving frontier slowly moving inland and eastward. Instead, the available data suggest a series of overlapping frontiers that were relatively

---

[129] Smallwood, *Saltwater Slavery*, 35–6, 52–3, 63. For the idea of a prolonged middle passage, see, Miller, *Way of Death*, 189–200.

fluid and therefore allowed large numbers of people to be seized on the coast, who, in theory, were inside the frontier and within "protected" zones. Frontiers were not static and were under constant reconfiguration through the slaving activities of both Portuguese and African agents. There were many frontiers, some of which corresponded to physical space, whereas others referred to the idea of a person being an insider or an outsider. Anyone who did not share the same language, religion, habits, and political affiliation was an outsider, that is, potentially subject to enslavement. Recognizing that chronic instability is essential to understanding how the slave trade was organized and who was involved in the commerce, as well as the nature of societies in the areas affected by the perpetual redefining of the "frontier" in terms of who could be enslaved and how. Also, if people were enslaved in regions close to the coast, not far from their communities, we have to readdress the vision that African slaves waiting for embarkation at the port were removed from the "physical and social landscape with which they were familiar."[130] For many of the people captured in and around Benguela, they were enslaved in familiar territories, where they knew the languages and customs.

The trans-Atlantic slave trade affected demography, political and economic life, but more than anything it disrupted social organizations and increased a disregard for human life. Hundreds of thousands of people were exported from the port of Benguela as if they were legally enslaved, without a chance to tell their story or challenge their fate. They were enslaved because the societies where they lived were transformed by the Atlantic demand. Judicial systems were corrupted, rulers co-opted, and institutions that were there to protect them had been seized by the colonial state or corrupted by the pressure of the trans-Atlantic slave trade. Societies responded to these pressures by transforming and reshaping old institutions, doing their best to protect insiders while responding to the demands of the new order. In the process, they attacked outsiders while reinforcing differences and political fragmentation, which will be analyzed further in Chapter 5.

---

[130] Smallwood, *Saltwater Slavery*, 54–5, 57

5

Political Reconfiguration of the Benguela Hinterland, 1600–1850

As has been discussed in previous chapters, societies located in and around Benguela were affected by the trans-Atlantic slave trade, which brought about the collapse of existing polities, the imposition of Portuguese colonialism, the redirection of trade routes, new patterns of consumption, modified ideas about right and wrong, transformed economies, and new legislation. The world people experienced before the arrival of the Portuguese and the expansion of the Atlantic market no longer existed. Societies mutated and changed themselves to survive in the new order.

After discussing the importance of Benguela in the South Atlantic world and the mechanisms of enslavement in the port town and its hinterland, this chapter explores the changes in the political organization of societies in the interior of Benguela, including regions nominally under Portuguese control, such as Caconda, and territories outside Portuguese imperial claims. The focus will be on the hinterland and not on the coast, which will allow an analysis of the effects of the trans-Atlantic slave trade inland, including the expansion of creolization. As seen in the first two chapters of this book, the presence of the Portuguese on the littoral led to a series of diplomatic treaties signed with local leaders, which in many ways incorporated local institutions such as *undar* and the *mucanos* tribunal, showing how adaptation and accommodation worked both ways, with Europeans adapting African venues of power and litigation. For some rulers, treaties with the Portuguese represented the end of an autonomous life, whereas others managed to negotiate the continued existence of their states throughout the centuries, although dependent on colonial power. While some rulers declared vassalage, others migrated in search of a new place where they could live alongside their subjects away from

Portuguese control. Thus, from the seventeenth to the mid–nineteenth centuries, political life changed dramatically in the interior of Benguela, and in this chapter I will explore this process. The interior of Benguela faced violent turmoil associated with expansion of the slave trade since its inception; thus the "fall of the kings" was not limited to the mid–nineteenth century, as Jan Vansina proposed.[1] In fact, rulers were killed, removed from power, and co-opted into the trans-Atlantic slave trade from the early seventeenth century. The trans-Atlantic slave trade disrupted political and economic lives along the coast, as seen in Chapters 1 and 2. It favored the spread of violence and provoked changes in the way criminals were punished under *sobado* codes. It also created new patterns of consumption with the adoption of manioc and corn in local diets and the widespread commercialization of Asian textiles and Brazilian alcohol in the central highlands. Yet, in West Central African historiography, the damage inflicted by the Atlantic economy has been underestimated and sometimes reduced to demographic loss, which could be quickly recuperated through natural reproduction or migration. Throughout this chapter I will explore how old states and chiefdoms collapsed and new states emerged in the context of violence, altering the political landscape and reinforcing political fragmentation. A constant level of competition threatened alliances between African rulers and imposed fragmented polities with different degrees of connection to the colonial state and the trans-Atlantic slave trade. Migration and political reorganization affected the way people associated themselves with their homelands and their rulers, ultimately transforming identities.

In the 1980s, two influential studies challenged the understanding of the destructive force of the trans-Atlantic commerce in West Central Africa. In 1980, John Thornton argued that the trans-Atlantic slave trade did not have an impact on agricultural production and natural reproduction of the populations in West Central Africa because women were retained while men exported, allowing the population in the central highlands to recuperate the demographic loss through natural reproduction. In the same decade, Joseph Miller's studies confirmed Thornton's interpretation. According to Miller, diseases and environmental changes had provoked major political and demographic reconfigurations rather

---

[1] Jan Vansina, *Kingdoms of the Savanna* (Madison: University of Wisconsin Press, 1968), 208–44; Miller later stated that the collapse of old elites and their replacement with military leaders in the central highlands took place at the end of the eighteenth century. See Joseph Miller, "Angola Central e Sul por volta de 1840," *Estudos Afro-Asiaticos* 32 (1997), 16–18.

than the Atlantic demand for human beings.[2] Thornton's and Miller's contributions were strongly focused on demographic interpretation rather than on exploring the social and political ramifications of the region's insertion in the Atlantic economy. They overlooked the expansion of slavery within West Central Africa and how it accelerated social changes and political reorganization. Indeed, their works did not focus on Benguela and its interior, nor did they explore the role of external demand, a crucial aspect to understanding how war and colonial expansion changed over time and were intimately linked to slave procurement. This chapter revisits this three-decade-old debate, focusing on Benguela's interior to bring a new interpretation of the impact of the slave trade on the territory.

Earlier Portuguese contacts in the seventeenth century probably occurred during a period of political reconfiguration in the interior. While farming and cattle-herding groups could incorporate or be incorporated into other groups depending on local politics and environmental crises, the presence of the Portuguese along the coast was another factor leading to social and political rearrangement. Migrations and resettlement that predated the trans-Atlantic slave trade were accelerated by the Atlantic commerce. Some people who inhabited the coast moved inland in search of protection. The interior of Benguela was a land of migration, relocation, and change between 1600 and 1850. The archeologist Carlos Ervedosa explained how the Kwandu (a Khoe-speaking group in Angola, also identified as Ovakwambundu and Moquando/Mucuando in ethnologic studies and primary sources) went through a slow process of migration inland during the nineteenth century.[3] In the eighteenth century,

---

[2] John Thornton, "The Slave Trade in Eighteenth Century Angola: Effects of Demographic Structure," *Canadian Journal of African Studies* 14, no. 3 (1980): 417–27; Joseph C. Miller, "The Significance of Drought, Disease and Famine in the Agriculturally Marginal Zones of West-Central Africa," *Journal of African History* 23, no. 1 (1982), 17–61; and Joseph C. Miller, *Way of Death: Merchant Capitalism and the Angolan Slave Trade, 1730–1830* (Madison: University of Wisconsin Press, 1988).

[3] Carlos Ervedosa, *Arqueologia Angolana* (Lisbon: Edições 70, 1980), 164. For more on the Kwandu and its differentiation from other Khoe groups, as well as from Umbundu-speaking neighbors, see A. Machado Cruz, "O Povo Ovakwambundo," *Boletim do Instituto de Investigação Científica de Angola* 4, no. 2 (1967): 67–88; and Carlos Estermann, "Les Twa du Sud-Ouest de l'Angola," *Anthropos* 57 (1962): 467–74. I am very grateful to Beatrix Heintze's help with the ethnography of the Khoe groups from Angola. For changes that predate the Portuguese arrival and the role of Imbangala raids, see John Thornton, "The African Experience of the '20s and Odd Negroes' Arriving in Virginia in 1619," *William and Mary Quarterly* 55, no. 3, Third Series (1998): 421–34; and Jan Vansina, *How Societies are Born: Governance in West Central Africa before 1600* (Charlottesville: University of Virginia Press, 2004), 190–7.

the Kwandu were living along the coast south of Benguela between the Cabo Negro and Tiger Bay; in the nineteenth century, they moved inland, probably seeking protection from the raids and illegal embarkation of slaves from this region. Decimated and incorporated by other groups, few Kwandu survived the early years of twentieth-century colonialism.[4] The changes that affected the southern coast of West Central Africa had the same impact on other groups around Benguela and its interior. The interaction with Portuguese colonialism and Atlantic commerce led to the disappearance of some states and peoples. They were replaced by new polities under the rule of militaristic groups who relied on their ability to recruit unprotected people. Some states that had already consolidated by the mid–seventeenth century, such as the Wambu, managed to survive until the mid–nineteenth century. Others, such as Peringue, the first ruler to enter into contact with the Portuguese in the seventeenth century, did not have the same fate. Kakonda and Mbailundu, for example, negotiated their continued existence with the Portuguese colony of Benguela.[5]

People who lived in the interior of Benguela, between the littoral and the highlands, as well as in the central plateau, did not perceive themselves as members of a single community. The association with a state and ruler was extremely important in the process of how people thought of themselves as members of a community. Identities were formed and created in association with a power structure based on a series of assumptions, such as protection and rights, that members shared. Yet this was a territory characterized by population mobility under reconfigurations to accommodate the level of violence intrinsic to colonialism and processes of enslavements explored in earlier chapters. People who were subjects of Kakonda, Mbailundu, or Viye felt protected by the power of their rulers, who relied on military force but also on the connection with their ancestors and the ability to communicate with spiritual figures. These cultural factors contributed to the development of small political units, although this allegiance could change over time in reaction to a moment of crisis or external threat. Yet membership in a state or chiefdom was seen as a source of security. Luso-Africans were alienated from local states and therefore were vulnerable to enslavement, as seen in several examples explored in Chapter 4. As Joseph Miller explained, "[M]ost central

---

[4] Bernard Clist and Raymond Lanfranchi, "Contribution a l'étude de la sedentarisation en République Populaire d'Angola," *Leba* 7 (1992) : 254.

[5] Joseph C. Miller, *Kings and Kinsmen: Early Mbundu States in Angola* (Oxford, UK: Clarendon Press, 1976), 80–90; Gladwyn M. Childs, "Chronology of the Ovimbundu Kingdoms," *Journal of African History* 11 (1970): 241–8.

Africans had thought of themselves primarily in terms of social identities constructed out of family and other local communities," not necessarily as members of an abstract political organization. In fact, most of the chiefdoms were very small, representing a combination of a few villages with the power of the leader or the chief/*soba* limited to its vicinity.[6] Yet these societies did not necessarily evolve into a dynastic web, to use Vansina's term, with a centralized pan-Ovimbundu state emerging after 1600 to unify smaller communities or chiefdoms. By 1850, an important number of people continued to live in small-scale polities in the interior of Benguela, although some centralized and military states had been formed in previous decades. This does not mean that a sense of identity or ethnicity was a divisive force, but as in the twentieth century, it was used by the colonial power to increase conflict among locals and exacerbate disputes between *sobas*. Yet it becomes clear that ethnicities were not invented in the twentieth century but were created historically.[7]

The chapter starts with the foundation of the first fortress of Caconda, in the lands of the *sobeta* Bongo, 180 km inland of the port of Benguela, the first administrative, military, and commercial outlet established in the hinterland. It follows the transfer of the *presídio* in the 1760s to the lands of Katala and stresses its relations with other regional powers around the colonial fortress. The chapter also analyzes the population of the fortress and traces its parallel to Benguela's colonial society. A fourth section presents what is known about the volatile political changes among many smaller polities near Caconda and examines the consequences of warfare and Atlantic pressure over political structures and ruling elites. The last section discusses the emergence of three states directly involved in the slave trade, Wambu, Mbailundu, and Viye, examining their roles in the ongoing shifts and political developments in Benguela's hinterland.

---

[6] Joseph C. Miller, "Central Africans during the Era of the Slave Trade, c. 1490s-1850s," in *Central Africans and Cultural Transformations in the American Diaspora*, ed. Linda Heywood (Cambridge University Press, 2001), 22. For more on the development of political unities in West Central Africa, see Vansina, *How Societies are Born*, 226–44, 259–60. For more on the problematic use of the term *soba*, originally *kimbundu*, to rulers in the interior of Benguela, see Joseph C. Miller, *Kings and Kinsmen: Early Mbundu States in Angola* (Oxford, UK: Clarendon Press, 1976), 302

[7] For scholars who claim that ethnicity was invented in the twentieth century, see Leroy Vail, "Introduction: Ethnicity in Southern African History," *The Creation of Tribalism in Southern Africa* (Berkeley: University of California Press, 1991), 1–19. The Yoruba, as a historical category, is an interesting case of comparison with the Ovimbundu. See Robin Law, *The Oyo Empire, c.1600-c.1836: A West African Imperialism in the Era of the Atlantic Slave* (Oxford, UK: Clarendon, 1977).

To emphasize the movement of people and their leaders during the seventeenth, eighteenth, and early nineteenth centuries, I chose to stress the absence of a single group identity. Political and social alliances were fluid and subject to change in the central highlands and along the coast before the mid–nineteenth century. Hermann Baumann stressed that the Umbundu-speaking group was not unified as a state in the past, although its members shared some common cultural traits.[8] Jan Vansina has made a similar comment about the limit of ethnic identities north of the Kwanza River, yet he insisted in portraying the inhabitants of the central highlands as a single group, Ovimbundu.[9] The fluid identities that prevailed for most of the period of the trans-Atlantic slave trade changed in the late nineteenth and early twentieth centuries; nonetheless, the notion of a single identity dominates the scholarship. Ferreira, for example, stated that "most Africans taken to Benguela were captives as a result of wars pitting Africans against each other,"[10] not recognizing that being African was not an identity people shared. Inhabitants of Benguela and its hinterlands saw themselves as Ndombe, Kakonda, Kilengues, and Viye, among others, but not as Africans. The work of missionaries and anthropologists helped to create stable identities that did not reflect how people had identified themselves in the previous decades and centuries. Twentieth-century colonialism, followed by the anticolonial and civil wars, helped to solidify how people identify themselves in Angola. The idea that an Ovimbundu ethnicity had existed since early times has shaped the way that politicians, Angolans, and historians have viewed and continue to read the past. The term "Ovimbundu" or "Ovi-Umbundu" is not found in the Portuguese colonial records analyzed here. António Cadornega, in the seventeenth century, described people as "Quimbundu," in contrast to the northern "Ambundu."[11] Most contemporary travelers and observers, however, referred to village or chiefdoms ethnonyms or used the term *Nano* when

---

[8] Hermann Baumann, *Die Völker Afrikas und ihre traditionellen Kulturen* (Franz Steiner Verlag, 1979), 1, 504. I am grateful to Beatriz Heintze for help with and translation of the German original to Portuguese.

[9] Jan Vansina, *Paths in the Rainforest: Toward a History of Political Tradition in Equatorial Africa* (Madison: University of Wisconsin Press, 1990), 20; Vansina, *Kingdoms of the Savanna*, 197–201.

[10] Roquinaldo Ferreira, "Slaving and Resistance to Slaving in West Central Africa," in *The Cambridge World History of Slavery. AD 1420–AD 1804*, vol. 3, ed. David Eltis and Stanley L Engerman (New York: Cambridge University Press, 2011), 121.

[11] António de Oliveira de Cadornega, *História Geral das Guerras Angolanas, 1680–1681* (Lisboa: Agência-Geral das Colónias, 1972), 3, 249–50. See also Gladwyn M. Childs, *Umbundu Kinship and Character* (Oxford University Press, 1949), 272.

describing those who lived in the highlands.[12] For this reason, I avoid the term, even if the descendants of the people identified here as Viye or Mbailundu prefer to call themselves Ovimbundu in the twenty-first century. The conviction held by many of those who now believe they are Ovimbundu is a result of intense interaction among different groups throughout a long period of time, and as I will explore in this chapter, this unified identity was not employed during the era of the trans-Atlantic slave trade.

The idea of static and ahistorical ethnic groups throughout the African continent has led to decades of conflicts in the twentieth century. In the past, people changed political affiliation and assumed new identities as Wambu, Kakonda, or Mbailundu without having to prove their family origins or show birth certificates. One could become part of a larger group when it was convenient and could always change this affiliation as many times as necessary. This process was not the case in early twentieth-century Angola when colonized people needed identity cards with their "tribe" listed. In the same way that a Portuguese exile could migrate to West Central Africa in the early eighteenth century and reinvent himself as a legitimate colonial authority, many Ndombe or Kakonda reinvented themselves as agents of the colonial state and were seen as Portuguese by their peers. Identity was fluid and unstable and defined, among many other features, by language use, as well as dressing and housing styles. Migrants from the littoral also could assume new identities as subject of headmen in the interior.[13] In this way, identity reconfiguration was

---

[12] At least by the mid–nineteenth century the term *Nano* was employed to designate those from the central highlands. See Arquivo Histórico Nacional de Angola (AHNA), cod. 3160, 1854.

[13] The literature on changing identity in Africa is vast. I am influenced by Vail (ed.), *The Creation of Tribalism in Southern Africa*; Eric Hobsbawm and Terence Ranger (eds.), *The Invention of Tradition* (Cambridge University Press, 1992); Robin Law, *The Oyo Empire, c.1600–c.1836: A West African Imperialism in the Era of the Atlantic Slave Trade* (Oxford, UK: Clarendon Press, 1977); G. Ugo Nwokeji, *The Slave Trade and Culture in the Bight of Biafra: An African Society in the Atlantic World* (New York: Cambridge University Press, 2010); Peter Mark, *"Portuguese" Style and Luso-African Identity: Precolonial Senegambia, Sixteenth-Nineteenth Centuries* (Bloomington: Indiana University Press, 2002); and Toby Green, *The Rise of the Trans-Atlantic Slave Trade in Western Africa, 1300–1589* (Cambridge University Press, 2011). For more on Central Africans who appropriated Lusophone culture, see Beatrix Heintze, *Pioneiros Africanos: Caravanas de Carregadores na África Centro-Ocidental: entre 1850 e 1890* (Lisbon: Caminho, 2004), chap. 7; and Joseph C. Miller, *Way of Death: Merchant Capitalism and the Angolan Slave Trade, 1730–1830* (Madison: University of Wisconsin Press, 1988), 246–7; Linda M. Heywood and John Thornton, *Central Africans, Atlantic Creoles, and the Making of the Foundation of the Americas, 1585–1660* (New York: Cambridge University Press, 2007).

a constant process in Benguela and its hinterland during the era of the trans-Atlantic slave trade. People assumed new allegiances in search of protection and to inscribe themselves into new communities, forging new social, political, and economic networks. Belonging to a community, as seen in Chapter 4, protected people from raids, warfare, and eventually, enslavement. Yet this identity was fluid and subject to change depending on a series of variations.

Although I cannot know what people called themselves in the past, in this text I follow the names used in the historical records. Aware of the limitations of colonial documents, I realize that records were collected and produced mostly by outsiders. As in the twentieth century, colonial agents labeled people they encountered, whether in hostile or collaborative settings, and created new collective identities. Although often the fruit of violence, I assume that Portuguese agents relied on the information provided by the local population to name territories, rulers, and people. Still, the historical documents drag the historian toward the point of view of those who wrote the records, who were probably settled in Benguela or Luanda, far from the hinterland. Some letters, however, were written by colonial agents born on the African continent, bilingual individuals who circulated easily in the existing and competing cultures that were present in the region of Benguela. Struggling with the limitations of the primary sources, this chapter is about changes in the interior of Benguela and how they were related to expansion of the trans-Atlantic slave trade and colonialism inland. As I will show, the trans-Atlantic slave trade had a profound and dramatic effect on how people organized themselves politically and how they perceived and classified the world around them. Caconda plays a central role in this chapter as the site of intense cultural exchanges between foreigners and the local population. The study of Caconda and the interior shows how different cultures interacted in a situation not different from the port of Benguela in a process known as "creolization."[14] Although the term has been used almost exclusively

---

[14] Among others, see James Sweet, *Recreating Africa: Culture, Kinship, and Religion in the African-Portuguese World, 1441–1770* (Chapel Hill: University of North Carolina Press, 2003), 227–30; Walter Hawthorne, *From Africa to Brazil: Culture, Identity, and an Atlantic Slave Trade, 1600–1830* (New York: Cambridge University Press, 2010), 14–16; Paul E. Lovejoy, "Ethnic Designations of the Slave Trade and Reconsiderations of the History of Trans-Atlantic Slavery," in *Trans-Atlantic Dimensions of Ethnicity in the African Diaspora*, ed. Paul E. Lovejoy and David Trotman (London: Continuum, 2003), 9–42; Green, *The Rise of the Trans-Atlantic Slave Trade in Western Africa, 1300–1589*. This process continued in the Americas, when transplanted Africans had to reconstitute their respective communities. See James H Sweet, *Domingos Álvares, African Healing, and*

to culture appropriation of Africans in the diaspora, I will employ it to describe processes of cultural exchange among Africans, Europeans, and Brazilian individuals in Benguela's hinterland.

The First Caconda, ca. 1680–1750

From the early seventeenth century, the Portuguese intended to expand control over the interior. The relationship between the highland political authorities and the Portuguese invaders along the Benguela coast goes back to the seventeenth century when caravans brought ivory, animal skins, and slaves from the polities located inland.[15] At the littoral, traders from the interior acquired salt and dried fish. Eventually, they also consumed imported goods introduced by Europeans. The *jaga* of Kakonda challenged the Portuguese who ventured inland, as seen in Chapter 2. The actions of the ruler of Kakonda, as well as others, prevented the Portuguese from establishing settlements far from the coast. In 1629, soldiers in Benguela maintained regular contact with Kakonda, which was considered an ally to the Portuguese Crown, although the nature of this relationship is not clear from the documents because Kakonda only became a vassal in 1681.[16]

Facing difficulties in acquiring slaves in sufficient numbers in the interior of Luanda, in part due to the resistance of the inland rulers of Matamba and Kasanje, Portuguese agents sought alternative sources of slaves. One of the solutions was to establish political and commercial alliances with the *jaga* of Kakonda, who controlled the trade in slaves.[17] Located in the

---

the *Intellectual History of the Atlantic World* (Chapel Hill: University of North Carolina Press, 2011); Karen B. Graubart, "'So Color de una Confradía': Catholic Confraternities and the Development of Afro-Peruvian Ethnicities in Early Colonial Peru," *Slavery & Abolition* (2012): 1–22; and Linda M. Heywood and John Thornton, *Central Africans and Cultural Transformations in the American Diaspora* (Cambridge University Press, 2001).

[15] Ralph Delgado, *Ao Sul do Cuanza (Ocupação e Aproveitamento do Antigo Reino de Benguela* (Lisbon: Beleza, 1944), 230–1. See also Linda Heywood, *Contested Power in Angola, 1840s to the Present* (University of Rochester Press, 2000), 2; Miller, *Way of Death*, 28–30.

[16] Beatrix Heintze, *Fontes para a História de Angola do Século XVII* (Stuttgart: F. Steiner Verlag Wiesbaden, 1985), 2, 303.

[17] Rosa Cruz e Silva, "Saga of Kakonda and Kilengues," in *Enslaving Connections: Changing Cultures of Africa and Brazil during the Era of Slavery*, ed. José C. Curto and Paul E. Lovejoy (New York: Humanity Books, 2004), 245–60. For more on the relationships with the *jaga* of Kakonda, see Torres, *Memórias contendo a Biographia*, 211. On the initial conflicts between the ruler of Kakonda and the Portuguese, see Jan Vansina, *Kingdoms of the Savanna* (Madison: University of Wisconsin Press, 1966), 181–2; and Ralph Delgado,

outskirts of the central highland, the *jaga* of Kakonda was willing to trade with the Portuguese, although he resisted political control. In 1659, he requested that the captain-major of Benguela provide protection against a neighboring power. The unnamed headman was defeated by Portuguese and Kakonda forces, which resulted in the killing of men, the capture of women, and the appropriation of cattle and grains.[18] The military alliance between the *jaga* and the colony, however, was short-lived. In November 1672, Governor Francisco da Távora of Angola reported that the *jaga* of Kakonda, with the support of its neighbors, organized attacks on caravans in order to steal goods from itinerant traders known as *pombeiros*. The only solution, according to the governor, was to attack and punish the *jaga*, along with any headmen who had supported him.[19]

After years of conflict, the *jaga* of Kakonda declared vassalage in 1681 and was forced to compensate the Crown for the costs of the war. With his defeat, the Portuguese Crown laid claim to land close to the Lutira River, where the *jaga*'s tributary, the *sobeta* of Bongo, lived with his people. In 1682, the first Portuguese *presídio* in the interior of Benguela was raised at that location. The Caconda fortress was established in the land of the ruler Bongo as an administrative and military center where caravans and traders gathered and paid taxes. In 1684, regretting the presence of the Portuguese settlement, and with the support of Kakonda, Bongo organized an attack on the Portuguese forces, which resulted in the fort's destruction.[20] The Portuguese then launched another expedition with troops from Benguela. A new fortress was established, and the ruler of Bongo was expelled from his lands and fled to the interior, indicating how rulers withdraw from regions where Portuguese agents were in search of protection. Migration, here, can be seen as a direct

---

O Reino de Benguela: Do Descobrimento à Criação do Governo Subalterno ([S.l: s.n.], 1945), 120–122.

[18] Delgado, *Reino de Benguela*, 213–5.

[19] Arquivo Histórico Ultramarino (AHU), Angola, caixa 10, doc. 80, November 29, 1672. AHU, Angola, caixa 11, doc. 4, March 7, 1674. On this revolt, see also Pascoal Leite de Aguiar, *Administração Colonial Portuguesa no Congo, em Angola e em Benguela* (Lisbon: Sociedade Histórica da Independência de Portugal, 2006), 1, 195–6. On *pombeiros*, see Jan Vansina, "Long-Distance Trade-Routes in Central Africa," *Journal of African History* 3, no. 3 (1962): 378.

[20] For information on the construction of the first fortress of Caconda, see Torres, *Memórias Contendo a Biographia*, 211–13. See also Delgado, *Ao Sul do Cuanza*, 231; Aguiar, *Administração Colonial*, 1, 261; and Mariana P. Candido, "Trade, Slavery and Migration in the Interior of Benguela: The Case of the Caconda, 1830–1870," in *Angola on the Move: Transport Routes, Communications, and History*, eds. Beatrix Heintze and Achim von Oppen (Frankfurt am Main: Lembeck, 2008), 63.

consequence of the growing pressure of the trans-Atlantic slave trade in the late seventeenth century. The location of the Portuguese fortress of Caconda was "in the worst place in the world," according to Governor Francisco Inocêncio de Sousa Coutinho decades later.[21] The reconstruction of the fortress was met with resistance from the ruler of Kakonda, who saw it as an attempt to expand Portuguese control beyond the coast. Located 40 légoas, or almost 180 km, from Benguela, the fortress relied on the presence of fifty soldiers and six masons in charge of building a permanent fort to protect the garrison from attacks. The territory in between Benguela and Caconda was not under Portuguese control, which shows that the Portuguese notion of colonial control was not based on a continuous expansion into new adjacent territory but rather on securing pockets in a landscape occupied by competing powers.

The *jaga* of Kakonda challenged Portuguese power and attacked the fortress on several occasions in a clear effort to resist the new order and the pressure of the Atlantic world. Although after he signed the vassalage treaties in 1681 the ruler was often called *soba*, during the conflicts in the 1688, he was again called *jaga*, to emphasize his rebelliousness and resistance to Portuguese conquest, as discussed in Chapter 1. After hours of struggle in February 1688, the captain of the fortress, Manoel da Rocha, waved a white flag and capitulated. The ruler of Kakonda requested the presence of Captain Rocha, who left the fortress accompanied by three soldiers. Portuguese documents report that as soon as both sides met outside the fortress walls, the *jaga* beheaded Captain Rocha and spared the lives of lower-ranking military, who returned to the fortress to retell the events. The witnesses mentioned that while sitting on the head of Captain Rocha, the *jaga* Kakonda declared war on the Portuguese and ordered an invasion of the fortress. In the conflict, slaves, firearms, gunpowder, and imported commodities were seized. The ruler also apprehended three images of Jesus and the Virgin Mary, the silver Eucharistic chalice, and sacerdotal vestments. He was seen drinking from the chalice and wearing the religious outfit. The King of Portugal, Pedro II, authorized a "just war" to punish Kakonda, although he had difficulties recruiting troops. The slaves of residents of Luanda resisted embarking to fight in the interior of Benguela, assuming that they were heading to Brazil.[22] This conflict in the early months of 1688 revealed

---

[21] Biblioteca Nacional, Lisboa (BNL), cod. 8553, fl. 92–92v., August 14, 1768.
[22] AHU, Angola, caixa 13, doc. 51, February 7, 1688; and AHU, cod. 545, fl. 45, April 3, 1688.

how the Portuguese presence and Catholicism were intertwined and were seen as such by the local authorities. The colonial forces apprehended the religious paraphernalia because its ownership by Kakonda was seen as a menace to the colonial order. At the same time, Kakonda's actions indicated the anxiety societies faced as the growing violence engulfed their lives and institutions. In March 1688, colonial troops coming from Benguela arrived close to the now-abandoned fortress of Caconda, but the ruler had already fled and found refuge in the region of Kikoa, where a well-located fortress built of stones protected his people. The spread of violence led rulers to adjust to the new order, including importing weapons and building defensive mechanisms such as walls and palisades. Facing a possible defeat, the governor of Angola, Luis Lobo da Silva, requested *guerra preta* ("soldiers") from Portuguese vassals in the interior of Luanda. The troops attacked the state of Kakonda on April 9, 1688. In the conflict, a large number of captives and cattle were taken, although the ruler was spared.

The accounts of this event offer insight into life on the outskirts of the central plateau at the end of the seventeenth century. The ruler of Kakonda certainly was strong, and he was able to rely on a professional army. His attacks on the fortress show his ability to organize his troops and also his interest in weapons, gunpowder, and imported commodities. Although emphasizing Portuguese strength, the accounts reveal the weakness of the inland garrison and its difficulty in protecting itself against neighboring headmen. Capture of cattle and people plays an important role in the attacks. While people could easily be incorporated into other states or sold to trans-Atlantic slave traders already established in Benguela, cattle were prized possessions. Inhabitants of the interior of Benguela were agropastoralists who enjoyed the multipurpose role of cattle. Besides providing meat and fertilizing agricultural lands, cattle represented wealth and prestige and could be exchanged. Given the central function of herding in the societies that inhabited Benguela's littoral and interior, cattle also were vulnerable to pillage, as several raids in the seventeenth, eighteenth, and nineteenth centuries indicate.[23] The episode at Kakonda also reveals how African rulers resisted the advance of the trans-Atlantic slave trade, perhaps not with perfect strategies, yet with those available in moments of turmoil.

---

[23] AHU, Angola, caixa 13, doc. 89, March 2, 1689. See also Wilfrid D. Hambly, *The Ovimbundu of Angola* (Chicago: Field Museum of Natural History, 1937), 153–4; Vansina, *How Societies*, 81–9, 129–31; Linda Heywood, "Production, Trade and Power: The Political Economy of

Societies eventually adjusted to the encroaching changes and the pressures of the trans-Atlantic slave trade. The ruler of Kakonda declared vassalage, for example, perhaps assuming that this status would protect him and his subjects. In 1691, he requested safe conduct to travel to Benguela to renegotiate the terms of Portuguese penetration inland. Despite the pass, the governor of Benguela arrested the ruler and sent him to Luanda, where he died in prison.[24] The conflict with Kakonda in the late seventeenth century highlights the vulnerability of the Portuguese presence in the interior. Unable to maintain cordial relationships with the vassals, Portuguese forces were constantly attacked by authorities who disputed its presence and the violence it generated. Although the relationship with Kakonda was the major conflict in the interior in the seventeenth century, it was not the only one. Colonial official correspondence constantly refers to clashes between Portuguese agents and local rulers who had different perceptions and understandings of politics in the region. These accounts describe several polities, sometime in very confusing narratives, that stress the mobility of population, the short span of some chiefdoms, and how African rulers resisted the Portuguese presence and the pressures of the trans-Atlantic slave trade.

In the last years of the seventeenth century, Governor Luís César de Menezes described two powerful rulers in the interior of Benguela, *Jaga* Hiamba and his sister Nana Ambundu. Colonial historian Ralph Delgado identified Hiamba as Huambu (Wambu).[25] As with Kakonda earlier, neither Hiamba nor Nana Ambundu welcomed the Portuguese presence in the lands of Hanya, and both threatened Portuguese agents. Located around the first fortress of Caconda, both rulers were probably not direct relatives but allies in preventing the advance of the Portuguese inland. They challenged Portuguese claims of territorial control and

Central Angola, 1850–1930," PhD dissertation, Columbia University, 1984, 27–8. For cattle's importance on other regions, see Norman Etherington, *The Great Treks: The Transformation of Southern Africa, 1815–1854* (Harlow, UK: Longman, 2001), 10–18; and John Comaroff and Jean Comaroff, "Godly Beasts, Beastly Goods: Cattle and Commodities in a South African Context," *American Ethnologist* 17, no. 2 (1990): 195–216.

[24] AHU, cod. 545, fl. 53v., February 17, 1691. This conflict between the ruler of Kakonda and the Portuguese colonial force is described by later chroniclers such as Elias Alexandre da Silva Corrêa, *História de Angola* (Lisbon: Ática, 1937), 1, 305–9; and Torres, *Memórias contendo a biographia*, 213–4. This episode is also described by Delgado, *Ao Sul do Cuanza*, 1, 230–231; and Joseph C. Miller, "Angola Central e Sul por volta de 1840," *Estudos Afro-Asiáticos* 32 (1997), 23.

[25] See Delgado, *Ao Sul do Cuanza*, 1, 309. If Hiamba is Wambu as Delgado claims, by the 1780s, when Pinheiro Furtado drew his map, the *soba* had relocated to lands far from the first Caconda fortress. See *Carta Geográfica*.

made full use of their trained armies to block colonial conquest. In the first few years of the eighteenth century, Nana Ambundu was defeated by the forces of the captain-major of Caconda, António de Faria, and forced to declare vassalage. However, Hiamba (Wambu?), who continued to be called a *jaga* in Portuguese documents, resisted Portuguese advances. Regardless of their different approaches to Portuguese forces, both moved away from the jurisdiction of Caconda, trying to physically remove themselves from Portuguese contact and the actions of colonial officials. Hiamba claimed to be the lord of his land and, along with his subjects, migrated toward the land of *soba* Kanguengo or Invagando, depending on the source. Invagando (Kanguengo) offered Hiamba and Nana Ambundu asylum. Joining forces, Hiamba and the neighboring headman of Kanguengo raided the lands of neighbors, some vassals of the Portuguese Crown, in a clear retaliation and condemnation of rulers who allied themselves with the colonial power. Incapable of punishing Himba, the Portuguese sent troops to control Kanguembo and avoid the strong alliance. The Portuguese army captured more than fifty-five people and 1,000 cows. Days later, Hiamba, the former *jaga*, now called *soba* in the official correspondence, visited the fortress of Caconda and declared vassalage to the captain-major.[26]

Nana Ambundu and Kanguengo vanished from the records after these accounts. Perhaps they lost their place of prominence in the documentation and continued to exist independently, away from the colonial eye. The fact is that I was unable to find any more information about these polities for later years. They seem to have been strong leaders at the end of the seventeenth century who disappeared in the aftermath of establishment of the Portuguese fortress of Caconda, probably engulfed in cycles of warfare that accompanied the Portuguese penetration. Not necessarily all their subjects were killed or enslaved, but the competition of clashing powers resulted in the migration of groups of refugees who had lost their rulers.[27] The trans-Atlantic slave trade did not have a minimal impact on

[26] The documents are dated from 1701 and 1703 but refer to episodes that took place in the last three years of the seventeenth century when Luís de Cesar Meneses was governor of Angola. AHU, Angola, caixa 16, doc. 27, September 4, 1701; AHU, Angola, caixa 17, doc. 58, October 19, 1703. For more on this event, see Corrêa, *História de Angola*, 1, 327–30; and Torres, *Memória Contendo a Biografia*, 227–8, who emphasized the Portuguese victory. Ralph Delgado dedicated five pages to the events involving Hiamba and Nana Ambundo. See Delgado, *O Reino de Benguela*, 229–33. On Invagando, see Delgado, *Ao Sul do Cuanza*, 1, 513–14.

[27] For similar cases in southern Africa but not necessarily for the same historical period, see Etherington, *The Great Treks*, 27–34; Julian Cobbing, "The Mfecane as Alibi: Thoughts

this region. Old states started to collapse as soon as the trans-Atlantic slave trade became the major economic force in the port of Benguela. The stability that Vansina interpreted as only being disrupted in the 1840s[28] reached the interior of Benguela by the mid–seventeenth century. The same happened to the *soba* of Kakonda, who was regarded as a powerful ruler during the seventeenth century. Although he continued to exist in later periods, he and his subjects were no longer a threat to Portuguese colonialism. Adapting to the demands of commerce, the ruler and his subjects became invested in expansion of the trans-Atlantic slave trade and, in the process, lost their autonomy. Erased from later accounts, as with most defeated people in history, the existence of some of these rulers is only registered in Portuguese colonial documents and absent from major early twentieth-century works on the Ovimbundu group based on oral recollection.[29] They were literally forgotten.

By the early eighteenth century, other leaders lived around the fortress of Caconda, such as Anaquibenga, who was described as settled with his people in the lands around the fortress.[30] The leader, Ngando ya Kitata, was powerful enough to disrupt trade. In 1719, he ordered attacks on itinerant traders, stealing goods and interrupting commerce.[31] Another nearby headman, Kambuinda, attacked the Portuguese fortress of Caconda, killing between 100 and 200 people who lived outside the walls. Kambuinda was caught, and the captain-major of Caconda suggested his sale to slave traders and shipment to Brazil. Three *makotas* ("elders who advised the ruler") were beheaded, and 23 captives, 400 cattle, and more than 100 sheep were sent to Benguela as the royal fifth. The captain recognized that although the booty of war was large, "everybody stole [more than was accounted for in the royal fifth] during the conflict."[32] As a result of this attack and many others perpetrated by the

on Dithankong and Mbolompo," *Journal of African History* 29, no. 3 (1988): 487–519; and Allen Isaacman, "Chikunda Transfontiersmen and Transnational Migrations in Pre-Colonial South Central Africa, ca. 1850–1900," *Zambezia* 27, no. 2 (2000): 109–38. See also Allen F. Isaacman and Barbara Isaacman, *Slavery and Beyond: The Making of Men and Chikunda Ethnic Identities in the Unstable World of South-Central Africa, 1750–1920* (Portsmouth, NH: Heinemann, 2004).

[28] Vansina, *Kingdoms of the Savanna*, 208–14.

[29] Among others, see Hambly, *The Ovimbundu*; and Merran McCulloch, *The Ovimbundu of Angola* (London: International African Institute, 1952).

[30] AHU, Angola, caixa 17, doc. 30, June 20, 1703; and AHU, Angola, caixa 18, doc. 3, February 27, 1705.

[31] Torres, *Memoria contendo a biografia*, 233–4; and Delgado, *Ao Sul do Cuanza*, 1, 514.

[32] AHU, caixa 20, doc. 98, April 26, 1719. Torres, *Memoria contendo a biografia*, 241–3.

captain-major of Caconda, José da Nóbrega de Vasconcelos, the population living around the fortress refused to cooperate with the Portuguese agents. Rulers did not provide soldiers, refused to open trade routes to troops, and attacked Portuguese soldiers whenever they were in a vulnerable position. The *soba* of Kiombela, for example, had gathered his forces to raid the fortress in 1721 but eventually subjugated himself and his subjects to Caconda's control.[33] Even if saved from the threats of Kiombela, the troops who lived in Caconda faced starvation because none of the neighbors was willing to provide food. To overcome the situation, in 1722 some soldiers, among them Lourenço de Matos Coutinho, raided the chiefdoms of Maluzes and Lungarinho, located northeast of the fortress, and obtained enough food to feed the troops.[34] These accounts show the fragility of the garrison of Caconda, which was subjected to raids and attacks from neighboring headmen and forced to negotiate the terms of its relationship with African rulers. References to several rulers, states, and chiefdoms around Caconda may seem confusing, yet it indicates the presence of different polities in the interior of Benguela with a wide variety of scale and status of unification and tolerance of the colonial state. Conflict and competition may predate the construction of the *presídio* of Caconda, but its existence changed the dynamics among the leaders located on the outskirts of the central plateau. A new force, the Portuguese garrison, was seen by the existing powers as both an ally and a menace. And the fortress represented the expansion of the trans-Atlantic slave trade inland.

Establishing a fortress inland changed the relationship between the Portuguese and local groups, or as Walter Rodney and George Brooks have explored in relation to West Africa, its presence altered the power balance between strangers and landlords.[35] For over a century, Portuguese agents had been signing treaties with local authorities and forging alliances with political elites, yet for the first time they guaranteed access

---

[33] AHU, caixa 25, doc. 65, January 21, 1731; AHU, caixa 22, doc. 99, June 8, 1725; AHU, caixa 21, doc. 81, August 3, 1722; AHU, caixa 21, doc. 53, September 6, 1721; and AHU, caixa 26, doc. 10, January 25, 1732. See also Torres, *Memoria contendo a biografia*, 245.

[34] AHU, caixa 29, doc. 24, March 2, 1736.

[35] George E. Brooks, *Landlords and Strangers: Ecology, Society, and Trade in Western Africa, 1000–1630* (Boulder, CO: Westview Press, 1993); Walter Rodney, *History of the Upper Guinea Coast: 1545–1800* (New York: Monthly Review Press, 1980). Jan Vansina makes similar remarks about landlords in West Central Africa. See Jan Vansina, *Paths in the Rainforests: Toward a History of Political Tradition in Equatorial Africa* (Madison: University of Wisconsin Press, 1990), 205–7.

to an inland territory, which facilitated sending armed expeditions and allowed them to dream about controlling trade routes. The first fortress of Caconda was located near the river Coporolo, which fertilized the surrounding lands, already occupied by farmers and herders. Located on higher ground, it was particularly suitable for defensive observations. The supply of water and trade networks secured the survival of anyone who settled there, which explains the existence of different chiefdoms, such as Bongo, as well as other leaders who took advantage of the geographic location to raid neighboring areas. Demographic concentration also meant conflicts over land, people, and cattle. Groups that managed to accumulate cattle herds and dependents allied with other powerful neighbors and challenged old leaders. Although certain accounts emphasize peace around Caconda after 1722, several episodes of violence were recorded.[36]

Kahumba, a runaway slave of a Luanda resident, rose to become a new leader in the interior of Benguela, close to Caconda. A product of the trans-Atlantic slave trade, Kahumba had served as a slave in Luanda or probably was a trusted slave who acted as a *pombeiro* transporting slaves and commodities to and from the coast. After running away, he found refuge near the fortress of Caconda and recreated himself as a ruler or landlord, not as a slave any longer. Relying on his connections and the commodities he transported, in a few years he became powerful in the interior of Benguela and controlled more than twenty *libatas* ("settlements of several huts"). He traded, probably in slaves, controlled a large number of dependents, including wives, and guaranteed order. With the support of professional soldiers, he attacked Portuguese and itinerant traders, resisting their penetration into his territory. In the 1730s, Kahumba had the support of the *soba* of Luceque or Luqueco, who, in the 1630s, was considered to be one of the most powerful rulers in the interior of Benguela, although it is not clear if that was still true 100 years later.[37] The army in Benguela eventually attacked both Kahumba and Luceque. Luceque relocated to the interior of Ngangela, looking for a

---

[36] For the emphasis on peace, see Francisco Travassos Valdez, *Six Years of a Traveller's Life in Western Africa* (London: Hurst and Blackett, 1861), 325; and Torres, *Memórias contendo a Biographia*, 242. For more on the importance of location in settlement decisions in West Central Africa, see Jan Vansina, *How Societies Are Born: Governance in West Central Africa Before 1600* (Charlottesville: University of Virginia Press, 2004), 210–11.

[37] AHU, caixa 27, doc. 157, November 13, 1734. On Luceque, see Heintze, *Fontes Para a História*, 2, 304. On the ability of *pombeiros* to accumulate wealth and power, see Heintze, *Pioneiros Africanos*, chap. 4.

powerful ruler who could protect him and his people, showing once more how migration was seen perhaps as the only effective way to resist the advances of the trans-Atlantic slave trade and colonialism.[38] Kahumba moved toward the coast, yet he and 300 of his people were apprehended by the *soba* of Bambe, an old ally of the Portuguese, who sent sixty-six captives, including men, women, and children, to Benguela.[39] Kahumba probably was murdered because the governor of Benguela, referring to him, stated that "a strong black man dies fighting or runs away. Only those who cannot run, stay in their *libatas*."[40] Thus more than forty years after the opening of the first fortress of Caconda, the Portuguese presence continued to be challenged by local authorities, who opposed the colonial expansionist claims and the Atlantic pressure. These small-scale resistances and reactions emphasize how political allegiance was understood in local terms rather than as a pan-ethnic process. Heads of lineages and chiefdoms withstood external pressures in the best way they could, allying themselves when convenient but also removing themselves from political support or even physically migrating when the threat was too great. None of these polities claimed political or even cultural unity. Colonialism and the slave trade became endemic forces that had long-lasting consequences for small chiefdoms and larger polities, which disappeared or survived based on the relationships they established with colonial men on the spot and neighboring rulers.

Seventeenth- and early-eighteenth-century accounts demonstrate the movement of distinct groups in the interior and the widespread use of violence by those involved. Instability led to the replacement of old authorities and the emergence of new ones, including ephemeral ones such as Kahumba, the Luanda runaway slave turned into *soba*, who could last a few years or decades in power depending on their ability to recruit dependents and allies. While the trade in slaves could be a way to gaining greater access to firearms and gunpowder, the export of captives of war diminished the chances of a new leader to increase the number of dependents under his control. Some states, such as Luceque, however, managed to survive despite the violence and instability in part because

---

[38] "Ngangela" was a derogatory Umbundu term used to refer to the inhabitants of the southeast territories, including Luimbe, Luceque, and Mbunda. See McCulloch, *The Ovimbundu of Angola*, 3; Miller, *Way of Death*, 23–8, and Miller, "Central Africa," 47–8.

[39] AHU, caixa 27, doc. 156, December 20, 1734. For the Bambe alliance with the Portuguese after the 1620s, see Heintze, *Fontes para a História*, 2, 304.

[40] AHU, caixa 27, doc. 157, November 13, 1734.

its leader migrated when confronted by Portuguese colonial armies.[41] Luceque, by the end of the eighteenth century, was a powerful state that collected revenue from the travelers who used its ferry canoe to cross the River Kutado.[42] Smaller polities were raided by stronger ones, which could incorporate slaves as dependents or sell them to itinerant traders. The growing demand of the Atlantic market as well as the expansion of a slave society in the colonial town of Benguela gave an extra push to warfare. Conflicts intimately linked to expansion of the trans-Atlantic slave trade produced a large number of captives who were acquired by Portuguese soldiers and other traders around the fortress of Caconda. Slave coffles, the *libambos*, descended the plateau, following the return of colonial armies to Benguela and were sold to traders located at the port.[43] Yet most of the slave trade was not under the control of the Portuguese and was negotiated in markets controlled by *sobas*, where coastal traders and their agents were not necessarily welcome, as seen in Chapter 4.

Despite its location in a fertile area, the fortress of Caconda and the region around it were affected by a series of droughts from 1715 to 1725 that accelerated disputes over resources.[44] In 1719, the *soba* of Kambuinda, located close to the fortress of Caconda, attacked traders and invaded the Portuguese *presídio*, stealing foodstuffs, probably as a consequence of hunger. Following the Kambuinda raids, the rulers of Gando-ia-Kitata and Kiambela also attacked the Portuguese fortress. In those raids, cattle and people were seized, showing how the early eighteenth century continued to be a period of instability in Benguela's hinterland. Moreover, famine and drought were connected to the pressure

---

[41] Redinha identifies Luceque as an "Umbundu element of lesser importance"; Redinha, *Distribuição Étnica*, 16. For more on Luceque strength, see Delgado, *Ao Sul do Cuanza*, 1, 511–3. On the replacement of old elites for new ones, see Miller, *Kings and Kinsmen*, 167–75.

[42] Francisco José de Lacerda e Almeida, et al., *Lacerda's Journey to Cazembe in 1798* (London: John Murray, 1873), 22.

[43] José C. Curto, "Luso-Brazilian Alcohol and the Slave Trade at Benguela and Its Hinterland, c. 1617–1830," in *Négoce Blanc en Afrique Noire: L'évolution du commerce à longue distance en Afrique noire du 18e au 20e siècles,* ed. H. Bonin and M. Cahen (Paris: Publications de la Société française d'histoire d'outre-mer, 2001), 355. For a similar case in Cape Colony, see Cobbing, "Mfecane as Alibi," 494–5; Pamela Scully, *Liberating the Family?: Gender and British Slave Emancipation in the Rural Western Cape, South Africa, 1823–1853* (Portsmouth, NH: Heinemann, 1997), 20–6; Robert Ross, *Cape of Torments: Slavery and Resistance in South Africa* (London: Routledge & Kegan Paul, 1983); Wayne Dooling, *Slavery, Emancipation and Colonial rule in South Africa* (Athens: Ohio University Press, 2008).

[44] Miller, *Way of Death*, 150

of trans-Atlantic slavers and their agents inland.[45] In 1738, a military expedition launched against the *soba* of Kakonda resulted in the apprehension of at least 340 people because sixty-eight were sent to Benguela as part of the royal fifth. Apparently these people were identified by their place of origin, as Kitete (Quitete in Portuguese), Sumbe (Sumba), or Quilengues, and six were labeled Ussoa.[46] Descriptions of the population around the fortress of Caconda in the first eighty years of the foundation of the *presídio* emphasize the existence of several competing headmen on the outskirts of the highlands. Portuguese sources identify people based on their political affiliation, which may correspond with how people identified themselves. If so, by the early eighteenth century, there was no sense of an entrenched ethnic identity. People were identified based on the land they lived on, or on their political allegiance, or even by the name of their ruler. Alliances could shift due to power struggles, which were strongly influenced by the Atlantic demand for slaves. In fact, slave raiding was at the core of political reorganization in the highlands, allowing new leaders to profit from the sale of human beings and to acquire more weapons and ammunition, as well as other imported commodities, creating a cycle of violence and dependence on the trans-Atlantic slave trade. The consequence of the slave trade was the emergence of societies deeply involved in the Atlantic commercial networks and the products, violence, and ideas it generated. However, this was a dangerous association with dramatic repercussions. In 1755, for example, the ruler of Kabunda raided people around the fortress of Caconda, probably perceiving them as easy targets and potential slaves who could generate imported commodities. In retaliation, a Portuguese army detachment was sent from Benguela to subjugate Kabunda. More than 2,000 Kabunda subjects were captured alive, showing once again that the slave trade was not restricted to small numbers of captives. More than 600 were sent to Benguela as the royal fifths to be sold in the public market.[47] The trans-Atlantic slave trade had dramatic consequences for Kabunda and its subjects.

[45] AHU, Angola, caixa 20, doc. 98, April 26, 1719; and Delgado, *O Reino de Benguela*, 256–9; Miller, "Angola Central e Sul," 25. See also Joseph C. Miller, "The Significance of Drought, Disease and Famine in the Agriculturally Marginal Zones of West-Central Africa," *Journal of African History* 23, no. 1 (1982): 22–3.

[46] Miller, *Way of Death*, xii–xiii.

[47] Instituto Histórico Geográfico Brasileiro (IHGB), DL29,17, "Noticia Geral dos Costumes da Provincia de Bihé," fl. 2v. For the 1755 Kabunda attacks, see AHU, Angola, caixa 40, doc. 71, January 22, 1756; AHU, Angola, caixa 40A, doc. 130, April 20, 1756. Torres, *Memoria contendo a biografia*, 257; and Miller, *Way of Death*, 17.

Colonial accounts emphasize disputes and raids for slaves and cattle as common practices in the area around the fortress of Caconda in the first 150 years of Portuguese early colonialism. The activities of rulers and slavers produced new attacks, counterattacks, migrations, and new alliances. Rulers and people who were raided eventually raided others as well, showing how enslavement became endemic, and the trans-Atlantic slave trade altered the political and economic organization of the polities in the region. Positions shifted according to military conditions and strategic associations, and everybody was affected by the trans-Atlantic slave trade. Initially, Portuguese and Brazilian-born major merchants remained on the coast, relatively safe, waiting for captives to be transported to the Americas, whereas local rulers and traders, including many Luso-Africans as well as colonial officials, perpetrated violence against vulnerable people. Kidnapping, warfare, and other acts of violence were part of this new reorientation of the economy, which emphasized exports of human beings and generated frequent cycles of violence intimately linked to the Atlantic economy.

The fortification at Caconda demonstrated changes in the Portuguese expansionist efforts in the seventeenth century. Rather than limiting themselves to the coast, as they had done in West Africa, the men on the spot became more involved in the processes of enslavement and with territorial expansion of the colony. These actions might explain the growing number of people exported from Benguela in the late seventeenth and early eighteenth centuries who were found in Lima, Havana, Salvador, Cartagena, Mariana, and Rio de Janeiro, among other destinations. The Portuguese effort to occupy territory inland, even if it failed, reinforced the idea that Benguela was a profitable colony intimately linked to the Atlantic market. Societies in the hinterland were forced to rearticulate their relationship with colonial agents in order to resist the pressure and demands from the coast.

The New Fortress at Caconda, ca. 1760–1850

As seen in Chapter 2, new approaches to colonialism and expansionism emanating from Lisbon arrived in Benguela in the 1760s. The governor of Angola, Sousa Coutinho, transferred the *presídio* of Caconda further east to the lands of the *soba* of Katala in 1769, around 40 km inland from the previous location, in order to guarantee control of trade routes. The Portuguese army defeated the headman of Katala in a confrontation and then established a military and trading post in his territory. According to Sousa Coutinho, the new Caconda was located a few days away from its previous place.... [T]he artillery, ammunition, and troops were transferred to the new location between the months of January and July, by the end of which the *presídio* already had a fence of poles and mud, a church, and a treasury.[48]

The governor hoped that "the quality of the air and soil, and the abundance of cattle would transform it into a populous village."[49] The new location was between the Sucula and Cabala rivers, both tributary streams of the Catape River, and located some 220 km from the coast.[50] Metropolitan authorities believed that the new fortress offered a second chance for the Portuguese Crown to try to control the movement of itinerant traders, the *pombeiros*. Merchants coming from the inland territories had to stop in Caconda to pay taxes, which motivated itinerant traders to try alternative routes as soon as the fortress was opened.

A few months after relocation of the soldiers, the Portuguese army initiated a series of attacks against the powerful states in the central highlands that had remained free of Portuguese control until the mid–eighteenth century. Territories that were almost absent from colonial documents were suddenly under scrutiny by the Portuguese. Reports and accounts started to mention Mbailundu, Viye, and Wambu with greater frequency. Inserting themselves into internal political clashes, Portuguese colonial administrators supported the replacement of old political elites with new economic powers who were allied with Portuguese interests and deeply committed to the slave trade. The new political elites became vassals of the Portuguese Crown, which resulted in stronger trade partnerships but also in more conflict. Portuguese officers visited the states in the central plateau and, along with Luso-African traders and a few priests who traveled inland, spread knowledge of the Portuguese and access to the Atlantic economy. The new heads of state were intrinsically linked to the trans-Atlantic slave trade and the Portuguese presence on the coast.[51] In the new *presídio*, a Portuguese settlement was created with the construction of official buildings and a Catholic church called Nossa Senhora da Conceição de Caconda, which is still standing. Although a

---

[48] Biblioteca Nacional, Lisboa (BNL), cod. 8553, fl. 92–92v., August 14, 1768.

[49] AHU, Angola, caixa 53, doc. 71, October 18, 1769.

[50] Delgado, *Ao Sul do Cuanza*, 230–1; Luiz Keiling, *Quarenta anos de África* (Braga: Edição das Missões de Angola e Congo, 1934), 9; and Heywood, "Production, Trade and Power," 117.

[51] Curto, "Luso-Brazilian Alcohol," 358; Miller, "Angola Central e Sul," 26–34. See also Linda Heywood, "Portuguese into African: The Eighteenth-Century Central African Background to Atlantic Creole Cultures," in *Central Africans and Cultural Transformations in the American Diaspora* (Cambridge University Press, 2001), 98.

IMAGE 6. Nossa Senhora da Conceição, Caconda. (Photo by Mariana P. Candido.)

church existed in the first fortress of Caconda and was transferred to the new *presídio* in 1769, parish records have not been located.[52] Baptismal records from 1772 onward, with some gaps owing to the absence of priests and missing books, reveal a little bit about Caconda's population, a topic that will be analyzed in further detail in the next section of this chapter.

With the establishment of Caconda in the lands of Katala, colonial knowledge about the region increased. Expeditions were sent to find the route to the Sena River and the colony of Mozambique. New markets also were reached, thanks to alliances established with neighboring headmen. By the 1770s, slave coffles from Humbe, in the south, as well as slaves from other inland markets crossed the territory of Caconda en route to Benguela.[53] The *presídio* of Caconda also was a place where rulers from the interior sent their ambassadors to discuss their relationships with Portuguese forces. In 1777, the captain-major of Caconda, José de Lemos Chaves, reported a visit from the ambassador of Wambu, who came to discuss a peaceful trade relationship with the Portuguese and promised protection to itinerant traders coming from the coast in exchange for imported commodities and trade advantages.[54] The fortress also was a place where noncooperative headmen were punished, such as the case of Kalukembe. Arrested in 1800, he was imprisoned in the fortress of Caconda for insubordination and participation in attacks on the fortress. After his removal from power, a new and more cooperative ruler was put in his place.[55] Years later, the son of the *soba* killed by the Portuguese forces assumed the position of his father. Ascending to the position of his deceased father, the new ruler resisted Portuguese advances and forbade the entrance of colonial soldiers in his territory.[56]

By the end of the eighteenth century, Caconda had become an important commercial entrepôt on the fringes of the densely populated central highlands. It comprised an extensive territory centered on the fortress,

[52] IHGB, DL32,02.13, "Oficio do Vigario Giovani Antonio Pereira Carneiro," 1797. See also Arquivo do Arçobispado de Luanda (AAL), Caconda, Livro de Batismo, 1762 [refers to 1772].

[53] AHNA, cod. 80, fl. 43v., January 15, 1772; for the importance of Caconda fortress and the internal market, see AHNA, cod. 440, fl. 2–4, July 14, 1791; and AHNA, cod. 441, fl. 3, fl. 3–5v., July 27, 1796. See also Candido, "Trade, Slavery and Migration," 63–84.

[54] AHNA, cod. 81, fl. 14v., April 18, 1777.

[55] AHNA, cod. 442, fl. 126v.–128, August 17, 1800; and AHNA, cod. 443, fl. 45, June 12, 1800. On the Kalukembe, see Alfred Hauenstein, "L'Ombala de Caluquembe," *Antropos* 58 (1963): 47–120.

[56] AHNA, cod. 508, fl. 105–106, July 1, 1827.

139 km wide and 100 km long, that also included several neighboring *sobas* who did not necessarily live under Portuguese control.[57] The size of the territory made control difficult, and the cooperation of allied *sobas* was a necessity for maintaining trading operations. Some Portuguese traders refused to live in the fortress, preferring the protection of local rulers, as already seen in Chapter 3. Pedro Joaquim Ignácio lived in the territory of Kamburo; Francisco António da Glórias and Jacome Manoel, from Portugal, and João da Fonseca Leal, from Rio de Janeiro, lived in Kitata; and Jorge do Porto Ribeiro settled in the *sobado* of Kalukembe, all of them "Africanizing" themselves in the eyes of metropolitan officials. Rio de Janeiro trader José António de Carvalho lived in Ngalangue, where he married into the royal family. All of them opted to live apart from the colonial settlement, among the "heathens without respecting the law and regulations," where they enjoyed trading privileges and maintained relationships as patrons or clients with local rulers.[58] Yet they also retained links with the colonial state, as subjects of the Portuguese Crown, helping to spread Portuguese culture and Catholicism, and they were committed to expansion of slave-trade activities. Although they rejected life in the forts and under colonial control and embraced local practices, as agents of creolization, these traders continued to represent the Portuguese state in the eyes of the populations that lived inland, miles away from Benguela.[59]

The goal of the colonial administrators was to maintain control over the territories under vassalage rather than expand territorial control to new lands. In an official letter sent to the governor of Benguela, the governor of Angola, Manoel de Almeida Vasconcelos, stated that

[s]ometimes it is necessary to make use of force and punish rulers involved in disturbance and robberies, showing who retained the power. [If force was used] ... even the arrogant ruler of Wambu could subject himself to the Crown and receive

---

[57] Alexandre José Botelho de Vasconcellos, "Descripção da Capitania de Benguella, suas Províncias, Povos, Rios mais caudelosos, Minas de Ferro, e Enxofre, e outras particularidades (1799)," *Annaes Marítimos e Coloniais* 4, no. 4 (1844): 147–52. For more traders who refused to live in Caconda, see António Silva Porto, *Viagens e Apontamentos de um Portuense em África* (Coimbra: Biblioteca Geral, 1986), 60–2.

[58] IHGB DL31,05, fl. 10, December 31, 1797. See also Roquinaldo Ferreira, "Biografia, Mobilidade e Cultura Atlântica: A Micro-Escala do Tráfico de Escravos em Benguela, séculos XVIII-XIX," *Tempo* 10, no. 20 (2006): 28; and MEM Santos, *Nos Caminhos de Africa: Serventia e Posse: Angola, Século XIX* (Lisbon: Instituto de Investigação Científica Tropical, 1998).

[59] A. J. R Russell-Wood, *A World on the Move: The Portuguese in Africa, Asia, and America, 1415–1808* (Manchester, UK: Carcanet, 1992), 103–5.

the royal stamp to guarantee his fidelity, which could be seen as a good example for his neighbors.[60]

The *sobado* of Kakonda, one of the strongest in the region in the early eighteenth century, still existed as a separate political entity at the end of the century but had lost its strength due to Portuguese occupation of the territory. The trans-Atlantic slave trade led to the decline of the *sobado* of Kakonda and the rise of new and stronger leaders such as the rulers of Kitata, Kalukembe, and Kingolo, located away from colonial forces but still involved in the Atlantic commerce.

The fortress of Caconda gained more importance during the Portuguese expeditions into Mbailundu (1773–4), known as the "Bailundu wars." Caconda became a key military point, gathering personnel, weapons, and later, captives of war sold as slaves in Benguela, but the ruler and the state that gave the name to the fortress were not militarily competitive anymore. The colonial officials sent an expedition that replaced the old Mbailundu ruler with a new one who was willing to send slave coffles to Caconda and receive Luso-African traders. Portuguese officials were sent to the Mbailundu *sobado*, and the importance of Caconda as an advance Portuguese colonial settlement increased at the expense of the Kakonda *sobado* as its population was slowly incorporated into the colonial fortress.[61] Growing stronger, the colonial power disturbed neighboring headmen who saw it as a political threat to their existence after witnessing the events in Mbailundu. Some *sobas* complained about the behavior of men on the spot stationed at the Caconda fortress, claiming that they used abusive power and excessive violence. Neighboring rulers also reported abuse, such as the case of the *soba* of Gutelo, a new authority in place in the 1820s, who denounced violent acts by soldiers and the captain of the fortress.[62] People who lived within the fortress limits also denounced the behavior of authorities, such as the case of the letter that Caconda residents sent to the governor regarding the rough behavior of Captain-Major João da Costa Frade.[63] Portuguese colonial officers were seen as the cause of violence and turmoil.

---

[60] AHNA, cod. 444, fl. 20v.–21, October 15, 1796.
[61] Delgado, *Ao Sul do Cuanza*, 1, 239; and W. G.. Clarence-Smith, "Capitalist Penetration among the Nyaneka of Southern Angola, 1760s to 1920s," *African Studies*, 37, no. 2 (1978): 163–76, information on 165.
[62] AHNA, cod. 220, fl. 81, September 15, 1825.
[63] AHNA, cod. 442, fl. 34v., April 15, 1797; and AHNA, cod. 442, fl. 38–38v., June 17, 1797.

Caconda functioned as a relay station, which explains the strong links established between the traders who lived there and elsewhere in the territory. Caravans from Benguela passed through Caconda on their way to the slave markets controlled by interior polities on the plateau, as did the *libambos* ("slave coffles") descending from the highlands to the coast.[64] The activities of Luso-African traders linked different points of the interior and maintained the flow of slaves from the highlands to the coast. Yet any disturbance in the *presídio*, such as the occasional raids organized by neighboring *sobas*, had the potential of interrupting the supply of captives from the highlands.[65] The demand for slaves along the coast and the relocation of the long-distance trade route toward Benguela created some interesting connections between Benguela residents and *sobas* in the highlands. Some of the new rulers that emerged in the highlands had strong links to people residing in Benguela. By the early nineteenth century, Gumba, a new headman who lived on the outskirts of the fortress of Caconda, was identified as a relative of dona Catarina Pereira Lisboa, a woman who lived in Benguela at the end of the eighteenth century, already mentioned in Chapter 2.[66] Dona Catarina Pereira Lisboa was one of the most important residents on the south side of the town of Benguela, linked to the trans-Atlantic slave trade and the colonial state. Besides her slaves and free dependents, it seems that dona Catarina also hosted occasional visitors from the interior because sources indicate that Gumba stayed with her when he was in Benguela. After being accused of clashing with Portuguese authorities, the headman Gumba apparently authorized the killing of two Caconda soldiers who entered his territory without permission. Although they searched everywhere in Caconda and in the compound of dona Catarina in Benguela, Portuguese authorities failed to locate Gumba.[67] Dona Catarina and Gumba were

---

[64] AHU, Angola, caixa 53, doc. 71, October, 18, 1769; also AHU, Angola, caixa 70, doc. 5, February 24, 1785; AHU, Angola, cod. 551, fl. 45–53, January 30, 1810; Torres, *Memórias contendo a Biographia*, 23. See also David Birmingham, *Trade and Conflict in Angola: The Mbundu and Their Neighbours under the Influence of the Portuguese, 1483–1790* (Oxford, UK: Clarendon Press, 1966), 138.

[65] The *sobas* of Wambu, Kitete, and Kipeio staged two raids in 1809 and seized a large number of free people and slaves and devastated cultivated fields of the *presídio*; see AHNA, cod. 445, fl. 34–34v., January 27, 1809; and AHNA, cod. 445, fl. 41, September 6, 1809.

[66] IHGB, DL32,02.02, "Relação de Manuel José de Silveira Teixeira sobre os moradores da cidade de São Felipe de Benguela separados por raça, idade, emprego, título de habitação, ofícios mecânicos e quantos mestres e aprendizes existem," 1797, fl. 9.

[67] AHNA, cod. 442, fl. 230–231 July 12, 1803; and AHNA, cod. 443, fl. 119, August 22, 1803; AHNA, cod. 443, fl. 112v., November 15, 1803.

a clear product of changing societies struggling to adjust to the demand of the Atlantic commerce, yet their experience also reveals how coastal merchants and inland political elites cooperated, bypassing Portuguese control.

Colonial power continued to be very fragile in the highlands during the nineteenth century, relying on the goodwill of local rulers to maintain stability outside the fortress walls. Kitata and Kalukembe, for example, raided the lands around the fortress of Quilengues and kidnapped a white woman *filha da terra* in 1803. A new captain-major was sent to the territory of the ruler of Kitata in part to exercise some influence over that leader but also to control commerce.[68] These conflicts also revealed how local rulers resisted the advances of the trans-Atlantic slave trade and colonialism. They employed armies, kidnapped colonial agents, and refused to pay tribute, employing the mechanisms they assumed to be the most effective in stopping the transformations they were facing and living. These strategies were not necessarily successful, yet they are evidence of African agency and resistance to expansion of the Atlantic economy.

Political transformations in the interior affected Caconda, which was an area characterized by the constant movement of people in the aftermath of raids and warfare. Waves of refugees entered the colonial fortress, seeking protection or better access to resources.[69] The captain-major of Caconda, Gonçalves, stated several times in 1829 and 1830 that the constant migration made it very difficult for him to calculate how many people lived in and around the fortress. On three different occasions he stated that people had relocated within Caconda's jurisdiction, indicating that these temporary movements became regular during his administration.[70] The increased mobility of populations probably started in the mid-1820s, when *sobetas* of the Kitata ruler asked permission to emigrate to Caconda. Threatened by the *soba* of Kitata with kidnapping, robbery, and murder, the minor

---

[68] AHNA, cod. 442, fl. 223v.–225, May 10, 1803. See also Delgado, *Ao Sul do Cuanza*, 1, 516–17.

[69] Jill Dias, "Novas Identidades Africanas em Angola no Contexto do Comércio Atlântico," in *Trânsitos Coloniais: Diálogos Críticos Luso-Brasileiros*, ed. Cristiana Bastos, Miguel Vale de Almeida, and Bela Feldman-Bianco (Lisbon: Imprensa de Ciências Sociais, 2002), 294–7; and a Santos, *Nos Caminhos de África*, 79.

[70] AHNA, cod. 508, fl. 156v., January 30, 1829; AHNA, cod. 509, fl. 15–16, January 17, 1830; and AHNA, cod. 509, fl. 34–34v., September 30, 1830. For more about Caconda, see René Pélissier, *História das campanhas de Angola: resistência e revoltas (1845–1941)*, 2 vols. (Lisbon: Estampa, 1997).

ruler requested Caconda's protection, which was followed by relocation, along with dependents and slaves.[71] Episodes such as this one
show how allegiances could shift. Old allies and tributaries could
become the prey of stronger states with organized armies, provoking
population mobility.

By the mid–nineteenth century, the area of the *presídio* shrank compared with its size at the end of the eighteenth century. By 1850, the
fortress territory comprised an area 44.4 km by 28 km, surrounded
by the Cabala and Sucula-Bingo rivers.[72] From its privileged position
at the top of a hill, the fortress was further protected by a wall and
relied on the defensive capacity of eight cannons facing the surrounding
valley. Within the fortification's walls, there were several warehouses
where trade goods were stored. Around the central square were found
the Nossa Senhora da Conceição Church, public buildings such as the
Chamber House (Casa da Câmara), the house of the captain-major, and
a cemetery (see Image 5). The remaining buildings were barracks for
soldiers, surrounded by orange trees. In the valley, several rulers maintained trade relationships with the population living within the fortress.
The ruler of Kamburo, for example, controlled a territory located two
days away from Caconda. *Sobados* such as Fende, Kalukembe, and
Kitata were closer, and a trip to those locations required a day's march.
Bongo, where the first fortress was located, required a six days' march
toward the territory of Mbailundu.[73] The region around Caconda was
the stage for many of the political changes associated with the intrusion
of the Atlantic economy inland, such as migration and the realignment
and reorganization of existing polities.

The Brazilian ban on slave imports in 1830 brought fear to the
Portuguese administrators stationed in Caconda, who assumed that
Luso-African traders would not use the fortress of Caconda anymore and
that the economy would collapse. Despite the treaty, the slave trade continued to operate smoothly along with the trade in "legitimate commodities," such as beeswax, gum-copal, orchilla weed, and later, rubber, until

---

[71] AHNA, cod. 508, fl. 117–118v., December 30, 1827. For a disturbance created by the
ruler of Kitata in the 1820s, see Delgado, *Ao Sul do Cuanza*, 1, 518.

[72] Eduardo Balsemão, "Concelho de Caconda," *Annaes do Conselho Ultramarino*, 3a Série
(1862), 47; and Delgado, *Ao Sul do Cuanza*, 1, 241.

[73] IHGB, DL31,05, December 31, 1797, "Relação Feita por João Costa Frade," fl. 10. For
more on the Fende and Caconda relationship, see AHNA, cod. 81, fl. 118–119v., January
30, 1779. See also Lopes de Lima, *Ensaios sobre a Statistica*, 3, 52.

1850.[74] In an 1840 geographic survey of Africa, Caconda was described as being

[v]ery hilly and very elevated; the air is consequently pure and salubrious, especially at Caconda, the climate which is represented to be delightful in the extreme. Portuguese invalids from Benguela and other places on the coast travel there for the recovery of their health; nor are they disappointed.[75]

Francisco Valdez, who visited the fortress in the 1850s, described the fortress as built of mud and brick. There were shops and the Nossa Senhora da Conceição Church, which still stands. Around 500 houses were built around the walls of the fortress, accommodating the traders who could not live within the fortress.[76] Considered a very healthy place, it was called the "granary of the interior" due to its production of corn, beans, manioc, potatoes, cotton, and wheat, showing how crops from the Americas had been adopted and altered the diet. Grapevines and manioc flour produced there were sent to different parts of the territory, including Benguela. Chickens, pigs, sheep, and cows complemented the diet.

Population of Caconda, ca. 1700–1850

Societies in the interior of Benguela were solidly connected to the Atlantic world despite the fact that they were located hundreds of kilometers inland. Their physical location did not protect them from the expansion of raids and enslavement. In fact, the population of Caconda was fundamental to the expansion of violence inland, linking the interior to the coast. Moreover, the mobility of its population and its connection to the colonial settlement on the coast pushed creolization inland. New identities were forged as *filhos da terra*, *mulato* and white, acted to protect allies of the colonial elites and members of the economic elites against enslavement.[77] Most of the men on the spot in Caconda were *filhos da*

---

[74] For more on this trade, see Delgado, *A Famosa e Histórica Benguela*, 101; and Candido, "Trade, Slavery, and Migration," 63–84. See also Achim von Oppen, *Terms of Trade and Terms of Trust* (Munster: LIT Verlag Münster, 1994), 62–77.

[75] James MacQueen, *A Geographical Survey of Africa* (London: Fellowes, 1840), 7. For more on the quality of the land and air, see Alvin W. Urquhart, "Patterns of Settlement and Subsistence in Southwestern Angola," PhD dissertation, University of California, Berkeley, 1962, 97–8; Lima *Ensaios sobre a statistica*, 3, 49–53, 146. Miller, *Way of Death*, 262.

[76] Valdez, *Six Years of a Traveller's Life*, 325–6.

[77] Green, *The Rise of the Trans-Atlantic Slave Trade in Western Africa, 1300–1589*, 271–5; Walter Hawthorne, *From Africa to Brazil: Culture, Identity, and an Atlantic Slave Trade, 1600–1830* (Cambridge University Press, 2010); Peter Mark, *"Portuguese" Style*

terra, locally born descendants of Portuguese men and local women, who entered the colonial state and occupied positions in the interior. Exposed to tropical diseases as children, they had built-in immunity to yellow fever and other tropical diseases and resisted malaria infection with lower levels of mortality than recently arrived Portuguese officials. One of these men was António de Faria, captain-major of the fortress of Caconda from 1701 to 1703. Son of Portuguese official João de Faria, António was born and raised in Benguela. Described as *pardo*,[78] tall and with curly hair, he was also very knowledgeable about the hinterland because he had participated in several attacks against African forces, such as the *jaga* of Kakonda, *soba* Anaquibenga, and Nana Ambundu.[79] Another *filho da terra* was the mixed-race António da Silva Guimarães, born in the *sobado* of Kitata and a soldier at the first fortress of Caconda.[80] Very little information is available about the population of the first fortress of Caconda. A Catholic church, Nossa Senhora da Conceição de Caconda, and a hospital to treat sick and injured soldiers were built in 1721.[81] Yet I was only able to locate parish records for the years after 1772, and they were from the new fortress of Caconda.

With the transfer of Caconda to the new location in the highlands, more information becomes available. Given its dual commercial and

---

and *Luso-African Identity: Precolonial Senegambia, Sixteenth–Nineteenth Centuries* (Bloomington: Indiana University Press, 2002).

[78] The term *pardo* has usually been translated as "mulatto." However, scholarship on slavery and race classifications is Brazil has shown that *pardo* was a juridical category to designate blacks and their descendants who had been born free, in this way removing them from any association with slavery. More research has to be done to analyze if the same applies to the Portuguese colonies in Africa. See, among others, Hebe Matos, *Das Cores do Silêncio: os Significados da liberdade no Sudeste escravista, Brasil Século XIX* (Rio de Janeiro: Nova Fronteira, 1998); and Larissa Moreira Viana, *O Idioma da Mestiçagem: as Irmandades de Pardos na América Portuguesa* (Campinas: UNICAMP, 2007).

[79] AHU, caixa 17, doc. 51, August 3, 1703; AHU, Angola, caixa 16, doc. 27, September 4, 1701; AHU, caixa 18, doc. 3, February 27, 1705. For more on the role of *filhos da terra* in the colonial state, see Roquinaldo Ferreira, "'Ilhas Crioulas': O Significado Plural da Mestiçagem Cultural na África Atlântica," *Revista de História* 155, no. 2 (2006): 17–41; and Catarina Madeira Santos, "Luanda: A Colonial City between Africa and the Atlantic, Seventeenth and Eighteenth Centuries," in *Portuguese Colonial Cities in the Early Modern World*, ed. Liam Matthew Brockey (New York: Ashgate, 2010), 249–72; and José C. Curto, "'As If from a Free Womb': Baptismal Manumissions in the Conceição Parish, Luanda, 1778–1807," *Portuguese Studies Review* 10, no. 1 (2002): 36. For more on the role of tropical diseases in the emergence of a local elite, see John Robert McNeill, *Mosquito Empires: Ecology and War in the Greater Caribbean, 1620–1914* (New York: Cambridge University Press, 2010), 47–52.

[80] AAL, Caconda, Livro de Batismo, 1762 [but refers to 1772], fl. 2v., August 18, 1772.

[81] AHU, caixa 22, doc. 99, June 8, 1725

military purpose, the fortress attracted merchants and officials, who probably combined both activities. While scholarly knowledge about merchant communities and the social life of local populations is limited to coastal settlements in many parts of the African continent, in West Central Africa, an abundance of sources allows us to reconstruct the social life inland. Thus Caconda reveals how creolization was not restricted to the coast but also altered societies located in the hinterland. Some of the traders established in Caconda were born overseas, such as the case of Francisco Lourenço Borges, from the Azores, who had a daughter, Maria, with his slave Juliana.[82] Or the Rio de Janeiro trader Apolinário Fernandes de Oliveira, who married dona Vitória de Magalhães, who was born in Benguela. The couple lived in the fortress of Caconda, where they baptized their daughter, Luiza.[83] Dona Vitória was typical of Luso-African merchant women of Benguela, analyzed in Chapter 3, who probably relocated inland for business reasons. Her father was a Portuguese trader, and her mother, Anastácia, was a woman from the hinterland. With her Brazilian husband, she recreated the relationship of her parents, unifying trading elites and maintaining a space for her and her descendants as Luso-Africans allied to the Portuguese state. Few whites lived in Caconda, fewer than in Benguela, and the colonial state relied on people such as dona Vitória to maintain a colony in the Benguela hinterland.[84] It becomes clear that as in Benguela, foreign traders married into established Caconda families, and a Luso-African society emerged inland, with people adopting Christianity and Portuguese names to guarantee their place as colonial intermediaries. In the 1770s, for example, António José de Queirós, a soldier from Braga, Portugal, married dona Verônica Maria da Conceição, from Caconda-Velha, the first fortress. She was the daughter of a trader based in Caconda Velha, António da Silva Farinha, and his wife, dona Mariana Vieira de Freitas, who had been born in Benguela.[85] Women who were not the daughters of commercial elites were simply called *preta do sertão*, a black woman from the hinterland, or *preta gentio*, a heathen black woman, in the registers. Thus it is clear that in Caconda, as in Benguela, a local elite was

---

[82] AAL, Caconda, Livro de Batismo, 1762, fl. 3, August 19, 1772.

[83] AAL, Caconda, Livro de Batismo, 1762, fl. 3v., September 1, 1772. For more on the importance of mixed marriages for traders working or settled in the interior of Angola, see Miller, *Way of Death*, 248–9.

[84] Candido, *Frontera de la Esclavización*, 117–55. See also Heywood, "Portuguese into African," 95–8.

[85] AAL, Caconda, Livro de Batismo, 1762, fl. 9v. and 10, October 25, 1772.

formed, composed of descendants of foreign traders and well-placed native women, who became essential to the colonial state. Comfortable in the Portuguese spaces, in the *sobados*, and in markets outside the Portuguese zone, local women and their children were auxiliaries in the expansion of trade and the domination of Atlantic merchants. Thus, as in Benguela, Portuguese colonialism imposed new ideas and practices in the hinterland, including Catholic baptism and marriage. Colonialism introduced new classifications, such as white, *mulato*, or black; heathen or Catholic; and Portuguese or African, all categories that were associated with a new social hierarchy. For local rulers and their allies, these classifications could represent political legitimacy and power in the geopolitics of the hinterland.[86] In baptism records of Caconda, donas were recorded without any mention of their skin color, unlike other women. As with their male counterparts, the color of the donas' and the *filhos da terra* who were colonial agents mattered less in the eyes of the Portuguese than their social and economic position. In a world of increasing racial hierarchies and expanding violence, the notion of being colorless, or *filho da terra*, and dona became a marker and a protection, differentiating Luso-Africans from other West Central Africans, who were considered to be *gentio* ("heathens").[87]

Women who lived in Caconda did not necessarily have the company of their husbands. Some women stayed in Caconda, representing the interests of their partners who were established elsewhere. Some also organized the trade, such as dona Ana José Aranha. In the late eighteenth century, she was a widow based in Caconda who acted as a slave trader. In her compound lived 266 dependents, including twenty-one adult male slaves and fourteen boys and young men. Besides 182 free individuals and her male slaves, dona Aranha owned thirty-six adult women slaves

---

[86] Meredith McKittrick, *To Dwell Secure: Generation, Christianity, and Colonialism in Ovamboland* (Portsmouth, NH: Heinemann, 2002), 8. For the role of the Catholic Church as an institution promoting transculturalization in Angola, see Linda Heywood, "The Angolan-Afro-Brazilian Cultural Connections," *Slavery and Abolition* 20, no. 1 (1999): 9–23. For a different interpretation of the effects of Christianity in West Central Africa, see Sweet, *Recreating Africa*.

[87] I am influenced by the ideas of Toby Green, James Sweet, Mariza de Carvalho Soares, and Karen Graubart on how assuming new identities protected people. Graubart, "'So Color de una Confradía': Catholic Confraternities and the Development of Afro-Peruvian Ethnicities in Early Colonial Peru"; Mariza de Carvalho Soares, "A 'Nação' que se tem e a 'terra' de onde se vem: Categorias de Inserção Social de Africanos no Império Português, século XVIII," *Estudos Afro-Asiáticos* 26, no. 2 (2004): 303–30; Green, *The Rise of the Trans-Atlantic Slave Trade in Western Africa, 1300–1589*, 274–7; Sweet, *Domingos Álvares, African Healing, and the Intellectual History of the Atlantic World*, 222–5.

and thirteen enslaved girls or young women.[88] She was so powerful that not only did she trade in slaves in the fortress of Caconda, but she also was in charge of the caravans descending from the plateau to the port of Benguela. For her protection and to guarantee that her slave coffles would arrive safely in Benguela, she employed security personnel recruited locally or from Portuguese troops who had deserted.[89] Based in Caconda, dona Aranha maintained trade relationships with the rulers of Kigolo and Kitata, buying some slaves there in the early nineteenth century. She was probably illiterate because she used the services of a representative based in Benguela who negotiated the sale of her slaves to Atlantic merchants and wrote letters on her behalf. Apparently, dona Aranha conducted her business alone, although other women acted in partnership with their husbands. In 1797, dona Lourença Santos was a forty-five-year-old woman who lived in Caconda, whereas her husband was settled in Luanda. She was probably his business partner, acquiring slaves in the interior and sending them to her husband. She also was one of the most powerful residents of Caconda. By the end of the eighteenth century, 347 people lived in her compound, most of them free. She also had four male adult slaves, fifteen women slaves, three boys, and five enslaved girls. Most of dona Lourença's dependents were composed of free women who probably worked in the fields cultivating corn and *massambala* ("sorghum"). She also had sixty-eight head of cattle and was one of the wealthiest proprietors settled in the fortress.[90] Corn, a crop of the New World, was one of the agricultural staples in dona Lourença's fields, showing how an imported crop was adopted into the local diet, which certainly led to social and cultural changes.[91]

Also in the Portuguese fortress lived dona Luzia Ferreira Gomes, a slave trader who sent slave coffles to Benguela in the early nineteenth century.[92] At the end of the eighteenth century, she was a sixty-two-year-old widow who was identified as a *parda*, which can indicate a free black woman or a mixed-race. She owned seven male slaves and nine female

---

[88] See IHGB, DL31,05, fl. 4v.–5.

[89] AHNA, cod. 443, fl. 108–108v., March 23, 1802; AHNA, cod. 443, fl. 109, April 23, 1802; AHNA, cod. 443, fl. 109v., June 15, 1802. AHNA, cod. 443, fl. 138v. August 7, 1806.

[90] IHGB, DL31,05, fl. 5.

[91] For how the adoption of new crops led to social and religious changes, see Jan Vansina, "Finding Food and the History of Precolonial Equatorial Africa: A Plea," *African Economic History* 7 (1979): 9–20; and Adriano Parreira, *Economia e Sociedade em Angola na Época da Rainha Jinga (século XVII)* (Lisbon: Estampa, 1990), 39–51.

[92] AHNA, cod. 443, fl. 99, November 20, 1801.

slaves. In her compound also lived 124 free dependents. They produced corn, beans, and sorghum and tended fifty-four head of cattle.[93] Corn and sorghum were cultivated, eaten as grains, and also processed to be consumed. Corn or sorghum flour could be mixed with water or eggs and baked and consumed as bread (*jimbolo*); by adding honey, the flour could be fried and prepared as dumplings known as *matete*. The flour also could be fermented to make a powerful alcoholic drink called *quissangua*.[94] Some of the prosperous women, such as dona Joana de Magalhães, a forty-two-year-old widow, lived on the proceeds of agricultural production, for which purpose she employed slaves and free people. Dona Joana relied on the labor of sixty dependents, including fourteen slaves who worked on her land. Most of her dependents were free women who probably cultivated corn, beans, and sorghum for sale.[95] In the interior, these women reproduced the coastal practice of allying themselves with foreign traders, acting as business partners, translators, and brokers who received imported commodities and exchanged them for slaves in the interior.[96] Thus the society that emerged in Caconda in the era of the slave trade reflected the coastal developments in Benguela and other African ports, although it was located miles away from the littoral. Economy and society were directed toward the Atlantic market, heavily based on the exchange of slaves and imported commodities. Given its connections with different markets, Caconda attracted people from independent states and as well as those who were vassals of the Portuguese, who visited its urban center and accelerated cultural exchanges and contacts between people of different backgrounds.

Widely known as a healthy place, free of mosquitoes, and with many possibilities for lucrative trade, Caconda attracted traders from elsewhere, such as the Portuguese António José Coelho, who transported imported goods inland and slaves to the coast. By 1798, he was a forty-eight-year-old single white man who maintained a trade network with the deeper

---

[93] IHGB, DL31,05, fl. 6, December 31, 1797. Decades later, these were still the most important crops cultivated in Caconda. See AHNA, cod. 445, fl. 46v.–47, January 12, 1810; and AHNA, cod. 508, fl. 110v., August 31, 1827.

[94] Hermenegildo Capelo and Roberto Ivens, *From Benguella to the Territory of Yacca* (London: Gilbert & Rivington, 1882), 1, 365. For more on *quissangua*, see Isabel de Castro Henriques, *Percursos da Modernidade em Angola* (Lisbon: Instituto de Investigação Científica Tropical, 1997), 294, and José C. Curto, *Enslaving Spirits: The Portuguese-Brazilian Alcohol Trade at Luanda and Its Hinterland, c. 1550–1830* (Leiden: Brill, 2004), 19–41.

[95] IHGB, DL31,05, fl. 5v.–6.

[96] Miller, *Way of Death*, 296.

interior, as well as with Benguela, where he sold slaves and other goods. Coelho, as was also the case with some of Caconda's other residents, also engaged in food production.[97] Coelho had twenty-two slaves, sixteen of whom were females. Three free men and seven free women also lived on his property, probably working alongside his slaves in corn and bean production. Even though he was identified as single, three of his sons and one daughter also lived on his property, without mention of their mothers. The free men listed as Coelho's dependents performed some of the typical activities practiced in Caconda by the local population. They were shoemakers, carpenters, blacksmiths, and tailors.[98] The profits of the slave trade attracted many individuals who started businesses in Benguela and later relocated to Caconda.[99] This seems to be the case with Joaquim de Santa Ana, a Luso-African trader who by the early nineteenth century left Benguela in search of closer contact with the interior markets. Established in Caconda, he maintained business relationships in Kitata. In 1803, after the *soba* of Kitata could not or would not provide him with enough slaves for the goods he had given him in advance, Joaquim Santa Ana kidnapped some free subjects of the *soba* of Kitata, in a case that seems to indicate pawnship because it appears that these free people were put under Santa Ana's care as collateral. Yet Santa Ana sold the pawns to Benguela traders, creating a conflict that required intervention by the colonial state.[100]

Some traders managed to stay in Caconda for decades. They maintained their businesses, married local women, and raised large families, although always complaining about their economic situation.[101] This situation seems to have been the case for José de Lemos Chaves, who was the captain-major of Caconda in 1777. In 1799, he was married to

---

[97] AHNA, cod. 441, fl. 59–59v., May 25, 1798. AHNA, cod. 442, fl. 60–61v., May 26, 1798. For Coelho's trade with Benguela, see AHU, Angola, caixa 88, doc. 3, May 15, 1798; and AHU, Angola, caixa 88, doc. 5, May 25, 1798.

[98] IHGB, DL31,05, fl. 9v., 1797.

[99] Delgado, *Ao Sul do Cuanza*, 1, 572–5.

[100] AHNA, cod. 442, fl. 217v.–218, February 12, 1803; and AHNA, cod. 443, fl. 114v., January 9, 1803. For more on pawnship, see Paul E. Lovejoy and David Richardson, "The Business of Slaving: Pawnship in Western Africa, c. 1600–1810," *Journal of African History* 42, no. 1 (2001): 67–89; and Paul E. Lovejoy, *Transformations in Slavery: A History of Slavery in Africa* (Cambridge University Press, 2000), 13–14. See also Jan Vansina, "Ambaca Society and the Slave Trade, c. 1760–1845," *Journal of African History* 46, 1 (2005), 1–27; and Miller, "Slaves, Slavers and Social Change," 14–15.

[101] Joaquim Rodrigues Graça, "Expedição ao Muatayânvua," *Boletim da Sociedade de Geografia de Lisboa* 9, no. 8 (1890): 395; Henriques, *Percursos da Modernidade em Angola*, 127; and Santos, *Viagens e Apontamentos*, 47–8.

dona Rosa de Espírito Santo, and they had a son named Mateus and a daughter named Victória.[102] By 1836, a João de Lemos Chaves, probably his son, baptized three children with two different women. He had two sons with dona Clara Lobo Filho and a daughter with Isabel, who was probably his slave because he freed their daughter.[103] Locally born *filhos da terra* tended to live longer than recently arrived Portuguese, such as Portuguese traders Francisco Teixeira Carneiro, António Duarte Ferreira, and Luís Lopes de Andrade, who perished on one of their journeys to the interior just a few months after arriving in Benguela.[104] Others acquired wealth and power from their activities in the interior, as in the case of the Caconda-born Francisco José Coimbra, who established himself as a client of the ruler of Viye. Coimbra profited from the slave trade, accumulating some wealth and advancing in the military hierarchy. By the mid–nineteenth century, he achieved the post of commandant of Viye.[105] Yet wealth was relative. Lieutenant Vítor dos Santos Maia, who served in Caconda, owned the modest number of three slaves, two men and a woman, at the time of his death in the mid–nineteenth century.[106]

The profile of the population of Caconda demonstrates the links between this inland *presídio* and the South Atlantic world. Overseas traders and merchants born in Benguela moved to the inland fortress in search of business opportunities. People of different backgrounds interacted within and outside the fortress walls. Rulers visited the *presídio*

---

[102] AAL, Benguela, Livro de Batismo [although the register refers to Caconda], fl. 140, August 27, 1799, and fl. 223, December 29, 1805.

[103] AHNA, cod. 81, fl. 14v., April 18, 1777. AAL, Caconda, Livro de Batismo, 1771–1836, fl. 116v., January 16, 1836. For more on men's control over women's labor, see Lovejoy, *Transformations in Slavery*, 14–15; Paul E. Lovejoy, "Concubinage and the Status of Women Slaves in Early Colonial Northern Nigeria," *Journal of African History* 29, no. 2 (1988): 245–66; Martin A. Klein, "Slavery, the International Labor Market, and the Emancipation of Slaves in the Nineteenth Century," *Slavery and Abolition* 15, no. 2 (1994): 197–220; and Richard Roberts, "Women's Work and Women's Property: Household Social Relations in the Maraka Textile Industry of the Nineteenth Century," *Comparative Studies in Society and History* 26, no. 2 (1984): 229–50. For information on polygamous relationships as a way to guarantee political and social control, see Nakanyike B. Musisi, "Women, 'Elite Polygyny,' and Buganda State Formation," *Signs* 16, no. 4 (1991), 757–86.

[104] Arquivo Nacional da Torre do Tombo (ANTT), FF, JU, África, Mc. 3 doc. 11, 1769; ANTT, FF, JU, África, Mc. 16 doc. 1, 1794; and ANTT, FF, JU, África, MC 10, doc. 12, 1756.

[105] Graça, "Expedição ao Muatayânvua," 384. For the recruitment of mixed-race, see AHU, Angola, caixa 69, doc. 47, December 15, 1784; AHU, Angola, caixa 77, doc. 86, 1792; and Silva Corrêa, *História de Angola*, 1, 72–4.

[106] AHNA, cod. 444, fl. 176v.–177, October 24, 1848.

with their subjects. In moments of political readjustment or warfare, they could even request to live within the jurisdiction for protection. As people moved, they adjusted to new political relationships, and at the same time they influenced cultural and social practices. Ongoing contact inevitably led to the amalgamation of cultures and the transformation of old and the emergence of new identities. When convenient, the inhabitants of Caconda adopted a Portuguese identity associated with being baptized and having a Catholic name, dressing in Western fashion, wearing shoes or trousers, and living in the colonial settlement. René Pélissier claims that the residents of the fortress were "re-bantunized mestizos."[107] Yet this identity could be dropped at any point.

The nature of society at Caconda reveals how the trans-Atlantic slave trade affected trade and social relationships inland despite a historiography that minimizes its effects. Wealthy men were able to accumulate a large number of dependents and many wives, as was characteristic of the local societies. Powerful women recruited free and enslaved men. Dependents cultivated fields supplying caravans with flour, vegetables, and alcohol. Local women and their children, similar to what happened in Benguela and other African ports, joined this colonial society and gave shape to a Luso-African community inland.[108] The population in the fortress of Caconda, as well as in neighboring states, was linked to the Atlantic economy and was profoundly affected by it. The trans-Atlantic slave trade introduced new eating habits, such as the adoption of corn and manioc; changed the institution of marriage, spreading polygamy; and imposed a new culture, expressed in the use of Portuguese language inland and the perception that Catholicism could protect people and favored their insertion into colonial society. People who lived miles

---

[107] Pélissier, *História das campanhas de Angola*, 1, 67. For more on Luso-Africans, see Miller, *Way of Death*, 244–51; Mark, *"Portuguese" Style*; George E. Brooks, *Eurafricans in Western Africa* (Athens: Ohio University Press, 2003); Silke Strickrodt, "'Afro-Brazilians' of the Western Slave Coast in the Nineteenth Century," in *Enslaving Connections: Western Africa and Brazil during the Era of the Slavery*, ed. J. Curto and P. Lovejoy (Amherst, NY: Humanity Books, 2003), 213–24; Peter Mark "The Evolution of Identity: Luso-Africans on the Upper Guinea Coast from the Sixteenth to the Early Nineteenth Century," *Journal of African History* 40, no. 2 (1999), 173–91; and Philip Havik, "Women and Trade in the Guinea Bissau Region: The Role of African and Luso-African Women in Trade Networks from the Early 16th to the Mid-19th Century," *Studia* 52 (1994): 83–120.

[108] See Miller, *Way of Death*, 42–3; Linda M. Heywood and John K. Thornton, *Central Africans, Atlantic Creoles, and the Making of the Foundation of the Americas, 1585–1660* (New York: Cambridge University Press, 2007); and Ferreira, "Ilhas Crioulas," 17–41.

away from the coast baptized their children and identified themselves as Christian, nominally or not. They were part of the expanding Luso-African community, which maintained strong links to the colonial posts in a clear indication that creolization moved inland. They participated actively in the Atlantic trade and were connected to internal markets. The population of Caconda, although located in the highlands, developed in parallel to those in African ports such as Luanda, Lagos, and Ouidah, as well as other societies across the Atlantic, such as Lisbon, Rio de Janeiro, and Salvador.

Political Reconfigurations in the Interior of Benguela

The interior of Benguela included more territories than the fortress of Caconda, including many vassal and autonomous polities. This section explores the political landscape in Benguela's hinterland and demonstrates how the trans-Atlantic slave trade provoked political changes. Demand for slaves led to social disruption and expansion of conflicts around Caconda. As seen in previous chapters, local states and colonial authorities engaged in warfare but also kidnapped individuals with the collusion of corrupt institutions to generate large numbers of slaves. Enslavement and slavery itself spread and became a common feature of the colony of Benguela and neighboring states, connecting capture of slaves, the slave trade, and the use of slave labor. The spread of warfare was intimately related to episodes of droughts and famines and favored political reconfiguration in the hinterland of Benguela from the seventeenth to the mid–nineteenth centuries. In sum, environmental changes are seen as human-induced rather than naturally created and part of ongoing climatic shifts.[109]

Few seventeenth-century accounts described the interior owing to the limitations that kept Portuguese from traveling inland. According to the description of the Capuchin missionary Antonio Cavazzi, who lived in Angola from 1654 to 1667, there were ten provinces south of the Kwanza River. He listed Kissama, Sumbe, and Benguela, territories that

---

[109] Lovejoy, *Transformations in Slavery*, 22–3, 76–80, 127–39. See also Robert W. Harms, *River of Wealth, River of Sorrow: The Central Zaire Basin in the Era of the Slave and Ivory Trade, 1500–1891* (New Haven, CT: Yale University Press, 1981), 29–36; Miller, "Slaves, Slavers and Social Change," 10; and Heywood, "Production, Trade and Power," 56–7. For a different opinion on drought and disease, see Joseph C. Miller, "The Significance of Drought, Disease and Famine in the Agriculturally Marginal Zones of West-Central Africa," *Journal of African History* 23, no. 1 (1982): 17–61.

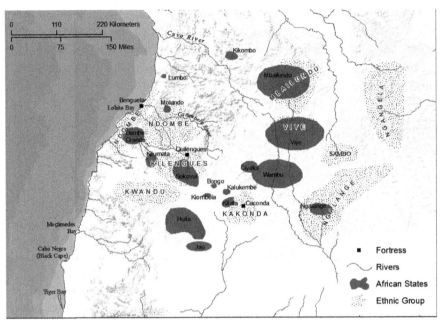

MAP 4. Benguela and its interior. Map by Tsering Wangyal Shawa, Princeton's GIS and Map Librarian.

were located along the coast. In the interior, there were Nsele (Chela), Rimba, Upper Bembe, Lower Bembe, Haku, Kabeso, and Libolo. Each one of them was under a single ruler, which Cavazzi called a "governor," who controlled subordinate leaders or *sobas*.[110] His account recognizes political organization and centralization that predated the arrival of the Europeans. All these territories were located northeast of Benguela, in the interior of Benguela Velha, such as the case of Hako or Libolo.[111] Thus much of the interior that was known by the mid–seventeenth century was very close to the southern margin of the Kwanza River. The region south of the Cuvo River, mainly the hinterland of the colony of Benguela, remained unknown. However, the situation started to change

[110] Giovanni Antonio Cavazzi, *Descrição Histórica dos Três Reinos do Congo, Matamba e Angola* (Lisbon: Junta de Investigações do Ultramar, 1965), 2, 250, L. V, para. 108. John K. Thornton located all these states in *Africa and Africans in the Making of the Atlantic World, 1400–1800* (New York: Cambridge University Press, 1998), see map 3 and the corresponding notes on pages xxxv and xxxvi.

[111] Heintze, *Fontes para a História*, 1, 328–9, and Cadornega, *História Geral*, 1, 52.

in the seventeenth century, especially after the opening of the first fortress of Caconda. Other accounts reveal the movement of political states, or of titles, away from the coast. In 1627, for example, the state of Kikombo was a coastal polity, south of Sumbe. By the end of the seventeenth century, it had many tributary states and had expanded to the provinces of Kissama, along the littoral, and inland toward Libolo. Colonel Pinheiro Machado Furtado produced a map between 1786 and 1790 in which he identified Kikombo miles inland, along the Cuvo River, not in the littoral anymore, as can be seen on the map of states in the hinterland of Benguela.[112] It seems that the Kikombo people migrated inland from the early seventeenth century to the end of the eighteenth century. Perhaps the ruler of the Kikombo or his subjects moved away from the coast in response to the expansion of colonialism and Atlantic commerce.

It should not be surprising that the slave trade provoked political convulsions throughout the region and pushed people inland. One of the features of political organization on the African continent during the era of the trans-Atlantic slave trade was an increase in the number of small polities as part of the collapse of larger states. Thus it seems plausible that rulers who administered coastal states moved inland with their subjects in search of peace and stability. Although there is no explanation in the available records for the new location of Kikombo by the late eighteenth century, the growing violence explored in Chapters 2 and 3 might explain why leaders retreated inland. Yet we should not assume that the Kikombo state in the late eighteenth century reflects the same structure as in the 1630s. More than 150 years passed between the two records, and the leader and his subjects of the 1630s were all dead by the late eighteenth century. However, it shows the methodologic problems of employing a 1790 map to understand where people and states were located in previous centuries; it cannot be assumed that eighteenth-, nineteenth-, or twentieth-century place names were stable and static. Frontiers of states were not fixed and were under constant adjustment in part because the history of this region during the period from 1600 to 1850 was marked by conflict and negotiation. Although central authorities tried to define

---

[112] *Carta Geografica da Costa Ocidental da Africa: Desenhadao pelo Tenente Coronel Eng. L. C. C. Pinheiro Furtado em 1790. Gravada em Pariz por Ordem do Major Cap Carlos Feo Cardoso de CastelloBranco e Torre em 1825.* Reproduced in João Carlos Feo Cardoso de Castello Branco e Torres, *Memórias contendo a biographia do vice almirante Luiz da Motta Feo e Torres* (Paris: Fantin, 1825); and also in António de Oliveira de Cadornega, *História Geral Das Guerras Angolanas, 1680–1681* (Lisbon: Agência-Geral das Colónias, 1942), 3, map after p. 422.

the territorial limits, subjects, outsiders, and events such as warfare and state expansion constantly challenged borders. In sum, the geographic locations of states in the interior of Benguela before the 1850s were not permanent and were defined historically, which has profound consequences on the way people identified themselves.[113]

In 1629, Luis Leitão Sotomaior, superintendent of the treasury of Benguela, described the population around Benguela. According to him, Biasisongo (Bisansongo) and Kisange were lands outside the village of Benguela, where independent leaders ruled their subjects.[114] Yet later chronicles did not mention Bisansongo, as if it had disappeared or was incorporated as tributary of another state, although Kisange (or Quisange) continued to be mentioned by other travelers, especially in the eighteenth century, as part of the state of Kibula.[115] Since Biasisongo was close to the first Benguela settlement in the early seventeenth century, perhaps it was incorporated into Benguela when that village expanded inland, and the ruler and his subjects were absorbed or forced to move away. The names Biasisongo and Bisansongo seem to have disappeared from colonial documents as political entities in the interior of Benguela, demonstrating the destructive power of Portuguese colonialism and the trans-Atlantic slave trade that shifted alliances and led to the erasure of states and peoples. Kisange continued to exist as a state in the late eighteenth century, as seen in the territorial designation on the map made by Pinheiro Furtado.[116] The flight inland of coastal populations, such as the Kikombo, and their incorporation into stronger groups were responses to slave raids and colonial conquest. Pressed between the Portuguese and powerful groups in the interior, coastal populations who survived raids and confrontations were forced to split into smaller groups, move to new territories, and at times join other polities or integrate into other communities. Sometimes they did all of the above in order to survive, leading to the disappearance of some groups and the expansion of others. Resistance to trans-Atlantic

---

[113] See Lovejoy, *Transformations in Slavery*, 68–70; and Cobbing, "Mfecane as Alibi," 506–7. For the idea of frontiers, see Igor Kopytoff, *The African Frontier: The Reproduction of Traditional African Societies* (Bloomington: Indiana University Press, 1987), 3–83. For the political effects of the trans-Atlantic slave trade on Mbundu polities north of Kwanza River, see Miller, *Kings and Kinsmen*, 167–75.

[114] Heintze, *Fontes Para a História*, 303. See Thornton, *Africa and Africans*, xxxvi; and Ralph Delgado, *História de Angola* (Luanda: Banco de Angola, 1948), 2, 125.

[115] Delgado, *Ao Sul do Cuanza*, 1, 524–5, 677–8 (doc. 112).

[116] Almeida, *Lacerda's Journey*, 24–5. See also Mário António Fernandes de Oliveira, *Angolana* (Luanda: Instituto de Investigação Científica, 1968), 1, 280.

pressures and changes assumed different forms, and rulers and subjects employed the tools available to survive.

In the 1620s, officer Sotomaior also described the state of Kilumata (Quitumata or Quitomata in different sources), located inland from Benguela. Kilumata continued to be described by travelers and explorers in the late eighteenth century.[117] Knowledge about the territory and its people expanded in a few decades in the seventeenth century. António Cadornega, writing at the end of the seventeenth century, added information about the territories beyond the coast. He mentioned that the area between Benguela and the central highlands was called "Quilengues," where several *sobas* ruled.[118] Sotomaior's and Cadornega's accounts show how political power was splintered among different polities who competed for resources, with their size and borders changing over time. Cadornega identified those who lived in the central highlands as "Quimbundos," people called today "Ovi-Mbundu," making a clear distinction between the populations of the coast and the highlands.[119] In the 1850s, Hungarian traveler László Magyar also employed the term "Quimbundu" to refer to those who lived in the highlands. Both accounts emphasized the presence of multiple political states among the people who lived in the highlands.[120] Confusingly, in the twenty-first century, "Kimbundu" is the designation applied to the language of those who live in the interior of Luanda, north of the Kwanza River, not south, as before the 1850s.

It is evident that not all groups in the interior of Benguela were known to Cadornega. Since he was based in Luanda and Massangano, his description of the hinterland was based on the accounts of traders, soldiers, and others who had visited the lands south of the Kwanza. Although limited, Sotomaior's and Cadornega's accounts from the seventeenth century describe the interior of Benguela as place where many chiefdoms and states of varying sizes coexisted. The Atlantic commerce, allied with

---

[117] Heintze, *Fontes Para a História*, 304. See also Almeida, *Lacerda's Journey to Cazembe*, 24; and Thornton, *Africa and Africans*, xxxvi.

[118] Heintze, *Fontes Para a História*, 181, 304; and Cadornega, *História Geral*, 3, 168, 172. See also Vansina, *How Societies Are Born*, 144–7. For more on Huíla, see Clarence-Smith, "Capitalist Penetration," 275–81.

[119] Cadornega, *História Geral*, 3, 249–50. See also Childs, *Umbundu Kinship*, 272.

[120] László Magyar, *Reisen in Sud-Afrika in den Jahren 1849 bis 1857* (Berlin: Pest, Lauffer & Stolp, 1859), chaps. 7 and 8. I would like to express my gratitude to Maria da Conceição Neto, who kindly made the manuscript of the Portuguese translation available to me. The Portuguese title is Ladislau Magyar, *Viagens no Interior da África Meridional (1849–1857)*. Chapters 7 and 8 are entitled, "A Nação dos Quimbundos e seus Costumes" and "Impostos, Crimes e Castigos." All the following references refer to the Portuguese translation.

internal factors such as droughts, propelled migration inland away from the coast. The population shifts led to political reconfigurations based on competition for new resources and markets, linked to expansion of the trans-Atlantic slave trade. In this interpretation, the trans-Atlantic slave trade is seen as a major event in this region that provoked social, economic, and political transformations. Moving away from a demographic approach that emphasizes continuities, the collapse of old states and the emergence of new political entities are understood here as a direct effect of the cycles of violence and population turmoil imposed by the Atlantic pressure for captives.[121] Some of the states and their political leaders described in seventeenth-century accounts continued to exist centuries later, such as Wambu and Kitata. Yet most of them disappeared in subsequent centuries owing to Portuguese colonial expansion and territorial conquest, indicating the destructive impact of the trans-Atlantic slave trade. The *soba* of Peringue, based in Benguela, and the ruler located in the port of Kikombo both vanished from Portuguese accounts in the eighteenth century, although on Furtado's map of 1790, Peringue is located living in the interior north of Quilengues, not along the coast.[122]

Not all states and chiefdoms described in seventeenth-century accounts collapsed. Some grew stronger in the eighteenth century, as with the case of Sokoval, which profited from the political instability inland. In the late 1680s, the *soba* of Sokoval was expanding his political control over smaller polities such as Kayoquela and Katira, all located in the Quilengues region. Although Katira was mentioned in later accounts, Kayoquela is not, which may indicate that Sokoval overpowered its leader, erasing its existence from future oral and written documents. The growing power of Sokoval led people to reorganize, joining other groups or splitting into smaller unities. Weaker rulers, in search of protection, requested to relocate under his control with their people. Kabongo was one of the *sobas* who moved voluntarily under Sokoval's control, whereas Ngola Jimbo resisted and was eventually defeated by the Sokoval, who appropriated people and cattle, accelerating the process of accumulation of wealth that

[121] For studies that minimize the effects of the trans-Atlantic slave trade in the region, see Miller, *Way of Death*; John Thornton, "The Slave Trade in Eighteenth Century Angola: Effects on Demographic Structures," *Canadian Journal of African Studies* 14, no. 3 (1980): 417–27; and Thornton, "Sexual Demography."

[122] Cadornega, *História Geral*, 249–50. For places mentioned in other documents, see AHU, Angola, caixa 4, doc. 57, September 13, 1645; and AHU, Angola, caixa 4, doc. 58, December 4, 1645; AHU, caixa 16, doc. 27, July, 1705; and AHU, caixa 18, doc. 14, June and July 1705. Cadornega called the *soba* of Benguela Kasindi, not Peringue, the name used in most Portuguese accounts. See Cadornega, *História Geral*, 250.

inevitably resulted in growing power.[123] Sokoval's increasing power at
the end of the seventeenth century consolidated in the eighteenth century
probably because one of the routes linking the new fortress of Caconda
to Benguela was under Sokoval's control.

Sokoval's expanding dominance was documented by different colonial
agents, although the evidence might seem confusing or repetitive. In this
region of the African continent, a new leader assumed the relationships
and titles of his predecessor in what is known as "positional succession."
This institution, which allowed the continuation of kinship relations
known as "perpetual kinship," brought dynastic stability to a region characterized by change. Yet these institutions created a series of problems for
historians who tried to understand political succession and change. Since
any new leader assumed the social identity of his predecessor, it creates
a false sense of political continuity. Probably aware of the characteristics
of political life in the region, Portuguese colonial authorities employed
the same title and territorial name to refer to rulers, although they clearly
do not indicate that the same person was in power.[124] Thus the ruler of
Sokoval mentioned in the historical documents in the seventeenth century
is different from the Sokoval leader of the eighteenth century, although
it is difficult to determine the differences between them. In the same way
that the political elite of Sokoval incorporated clients and minor polities,
discontented people had the option to move out of the state and relocate
elsewhere, although people in political opposition could be enslaved and
sold to trans-Atlantic traders, as seen in Kongo.[125]

In 1755, colonial agent Domingos da Fonseca Negrão was sent on
an exploratory mission to the interior of Benguela. With his soldiers, he
crossed the land of the *soba* of Sokoval, described as the ruler who controlled most of the territory in Kilengues.[126] Other accounts from the end

---

[123]   AHU, Angola, caixa 17, doc. 30, June 20, 1703. Joseph Miller discusses wealth in people or human capital as a central feature of political-economic system in West Central
Africa. See Miller, *Way of Death*, 42–54.

[124]   For more on positional succession and perpetual kinship as key characteristics of political
life in West Central Africa, see, among others, Miller, "The Imbangala," 549–74; Beatrix
Heintze, "Translocal Kinship Relations in Central African Politics of the 19th Century," in
Translocality: The Study of Globalising Processes from a Southern Perspective, ed. Ulrike
Freitag and Achim von Oppen (Leiden: Brill, 2010), 179–204; and Miller, *Kings and
Kinsmen*, 209. See also Jan Vansina, "Government in Kasai before the Lunda," *International
Journal of African Historical Studies* 31, no. 1 (1998): 1–22; and J. Jeffrey Hoover, "Mythe et
Remous Historique: A Lunda Response to De Heusche," *History in Africa* 5 (1978): 63–80.

[125]   Lovejoy, *Transformations in Slavery*, 88–9.

[126]   IHGB, DL106,15, "Apontamento sobre a Viagem feita pelo Exército ao Reino de
Benguela sob o Comando de Domingos da Fonseca Negrão," 1755, fl. 1–8v.

of the eighteenth century emphasize the central position that the ruler of Sokoval played in trade and the expansion of Portuguese colonialism. One of the most powerful states in Benguela's hinterland, Sokoval shared the region of Quilengues with the rulers of Tunda and Kabelo, although their relationship with the ruler of Sokoval is not clear from the accounts.[127] The political power of Sokoval was based in its ability to recruit soldiers, who engaged in enslaving raids around the territory and sold captives to coastal traders.[128] In 1769, a Portuguese fortress was established in the territory, creating the *presídio* of Quilengues, a gateway to the Huíla highlands, suggesting the strong alliance between the ruler of Sokoval and the colonial power in Benguela. In 1808, the new ruler of Sokoval received military support from the captain-major of the fortress of Quilengues, located not far from his territory. The captain-major of Quilengues, Miguel António da Silva, provided gunpowder and firearms to Sokoval in order to maintain "peaceful" connections. By then, Sokoval was an expansionist state, raiding neighbors, capturing outsiders, and selling them to Luso-African traders coming from the fortresses of Quilengues and Caconda.[129] In 1814, Sokoval also was raiding the Ndombe in the littoral around Benguela and the areas identified by the Portuguese as Dombe Grande in the Kizamba.[130] The consolidation and growth of the state of Sokoval were linked to expansion of the Atlantic market. Imported gunpowder and weapons fueled conflicts that resulted in captives of war. Accumulation of imported commodities became an avenue for old political elites to remain in power, as well as for new warrior and economic elites to challenge the established ruling class.[131]

Accounts from the eighteenth century also highlight the geographic proximity between states, indicating that negotiation was a feature of daily political life. In a few days in 1755, Domingos da Fonseca Negrão crossed several different territories. He visited the lands of the *soba* of Guimbo in the jurisdiction of the old Caconda fortresses, and in two days he reached the territory of the ruler of Kalukembe. After Kalukembe, he marched for two more days until he arrived in Kitata. He spent twelve

---

[127] AHU, Angola, caixa 61, doc. 83, July 28, 1778; and AHU, Angola, caixa 71, doc. 60, November 15, 1786; AHU, caixa 87, doc. 5, January 2, 1798.

[128] AHNA, cod. 442, fl. 64, August 29, 1798; and AHNA, cod. 442, fl. 72v.–73, January 3, 1799; and AHNA, cod. 443, fl. 4, August 11, 1796. AHNA, cod. 443, fl. 123–124, December 9, 1803.

[129] AHNA, cod. 445, fl. 8v.–9, February 20, 1808. For more on the fortress of Quilengues, see Delgado, *Ao Sul do Cuanza*, 281–308.

[130] AHNA, cod. 446, fl. 5–5v., August 27, 1814.

[131] Vansina, *Paths in the Rainforest*, 235–7; Lovejoy, *Transformations in Slavery*, 276–88.

days in Kitata, gathering information, porters, and soldiers. After Kitata, Negrão visited Kingolo. He described Kingolo as a sparsely populated, fortified village, indicating that its population had built protection against raiding parties. In 1806, traders Caetano Pestana and Inácio Rodrigues de Sá were settled in Kingolo and maintained contact with the fortress of Caconda. In the lands of Kingolo lived the *soba* of Malanka, a relative of the ruler because one of the relatives of the *soba* of Malanka was married to the *soba* of Kingolo.[132] Providing a wealth of data on rivers and the distance of his march, Negrão's account describes several rulers and the interactions between people who lived around the fortress of Caconda. The marriage between the royal families of Malanka and Kingolo indicates a common pattern of intermarriage as political alliance. Although reports of warfare reveal disputes in the region, political leaders relied on marriage to form partnerships between competing groups and to avoid warfare. Marriage outside the initial groups shows the importance of interaction and diplomacy. The description of Domingos da Fonseca Negrão caught my attention because it is very different from the early twentieth-century maps of the interior of Benguela. Yet the multiplicity of states described, some of them mentioned in earlier sources, portrays a seventeenth- and eighteenth-century landscape where political alignments were in constant flux due to the impact of the trans-Atlantic slave trade.[133]

The mid-eighteenth-century report on the interior expanded knowledge about the populations and states in the central highlands and was the result in part of the expansion of Portuguese colonialism and settlement of the new fortress of Caconda, as discussed earlier. Leaders of the Sokoval, Kalukembe, Kitumata, Kitata, and Kingolo, located around the fortresses of Caconda and Quilengues throughout this period, were successful in consolidating their power. Relying on their ability to participate in long-distance trade, organize inland markets for itinerant traders, and tax commercial operations within their limits, they attracted subjects of chiefdoms and states that had collapsed previously, further expanding

---

[132] IHGB, DL106,15, "Apontamento sobre a Viagem feita pelo Exército ao Reino de Benguela sob o Comando de Domingos da Fonseca Negrão," 1755, fl. 1–8v. See also Delgado, *Ao Sul do Cuanza*, 1, 522–3.

[133] IHGB, DL106,15, "Apontamento sobre a Viagem feita pelo Exército ao Reino de Benguela sob o Comando de Domingos da Fonseca Negrão," 1755, fl. 1–8v. See Childs, *Umbundu Kinship*, map, "Tribal Divisions and History of the Ovimbundu," before p. 167; and Carlos Estermann, *The Ethnography of Southwestern Angola* (New York: Africana Publishing, 1976), maps before p. 205; and "Ethnological Map of Angola," in Redinha, *Distribuição Étnica*. For similar contexts of landscape change, see Etherington, *The Great Treks*, 5–7.

their authority with the incorporation of dependents. Slaves were offered to *pombeiros* who visited their markets in exchange for alcohol, textiles, and gunpowder, among many other imported goods. The disputes among these states created enough violence and raids to generate captives of war and, in a vicious cycle, attracted caravans crossing their territories in search of slaves for the international trade.[134]

By 1764, the Portuguese Crown continued to sign vassalage treaties, attracting new commercial partners. The rulers of Kambuinda, Kambibe, Mipua, Kipia Pirua, Sokoval, Muila Huíla, Kipungo, Luceque, Mosanjeracata, Fende, Katala, Kitata, Kingolo, Kandumbo, Auzamba, Mbailundu, Kiombela, Tinde and Kibonga were some of the heads of state who signed treaties with the colonial state, although most of these relationships were short-lived. The rulers of Luceque, Kitata, Kingolo, and Tinde, for example, removed themselves from Portuguese control after a few decades due to their discontent with paying taxes and supplying troops to the colonial army.[135] It is not clear if all vassals received official Portuguese advisers and priests, but some did. The ruler of Kitata, for example, had declared vassalage in 1756 to the captain-major of the fortress of Caconda. The trade and the internal market were prosperous and attractive enough to justify the foundation of Vila Viçosa, a short-lived Portuguese colony in the territory of the *soba* of Kitata. A Catholic chapel named after Nossa Senhora de Santa Ana was built to represent the expansion of Catholicism and Portuguese colonialism. Between August 1767 and September 1769, the priest Manoel Lourenço Vieira performed fifty-seven baptisms. After 1769, more baptisms were carried out, but a fire struck the church sometime between 1769 and 1774, and the records were lost.[136] From the available evidence we can gain some insight into the Luso-African population that settled in Kitata in close connection to Benguela and Caconda. In 1767, Sebastião, a three-month-old boy, was baptized. Son of the Benguela-born trader Domingos Rodrigues de Sá and his wife, Ana, "from the heathens of this hinterland," Sebastião and his parents represented the expansion of Portuguese colonialism inland.[137] Kitata's importance was such that it

---

[134] See the reports of the captain-major of Quilengues and Caconda at the end of the eighteenth century referring to most of these states. Among others, see AHNA, cod. 443, fl. 7–7v., September 22, 1796. See also AHNA, cod. 443, fl. 26–27, March 28, 1798. See also Lovejoy, *Transformations in Slavery*, 112–33.

[135] Delgado, *O Reino de Benguela*, 294–5; and Delgado, *Ao Sul do Cuanza*, 1, 511–27.

[136] AAL, Caconda, Livro de Batismo, 1771–1836, fl. 22, February 3, 1774. See also Delgado, *Ao Sul do Cuanza*, 1, 515.

[137] AAL, Caconda, Livro de Batismo, 1771–1836, fl. 7v., September 13, 1767.

attracted traders from overseas such as Jacome Manoel from Portugal and João da Fonseca Leal from Brazil. The priest Vieira baptized Luís, the legitimate son of a Portuguese trader from Braga, Jacome Manoel, and his wife, Rita da Silva, a free black woman from the central highlands.[138] In 1769, Rio de Janeiro–born trader João da Fonseca Leal and Isabel de Araújo Barros, from Kipeio, brought their son, Bernardo, to be baptized in the parish of Santa Ana in Kitata. Bernardo was born two years before, but because of the lack of priests, his parents waited until 1769 to baptize him.[139] People living miles inland had become part of a new culture, mixing local and foreign practices and embracing Portuguese values. Similar to the case of Ambaca in the interior of Luanda, people living in Kitata received the religious sacraments associated with Catholicism, even if they consulted *ngangas* ("local healers"), thus combining Christianity with local spiritual practices. As this example from Kitata reveals, the spread of Portuguese names illustrates the penetration of Portuguese culture inland, probably associated with wealth and links to the Atlantic economy. Creolization moved inland and away from areas nominally under Portuguese control, such as Benguela and Caconda.[140]

In the same year, however, Governor Sousa Coutinho founded a new settlement in Kipeio, where Isabel de Araújo Barros was from. Named "Passo de Souza" by the Portuguese empire, the territory of Kipeio had fertile soil. It is not clear if a church was built there, but the Portuguese settlement was short-lived.[141] Although the colonial enterprise had a short duration in Kipeio, in Kitata, Portuguese agents continued to be appointed by the end of the eighteenth century. In 1797, trader Luís Santos Amaral was nominated captain-major of Quitata, the new colony, although his authority was not recognized by the captain-major of

---

[138] AAL, Caconda, Livro de Batismo, 1771–1836, fl. 7, August, 17, 1767.

[139] AAL, Caconda, Livro de Batismo, 1771–1836, 20v., February 28, 1769.

[140] Linda M. Heywood, "Portuguese into African: The Eighteenth Century Central African Background to Atlantic Creole Culture," in *Central Africans and Cultural Transformations in the American Diaspora*, ed. Linda Heywood (New York: Cambridge University Press, 2002), 91–114; Kalle Kananoja, "Healers, Idolaters, and Good Christians: A Case Study of Creolization and Popular Religion in Mid-Eighteenth Century Angola," *International Journal of African Historical Studies* 43, no. 3 (2010): 443–65; Linda M. Heywood and John K. Thornton, *Central Africans, Atlantic Creoles, and the Making of the Foundation of the Americas, 1585–1660* (New York: Cambridge University Press, 2007), 208–10. For more on Ambaca and its Luso-African population, see Jan Vansina, "Ambaca Society and the Slave Trade, c. 1760–1845," *Journal of African History* 46, no. 1 (2005): 1–27.

[141] Delgado, *Ao Sul do Cuanza*, 1, 310.

the fortress of Caconda, which had controlled and taxed trade from the state of Kitata before 1797.[142] The colony of Quitata was abandoned in part because of the refusal of the captains-major of Caconda to give up control over trade there.[143]

The available historical records indicate an eighteenth century marked by migration and conflict but also by communication among different groups and interaction between states in the highlands and Portuguese agents located on the coast and in autonomous states inland. Instability brought migration and forced groups of refugees to insert themselves into stronger communities and adopt new ideas and lifestyles. Thus the pressure of expanding Atlantic commerce also required that people recreate themselves and assume new political allegiances in order to adjust to the new economic and political environment. While people along the coast could relocate to Benguela and assume a culture characterized by the adoption, in varying degrees, of Portuguese culture and language, people in the highlands also could move into the fortress of Caconda and reinvent themselves as intermediaries, or what scholars call "Luso-Africans."[144] In the same way that some people selected the parts of Portuguese culture that seemed valid and important, other groups of immigrants could follow the same process while relocating into a stronger African state. The seventeenth and eighteenth centuries were a period of change seen in the emergence of new groups. New states also were brought into the Portuguese sphere of influence, forcing local elites to adjust to the new economic and political environment. Yet it was not unique. Other regions of the African continent experienced transformations due to internal and external factors, showing that the unstable political history of the Benguela hinterland was far from unusual.[145] In Benguela, however, such political reorganizations emphasized the destructive effects of the trans-Atlantic slave trade.

By the late eighteenth century, more than twenty states were identified as close to the lands of the *soba* of Sokoval, among them Kipungo, yet these were not tributaries to Sokoval but were autonomous states. Between the coast and the territory of Sokoval, there were another twenty-one

---

[142] AHU, Angola, caixa 105, doc. 19, December 18, 1798; Delgado, *Ao Sul do Cuanza*, 1, 676–7 (doc. 111). For more on Santos Amaral, see Candido, *Fronteras de la Esclavización*, 51–2.

[143] AHNA, cod. 441, fl. 44–48, January 2, 1798. See also AHNA, cod. 442, fl. 59, April 24, 1798; and Delgado, *Ao Sul do Cuanza*, 1, 516–7.

[144] See Heywood and Thornton, *Central Africans*, 49–107.

[145] See Lovejoy, *Transformations in Slavery*, 68–90; Etherington, *The Great Treks*, 10–44.

polities of different sizes, including the Khoe group Kwadi (Mocoroca in the Portuguese documents) close to the Cabo Negro. Between the fortresses of Quilengues and Caconda, there were another twenty-three polities. South of Humbe lived the Kung, a Khoisan group that spoke a "language with clicks and were red; they lived in an unknown remote territory."[146] Many more groups, mainly hunters and gatherers, lived in this region and remained outside the knowledge of the colonial authorities. The multiplicity of groups helps us to understand the raids and invasions described in Chapter 4 and puts them in the context of political reorganization. Rulers such as the *soba* of Kipia, who was apparently powerful from 1800 to 1806, disappeared from the documentation afterward, showing the brief existence of some states and their rulers or perhaps indicating their ability to avoid contact with Portuguese agents.[147] Accounts described political structures that favored centralization, in the person of the *soba* and his council of elders, the *makotas*, such as the case of Sokoval. Yet most of the residents did not live in the center of power but rather around the settlements or in small communities where they raised cattle and cultivated the fields. Even for those who lived under a powerful state, if geographically distant from the center of power, households could easily move away from the state if they became unhappy with taxation or with a ruler who had lost his power and ability to protect his subjects. The migrations described in the accounts of the men on the spot stationed in the fortresses of Caconda and Quilengues could be the result of households and smaller groups moving away from power centers in search of alternative protection. In a sense, pastoral and forager groups

---

[146] IHGB, DL32,02.01, "Relação dos sobas Potentados, souvetas seus vassalos e sobas agregados pelos nomes das suas terrras," 1798, fl. 3v. For more on the Kwadi and !Kung, see Estermann, *The Ethnography of Southwestern Angola*, vol. I. See also E. Westphal, "A Re-Classification of Southern African Non-Bantu Languages," *Journal of African Languages* 1 (1962); Carlos Estermann, "Quelques Observations sur les Bochimans !Kung de l'Angola Méridionale," *Anthropos* 41–4 (1946–1949); Alan Barnard, *Hunters and Herders of Southern Africa: A Comparative Ethnography of the Khoisan Peoples* (Cambridge University Press, 1992), 131–2; and Christopher Ehret, "The First Spread of Food Production to Southern Africa," in *The Archaeological and Linguistic Reconstruction of African History*, ed. Christopher Ehret and Merrick Posnansky (Berkeley: University of California Press, 1982), 167–8. For details on the Kwadi language, see E. O. J. Westphal, "The Linguistic Prehistory of Southern Africa: Bush, Kwadi, Hottentot, and Bantu Linguistic Relationships," *Africa: Journal of the International African Institute* 33, no. 3 (1963), 247–8. Alberto Machado Cruz, however, identified this group as the Kwepe. See his "O Povo Ovakwambundu," *Boletim do Instituto de Investigação Científica de Angola* 4, no. 2 (1967): 67–8.

[147] AHNA, cod. 443, fl. 42–43v., March 7, 1800; Delgado, *Ao Sul do Cuanza*, 1, 284–5. For similar cases, see Vansina, *Paths in the Rainforest*, 220–9.

such as the Kwadi had an advantage in moments of turmoil. They could relocate elsewhere without compromising much of their lifestyle, a more difficult option for farmers who had invested time and resources in land cultivation. Competing forces existed within many of these interior polities, where there was a constant struggle between state centralization at the core and food production and cattle raising in the outer regions.[148]

The prospects of profiting from doing business with slave traders turned old allies against each other. It also changed the power balance in response to pressures from the slave trade. In 1810, the growing power of some groups of hunters and gatherers along the coast challenged settled groups. In 1811, for example, a group of agropastoral Kwandu (Moquandos in the sources) raided the fortress of Quilengues. Small groups of Kwandu were helped by Humbe forces, coming from the southwest, known as a region with abundant ivory and slaves. Their main goal was to steal cattle and firearms from people living around the fortress of Quilengues.[149] In the same year, the Ndombe, also an agropastoral group from the coast, attacked the *soba* of Lumbombe, who was settled on land around Quilengues.[150] The actions of these coastal groups moving eastward shows how the growing access to imported goods allowed littoral groups, even those considered to be acephalous, such as the Kwandu, to raid centralized societies located inland. These attacks allowed coastal groups to secure access to cattle or higher land as a defensive strategy against Atlantic traders, patterns of conflict and migration similar to that taking place in the Upper Guinea and central Zaire basin. Decentralized societies, rather than centralized ones, had an advantage in resisting raids and political annexation.[151] Increasing internal competition led small groups

---

[148] See Harms, *River of Wealth*, 143–59; and Comaroff and Comaroff, "Godly Beasts, Beastly Goods," 195–216. For a different interpretation that focuses on a state's ability to control subjects, see Linda Heywood and John Thornton, "African Fiscal Systems as Sources for Demographic History: The Case of Central Angola, 1799–1920," *Journal of African History* 29, no. 2 (1988): 213–28.

[149] AHNA, cod. 445, fl. 11v.–112, December 1, 1811. For more on the Kwandu, see Estermann, "Les Twa du Sud-ouest de l'Angola"; and Carlos L. Medeiros, "Kwandu Law: the Evolution of a Juridical System among an Herero People of South-west Angola," *Journal of African Law* 28, nos. 1–2 (1984): 80–9.

[150] AHNA, cod. fl. 115v.–122, June 22, 1811. For more on the conflicts around the fortress of Quilengues, see Delgado, *Ao Sul do Cuanza*, 1, 286–9; Pélissier, *História das campanhas de Angola*.

[151] Harms, *River of Wealth*, 111–25. On the role of decentralized societies in raids, see also Walter Hawthorne, *Planting Rice and Harvesting Slaves: Transformations along the Guinea-Bissau Coast, 1400–1900* (Portsmouth, NH: Heinemann, 2003), 91–110; and Green, *The Rise of the Trans-Atlantic Slave Trade*, 258–9.

to separate from the initial community and migrate to new regions, reinforcing political fragmentation as a survival strategy. These migrations
could result from clashes with the previous occupants, provoking restruc-
turing of settlements and the emergence of new leaders, although some
were ephemeral, and conflict did not necessarily lead to centralization.
The Kwandu, for example, attached themselves to an agricultural group,
the Munda, mixing their nomadic pastoralist lifestyle with their host's
sedentary farmers' practices.[152] In the case of the attacks on Quilengues,
it is not clear whether the attackers retreated to the littoral after the raids
or were incorporated into existing states. Caught between trans-Atlantic
slavers and strong states such as Sokoval, coastal agropastoral populations organized into small communities and struggled against the actions
of expansionist states, each plundering labor and cattle. Organization
into small-scale political groups reinforced fragmentation rather than
unity in this region. People did not see themselves as members of a single
community.

Raids perpetrated by states under Caconda's jurisdiction against other
vassal states emphasized the absence of political unity or even a sense of
belonging to the same cultural group or community. In 1817, for example,
the *sobas* of Kitata and Kalukembe, located just outside the fortresses,
raided westward toward the coast, invading the territory of the Ndombe,
destroying crops, and seizing people and cattle. The governor of Benguela
intervened, fearing the lack of control of the captain-major of Caconda
over its neighboring communities, which were kidnapping fellow vassals of the Portuguese Crown. The Ndombe had a long history of links
with the colony of Benguela and were, to a certain degree, exposed to
Lusophone culture.[153] Their enslavement was seen as a threat to those
who lived around Benguela. A few years later, in the early 1820s, Kitata
and Kitete were raiding other rulers around the fortress of Caconda.[154]
In 1829, it was the turn of the Ndombe to raid and seize cattle and goats
from neighbors of the fortress of Caconda.[155] Neighboring rulers refused
to pay tribute to Caconda in 1830 perhaps because of their growing
power and the absence of any real advantage to them. Only the rulers
of Kimungo and Kibonga paid the annual tribute, whereas the rulers of
Bambo, Kauco, Luceque, Mallanka, Kalukembe, and Kingolo refused to

[152] Medeiros, "Kwandu Law," 83–4.
[153] AHNA, cod. 155, fl. 5v.–6 v., August 29, 1817. For more on the Ndombe, see Candido,
"Slave Trade and New Identities in Benguela."
[154] AHNA, cod. 508, fl. 8, September 6, 1823.
[155] AHNA, cod. 220, fl. 185v., October 1, 1830.

do so.[156] These reports make clear the division among the states around the fortress of Caconda, which negotiated their relationships with the *presídio* individually rather than in coalition. Competition and dispute for more subjects, slaves, and imported commodities prevented alliances and reinforced political fragmentation. In the 1840s, new rulers showed up in Portuguese correspondence, such as the rulers of Vatalla and Handa in the Dombe Grande.[157] After suffering attacks, the ruler of Vatalla requested protection from an unnamed ruler in the Quilengues region.[158]

These changes did not happen in a vacuum. As seen in Chapter 3, the British pressure to bring slave exports to an end created tension among inland states, rulers and administrators, traders, and colonial officials. In 1827, the fear that the slave trade would end by 1830, as the agreement signed between Brazil and Britain stated, led to the spread of violence in order to secure an increasing number of captives to feed the dying trans-Atlantic slave trade. Small states joined forces and raided areas between the town of Benguela and the fortress of Caconda. The *sobas* of Kitete and Kitata recruited the support of smaller rulers, such as those of Fundi, Ica, and Bengo, and organized raids to kidnap people and steal from itinerant traders.[159] With abolition of the slave trade, the Portuguese Crown revoked its monopoly on the trade of ivory, wax, and other natural resources, yet the slave trade intensified in the port of Benguela in part because of the difficulty in patrolling the adjacent waters. The rulers of Dombe Grande raided regions neighboring Benguela, seizing people and selling them to illegal slave traders. Ports south of Benguela, such as Moçâmedes, became sites of illegal slave exports and the sale of ivory descending from the Huíla highlands.[160]

In 1850, probably responding to the fear of changes in the trans-Atlantic slave trade, rulers under the fortresses of Dombe Grande and Quilengues raided the areas around Moçâmedes, destroying the village of Giraulo, seizing most of the people and cattle, and provoking migrations of those who were spared. The land was abandoned and the ruler killed.[161] The instability and violence propelled young men, probably soldiers, to leave

---

[156] AHNA, cod. 509, fl. 15v.–16, January 17, 1830.
[157] AHNA, cod. 545, fl. 18–21, April 30, 1843; Pélissier, *História das campanhas de Angola*, 1, 66.
[158] AHNA, cod. 460, fl. 7v., September 24, 1846.
[159] AHNA, cod. 449, fl. 116v.–118, October 18, 1827. For more on conflicts around the fortress of Caconda, see Delgado, *Ao Sul do Cuanza*, 1, 248–9.
[160] Clarence-Smith, "Capitalist Penetration," 166–7; Santos, *Nos Caminhos de Africa*.
[161] AHNA, cod. 453, fl. 93v.–94, November 29, 1850; Pélissier, *História das campanhas de Angola*, 1, 66.

their homeland in search of wealth and power. In the early months of 1851, young men from Hanya abandoned their homeland and pillaged villages in the interior of Catumbela, recruiting more young men to join forces and apprehending women and cattle.[162] People who were captured could be incorporated into the group as dependents or as slaves or sold to traders who visited the port of Catumbela periodically during the 1840s and 1850s looking for African slaves.[163] The death in the early 1840s of the *soba* Francisco Pedro de Moraes, ruler of Katumbela, created a political vacuum that resulted in raids in the interior and exports of slaves from the port. The enthronement of his successor, António Pedro de Moraes, was attended by the interim governor of Benguela, José Vieira Meneses. Interestingly, he did not assume the name of his predecessor, as was the custom with positional succession. Perhaps Portuguese officials assigned him a Portuguese name that differentiated him from the previous *soba* but was not necessarily recognized by the ruler and his subjects. The interim governor offered the new ruler tobacco to cement the alliance and guarantee peace.[164] In 1846, *soba* António Pedro de Moraes visited Benguela and reiterated his fidelity to the Portuguese Crown. He returned two years later for his *undamento*, the ceremony where the new ruler committed himself to the vassalage in the eyes of his subjects and the colonial state. He also was baptized in the Nossa Senhora do Pópulo Church.[165]

The disturbances in the interior were rooted in the demands coming from traders and colonial agents in Benguela for more labor, cattle, and foodstuffs. The damage inflicted by the Atlantic economy has been underestimated in West Central African historiography,[166] but examples from

---

[162] AHNA, cod. 453, fl. 120, March 31, 1851. For the incorporation of women, see Heywood, "Production, Trade and Power," 40–1.

[163] AHNA, cod. 454, fl. 10v.–11, April 8, 1843; AHNA, cod. 453, fl. 76v.–77, April 1, 1850; AHNA, cod. 456, fl. 8, April 4, 1844, and fl. 138v., November 26, 1844; AHNA, cod. 463, fl. 55, January 17, 1848.

[164] AHNA, cod. 454, fl. 54v., August 25, 1843, and fl. 128v., January 7, 1844.

[165] AHNA, cod. 461, fl. 10v., September 17, 1846; AHNA, cod. 461, fl. 81, October 7, 1848. For more on *undamento*, see Beatrix Heintze, "Ngonga a Mwiza: um Sobado Angolano sob Domínio Português no Século XVII," *Revista Internacional de Estudos Africanos* 8–9 (1988): 221–3; Carlos Couto, *Os Capitães-Mores em Angola no século XVIII* (Lisbon: Instituto de Investigação Científica de Angola, 1972), 252–5. On the etymology of the term, see Ana Paula Tavares and Catarina Madeira Santos, *Africæ monumenta: Arquivo Caculo Cacahenda* (Lisbon: Instituto de Investigação Científica Tropical, 2002), 410; Heintze, *Fontes*, 1, 129; and Valentim Alexandre and Jill Dias, *O Império Africano: 1825–1890* (Lisbon: Estampa, 1998), 356–7.

[166] Miller, *Way of Death*; and Thornton, "The Slave Trade in Eighteenth Century Angola," 417–27.

the interior of Benguela reveal the disruptive effects of the trans-Atlantic slave trade on local societies, along the coast and inland. The loss of labor that resulted from the flight from fertile lands impaired cultivation. Raids targeted cattle but also resulted in the destruction of fields, affecting the nutrition of pastoral and agropastoral communities. Survivors joined other groups such as the Kitata or Kalukembe or moved into other states further inland, such as Viye, Mbailundu, and Wambu. States grew from the arrival of refugees and from incorporation of the population of weaker states, leading to the concentration of people and power in fewer hands. Drought, famine, migration, and the emergence of new states in the late eighteenth and early nineteenth centuries were aspects of the same processes unleashed by the Atlantic economy and can only be understood in a context of expanding violence.

The Highland States: Wambu, Mbailundu, and Viye

The people who would later come to know themselves as Ovimbundu lived under different polities that maintained complex regional relations. Their states, rulers, and elites sustained trade networks with regional and distant powers located in the northeast and southeast that resulted in their adoption of ideas coming from elsewhere, such as Lunda titles.[167] They were increasingly affected by commerce with the colony of Benguela, and in fact, Portuguese colonial authorities played an important role in the replacement of old political elites with military rulers who had deeper connections to the slave trade. Visitors recorded striking variations among the states in the highlands, ranging from highly centralized such as Viye to small communities organized as autonomous villages that were dotted over the landscape. Linda Heywood states that identity in this region was associated with a political entity, and "although the kingdoms were not politically unified, they had a common set of political traditions and cultural beliefs and an ethno-linguistic identity which set their peoples apart from their non-Umbundu speaking neighbors."[168] Yet, in contemporary Angola, and even in academic studies, the idea of a common Ovimbundu ancestry rooted in earlier times persists, with expressions such as "Ovimbundu raiders" or "Ovimbundu people" widely used despite their anachronism.[169] The historical evidence, however, indicates

---

[167] Jan Vansina, "It Never Happened: Kinguri's Exodus and Its Consequences," *History in Africa*, 25 (1998): 400–1.

[168] Heywood, *Contested Power in Angola*, 2.

[169] David Birmingham, *Central Africa to 1870: Zambezia, Zaire and the South Atlantic* (Cambridge University Press, 1981), 83–7; Jan Vansina, "Log-Distance Trade Routes

that political and social fragmentation was a reality that threatened rulers and their subjects, and a collective sense of Ovimbundu was not present before 1850. This chapter highlights the fact that what is known today as Ovimbundu, an ethnicity in central Angola with a distinct language and culture, was not recognized in the period under study. In this section I will focus on the highland states of Wambu, Mbailundu, and Viye to show that they were independent and competing states during the era of the trans-Atlantic slave trade. This section emphasizes Wambu, Mbailundu, and Viye defense mechanisms against raids and warfare organized by other polities and the Portuguese colonial army, offering a new interpretation of how identity was centered on allegiance to small political groupings and was not necessarily related to shared cultural practices. The Atlantic economy demanded slaves for imported commodities that were prized by the highland elites, resulting in their deep involvement in slaving activities, perpetuating political fragmentation in the region.

Most seventeenth- and early-eighteenth-century evidence does not refer to the main states in the central highlands, which might indicate that they were not established yet or, most probably, that they had not attracted the attention of Portuguese agents. By the late seventeenth century, Cadornega mentioned Wambu as a powerful *soba* in the interior of Benguela.[170] In 1728, the captain of Benguela, Francisco de Sousa da Fonseca, launched a punitive war against an unidentified Wambu tributary, which led Wambu forces to react to protect a dependent ruler. In the conflict, six colonial soldiers were killed. Wambu forces also disregarded Portuguese authority and moved toward the coast and captured cattle belonging to residents of Benguela in a clear indication of resistance to the Portuguese presence.[171] The governor of Angola punished the captain of Benguela by removing him from his position as the highest colonial authority in Benguela. He was held responsible for Wambu's combative actions and the loss of residents and traders. His removal, however, did not bring an end to the conflict between the Portuguese and communities

---

in Central Africa," *Journal of African History* 3 (1962), 375–90; Vansina, *Kingdom of the Savana*; Maria Emilia Madeira Santos, *Nos Caminhos da Africa: Serventia e Posse* (Lisbon: IICT, 1998); T. J. Desch Obi, *Fighting for Honor: The History of African Martial Art Traditions in the Atlantic World* (Columbia: University of South Carolina, 2008), 48–50; Heywood and Thornton, *Central Africans*, 94.

[170] Cadornega, *História Geral*, 3, 250.

[171] AHU, caixa 24, doc. 41, June 21, 1728. See also Pascoal Leite de Aguiar, *Administração Colonial Portuguesa no Congo, em Angola e em Benguela* (Lisbon: Sociedade Histórica da Independência de Portugal, 2006), 120–1; Delgado, *Reino de Benguela*, 260–1. For later attacks of Wambu forces in search of cattle, see Heywood, "Production, Trade and Power," 26–32.

located in the central highlands. The newly appointed governor soon organized more expeditions to avenge the Crown and the residents, hoping to salvage Portuguese authority. Although no sources explain the motivations of the ruler of Wambu, from the Portuguese sources we can assume that Wambu was protecting its territory and regional power. A strong political entity in the highlands by the 1720s, the prominence of the state of Wambu was the result of new warrior leaders who engaged in raids and enslaved neighboring villagers.[172] The rise of Wambu in the early eighteenth century might be linked to drought in the region in the late 1710s, which led to political revolution and the emergence of new leaders who were better able to address people's needs. People tried to defend themselves in times of ecological crises and slave raids by moving to more prosperous regions with stronger rulers. Competition also resulted in power struggles within states, such as happened to the founder of the state of Wambu, Ngola Ciluanji, who was succeeded by the *jaga* Wambu Kalunga.[173]

By the second half of the eighteenth century, Wambu shared power with other polities located in the central highlands that colonial authorities were not aware of in part because they were focused on occupying new territory with the construction of the new fortress of Caconda. There is no doubt that the expansion of slave exports led to the emergence of new states and the opening of new trade routes, which attracted new leaders and business elites. Colonial expeditions sent at the end of the eighteenth century also helped to expand knowledge about the interior and its population. In 1798, Francisco José de Lacerda e Almeida wrote an account of his journey to Cazembe. According to him, the Benguela highlands were ruled by four *sobas* (Mbailundu, Wambu, Kitata, and Ngalangue). Curiously, he did not mention Viye, another powerful state. In the outskirts of the highlands, there were several rulers, such as Kipungo and Sambo, clearly described as smaller polities or chiefdoms. The rulers of Kilumata, Lombimbe, Kilengues, Bembe, Kipungo, and Sambo were located to the south, nearly reaching Humbe territory.[174]

---

[172] Miller, "Angola Central e Sul por volta de 1840," 22; Gladwyn M. Childs, "The Kingdom of Wambu (Huambo): A Tentative Chronology," *Journal of African History* 5, no. 3 (1964): 367–79; and Heywood, "Production, Trade and Power," 15.

[173] On the difficulties of reconstructing the history of African states through Portuguese sources, see Beatrix Heintze, "The Extraordinary Journey of the *Jaga* Through the Centuries: Critical Approaches to Precolonial Angolan Historical Sources," *History in Africa* 34 (2007): 69–70.

[174] Almeida, *Lacerda's Journey*, 24. For more on this expeditions, see Torres, *Memórias Contendo a Biographia*, 300–1.

Lacerda's account confirms the genealogies of foundation recorded later by missionary and anthropologist Gladwyn Childs, stressing the mid–eighteenth century as the moment when the state of Mbailundu was founded. In the twentieth century, however, Mbailundu, Viye, and Wambu had traditions of origins different from those collected by the end of the eighteenth century, stressing the problems associated with relying on the works of missionaries and anthropologists to reconstruct earlier histories. The variety of legends that justified their presence in the territory and their claims to power reinforced the idea of competing states coexisting in the hinterland in the eighteenth and nineteenth centuries.[175] Thus we can assume that by the late eighteenth century, the people who inhabited the central highlands had not formed a united ethnic or political entity as their southern neighbors in the Huíla highlands had.[176]

By the 1770s, the Wambu territory was an alternate route for traders who were avoiding the fortress of Caconda because they were unwilling to pay taxes and otherwise obey Portuguese control. Luso-African traders searched for routes that did not cross the area around the Portuguese fortress of Caconda or Quilengues. One of the alternative routes was through Kiaka, a tributary of Wambu that received caravans from different regions. Given its participation in the trade, Kiaka and Portuguese armies entered into conflicts in 1773 and 1774.[177] Kiaka's location in the central highlands, close to the fortress of Caconda on the way to the markets of Viye and Mbailundu, made it an attractive zone that Portuguese authorities wanted to control. Traders who visited Wambu in 1795 identified between twenty and twenty-two tributaries of Wambu, including the chiefdoms of Kambundu, Kicalla, and Kiaka. Eight *sobas* ruled over 311 villages where many Luso-Africans resided.[178] In 1800, to guarantee his share of trade and control, the ruler of Wambu confiscated the goods of traders who crossed his territory without his authorization in a struggle with Caconda authorities and merchants over routes and markets. This triggered conflicts with neighboring *sobas*, who also participated in the trade, such as Kalukembe, and Luso-African traders established in the fortress of Caconda. Some of the subjects of the ruler of Wambu

---

[175] Childs, "Chronology," 241–8.

[176] Clarence-Smith, "Capitalist Penetration," 163–4.

[177] Deolinda Barrocas and Maria de Jesus Sousa, "As Populações do Hinterland the Benguela e a Passagem das Caravanas Comerciais (1846–1860)," in *II Reunião Internacional de História da África* (São Paulo: CEA/USP/SDG Marinha, 1996), 96. For more on Kiaka, see Delgado, *Ao Sul do Cuanza*, 1, 526–7.

[178] IHGB, DL22,02.01, "Relação dos Sobas Potentados," 1798, fl. 5. See also Heywood and Thornton, "African Fiscal Systems."

requested protection from the captain-major of Caconda and were granted permission to settle within and around the fortress.[179] Conflicts such as this show the power of Wambu but also stress the absence of a core alliance among central highland rulers. Moreover, such conflicts suggest that population increase did not necessarily happen because even strong states lost population, an argument that has led Linda Heywood and John Thornton to minimize the impact of the trans-Atlantic slave trade on the central highlands. Although communities might appear to be stable, migrations disrupted commerce and affected how people organized themselves. Refugees could be assimilated or driven off, generating conflicts between newcomers and predecessors similar to those in other parts of southern and central Africa.[180]

By the first decades of the nineteenth century, Wambu had become a strong political power in the highlands. In 1801, the Portuguese appointed Manoel Teixeira as the first captain-major, assigned to increase the Portuguese military and political presence inland and to defend the interests of the Portuguese Crown.[181] In 1808, the ruler of Wambu joined forces with seven other *sobas* and destroyed the Fende territory. Although a colonial officer, the captain-major did not have much authority. To bring the conflict to an end, Captain Teixeira visited the ruler of Wambu to negotiate a peace treaty. It is not clear from the account how many people were captured in Fende or the fate of the state after the war.[182] A few months later, in January 1809, the *soba* of Wambu joined forces with the rulers of the smaller powers of Kipeio and Kitete and raided the lands around the fortress of Caconda. The Luso-African trader Sebastião de Abreu Leite and everyone who lived in his compound were killed, showing how the violence of raiders did not spare allies of the colonial state. In fact, as explored in Chapter 4, *pombeiros* and Luso-Africans could be targeted exactly because of their association with the Atlantic market and the spread of violence. Besides the people killed and seized, the agricultural land around the fortress of Caconda was burned. The captain-major

---

[179] AHNA, cod. 442, fl. 153v.–155, January 18, 1800. See also Delgado, *Ao Sul do Cuanza*, 1, 312–33.

[180] Harms, *River of Wealth*, 129–33; Cobbing, "Mfecane as Alibi"; Etherington, *The Great Treks*, 294–300. For a different interpretation that stresses population growth in Wambu between 1799 and 1850, based on data collected by Magyar in the 1860s, see Heywood and Thornton, "African Fiscal Systems," 225. John Thornton has also claimed population growth in the era of the slave trade. See his "Slave Trade in the Eighteenth Century," 417–27.

[181] AHU, caixa 102, doc. 31, October 30, 1801.

[182] AHNA, cod. 445, fl. 9v., March 4, 1808, and cod. 445 fl. 10v., April 1, 1808.

of Caconda reported that most residents around the fortress had lost property and suffered damages, emphasizing the destructive effects of raids.[183] The attacks by Wambu probably affected former Wambu subjects who had migrated to Caconda in the early nineteenth century. As someone who had received very little attention in the Portuguese records of the eighteenth century, the ruler of Wambu became a major expansionist force by the early nineteenth century.

Wambu's expansion clashed with the Portuguese colonial agenda. The governor of Benguela, by 1814, identified Wambu, Viye, Mbailundu, and Ngalangue as the major political forces in the highlands. Their military power was seen a threat to the fortress of Caconda.[184] In the late 1810s, the ruler of Wambu organized expeditions against the lands of Kungo in the margins of the Catumbela River, where the *soba* Francisco de Moraes ruled. A vassal of the Portuguese Crown, as seen in the preceding section, Francisco de Moraes requested support from the troops in Benguela in protecting his people against Wambu advances.[185] In the 1820s, the new *soba* of Wambu sent an emissary to the fortress of Caconda and requested vassalage, an act that was apparently just an excuse to enter the fortress because the captain-major reported that rather than signing the treaty, the *soba* seized people and commodities from the Portuguese fortress.[186] In 1828, the same ruler sent armies to raid the littoral, and in the region around the colonial fortress of Dombe Grande, in Kizamba, "[H]e was very successful, acquiring a vast number of slaves."[187] These events demonstrate how inland states resisted the advance of Portuguese territorial conquest and the pressures of the Atlantic commerce, raiding neighboring areas and selling the captives to itinerant traders who visit their markets. The power of the Wambu was enough to scare the smaller

[183] AHNA, cod. 445, fl. 33–34v., 27 de Janeiro de 1809. The accounts indicated that Wambu did not control Kipeio, although Ralph Delgado claimed that Kipeio was part of Wambu territory. See Delgado, *Ao Sul do Cuanza*, 1, 310–4. For more on the vulnerability of Luso-Africans, see Green, *Rise of the Trans-Atlantic Slave Trade*, 282–3.

[184] AHNA, cod. 446, fl. 2v., August 24, 1814.

[185] AHNA, cod. 446, fl. 175v.–176, March 24, 1818. See also Delgado, *Ao Sul do Cuanza*, 1, 315.

[186] AHNA, cod. 447, fl. 223v.–224, August 25, 1821; AHNA, cod. 508, fl. 112v.–113, October 20, 1827, and fl. 122–123, February 13, 1828; AHNA, cod. 508, 178v.–179, September 11, 1829; AHNA, cod, 509, fl. 60v.–1, January 17, 1830. See also Delgado, *Ao Sul do Cuanza*, 1, 315; and Pélissier, *História das campanhas de Angola*.

[187] AHNA, cod. 449, fl. 128, February 29, 1828. For the incorporation of slaves as a possible explanation for demographic growth, see Heywood and Thornton, "African Fiscal Systems," 225. However, it is not clear if these slaves worked domestically or were exported.

states. In 1825, the governor of Benguela threatened to request the help of the *sobas* of Wambu and Mbailundu to punish the ruler of Kitata, who had decided to challenge the authority of the captain-major of Caconda. The *soba* of Kitata retreated, fearing Wambu's power, and allowed the presence of traders in his territory. He also agreed to pay the annual tribute, yet Wambu forces continued to raid decentralized polities around the fortress of Quilengues in 1836.[188]

The growing power of Wambu allowed the rulers there to decide who could trade in their territories. By the 1840s, there was a new ruler in Wambu named Kapoko. He sent a letter to the governor of Benguela and requested that a literate trader be sent to his market. He provided a young girl as a slave to guarantee that the governor of Benguela would help him with his request, basically offering a slave in exchange for a literate *pombeiro*. Yet, in 1847, Kapoko raided his neighbors, some of them vassals of the Portuguese Crown, putting the governor in a difficult situation.[189] Reports about the state of Wambu indicated commercial operations with the colony of Benguela, where the ruler sent wax, ivory, and agricultural products such as beans, pumpkins, manioc, and corn, besides slaves. Wambu also maintained trading relations with Kipungo and Gambos in order to acquire cattle. The fertility of the land facilitated expansion of the settlement. The acquisition of weapons and gunpowder in the markets of Caconda and Benguela supported further warfare. Oral traditions collected in the early twentieth century emphasized the importance of a warrior ruler and recollected the actions of Wambu armies over neighboring territories such as Kiaka, which eventually became tributaries.[190] Evidence suggests continual competition among the highland states.

While seventeenth-century reports mentioned Wambu, Mbailundu remained outside the Portuguese zone for a longer period, although Ralph Delgado indicates trade between Luanda and Mbailundu in the seventeenth century.[191] Oral traditions suggest that it was founded in the eighteenth century by an immigrant named Katiavala, from Kibala, located in the north.[192] The rulers of Mbailundu are mentioned in accounts from

---

[188] AHNA, cod. 449, fl. 68, January 19, 1826, and fl. 137v., June 9, 1828. Alexandre and Dias, *O Império Africano*.

[189] AHNA, cod. 509, fl. 277v.–278, November 14, 1838. See also AHNA, cod. 462, fl. 128, August 31, 1848, and fl. 133–133v., October 4, 1848; AHNA, cod. 463, fl. 131–31v., August 28, 1848; AHNA, cod. 510, fl. 9v.–10, May 19, 1847. See also Delgado, *Ao Sul do Cuanza*, 1, 604–5 (doc. 69); and Pélissier, *História das campanhas de Angola*, 1, 67.

[190] Childs, *Umbundu Kinship*, 176; and Heywood, "Production, Trade and Power," 39.

[191] Delgado, *Ao Sul do Cuanza*, 1, 377.

[192] Childs, *Umbundu Kinship*, 171; Vansina, *How Societies Are Born*, 180; Keiling, *Quarenta Anos*, 59–61.

different eras, pointing to the ability of the highlands rulers to maintain a strong state despite warfare. In the 1770s it was seen as a powerful state with commercial elites who participated in long-distance caravans and took part in markets organized in the Dondo at the Kwanza River.[193] In order to tax the trade, the Portuguese Crown sent armies to attack Mbailundu with the goal of imposing vassalage. From 1770 to 1775, the Portuguese sent several military expeditions to Mbailundu, hoping to defeat the ruler and replace him with a leader who would cooperate with the colony of Benguela. Known as the "Bailundu wars," these expeditions enabled the Portuguese Crown to force vassalage treaties over several rulers, including the ruler of Mbailundu.

By 1788, the governor of Angola, Barão de Moçâmedes, believed that Mbailundu's power was in decline, though he was proven wrong when it continued to be a strong force until the early twentieth century.[194] Yet control over Mbailundu in the late eighteenth century changed the relationship between the states in the central highlands and the Portuguese colony of Benguela. Other rulers came under Portuguese control, although the ruler of Mbailundu was identified as the most powerful one. In the late eighteenth century, the ruler of Mbailundu controlled forty tributaries, among them Katira, Kangenge, and Kitushe. Still, he was surrounded by neighboring states that were not Portuguese dependents, such as Kengue and Ondura, which had six tributaries. After the "Bailundu wars" in the 1770s, the fortress of Caconda acquired more importance as a trading center in the interior, and the number of slaves exported from the port of Benguela increased by the end of the century.[195]

In another account from 1798, the recently nominated captain-major of Mbailundu, António José Fernandes, described the state as centralized under a single ruler, the *soba*, who relied on the information provided by his twenty-one *kicanzo*. *Kicanzo* were the lands administrators of tributaries (*sobetas*) and were in charge of governing the village territories.[196]

[193] AHNA, cod. 80, fl. 115v., August 27, 1772; Pélissier, *História das campanhas de Angola*, 1, 70.

[194] AHNA, cod. 82, fl. 115v.–116, January 10, 1788. Torres, *Memórias contendo a Biographia*, 268. For more on the conflicts, see AHU, Angola, caixa 62, doc. 4, May 22, 1779; AHU, Angola, caixa 74, doc. 49, November 10, 1789; and Delgado, *Ao Sul do Cuanza*, 1, 377–80. For Mbailundu strength in the twentieth century, see Heywood, *Contested Power*, 28–33.

[195] IHGB, DL32,02.01, fl. 5v.; Corrêa, *História de Angola*, 1, 62–7; and Miller, "Angola Central e Sul," 30–1.

[196] IHGB, DL32,02.05, "Relação de António José Fernandes, capitão-mor, a Alexandre José Botelho de Vasconcelos, Governador de Benguela, dos moradores e de seus filhos desta Província de Bailundu," March 3, 1798, fl. 36–36v.

The ruler of Mbailundu ensured that the state was protected but relied on the *sobetas* for the collection of taxes, land distribution, and control over households. Through this institution, the ruler was able to expand by attracting smaller states whose rulers could maintain control under Mbailundu's rule. The growing power of Mbailundu is reflected in the large number of smaller states that were incorporated as dependents. In the 1790s, for example, the state of Kipaka was part of Mbailundu. Alliances between a strong military power such as Mbailundu and smaller polities allowed the spread of professional armies by incorporating new soldiers into Mbailundu forces. Mbailundu's increasing power also gained from the growth in the labor force that carried out agricultural production, cattle, and hunting activities.[197]

The ruler of Mbailundu also hosted soldiers who had deserted the colonial states, such as Luanda-born soldier Manuel de Brito Santos, who was trading in the Mbailundu until he was kidnapped and sold as a slave. A Luso-African trader from Benguela, Bartolomeu Gonçalves bought Santos and transported him to Benguela, as shown in Chapter 4.[198] Colonial officials also were appointed to positions there, such as the case of trader Manoel José da Costa Arouca, nominated captain-major of Mbailundu in 1800 to substitute for António José Fernandes. Although removed from colonial administration, Fernandes remained in Mbailundu at least until 1813, acting as trader, sending slave coffles to Benguela, and exercising political and economic influence over the Mbailundu elite. Portuguese colonial agents stationed in the inland *sobados* reported changes of heads of state and episodes of war but rarely mentioned any details about the population and social life.[199] The ruler of Mbailundu constantly sent letters to the governor of Benguela requesting weapons, ammunition, and paper, showing how literacy was appropriated and valued as an important skill. In exchange for imported commodities, he sent his army to impose order over the states of Kibula, Lumbo, and Kisange, as the governor of Benguela had requested. Besides his military power, he offered an adult man and a young boy as "presents" to the governor, an example of trade disguised as a gift exchange.[200] The relationship

---

[197] AHNA, cod. 441, fl. 44–8, January 2, 1798; Lopes de Lima, *Ensaios sobre a Statistica*, 54–6. See also Miller, "Angola Central e Sul," 31. Childs also listed Ngalanga as a tributary of Mbailundu in his *Umbundu Kinship*, 168.

[198] AHNA, cod. 442, fl. 137v., September 17, 1800, and fl. 144–145, October 19, 1800.

[199] AHNA, cod. 443, fl. 46, July 23, 1800; and AHU, Angola. caixa 115, doc. 24, February 14, 1806.

[200] Delgado, *Ao Sul do Cuanza*, 1, 623–4 (docs. 82 and 83). For more on the incorporation of writing and diplomatic correspondence among West Central African rulers,

of cooperation between the colony and Mbailundu resulted in unequal advantages for those involved. The Portuguese colonial state increased its revenue and territorial claims. Luso-African itinerant traders were welcomed at Mbailundu, increasing the number of captives from the interior who were arriving in Benguela by the turn of the nineteenth century. The ruler of Mbailundu grew in importance in the geopolitics of the interior as his access to imported commodities attracted itinerant traders from all over the interior to his markets and smaller polities searched for protection and alliance. These advantages, however, were short-lived because the Portuguese colonial state subjugated the Mbailundu in the early twentieth century.

The alliance with the colony of Benguela also is seen in the arrival of coastal traders and their agents bringing imported commodities to the markets of Mbailundu. It is difficult to know the nationalities of all the traders who were stationed in Mbailundu. For instance, António Mendes, who was sending caravans to Benguela by 1801, might or might not have been born in Africa but was clearly a Luso-African who had adopted some colonial values. His Christian name might indicate that he had been baptized. The *soba* also received personal gifts or tribute from Portuguese authorities. In 1812, the newly enthroned Dom Lourenço Ferreira da Cunha received gunpowder and firearms from the governor of Benguela.[201] The alliance with the Portuguese brought greater power to the Mbailundu ruler, allowing him to conquer new territories. In 1814, Dom Lourenço Ferreira da Cunha occupied the lands of Kimbarandongo, in Luculo, and Monguia, in the Bimbe, acquiring a large number of captives who were sent to Benguela.[202] Yet each new ruler had to declare vassalage to the Portuguese. In 1821, when a new *soba* of Mbailundu was enthroned, he was invited to travel to Benguela to be baptized and attend the ceremony of *undamento*. This visit certainly was an opportunity to display his wealth and power when traveling to the coast.[203] Mbailundu

see Ana Paula Tavares, "A Escrita em Angola: Comunicação e Ruído entre as Diferentes Sociedades em Presença," in *Angola on the Move: Transport Routes, Communications and History*, ed. Beatrix Heintze and Achim Von Oppen (Frankfurt: Lembeck, 2008), 163–73; Catarina Madeira Santos, "Écrire le Pouvoir en Angola. Les archives Ndembu (XVIIe–XXe siècles)," *Annales. Histoire, Sciences Sociales* 4 (2009): 767–95. An earlier version of this article was published in Portuguese as "Escrever o Poder. Os Autos de Vassalagem e a Vulgarização da Escrita entre as Elites Africanas Ndembu," *Revista de História* 155, no. 2 (2006): 81–95.

[201] AHNA, cod. 443, fl. 89v., May 29, 1801.
[202] AHNA. cod. 446, fl. 13, October 19, 1814.
[203] AHNA, cod. 156, fl. 44v.–45, March 27, 1821.

continued to be an important ally of the Portuguese in later decades, providing soldiers to the Portuguese army and regularly being in command of punitive colonial wars against Wambu and Viye for periods that go beyond the scope of this book. This alliance was eventually fatal because it resulted in territorial control by the Portuguese in the early twentieth century and had no real lasting advantage to the rulers and subjects of Mbailundu. By 1850, Magyar estimated that the population was around 450,000.[204]

The last of the major highlands powers that will receive attention in this chapter is the state of Viye. Located northeast of the fortress of Caconda, further east than the states of Wambu and Mbailundu, the *sobado* of Viye seems to have been founded after a schism in a previous state. According to the tradition recorded by colonial officer José Nepomuceno Correia in 1797, the founder of Viye was subordinate to the chiefdoms of Songo, near the Kwanza River.[205] Groups of Songo migrated south, either physically or just as a name, and founded Viye. In 1797, João Napumoceno Correia distinguished the population that inhabited the Viye from its Wambu and Mbailundu neighbors, claiming that originally they spoke a different language, not Umbundu, although it is not clear whether this language was the Kimbundu that was spoken in the north.[206] In the process of migration, people who became identified as Viye incorporated the language, customs, and clothing of their neighbors, who later were identified as Ovimbundu. Correia's account describes a process of cultural transformation that can be called "creolization," where prior to the end of the eighteenth century, people identified as Viye assumed a new language and culture that was similar to that of their neighbors. This change might be linked to their migration to a new land and their attempts to forge new alliances, but it clearly indicates the fluidity of identities in pre-twentieth-century West Central Africa. The case of Viye shows how signs associated with a group's identity, such as language and clothing

[204] McCulloch, *The Ovimbundu of Angola*, 4; and Heywood and Thornton, "African Fiscal Systems," 223–4. For more on Mbailundu after 1850, see Alexandre and Dias, *O Império Africano*, 398; and Pélissier, *História das campanhas de Angola*, 1, 77–89.

[205] IHGB, DL29,17. "Notícia Geral dos Costumes da Provincia do Bihe, em Benguela, por João Nepomuceno Correia," 1797, fl. 1. This tradition is similar to the one collected by Magyar in the 1850s. See Vansina, *How Societies Are Born*, 180–1; and Childs, *Umbundu Kinship*, 173. Missionary Keiling claimed that Viye was part of the Humbe state, southeast of Benguela; see Keiling, *Quarenta Anos*, 19–20. For a reconstruction of the state of Viye after the 1850s, see Heywood, "Production, Trade and Power," 45–54.

[206] IHGB, DL29,17, fl. 1. For the confusion between the terms "Kimbundu" and "Umbundu," see Redinha, *Distribuição Étnica*, 5–6.

styles, were subject to change when convenient. It also challenges the idea of ethnic origins being rooted in earlier centuries when populations were migrating and adopting new cultures in this region, a process intimately linked with expansion of the trans-Atlantic slave trade. In the mid–nineteenth century, traders Silva Porto and Magyar also presented different versions of the origin of Viye, which may indicate adaptation of the myth of origin to justify land claims and regional power.[207] Yet, in most accounts, Viye is portrayed as state founded by immigrants who were relocating after clashes with an Ambundu polity in the north in a process of cultural exchanges and creolization of old and new practices.

Viye came to the attention of the Portuguese in 1755, when Domingos da Fonseca Negrão explored the interior of Benguela. While in Viye, Negrão ordered the arrest of the *soba*.[208] Sometime before 1772, a *filho* (which can be translated as either "son" or "subject") of the removed ruler requested Portuguese help. He wanted Portuguese support for his claim to power. The captain-major of Caconda, José Vieira de Araújo, perceiving an opportunity to establish a favorable ruler in Viye, offered trade advantages if a treaty of vassalage was signed. Captain-major Francisco José Coimbra, an Afro-Goan, was sent to represent Portuguese interests, revealing how people of different backgrounds interacted in Benguela's hinterland.[209] The Viye contender went to Benguela, where he was baptized and received the name by which he was referred to in the official correspondence, Dom António de Alencastro. Allied with the Portuguese Crown, Dom Alencastro returned to the highlands, removed the *soba*, Minuio, from power, and ruled Viye until 1813. This case also stresses the direct involvement of the Portuguese colonial state in the politics of the interior and demonstrates how the trans-Atlantic slave trade accelerated political changes.

By the end of the eighteenth century, Viye had several tributary states, including Kabanda, Kapollo, Kakiongo, Gambos, and Kitungo.[210] Yet travelers who visited the region three years later named other tributaries, Guruca, Cunhaco, Trumba, and Candavita, which may indicate either their incorrect observation or political rearrangement.[211] More than twenty

[207] Porto, *Viagens e Apontamentos de um Portuense em África* (UC Biblioteca Geral 1, 1986), 165–71; and Childs, "Chronology of Ovimbundu Kingdoms," 241–8.

[208] IHGB, DL106,15, fl. 1–8v.

[209] AHNA, cod. 81, fl. 55–55v., March 7, 1778. See also Pélissier, *História das campanhas de Angola*, 1, 70.

[210] IHGB, DL29,17, 9v.–10. For more on Viye, see Santos, *Nos Caminhos e África*, 93–7.

[211] IHGB, DL32.02.01, fl. 6–6v.

autonomous rulers and headmen lived around Viye, including Kajungo, which itself had eleven tributaries; the *soba* Kikicocumulinda, with five tributaries; and the rulers of Munhemba, Kapumba, and Anguruca. The last one, the ruler of Anguruca, was perceived as a very powerful ruler with many dependents and tributary states.[212] Curiously, neither report mentioned Ndulu (Andulo, Ondulo, or Ondura), a powerful state by the end of the nineteenth century that was located nearby Viye, which Childs considered to be one of the oldest states in the region, indicating that Ndulu was not necessarily consolidated by the end of the eighteenth century despite twentieth-century accounts that claim ancestry in the land. By the mid–nineteenth century, however, trader Silva Porto mentioned Ndulu.[213] The case of Ndulu's foundation addresses the difficulties of writing the political history of the region relying exclusively in oral traditions.

Viye maintained close contact with the Mbailundu and Wambu, as seen in Viye's incorporation of language and technology from the other territories, such as knowledge about firearms.[214] Less powerful than Mbailundu and Wambu by the end of the eighteenth century, Viye's ruling class avoided conflicts in distant lands, and captives were sold in the market located within the state. Subjects paid taxes in cattle and chickens; grains such as wheat and barley; and corn, beans, potatoes, manioc, and pumpkins. Lettuce, cabbage, rosemary, onions, and garlic also were produced. Fruits such as oranges, limes, bananas, and figs were eaten. Women baked bread and produced alcohol made of corn and honey.[215]

Similar to Mbailundu, the markets of Viye attracted soldiers who had deserted the Benguela army and relocated to the interior under the protection of local rulers. Viye residents Manuel do Nascimento, a white soldier, and Manuel Ruiz Mendes, Caetano Simões, and António da Silva Lisboa, all called *pardos*, were identified as soldiers who had deserted and who engaged in trade in 1800.[216] Its location made Viye attractive.

---

[212] AHNA, cod. 441, fl. 44–8, January 2, 1798; and IHGB, DL32,02.01, fl. 6–6v.

[213] Graça, "Expedição ao Muatayânvua," 385–6. For Silva Porto's account, see BSGL, res. 1, pasta E, 2, "Memorial dos Mucanos" [pages not numbered], "July 28, 1850." See also Childs, *Umbundu Kinship*, 170; and Vansina, *How Societies Are Born*, 181.

[214] IHGB, DL29,17, fl. 5. For the difference between the language spoken in Viye and other groups in the highlands, see J. Torrend, *A Comparative Grammar of the South-African Bantu Languages* (London: Kegan Paul, 1891), 30–1.

[215] IHGB, DL29,17, fl. 7v.–8. Decades later, the territory of Viye continued to be seen as very productive; see Lopes Lima, *Ensaios sobre a statistica*, 16, 46–7.

[216] AHNA, cod. 443, fl. 56, October 18, 1800; AHNA, cod. 443, fl. 70, March 7, 1801. For more on *pardos*, see n. 81.

From there it was relatively easy to travel to markets further inland, such as Ngangela and Lovar, and to the fortresses of Pedras Negras, located in Pungo Ndongo in the interior of Luanda. In 1802, more soldiers deserted and relocated to Viye, such as the Manuel Peres, a tailor who lived in the compound of the trader Vitorino.[217] Violence in the highlands and commercial disputes sometimes resulted in the murder of itinerant traders. In 1806, trader Basílio António de Gouveia, resident of Mbailundu, attacked the caravan of António Manuel Luís, a *pombeiro* who was bringing imported commodities from Benguela to Viye. The governor of Benguela sent a letter to the *soba* of Mbailundu requesting his cooperation in arresting Gouveia. As a reward for capturing Gouveia, the *soba* received a barrel of gunpowder and two barrels of *aguardente*, Brazilian sugar cane–based alcohol, revealing the connection between alliances, access to imported commodities, and the potential expansion of conflict.[218]

In actions that mirrored its increased role in Wambu and Mbailundu, the Portuguese Crown appointed a captain-major as the colonial officer responsible for defending and representing the interests of the Portuguese state. As in previous cases, the officer did not have effective control over state affairs and relied on the cooperation of the ruler and local elites to reside within the borders of the state. Different captains-major in Viye mentioned the same problems between 1798 and 1813.[219] While reporting on Viye in 1810, the captain-major stated that the *soba* ruled and he simply followed orders. He had no control over soldiers who deserted or convicts, the *degredados*, who lived in the *sobado*. He also said that he was incapable of listing all the tributaries due to his limited knowledge.[220] Even if Viye was considered a vassal of the Portuguese Crown, it is clear that its control was very limited, and the *soba* acted as an autonomous ruler. In 1813, a new *soba* was enthroned, Dom João Nepomuceno. Colonial officials appointed to the position of captain-major of Viye included Francisco José Coimbra, born in the fortress of Caconda; Pompílio Pompeu do Carpo; and eventually, the famous Portuguese trader Silva Porto in 1848.[221]

---

[217] AHNA, cod. 443, fl. 102, January 23, 1802; for the trade route connections, see Lopes Lima, *Ensaios sobre a statistica*, 17; Almeida, *Lacerda's Journey to Cazembe*, 24. See also Delgado, *Ao Sul do Cuanza*, 1, 339; and Alexandre and Dias, *O Império Africano*, 400.

[218] AHNA, cod. 443, fl. 143, December 16, 1806. For more on Viye's economic attraction, see Isabel de Castro Henriques, *Percursos da modernidade em Angola* (Lisbon: Instituto de Investigação Científica Tropical, 1997), 396–7.

[219] Delgado, *Ao Sul do Cuanza*, 1, 607–11 (docs. 72 and 74).

[220] AHNA, cod. 445, fl. 56–58, April 21, 1810.

[221] Delgado, *Ao Sul do Cuanza*, 1, 341–2. For more on Francisco José Coimbra, see Heintze, *Pioneiros Africanos*, chap. 2.

By the late 1840s, around 80,000 people lived in Viye. They cultivated corn, beans, pumpkins, and manioc, indicating how the Atlantic market had altered agriculture and diet in the highlands. They also hunted elephants and raised cattle. Others engaged in long-distance trade with the interior and the town of Benguela. The primary trade goods were wax, ivory, and slaves. Four minor rulers lived under Viye's control in the 1840s: Kanhete, Pulumba, Kipende, and Kabalango. It is not clear what happened to the many tributaries listed in previous decades.[222] By 1847, Kingula ruled the Viye state, and although he was not baptized, he used the Catholic name of Dom António de Lencastre, the first ruler of Viye who had signed vassalage treaties with the Portuguese in the 1770s. His adoption of the name of an earlier ruler was an unmistakable bid to claim kinship and to legitimize his power.[223] Merchants continued to live in Viye until mid–nineteenth century, such as Manoel Francisco de Sousa, who died there before February 14, 1849, Silva Porto, and Magyar, among others.[224] When living in Viye in the 1840s, Silva Porto reported a multiplicity of headmen living close to him. The headman of Dumbo and the *soba* of Kipupire, for example, were mentioned in Silva Porto's diaries but had never been mentioned in other documents before.[225]

In Viye, similar to other states in the highlands, political alliances changed overnight. The *sobetas* of Kakemgue, Donde, Kamessi, and Kapango, which were vassals of Viye, in 1847 slipped from its control and requested protection to the ruler of Mbailundu.[226] The state of Mbailundu was alleged to be invincible in the hinterland, and the *sobetas* took advantage of changes in the geopolitics of the highlands to improve their own positions. By 1849, Hungarian trader László Magyar moved into Viye, and noticing how easy it was for people to migrate and resettle in new lands, he commented, "[I]nhabitants can easily abandon a village and settle in a new place near to or far from the abandoned one; usually the new place is given a new name."[227] Migration was a feature of life in societies disrupted by the trans-Atlantic slave trade.

---

[222] AHNA, cod. 462, fl. 29v.–33v., November 26, 1849. See also Henriques, *Percursos da modernidade*, 397.

[223] Delgado, *Ao Sul do Cuanza*, 1, 347. For the importance of perpetual kinship and positional succession in the regions, see Vansina, *Kingdoms of the Savanna*, 82.

[224] AHNA, cod. 444, fl. 184v.–185, February 14, 1849. See also Santos, *Nos caminhos de Africa*, 79; Heywood and Thornton, "African Fiscal Systems," 214–5.

[225] See BSGL, res. 1, pasta E, 2, "Memorial dos Mucanos" [pages not numbered], "July 28, 1850," "August 17, 1851."

[226] AHNA, cod. 462, fl. 29v., November 4, 1847. See also Delgado, *Ao Sul do Cuanza*, 1, 346.

[227] Heywood and Thornton, "African Fiscal Systems," 214. Missionary/ethnographer Carlos Estermann also mentioned migrations of whole groups or parts of groups; Estermann, *Ethnography*, 2, 27–30.

Other groups who lived in the central plateau of Benguela and beyond, such as the Ngalangue, remained outside Portuguese control for much of the seventeenth, eighteenth, and early nineteenth centuries. Feared by Luso-African traders and authorities located in Caconda, people of Ngalangue were perceived as savages, dangerous and distrustful, in part because of their military power, seen in their ability to resist various colonial attacks.[228] Baptism records indicate that the *soba* of Ngalangue received a priest in his territory and was willing to let his subjects to be baptized at the end of the eighteenth century.[229] While it is not surprising to find Brazilian traders in Ngalangue, such as António Francisco da Conceição, it is interesting to see many subjects of Ngalangue baptizing their children. António Francisco da Conceição, born in the town of Maragogipe in Bahia, and Theresa, from Ngalangue, baptized their son Manuel.[230] Others who sought the priest, Francisco José de Oliveira Rodrigues, were the couple Vitorino da Rocha and Quitéria, a Luso-African couple born in Ngalangue. They named a colonial officer, Sergeant Lourenço Tavares, and Teresa de Oliveira, also from Ngalangue, as the godparents of their daughter, Lourença, purposefully or not, choosing the feminine version of her godfather's name.[231] In the parish records, there is no evidence of the baptism of adults, which indicates that the Catholic church assumed that all subjects of the *sobas* who declared vassalage were Catholics, a clear advantage in a period of intense violence and slaving. Moreover, it stressed the expansion of creolization into areas outside the control of the Portuguese Crown, where people living under an autonomous ruler chose to baptize their children if this could be used as a mechanism of protection against the widespread violence.

By the early nineteenth century, traders stationed among the population in Ngalangue continued to baptize their children when priests visited the *sobado*. In 1802, in consequence of some years without a priest, trader Francisco Gonçalves Rodrigues and his wife, dona Francisca Teresa de Oliveira, baptized two sons registered as legitimate children, indicating that the couple was married in the Catholic church. Francisco Gonçalves, however, maintained more than one family, and he made sure that all his children were baptized. Besides the two sons with dona Francisca Teresa de Oliveira, he baptized a son with dona Francisca da

---

[228] AHNA, cod. 155, fl. 2v.–4v., May 2, 1817. Santos, *Nos caminhos de Africa*, 451–70.
[229] Some of the baptisms in the states around the fortress of Caconda were recorded in the books of the parish of Nossa Senhora da Conceição in Caconda. See AAL, Caconda, Livro de Batismo, 1771–1836, for example.
[230] AAL, Caconda, Livro de Batismo, 1771–1836, fl. 32, November 17, 1780.
[231] AAL, Caconda, Livro de Batismo, 1771–1836, fl. 29v., August 22, 1779.

Fonseca; a daughter with Lucrécia, a free black woman from the hinterland; and a second daughter with a black woman called Teresa. On the same day, he also registered two other daughters born from two different black free women, Rosa and Maria, as well as a son with Micaela, another free woman.[232] It is clear that Francisco Gonçalves Rodrigues maintained polygamous relationships, probably not that different from other men who lived in Ngalangue. The demographic imbalance that the trans-Atlantic slave trade provoked left more women than men in West Central Africa and influenced the ability of wealthy men to have more than one spouse. It is not clear where Francisco Gonçalves Rodrigues was born. Foreigner or not, he adjusted to local patterns of marriage, which among other things allowed wealthy men to have more than one wife.[233] Although the Portuguese Crown nominated captains-major and caravans from Ngalangue arrived in Caconda and Benguela, Ngalangue remained outside colonial control and attacked the fortress of Caconda on several occasions.[234] Yet its population adopted values associated with the Portuguese presence, indicating that creolization was connected to expansion of the trans-Atlantic slave trade.

It becomes apparent from the accounts available before 1850 that multiple political powers existed in the interior of Benguela. Accounts of conflict, warfare, and competition more likely suggest the lack of an overarching ethnic identity that unified the population in the central highlands. People identified themselves with a territory and a political leader, which explains competition and raids within the so-called Ovimbundu states. As McCulloch stated, Ovimbundu "seems to have been adopted as a tribal name in fairly recent times, the various groups being formerly know separately as Mbailundu, Ciyaka, Viye, etc."[235] Although missionaries later insisted on cultural unity, the fact that people spoke closely related languages did not prevent competition among rulers and their subjects. The political instability imposed by the trans-Atlantic slave

---

[232] AAL, Caconda, Livro de Batismo, 1771–1836, fl. 53v.–54, August 3, 1802.

[233] Thornton, "The Slave Trade in Eighteenth Century Angola," 417–27; and Mariana P. Candido, "Women, Concubinage and Slavery in Benguela, ca. 1750–1850," paper presented at the Canadian African Studies Association, Ottawa, May 2010. For cases outside the African continent, see Robert McCaa, "Marriageways in Mexico and Spain, 1500–1900," *Continuity and Change* 9, no. 1 (1994): 11–43.

[234] AHU, Angola, caixa 71, doc. 60, November 15, 1786; AHU, Angola, caixa 123, doc. 15, March 10, 1811; AHU, Angola, caixa 126, doc. 8, February 16, 1813; and AHU, Angola, caixa 129, doc. 47, October 5, 1814; see also Delgado, *Ao Sul do Cuanza*, 1, 408–9.

[235] McCulloch, *Ovimbundu*, 1. See also Heywood, *Contested Power*, 12–16.

trade pressure helped to explain the transformation in the interior of Benguela. Rather than the emergence of large empires, states of different sizes coexisted in this region, competing for resources. These local differences were important for those involved, even those exported to the Americas. While the majority of people from the Benguela hinterland were identified as "benguela" in Brazil, Peru, Colombia, and Cuba during the era of the trans-Atlantic slave trade, when given the opportunity to identify themselves, they relied on more particular identities. These can be seen in the case of people living in Mariana in the early eighteenth century who claimed to be ganguela, or Nganguela, differentiating themselves from the benguelas.[236] Or even the cases of freed slaves in the Mixed Commission files in Rio de Janeiro who self-identified themselves as Viye, Mbailundu, Wambu, Kakonda, and Ndombe, among many more localized identities.[237] The list compiled by Mary Karasch further reveals the existence of specific identities in nineteenth-century Rio, such as Kitata, Kalukembe, Kitete, Mbailundu, and Wambu, all from the interior of Benguela.[238] These examples show how identity was elaborated in terms of lineage, village, and small-scale communities rather than a pan-ethnicity shared by most inhabitants of the central highlands.

Descriptions of conflicts among states and populations in the hinterland are sometimes confusing in the Portuguese accounts. The documents challenge the boundaries between ethnic groups that missionaries and Portuguese administrators so carefully elaborated in the twentieth century. People in the highlands did not develop a historical narrative of becoming Ovimbundu but of being Viye, Mbailundu, or Wambu, among many other polities that existed in the highlands. Oral traditions emphasize difference and conflict, corroborating the Portuguese written accounts.[239] It was the missionaries, anthropologists, and historians who created a historical narrative for the Ovimbundu, claiming a long idea

---

[236] For Nganguelas in 1720s, see Mariana, Minas Gerais, "Arquivo da Câmara Municipal de Mariana; Minas Gerais, cod. 166, 1723, fl. 11, fl. 37, 42, fl, 59, 62, 63, 64, 70, 71, 74, 76, 78. 83, 92, 96, 100, 103. 110, 115; cod. 150 (1725) also contains several Nganguelas, including fl. 8, 20v., 38v., 40, 52v., 56, 56v. I am grateful to Kássia Pereira da Costa and Ana Eliza Santos Rodrigues, who helped me in locating these cases.

[237] ANRJ, cod. 184, vol. 3, Escravos Emancipados, ID 490, 523, 857, 1707 (Viye or Bihe), 1267, 1280, 1324, 1327, 1331, 1347, 1363, 1364, 1366, 1368, 1376, 1389, 1411, 1414 (Wambu) 1226 (Bailundu), 1217 (Caconda), 1570, 1572 (Ndombe).

[238] The list of ethnonyms suggests the multiple layers of identity of the African population in Rio de Janeiro in the first half of the nineteenth century. Mary C. Karasch, *A vida dos Escravos no Rio de Janeiro, 1808–1850* (São Paulo: Companhia das Letras, 2000), 488–92.

[239] See, for example, Childs, *Umbundu Kinship*, 169–81.

of unity. Any attempt to obliterate political differences denies the history of violence and competition within the region before 1850 and risks eradicating the political and social impact of the trans-Atlantic slave trade on the Benguela highlands. Moreover, emphasizing unity purges the process by which current Angolan ethnicities were historically constructed and does not relate to pre-1850 events. The fact is that no person from West Central Africa saw herself or himself as Ovimbundu during the era of the trans-Atlantic slave trade. People saw themselves as subjects of Sokoval, Kakonda, Mbailundu, Wambu, or Viye, among many other identifiers.

In the twentieth century, the Wambu, Mbailundu, and Viye became Ovimbundu. Yet, claiming this identity in West Central Africa prior to 1850 is a historical anachronism. In the twentieth century, their neighbors, such as the Nganguela, were classified as part of the Ganguela ethnic group. People who lived in Humbe, who maintained commercial links with the highlands, were identified as Nyaneka.[240] In previous centuries, people who lived in the interior of Benguela were members of different ethnic and linguistic groups, although they had maintained intense contact, both peaceful and adversarial. Historical maps of West Central Africa show a multiplicity of unfamiliar names designating peoples and territories. Powerful states existed in the interior of Benguela, but their leaders never pulled their subjects together or gave up their separate powers to form a regional power that unified people under a single leader with a single resistance to Portuguese advances.

Conclusion

The history of the interior of Benguela during the seventeenth, eighteenth, and early nineteenth centuries can only be understood by studying both the colonial zone on the coast and the Portuguese *presídios* inland. Trade networks were linked to the port controlled by Portuguese forces, and political and economic influences emanating from Benguela shaped the way people organized those networks. The demand for slaves generated intense violence and a sense of insecurity throughout the period analyzed. The trans-Atlantic slave trade provoked changes in political

---

[240] Redinha, *Distribuição Étnica*, 15–18. For more on the creation of ethnicities in the late nineteenth and early twentieth centuries, see the articles in Vail, *The Creation of Tribalism*, 1–16. Vansina also notes the multiplicity and fluidity of ethnic designations in Eastern Angola. See Vansina, *How Societies Are Born*, 215.

organization, as well as how identity was understood. In the end, violence and schism proved to be important in the way people organized themselves. Luso-African traders and colonial officials spread Portuguese customs and Catholicism beyond the littoral, accelerating creolization away from the coast. The fortress of Caconda operated like a funnel linking the interior to the coast, although other routes continued to operate, and its existence was contested by local authorities who lived in the region and resisted expansion of the trans-Atlantic slave trade.

The society that emerged in Caconda reflected the Atlantic economy and other African ports and was profoundly affected by creolization. A colonial outpost, it attracted people, favoring cultural exchange and the elaboration of new codes. Coercion was employed to force people to submit to colonialism and Catholicism, but violence and instability also pushed vulnerable people to move closer to the fortress and to adopt values that could provide a sense of protection in a region characterized by turmoil and warfare. The interior of Benguela was marked by migrations in the seventeenth, eighteenth, and nineteenth centuries. The fundamental causes of violence and conflict in the interior of Benguela cannot be understood without considering the role of the trans-Atlantic slave trade and Atlantic merchants. The need for labor in the Americas, as well as in the colonial centers in West Central Africa, provoked raids, warfare, and its consequent displacement, hunger, and instability. People did not migrate along with their leaders but as groups of refugees in search of new land and safety. When rulers survived conflict, they migrated also, gathering people from different backgrounds, amalgamating people who spoke different languages or had conflicting conceptions of power. Thus creolization was nothing new for people who lived in the interior of Benguela. People changed political affiliations, lifestyles, and geographic locations for different reasons. Sometimes it was a negative experience such as warfare or drought and sometimes a positive goal such as seeking a trade advantage or as a result of marriage or a search for a better life. Changing location usually meant assuming a new affiliation to a territory, a leader, and fellow neighbors. New ideas and languages also could be incorporated. In most cases, the homeland was not far away, and people did not cut links with former neighbors.

Large states existed in the interior of Benguela before the end of the eighteenth century. Viye, Wambu, and Mbailundu were not the first ones. It is evident from the earliest accounts of political structures in the region that people organized themselves into states with different degrees of centralization. The older state of Kakonda, for example, demonstrates the ability of leaders to sustain their territories on a surplus extracted from agriculture, cattle, and trade in a fashion not different from more recent states. Some of these polities, such as Viye, were formed by migrant populations, although a few exceptions evolved more or less in one place. Some were ephemeral and did not last more than a few years. Others endured for centuries, such as Mbailundu and Wambu, although changing in form. Those which survived were mainly located in the central highlands, far away from the coast and the pervasive power of the Atlantic traders – states that resisted Portuguese colonialism adopted firearms, relied on professional armies, and were engaged in slave trade. Integrated into long-distance trade networks, most had inland markets where they attracted itinerant traders and taxed commercial operations. Their ability to be successful in the late eighteenth and early nineteenth centuries reflects the number of slaves exported from the port of Benguela.

The highland states were not created to meet the demands of the trans-Atlantic slave trade, but they certainly profited from the commerce in human beings. They sought to benefit from the opportunity presented by the Atlantic market to acquire goods associated with political and social capital. They seized people and gained power from their ability to connect the interior to the Atlantic shore. On some occasions they joined forces with Portuguese colonial agents. At other times rulers clashed with the colonial state. Viye, Mbailundu, Kitata, Kakonda, Kalukembe, Wambu, and Humbe raided each other. Sometimes they formed an alliance against Portuguese forces. More often, however, they relied on the colonial support of Portuguese armies to raid neighbors. The idea of an Ovimbundu people as an essentially anticolonial regime gained force in the second half of the twentieth century with the awakening of Ovimbundu nationalism. Yet this development is a simplification of a very long relationship with Portuguese agents. As the case of the interior of Benguela demonstrates, the trans-Atlantic slave trade had a devastating effect in this region of West Central Africa and forced successive rearticulations with Portuguese imperialism.

Conclusion

People in Benguela and Luanda often question me about my motivations for studying the history of the trans-Atlantic slave trade and its impact on societies in Benguela and its hinterland. Most assume that it is a dead topic, with no relevance to their current situation, with Angola still recovering from a long civil war with a newly emerging economy. In Benguela, Caconda, Dombe Grande, and Quilengues, most people want to share with me their experiences under colonialism, including forced labor. Yet, even if most Angolans could not acknowledge the trans-Atlantic slave trade as a major agent of change in the region, the stories they shared with me revealed how societies were profoundly affected by it. The 300 years of contact and exploitation facilitated Portuguese claims to the modern territory of Angola in the Berlin Conference (1884–5). However, the Berlin Conference did not mark the beginning of colonialism in Benguela. Indeed, Benguela had been a colony for over 200 years, and many of the features of twentieth-century colonialism in Africa, such as the incorporation of local authorities, the creation of chiefs, the use of forced labor for building infrastructure, the displacement of host populations, and the classification of people, for example, had already been employed. In sum, Portuguese colonialism in Angola did not start at the end of the nineteenth century, but in the 1500s with the first attempts to impose territorial control, extract taxes, and set up a colonial bureaucracy. As we have seen, the first encounters of Portuguese agents with the local Ndombe were already shaped by mineral interests and resulted in the enslavement of Africans.

The history of the port of Benguela and its interior reveals the effects of the trans-Atlantic slave trade on one of the southern ports of Africa. The rise and consolidation of the port of Benguela within the Atlantic world can only be understood in relationship to the foundation of a Portuguese colony on the coast and a series of fortresses inland. The establishment of the colony shifted the direction of trade routes, increased violence, and favored the spread of slave raids and the slave trade. In that moment of change and insertion into a new economic system, violence was key to generating enough captives to meet the demands of Atlantic slavers. In fact, violence is seen in this study as fundamental to colonialism and territorial occupation, and its continuity provoked political reorganization, economic reorientation, and altered social and cultural values, creating new groups and practices. Groups and chiefdoms were overpowered by stronger neighbors who literally incorporated them, resulting in their eventual disappearance from collective memory. The rise of states such as Wambu, Viye, and Mbailundu, for example, was intimately related to the spread of warfare, political instability, and violence in Benguela's hinterland. The formation of new social groups, such as the *filhos da terra* and *donas*, was part of the same process, directly linked to the expansion of violence and the trans-Atlantic slave trade. Thus changes in the interior of Benguela during the seventeenth, eighteenth, and early nineteenth centuries cannot be disassociated from expansion of the trans-Atlantic slave trade and Portuguese colonialism. Even moments of environmental crisis were human-made, on many occasions as a direct result of raids, population displacement, and assaults on cultivated lands. Migration, famine, drought, and epidemics did not happen in a vacuum and in many ways were related to the actions of violence. Indeed, many of these features continued when Europeans decided that transporting Africans to the Americas was morally wrong. The slave trade and slavery did not come to an end with closure of the Brazilian market in 1850 but continued after the Atlantic exports ended. New plantations were established along the coast and made use of slave labor under a different name, *trabalho forçado*, or coerced labor.[1] Portuguese colonialism continued and gained a new impetus after the Berlin Conference. It is important to stress,

---

[1] W. G Clarence-Smith, *Slaves, Peasants, and Capitalists in Southern Angola, 1840–1926* (Cambridge University Press, 1979); Mariana P. Candido, "Trade, Slavery and Migration in the Interior of Benguela: The Case of the Caconda, 1830–1870," in *Angola on the Move: Transport Routes, Communications, and History*, ed. Beatriz Heintze (Frankfurt: Lembeck, 2008), 63–84; Augusto Nascimento and Alfredo Gomes Dias, "A Importação de Libertos em São Tomé no Terceiro Quartel de Oitocentos," *Revista de História Económica e Social* 25 (1989): 1–70; and Mariana P. Candido, "Between Slavery and Freedom: the Displacement of West Central Africans to São Tomé after the End of the Trans-Atlantic Slave Trade," paper presented at the conference "Affranchis et Descendants d'affranchis

however, that the population living in Benguela and its interior had been exposed to an early form of Portuguese imperialism beginning in the seventeenth century.

As the first full-length history of Benguela and its hinterland to appear in English, this book engages with studies on the effects of the trans-Atlantic slave trade in Africa, the role of Europeans and Africans in slaving and slave exports, and social and political changes in West Central Africa from 1600 to 1850. The central question is the importance of Benguela in the developing commerce in the Atlantic Ocean, although other important debates are also covered, such as the role of Portuguese colonialism, the effects of climate and disease, the emergence of new social and political groups, the nature of slavery in African societies, and the formation of new identities.

The Portuguese interest in the central highlands and the peoples south of the Kwanza River started in the fifteenth century. Reports of mines and a high demographic concentration attracted the attention of Portuguese authorities in Lisbon and Luanda. The first expeditions were not able to find the precise location of mines but mentioned the use of copper in the production of tools and jewelry. An important mineral in the nascent sugar industry, as well currency in the trade networks in India, copper was a desirable mineral. Control of copper mines, as well as other minerals, could represent a shift in the position of Portugal in the world. During the seventeenth century, the Portuguese Crown imported silver from the Spanish colonies and copper from Sweden. The Portuguese Crown's avarice for silver explains the initial export of slaves from Benguela to Spanish America. Although Portuguese colonial documents do not make any reference to the export of slaves from Benguela, there were Africans identified as coming from this port present in Havana and Lima, in Spanish America, in Salvador and Mariana, and in Brazil by the late seventeenth and early eighteenth centuries. Their presence in the New World reveals that traders based in Benguela were already taking part in the trans-Atlantic slave trade. Moreover, their presence challenges the current *Trans-Atlantic Slave Trade Database* estimates, demonstrating that contraband and illegal exports were features of the early trans-Atlantic slave trade, as Antonio Mendes and Toby Green have shown.[2] Yet, despite the

---

dans le Monde Atlantique du XVe au XIXe siècle: Status Juridiques, Insertions Sociales et Identités Culturelles," Bordeaux, France, 2009.

[2] António de Almeida Mendes, "The Foundations of the System: A Reassessment on the Slave Trade to the Americas in the Sixteenth and Seventeenth Centuries," in *Extending the Frontiers: Essays on the New Transatlantic Slave Trade Database*, ed. David Eltis

absence of records, people who were known as Benguelas were present
in different parts of the Americas, indicating the importance of the port
and its insertion into the Atlantic system. Integrated into the Atlantic
world, Benguela attracted the attention of Dutch, French, and English
traders who visited the port town at different times. During the wars that
affected Europe in the seventeenth century, Dutch merchants invaded
and occupied Benguela for nearly 10 years. Decades later, in the early
eighteenth century, French forces invaded the port in search of minerals
and slaves, before they advanced in other Atlantic ports such as Rio de
Janeiro. The English never made a real threat, although English ships
were seen at times in the eighteenth century. Thus the history of Benguela
should be seen from an Atlantic perspective, inserted into the context of
the growing expansion of the trans-Atlantic slave trade and European
rivalry for markets and African ports.

Located fewer than 600 km south of the Portuguese capital of Luanda,
Benguela was in a privileged position for traders and administrators who
were seeking autonomy from the Portuguese authorities. The region of
Kissama, between Luanda and Benguela, was autonomous and prevented
overland communication between the two colonies. Authorities had to
rely on a maritime route, yet ocean currents and winds in that part of
the South Atlantic favored sailing north, not south. The prevailing ocean
currents allowed the men on the spot to avoid official supervision, which
resulted in smuggling, illegal actions, and weak legislation. The expansion of trade in the eighteenth century was met with the need to send
more troops and colonial officials to enforce Portuguese control. A small
state in Europe with a large overseas empire, the Portuguese Crown relied
on the use of convict labor to strengthen its colonial presence. Known
as the "white man's grave," exile in Benguela was almost a death sentence. Outlaws from Portugal and Brazil were employed from the seventeenth century in colonial armies. During the eighteenth century, they
also were appointed as captains and soldiers in the Portuguese fortresses
located inland. Convicts and *filhos da terra*, descendants of Portuguese
and Brazilian fathers and local African mothers, occupied key positions
in the administration of the port of Benguela and its hinterland. Not necessarily committed to the Portuguese empire and with strong personal
and commercial links to African states, these agents were a menace to

and David Richardson (New Haven, CT: Yale University Press, 2008), 63–94; and Toby
Green, *The Rise of the Trans-Atlantic Slave Trade in Western Africa, 1300–1589* (New
York: Cambridge University Press, 2011), 214–16.

colonialism, yet they represented the colonial state in the region. They smuggled goods, defrauded the Crown, and declared wars against those they were supposed to protect. The growing demand for slaves corrupted commercial alliances, judicial codes, and colonial officials. Although legislation was in place to protect those who sided with Portuguese colonialism and declared vassalage, there were continuous disputes between the colony of Benguela and African rulers who had declared vassalage to the Crown.

This study emphasized the political and social effects of the slave trade on the African continent, moving away from a literature centered on demographic analysis and a quantitative approach. Valuable and useful, the emphasis on numbers has overshadowed the importance of Benguela in the trans-Atlantic slave trade and ignored a wide-ranging set of transformations that took place, including new naming practices and identities and accelerated cultural mixing. When confronted with political organizations they could not understand, Portuguese officials relied on previous experience and labeled them with terms employed north of the Kwanza. *Jagas*, for example, represented the other, the unknown, and, by definition, those who were strangers and did not accept Portuguese presence. Based on their earlier encounters in the region of Kongo and Angola, *jagas* were assumed to be cannibals, and as such, they were suitable for enslavement. This was the first of a series of naming practices introduced by Portuguese colonial agents that profoundly affected people who lived in Benguela and its hinterland and targeted them as potential captives destined for the trans-Atlantic slave trade. The continuous pressure for slaves led to the expansion of violence and slaving raids, which required the use of mechanisms to protect *filhos da terra* and free blacks allied with Portuguese colonialism. In the same way that African states regulated who could or could not be enslaved, the Portuguese Crown relied on its legal code, *Ordenações Filipinas*, and the idea of a "just war" to determine and judge the legality of enslavement. Colonialism introduced new legislation and protections to those seen as allies. Vassals who had been captured could contest their enslavement and regain their freedom. In the process, however, they legitimized the role of Portuguese colonial officials as arbitrators and slavery as a legal institution. Their agency in claiming their freedom, ironically, reinforced violence toward nonvassals, and those who were not allies of the colonial regime were regarded to be potential and legitimate slaves.

The expansion of the colonial bureaucracy in the eighteenth century resulted in the appointment of officials who supervised claims of original freedom. Yet the judicial apparatus of the Portuguese empire only worked in collaboration with men on the spot committed to respect the law. Some officials were invested in enforcing the law, whereas others were involved in the slave trade and committed to warfare, raids, and other episodes of violence against neighboring populations. Unlike in other ports along the African coast, where Europeans were limited to the port towns, in Benguela, Portuguese and Brazilian agents traveled inland, lived under the protection of African rulers, and on many occasions were directly responsible for the enslavement of Africans. Their actions were not limited to providing credit as they were also active agents of capture and enslavement.

In order to be more effective and familiar to the local population, colonial officers incorporated several elements of African political life, such as the practice of *undar* and the *mucano* tribunals. Local institutions associated with the transfer of political power and conflict resolution, both were adapted by the colonial regime to legitimatize the rise of new authorities and to facilitate case litigation and solution, revealing that creolization, or cultural mixing, was key to the expansion of colonialism. Additionally, Portuguese authorities consulted local healers, married into elite families, and adopted a series of local values and practices. At the same time, the Ndombe, Kakonda, Kilengue, and others adjusted to European fashion, cultivated manioc and corn, drank Brazilian-produced *cachaça*, and baptized their children in the Catholic Church. All actors, Europeans and Africans, incorporated the values that were useful, adopted what was relevant from each other's culture, and gave shape to a new culture born in the context of the growing trans-Atlantic slave export and violence.

In sum, the trans-Atlantic slave trade provoked more than a demographic drain. It altered social practices and notions of legality and morality and introduced new categories of classification, such as vassal or *jagas*; white, *mulato*, or black; free or slave; Catholic or heathen. It also provoked the expansion of slave labor in colonial centers because slaves worked in domestic spaces and in agricultural fields and were employed as porters, blacksmiths, sailors, hairdressers, street vendors, and many other productive tasks. The colonial elite had relatively few members and was forced to rely on the labor of men and women who were frequently subjected to violence. Slaves contributed to the formation of a multicultural port town where many languages were spoken and people of different cultural backgrounds interacted. The trans-Atlantic slave trade also brought about the formation of a new local elite composed of powerful merchant women, known as *donas*, and their children, classified as *mulatos, pardos,* or *filhos da terra.* As both slave owners and slave traders, people in the elite were intimately involved with slaving practices and the colonial state. Commerce generated wealth and social prestige and increased economic disparities and disregard for human life. Allied with foreign merchants, Luso-Africans spread the Portuguese language and ideas inland, becoming key agents of colonialism. I stress the participation of women in economic and service activities, showing that many took advantage of the presence of foreign traders to advance their own economic and social status.

The trans-Atlantic slave trade also led to increased political instability, as reflected in the disappearance of some states and the emergence of new ones. The interior of Benguela suffered intense political rearrangements as a result of the displacement of waves of refugees escaping from war zones. Weak leaders, unable to protect their subjects, were replaced by occupying powers or new military elites. As part of the Atlantic demand for captives of war, violence spread, and a significant number of people were enslaved in regions not far from the coast, including areas that maintained strong contacts with the colony of Benguela. As explored throughout this book, the slaving frontier did not simply move inland from Benguela. In fact, the Portuguese presence and the continuity of cycles of violence favored the capture of coastal inhabitants, many of whom were kidnapped or tricked by people they knew. Those captured close to the coast had already been exposed to the forces of colonialism, probably knew some Portuguese, and as many of the cases explored in Chapter 4 have shown, were already familiar with Catholicism. The effect on the coastal population was devastating, resulting in the collapse of many states and chiefdoms and the migration of unprotected subjects, who relocated inland or moved southward away from the tentacles of the Portuguese forces. In many cases, they ended up enslaved by local rulers.

The pressure of the trans-Atlantic slave trade reinforced political fragmentation, emphasizing rivalry and competition and making it very difficult for local leaders to join forces because their power was based on enslaving outsiders and expanding their domain over their neighbors. Competition and conflict emphasized difference rather than unity and weakened local states as they faced Portuguese colonialist expansion. These political transformations affected how people identified themselves and perceived others as distinct and subject to enslavement. People identified themselves as members of a state or subjects of a ruler. Identity was situational and subject to change. In moments of crisis, populations relocated to safer areas under the protection of new rulers and incorporated new values in order to survive. In the centuries of turmoil provoked by the trans-Atlantic slave trade, it was essential to protect oneself and one's relatives and friends from raids and kidnapping, even if that meant breaking away from one's land of origin and becoming an immigrant in a new land. Belonging to a state or chiefdom overlapped with how people conceived identity and could change overnight. The study of Benguela's interior before 1850 shows that certain groups that exist in modern Angola were a product of historical events. The Ovimbundu, the largest ethnic group in Angola in the twentieth and early twenty-first centuries, did not exist as a unified and centralized entity during the period under study. During the era of the trans-Atlantic slave trade, people identified themselves with smaller political unities, such as Mbailundu, Sokoval, Kakonda, Viye, and Wambu, among others. The sense of a larger community that went beyond political boundaries did not exist in the past, and an emphasis on other traits such as common language and culture do not seem to have existed, which explains the many conflicts and raids in the eighteenth and nineteenth centuries. Different political allegiances were reason enough to justify the capture or enslavement of each other and weakened any sense of unity.

In the early twentieth century, however, anthropologists saw similarities among these peoples and grouped them into larger groups, such as Ovimbundu, Nyaneka, and Nganguela. Groups that had lived in conflict for decades or centuries were unified according to language, custom, and marriage practices, characteristics that had previously been less important. The emergence of these large ethnic groups in the twentieth century erased a past of competition and rivalry. A fluid notion of identity, associated with position rather than birth, gave space to European ideas of nations. Identity, which had previously been associated with a political leader, became fixed to a territory, language, or lifestyle. The anachronism of ascribing twentieth-century ethnic identities to the groups that lived in the Benguela hinterland in the seventeenth, eighteenth, and early nineteenth centuries erased the historic reality of migration and conflict in order to emphasize unity among people who had never seen themselves as one ethnicity or group in previous centuries. Later political leaders reinforced this notion and helped to crystallize identities as a feature that was biological and primordial. Eventually, historians also perpetuated ideas of a common shared past, letting current notions of identity and rivalry influence how we understand the Angolan past. The study of pre-1850 Benguela and its hinterland shows that people did not see themselves as part of a single collective imagination, to use Jan

Vansina's words,[3] but as inhabitants of a region pulverized by different and competing powers. In the seventeenth, eighteenth, and early nineteenth centuries, the people who inhabited the land between the coast and the highlands lived under a variety of polities, some more centralized than others, and competed among themselves for resources and access to the Atlantic market. The pressures of the trans-Atlantic slave trade and the commodities it generated accelerated competition, dispute, and fragmentation among neighbors and made them vulnerable to the set of categories introduced by colonialism.

The history of Benguela examines the transformations of Portuguese imperialism before the nineteenth century and the establishment of bilateral connections in the Atlantic. Integrated into the Atlantic economy, the inhabitants of Benguela and Caconda maintained strong links with Brazil. Most of the people who were exported from Benguela landed in Brazilian ports and represented an important component of the African population in Brazil. The geographic area and the colonial urban center, which still stands in Benguela, were an embodiment of imperialism, where a small elite lived in a protected space and maintained itself through the labor of the indigenous population. The local elite profited from the sale of African slaves, yet their economic gains were gone after a few years and did not bring any lasting advantage. The people they captured and sold produced material goods that were used in exchange for more human beings, as well as the wealth to maintain the Portuguese overseas empire and, later, the Brazilian empire. A study of Benguela and its interior reveals how the trans-Atlantic slave trade affected African societies. More than human beings reduced to export numbers, societies lost political and economic independence and faced centuries of turmoil. That history also opened the door for Portuguese imperialists to use the old signed treaties of vassalage as proof of their later claims to colonial power in Angola. In the end, the events of twentieth-century Angola can be seen as a part of the transformations Benguela and its hinterland faced beginning in the late sixteenth century.

---

[3] Jan Vansina, *How Societies Are Born: Governance in West Central Africa before 1600* (Charlottesville: University of Virginia Press, 2004), 268–71.

Bibliography

Archival References

Angola

Arquivo Histórico Nacional de Angola (AHNA)
Arquivo do Arçobispado de Luanda (AAL)
Biblioteca da Província de Benguela (BPB)
Biblioteca Municipal de Luanda (BML)

Brazil

Arquivo da Câmara Municipal de Mariana/Minas Gerais (ACMM)
Arquivo da Cúria Metropolitana do Rio de Janeiro (ACMRJ)
Instituto Histórico e Geográfico Brasileiro (IHGB)
Arquivo Histórico Nacional (AHNRJ)
Biblioteca Nacional do Rio de Janeiro (BNRJ)

Portugal

Arquivo Histórico Militar (AHM)
Arquivo Histórico Ministério de Obras Públicas (AHMOP)
Arquivo Histórico Ultramarino (AHU)
Arquivo Nacional da Torre do Tombo (ANTT)
Biblioteca Nacional (BNL)
Biblioteca da Sociedade de Geografia de Lisboa (BSGL)

Canada

The United Church of Canada Archives

Published Primary Sources

"Angola no Fim do Século XVII." *Boletim da Sociedade de Geografia de Lisboa* 6 (1886): 284–304.

Almanak Statistico da Provincia de Angola e suas dependencies para o ano de 1852. Luanda: Imprensa do Governo, 1851.

Almeida, Francisco Tavares de. *Memória Justificativa do ex-Governador de Benguela.* Lisbon: Revista Universal, 1852.

"Auto de Undamento e Vassalagem que prestou o soba Iundo Aquembi em 1838," *Angola, Mensário Administrativo* 7 (1948): 39–41.

Benguela e seu sertão, 1617–1622. Lisbon: Imprensa Nacional, 1881.

Blake, John W. *Europeans in West Africa: 1450–1560.* London: The Hakluyt Society, 1942.

Boletim Geral do Governo da Provincia de Angola.

Bowdich, T. Edward. *Account of Discoveries of the Portuguese in the Interior of Angola and Mozambique.* London: John Booth, 1824.

Brásio, António. *Monumenta Missionária Africana,* 11 vols. Lisbon: Agência do Ultramar, 1953.

Brito, Domingo de Abreu e. *Inquérito da Vida administrativa e Economica de Angola.* Coimbra: Imprensa da Universidade, 1931.

Cadornega, António de Oliveira. *História Geral das Guerras Angolanas,* 3 vols. Lisbon: Agência Geral do Ultramar, 1972 [1680].

Capelo, Hermenegildo, and Roberto Ivens. *De Benguella às terras de Iacca,* 2 vols. Lisbon: Imprensa Nacional, 1881.

Carvalho, Henrique Augusto Dias de. *Expedição Portuguêza ao Muatiânvua,* 2 vols. Lisbon: Imprensa Nacional, 1894.

Cavazzi, Giovanni Antonio. *Descrição Histórica dos Três Reinos do Congo, Matamba e Angola.* Lisbon: Junta de Investigações do Ultramar, 1965.

Coleção das Leyes, Decretos e alvarás que comprehende o feliz reinado del rey fidelisimo D. José I Nosso Senhor desde o ano de 1761 ate o de 1769. Lisbon: Officina de Antonio Rodrigues Galhardo, 1776.

Cordeiro, Luciano. *Viagens e Explorações e Conquistas dos Portuguezes.* Lisbon: Imprensa Nacional, 1881.

"Do Surgião Mor do Reino de Benguela, Bernando Pinto (16 de Dezembro de 1649)." *Arquivos de Angola* 9, no. 35 (1952): 11–12.

Douville, J. B. *Voyage au Congo et dans l'interieur de l'Afrique Equinoxiale, fait dans les années 1828, 1829, 1830,* 3 vols. Paris: Jules Renouard, 1832.

Encyclopaedia Americana, vol. 2. Philadelphia: Lea & Blanchard, 1844.

Felner, Alfredo de Albuquerque. *Angola: Apontamentos sobre a Colonização dos Planaltos e Litoral do Sul de Angola,* 3 vols. Lisbon: Agência do Ultramar, 1940.

Gama, Antônio de Saldanha. *Memoria sobre as colonias de Portugal situadas na costa occidental d'Africa.* Paris: Casimir, 1839.

Graça, Joaquim Rodrigues. "Expedição ao Muatayânvua." *Boletim da Sociedade de Geografia de Lisboa* 9 série 8 (1890): 365–468.

Lacerda, Paulo Martins. "Notícia da Cidade de S. Filipe de Benguela e dos costumes dos gentios habitantes daquele sertão." *Annaes Maritimos e Coloniais* 12, no 5 Serie (1845): 486–91.

Lopes de Lima, José Joaquim. *Ensaios sobre a statistica d'Angola e Benguella e suas dependencies na costa Occidental d'Africa ao sul do Equador.* Lisbon: Imprensa Nacional, 1844.

MacQueen, James. *A Geographical Survey of Africa.* London: Fellowes, 1840.

Magyar, László. *Reisen in Sud-Afrika in den Jahren 1849 bis 1857.* Berlin: Pest, Lauffer & Stolp, 1859.

Mello, D. Miguel Antonio de. "Relatório do Governador de Angola D. Miguel Antonio de Melo." *Boletim da Sociedade de Geografia de Lisboa* 8, 5a serie (1885): 548–64.

The Missionary Review of the World. 1882.

Monteiro, Joachim John. *Angola and the River Congo.* New York: Macmillan, 1876.

Omboni, T. *Viaggi Nell'Africa Occidentale: Gia Medico di Consiglio Nel Regno d'Angola e Sue Dipendenze Membro Della R. Accademia Peloritana di Messina.* Milan: Civelli, 1846.

Ordenações Filipinas, Livro I. Brasília: Senado Federal, 2004.

"Não estivessem sujeitos a viver unidos em sociedade em religião, em justiça, e em indústria, será imediatamente preso e remetido para esta capital." *Arquivo de Angola* 1, no. 1 (1936).

Porto, António Silva. *Viagens e Apontamentos de um Portuense em África.* Coimbra: Biblioteca Geral, 1986.

Purdy, John. *The New Sailing Directory for the Ethiopic or Southern Atlantic Ocean.* London: R. H. Laurie, 1844.

Ravenstein, E. G. *The Strange Adventures of Andrew Battell of Leigh in Angola and Adjoining Regions.* London: The Haklut Society, 1901.

Santos, Joaquim Lopes dos. *Memória da Violência Praticada pelo governador de Benguela, João Antônio Pusich, contra o alferes Joaquim Lopes dos Santos.* Rio de Janeiro: Na Imprensa Nacional, 1824.

Silva Corrêa, Elias Alexandre da. *História de Angola,* 2 vols. Lisbon: Ática, 1937.

Tams, George. *Visita as Possessões Portuguesas na costa occidental d'Africa,* 2 vols. Porto: Tipografia do Calvario, 1850.

Visit to the Portuguese Possessions in South-Western Africa, 2 vols. London: T. C. Newby, 1845.

Torres, J. C. Feo Cardoso de Castello e Branco e. *Memórias Contendo a Biographia do Vice Almirante Luiz da Motta Feo e Torres.* Paris: Fantin Livreiro, 1825.

Valdez, Francisco Travassos. *Six Years of a Traveller's Life in Western Africa.* London: Hurst and Blackett, 1861.

Zucchelli, Antonio. *Relazioni del Viaggio e Missione di Congo nell'Etiopia inferiore Occidentale.* Venice: Bartolomeo Giavarina, 1712.

Books and Articles

Aguiar, Pascoal Leite de. *Administração Colonial Portuguesa no Congo, em Angola e em Benguela.* Lisbon: Sociedade Histórica da Independência de Portugal, 2006.

Alencastro, Luiz Felipe de. "The Apprenticeship of Colonization." In *Slavery and the Rise of the Atlantic System*, ed. Barbara L. Solow. Cambridge: Cambridge University Press, 1991, 151–76.

"Continental Drift: The Independence of Brazil (1822), Portugal and Africa." In *From Slave Trade to Empire: Europe and the Colonization of Black Africa, 1780–1880s*, ed. Olivier Pétré-Grenouilleau. New York: Routledge, 2004, 98–109.

"The Economic Network of Portugal's Atlantic World," In *Portuguese Oceanic Expansion, 1400–1800*, eds. Francisco Bethencourt and Diogo Ramada Curto. New York: Cambridge University Press, 2007, 109–136.

Trato dos Viventes: Formação do Brasil no Atlântico Sul, Séculos XVI e XVII. São Paulo: Companhia das Letras, 2000.

Alexandre, Valentim, and Jill Dias. *O Império Africano, 1825–1890.* Lisbon: Estampa, 1998.

Allen, Carolyn. "Creole: The Problems of Definition." In *Questioning Creole: Creolisation Discourses in Caribbean Culture*, eds. Verene Shepard and Glen L. Richards. Kingston, Jamaica: Ian Randle Publishers, 2002.

Alpers, Edward. "The Mutapa and Malawi Political Systems to the Time of the Ngoni Invasions." In *Aspects of Central African History*, ed. Terence Ranger. London: Heinemann Educational Books, 1968, 1–28.

Amaral, Ilídio do. *O Reino Do Congo, Os Mbundu (ou Ambundos), O Reino dos "Ngola" (ou de Angola) e a Presença Portuguesa de Finais do Século XV a meados do Século XVI.* Lisbon: Instituto de Investigação Científica Tropical, 1996.

O Rio Cuanza (Angola), Da Barra a Cambambe: Reconstituição de Aspectos Geográficos e Acontecimentos Históricos dos Séculos XVI e XVII. Lisbon: Ministério da Ciência e da Tecnologia, 2000.

Ames, Glenn J. "An African Eldorado? The Portuguese Quest for Wealth and Power in Mozambique and the Rios de Cuama, c. 1661–1683." *International Journal of African Historical Studies* 31, no. 1 (1998): 91–110.

Anderson, Benedict. *Imagined Communities: Reflections on the Origin and Spread of Nationalism.* London: Verso, 1983.

Antônio, Mário. *Luanda, Ilha Crioula.* Lisbon: Agência do Ultramar, 1968.

Antunes, Cátia, and Filipa Ribeiro Da Silva. "Cross-Cultural Entrepreneurship in the Atlantic: Africans, Dutch and Sephardic Jews in Western Africa, 1580–1674." *Itinerario* 35, no. 1 (2011): 49–76.

Aparício, Maria Alexandra. "Política de Boa Vizinhança: os Chefes Locais e os Europeus em Meados do século XIX. O Caso do Dombe Grande." In *II Reunião Internacional História de Angola.* São Paulo: CEA-USP/SDG-Marinha/CAPES, 1997, 109–16.

Araujo, Ana Lucia. *Public Memory of Slavery: Victims and Perpetrators in the South Atlantic.* Amherst, NY: Cambria Press, 2010.

Barnard, Alan. *Hunters and Herders of Southern Africa: A Comparative Ethnography of the Khoisan Peoples.* Cambridge: Cambridge University Press, 1992.

Barrocas, Deolinda, and Maria de Jesus Sousa. "As populações do hinterland the Benguela e a passagem das caravanas comerciais (1846–1860)." In *II*

Reunião Internacional de História da África. São Paulo: CEA/USP/SDG Marinha, 1996, 95–107.

Barry, Boubacar. *Senegambia and the Atlantic Slave Trade.* Cambridge: Cambridge University Press, 1998.

Barth, Frederik. *Los grupos étnicos y sus fronteras.* Mexico: Fondo de Cultura Económica, 1976.

Bay, Edna G. *Wives of the Leopard: Gender, Politics, and Culture in the Kingdom of Dahomey.* Charlottesville: University of Virginia Press, 1998.

Bazin, Jean. "War and Servitude in Segou." *Economy and Society* 3 (1974): 107–44.

Beckles, Hilary. *Natural Rebels: A Social History of Enslaved Black Women in Barbados.* New Brunswick, NJ: Rutgers University Press, 1989.

Bellini, Ligia. "Notas sobre Cultura, Política e Sociedade no mundo Português do séc. XVI." *Tempo* 7 (1999): 1–18.

Bender, Gerald J. *Angola under the Portuguese: The Myth and the Reality.* London: Heinemann, 1978.

Benton, Lauren. *Law and Colonial Cultures: Legal Regimes in World History, 1400–1900.* New York: Cambridge University Press, 2002.

"Legal Regime of the South Atlantic World, 1400–1750: Jurisdictional Complexity as Institutional Order." *Journal of World History* 11, no. 1 (2000): 27–56.

Bergad, Laird W. *The Comparative Histories of Slavery in Brazil, Cuba and the United States.* New York: Cambridge University Press, 2007.

Berlin, Ira. "From Creoles to African: Atlantic Creoles and the Origins of African-American Society in Mainland North America." *William and Mary Quarterly* 53, no. 2, 3rd series, (1996): 251–88.

Generations of Captivity: A History of African-American Slaves. Cambridge, MA: Harvard University Press, 2003.

"Time, Space, and the Evolution of Afro-American Society on British Mainland North America." *American Historical Review* 85, no. 1 (1980): 44–78.

Bethell, Leslie. *The Abolition of the Brazilian Slave Trade, 1807–1869.* Cambridge: Cambridge University Press, 1970.

Bicalho, Maria Fernanda. "As Câmaras Municipais no Império Português: O exemplo do Rio de Janeiro." *Revista Brasileira da História* 18, no. 36 (1998): 251–80.

Birmingham, David. *Central Angola to 1870: Zambezia, Zaire, and the South Atlantic.* Cambridge: Cambridge University Press, 1981.

"The Date and Significance of the Imbangala Invasion of Angola." *Journal of African History* 62, no. 2 (1965): 143–52.

Portugal and Africa. New York: Palgrave Macmillan, 1999.

The Portuguese Conquest of Angola. Oxford University Press, 1965.

Trade and Conflict in Angola. Oxford University Press, 1966.

Bittencourt, Marcelo. *Dos jornais às armas: trajectórias da contestação angolana.* Lisbon: Vega Editora, 1999.

Bolota, Abel Augusto. *Benguela, Mãe de Cidades.* Benguela: Câmara Municipal de Benguela, 1967.

Bontick, François. "Un Mausolée pour les Jaga." *Cahier d'Études Africaines* 20, no. 3 (1980): 387–9.

Bourdieu, Pierre. *Outline of a Theory of Practice*. Cambridge: Cambridge University Press, 2004.

Pascalian Meditations. Stanford, CA: Stanford University Press, 2000.

Bowser, Frederick P. *The African Slave in Colonial Peru*. Stanford, CA: Stanford University Press, 1974.

Boxer, Charles R. "Brazilian Gold and British Traders in the First Half of the 18th Century." *Hispanic American Historical Review* 49, no. 3 (1969): 545–72.

The Golden Age of Brazil, 1695–1750. Berkeley: University of California Press, 1962.

A Idade de Ouro do Brasil: Dores de Crescimento de uma Sociedade Colonial. Rio de Janeiro: Nova Fronteira, 2000.

O Império Marítimo Português. Rio de Janeiro: São Paulo, 2002.

A Mulher na Expansão Ultramarina Ibérica. Lisbon: Horizonte, 1977.

Race Relations in the Portuguese Colonial Empire, 1415–1825. Oxford University Press, 1963.

Brásio, Antônio. "As Misericórdias de Angola." *Studia* 4 (1959): 106–49.

Brathwaite, Kamau. *The Development of Creole Society in Jamaica, 1770–1820*. Oxford, UK: Clarendon Press, 1971.

Burke, Peter, ed. *New Perspectives on Historical Writing*. University Park: Pennsylvania State University Press, 2001.

Candido, Mariana P. "African Freedom Suits and Portuguese Vassal Status: Legal Mechanisms for Fighting Enslavement in Benguela, Angola, 1800–1850." *Slavery and Abolition* 32 (2011): 447–59.

"Different Slave Journeys: Enslaved African Seamen on Board of Portuguese Ships, c.1760–1820s." *Slavery & Abolition* 31, no. 3 (2010): 395–409.

"Merchants and the Business of the Slave Trade at Benguela, 1750–1850." *African Economic History* 35, no. 1 (2007): 1–30.

"Slave Trade and New Identities in Benguela, 1700–1860." *Portuguese Studies Review* 19, no. 1–2 (2011): 59–7.

"Trade, Slavery and Migration in the Interior of Benguela: The Case of the Caconda, 1830–1870." In *Angola on the Move: Transport Routes, Communications, and History*, ed. Beatrix Heintze and Achim von Oppen. Frankfurt: Otto Lemberck, 2008, 63–84.

"Trans-Atlantic Links: Benguela and Bahia, 1700–1850." In *Paths of the Atlantic Slave Trade. Interactions, Identities and Images*, ed. Ana Lúcia Araújo. Amherst, NY: Cambria, 2011, 239–72.

Capela, José. *Donas, Senhores e Escravos*. Porto: Afrontamento, 1995.

Carney, Judith. "With Grains in Her Hair': Rice in Colonial Brazil." *Slavery & Abolition* 25, no. 1 (2004): 1–27.

Carreira, António. *As Companhias Pombalinas de Grão Pará e Maranhão e Pernambuco e Paraíba*. Lisbon: Presença, 1983.

Chambouleyron, Rafael. "Plantações, sesmarias e vilas. Uma reflexão sobra a ocupação da Amazônia seiscentista." *Nuevo Mundo Mundos Nuevos* (2006); available at http://nuevomundo.revues.org/2260.

Childs, Gladwyn M. "Chronology of the Ovimbundu Kingdoms." *Journal of African History* 11 (1970): 241–8.

"The Kingdom of Wambu (Huambo): A Tentative Chronology." *Journal of African History* 5, no. 3 (1964): 367–79.

"Peoples of Angola in the Seventeenth Century According to Cadornega." *Journal of African History* 1, no. 2 (1960): 271–9.

Umbundu Kinship and Character. Oxford University Press, 1949.

Clarence-Smith, W. G. "Capitalist Penetration among the Nyaneka of Southern Angola, 1760 to 1920s." *African Studies* 37, no. 2 (1978): 163–76.

Slaves, Peasants, and Capitalists in Southern Angola, 1840–1926. Cambridge: Cambridge University Press, 1979.

The Third Portuguese Empire, 1825–1975. Manchester: Manchester University Press, 1985.

Clist, Bernard, and Raymond Lanfranchi. "Contribution a L'étude de la sedentarisation en République Populaire d'Angola." *Leba* 7 (1992): 245–67.

Coates, Timothy J. *Convicts and Orphans: Forced and State-Sponsored Colonizers in the Portuguese Empire, 1550–1755*. Stanford, CA: Stanford University Press, 2001.

Cobbing, Julian. "The Mfecane as Alibi: Thoughts on Dithankong and Mbolompo." *Journal of African History* 29, no. 3 (1988): 487–519.

Comaroff, John, and Jean Comaroff. *Ethnography and the Historical Imagination*. Boulder, CO: Westview Press, 1992.

"Godly Beasts, Beastly Goods: Cattle and Commodities in a South African Context." *American Ethnologist* 17, no. 2 (1990): 195–216.

Cooper, Frederick. *Colonialism in Question: Theory, Knowledge, History*. Berkeley: University of California Press, 2005.

Plantation Slavery on the East Coast of Africa. Portsmouth, NH: Heinemann, 1997.

Corcuera de Mancera, Sonia. *Voces y Silencios en la Historia. Siglos XIX e XX*. Mexico: Fondo de Cultura Económica, 1997.

Cordell, Dennis. "The Myth of Inevitability and Invincibility. Resistance to Slavery and the Slave Trade in Central Africa, 1850–1910." In *Fighting the Slave Trade: West African Strategies*, ed. Sylviane A. Diouf. Athens: Ohio University Press, 2003, 31–49.

Corrado, Jacopo. *The Creole elite and the Rise of Angolan Protonationalism: 1870–1920*. Amherst, NY: Cambria Press, 2008.

Costa, Maria Leonor Freire. *Império e Grupos Mercantis: Entre o Oriente e o Atlântico (Séc. XVII)*. Lisbon: Livro Horizonte, 2002.

Costa e Silva, Alberto. *Manilha e o Libambo: A África e a Escravidão, de 1500–1700*. Rio de Janeiro: Nova Fronteira, 2002.

Couto, Carlos. *Os Capitães-Mores em Angola*. Lisbon: Instituto de Investigação Científica e Tropical, 1972.

"Regimento de Governo Subalterno de Benguela." *Studia* 45 (1981): 285–94.

Crowder, Michael. "Indirect Rule: French and British Style." *Africa: Journal of the International African Institute* 34, no. 3 (1964): 197–205

Cruz, Alberto Machado. "O Povo Ovakwambundo." *Boletim do Instituto de Investigação Científica de Angola* 4, no. 2 (1967): 67–88.

Cunha, Manuela C. da *Negros estrangeiros. Os Escravos Libertos e a sua volta à África*. São Paulo: Brasiliense, 1985.

Cunha, Manuela C. da, and Francisco Salzano. *História dos Índios no Brasil*. São Paulo: Companhia das Letras, 1992.

Curtin, Philip D. *Africa Remembered: Narratives by West Africans from the Era of the Slave Trade*. Long Grove, IL: Waveland Press, 1997.

The Atlantic Slave Trade. A Census. Madison: University of Wisconsin Press, 1969.

Cross-Cultural Trade in World History. Cambridge: Cambridge University Press, 1984.

Disease and Empire. Cambridge: Cambridge University Press, 1998.

Economic Change in Precolonial Africa: Senegambia in the Era of the Slave Trade. Madison: University of Wisconsin Press, 1975.

Curto, José C. "The Anatomy of a Demographic Explosion: Luanda, 1844–1850." *International Journal of African Historical Studies* 32 (1999): 381–405.

"As If From a Free Womb: Baptism Manumissions in the Conceição Parish, Luanda, 1778–1807." *Portuguese Studies Review* 10, no. 1 (2002): 26–57.

"Un Butin Illégitime: Razzias d'esclaves et Relations Luso-Africaines dans la Région des Fleuves Kwanza et Kwango en 1805." In *Déraison, Esclavage et Droit: Les Fondements idéologiques et juridiques de la traite négrière et de l'esclavage*, eds. Isabel C. Henriques and Louis Sala-Molins. Paris: Éditions UNESCO, 2002, 315–27.

Enslaving Spirits: The Portuguese Brazilian Alcohol Trade at Luanda and its Hinterland, c. 1550–1830. Leiden: Brill Academic Publishers, 2004.

"Experiences of Enslavement in West Central Africa." *Social History* 41, no. 82 (2008): 381–415.

"The Legal Portuguese Slave Trade from Benguela, Angola, 1730–1828: A Quantitative Re-appraisal." *África* 17, no. 1 (1993–1994): 101–16.

"Luso-Brazilian Alcohol and the Legal Slave Trade at Benguela and Its Hinterland, c. 1617–1830." In *Négoce Blanc en Afrique Noire: L'évolution du commerce à longue distance en Afrique noire du 18e au 20e siècles*, eds. H. Bonin and M. Cahen. Paris: Publications de la Société française d'histoire d'outre-mer, 2001, 351–69.

"Resistência à escravidão na África: O caso dos escravos fugitivos recapturados em Angola, 1846–1876." *Afro-Ásia* 33 (2005): 67–88.

"A Restituição de 10.000 súbditos ndongo 'roubados' na Angola de meados do século XVII: Uma análise preliminar." In *Escravatura e Transformações Culturais: África-Brasil-Caraíbas*, ed. Isabel C. Henriques. Lisbon: Editora Vulgata, 2002, 185–208..

"The Story of Nbena, 1817–1820: Unlawful Enslavement and the Concept of 'Original Freedom' in Angola." In *Trans-Atlantic Dimensions of Ethnicity in the African Diaspora*, eds. Paul E. Lovejoy and David V. Trotman. London: Continuum, 2003, 43–64.

"Struggling Against Enslavement: The Case of José Manuel in Benguela, 1816–20." *Canadian Journal of African Studies* 39, no. 1, (2005): 96–122.

Davis, Natalie Zemon. *Fiction in the Archives: Pardon Tales and their Tellers in Sixteenth Century France*. Stanford, CA: Stanford University Press, 1987.

DeCorse, Christopher R. *An Archaeology of Elmina: Africans and Europeans on the Gold Coast, 1400–1900.* Washington, DC: Smithsonian Institution Press, 2001.

Delgado, Ralph. *A Famosa e Histórica Benguela. Catálogo dos Governadores (1779 a 1940).* Lisbon: Cosmos, 1944.

O Reino de Benguela: Do Descobrimento a criação do Governo Subalterno. Lisbon: Imprensa Beleza, 1945.

Ao Sul do Cuanza. Ocupação e Aproveitamento do Antigo Reino de Benguela, 2 vols. Lisbon: n.p., 1944.

Desch Obi, T. J. *Fighting for Honor: The History of African Martial Art Traditions in the Atlantic World.* Columbia: University of South Carolina Press, 2008.

Dias, Jill R. "Famine and Disease in the History of Angola c. 1830–1930." *Journal of African History* 22, no. 3 (1981): 349–78.

"Novas Identidades Africanas em Angola no Contexto do Comércio Atlântico." In *Trânsitos Coloniais: Diálogos Críticos Luso-Brasileiros,* eds. Cristiana Bastos and Miguel Vale de Almeida e Bela Feldman-Bianco. Lisbon: Imprensa de Ciências Sociais, 2002.

"Uma Questão de Identidade: Respostas Intelectuais às Transformações Econômicas no Seio da Elite Crioula da Angola Portuguesa entre 1870 e 1930." *Revista Internacional de Estudos Africanos* 1 (1984): 61–94.

Diffie, Bailey W. *Foundations of the Portuguese Empire, 1415–1580, Europe and the World in the Age of Expansion.* Minneapolis: University of Minnesota Press, 1977.

Diptee, Audra. *From Africa to Jamaica: The Making of an Atlantic Slave Society, 1775–1807.* Gainesville: University Press of Florida, 2010.

Domingues, Angela. "O Conceito de Guerra Justa e Resgate e os Ameríndios do Norte do Brasil." In *Brasil: Colonização e Escravidão,* ed. Maria Beatriz Nizza da Silva. Rio de Janeiro: Nova Fronteira, 1999, 45–56.

Quando os Índios eram Vassalos. Colonização e Relação de Poder no Norte do Brasil da segunda metdade do Século XVIII. Lisbon: Comissão Nacional para as Comemorações dos Descobrimentos Portugueses, 2000.

Dooling, Wayne. *Slavery, Emancipation and Colonial Rule in South Africa.* Athens: Ohio University Press, 2007.

Ehret, Christopher. "The First Spread of Food Production to Southern Africa." In *The Archaeological and Linguistic Reconstruction of African History,* eds. Christopher Ehret and Merrick Posnansky. Berkeley: University of California Press, 1982.

Elbl, Ivana. "Cross-Cultural Trade and Diplomacy: Portuguese Relations with West Africa, 1441–1521." *Journal of World History* 3, no. 2 (1992): 165–204.

"'Men without Wives': Sexual Arrangements in the Early Portuguese Expansion in West Africa." In *Desire and Discipline: Sex and Sexuality in the Premodern West,* eds. Jacqueline Murray and Konrad Eisenbichler. Toronto: University of Toronto Press, 1996, 61–86.

Eldredge, Elizabeth, and Fred Morton. *Slavery in South Africa: Captive Labor on the Dutch Frontier.* Boulder, CO: Westview Press, 1994.

Elliot, John. *Empires of the Atlantic World: Britain and Spain in the America, 1492–1830.* New Haven, CT: Yale University Press, 2006.

Eltis, David. *Economic Growth and the Ending of the Transatlantic Slave Trade.* New York: Oxford University Press, 1987.

"Fluctuations in the Age and Sex Ratios of Slaves in the Nineteenth Century Transatlantic Slave Traffic." *Slavery and Abolition* 7, no. 3 (1986): 257–72.

"The Volume and Structure of the Transatlantic Slave Trade: A Reassessment." *William and Mary Quarterly* 58, no. 1 (2001): 17–46.

Eltis, David, and Stanley Engerman. "Was the Slave Trade Dominated by Men?" *Journal of Interdisciplinary History* 23, no. 2 (1992): 237–57.

Eltis, David, and David Richardson. "A New Assessment of the Transatlantic Slave Trade." In *Extending the Frontiers: Essays on the New Transatlantic Slave Trade Database.* New Haven, CT: Yale University Press, 2008.

Eltis, David, and David Richardson, eds. *Extending the Frontiers: Essays on the New Transatlantic Slave Trade Database.* New Haven, CT: Yale University Press, 2008.

Eltis, David, Philip Morgan, and David Richardson. "Agency and Diaspora in Atlantic History: Reassessing the African Contribution to Rice Cultivation in the Americas." *American Historical Review* 112, no. 5 (2007): 1329–58.

Ennaji, Mohammed. *Serving the Master: Slavery and Society in 19th Century Morocco,* trans. Seth Graebner. New York: St. Martin's Press, 1998.

Ervedosa, Carlos. *Arqueologia Angolana.* Lisbon: Edições 70, 1980.

Estermann, Carlos. *The Ethnography of Southwestern Angola.* New York: Africana Publishing, 1976.

"Les Twa du Sud-Ouest de l'Angola." *Anthropos* 57 (1962): 467–74.

Esteves, Maria Luisa. "Para o Estudo do Tráfico de Escravos de Angola (1640–1668)." *Studia* 50 (1991): 79–108.

Etherington, Norman. *The Great Treks: The Transformation of Southern Africa, 1815–1854.* Harlow, UK: Longman, 2001.

Fage, John D. "Slavery and the Slave Trade in the Context of African History." *Journal of African History* 10, no. 3 (1969): 393–404.

Falola, Toyin, and Kevin D. Roberts, eds. *The Atlantic World, 1450–2000.* Bloomington: Indiana University Press, 2008.

Falola, Toyin, and Paul E. Lovejoy, eds. *Pawnship in Africa: Debt Bondage in Historical Perspective.* Boulder, CO: Westview Press, 1994.

Feinberg, Harvey M. *Africans and Europeans in West Africa: Elminans and Dutchmen on the Gold Coast during the Eighteenth Century.* Philadelphia: American Philosophical Society, 1989.

Fernandes, Paulo Jorges, Filipe Roberto de Meneses, and Manoel Baiôa. "The Political History of Nineteenth Century Portugal." *E-Journal of Portuguese History* 1, no. 1 (2003); available at www.brown.edu/Departments/Portuguese_Brazilian_Studies/ejph/.

Ferreira, Roquinaldo A. "Atlantic Microhistories: Mobility, Personal Ties, and Slaving in the Black Atlantic World (Angola and Brazil)." In *Cultures of the Lusophone Black Atlantic,* eds. Nancy Priscilla Naro, Roger Sansi-Roca, and David H. Treece. New York: Palgrave, 2007, 99–128.

"O Brasil e a Arte da Guerra em Angola (sécs XVII e XVIII)." *Estudos Historicos* 39 (2007): 3–23.

"'Ilhas Crioulas': O Significado Plural da Mestiçagem Cultural na África Atlântica." *Revista de História* 155, no. 2 (2006): 17–41.

"Fontes para o estudo da escravidão em Angola: Luanda e Icolo e Bengo no pós-tráfico de escravos." In *Construindo o passado Angolano: As fontes e a sua interpretação. Actas do II Seminário internacional sobre a história de Angola*. Lisbon: Comissão Nacional para as Comemorações dos Descobrimentos Portugueses, 2000, 667–80.

"Slaving and Resistance to Slaving in West Central Africa." In *The Cambridge World History of Slavery. AD 1420–AD 1804*, vol. 3, eds. David Eltis and Stanley L. Engerman. New York: Cambridge University Press, 2011, 111–30.

"The Supply and Deployment of Horses in Angola Warfare (17th and 18th Century)." In *Angola on the Move: Transport Routes, Communications and History*, eds. Beatrix Heintze and Achim Von Oppen. Frankfurt: Lembeck, 2008, 41–51.

Figueira, Luis. *África Bantu: Raças e tribus de Angola*. Lisbon: Fernandes, 1938.

Florentino, Manolo. *Em Costas Negras. Uma Historia do Trafico de escravos entre a Africa e o Rio de Janeiro*. São Paulo: Companhia das Letras, 1997.

Foucault, Michel. *La Arqueología del Saber*. Buenos Aires: Siglo XXI, 2002.

Fraginals, Manuel Moreno. *The Sugarmill: The Socioeconomic Complex of Sugar in Cuba, 1760–1860*. New York: Monthly Review, 1976.

Freudenthal, Aida. *Arimos e Fazendas. A Transição agrária em Angola*. Luanda: Chá de Caxinde, 2005.

Fuente, Alejandro de la. "Denominaciones Étnicas de los Esclavos Introducidos em Cuba, Siglos XVI y XVII." *Annales del Caribe* 6 (1986): 75–96.

"Introducción al Estudio de la Trata de Cuba, Siglos XVI y XVII." *Santiago* 61 (1986): 155–208.

"Slaves and the Creation of Legal Rights in Cuba: Coartación and Papel." *Hispanic American Historical Review* 87, no. 4 (2007): 659–92.

Fynn, J. K. *Asante and Its Neighbours, 1700–1807*. Evanston, IL: Northwestern University Press, 1971.

Geggus, David. "The French Slave Trade: An Overview." *William and Mary Quarterly* 58, no. 1 (2001): 119–38.

Genovese, Eugene D. *Roll, Jordan, Roll: The World the Slaves Made*. New York: Vintage Books, 1976.

Gikandi, Simon. *Slavery and the Culture of Taste*. Princeton, NJ: Princeton University Press, 2011.

Gilroy, Paul. *The Black Atlantic: Modernity and Double Consciousness*. Cambridge, MA: Harvard University Press, 1993.

Goodwin, Stefan. *African Legacy of Urbanization: Unfolding Saga of a Continent*. Lanham, MD: Lexington Books, 2008.

Graubart, Karen B. "Indecent Living: Indigenous Women and the Politics of Representation in Early Colonial Peru." *Colonial Latin American Review* 9, no. 2 (2000): 213–35.

Green, Toby. *The Rise of the Trans-Atlantic Slave Trade in Western Africa, 1300–1589*. Cambridge: Cambridge University Press, 2011.

Grinberg, Keila. *Liberata – a lei da Ambiguade: as Ações de Liberdade da Corte de Apelação do Rio de Janeiro no século XIX*. Rio de Janeiro: Relume Dumará, 1994.

"Slavery, Manumission and the Law in the Nineteenth-Century Brazil: Reflections on the Law of 1831 and the 'Principle of Liberty' on the Southern

Frontier of the Brazilian Empire." *European Review of History* 16, no. 3 (2009): 401–11.

Guelke, Leonard. "The Anatomy of a Colonial Settler Population: Cape Colony, 1657–1750." In *Families in the Expansion of Europe, 1500–1800*, ed. Maria Beatriz Nizza da Silva. Aldershot, UK: Ashgate, 1998, 293–313.

Guy, Jeff. "Analysing Pre-Capitalist Societies in Southern Africa." *Journal of Southern African Studies* 14, no. 1 (1987): 18–37.

Hall, Gwendolyn Midlo. *Africans in Colonial Louisiana: The Development of Afro-Creole Culture in the Eighteenth Century*. Baton Rouge: Louisiana State University Press, 1992.

Hambly, Wilfrid D. *The Ovimbundu of Angola*. Chicago: Field Museum of Natural History, 1937.

Harms, Robert W. *River of Wealth, River of Sorrow: The Central Zaire Basin in the Era of the Slave and Ivory Trade, 1500–1891*. New Haven, CT: Yale University Press, 1981.

Hauenstein, A. "Noms accompagnés de proverbes, chez les Ovimbundu et les Humbi du Sud de l'Angola." *Anthropos* 57, nos. 1–2 (1962): 97–120.

Havik, Philip J. *Silences and Soundbites: The Gendered Dynamics of Trade and Brokerage in the Pre-Colonial Guinea Bissau Region*. Munster: Lit. Verlag, 2004.

"Women and Trade in the Guinea Bissau Region: The Role of African and Luso-African Women in Trade Networks from the early 16th to the mid-19th century." *Studia* 52 (1994): 83–120.

Hawthorne, Walter. *From Africa to Brazil: Culture, Identity, and an Atlantic Slave Trade, 1600–1830*. New York: Cambridge University Press, 2010.

"From 'Black Rice' to 'Brown': Rethinking the History of Risiculture in the Seventeenth and Eighteenth Century Atlantic." *American Historical Review* 115, no. 1 (2010): 151–63.

"Strategies of the Decentralized: Defending Communities from Slave Raiders in Coastal Guinea-Bissau, 1450–1815." In *Fighting the Slave Trade: West African Strategies*, ed. Silviane Diouf. Athens: Ohio University Press, 2003, 152–69.

Planting Rice and Harvesting Slaves: Transformations Along the Guinea-Bissau Coast, 1400–1900. Portsmouth, NH: Heinemann, 2003.

Heintze, Beatrix. "Angola nas Garras do Tráfico de Escravos: As Guerras Angolanas do Ndongo (1611–1630)." *Revista Internacional de Estudos Africanos* 1 (1984): 11–59.

Angola nos Séculos XVI e XVII. Estudos sobre Fontes, Métodos e História. Luanda: Kilombelombe, 2007.

"Angolan Vassal Tributes of the Seventeenth Century." *Revista de História Económica e Social* 6 (1980): 57–78.

Asilo Ameaçado: Oportunidades e Consequências da Fuga de Escravos Em Angola no Século XVII. Luanda: Museu Nacional da Escravatura, 1995.

"Contra as Teorias Simplificadoras. O 'Canibalismo' na Antropologia e História da Angola." In *Portugal não é um País Pequeno. Contar o "Império" na Pós-Colonidade*, ed. Manuela Ribeiro Sanches. Lisbon: Cotovia, 2006, 215–28.

"Ethnographic Appropriations: German Exploration and Fieldwork in West-Central Africa." *History in Africa* 26 (1999): 69–128.

Fontes para a História de Angola do Século XVII, 2 vols. Stuttgart: F. Steiner Verlag Wiesbaden, 1985–1988.

"Historical Notes on the Kisama of Angola." *Journal of African History* 13, no. 3 (1972): 407–18.

"Luso-African Feudalism in Angola? The Vassal Treaties of the 16th to the 18th Century." *Separata da Revista Portuguesa de História* 18 (1980): 111–31.

"A Lusofonia no interior da África Central na era pré-colonial. Um contributo para a sua História e Compreensão na Actualidade." *Cadernos de Estudos Africanos* 6–7 (2006): 179–207.

"Ngonga a Mwiza: um Sobado Angolano sob Domínio Português no Século XVII." *Revista Internacional de Estudos Africanos* 8–9 (1988): 221–33.

Pioneiros Africanos: Caravanas de carregadores na África Centro-Ocidental : entre 1850 e 1890. Lisbon: Caminho, 2004.

"Propaganda Concerning 'Man Eaters' in West Central Africa in the Second Half of the Nineteenth Century." *Paideuma* 49 (2003): 125–35.

"Translocal Kinship Relations in Central African Politics of the 19th Century." In *Translocality. The Study of Globalising Processes from a Southern Perspective*, eds. Ulrike Freitag and Achim von Oppen. Leiden: Brill, 2010, 179–204.

"Written Sources and African History: A Plea for the Primary Source. The Angola Manuscript Collection of Fernão de Sousa." *History in Africa* 9 (1982): 77–103.

Henriques, Isabel Castro. *Percursos da Modernidade em Angola. Dinâmicas Comercias e Transformações Sociais no Século XIX.* Lisbon: Instituto de Investigação Científica Tropical, 1997.

Herlin, Susan. "Brazil and the Commercialization of Kongo." In *Enslaving Connections: Changing Cultures of Africa and Brazil during the Era of Slavery*, eds. José Curto and Paul Lovejoy. Amherst, NY: Humanity Books, 2004, 255–77.

Hespanha, António Manuel, and Catarina Madeira Santos. "Os Poderes num Império Oceânico." In *Historia de Portugal, O Antigo Regime*, ed. Antonio Manuel Hespanha. Lisbon: Estampa, 1993, 395–413.

Heywood, Linda M. "The Angolan-Afro-Brazilian Cultural Connections." *Slavery & Abolition* 20, no. 1 (1999): 9–23.

Contested Power in Angola. Rochester, NY: University of Rochester Press, 2000.

"Portuguese into African: The Eighteenth-Century Central African Background to Atlantic Creole Cultures." In *Central Africans and Cultural Transformations in the American Diaspora*, ed. Linda M. Heywood. Cambridge: Cambridge University Press, 2002, 91–115.

"Slavery in its Transformation in the Kingdom of Kongo: 1491–1800." *Journal of African History* 50 (2009): 1–22.

Heywood, Linda, and John Thornton. "African Fiscal Systems as Sources for Demographic History: the case of central Angola, 1799–1920." *Journal of African History* 29, no. 2 (1988), 213–28.

"Central African Leadership and the Appropriation of European Culture." In *The Atlantic World and Virginia, 1550–1624*, ed. Peter C. Mancall. Chapel Hill: University of North Carolina Press, 2007, 194–224.

Central Africans, Atlantic Creoles, and the Foundation of the Americas, 1585–1660. New York: Cambridge University Press, 2007.

Higgins, Kathleen. *Licentious Liberty in a Brazilian Gold-Mining Region*. University Park: Pennsylvania State University Press, 1999.

Hilton, Anne. "The Jaga Reconsidered." *Journal of African History* 22, no. 2 (1981): 191–202.

The Kingdom of Kongo. Oxford, UK: Clarendon Press, 1985.

Hobsbawm, Eric. *Nations and Nationalism Since 1780: Programme, Myth, Reality*. Cambridge: Cambridge University Press, 1992.

"History from Below: Some Reflections." In *History from Below: Studies in Popular Protest and Popular Ideology in Honour of George Rude*, ed. Frederick Krantz. Montreal: Concordia University, 1985.

Hobsbawm, Eric, and Terence Ranger, eds. *The Invention of Tradition*. Cambridge: Cambridge University Press, 1992.

Hopkins, Terence K., and Immanuel Wallerstein. "Commodity Chains in the World-Economy Prior to 1800." *Review (Fernand Braudel Center)* 10, no. 1 (1986): 157–70.

Hoover, Jeffrey J. "Mythe et Remous Historique: A Lunda Response to De Heusche." *History in Africa* 5 (1978): 63–80.

Hyam, Ronald. *Empire and Sexuality: The British Experience*. Manchester: Manchester University Press, 1992.

Inikori, Joseph. *Forced Migrations: The Impact of the Export Slave Trade on African Societies*. London: Holmes & Meier, 1982.

Isaacman, Allen. "Chikunda Transfontiersmen and Transnational Migrations in Pre-Colonial South Central Africa, ca. 1850–1900." *Zambezia* 27, no. 2 (2000): 109–38.

Mozambique: From Colonialism to Revolution, 1900–1982. Boulder, CO: Westview Press, 1983.

Mozambique: The Africanization of a European Institution: The Zambezi Prazos, 1750–1902. Madison: University of Wisconsin Press, 1972.

Isaacman, Allen, and Barbara Isaacman. *Slavery and Beyond: The Making of Men and Chikunda Ethnic Identities in the Unstable World of South-Central Africa, 1750–1920*. Portsmouth, NH: Heinemann, 2004.

Johnson, Sherry. *The Social Transformation of Eighteenth Century Cuba*. Gainesville: University Press of Florida, 2001.

Jones, Hilary. "From Mariage à la Mode to Weddings at Town Hall: Marriage, Colonialism, and Mixed-Race Society in Nineteenth-Century Senegal." *International Journal of African Historical Studies* 38, no. 1 (2005): 27–48.

Kanya-Forstner,. Alexander Sydney. "French Missions to the Central Sudan in the 1890s: The Role of Algerian Agents and Interpreters." *Paideuma* 40 (1994): 15–32.

Karasch, Mary. "From Portage to Proprietorship: African Occupations in Rio de Janeiro, 1880–1850." In *Race and Slavery in the Western Hemisphere:*

Quantitative Studies, eds. Stanley Engerman and Eugene Genovese. Princeton, NJ: Princeton University Press, 1975, 369–94..

"As Mulheres Livres de Cor no Brasil, 1779/1832." *Revista da Sociedade Brasileira de Pesquisa Historica* 15 (1998): 3–20.

Slave Life in Rio de Janeiro, 1808–1850. Princeton, NJ: Princeton University Press, 1987.

Kea, R. A. "Firearms and Warfare on the Gold and Slave Coasts from the Sixteenth to the Nineteenth Centuries." *Journal of African History* 12, no. 2 (1971): 185–213.

Keiling, Luiz Alfredo. *Quarenta Anos de Africa.* Braga: Edição das Missões de Angola e Congo, 1934.

Kelly, Kenneth G. "Change and Continuity in Coastal Benin." In *West Africa during the Atlantic Slave Trade: Archaeological Perspectives*, ed. Christopher DeCorse. New York: Leicester University Press, 2001, 81–101.

Klein, Herbert. *The Atlantic Slave Trade.* New York: Cambridge University Press, 1999.

"The Portuguese Slave Trade from Angola in the Eighteenth Century." *Journal of Economic History* 32, no. 4 (1972): 7–32.

"The Trade in African Slaves to Rio de Janeiro, 1795–1811: Estimates of Mortality and Patterns of Voyages." *Journal of African History* 10, no. 4 (1969): 533–49.

Klein, Herbert, and Francisco de la Luna. *Slavery in Brazil.* New York: Cambridge University Press, 2010.

Klein, Martin A. *Slavery and Colonial Rule in French West Africa.* Cambridge: Cambridge University Press, 1998.

"Slavery, the International Labor Market and the Emancipation of Slaves in the Nineteenth Century." *Slavery & Abolition* 15, no. 2 (1994): 197–220.

"Social and Economic Factors in the Muslim Revolution in Senegambia." *Journal of African History* 13, no. 3 (1972): 419–41.

Kopytoff, Igor. *The African Frontier: The Reproduction of Traditional African Societies.* Bloomington: Indiana University Press, 1987.

"Permutations in Patrimonialism and Populism: The Aghem Chiefdoms of Western Cameroon." In *Beyond Chiefdoms: Pathways to Complexity in Africa*, ed. Susan K. McIntosh. Cambridge: Cambridge University Press, 2005, 88–96.

Lara, Silvia H. *Campos da Violência: Escravos e Senhores na Capitania do Rio de Janeiro, 1750–1808.* São Paulo: Paz e Terra, 1988.

"Palmares, Cuacu e as Perspectivas de Liberdade." In *Trabalho Livre, Trabalho Escravo*, eds. Douglas Cole Libby and Júnia Ferreira Furtado. São Paulo: Annablume, 2006, 361–81.

"The Signs of Color: Women's Dress and Racial Relations in Salvador and Rio de Janeiro, ca. 1750–1815." *Colonial Latin American Review* 6, no. 2 (1997): 205–24.

"Do Singular ao Plural: Palmares, Capitães do Mato e o Governo dos Escravos." In *Liberdade por um fio, História dos Quilombos no Brasil*, eds. João José Reis and Flávio Gomes dos Santos. São Paulo: Companhia das Letras, 1996, 81–109.

Law, Robin. "Human Sacrifice in Pre-colonial West Africa," *African Affairs* 84, no. 334 (1985): 53–87.

    Ouidah, The Social History of a West African Slaving 'Port', 1727–1892. Athens: Ohio University Press, 2004.

    "Slave-Raiders and Middlemen, Monopolists and Free Traders: The Supply of Slaves for the Atlantic Trade in Dahomey, c. 1715–1850." *Journal of African History* 30 (1989): 45–68.

    The Oyo Empire, C.1600–C.1836: A West African Imperialism in the Era of the Atlantic Slave Trade. Oxford, UK: Clarendon Press, 1977.

Law, Robin, and Paul E. Lovejoy, eds. *The Biography of Mohammah Gardo Baquaqua: His Passage from Slavery to Freedom in Africa and America.* Princeton, NJ: Markus Wiener, 2001.

Lawrance, Benjamin N., Emily Osborn, and Richard L. Roberts, eds. *Intermediaries, Interpreters, and Clerks: African Employees in the Making of Colonial Africa.* Madison: University of Wisconsin Press, 2006.

Lawton, Richard. "Introduction." In *The Census and Social Structure. An Interpretative Guide to Nineteenth Century Censuses for England and Wales*, ed. R. Lawton. London: Frank Cass, 1978.

Le Goff, Jacques, and Pierre Nora, eds. *Constructing the Past: Essays in Historical Methodology.* Cambridge: Cambridge University Press, 1985.

Lindsay, Lisa A. *Captives as Commodities: The Transatlantic Slave Trade.* Upper Saddle River, NJ: Pearson Prentice-Hall, 2007.

Lovejoy, Paul E. *Transformations in Slavery: A History of Slavery in Africa*, 3rd ed. Cambridge: Cambridge University Press, 2011.

    "Concubinage and the Status of Women Slaves in Early Colonial Northern Nigeria." *Journal of African History* 29, no. 2 (1988): 245–66.

    "Identifying Enslaved Africans in the African Diaspora." In *Identity in the Shadow of Slavery*, ed. Paul Lovejoy. London: Cassell Academic, 2000, 1–29.

    "The Impact of the Atlantic Slave Trade on Africa: A Review of the Literature." *Journal of African History* 30 (1989): 1–30.

    "Plantations in the Economy of the Sokoto Caliphate." *Journal of African History* 19, no. 3 (1978): 341–68.

    Salt of the Desert Sun: A History of Salt Production and Trade in the Central Sudan. Cambridge: Cambridge University Press, 1986.

    Transformations in Slavery: A History of Slavery in Africa. New York: Cambridge University Press, 2000.

    "The Urban Background of Enslaved Muslims in the Americas." *Slavery & Abolition* 26, no. 3 (2005), 349–76.

Lovejoy, Paul E., ed. *Identity in the Shadow of Slavery.* London: Cassell Academic, 2000.

Lovejoy, Paul E., and David Richardson. "The Business of Slaving: Pawnship in Western Africa, c.1600–1810." *Journal of African History* 42, no. 1 (2001): 67–89.

    "Trust, Pawnship and Atlantic History: The Institutional Foundations of the Old Calabar Slave Trade." *American Historical Review* 102 (1999): 333–55.

Lovejoy, Paul E., and David Trotman. "Enslaved Africans and their Expectations of Slave Life in the Americas: Toward a Reconsideration of Models of

'Creolisation.'" In *Questioning Creole: Creolisation Discourses in Caribbean Culture*, eds. Verene Shepard and Glen L. Richards. Kingston, Jamaica: Ian Randle, 2002, 67–91.

Mamdani, Mahmood. *Citizen and Subject*. Princeton, NJ: Princeton University Press, 1996.

Mancall, Peter C. *The Atlantic World and Virginia, 1550–1624*. Chapel Hill: University of North Carolina Press, 2007.

Mann, Kristin. *Marrying Well: Marriage, Status and Social Change among the Educated Elite of Colonial Lagos*. Cambridge: Cambridge University Press, 1985.

Slavery and the Birth of an African City: Lagos, 1760–1900. Bloomington: Indiana University Press, 2007.

Manning, Patrick. *Slavery and African Life: Occidental, Oriental, and African Slave Trades*. Cambridge: Cambridge University Press, 1990.

Slavery, Colonialism and Economic Growth in Dahomey, 1640–1960. Cambridge: Cambridge University Press, 1982.

Mark, Peter. "The Evolution of Identity: Luso-Africans on the Upper Guinea Coast from the Sixteenth to the Early Nineteenth Century." *Journal of African History* 40, no. 2 (1999): 173–91.

"Portuguese" Style and Luso-African Identity: Precolonial Senegambia, Sixteenth-Nineteenth Centuries. Bloomington: Indiana University Press, 2002.

Marques, João Pedro. *Os Sons do Silêncio: O Portugal de Oitocentos e a Abolição do Tráfico de Escravos*. Lisbon: Imprensa da Ciências Sociais, 1999.

Martin, Phyllis. *The External Trade of the Loango Coast, 1576–1870*. Oxford, UK: Clarendon Press, 1972.

Matos, Raimundo José da Cunha. *Compêndio Histórico das Possessões de Portugal na África*. Rio de Janeiro: Arquivo Histórico Nacional, 1963.

Mattos, Hebe M. "'Black Troops' and Hierarchies of Color in the Portuguese Atlantic World: The Case of Henrique Dias and His Black Regiment." *Luso-Brazilian Review* 45, no. 1 (2008): 6–29.

Das Cores do Silêncio: Os Significados da liberdade no Sudeste escravista, Brasil Século XIX. Rio de Janeiro: Nova Fronteira, 1998.

"A Escravidão Moderna nos Quadros do Império Português: o Antigo Regime em perspectiva Atlântica." In *O Antigo Regime nos Trópicos: a dinâmica imperial portuguesa (sec. XVI–XVIII)*, eds. João Fragoso, Maria Fernanda Bicalho, and Maria Fátima Gouveia. Rio de Janeiro: Civilização Brasileira, 2001, 141–62.

Mauro, Frédéric. *Portugal, o Brasil e o Atlântico*. Lisbon: Estampa, 1997.

Le Portugal, le Bresil et L' Atlantique au XVII siecle (1570–1670). Lisbon: Fundação Calouste Gulbenkian, 1983.

McCaa, Robert. "Marriageways in Mexico and Spain, 1500–1900." *Continuity and Change* 9, no. 1 (1994): 11–43.

McClintock, Anne. *Imperial Leather: Race, Gender and Sexuality in the Colonial Context*. New York: Routledge, 1995.

McCulloch, Merran. *The Ovimbundu of Angola*. London: International African Institute, 1952.

McIntosh, Susan Keech, ed. *Beyond Chiefdoms: Pathways to Complexity in Africa*. Cambridge: Cambridge University Press, 1999.

McKittrick, Meredith. *To Dwell and Secure: Generation, Christianity, and Colonialism in Ovamboland*. Portsmouth, NH: Heinemann, 2002.

McKnight, Kathryn Joy. "Confronted Rituals: Spanish Colonial and Angolan Maroon Executions in Cartagena de Indias (1634)." *Journal of Colonialism and Colonial History* 5, no. 3 (2004).

McNeill, John Robert. *Mosquito Empires: Ecology and War in the Greater Caribbean, 1620–1914*. New York: Cambridge University Press, 2010.

Medeiros, Carlos L. "Kwandu Law: The Evolution of a Juridical System among an Herero people of South-west Angola." *Journal of African Law* 28, nos. 1–2 (1984): 80–9.

Medina, João, and Isabel de Castro Henriques. *A Rota dos Escravos: Angola e a Rede do Comércio Negreiro*. Lisbon: Cegia, 1996.

Meillassoux, Claude. *Mujeres, Graneros y Capitales: Economía Doméstica y Capitalismo*. Mexico: Siglo XXI, 1977.

Mello, Evaldo Cabral de. *O Nome e o Sangue. Uma parábolda genealógica no Pernambuco Colonial*. São Paulo: Companhia de Bolso, 2009.

Metcalf, Alida C. *Go-Betweens and the Colonization of Brazil, 1500–1600*. Austin: University of Texas Press, 2005.

Miller, Joseph C. "Angola Central e Sul por Volta de 1840." *Estudos Afro-Asiáticos* 32 (1997): 7–54.

"Central Africa during the Era of the Slave Trade." In *Central Africans and Cultural Transformations in the American Diaspora*, ed. Linda Heywood. New York: Cambridge University Press, 2001, 21–69.

"The Imbangala and the Chronology of Early Central African History." *Journal of African History* 13, no. 14 (1972): 549–74.

Kings and Kinsmen: Early Mbundu States in Angola. Oxford, UK: Clarendon Press, 1976.

"Legal Portuguese Slaving from Angola: Some Preliminary Indications of Volume and Direction." *Revue Française d'Histoire d'Outre Mer* 62, nos. 1–2 (1975): 150–2.

"The Numbers, Origins, and Destinations of Slaves in the Eighteenth-Century Angolan Slave Trade." In *The Atlantic Slave Trade: Effects on Economies, Societies, and People in Africa, the Americas, and Europe*, eds. Joseph Inikori and Stanley L. Engerman. Durham, NC: Duke University Press, 1992, 7–115.

"The Paradoxes of Impoverishment in the Atlantic Zone." In *History of Central Africa*, eds. David Birmingham and Phyllis Martin. London: Longman, 1983, 118–59.

"Requiem for the Jaga." *Cahiers d'Etudes Africaines* 13, no. 49 (1973): 121–49.

"The Significance of Drought, Disease and Famine in the Agriculturally Marginal Zones of West Central Africa." *Journal of African History* 23, no. 1 (1982): 17–61.

"Some Aspects of the Commercial Organization of Slaving at Luanda, Angola – 1760–1830." In *The Uncommon Market: Essays in the Economic History of the Atlantic Slave Trade*, eds. Henry Gemery and Jan Hogendorn. New York: Academic Press, 1979, 77–106.

Way of Death: Merchant Capitalism and the Angolan Slave Trade, 1730–1830. Madison: University of Wisconsin Press, 1988.

Miranda, Carlos Alberto Cunha. *A Arte de Curar nos Tempos da Colônia: Limites e Espaços da Cura*. Recife: Secretaria de Cultura, 2004.

Morgan, Jennifer L. "'Some Could Suckle over Their Shoulder': Male Travelers, Female Bodies, and the Gendering of Racial Ideology, 1500–1700." *William and Mary Quarterly* 54, no. 1 (1997): 167–92.

Mulvey, Patricia. "Slave Confraternities in Brazil: Their Role in Colonial Society." *The Americas* 39, no. 1 (1982): 39–68.

Musisi, Nakanyike B. "Women, 'Elite Polygyny,' and Buganda State Formation." *Signs* 16, no. 4 (1991): 757–86.

Nazzari, Muriel. "Concubinage in Colonial Brazil: The Inequalities of Race, Class and Gender." *Journal of Family History* 21 (1996): 107–21.

Neto, Maria da Conceição. "Ideologias, Contradições e Mistificações da Colonização de Angola no Século XX." *Lusotopie* (1997): 327–59.

Newitt, M. D. D. *A History of Portuguese Overseas Expansion, 1400–1668*. New York: Routledge, 2005.

Newson, Linda A., and Susie Minchin. *From Capture to Sale: The Portuguese Slave Trade to Spanish South America in the Early Seventeenth Century*. Leiden: Brill, 2007.

Novais, Fernando A. *Estrutura e Dinâmica do Antigo sistema Colonial (séculos XVI-XVIII)*. São Paulo: CEBRAP, 1974.

Núñez, Benjamin. *Dictionary of Portuguese-African Civilization*. London: Hans Zell, 1995.

Nwokeji, G. Ugo. *The Slave Trade and Culture in the Bight of Biafra: An African Society in the Atlantic World*. Cambridge: Cambridge University Press, 2010.

Olival, Fernanda de. "Mercado de Hábitos e Serviços em Portugal (séculos XVII–XVIII)." *Análise Social* 38, no. 168 (2003): 743–69.

As Ordens Militares e o Estado Moderno: Honra, Mercê e Venalidade em Portugal (1641–1789). Lisbon: Estar, 2001.

Oliveira Marquês, Antônio Henrique R. de. *History of Portugal*, 2 vols. New York: Columbia University Press, 1972.

Oppen, Achim von. *Terms of Trade and Terms of Trust*. Munster: LIT Verlag Münster, 1994.

Pantoja, Selma. "A Dimensão Atlântica das Quitandeiras." In *Diálogos Oceânicos: Minas Gerais e as Novas Abordagens para uma História do Império Ultramarino Português*, ed. Júnia F. Furtado. Belo Horizonte: UFMG, 2001, 45–68.

"Gênero e Comércio: As Traficantes de Escravos na Região de Angola." *Travessias* 4–5 (2004): 79–97.

"As Fontes Escritas do Século XVII e o Estudo da Representação do Feminino em Luanda." In *Construindo o Passado Angolano: As fontes e a sua interpretação. Actas do II Seminário internacional sobre a história de Angola*. Lisbon: Comissão Nacional para as Comemorações dos Descobrimentos Portugueses, 2000, 583–96.

"Inquisição, Degredo e Mestiçagem em Angola no século XVII." *Revista Lusófona de Ciência das Religiões* 3, nos. 5–6 (2004): 117–36.

"Women's Work in the Fairs and Markets of Luanda." In *Women in the Portuguese Colonial Empire: The Theater of Shadows*, ed. Clara Sarmento. Newcastle-upon-Tyne, UK: Cambridge Scholars Publishing, 2008, 81–93.

"Três Leituras e Duas Cidades: Luanda e Rio de Janeiro nos Setencentos." In *Angola e Brasil nas Rotas do Atlântico Sul*, eds. Selma Pantoja and José Flávio Sombra Saraiva. Rio de Janeiro: Bertrand Brasil, 1999, 99–126.

Parreira, Adriano A. T. *Economia e Sociedade em Angola na Época da Rainha Jinga, Século XVII*. Lisbon: Editorial Estampa, 1990.

"A Primeira Conquista de Benguela." *História* 12, no. 128 (1990): 64–8.

Patterson, Orlando. *Slavery and Social Death: A Comparative Study*. Cambridge, MA: Harvard University Press, 1982.

Peabody, Sue. *"There Are No Slaves in France": The Political Culture of Race and Slavery in the Ancien Régime*. New York: Oxford University Press, 1996.

Pena, Eduardo S. *Pajens da Casa Imperial: Jurisconsultos, Escravidão e a Lei de 1871*. Campinas: Ed. Unicamp, 2001.

Perrone-Moisés, Beatriz. "A Guerra Justa em Portugal no Séc. XVI." *Sociedade Brasileira de Pesquisa Histórica* 5 (1989–90): 5–10.

Pieroni, Geraldo. *Vadios e Ciganos, Heréticos e Bruxas: Degredados no Brasil Colônia*. Rio de Janeiro: Bertrand, 2000.

Os Excluídos do Reino. Brasília: Editora UNB, 2000.

Pimenta, Tania Salgado. "Barbeiros-Sangradores e Curandeiros no Brasil (1808–28)." *História, Ciências e Saúde* 2 (1998): 349–72.

Pinto, Luís Joaquim Marques Pais. "Arqueologia da Faixa Sedimenral de Benguela: A Idade da Pedra e do Ferro." *Leba* 7 (1992): 203–20.

Pinto, Paulo Jorge de Sousa. "Em Torno de um Problema de Identidade: Os 'Jagas' na História do Congo e Angola." *Mare Liberum* 18–19 (1999–2000): 193–241.

Postman, Johannes M. *The Dutch in the Atlantic Slave Trade, 1600–1815*. Cambridge: Cambridge University Press, 1990.

Raman, Bhavani. "The Familial World of the Company's Kacceri in Early Colonial Madras." *Journal of Colonialism & Colonial History* 9 (2) (2008), 1–N_A. http://search.proquest.com/docview/210657799?accountid=13314

Raposo, Luis. *Marcas de Escravos: Listas de escravos emancipados vindos a bordo de navios negreiros (1839–1841)*. Rio de Janeiro: Arquivo Nacional, 1990.

Ratelband, Klaas. *Os Holandeses no Brasil e na costa africana: Angola, Kongo e São Tomé, 1600–1650*. Lisbon: Vega, 2003.

Rebelo, Manuel dos Anjos da Silva. *Relações entre Brasil e Angola, 1808–1830*. Lisbon: Agência Geral do Ultramar, 1970.

Redinha, José. *Distribuição Étnica de Angola: Introdução, Registo Étnico*. Luanda: Centro de Informação e Turismo de Angola, 1962.

Ribeiro, Márcia Moisés. "Nem Nobre, Nem Mecânico: A Trajetória Social de um Cirurgião na América Portuguesa do Século XVIII." *Almanack Braziliense* 2 (2005): 64–75.

Ricoeur, Paul. *Time and Narrative*. The University of Chicago Press, 1984.

Rigby, Nigel. "Sober Cannibals and Drunken Christians: Colonial Encounters of the Cannibal Kind." *Journal of Commonwealth Literature* 27 (1992): 171–82.

Roberts, Richard. "Women's Work and Women's Property: Household Social Relations in the Maraka Textile Industry of the Nineteenth Century." *Comparative Studies in Society and History* 26, no. 2 (1984): 229–50.

Robertson, Claire, and Martin Klein, eds. *Women and Slavery in Africa*. Madison: University of Wisconsin Press, 1983.

Rodney, Walter. *How Europe Underdeveloped Africa*. Washington, DC: Howard University Press, 1974.

History of the Upper Guinea Coast: 1545–1800. New York: Monthly Review Press, 1980.

Rodrigues, José H. *Brasil e África: outro horizonte*. Rio de Janeiro: Civilização Brasileira, 1961.

Ross, Robert. *Cape of Torments: Slavery and Resistance in South Africa*. London: Routledge & Kegan Paul, 1983.

Russell-Wood, A. J. R. *The Black Man in Slavery and Freedom in Colonial Brazil*. New York: St. Martin's Press, 1982.

Fidalgos and Philanthropists: The Santa Casa da Misericórdia of Bahia, 1550–1755. Berkeley: University of California Press, 1968.

"Iberian Expansion and the Issue of Black Slavery: Changing Portuguese Attitudes, 1440–1770." *American Historical Review* 83, no. 1 (1978): 16–42.

"Patterns of Settlement in the Portuguese Empire, 1400–1800." In *Portuguese Oceanic Expansion, 1400–1800*, eds. Francisco Bethencourt and Diogo Ramada Curto. New York: Cambridge University Press, 2007, 161–96.

A World on the Move: The Portuguese in Africa, Asia, and America, 1415–1808. Manchester, UK: Carcanet, 1992.

Sá, Isabel dos Guimarães. "Ecclesiastical Structures and Religious Action." In *Portuguese Oceanic Expansion, 1400–1800*, eds. Francisco Bethencourt and Diogo Ramada Curto. Cambridge: Cambridge University Press, 2007, 255–80.

Santos, Catarina Madeira. "Écrire le pouvoir en Angola: Les archives ndembu (XVIIe–XXe siècles)." *Annales. Histoire, Sciences Sociales* 64, no. 4 (2009): 767–95.

"Entre Deux Droits: Les Lumières en Angola (1750–v.1800)." *Annales. Histoire, Sciences Sociales* 60, no. 4 (2005): 817–48.

"Escrever o Poder: Os Autos de Vassalagem e a Vulgarização da Escrita entre as Elites Africanas Ndembu." *Revista de História* 155, no. 2 (2006): 81–95.

"Luanda: A Colonial City between Africa and the Atlantic, Seventeenth and Eighteenth Centuries." In *Portuguese Colonial Cities in the Early Modern World*, ed. Liam Matthew Brockey. New York: Ashgate, 2009, 249–72.

Santos, Corcino M. Dos. "Relações de Angola com o Rio de Janeiro (1736–1808)." *Estudos Históricos* 12 (1973): 7–68.

Santos, Maria Emilia Madeira. "Os Africanos e o mar: Conhecimento e Práticas à Época da chegada dos Portugueses." *Africa: Revista do Centro de Estudos Africanos* 20–21 (1997–8): 79–92.

"Abolição do tráfico de Escravos e Reconversão da Economia de Angola: Um confronto participado por brasileiros." *Studia* 52 (1994): 221–44.

Nos Caminhos de África: Serventia e Posse, Angola século XIX. Lisbon: Instituto de Investigação Científica Tropical, 1998.

Problema da Segurança das Rotas e a Concorrência Luso-Holandesa antes de 1620. Coimbra: Universidade de Coimbra, 1985.

Santos, Maria Emília Madeira, ed. *Textos para a História da África Austral (século XVIII).* Lisbon: Publicações Alfa, 1989.

ed. *Viagens e Apontamentos de um Portuense em África.* Coimbra: Biblioteca Geral da Universidade de Coimbra, 1986.

Saunders, A. C. de C. M. *História Social dos Escravos e Libertos Negros em Portugal (1441–1555).* Lisbon: Imprensa Nacional, 1994.

Schmidt, Elizabeth. "Farmers, Hunters, and Gold-Washers: A Reevaluation of Women's Roles in Precolonial and Colonial Zimbabwe." *African Economic History* 17 (1988): 45–80.

Peasants, Traders and Wives: Shona Women in the History of Zimbabwe, 1870–1939. Portsmouth, NH: Heinemann, 1992.

Schwartz, Stuart B. "'A Commonwealth within Itself': The Early Brazilian Sugar Industry, 1550–1670." *Revista de Indias* 65, no. 233 (2005): 79–116.

"The Economy of the Portuguese Empire." In *Portuguese Oceanic Expansion, 1400–1800*, eds. Francisco Bethencourt and Diogo Ramada Curto. New York: Cambridge University Press, 2007, 19–48.

"Luso-Spanish Relations in Hapsburg Brazil, 1580–1640." *The Americas* 25, no. 1 (1968): 33–48.

"Prata, Açúcar e Escravos: de como o império restaurou Portugal." *Tempo* 12, no. 24 (2008): 201–23.

Sugar Plantations in the Formation of Brazilian Society: Bahia, 1550–1835. New York: Cambridge University Press, 1986.

Scott, Rebecca J. "Paper Thin: Freedom and Re-Enslavement in the Diaspora of the Haitian Revolution." *Law and History Review* 29, no. 4 (2011): 1061–87.

"'She ... Refuses to Deliver Up Herself as the Slave of Your Petitioner': Émigrés, Enslavement, and the 1808 Louisiana Digest of the Civil Laws." *Tulane European & Civil Law Forum* 24 (2009): 115–36.

Scully, Pamela. *Liberating the Family? Gender and British Slave Emancipation in the Rural Western Cape, South Africa, 1823–1853.* Portsmouth, NH: Heinemann, 1997.

"Malintzin, Pocahontas, and Krotoa: Indigenous Women and Myth Models of the Atlantic World." *Journal of Colonialism and Colonial History* 6, no. 3 (2005).

Searing, James F. *West African Slavery and Atlantic Commerce: The Senegal River Valley, 1700–1860.* New York: Cambridge University Press, 2003.

Sebestyén, Evá, Jan Vansina, and Manoel Correia Leitão. "Angola's Eastern Hinterland in the 1750s: A Text Edition and Translation of Manoel Correia Leitão's 'Voyage' (1755–1756)." *History in Africa* 26 (1999): 299–364.

Shumway, Rebecca. *The Fante and the Transatlantic Slave Trade.* Rochester, NY: University Rochester Press, 2011.

Silva, Manuel dos Anjos da Rebelo. *Relações entre Angola e Brasil (1808–1830).* Lisbon: Agência-Geral do Ultramar, 1970.

Silva, Rosa Cruz e. "The Saga of Kakonda and Kilengues: Relations between Benguela and Its Interior, 1791–1796." In *Enslaving Connections: Changing*

Cultures of Africa and Brazil during the Era of Slavery, eds. José C. Curto and Paul E. Lovejoy. Amherst, NY: Humanity Books, 2004, 245–59.

Smallwood, Stephanie. *Saltwater Slavery: A Middle Passage from Africa to American Diaspora*. Cambridge, MA: Harvard University Press, 2007.

Soares, Mariza de Carvalho. "A Biografia de Ignácio Montes: O Escravo que virou Rei." In *Retratos do Império: Trajetórias Individuais no Mundo Português nos séculos XVI a XIX*, eds. Ronaldo Vainfas, R. Santos, and G. Neves. Niterói: Eduff, 2006, 47–68.

"Descobrindo a Guiné no Brasil Colonial." *Revista do Instituto Historico Geografico Brasileiro* 161, no. 407 (2000): 71–94.

Devotos da Cor. Rio de Janeiro: Civilização Brasileira, 2000.

"Indícios para o traçado das Rotas Terrestres de Escravos na Baía do Benim, século XVIII." In *Rotas Atlânticas da Diáspora Africana: da Baía do Benim ao Rio de Janeiro*. Niterói: Eduff, 2007.

"A Nação que se tem e a Terra de onde se vem: Categorias de Inserção Social de Africanos no Império Português, Século XVIII." *Estudos Afro-Asiáticos* 26, no. 2 (2004): 303–30.

"O Vinho e a Farinha, 'Zonas de Sombra' na Economia Atlântica no século XVIII." *Populaçaõ e Sociedade* 16 (2008)): 215–32.

Socolow, Susan Migden. "Marriage, Birth and Inheritance: The Merchants of Eighteenth-Century Buenos Aires." *Hispanic American Historical Review* 60, no. 3 (1980): 387–406.

Sommerdyk, Stacey. "Rivalry on the Loango Coast: A Re-examination of the Dutch in the Atlantic Slave Trade." In *Trabalho Forçado Africano: O Caminho de Ida*, ed. Arlindo Manuel Caldeira. Porto: CEAUP, 2009, 105–18.

Sousa, Laura de Mello e. *Desclassificados do Ouro: A Pobreza Mineira no Século XVIII*. Rio de Janeiro: Graal, 1985.

Sparks, Randy J. "Two Princes of Calabar: An Atlantic Odyssey from Slavery to Freedom." *William and Mary Quarterly* 59, no. 3 (2002): 555–84.

The Two Princes of Calabar: An Eighteenth-Century Atlantic Odyssey. Cambridge, MA: Harvard University Press, 2004.

Stilwell, Sean. *Paradoxes of Power: The Kano "Mamluks" and Male Royal Slavery in the Sokoto Caliphate, 1804–1903*. Portsmouth, NH: Heinemann, 2004.

Stoler, Ann Laura. *Carnal Knowledge and Imperial Power: Race and the Intimate in Colonial Rule*. Berkeley: University of California Press, 2002.

Along the Archival Grain: Epistemic Anxieties and Colonial Common Sense. Princeton, NJ: Princeton University Press, 2009.

St. Clair, William. *The Door of No Return: The History of Cape Coast Castle and the Atlantic Slave Trade*. New York: BlueBridge, 2007.

Strickrodt, Silke. "'Afro-Brazilians' of the Western Slave Coast in the Nineteenth Century." In *Enslaving Connections: Western Africa and Brazil during the Era of the Slavery*, eds. J. Curto and P. Lovejoy. Amherst, NY: Humanity Books, 2003, 213–24.

Subrahmanyam, Sanjay. "Holding the World in Balance: The Connected Histories of the Iberian Overseas Empires, 1500–1640." *American Historical Review* 112, no. 5 (2007): 1359–86.

Subtil, José. "Os Ministros do Rei no Poder Local, Ilhas e Ultramar (1772–1826)." *Penélope* 27 (2002): 37–58.

Sweet, James H. *Domingos Alvares, African Healing, and the Intellectual History of the Atlantic World*. Chapel Hill: University of North Carolina Press, 2011.

"African Identity and Slave Resistance in the Portuguese Atlantic." In *The Atlantic World and Virginia, 1550–1624*, ed. Peter C. Mancall. Chapel Hill: University of North Carolina Press, 2007, 225–48.

"Manumission in Rio de Janeiro, 1749–54: An African Perspective." *Slavery & Abolition* 24 (2003): 54–70.

Recreating Africa: Culture, Kinship, and Religion in the African-Portuguese World, 1441–1770. Chapel Hill: University of North Carolina Press, 2003.

Taunay, Affonso de E. *Subsídios para a história do tráfico africano no Brasil*. São Paulo: Imprensa Oficial do Estado, 1941.

Tavares, Ana Paula. "A Escrita em Angola: Comunicação e Ruído entre as Diferentes Sociedades em Presença." In *Angola on the Move: Transport Routes, Communications and History*, eds. B. Heintze and A. van Oppen. Frankfurt-am-Main: Lembeck, 2008, 163–73.

Tavares, Ana Paula, and Catarina Madeira Santos. *Africæ monumenta: Arquivo Caculo Cacahenda*. Lisbon: Instituto de Investigação Científica Tropical, 2002.

Thom, Martin. *Republics, Nations and Tribes*. New York: Verso, 1995.

Thornton, John K. *Africa and Africans in the Making of the Atlantic World, 1400–1800*. New York: Cambridge University Press, 1998.

"African Dimensions of the Stono Rebellion." *American Historical Review* 96, no. 4 (1991): 1101–13.

"The African Experience of the '20s and Odd Negroes' Arriving in Virginia in 1619." *William and Mary Quarterly* 55 (1998): 421–34.

"African Political Ethics and the Slave Trade." In *Abolitionism and Imperialism in Britain, Africa, and the Atlantic*, ed. Derek R. Peterson. Athens: Ohio University Press, 2010, 38–62.

"The Art of War in Angola, 1575–1680." *Comparative Studies in Society and History* 30 (1988): 360–78.

"Cannibals, Witches, and Slave Traders in the Atlantic World." *William and Mary Quarterly* 60, no. 2 (2003): 273–94.

"Demography and History in the Kingdom of Kongo, 1550–1750." *Journal of African History* 18 (1977): 507–30.

"The Development of an African Catholic Church in the Kingdom of Kongo, 1491–1750." *Journal of African History* 25, no. 2 (1984): 147–67.

"'I am the Subject of the King of Congo': African Ideology in the Haitian Revolution." *Journal of World History* 4 (1993): 181–214.

The Kingdom of Kongo: Civil War and Transition, 1641–1718. Madison: University of Wisconsin Press, 1983.

The Kongolese Saint Anthony: Dona Beatriz Kimpa Vita and the Antonian Movement, 1684–1706. Cambridge: Cambridge University Press, 1998.

"On the Trail of Voodoo: African Christianity in Africa and the Americas." *The Americas* 44 (1988): 261–78.

"The Slave Trade in Eighteenth Century Angola: Effects on Demographic Structures." *Canadian Journal of African Studies* 14, no. 3 (1980): 417–27.

Warfare in Atlantic Africa, 1500–1800. London: UCL Press, 1999.

Urquhart, Alvin W. *Patterns of Settlement and Subsistence in Southwestern Angola.* Washington, DC: National Academy Press, 1963.

Vail, Leroy, ed. *The Creation of Tribalism in Southern Africa.* Berkeley: University of California Press, 1989.

Vainfas, Ronaldo. "Guerra Declarada e Paz fingida na Restauração Portuguesa." *Tempo* 14, no. 27 (2009): 82–100.

Valladares, R. "El Brasil y las Índias espanolas durante la sublevacion (1640–68)." *Cuadernos de História Moderna* 14 (1993): 151–72.

Vansina, Jan. "Ambaca Society and the Slave Trade, c. 1760–1845." *Journal of African History* 46, no. 1 (2005): 1–27.

"Finding Food and the History of Precolonial Equatorial Africa: A Plea." *African Economic History* 7 (1970): 9–20.

"Foundation of the Kingdom of Kasanje." *Journal of African History* 4, no. 3 (1963): 355–74.

"Government in Kasai before the Lunda." *International Journal of African Historical Studies* 31, no. 1 (1998): 1–22.

How Societies are Born: Governance in West Central Africa before 1600. Charlottesville: University of Virginia Press, 2004.

Kingdoms of the Savanna: A History of Central African States until European Occupation. Madison: University of Wisconsin Press, 1970.

Living with Africa. Madison: University of Wisconsin Press, 1994.

"On Ravenstein's Edition of Battell's Adventures in Angola and Loango." *History in Africa* 34 (2007): 321–47.

Paths in the Rainforest: Toward a History of Political Tradition in Equatorial Africa. Madison: University of Wisconsin Press, 1990.

"Pathways of Political Development in Equatorial Africa and Neo-evolutionary Theory." In *Beyond Chiefdoms, Pathways to Complexity in Africa*, ed. Susan K. McIntosh. Cambridge: Cambridge University Press, 2005, 166–72.

"Portuguese vs. Kimbundu: Language Use in the Colony of Angola (1575–c. 1845)." *Bulletin des Séances/Mededelingen der Zittingen* 47 (2001–2003): 267–81.

Venâncio, José Carlos. *A Economia de Luanda e Hinterland no Século XVII: Um estudo de Sociologia Histórica.* Lisbon: Estampa, 1996.

Verger, Pierre. "The Influence of Africa on Brazil and of Brazil on Africa." *Journal of African History* 3 (1962): 49–67.

Flux et Reflux de la traite des Negres entre le Golfe de Benin et Bahia de Todos os Santos, du XVIIe au XIXe siècle. Paris: Mouton, 1968.

Viana, Larissa Moreira. *O Idioma da Mestiçagem: As Irmandades de Pardos na América Portuguesa.* Campinas: UNICAMP, 2007.

Viana, Luís Filho. *O Negro na Bahia.* São Paulo: Martins, 1976.

Wallerstein, Immanuel. *World-Systems Analysis: An Introduction.* Durham, NC: Duke University Press, 2004.

Bibliography

Westphal, E. O. J. "The Linguistic Prehistory of Southern Africa: Bush, Kwadi, Hottentot, and Bantu Linguistic Relationships." *Africa: Journal of the International African Institute* 33, no. 3 (1963): 237–65.

"A Reclassification of Southern African Non-Bantu Languages," *Journal of African Languages* 1 (1962): 1–18

Wheeler, Douglas L. "The Portuguese Army in Angola." *Journal of Modern African Studies* 7, no. 3 (1969): 425–39.

White, Hayden V. *Metahistory: The Historical Imagination in Nineteenth-century Europe*. Baltimore, MD: Johns Hopkins University Press, 1973.

White, Luise. *Speaking with Vampires: Rumor and History in Colonial Africa*. Berkeley: University of California Press, 2000.

Willis, Justin. "'Men on the Spot': Labor and the Colonial State in British East Africa: The Mombasa Water Supply, 1911–1917." *International Journal of African Historical Studies* 28, no. 1 (1995): 25–48.

Wright, Marcia. *Strategies of Slaves and Women: Life-Stories from East/Central Africa*. New York: Lilian Barber Press, 1993.

Xavier, Regina. *A Conquista da Liberdade: Libertos em Campinas na Segunda metade do Século XIX*. Campinas: UNICAMP, 1997.

Unpublished Dissertations and Papers

Bezerra, Nielson. "Mosaicos da Escravidão: Identidades Africanas e Conexões Atlânticas no Recôncavo da Guanabara (1780–1840)."PhD dissertation, Universidade Federal Fluminense, 2010.

Candido, Mariana P. "Enslaving Frontiers: Slavery, Trade and Identity in Benguela, 1780–1850." PhD dissertation, York University, 2006.

"Women, Concubinage and Slavery in Benguela, ca. 1750–1850." Paper presented at the Canadian African Studies Association, Ottawa, Canada, May 2010.

"Between Slavery and Freedom: the Displacement of West Central Africans to São Tomé after the end of the Transatlantic Slave Trade." Paper presented at the conference "Affranchis et Descendants d'affranchis dans le Monde Atlantique du XVe au XIXe siècle: Status Juridiques, Insertions Sociales et Identités Culturelles," Bordeaux, france, 2009.

Curto, José C. "Movers of Slaves: The Brazilian Community in Benguela (Angola), c. 1722–1832." Unpublished paper presented at the International Symposium "Angola on the Move: Transport Routes, Communications, and History," Berlin, November 2003.

Daddi Addoun, Yacine. "Abolition de l'esclavage en Algérie: 1816–1871." PhD dissertation, York University, 2010.

Ferreira, Roquinaldo Amaral. "Transforming Atlantic Slaving: Trade, Warfare and Territorial Control in Angola, 1650–1800." PhD dissertation, University of California, Los Angeles, 2003.

"Dos Sertões ao Atlântico: Tráfico Ilegal de Escravos e Comércio Lícito em Angola, 1830–1860." MA thesis, Universidade Federal do Rio de Janeiro, 1996.

Heywood, Linda M. "Production, Trade and Power The Political Economy of Central Angola, 1850–1930." PhD dissertation, Columbia University, New York, 1984.

Miguel, Contança do Nascimento da Rosa Ferreira de Ceita. "A Vida e a Obra do Portuense Silva Porto no reino Ovimbundu–Bié." MA thesis, Universidade do Porto, 2001.

Pantoja, Selma. "Encontros nas Terras de Além-Mar: os Espaços Urbanos do Rio de Janeiro, Luanda e Ilha de Moçambique na era da Ilustração." PhD dissertation, Universidade de São Paulo, 1994.

Ojo, Olatunji. "Warfare, Slavery and the Transformation of Eastern Yorubaland c.1820–1900." PhD dissertation, York University, 2003.

Rodrigues, Eugénia. "Portugueses e Africanos nos Rios de Sena: Os prazos da Coroa nos séculos XVII e XVIII." PhD dissertation, Universidade Nova de Lisboa, 2002.

Silva, Daniel B. Domingues da. "Crossroads: Slave Frontiers of Angola, c. 1780–1867." PhD dissertation, Emory University, 2011.

Sommerdyk, Stacey. "Trade and Merchant Community of the Loango Coast in the Eighteenth Century." PhD dissertation, Hull University, 2011

Vieira, Maria Eugénia Martins. "Registro de Cartas de Guia de Degredados para Angola (1712–1757), Análise de um Códice do Arquivo da Câmara Municipal de Luanda." BA major research paper, Universidade de Lisboa, 1966.

Index

Note to index: An n following a page number indicates a note on that page.

abolition of slave trade, 4, 111, 119, 167, 314
administrative reform, 103–4
adultery, enslavement as punishment for, 230–32
Africanization, 114–15, 124, 128–29
agency, 18
agricultural production
demographic data on, 84–85
by Ndombe, 84–85
slaves as fieldworkers, 318
at Viye, 304, 306, See also crops
agro-pastoralism, 8, 288
Albano, 221, 235
Albuquerque, Paulo Caetano de, 94, 96, 114
alcohol
cachaça, 107, 127, 143, 161, 170
and change in drinking habits, 170
slaves exchanged for, 284
as status marker, 232
Alencastro, António de, 303
Afonso VI (Portugal), 156–57
Almeida, Manoel Joaquim Pinto de, 111, 223
Amaral, Luís Santos, 285–86
Ambuila, Sumbe, 63
Ambundu, 242, 303
Ambundu, Nana, 249–50, 267
Anaquibenga, 251, 267

Andrade, Joaquim Vieira de, 181, 205–7
Andrade, José de, 136
Andrade, Luís Lopes de, 273
Angola
jagas in, 317
separation of Benguela from, 42–43
slave trade with Benguela, 153
as source of troops, 43
twentieth-century wars in, 23
Anguruca, 304
animal skins, 153, 189, 245
Anjos, António Lopes, 111
Aragão, Baltasar Rebelo de, 58
Aranha, Ana José, 269–70
Araújo, José Vieira de, 303
arimos (farms of local residents), 114, 115–16
Arouca, Manoel José da Costa, 171–73, 300
asiento of 1594, 20, 155
Assunção, Juliana Maria de, 137
Auzamba, 284
Azeredo, José Pinto de, 115

Baía das Vacas (Cattle Bay), 44
Bailundu wars, 262, 299
Bambe, 254
Bambo, 289–90
Bandeira, Francisco José, 220

baptism, 87, 128, 130
  in hinterland, 284–85
  importance of godparents, 120
  as not protection against enslavement,
    227
  spread to central plateau, 307–8
baracoons (holding cells), 111–12, 169
barbers, 63, 104
Barbosa, José de Oliveira, 217
Barriga, Manuel, 71
Barros, António José de, 132
Barros, Isabel de Araújo, 285
Barros, Maria Domingos de, 118, 225
Barros, Vicente de, 223
Battell, Andrew, 40, 57–58
Baumann, Hermann, 242
beads, 143, 170
  use in barter, 41
  use in fashion, 41
Beattie, Peter, 173–49
beeswax, 112, 121, 168, 174, 189, 216,
    265–66, 290, 306
Beltran, Luís, 157
Bembe, 95, 176, 294
Bengo, 212
Benguela
  administrative control of, 95
  commodities introduced into, 143
  Dutch attack and occupation of, 67–69
  early integration into Atlantic economy,
    189
  expansion of colonialism in, 140
  migrations after abolition of slave trade,
    22–23
  natural resources of, 66, 143
  overview of, 3–4
  population of, 6, 78, 107
  Portuguese regain from Dutch, 69–70
  relations with neighboring rulers, 56,
    65, 72
  relative autonomy of, 6–7
  sea/land routes to, 6
  separation from Angola, 42–43, 63.
    See also Benguela, colonization
    of; Benguela, early history of;
    Benguela-Velha
Benguela, colonization of, 70–76
  building of Nossa Senhora do Pópulo
    Church, 96–97
  consolidation of slave trade, 73
  defensive fortifications, 96
  development of trade, 72

  expansion of bureaucracy, 73
  foreign incursions into, 73–76
  military forces, 73
  territorial expansion, 72
Benguela, early history of
  beginnings of slave trade, 48
  conflicts, 38
  contact with Portugal, 33
  conversions to Catholicism, 34–35, 53,
    62–63
  development as port, 48–49
  early Portuguese settlement, 44–50
  expansion patterns, 57
  fortress established, 86, 91
  founding of, 44, 44n.43
  initial settlement, 61–62
  lack of military forces, 63
  local trade, 46–47, 87
  medical care, 63–64
  as part of "imagined community" of
    Portuguese empire, 43
  political organization, 35
  power vacuum after death of Cerveira
    Pereira, 64
  search for copper mines, 47–48
  slave exports before 1640s, 69
  slave population in, 121
  slave trade in, 86
  under Soares Lasso, 64–66
  treaties, differing views on, 38.
    See also jagas; Pereira, Manoel
    Cerveira; vassalage
Benguela, Francisco, 157
Benguela, José, 158–59
Benguela, Manoel Pires Jucele, 178
Benguela-Velha, 32
  abandonment of, 38, 40
  early accounts of, 40–42
  early expeditions to, 37–40
  redevelopment of interest in, 42–44
  style of dress in, 41
Berlin Conference, 313
Biasisongo (Bisansongo), 278
bilateral relationship, 68, 85, 106, 110,
    153, 173–49, 189–90, 321
Bimbe, 301
Birmingham, David, 146–47
blacksmiths, 116, 272, 318
Bongo, 180–81, 246, 265
Borges, Francisco Lourenço, 268
Botapouco, Elias António, 110
Botelho, Alexandre José, 216

Bourdieu, Pierre, 108, *121*, 207
Bowdich, Edward, 173–74
brasileiros, 70, 83–84, 165–66
Brazil
    abolition of slave trade by, 4, 314
    consolidation of relationship with
        Benguela, 110–11
    early presence of slaves from Benguela
        in, 315
    manioc flour imported from, 154
    Portuguese Crown exile to, 110
Brazilian party, 110–11
bribes, slaves used for political, 230
British, abolition of slave trade by, 167
Brito, Domingos Abreu de, 40, 42
Brooks, George, 252
building techniques, 46
bureaucracy, 91

Cabinda, 152
cachaça, 107, 127, 143, 161, 170
cacimbo (cooler, dry season), 44
Caconda, 89, 97, 171
    creolization at, 268–69
    filhos da terra at, 266–67
    officials, involvement in slave trade, 188
    population of, 1700–1850, 266–75
    slaves from area between, and coast, 197
    social classification at, 269
    social life at, 267–69
    and taxation, 179–80
    traders in, 271–73
    vulnerability to attacks, 210–12
    women in, 269–71. *See also* Caconda,
        first fortress; Caconda, second
        fortress 1760–1850
Caconda, first fortress, 245–57
    attacks on, 247–48
    attacks on area surrounding, 253–54
    Catholic church in, 267
    challenges to Portuguese claims in area
        of, 249–50
    changing dynamics among leaders on
        outskirts of, 249–50
    demographic concentration as cause of
        conflict at, 253
    destruction of, 246
    establishment of, 73, 246
    famine and drought at, 255–56
    food shortages at, 252
    hospital in, 267
    identity of persons in area of, 256

    increase in violence tied to slave trade
        at, 257
    location of, 247, 253
    rebuilding of, 246–47
    as rely station, 263
    slave raids in area of, 256
    vulnerability of, 249
Caconda, second fortress, 1760–1850,
        257–66
    agriculture at, 270, 271
    attacks on, 297
    Catholic church at, 258–60
    commercial activity at, 269–71
    continuance of slave trade after
        abolition, 265–66
    cooperation with coastal merchants,
        263–64
    creation of new vassals in area
        surrounding, 258
    creolization of, 311
    descriptions of, during 1850s, 265, 266
    diet at, 266, 270, 271
    effect on routes of *pombeiros*, 258
    effects of political transformation of
        interior on, 264–65
    extent of territory of, 260–61
    fluidity of identity at, 274
    importance during Bailundu Wars, 262
    location of, 257–58
    punishment of noncooperative headmen
        at, 260
    resistance to slave trade/colonialism at,
        264
    trader preference no to live at, 261
    and tribute, 289–90
Cadornega, António de Oliveira, 50,
        50n.68, 59, 150, 242, 279
Cafuxe, 59n.101
Calabar, 152
Calado, Jerônimo Rodriguez, 68
Caldas, Joaquim da Silva, 111
Camelo, Diogo Vaz, 82
Camlocoxo, 133
Candavita, 303
cannibals, 57, 58
Cão, Diogo, 37
Caparica, Luis Rodrigues, 225–26
Cape Town, 116–17
captain major, rank of, 106
captaincy system, 38–39
Cardoso, Bento Banha, 64
Cardoso, João, 68

Carneiro, Francisco Teixeira, 273
carpenters, 116, 272
Carpo, Pompílio Pompeu do, 305
Carvalho, António de, 119, 133
Carvalho, António Joaquim de, 226
Carvalho, Apolinário Francisco de, 205
Carvalho, João Teixeira de, 114, 131
Carvalho, José António de, 261
Carvalho, José de, 161
Carvalho, Mariana António de, 169
Castro Henriques, Isabel de, 60, 145
Castro, Martinho de Melo e, 180
Catholicism
    conversion to, 34–35, 53, 62–63
    spread into central plateau, 307–8
    spread into hinterland, 284–85
cattle, 44, 45–46n.48, 248, 298
Cattle Bay (Baía das Vacas), 8
Catumbela, 210, 290–91
Cavazzi, Antonio, 275–76
Cavazzi, Giovanni Antonio, 49
Cbo Kalunda, 48
cemeteries, for slaves, 119
census, first, 107
Chaves, João de Lemos, 273
Chaves, José de Lemos, 260, 272–73
children
    as captives, 180, 206, 209–10
    slaves, as domestic workers, 117
Childs, Gladwyn, 295
Christianity
    expectation of conversion to, 53
    religious conversion, 34–35, 43, 53, 62–63
    resistance to conversion to, 61
Ciluanji, Ngola, 294
classification categories, 318
    pardo, 267, 267n.78, 304
    soba/jaga, 54–55
    white/mixed race/black, 139
climate, 44, 80
cloth/clothing
    exchanged for slaves, 187
    imported, 143, 173, 189
Coelho, António José, 271–72
Coelho, João, 127
coerced labor *(trabalho forçado)*, 314
cohabitation, 80
Coimbra, Francisco José, 273, 303, 305
Colaço, Andrade, 201
colonial officials. *See* Portuguese officials, role in slaving activities

commodities, imported
    dependence on, 9, 189
    slaves exchanged for, 169–70.
        See also alcohol; cloth/clothing; gunpowder; textiles; weapons
Conceição, António Francisco da, 307
Conceição, Marcos Vaz da, 137
Conceição, Verônica Maria da, 268
concubinage, 119–20, 130, 131–32
Conspiracy of Minas Gerais (Inconfidência Mineira), 126
consumption, changes in, 14, 145
contraband, 74, 147
convicts. *See degredados* (convicts)
Cooper, Frederick, 43, 77–78
copper, 36
    exports, 112
    jewelry made from, 41, 153
    mining of, 40, 315
    uses of, 47
Cordeiro, Francisco José, 171–73
corn, 105, 270, 271
Corrêa, Elias Alexandre da Silva, 98, 175
Correia, João Nepomuceno, 228–29, 302, 305
cosmology, African, 115
Costa, António José da, 216
Costa, Diogo da, 37–38
Costa, Jacinto José da, 109
Coutinho, Francisco Inocêncio de Sousa, 151, 163–64, 179, 192, 247, 257–58, 285
Couto, Manuel Rodriguez de, 72
credit, 145, 162
creolization, 123–25
    in Caconda, 268–69
    in central plateau, 307–8
    as cultural adaptation, 52
    in hinterlands, 285
    significance of, 12–13
    as two-way process, 10–12, 138, 140
    in Viye, 302
criminals. *See degredados* (convicts)
crioulo, 119, 122–23, 211–12
crops
    from Americas, 266
    from Brazil, 105
    destruction of, 10, 77, 84, 96, 112
Cruz, Angelo da, 85
Cruz, Fortunato José da, 132
Cuba, 156, 157–58, 165, 315
cultural transformation, 7

gender relations, changes in, 7
new social groups, 7
overview of, 7, 10–12
transformed family composition, 7
Cunha, Lourenço Ferreira da, 301
Cunhaco, 303
Curtin, Philip, 143
Curto, José, 145, 170, 218
customs officials, 104

decentralization, 57, 97, 288
degredados (convicts)
administrative positions, 130–31,
316–17
banned from trade in interior, 205
exiles, 82, 96, 232
protection by colonial state, 128
role in settlement of Benguela, 77,
82–83, 92
Delgado, Ralph, 2, 22, 122, 151, 249, 298
demographic data
colonial use of, 108–9
gender imbalance, 80, 83, 308
use in analyses, 317. *See also* population;
quantitative analysis, shortcomings
of
Dias, Jill, 145
Dias, José Vieira, 126
diet, adoption of new foodstuffs, 14, 87,
266, 270, 271
disease, 86, 102–3
effect on European population, 77,
78–80, 109, 112
effect on local population, 109–10, 267
d'Oliveira, Aurélio, 167–68
Dombe Grande da Kizamba, 94, 109,
212–13, 282, 290, 297
domestics, slaves as, 115, 117, 119, 318
Domingues, José Joaquim, 225
donas, 12, 135, 318–19
Donde, 302–3
Douville, Jean Baptiste, 111, 167, 231–32
dress
of *filhos da terra*, 81
in highlands, 173–74
as identity marker, 243, 274
introduction of new styles, 101
of Luso-Africans, 234
as status marker, 129
style in Benguela-Velha, 41
drought, 94, 109, 112, 275
Dumbo, 306

Dutch, attack/occupation of Benguela,
67–70, 74–75, 157, 316

elites
colonial, 318
local, 82, 318–19, 321
political, 14, 258, 263–64
Elmina, fortress at, 3, 8, 75, 152
Eltis, David, 143–44
Endalanbondos, 40
England, incursions into Benguela, 75, 316
enlightenment ideas, spread of
entambe (wake), 128, 128n.139
environmental crises
as man-made, 94, 96, 275
responses to, 294
Ervedosa, Carlos, 239–40

Fage, J. D., 143
famine, 77, 84, 96, 211, 275
Faria, António de, 250, 267
feiras, 185, 189
Felipe II (Portugal), 40, 42, 150
Fende, 133, 179, 204–5, 265, 284, 296
Fernandes, António José, 299, 300
Fernandes, Mariana, 131
Ferreira, António Duarte, 273
Ferreira, Matias, 132
Ferreira, Pedro Nolasco, 103–4
Ferreira, Roquinaldo, 49, 115, 145, 157,
158, 192, 199, 207, 218, 227–28,
242
Figuereiro, Henrique de, 96
Filho, Clara Lobo, 273
filhos da terra, 316–17
administrative positions, 130–31,
316–17
banned from trade in interior, 205
in Caconda, 266–67
classification as, 138
demographic data, 11, 81–82, 83–84
dress of, 81
fines, enslavement as result of inability to
pay, 232
firearms. *See* weapons
fiscal reform, 103–4
fish, dried, 245
fishing, 32
Fonseca, Francisca da, 307–8
Fonseca, Francisco de Sousa da,
293–94
Fonseca, Leonor de Carvalho, 217

food, reliance of local population for, 50, 84

foragers, 287–88

Foucault, Michel, 23

Frade, João da Costa, 262

fragmentation, political, 279, 288–90, 319–20

France, incursions into Benguela, 74–76, 86, 160, 316

Freira, António, 125–26

Freitas, António de, 115

Fuente, Alejandro de la, 158

Fundi, 212

Furtado, Luis Candido, 199

Furtado, Pinheiro Machado, 277, 278

Galiano, José Velascao, 184

Gambos, 298, 303

Ganda, 180–81

Ganguela ethnic group (see Nganguela), 310

Ganguela, Maria, 157–58

Gaspar, Joanes, 23, 226

gender imbalance, 80, 83, 308

gift exchange, as source of slaves, 186–87

Gil, André Ferreira, 131

Glórias, Francisco António da, 171, 261

Góes, António Jorge de, 177

gold, 40, 159, 165

Gomes, André da Fonseca, 79

Gomes, Luzia Ferreira, 270–71

Gonçalves, Aguida, 107

Gonçalves, Bartolomeu, 300

Gonçalves, Jonuel, 148

Gonçalves, Manoel, 216

Gonçalves, Manoel Pereira, 136

Gouveia, Basílio António de, 304

Green, Toby, 10, 12–13, 52, 115, 147, 315

guerra preta (black troops), 62, 71, 98

Guimarães, António da Silva, 267

Guimbo, 282

Guindagongo, 98

Gumba, 263–64

gum-copal, 168, 174, 265–66

gunpowder
    imports, 143, 189
    role in expansion of violence, 74, 232, 282, 298
    slaves exchanged for, 187, 254, 284
    as tribute, 57
    use to seal alliances, 282

Guruca, 303

Gutelo, 262

Gypsies, 80n.177

Handa, 290

Hapsburgs, 39

Hawthorne, Walter, 10, 115

healers, African, 115, 139, 285

health care, 63–64
    barber role in, 63, 104
    hospitals, 3, 91, 101, 267

Heintze, Beatrix, 59, 145

Henrique (King Infante), 37

Heywood, Linda, 48, 115, 292, 296

Hiamba, 249–50

Hilton, Anne, 36, 59–60

hinterland, commercial networks in interior
    commodity exchange, 173–74
    luxury goods, 174–75
    traders living in highlands, 171–73

hinterlands, 275–92
    Catholicism, spread into, 284–85
    colonial officials, role in slaving activities in, 181–83
    consequences of pressures of slave trade on, 279–80
    consolidation of power of states in, 280–82, 283–84
    creolization, spread into, 285
    cultural transformation of, 14
    fluidity of geographic locations of states, 277–78, 279
    foundation of new settlements in, 285–86
    geographical proximity of states in, 282–83
    identity of inhabitants of, 19, 256, 308–9
    lack of Portuguese control of, 89–90
    migrations, effect on political reorganization in, 286, 287–89
    multiplicity of autonomous groups in, 286–88
    political fragmentation in, 279, 288–90
    political organization, seventeenth century, 275–77
    and positional succession, 281
    relationship with colonial power, 312
    rise/collapse of states in, 16–17, 278, 280, 287, 312, 319
    role in slave trade, 312
    slave trade effect on power balance in, 288–89
    survival of states in, 312
    and vassalage treaties, 1764, 284–85

violence, increase due to abolition
of slave trade, 290–91.
See also Caconda
Hombiangymbe, 41
hospitals, 3, 91, 101, 267
housing
building materials, 46, 96, 105, 106–7
European *vs.* slave, 121
Huila, 284
Humbe, 173, 186, 260, 288, 310
hunters and gatherers, 46, 208–9, 287, 288
hunting, 32, 232

Iberian Crowns, unification of, 39–40, 155
identity, 18–19
basis of shared, 240–41
fluidity of, 12–13, 242–44, 274, 302–3,
319–20
of inhabitants in hinterland, 19, 256,
308–9
of inhabitants of Benguela, 18–19
twentieth-century ethnic, 320
Ignácia, Francisca Joaquina, 223–24
Ignácio, Pedro Joaquim, 171, 261
Ika, 212
Imbangalas, 40–41, 58, 59, 196
Inconfidência Mineira (Conspiracy of
Minas Gerais), 126
Inikori, Joseph, 10, 143–44
inland progression of slaving frontier,
reassessment of, 194–95, 197, 209,
235–36, 319
inquisidor da liberdade (freedom
inquisitor), 215–16, 217, 219
interior. *See* Caconda; hinterlands
intermarriage. *See* mixed marriage
internal raids, 228–29
ivory, 40, 112, 121, 189, 245, 290
amount of, 72
control of highland market for, 216
as impetus for reoccupation of
Benguela, 40
revocation of trade monopoly on,
168, 290
tusks, 72, 87, 156–57, 168, 174
Viye trade in, 306

jaga(s), 36–37
as cannibals, 57n.91, 203
as classification category, 54–55, 74
geographical location of, 59n.101
meaning of term, 57–61, 317
Jau people, 208

jewelry
copper, 41, 315
manufacture of, 50
pau de cacongo (aromatic wood), 66
as wealth marker, 129
Jews, 80n.177
João IV (Portugal), 70
Joint Crowns, 39–40, 156
end of, 70
José I (Portugal), 163
judicial cases, and enslavement, 199, 207
judicial reform, 103–4
judicial system, as mechanism of
enslavement, 197, 198
juizes de fora, 104
"just war"
against cannibals, 57
as enslavement mechanism, 65, 200–2,
203–4
legality of, 56, 317
under Soares Lasso, 65

Kabalango, 306
Kabanda, 303
Kabiunda, 99
Kabongo, 280–81
Kabunda, 98, 99
Kahumba, 253–54
Kajungo, 303–4
Kakamgue, 302–3
Kakiongo, 303
Kakoko, 97
Kakombao, 181
Kakonda
attacks against, 85, 162, 267
continued existence under Portuguese,
240, 311–12
decline of, 262
dependants of, 73
resistance to Portuguese, 72, 74, 245–46
sources of security in, 240
subjugation of, 65
vassalage of, 99, 246, 249
Kalukembe
attacks on, 95
changing alliances of, 208, 213
consolidation of power of, 283–84
distance from Caconda, 265
kidnapping of white woman, 264
Negrão at, 282
raids on Ndombe, 209, 221, 289
refusal to pay tribute, 289–90
revenge attack on, 207–8

Kalukembe (*cont.*)
  rise of, 262
  traders living at, 171, 221, 261
Kalunda, Cbo, 48
Kalunga, Wambu, 294
Kambamba, 65, 65n.123
Kambibe, 284
Kambuinda, 251, 284
Kambundu, 295
Kamburo, 171, 261, 265
Kamessi, 302–3
Kananoja, Kalle, 115
Kandumbo, 284
Kangenge, 299
Kangombe, 55n.85, 55–56
Kanhete, 306
Kanyangula, Olosoma, 134
Kapango, 302–3
Kapembe, 212–13
Kapiango, 97
Kapoko, 298
Kapollo, 303
Kapumba, 303–4
Karasch, Mary, 309
Kasanje, 245
Katala, 284
Katira, 74, 280, 299
Katumbela, 231
Kauco, 289–90
Kayoquela, 280
Kengue, 299
Khoe speakers, 239–40, 286–87
Kiaka, 180–81, 212, 295
Kiambela, 95–96, 201–2
Kibonga, 284, 289–90
Kibula, 300
Kicalla, 295
kicanzo, 299
kidnapping, 214–27
  administrative response to, 214–16
  colonial legislation on, 222–24, 227
  community members as agents of,
    221–22
  demand for slaves as impetus for,
    220–21, 225–26
  of free black soldiers, 222, 223
  kin as agents of, 220–21, 223
  legality of, challenges to, 222, 223, 227
  of Luso-Africans, 217, 218–19, 227,
    233–35
  and pawnship, 272
  prohibition on, 214

  of relative of African ruler, 225–26
  resistance to, 219
  social contacts as instrumental in
    resisting, 220, 221
  suits for freedom, 215
  of traders, 218–19, 227
  vulnerability of free persons, 197, 212,
    225
Kikicocumulinda, 303–4
Kikombo, 277, 280
Kilengues, 176, 294
Kilumata (Quitumata/Quitomata), 279,
    294
Kimbarandongo, 301
Kimboas, 231
Kimbundu, 279
Kimungo, 289–90
Kingolo, 262, 282–84, 289–90
Kingula, 306
Kiombela, 252, 284
Kipaka, 300
Kipeio, 210–12, 263, 285, 296–97
Kipende, 306
Kipia, 265n.65, 284, 287
Kipungo, 213, 284, 294, 298
Kipupire, 231, 306
Kisange (Quisange), 278, 300
Kissama, 6, 61, 66–67, 151–52, 316
Kitata
  attacks on, 298
  attacks on traders, 212
  consolidation of power of, 283–84
  distance from Caconda, 265
  effects of abolition of slave trade
    on, 290
  kidnapping of white woman, 264
  and migrations, 264–65
  Negrão at, 282–83
  raids on Ndombe, 209, 289
  raids on rulers around Caconda
    fortress, 289
  rise of, 262
  spread of Catholicism in, 284–85
  traders living at, 171, 221, 261
  vassalage of, 284
Kitata, Ngando ya, 251
Kitete, 210–12, 263, 289, 290, 296–97
Kitumata, 283–84
Kitumbela, 46, 56–57, 65
Kitungo, 303
Kitushe, 299
Kizamba, 65, 94

Kizemba, 178
Kongo, 8, 38, 60
    enslavement legislation in, 228
    enslavement of soldiers of, 230
    jagas in, 59–60, 317
    nzimbu shells as currency in, 36, 48, 153
    slaves as gift offerings in, 186–87
    as source of troops, 43
!Kung, 287
Kungo, 297
Kwadi (Mocoroca), 286–88
Kwandu, 46, 57, 208–9, 239–40, 288, 289

Lacerda e Almeida, Francisco José de,
    294–95
ladinos, 119
Lago, João Pereira do, 85
Lagos, 112, 116–17, 275
lançados, 211, 218
language use, 120–21, 137–38
Lasso, Lopo Soares, 64–66, 131, 176
Leal, João da Fonseca, 261, 285
legal code, 317
legal pluralism, 224
legality, slave trade effect on notions of,
    225
legitimacy
    of slavery and slave trade, 108, 224, 317
    of war *See* (just war)
Leiria, João de Alvelos, 183, 219–20
Leitão, Manuel de Magalhães, 67
Leite, Sebastião de Abreu, 296
Lemos, Nicolau de, 66, 68
Lencastre, António de, 179–80, 182, 204,
    306
libambos (slave coffles), 73, 168, 174, 188,
    255, 260, 263
Liberal Wars, 111
Libolo, 59n.101, 73
Lima, José Joaquim Lopes de, 102
Lima, Roque Vieira de, 82
Lisboa, António da Silva, 304
Lisboa, Catarina Pereira, 135, 263–64
literacy, 298, 300
Lombimbe, 294
Lovejoy, Paul, 10, 143–44, 193
Luanda, 275
    business-oriented unions in, 134–37
    difficulty of sailing to, 39, 151
    exile of criminals to Benguela, 82, 96
    population increase, 112
    and slave trade, 152, 162–63

slave trade, estimates of size of, 152
    trade with Benguela, 153
Lubando, 213
Luceque, 95, 213, 253–55, 284, 289–90
Luculo, 301
Luís, António Manuel, 305
Lumbo, 183, 300
Lumbombe, 288
Luso-Africans, 122–39
    and British anti-slavery patrols, 137
    in Caconda, 268–69
    and concubinage, 130, 131–32
    criminal exiles, 125–26
    and cultural exchange, 128
    education of children in Brazil, 127–28
    filhos da terra, 130–31
    foreign residents, 132
    itinerant traders from Brazil, 127
    kidnapping of, 197, 212
    language issues, 137–38
    local women as commercial partners for,
        134–37
    and marriage, 128–29
    and marriage with daughters of rulers,
        133–34
    military personnel from Brazil, 126
    political exiles, 126
    and slave trade, 92–94, 126–27
    social classification of, 11, 138–39
    social connections through marriage,
        136–37
    social regulations as barriers to,
        129–30
    vulnerability to enslavement, 210–11

Magalhães, Jacques de, 67
Magalhães, Joana de, 271
Magalhães, José Rodrigues, 127–28
Magalhães, Pedro José Correia de Quevedo
    Homem e, 106
Magalhães, Vitória de, 268
Magyar, László, 134, 231, 279, 302, 303,
    306
Maia, Vítor dos Santos, 273
Malanka, 97, 289–90
malaria, 62, 77, 80, 109–10, 267
Malheiro, Manuel Eleutério, 169
Mani Berro, 65
manioc, 84–85, 105, 154, 169–70
Manning, Patrick, 145
Manoel, Jacome, 261, 284–85
manumission, 118, 120, 127, 192

Maranhão, Companhia Geral do Grão
    Pará e, 161–62
Margarido, Alfredo, 60
marine route, 316
marriage
    attempt to make mandatory, 100
    of daughters of important rulers, 133–34
    and Luso-Africans, 128–29
    mixed, 93–94, 128–29, 139, 140
    social connections through, 136–37
Martin, Phyllis, 145
Massak, Luzia, 134
Matamba, 245
matrilineal society, slave/free distinction
    in, 192
Mbailundu, 171, 298–302
    alliance with Benguela, 300–2
    attacks on, 183–84, 210
    Bailundu Wars, 262
    centralization of, 299–300
    commodities, access to, 300, 301
    commodities, traded for slaves in, 173
    continued existence under Portuguese,
        240
    enslavement of Luso-African by soba
        of, 217
    founding of, 295, 298
    freeing of enslaved persons in, 216
    jagas in, 59n.101
    migrations to, 306
    military/political power of, 299–300
    population of, 302
    raids to increase power/prestige of ruler,
        229
    sources of security in, 240
    subjugation by colonial state, 301
    tributaries of, 299
    tribute as source of slaves, 187–88
    vassalage of, 284, 299, 301
    white traders at, 171–73
McCulloch, Merran, 308
measles, 109–10
mechanisms of enslavement
    capture along coast, 194–95, 197, 209,
        235–36, 319
    debt, 197, 222, 223–24, 229–30
    free blacks, vulnerability to, 191–94
    judicial cases, 199, 207
    judicial system, 197, 198
    "just war" *See* ("just war")
    kidnapping *See* (kidnapping)
    legal pluralism, 234

military-administrative sites,
    vulnerability to, 213
pressure of trans-Atlantic commerce on,
    210–12
protections against, 203, 317
raids by autonomous highland warlords,
    196–97
raids by Portuguese forces, 196, 197
raids by rulers on one another, 207–8
religious belief as justification for war,
    203–4
royal fifth as justification for, 204–5
tribute *See* (tribute)
trickery, 216, 221
and vassals, 204–7, 208–9
warfare and raids, 195, 199–214
witchcraft as, 230, 231
women and children, vulnerability to,
    209–10
meconnaissance, 121n.113
Mello, José da Assunção de, 166
Melo, João Rodrigues de Sá e, 182–83
Melo, Miguel António de, 182, 201
Melo, Pedro Neto de, 47n.57
men on the spot, 39n.26, 92
    persistence in slave trade after
        abolishment, 111–12
    relative autonomy of, 39
Mendes, António, 33, 147, 301, 315
Mendes, Joana, 169
Mendes, Manuel Ruiz, 304
Mendonca, Francisco Xavier de, 101–2
Meneses, Joaquim José de Andrade e
    Silva, 127
Meneses, José Vieira, 291
Menezes, Luís César de, 249–50
Mesquita, António José Pimental de
    Castro e, 106
migration
    Atlantic commerce effect on, 239–40
    from Benguela after abolition of slavery,
        22–23
    effect of pressure of slave trade on,
        246–47, 250, 253–54, 311
    and political reorganization in
        hinterlands, 286, 287–89
    as response to environmental
        crises, 294
Miller, Joseph, 12, 60, 77, 84, 99, 144–45,
    194–95, 202–3, 227, 238–39,
    240–41
Minas Gerais, 75, 126, 159, 165

mining in New World, effect on demand for slaves, 156
Minuio, 303
Mipua, 284
Miranda Henriques, Rodrigo de, 79
Mixed Commission, 309
mixed marriage, 93–94, 128–29, 139, 140, 283
mixed race, 130, 138–39
Moçâmedes, 290
Moçâmedes, Barão de, 299
Molundo, 65, 75–76
Monguia, 301
Moquimbas, 46
Moraes, Francisco Pedro de, 183, 226, 291, 297
mortality
    among Europeans, 11, 103
    among local population, 103
    among slaves, 103
    slave trade effect on notions of, 225
Mosanjeracata, 284
Moutinho, Maria Gomes, 220
mucano tribunal, 12, 214–15, 234
Muene Chele, 212–13
Muene Kalunga, 212–13
Muene Kizamba, 212–13
Muene Mama, 212–13
Mulundo, 98
Munda, 289
Munhemba, 303–4
Municipal Council, 104
murder
    enslavement as punishment for, 232
    of own slave, 232

naming practices, 54–56, 87, 317
Nano, 242–43
Napoleanic Wars, 110
Nascimento, Manuel do, 304
natural resources, revocation of trade monopoly on, 290
Ndombe
    and agricultural production, 84–85
    in Benguela, 94
    linguistic group of, 45n.45
    and pastoralism, 94
    raids by, 288, 289
    raids on, 209, 221, 289
    and slave trade, 196
    and trade with Benguela, 94
Ndongo, 38, 60

Ndulu, 304
Negrão, Domingos da Fonseca, 98, 281, 282–83, 303
Neves, Cristiana das, 137
Ngalangue, 171, 183–84, 210, 211, 229, 261, 307–8
ngangas (local healers), 285
Nganguela, 174, 312
Ngola, 8
Ngola Jimbo, 76, 280–81
Ngola people, 8
Ngombe, meaning of, 55n.85
Nguela, 213
Nóbrega, José da, 201–2, 251–52
Nogueira, José António, 173
Nojosa, Manoel de, 85
Noronha, António Manoel de, 185
Nossa Senhora da Conceição de Caconda church, 267
Nossa Senhora da Misericórdia hospital, 3
Nossa Senhora do Pópulo Church, 3, 96–97, 100–1
Novais, Paulo Dias de, 37
Nunes, João, 127, 166
Nyaneka, 310
nzimbu shells (Kongon currency), 36, 48, 153

Oliveira, António Francisco de, 161
Oliveira, Apolinário Fernandes de, 268
Oliveira, Francisca Teresa de, 307
Oliveira, Joaquim Aurélio de, 212, 223–24
Oliveira, Manoel, 183
ombaka, meaning of, 31–32
Ondura, 299
oral tradition, 22–23, 31, 251, 298, 304, 309
orchilla weed, 168, 265–66
Ordenações Filipinas, 317
original freedom, 204, 221
ostrich plumes, 66, 72
Ouidah, 112, 116–17, 152, 275
Overseas Council *(Conselho Ultramarino)*, 79, 130, 161, 162–63, 205, 214, 215
Ovimbundu, 16, 242–43, 279, 292–93, 302, 308–10, 312, 320.
    See also Mbailundu; Viye; Wambu

Pacheco, Francisca da Silveira, 101
Pais, Henrique, 35
palm oil, 84, 84n.187, 112

Pantoja, Pedro Leão de Aguilar, 126
paper, 143, 173, 187, 189, 300
Paraíba, 161–62
pardo classification, 267, 267n.78, 304
pastoralism, 94, 287–88
   agro-pastoralism, 8, 288
Patterson, Orlando, 18, 219
pau a pique (building technique), 46
pau de cacongo (aromatic wood), 66
pawnship, 272
Pedro II (Portugal), 247
Peixoto, Lopes, 37, 38
Pereira, Alberto António, 130
Pereira, José dos Santos, 191–92
Pereira, Manoel Cerveira, 8
   colonial Portuguese revolts
      against, 63
   conflict with Angola, 63
   conquest of Benguela, 175
   as governor/conqueror of Benguela,
      42–44
   and Kangombe, 55–56
   lack of military forces under, 63
   on New Christians, 80
   request for priest, 81
   sends slaves to Benguela, 150
Pereira, Paulo, 71
Peres, Manuel, 305
Peringue
   as both state and ruler, 8n.7
   classification of ruler as jaga/soba, 54
   grants Portuguese right to trade, 8
   migrations of, 45–46, 280
   provides troops to Portuguese, 98
   reaction to arrival of Portuguese, 45–46
   requests for asylum in after French
      attacks, 76
   survival of, 240
   vassal sobas in, 65
Pernambuco, 85
Peru, 155, 156, 157, 158, 315
Pestana, Caetano, 283
Pimentel, Belchior Raposo, 97, 130–31
Pinheiro, Vicente Borges, 74
Pinto, João José, 132
Pinto, Paulo Jorge de Souza, 59
Pirua, 284
plumes, 66, 72, 143, 189
plunder, 50–51, 289
political elites, 14, 258, 263–64
political fragmentation, 279, 288–90,
   319–20

political succession, 228–29
polygamy, 128, 308
   female, 131
pombeiros (itinerant traders), 74n.156
   attacks on, 212, 246, 251, 304
   enslavement of, 218–19
   new styles of dress adopted by, 101
   restrictions on, 174, 185, 205
   seizure of free blacks by, 216–17
   and slave trade, 162, 168–69
population
   of Benguela, 6, 78, 107
   decrease in Benguela, 112–13
   increase in Lagos, 112
   increase in Luanda, 112
   increase in slave, 119, 120–21
   of Mbailundu, 302
   slave, in Benguela, 121
   of Viye, 306
porters
   seizure of free black, 216–17
   slaves as, 116, 117–18, 318
Porto Amboim, 32
Porto Ribeiro, Jorge do, 171, 261
Portuguese language
   as lingua franca, 121, 138
   spread of, 13
Portuguese officials, role in slaving
      activities, 175–85, 317–18
   attempts at nonviolent resolution of
      disputes, 183
   black troops under leadership of,
      179–80
   captives from wars organized by,
      175–77, 179–80
   and end of slave trade, 184–85
   and increase in violence, 178–79,
      180–84
   misconduct of, 179, 180–83, 189–90
   relative autonomy of, 6–7
   strategies to prevent involvement in
      hinterland, 181–83
   and taxation, 179
positional succession, 281
preta do sertão (black woman from
      hinterland), 268
preta gentio (heathen black woman), 268
Principe, 75
prisoners of war. See war captives
public market (terreiro público), 105–6,
   115–16
Pulumba, 306

quantitative analysis, shortcomings of, 1,
    14, 16, 69, 108, 147, 198, 317
Queirós, António José de, 268
Quilengues, 137, 191–92, 279
    attacks by, 205–7
    attacks on, 213, 288, 289
    initial settlement, 44–45
    linguistic group of, 45n.45
    presidio of, 282
Quimbundu, 242, 279
Quintas, Manoel Pires das, 102
quitandeiras, 105
Quitata, 285–86

ransom, 191, 193, 222, 225
Regimento (government orders), 33
Reis, Francisco Xavier do, 127
Reis, Justiniano José dos, 111, 225–26
religion
    African practices, 115
    connection with colonial order, 247–48.
        See also baptism; Catholicism;
        Christianity
Remédio, Rita Maria dos, 136–37
Rio de Janeiro, 70, 275
    early accounts of Benguela slaves in, 159
    exile of Crown to, 110–11, 166
    French attacks on, 75
    as port of entry, 190
    and slave trade, 110–11, 161–62, 165
    sugar cane exports, 161
Rocha, Manoel da, 247
Rocha, Vitorino da, 307
Rodney, Walter, 10, 143, 252
Rodrigues, António José, 171
Rodrigues, Francisco Gonçalves, 307–8
Rodrigues, Francisco José de Oliveira, 307
Rodriguez, António, 68
Rosário, António do, 132
royal fifth, 179, 180, 184, 200–1, 251
rubber, 168, 265–66
runaway slaves, 55–56, 72, 125–26,
    253–54

Sá, Domingos Rodrigues de, 284
Sá, Inácio Rodrigues de, 283
Sá, Manoel A., 171–73
Sá, Salvador Correia de, 69–70, 71
Sacramento, António Leal do, 221–22
sailors, slaves as, 115, 119, 318
Saldanha, Bento Teixeira, 177
salt, 66–67, 104, 114, 153, 245

Salvador, 127, 190, 275
Sambo, 294
Sambu, 211
Santa Ana, Joaquim de, 272
Santa Casa da Misericórida hospital, 91,
    101
Santo, Rosa de Espírito, 272–73
Santos, Lourença, 270
Santos, Manoel Isidoro dos, 166
Santos, Manuel de Brito, 300
Santos, Marcelina Francisca dos, 136–37
São Felipe de Benguela, 44–45
São Tomé, 75, 314
Schwartz, Stuart, 47
Selema, António de Abreu, 71
senzalas, 105, 106–7, 115–16
servants, 53, 115, 117, 217
sexual abuse, 42, 122
shoemakers, 116, 272
Silva, Aguida Gonçalves da, 135
Silva, Álvaro de Barros e, 95–96, 203
Silva, Felipe de, 132
Silva, Hipólito Ferreira da, 166
Silva, Luis Lobo da, 248
Silva, Manoel da, 161
Silva, Manuel Francisco da, 133
Silva, Miguel António da, 282
Silva, Nuno Joaquim Pereira e, 107
Silva Porto, Antonio, 134, 139, 174, 231,
    232, 233, 303, 305, 306
Silva, Rita da, 285
silver, 40, 42
silver mining, in New World, 155, 315
Simões, Caetano, 304
Siqueira, Valentim Muniz de, 127
skin color, importance in defining roles, 92
slave coffles *(libambos)*, 73, 168, 174, 188,
    255, 260, 263
slave society, development of, 113–22
    cultural exchange, 114–15
    domestic workers, 115, 117, 119, 318
    increase in population, 119, 120–21
    local employment, 113–14, 115–16
    male skilled slaves, 118–19
    ownership as sign of prestige/wealth,
        117
    porters, 116, 117–18
slave trade
    abolition of, 4, 111, 119, 167, 314
    abolition of, persistence after, 111–12,
        169, 314
    commercial networks in interior, 171–75

slave trade (*cont.*)
  early trade, 154–60
  effects into twentieth century, 90
  effects of abolition of, 290
  estimates of size of, 152, 189
  expansion of, 7, 13–17
  impact on African society, 7, 8–10
  location of Benguela, importance in,
    151–52
  organization of, 160–70
  overview of, 7–8, 17–19
  Portuguese agents, role in slaving
    activities, 175–85
  seventeenth century, 150–51, 155,
    156–59
  slave ships, overloading, 167
  slave voyage, length of as favorable,
    152–53
  and violence *See* (violence)
slavery, reassessment of inland progression
  of slavery, 194–95, 197, 209,
    235–36, 319
smallpox, 103, 109–10, 112
Smallwood, Stephanie, 235
smuggling, 42, 73, 150, 160, 165
sobados, 35, 230–32
soba(s), 23, 35n.10, 53, 54–55
Sobral, José Dias de, 225–26
social death, slavery as, 18, 120, 219
Sokoval
  attacks on, 181, 205–7
  centralization in, 287
  changing alliances of, 208
  power of, 280–82, 283–84
  resistance to Portuguese, 74
  vassalage treaty, 284
soldiers
  enslavement in Kongo, 230
  guerra preta, 62, 71, 98
  kidnapping of free black, 222, 223
  reliance of local population for, 50, 179
Songo, 302
Sotomaior, Luis Leitão, 278, 279
Sousa, Fernão de, 49, 66–67, 175
Sousa, José de, 118
Sousa, Manoel Francisco de, 306
Sousa, Maria José da Silveira, 130
Souza, António de Almeida e, 161
Souza, António Rebello de Andrade
  Vasconcelos e, 119
Souza, Crispim de Silveira e, 166
Spanish colonies, 155–56

stamps, 173, 187
street vendors, 105–6, 318
Subrahmanyam, Sanjay, 62
sugar cane alcohol, 143
sugar industry
  effect on slave trade, 156, 165
  use of copper in, 47
Sweet, James, 52, 123
swords, 173, 187
syncretic, 128

tailors, 272
Tams, George, 102, 112, 121, 169
taverns, 107, 127
Távora, Francisco da, 246
taxes
  changes in system, 163
  in kind, 304
  royal fifth, 179, 180, 184, 200–1, 251
  from sale of slaves, 73
  from salt production, 104
  slaves used as payment for, 230
  tax invasion, 163–64
  used to pay military, 155
Teixeira, Francisco, 137
Teixeira, José da Silva, 119
Teixeira, Manoel, 296
tendala (translator), 63, 65, 68
terreiro público (public market), 105–6,
  115–16
textiles, 14, 173–74, 284
  Asian, 143, 189
  slaves exchanged for, 187, 284
  as status marker, 232
Thorton, John, 48, 99, 115, 144, 192,
  238–39, 296
Tinde, 284
tools, 32, 315
trabalho forçado (coerced labor), 314
trade
  in commodities, 143, 153, 173, 229
  development in early Benguela, 46–47,
    72
  internal, 87, 153–54
  revocation of monopoly on, 168, 290
  transformation of local, 7.
    See also alcohol; ivory; textiles
traders. *See pombeiros* (itinerant traders)
trading post *(feitoria)*, 155, 158
Trans-Atlantic Slave Trade Database, 147,
  149, 152, 315
treason, as mechanism for slavery, 230

treaties with Portuguese, consequences
of, 9
Treaty of Tordesilla, 39
tribute
as mechanism of enslavement, 195
payment by traders, 55
refusal to pay, 289–90
slaves as payment, 52, 185–88, 230
weapons as, 57
trickery, 216, 221
Trumba, 303

Umbundu language, 28–29, 31, 35, 92–93,
124, 138
discouraging use of, 137–38
as *lingua franca*, 121, 138
prohibition against, 137–38
Umbundu speakers, as not unified state,
214
undar, 12, 51–52, 301
Upper Guinea, 211, 218

Valdez, Francisco, 266
Valente, António José, 127, 164
Valente, Paulo, 82
Van Dunem, Simão, 85
Van Dunen, Baltasar, 156
Vansina, Jan, 16, 59, 192, 195, 241, 242,
251, 320–21
Vasconcelos, Alexandre Botelho de, 181
Vasconcelos, António de, 102
Vasconcelos, João da Cunha, 126
Vasconcelos, José Maria Doutel de Almeida
Machado, 106
Vasconcelos, Luis Mendes de, 63
Vasconcelos, Manoel de Almeida e,
151–52, 261–62
vassalage
colonial expansion as reason for,
50–61
in hinterlands, 1764, 258, 284–85
protection as reason for, 8–9, 53, 76,
86–87
resistance to, 12
undar ceremony, 12, 51–52
vassals
and mechanisms of enslavement, 204–7,
208–9
obligations of, 49–50, 52–53
as partners, 86
Vatalla, 290
Vieira, Manoel Lourenço, 284, 285

Vila Viçosa, 284
violence
consolidation of, 91
due to abolition of slave trade,
290–91
effect on defensive measures, 248
effect on political stability, 9–10
expansion, role of gunpowder/weapons
in, 57, 74, 77, 232, 248, 282, 298
expansion, of, due to slave trade, 17–18,
208, 220, 257, 314
as means of social control, 107–8
relationship with power, 15–16
use by colonial officials, 175–77, 178–79
use for social control, 107–8
against women, 80, 122
Viye, 171, 302–6
adultery, punishment of, 231
agriculture at, 304, 306
creolization in, 302
founding of, 302–3, 312
identity, fluidity of, 302–3
imported commodities in, 173
merchants in, 306
political alliances, fluidity of, 306
political marriage in, 134
political succession in, 228–29
population of, 306
raids against, 183–84
relative autonomy of, 305
slaves as payment to settle problems in,
229, 230
sources of security in, 240
taxation in, 304
trade at, 304–5, 306
tributaries of, 303, 306

Wambu, 293–98
as alternate trade route, 295–96
and commodities trade, 173, 229
consolidation/survival of, 240
military/political power of, 296–98
raids against, 183–84
resistance against colonial power,
210–12, 293–94, 297
slave raids by, 212, 263
slave raids to increase ruler power/
prestige, 229
and trade relations, 298
tributaries of, 295
war captives, 20, 154, 155–56, 189
wax. *See* beeswax

weapons
  imports, 189
  role in expansion of violence, 57, 74, 77,
    248, 282, 298
  slaves exchanged for, 187, 254
  as tribute, 57
  use to seal alliances, 282
weddings
  Catholic, 128, 139
  customary, 139. *See also* marriage
White, Hayden, 24
wild animals, trade in, 153
witchcraft, as mechanism for slavery,
  230, 231
women
  and agriculture, 270, 271
  and concubinage, 130, 131–32
  as domestic workers, 115, 117, 119, 318
  donas, 12, 135, 318–19

  economic roles of, 105, 107, 134–37,
    140, 318–19
  enslavement of, 180, 209–10
  enslavement of Luso-African, 217
  as intermediaries, 135, 136–37, 140
  lack of European in Benguela, 132–33,
    137
  role in slave trade, 269–70
  violence against, 80, 122.
    See also marriage

Xaucuri, 191

yellow fever, 77, 80, 103, 109–10, 267

Zamba, 97
Zenze, 59n.101
Zimba, 60
Zucchelli, Antonio, 74–75, 80, 150, 160

BOOKS IN THIS SERIES

1 *City Politics: A Study of Léopoldville, 1962–63*, J. S. La Fontaine
2 *Studies in Rural Capitalism in West Africa*, Polly Hill
3 *Land Policy in Buganda*, Henry W. West
4 *The Nigerian Military: A Sociological Analysis of Authority and Revolt, 1960–67*, Robin Luckham
5 *The Ghanaian Factory Worker: Industrial Man in Africa*, Margaret Peil
6 *Labour in the South African Gold Mines*, Francis Wilson
7 *The Price of Liberty: Personality and Politics in Colonial Nigeria*, Kenneth W. J. Post and George D. Jenkins
8 *Subsistence to Commercial Farming in Present Day Buganda: An Economic and Anthropological Survey*, Audrey I. Richards, Fort Sturrock, and Jean M. Fortt (eds.)
9 *Dependence and Opportunity: Political Change in Ahafo*, John Dunn and A. F. Robertson
10 *African Railwaymen: Solidarity and Opposition in an East African Labour Force*, R. D. Grillo
11 *Islam and Tribal Art in West Africa*, René A. Bravmann
12 *Modern and Traditional Elites in the Politics of Lagos*, P. D. Cole
13 *Asante in the Nineteenth Century: The Structure and Evolution of a Political Order*, Ivor Wilks
14 *Culture, Tradition and Society in the West African Novel*, Emmanuel Obiechina
15 *Saints and Politicians*, Donald B. Cruise O'Brien
16 *The Lions of Dagbon: Political Change in Northern Ghana*, Martin Staniland
17 *Politics of Decolonization: Kenya Europeans and the Land Issue 1960–1965*, Gary B. Wasserman
18 *Muslim Brotherhoods in Nineteenth-Century Africa*, B. G. Martin
19 *Warfare in the Sokoto Caliphate: Historical and Sociological Perspectives*, Joseph P. Smaldone
20 *Liberia and Sierra Leone: An Essay in Comparative Politics*, Christopher Clapham
21 *Adam Kok's Griquas: A Study in the Development of Stratification in South Africa*, Robert Ross
22 *Class, Power and Ideology in Ghana: The Railwaymen of Sekondi*, Richard Jeffries
23 *West African States: Failure and Promise*, John Dunn (ed.)

24 *Afrikaners of the Kalahari: White Minority in a Black State*, Margo Russell and Martin Russell

25 *A Modern History of Tanganyika*, John Iliffe

26 *A History of African Christianity 1950–1975*, Adrian Hastings

27 *Slaves, Peasants and Capitalists in Southern Angola, 1840–1926*, W. G. Clarence-Smith

28 *The Hidden Hippopotamus: Reappraised in African History: The Early Colonial Experience in Western Zambia*, Gwyn Prins

29 *Families Divided: The Impact of Migrant Labour in Lesotho*, Colin Murray

30 *Slavery, Colonialism and Economic Growth in Dahomey, 1640–1960*, Patrick Manning

31 *Kings, Commoners and Concessionaires: The Evolution and Dissolution of the Nineteenth-Century Swazi State*, Philip Bonner

32 *Oral Poetry and Somali Nationalism: The Case of Sayid Mahammad 'Abdille Hasan*, Said S. Samatar

33 *The Political Economy of Pondoland 1860–1930*, William Beinart

34 *Volkskapitalisme: Class, Capital and Ideology in the Development of Afrikaner Nationalism, 1934–1948*, Dan O'Meara

35 *The Settler Economies: Studies in the Economic History of Kenya and Rhodesia 1900–1963*, Paul Mosley

36 *Transformations in Slavery: A History of Slavery in Africa*, Paul E. Lovejoy

37 *Amilcar Cabral: Revolutionary Leadership and People's War*, Patrick Chabal

38 *Essays on the Political Economy of Rural Africa*, Robert H. Bates

39 *Ijeshas and Nigerians: The Incorporation of a Yoruba Kingdom, 1890s–1970s*, J. D. Y. Peel

40 *Black People and the South African War, 1899–1902*, Peter Warwick

41 *A History of Niger 1850–1960*, Finn Fuglestad

42 *Industrialisation and Trade Union Organization in South Africa, 1924–1955*, Stephen Ellis

43 *The Rising of the Red Shawls: A Revolt in Madagascar 1895–1899*, Stephen Ellis

44 *Slavery in Dutch South Africa*, Nigel Worden

45 *Law, Custom and Social Order: The Colonial Experience in Malawi and Zambia*, Martin Chanock

46 *Salt of the Desert Sun: A History of Salt Production and Trade in the Central Sudan*, Paul E. Lovejoy

47 *Marrying Well: Marriage, Status and Social Change among the Educated Elite in Colonial Lagos*, Kristin Mann

48 *Language and Colonial Power: The Appropriation of Swahili in the Former Belgian Congo, 1880–1938*, Johannes Fabian

49 *The Shell Money of the Slave Trade*, Jan Hogendorn and Marion Johnson

50 *Political Domination in Africa*, Patrick Chabal

51 *The Southern Marches of Imperial Ethiopia: Essays in History and Social Anthropology*, Donald Donham and Wendy James

52 *Islam and Urban Labor in Northern Nigeria: The Making of a Muslim Working Class*, Paul M. Lubeck

53 *Horn and Crescent: Cultural Change and Traditional Islam on the East African Coast, 1800–1900*, Randall L. Pouwels

54 *Capital and Labour on the Kimberley Diamond Fields, 1871–1890*, Robert Vicat Turrell

55 *National and Class Conflict in the Horn of Africa*, John Markakis

56 *Democracy and Prebendal Politics in Nigeria: The Rise and Fall of the Second Republic*, Richard A. Joseph

57 *Entrepreneurs and Parasites: The Struggle for Indigenous Capitalism in Zaïre*, Janet MacGaffey

58 *The African Poor: A History*, John Iliffe

59 *Palm Oil and Protest: An Economic History of the Ngwa Region, South-Eastern Nigeria, 1800–1980*, Susan M. Martin

60 *France and Islam in West Africa, 1860–1960*, Christopher Harrison

61 *Transformation and Continuity in Revolutionary Ethiopia*, Christopher Clapham

62 *Prelude to the Mahdiyya: Peasants and Traders in the Shendi Region, 1821–1885*, Anders Bjørkelo

63 *Wa and the Wala: Islam and Polity in Northwestern Ghana*, Ivor Wilks

64 *H. C. Bankole-Bright and Politics in Colonial Sierra Leone, 1919–1958*, Akintola Wyse

65 *Contemporary West African States*, Donald Cruise O'Brien, John Dunn, and Richard Rathbone (eds.)

66 *The Oromo of Ethiopia: A History, 1570–1860*, Mohammed Hassen

67 *Slavery and African Life: Occidental, Oriental, and African Slave Trades*, Patrick Manning

68 *Abraham Esau's War: A Black South African War in the Cape, 1899–1902*, Bill Nasson

69 *The Politics of Harmony: Land Dispute Strategies in Swaziland*, Laurel L. Rose

70 *Zimbabwe's Guerrilla War: Peasant Voices*, Norma J. Kriger

71 *Ethiopia: Power and Protest: Peasant Revolts in the Twentieth Century*, Gebru Tareke

72 *White Supremacy and Black Resistance in Pre-Industrial South Africa: The Making of the Colonial Order in the Eastern Cape, 1770–1865*, Clifton C. Crais

73 *The Elusive Granary: Herder, Farmer, and State in Northern Kenya*, Peter D. Little

74 *The Kanyok of Zaire: An Institutional and Ideological History to 1895*, John C. Yoder

75 *Pragmatism in the Age of Jihad: The Precolonial State of Bundu*, Michael A. Gomez

76 *Slow Death for Slavery: The Course of Abolition in Northern Nigeria, 1897–1936*, Paul E. Lovejoy and Jan S. Hogendorn

77 *West African Slavery and Atlantic Commerce: The Senegal River Valley, 1700–1860*, James F. Searing

78 *A South African Kingdom: The Pursuit of Security in Nineteenth-Century Lesotho*, Elizabeth A. Eldredge

79 *State and Society in Pre-colonial Asante*, T. C. McCaskie

80 *Islamic Society and State Power in Senegal: Disciples and Citizens in Fatick*, Leonardo A. Villalón

81 *Ethnic Pride and Racial Prejudice in Victorian Cape Town: Group Identity and Social Practice*, Vivian Bickford-Smith

82 *The Eritrean Struggle for Independence: Domination, Resistance and Nationalism, 1941–1993*, Ruth Iyob

83 *Corruption and State Politics in Sierra Leone*, William Reno

84 *The Culture of Politics in Modern Kenya*, Angelique Haugerud

85 *Africans: The History of a Continent*, John Iliffe

86 *From Slave Trade to 'Legitimate' Commerce: The Commercial Transition in Nineteenth-Century West Africa*, Robin Law (ed.)

87 *Leisure and Society in Colonial Brazzaville*, Phyllis Martin

88 *Kingship and State: The Buganda Dynasty*, Christopher Wrigley

89 *Decolonization and African Life: The Labour Question in French and British Africa*, Frederick Cooper

90 *Misreading the African Landscape: Society and Ecology in an African Forest Savannah Mosaic*, James Fairhead and Melissa Leach

91 *Peasant Revolution in Ethiopia: The Tigray People's Liberation Front, 1975–1991*, John Young

92 *Senegambia and the Atlantic Slave Trade*, Boubacar Barry

93 *Commerce and Economic Change in West Africa: The Oil Trade in the Nineteenth Century*, Martin Lynn

94 *Slavery and French Colonial Rule in West Africa: Senegal, Guinea and Mali*, Martin A. Klein

95 *East African Doctors: A History of the Modern Profession*, John Iliffe

96 *Middlemen of the Cameroons Rivers: The Duala and Their Hinterland, c.1600–1960*, Ralph Derrick, Ralph A. Austen, and Jonathan Derrick

97 *Masters and Servants on the Cape Eastern Frontier, 1760–1803*, Susan Newton-King

98 *Status and Respectability in the Cape Colony, 1750–1870: A Tragedy of Manners*, Robert Ross

99 *Slaves, Freedmen and Indentured Laborers in Colonial Mauritius*, Richard B. Allen

100 *Transformations in Slavery: A History of Slavery in Africa, 2nd Edition*, Paul E. Lovejoy

101 *The Peasant Cotton Revolution in West Africa: Côte d'Ivoire, 1880–1995*, Thomas J. Bassett

102 *Re-Imagining Rwanda: Conflict, Survival and Disinformation in the Late Twentieth Century*, Johan Pottier

103 *The Politics of Evil: Magic, State Power and the Political Imagination in South Africa*, Clifton Crais

104 *Transforming Mozambique: The Politics of Privatization, 1975–2000*, M. Anne Pitcher

105 *Guerrilla Veterans in Post-war Zimbabwe: Symbolic and Violent Politics, 1980–1987*, Norma J. Kriger

106 *An Economic History of Imperial Madagascar, 1750–1895: The Rise and Fall of an Island Empire*, Gwyn Campbell

107 *Honour in African History*, John Iliffe

108 *Africans: History of a Continent, 2nd Edition*, John Iliffe

109 *Guns, Race, and Power in Colonial South Africa*, William Kelleher Storey

110 *Islam and Social Change in French West Africa: History of an Emancipatory Community*, Sean Hanretta

111 *Defeating Mau Mau, Creating Kenya: Counterinsurgency, Civil War, and Decolonization*, Daniel Branch

112 *Christianity and Genocide in Rwanda*, Timothy Longman

113 *From Africa to Brazil: Culture, Identity, and an African Slave Trade, 1600–1830*, Walter Hawthorne

114 *Africa in the Time of Cholera: A History of Pandemics from 1817 to the Present*, Myron Echenberg

115 *A History of Race in Muslim West Africa, 1600–1960*, Bruce S. Hall

116 *Witchcraft and Colonial Rule in Kenya, 1900–1955*, Katherine Luongo

117 *Transformations in Slavery: A History of Slavery in Africa, 3rd Edition*, Paul E. Lovejoy

118 *The Rise of the Trans-Atlantic Slave Trade in Western Africa, 1300–1589*, Toby Green

119 *Party Politics and Economic Reform in Africa's Democracies*, M. Anne Pitcher

120 *Smugglers and Saints of the Sahara: Regional Connectivity in the Twentieth Century*, Judith Scheele

121 *Slaving and Cross-Cultural Trade in the Atlantic World: Angola and Brazil during the Era of the Slave Trade*, Roquinaldo Ferreira

122 *Ethnic Patriotism and the East African Revival*, Derek Peterson

123 *Black Morocco: A History of Slavery and Islam*, Chouki El Hamel